# INTERNATIONAL FINANCIAL MANAGEMENT



(Late) **Dr. V.A. Avadhani**

*M.A., Ph.D. (U.S.A.), M.A., L.L.B., C.A.I.I.B.*

* Retired Adviser in the Reserve Bank of India
* Former Director of Research and Training in Bombay Stock Exchange
* Former Adviser in Hyderabad Stock Exchange

Himalaya Publishing House

ISO 9001:2015 CERTIFIED

| | | |
|---|---|---|
| **First Edition** | : | **2006** |
| **Reprint** | : | **2007** |
| **Reprint** | : | **2008** |
| **Second Revised Edition** | : | **2011** |
| **Reprint** | : | **2013** |
| **Third Revised Edition** | : | **2017** |
| **Reprint** | : | **2019, 2023** |
| **Reprint** | : | **2025** |

**Published by** : Mrs. Meena Pandey
for **HIMALAYA PUBLISHING HOUSE PVT. LTD.,**
Vishal Industrial Estate, 1st Floor, Office No. 63/64,
Bhandup Village Road, Subhash Nagar (Opp. CEAT Tyres),
Nahur (W), Mumbai - 400 078. Phone: 022-35131464/65/66/67
E-mail: himpub@bharatmail.co.in; Website: www.himpub.com

**Branch Offices** :

**New Delhi** : "Pooja Apartments", 4-B, Murari Lal Street, Ansari Road, Darya Ganj, New Delhi - 110 002. Phone: 011-23270392, 23278631; Fax: 011-23256286

**Nagpur** : Kundanlal Chandak Industrial Estate, Ghat Road, Nagpur - 440 018. Mobile: 09325409992, 09325908881

**Bengaluru** : Plot No. 91-33, 2nd Main Road, Seshadripuram, Behind Nataraja Theatre, Bengaluru - 560 020. Phone: 080-41138821; Mobile: 09379847017, 09379847005

**Hyderabad** : No. 3-4-184, Lingampally, Besides Raghavendra Swamy Matham, Kachiguda, Hyderabad - 500 027. Phone: 040-27560041, 27550139

**Chennai** : No. 34/44, Motilal Street, T. Nagar, Chennai - 600 017. Mobile: 09380460419

**Pune** : "Laksha" Apartment, First Floor, No. 527, Mehunpura, Shaniwarpeth (Near Prabhat Theatre), Pune - 411 030. Phone: 020-24496323, 24496333; Mobile: 09370579333

**Cuttack** : Plot No 5F-755/4, Sector-9, CDA Markat Nagar, Cuttack - 753 014, Odisha. Mobile: 09338746007

**Kolkata** : 3, S.M. Bose Road, Near Gate No. 5, Agarpara Railway Station, North 24 Parganas, West Bengal - 700109. Mobile: 09674536325

**DTP by** : Sunanda

**Printed at** : Geetanjali Press Pvt. Ltd., Nagpur. On behalf of HPH (P).

# PREFACE

This book is intended for all students of Finance and Management, in all Management Institutes and Universities. The objectives of the book are to provide students with a conceptual framework of financial decisions taken in a multinational company and to familiarise the students with the unique economic fundamentals and financial factors which challenge the financial manager in the international context. The book covers the entire syllabus, as approved by UGC on the subject of International Financial Management.

With increasing globalisation and opening up of the economies to free market forces of competition and efficiency, the role of multinational trade and finance has grown by leaps and bounds in the last decade. This is particularly more relevant in the Indian context, where the rupee was made convertible on current account and export and import trade is growing both in absolute and relative terms. The scrips of many corporates in India are listed and traded in main foreign stock exchanges and Foreign Financial Institutions and Foreign Institutional Investors are operating in Indian financial markets both of equity and debt nature. Foreign capital flows and foreign investment are growing and gaining in importance. The international forces are throwing new challenges to the Finance Manager. It is in this context that the subject of International Financial Management has assumed vital importance to the students of Finance Management who will be the future financial managers operating in international markets, for goods, services and finance. This book is intended to cater to their requirements.

This book is presented in simple non-mathematical terms, easily understandable to the average students and lay executives of the corporates. This has the advantage of ***harmonising*** the finance function with the investment function of the Financial Manager on the one hand and integrating the domestic finance with international finance, on the other. The material is kept as brief as possible, yet with a comprehensive coverage of all the modules as approved by UGC and in accordance with their syllabus.

From time to time, it has been revised to incorporate changes in policy and empirical data. The author acknowledges all the faculty who have recommended changes and to the Himalaya Publishing House Pvt. Ltd.

**— Author**

# CONTENTS

## PART I

## BACKDROP OF INTERNATIONAL FINANCIAL MANAGEMENT



## PART II

## MANAGEMENT OF EXCHANGE AND INTEREST RATE EXPOSURE



## PART III

## MANAGEMENT OF RISKS IN INTERNATIONAL TRANSACTIONS

## PART IV

## MANAGEMENT OF INTERNATIONAL BUSINESS OPERATIONS AND PRACTICES



## PART V

## MANAGEMENT OF SHORT-TERM INTERNATIONAL FINANCING



## PART VI

## MANAGEMENT OF LONG-TERM INTERNATIONAL FINANCING

# BRIEF CONTENTS

# PART I

# BACKDROP OF INTERNATIONAL FINANCIAL MANAGEMENT

# INTRODUCTION TO INTERNATIONAL FINANCIAL MANAGEMENT

# 1

## Introduction

International Financial Management has assumed an important role in the Indian economy, with FDI's, FFIs and FIIs playing a key role in the stock and capital markets. The recent estimate is that FIIs hold about 18% of market capitalisation of the listed companies, in the Stock Exchanges in India. Many Indian corporates are listed and traded on Foreign Stock Exchanges. Many foreign banks were permitted to operate in India and Indian banks have become more globalised in their operations. Indian exports are growing at a rate of 12%, per annum as envisaged in the Tenth Plan. Nearly more than 50% of the manufacturing output in India is exported on an average. The total of exports and imports trade crossed U.S. $ 455 billion and its foreign exchange assets are also more than U.S. $ 300 billion. With such growing importance of global sector, the operations in International Finance are also growing faster than ever before.

World trade was estimated to grow in 2008 at a rate of 4% and that of the developing countries at 8% to 10%. The scope of expansion for International Financial Management has increased. India has a major role to play in the world trade and finance. Net capital flows into Emerging Market economies on non-official basis were estimated at U.S. $ 320 billion in 2014.

India has emerged as a Creditor Country among the IMF of members. World Bank is reported to be planning to issue rupee bonds in India to raise rupee resources. Indian rupee has shown strength and resilience that it was in demand in International Finance

Markets. Many big companies in India have become international market participants and are rated as domestic MNCs in addition to many MNCs of foreign origin in India: The above picture provides a brief overview of the importance of International Financial Management. Gross capital inflows into India Through FDI are NRIs continued to grow even in a Recession year of 2009.

## Objective

The object of this chapter is to develop linkages between the domestic economic and financial system and international financial system and to provide theoretical and analytical inputs necessary for a student of international financial management. The corporate executives have before them, the corporate goals for implementing the management function, finance function or marketing function. All these functions are interrelated and connected with the international financial system. The finance manager or the production manager operates at the corporate level in both domestic and foreign markets corresponding to the domestic and foreign sectors. If we start with the production function of a corporate entity and analyse the finance function of the manager, his operations in the foreign sector provide the link between the corporate sector, on the one hand, and the foreign sector, on the other. The mutual interactions between foreign sectors of various countries lead to the emergence of the international financial system. The foreign sectors are the cementing blocks of the international financial system and institutions operating in the international financial system are closely connected with the foreign sectors of the various economies. In this chapter an attempt has been made to trace back the operations in the international finance system from the international level to the national level through various financial institutions and banks and at the national level, from these institutions to the corporate units and the company managers. In view of global importance to operations of international trade and funds flow international financial management has assumed a vital role.

There are various facets of the international financial system (IFS) which are analysed in depth in the chapter. To start with, an important aspect of international financial system is international trade which accounts for the largest chunk of international commercial and financial relations and payments. Thus, a part of the treatment of this book is on the subject of international trade and finance, Balance of Payments and related aspects of international economic relations. Another aspect is the institutions and organisations in it under which banks, national and international financial institutions have all found a place in this book.

The sub-markets in the financial system such as in foreign currency, corresponding to short-term flow of funds as between countries' investments in foreign money markets and in foreign claims, etc., are reflected in financial flows as between countries through the flows of money payments and receipts. Thus, both international trade and international currency and exchange markets are closely connected and are dealt with. Yet another aspect of the international financial system is the role of term lending and foreign aid in the flows of trade between countries, corresponding to long-term flows as between countries. It is in this context that foreign trade and aid are discussed as important components of the international financial system as short-term and long-term wings of the operations of the International Financial Manager.

## Relevance to Management

As this book is intended for students and corporate executives, we should set out in the beginning itself the relevance of international finance to their day-to-day work. Domestic finance and international finance are next-door neighbours-both complementary and competitive- viewed either as sources or uses of funds.

Firstly, in a fast-growing world economy and world markets, it would be naïve for a corporate executive to confine himself to the domestic markets and domestic finance alone. The days of national autarky have gone by and we are in a world of interdependence. With a fast growing network of transport and communications, the world is getting closer and a finance manager can hardly ignore the forces operating on him from the international plane as much as from the domestic plane.

Secondly, as the operations and systems in domestic and international finance are different, the factors influencing them need to be studied separately.

Thirdly, in a world of competition and survival of the fittest, the managerial function involves choosing the right input mix both from home and abroad and the right output mix suitable for home and foreign markets and expose oneself to the winds of competition both at national and international levels. These aspects are clearly noticed in India, with the opening up of the economy since July 1991 through Economic and Financial Reforms.

It is to be conceded that the impact of the foreign sector on the activities of the corporate executive is more keenly felt in some lines than in others. Such lines are in exportable goods and services, finance, shipping, airways, tourism etc. If the corporate entity belongs to the sector of multinational companies, foreign-owned companies, subsidiaries or branches of foreign companies etc., international forces are relatively more important. At any rate, any management executive can ill-afford to be blind to the international economic and financial scene even if he is not directly involved in it as these forces operate on him in the modern world.

## Finance Function

The objective of the finance function of a manager may be set out in different ways. He may aim at optimising the value of his assets or minimising the worth of his liabilities. Put in differently, he may maximise his gross profits or net profits and minimise risks or aim at optimising the market value of his company's shares. Looked at from any angle, the management basically aims at economy, efficiency and productivity leading to greater profitability. For this purpose, he concentrates on the efficient management of cash and credit so far as the financial aspect is concerned. But more importantly, he has to consider the production function of which cash and credit are inputs. The finance function is also closely related to marketing function also, as the latter involves the use of cash and credit. The manager has to take into account the international forces in the preparation of plans and budgets for resource inflows and outflows and in input and output markets. In the raising of funds and use of such funds, the cost of alternative uses and sources have to be considered both at home and abroad. Finance Function is all pervading being related to all activities of the firm, and particularly to the Management.

In terms of the real sector or the financial sector, the manager has to observe the criteria of efficiency and productivity etc., in the input market and output market and in allocation of physical resources or financial resources. In the input and output markets as well as in financial markets, both domestic and foreign, forces have to be reckoned with.

## Input Market

In the input market, physical and financial inputs are fed into the productive system. Physical inputs relate to physical capital equipment, plant and machinery, raw materials, spare parts and intermediate (semi-finished) products, etc. They may come from domestic or foreign markets. Financial inputs relate to moneys spent on wages for labour or cash kept for current liabilities or contingencies. Such inputs can be secured both from domestic markets and foreign markets. As such, a cost calculus has to be made for the right mix of inputs and the right sources of supply of such inputs so as to minimise the costs for a given product mix. It is possible that some raw materials or spares are more cheaply available abroad than at home and due to free access to such markets the manager may plan for a mix of inputs at the least cost, subject to the technical feasibilities in the production function. The markets, both domestic and foreign, have to be assessed for these inputs in terms of costs and prices and alternative sources of supply explored. This is an area in international economics and finance. In the supply of financial inputs for production purposes one has to take into account the need for cash and credit and the relative proportions of each both from home and abroad and to assess their relative costs. Marginal costing of cash and credit is part of the wider subject of cash management. The cash component as an input in the production function is part of the subject of production management, while the overall management of all funds is in the domain of financial management.

In a subsidiary or branch of a foreign company, foreign sources play a more important role even in financial inputs. In more recent years, outsourcing in the I.T. and related areas has become important due to its cost reduction advantages. Such exercises relating to financial inputs have to be made after an assessment of cash inflows and outflows, both on current and capital accounts. On the capital account, sources and uses of funds for investment also become an important pre-requisite for planning for credit. These will be discussed below under sources and uses of funds.

## Output Market

In the output market, the sale of final and intermediate products can be made both in domestic and foreign markets and mix of them. International marketing and international finance are closely interlinked and flows of finance follow the flows of trade. Marketing is an important pre-requisite for trade. International trade and international finance are close complements. The costs of production and selling costs and the available margins both on domestic sales and foreign sales have to be considered. Here again, it is assumed that there is a free market in India and abroad or trading is possible subject to satisfying all the requirements of the government policy in this regard. A cost calculus has to be made for planning for the right mix of sales at home and abroad. For an assessment of the demand prospects abroad, we need to know the alternative sources of supply in such markets, demand and supply elasticities, costs and prices of such alternative sources, transport and selling costs etc., which are the subject of international economics and finance. In India due to the premium put on export sales by government policy, the cost calculus has to take into account this aspect also.

## Sources and Uses

At the micro level of a company, an analysis of the sources of funds reveals that broadly there are three categories of sources:

*(i)* Savings of the company which are its retained earnings,

*(ii)* External sources (domestic) from the capital and money markets such as banks, all-India or State-level financial institutions, government or the public and

*(iii)* Foreign sources, namely, markets, institutions and persons abroad. The last category can in turn be specified as follows:

- *(a)* Credit from private parties, *viz.*, trade credit, buyer's credit, etc.;
- *(b)* Foreign government credit, *viz.*, government to government line of credit, foreign aid or grants or loans;
- *(c)* Resources from international or inter-regional bodies such as IFC, IBRD, foreign banks or Euro-currency markets etc.; and
- *(d)* Non-resident individuals and institutions.

The same analysis holds good at the sectoral and national level. In fact, the emergence of international financial markets can be traced to this sectoral interdependence, including the foreign sector and intranational dependence. Basically, as no country is self-sufficient or autarkic but is dependent on other countries for something or the other, international economic and commercial relations emerge. These are referred to later in this chapter.

In a similar fashion, it would be appropriate to set out the pattern of use of funds of any company into various sectors of the economy, including the foreign sector. Dispensation of funds for current or capital expenditures in domestic markets and international markets can be separately set out. Such an analysis is particularly more relevant to multinational corporations and branches or subsidiaries of foreign companies in whose case foreign markets and foreign sources of supply play an important part. The head office or the holding company may spend a part of its funds in investment in the host country, make inward remittances for working capital or investment purposes and outward remittances for royalty and dividend, payments or technical fees.

## Macro View of Foreign Flows

RBI Company Finance Studies throw light on the macro-view of Foreign inflows and outflows in the Corporate Sector. These are published in RBI Bulletins regularly. A large number of smaller companies contribute larger foreign exchange earnings to the country. It is true that both expenditure and earnings on foreign account are concentrated in a small number of large foreign controlled Indian companies and multinational corporations, but they may not add much to the not accrual of foreign exchange. A large number of small companies do not operate on such a large scale, but add substantially to our net accrual of foreign exchange. In more recent years, the accrual of reserve is due to inflows on current account for services remittances and due to depreciation of dollar, and capital inflows for FDI, and NRE deposits.

## Sectoral Interdependence

International financial markets emerged out of the felt need to facilitate operations of nations arising out of the commercial and financial transactions with the rest of the world. This emergence can be attributed logically to: *(a)* Sectoral interdependence, and *(b)* National interdependence.

It would be apt to set out here the inter-relations between the micro-level operations of a finance manager with the macro-level working of the corporate sector and foreign sector. A finance manager is a micro unit in the corporate sector. The environment he faces is competition from other similar units in the corporate sector and as suppliers of inputs or as consumers of output. Besides, the corporate sector, in turn, is interlinked with all other sectors of the economy. The micro-level manager is thus faced with a total environment of the economy which includes foreign sector, and it is thus relevant to him to be familiar with the international financial system, which is the product of developments in the foreign sectors of all the world economies.

The corporate sector is a part of the total business sector having trading and manufacturing activities. The corporate sector is also connected with all sectors of the economy, namely, government sector, household sector and foreign sector either as suppliers of inputs or as consumers of output. Besides, all these domestic and foreign sectors are interconnected through the flow of funds and savings from one sector to the other. In each sector, there are both savers and investors. Only the household sector is a net saver in India. The household sector is also a supplier of factors of production such as labour, management, enterprise etc. For some time in the past, foreign sector was a net saver, as there was a net balance on current account of our balance of payments leading to the accretion to our foreign exchange reserves. We are running huge deficits in merchandise trade account for a long time which was offset by positive balance on the net invisible trade account. For some recent years, we are having a negative savings in the foreign sector leading to a loss of our foreign exchange reserves. If there is a net inflow of funds from abroad either as foreign credits, grants, etc., or borrowings from foreign governments, international bodies etc., there may be a positive balance, in the balance of payments and foreign savings would accrue. The surplus savings in some sectors would flow into other sectors with deficit. In the corporate sector where investment is invariably more than their available savings, the units have to depend on other sectors to finance them. These savings may flow directly from the government sector or household sector or indirectly through financial institutions, banks and other agencies. It would thus, be clear that the corporate sector is intricately connected with all other sectors of the economy either as suppliers of inputs of production or suppliers of factors of production, including land, labour, capital or enterprise or consumers of their products or services.

They are also connected with other sectors of the economy through inflow or outflow of funds or savings or financial assets-moneys or near money assets or financial flows.

Another aspect of interdependence of the various sectors of the economy is foreign private investment in the domestic economy or Indian investment abroad. The investment may take the form of

*(i)* Equity participation in Indian enterprises,

*(ii)* Investment in bonds or debentures,

*(iii)* Granting of loans or credits either on government to government basis or party to party basis in the private sector,

*(iv)* Joint ventures in third countries and

*(v)* Technical consultancy or know-how participation etc. Transfer of technology is also one of the aspects of the international commercial and financial relations which is necessary for a sustained rate of growth at the lowest possible cost and the highest level of productivity.

All the inputs of the corporate sector come either from the household sector as labour, capital or enterprise or from Government sector as infrastructure, land, electricity, water etc., or from agriculture or industry (business sector) as raw materials, intermediate products, spares parts etc.

Particularly more relevant for our discussion is the contribution of foreign sector towards inputs of the corporate sector in the form of physical capital, plant, machinery, spares, raw materials, etc., or financial inputs in the form of short-term credits or investment in financial assets, etc. The inflows into India are through FIIs for portfolio investment and through MNCs for direct investment in equity or debt forms.

Such interdependence between the corporate sector and other sectors is also noticed in the field of outputs. The main consumers of some products may in fact be the foreigners. Either in respect of consumer goods or capital goods, there is a good element of foreign demand, particularly from the less developed countries. In view of the vastness of our domestic markets, the executives of the corporate sector rarely explore the foreign markets, unless the products are export-oriented. With the projected expansion of the industry and limitations in the domestic markets, the present executives may have to think more in terms of foreign markets than of domestic markets. More recently, export-oriented industries and 100 per cent export units are being encouraged by the government in the light of the prevailing balance of payments difficulties of the country and increasing export shortfalls. Besides, the philosophy of the government is also veering round to the view of making our economy more competitive with a greater role allocated to the private sector. The recent trend to globalisation and opening up of the economy to free market forces make the foreign sector more relevant than before. The cost consciousness and competitiveness has increased in the Indian enterprise. In such an environment, the role of foreign sector can be hardly overemphasised when the chilly winds of competition and cost consciousness make the present executives of the corporate enterprise more alert and informed on both the domestic and external sectors. The foreign environment would be equally important and more challenging than the domestic market due to the ever changing scene of demand and supply forces, competition and cost price factors operating from all sides of the world. These may hopefully improve the efficiency of factors and lower the costs of production.

There is another reason why the foreign sector is more important to India, namely, the limits are already reached in the domestic markets and the scope for further expansion of markets lies abroad. Besides, there is the debt service burden which we carry due to our reliance on foreign credits during the last few decades of our planning. This burden can be discharged by a continuous flow of goods and services outside the country leading to an export surplus for the nation.

In the output market, the domestic household sector has been the main consumer in India, followed by the government sector which needs the output of the corporate sector both for capital formation and current consumption. Besides, the government with its contracting role in the economy has got less say in the affairs of the corporate sector today and is likely to become lesser in future due to their avowed policy of a greater role for the private sector in the years to come. The business sector comprising industry and agriculture continue to consume the products of the corporate sector as intermediates or raw materials for manufacture or further processing. These facts are brought out in any analysis of input-output matrix tables for the economy, brought out by the ISI and CSO.

## International Flow of Funds

We have seen that national economy of a country is composed of a number of sectors, including the foreign sector and the interdependence of these sectors either as suppliers of savings or of factors of production, or of other inputs in the productive process or as consumers of their output leads to economic, commercial and financial transactions as between these sectors. It is such transactions between the domestic sectors and foreign sector that gives rise to the international financial system.

An extension of this principle of mutual interdependence to the case of national economy of one country depending upon that of others lends further support to our thesis that emergence of international financial markets is the result of such interdependence and intra flow of funds. Thus, no modern nation/state is self-sufficient nor is it closed to external forces from other nations and states. This dependence is the result of the expanding civilisation and modern socio-economic systems. It is now well recognised that countries are interdependent in various degrees resulting in economic commercial and financial transactions among them. Such interdependence is a necessary but not a sufficient condition for the emergence of international financial markets. But the conquering of the distance and time by revolution in telecommunications, electronic media and information technology has brought the world together and led to a sufficient condition for emergence of International Financial Management, as an area of vital importance. More importance is given recently to globalisation and privatisation leading to greater international interdependence.

The interdependence of nations can be ascribed to the following factors:

(1) Differential factor endowments and natural endowments in different countries, leading to different production functions.

(2) Different stages of growth of industry, agriculture and other sectors in the economies of these countries, and different levels of savings and investment.

(3) Differentials in technological advancement, R&D, and economies of scale.

(4) Differences in habits, tastes and consumer preferences, leading to different demand functions.

(5) Differences in standards of living and incomes, leading to flow of funds through grants, loans etc.

## Conclusion

It would thus, be seen that the importance of international financial management can be traced to the sectoral and national interdependence which leads to international economic, commercial and financial relations as between countries. International trade, aid and financial flows account for the bulk of such transactions as between nations. The basic economic principles of efficiency, productivity and least cost optimisation process necessitate the use of inputs both domestic and foreign and flow of goods and services across national borders, provided there are no barriers to such flows. The result is the exchange of goods and services involving payments and receipts as between countries and exchange of one currency for another and borrowing and lending of money or near money assets across borders. These transactions and trading in foreign currencies, foreign assets or liabilities and foreign claims constitute the international financial system, and are the subject matter of International Financial Management.

❖ ❖ ❖

# INTERNATIONAL FINANCIAL ENVIRONMENT

# 2

International Financial Environment can be classified into economic, financial, political and social areas. Besides, the legal and accounting standards and regulatory frameworks vary from country to country. Global players have to face a dynamic environment of free market forces and fierce competition of cross border companies. Social and political environment should be receptive to the MNCs. For example, spirit of Swadeshi, self-sufficiency and protective walls against cross border trade are the anathema of globalisation. Political system should be oriented to private enterprise and freedom of operations. Controls of all kinds are to be dismantled and freedom of entry and exit and entry to foreign funds have to be ensured.

## Political System — Good Economics is Good Politics

With the deregulation and liberalisation of policies, a political will has been created for promotion of global operations. The controlled and protectionist regime disappeared with companies free to export and import and with free flow of funds. The governments would have a limited say in development of infrastructure and in enforcement of law and order situation in the country. The political equations and friendly relations are an important requisite for international financial flows, trade and investment.

With the emergence of free markets, the corporates have to readjust to the market mechanism. As regards the socio-political priorities, the quality and cost are the considerations and post-sales service has to be guaranteed. Pollution control, effective water and effluent treatment before discharge, conservation of energy etc. are some of the social responsibilities. Besides I.S.I. quality control, maintenance and an efficient distribution system with a network of centres for maintenance of continuous supply to the consumers and a guaranteed after sales service to consumers are absolutely necessary for global players.

## Social System

The environment comprises of the social habits, customs and tastes. Social priorities and responsibilities have to be looked into by the International Finance Managers, who have to observe an accepted code of corporate governance. Social system varies from country to country and some countries like India have multi-religious and mult-linguistic back grounds which have to be scrupulously honoured by the cross country players. The activities of MNCs like production, distribution, sales and advertisement, etc. impinge on the social priorities. Resource conservation, and quality and services standards, environmental concerns require to be observed. The health concerns and scarce resource depletion and maintenance of quality standards etc. are some of the environmental constraints. Socio-political system is thus a major environmental factor for international financial management. Social responsibility and good business ethics are essential parts of good corporate governance, which all global players have to observe. Good corporate governance is made mandatory to all listed companies in India by the SEBI.

## Information Technology

The global players will have to possess the latest technology and information systems of countries in which they operate. The role of capital and technology has to be emphasised in the global operations, as these players have to develop a R&D system and evolve the latest technologies to be introduced in the markets that they operate. Capital has to be very mobile to flow along with technology into areas and countries which promise high returns and good markets.

The economic factors like the GDP growth, labour expertise, interest rates and inflation and a host of other factors have to ensure economic stability and growth of the economy for global players to be attracted. Domestic corporates have to turn global by a series of structural changes, adoption to the new market forces and cost-price adjustments to suit the markets. Information Technology and new technologies have to be globally relevant and applicable.

## Financial Strength

The finance markets will be more volatile as foreign funds come in and go out, as per the winds of economic forces. The role of speculation and commercial gains become more prominent. Both, the domestic and foreign MNCs have to be attuned to the environments facing them and evince the expertise to meet the challenges of free market forces, where strength is the *sine-qua-non* of success. The weak ones will have to exit or strengthen themselves to meet the competition of MNCs with their superior management talent, latest technology and abundant financial resources. There will be only survival of the fittest and the market forces themselves will eliminate the weak and the sick in the international accounting standards and reporting standards, auditing standards high degree of transparency and disclosures are necessary for operation in financial markets.

## Legal and Economic System

International business transactions will involve the knowledge of the systems of law prevailing in the concerned countries. Similarly the currency volatility and its behaviour is yet another factor to be reckoned with in international business. If the economy is to be considered as open, it should have at least current account convertibility, free access to the markets and free inflow and outflow of funds across borders.

The parties to a transaction may be from two or more countries and the law of which country is to be observed in the event of a dispute is a major question. The parties must not only familiar with the laws of the country in question or the host country but also abide by it and be prepared to agree to the enforcement of a judgement obtained in a foreign court.

The factors which influence the choice of the legal system are similar to the choice of the economic system. Democracy, freedom of choice and importance of the private sector are the pillars on which economic system has to rely for the MNCs and global players to accept the country for their operations. Non-legal factors such as familiarity, convenience, patriotism and tradition also play a role in the choice of the legal system as acceptable.

The credibility of the legal systems, fairness and justice in the country, independence of the judiciary from executive wing of the government are some of the criteria of the choice of the legal system for an international contract. Then the next step is to consider which legal system is most closely connected with the contract. English being predominantly used in international transactions and London and New York being major financial centres, their courts are widely accepted for adjudication of international disputes in global financial contracts. Costing and accounting standards are also an important aspect of international contracts along with legal and regulatory framework.

## General Environment

Any corporate business unit faces global environment in various forms, particularly if it is an export industry, import dependent industry and import competing industry. Also, units in joint ventures, subsidiaries of foreign companies, and partly or wholly owned foreign companies face the global environment. The major global environmental factors are shown in this chart.

**Chart : 2.1**

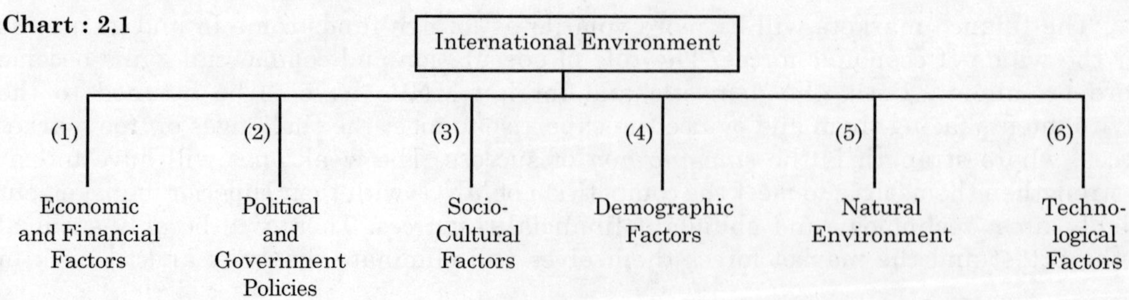

## Examples

**1. Economic and Financial Factors:** Recession, Depression or Boom conditions in other trading partners. Growth rates of GDP, inflation rates, interest rates, money supply growth rates, sectoral and industry growth rates, exchange rates, currency fluctuations are some examples of economic factors. Commodity prices and prices of crude oil minerals and metals and market conditions etc. are the other factors of economic nature. The conditions in financial markets, cost and availability of funds, interest rates and a host of similar forces are also part of the global environment. Rise in oil prices adversely affects many global players and recession in major developed countries like U.S.A. affects the exports and production of some of export dependent industries and growth of international trade. Depreciation of currency or appreciation influences the inflow and outflow of funds, trade and investment on a global scale as much as returns and interest rates.

**2. Political and Government Policies:** Stability in economic policies depend upon the political system and its stability. Political and economic factors are interrelated. Laws relating to ownership, foreign trade and foreign investment are all factors which influence global business. The legal system and the operation of laws and the dependability of courts and their efficiency are also a part of the environment for global operations. Political system has different organs, namely, executive (administrative machinery), legislature (parliament for making laws) and judiciary. The efficiency of the three organs and their mode of operations are factors to be reckoned with in all countries, whether it is a communist, socialist or capitalist system. Corruption of bureaucracy and red tapism and delays in delivery of justice in any country are deterrent to a larger flow of foreign private investment, into that country.

Government policies, including policies on industry, fiscal policy, trade and tariff policy and monetary policy have profound influence on global business. Policies on industry include those on foreign ownership, freedom of entry and price controls, which influence foreign investment and foreign trade. Policies of control dissuade free flows across borders whereas, free markets and deregulation and liberalisation policies attract flows of goods, funds etc.

Some governments impose minimum standards of quality, packaging, advertisement, health and environmental protection and for protection of the consuming public. Many countries have controls on drugs, cosmetics and food additives. But controls on investment and trade, licensing of industrial units, labour policies and lack of free entry and exit are the most significant factors affecting global business. The reservation to small scale industry and privileges attached to them are responsible for the success of "Nirma" brand soaps and detergents, in India.

**3. Social and Cultural Factors:** The social habits and customs of the consuming public, their tastes and preferences are some of the factors influencing global operations. Some cultural factors like traditions and customs play a role, as in the case of sale of family planning devices and the use of bio-gas for cooking in India, for which there is a social stigma. Nestle, a Swiss MNC, was reported to be manufacturing some forty varieties of instant coffee to suit the tastes of different countries.

Beliefs regarding colour is another example. Black is used by Muslim women for their burkha, while the same black is a symbol of mourning for the Hindu cultures.

While white indicates death and mourning in China and Korea, it is a symbol of happiness for some cultures in the West, as wedding gowns are made of white colour.

The perceptions of product attributes may vary from country to country so that, the method of packaging and promoting a product may vary, to suit the cultures, tastes and habits of the consumer in different nations. The mode of consumption of tuna varies in Europe and U.S. and therefore, the mode of its promotion and advertisement varies. The use of pesticides and chemicals for agricultural and horticultural products are banned for being imported products in the U.S. and the E.U. countries.

**4. Demographic Factors:** The demographic factors which influence the operations of MNCs are varied from country to country. Some of these are the size of the country population, and its growth rate, age composition, and sex composition of population, rural and urban proportions, language, religion, ethnicity, caste, literacy and educational levels, occupational status, wage levels of employment etc. Some of these influence the demand pattern and product mix, market size, advertisement and packaging, marketing strategies etc.

All these factors influence the business decisions and operations of global players. Although, domestic companies are also affected by these factors, the MNCs face greater adjustment and adaptation problems. As observed by Louis Stern, "Marketing personnel are to interface between company and society. In this position, they have the responsibility not merely for designing a competitive marketing strategy, but for sensitizing business to a social, as well as product demand of society."

Rapidly increasing population as in China and India, attract more foreign investment than the stagnant population. The flow of MNC funds is more to developing countries, as they have growth rates higher and market size larger. If labour is heterogeneous, there will be more personnel management problems. Cheap labour particularly skilled labour as in India attract more MNCs for their operations. Stagnant population growth and decline in birth rate as in USA forced Johnson and Johnson to find outlets for its products in India and other developing countries and diversify into female hygiene products.

**5. Natural Environment:** Natural environment encompasses natural resource endowments, weather, climatic conditions, ecological factors, infrastructural factors like power, water resources, air ways, ports, surface transport, etc. Geographical and climatic factors force a change in market mix and product mix of production and marketing strategies. These factors influence also, the location of certain industries and units. Cotton textiles is attracted to the availability of raw cotton and damp climatic conditions. Coal, steel and cement are located at places where raw materials and cheap labour are available. Insistence on conservation of energy, pollution control and the need for ecological balance, pose additional social responsibilities on business. The developed West particularly the USA, insist on certain hygienic packing and health safeguards for their markets and consumption of population. Environmental consideration and health grounds have been the main reasons for imposing tariff and non-tariff barriers by the western developed countries (USA and EC etc.), on the products of developing countries.

---

1. Louis L. Stern:"Consumer Protection Vs Self-Regulation", in *Journal of Marketing,* July 1971.

Natural environment varies from country to country and region to region. Multinational company which caters to the demand of so many nations has to attune its products, costs of products and marketing strategies etc. suitable to the concerned countries. The costs of Indian products being cheaper than in the African continent, the developed West can produce in India and market the products in the Africa. Many drug multinationals have to adopt their marketing strategies and product mix strategies to suit to the demands of the poor population and with low standards of living. The demands of rural India are different from those of the Metro centres.

**6. Technological Environment:** While natural environment is given and uncontrollable, the technological environment is adjustable and changeable to suit to the market and demand conditions. Quality is set by technology and competition forces the units to use the most cost effective and high quality standards for the production units. High cost of technology and consultancy of the developed West forces the poor African and Asian nations to attract Indian skills and technology to different countries at different stages of growth. Thus, Esso had adopted its gasoline formulations to suit the weather conditions prevailing in different markets.

The fast changes in technologies lead to high cost of transition from one stage to another. Machinery becomes outmoded fast. The product mix strategies and marketing strategies have to change and adapt themselves to the revolution in advertisement and packaging, the introduction of colour T.V. led to cable network and electronic marketing. Internet facilities and revolution in satellite communication facilities led to e-commerce, cellular phone facilities and the demand for telephone connections rose rapidly in the last few years.

The product mix of Hindustan Lever, Glaxo, Nestle, Ponds etc. has undergone so many changes that their turnover mix in 1990 was not the same as in 2000 AD. This is particularly true of their export products. New market and product opportunities are emerging and old technologies are replaced by new ones due to the progress of R&D efforts which is particularly true of the developed country MNCs.

## Factors in Environment

The chart showing the Factors in Global environment is presented below:

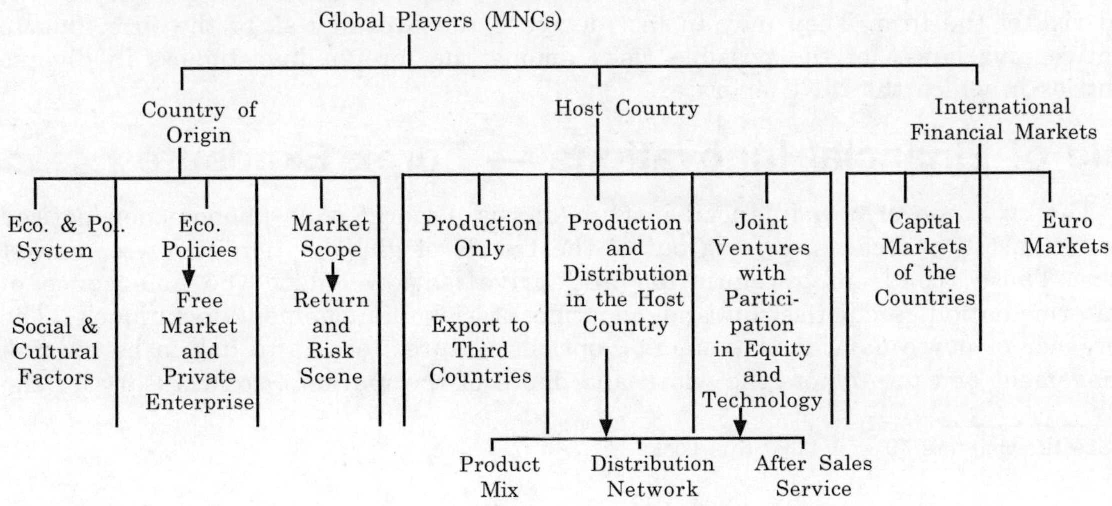

The global factors which influence the global players are the world output, world trade, boom and recessions in countries, political and cultural equations of the concerned countries, political system and stability of the system and conditions in the international Financial Markets, etc. For the funds to flow and investment to be made, the prime economic criteria is risk and return scenario. But more often, it is political equations, friendly economic ties, trading partnership etc., which count for foreign inflow of debt and equity funds along with technological flows. The social responsibilities which are thrusted on the foreign investors, tax system which the foreign investors have to face and the bureaucracy which they have to deal with all count equally on the risk-return scenario. Globalisation leads to integration of markets, opens up new challenges of competition in respect of costs and quality, increases the scale of operations and scope for upgradation of technology and modernisation. The markets become more volatile and tools of risk management have to be used discretely.

## Risks and Diversification

The existing evidence shows that the impact of foreign operations on firm's riskiness is to lower it, thereby suggesting that the MNCs should capture any opportunity for expanding their overseas operations. It would therefore, be necessary for the MNCs to question the use of risk premium to account for the added political and economic risks of overseas operations when evaluating prospective foreign investments. It is also wrong to consider that foreign investments are always more risky and hence, they will add to the total riskiness of the MNC. On the other hand, because of the negative covariance or zero covariance of the various country projects (following Markowitz theory) among themselves, the total net risk added to the domestic company will be less than the corresponding domestic investments; due to Markowitz diversification.[2]

Thus, the use of any risk premium ignores the fact that the risk of any overseas investment may be less than the average total risk of the firm. The automatic inclusion of premium for risk when evaluating a foreign project is not a necessary component of the exercise in project evaluation. In capital budgeting, any method of risk analysis for foreign investment should take into account both the components of risk, namely, systematic and unsystematic risks. But, that does not mean that they would increase the total risk of the firm. They may in fact decrease the overall risk of the firm, due to negative covariances of the possible risks among the foreign investments in diverse countries in which the MNC operate.

## Role of Financial Innovations — Forex Exposure

The evolution of new financial instruments is a world wide phenomenon noticed over the last two decades, arising out of the trends of globalisation and free market forces. These trends of deregulation and privatisation led to the emergence of disintermediation, securitisation and adoption of risk management technique's. The emergence of new financial instruments, options, futures, etc. is to help a better risk management and to promote the width and depth of the markets, so necessary for the

2. See the chapters 40 and 41 of this book.

globalised operations of MNCs. The derivative markets arising from these new instruments offer tools for diversification, risk reduction and adaptation to the new global environment. They offer hedge against the prevailing conditions in global markets, namely, volatility of exchange rates, interest rates, and of equity and commodity prices.

The increase of disintermediation trend led to greater reliance of the corporates on the selling and buying of securities and the emerging trend of securitisation is a worldwide phenomenon. Anomalies in the international debt markets gave opportunities of swaps to take advantage of arbitrage. The market imperfections are the basis for the growth of swaps and hedges. The emergence of financial derivatives is to provide a venue for risk reduction and hedges. The risks have increased due to globalisation, inter country differences in inflation rates, the currency and interest rate fluctuations, cross border flows of funds due to speculation. Many new financial instruments have emerged out of the felt need. The international savings imbalances led to the emergence of offshore funds and markets.

## Role of Securitisation

The issuers of securities raise funds from the market through debt or equity by creating the securities or claims on future money on the basis of book debt. This has replaced or supplemented the traditional source of funds by borrowing from banks and FIs. The process of securitisation, has increased in more recent years due to disintermediation created by economic and financial reforms and deregulation and privatisation leading to freer market forces. Such traded and liquid securities created by corporates include commercial paper, certificates of deposits, Euro notes, collateralised mortgage obligations, Eurobonds, pass through securities, participation certificates and credit card receivables. This method of borrowing is found to be cheaper and cost effective than borrowing from banks.

The securities markets offer the following services, which the banks also render to the MNCs:

(1) They offer a venue for meeting the surpluses with deficits of the savers and investors.

(2) They offer a return commensurate with risk.

(3) The risk is measured and made known for the benefit of investors by the credit rating agencies in the financial market.

(4) As there is a secondary market for them, liquidity is ensured. This does not control or monitor the end use of funds by the borrowers.

(5) This type of borrowing not only lowers the cost but frees the management from the control and monitoring by banks/FIs, who are the lenders.

The main objective of these inventions of new financial products is to cater to the felt need for hedging the international risk; increase competition among products, widen and deepen the market and thereby, increase the investors' choice. The basic risks are repackaged, the different segments of the market are integrated and the volume of trade increase in the international derivatives.

## Role of Banks — Interest Rate Exposure

The role of bankers has changed from just borrowing and lending to providers of a wide variety of services in the international capital markets as dealers and intermediaries in international deals, arbitrageurs, and for risk hedge. For example, bankers provide Forward Rate Agreements (FRA), which is an agreement guaranteeing a rate of interest in future say, with a duration of anything between 3 and 12 months. In this contract, there is no risk of default of principal as the gain or loss resulting from the change in market rates is simply paid or received in cash. The risk of interest rate volatility is covered by banks. To give an example, the corporate wants to lock in its future interest rate liability for any possible rise in rates. The corporate can purchase from a bank an FRA contract as protection against rise. The banker quotes a rate say of 8% for the specified period of January to March end. If the rate goes up to 9%, bank credits to the customer's account the difference of 1% on the agreed amount of principal. If the rate has fallen 7%, the company would have to pay to the bank the difference of 1% for the period of the contract on the agreed amount. The bank may cover this position by taking futures contracts or to forward transactions to hedge interest rate exposure.

There are many other such derivative instruments, a few of which are referred here, but detailed discussion on derivatives is seen in a separate chapter.

**1. Caps:** These will ensure that interest paid will not be more than a cap rate for the borrower. To achieve this, the seller of the cap agrees to make a payment equal to the difference between the floating rate and the cap rate whenever, the former is higher than the rate agreed upon.

**2. Collar:** The purchaser of a cap need not pay a fee. If instead, the cap seller agrees to take compensation in the form of a payment whenever, the floating rate falls below a set level, namely, the floor, a collar thus, sets a ceiling and a floor for the fluctuation in interest rates. The collar amounts to a simultaneous purchase of a call option and sale of a put option by the collar-purchaser. The collars are similar to range forward contracts in foreign exchange and mini-maxi transaction on interest rates. By providing these services the banks earn fees and the higher the risk they take the higher is the fee. The banks in turn cover these positions by corresponding opposite positions to other parties or other banks. Banks can make more money by trading on technology based instruments than the spread on traditional borrowing and lending operations. Besides, the banks can continue to lend to small businesses and smaller companies whose credit rating is poor and hence, cannot enter these markets but by providing guarantees to those who want to enter these markets for direct access of funds.

The corporates dealing in these new instruments have to scrutinise carefully their own asset-liability matching and the risk that they are prepared to take. They have to take into account the following factors in particular:

(1) Legal position of entering into such contracts.

(2) Costs and benefits of these transactions.

(3) Any additional exposure to risks.

(4) Assessment of the balance sheet structure to know the extent of additional gearing that can be secured.

(5) Manage the credit risk and other risks of the third parties, involved.

(6) Flexibility of reversing the transactions.

## Multinational Corporations (MNCs)

The role of multinational corporations in the pattern of world production and trade has been increasing over the decades. As estimated by the Brandt Commission, they now control about one-third of the world production and the intra-national branch transfers of these MNCs would work out to about one-fourth of the world sales. The bulk of private investment is accounted for by the MNCs. The induction of latest technology and exploitation of the natural resources in the developing countries may be mainly due to the enterprise of multinational corporations. The oligopoly situation in their operations can be gleaned from the concentration of their productive capacity in the big 50 MNCs.[3]

## Definition

By definition, a multinational corporation is an enterprise which has "managerial headquarters located in one country while the enterprise carries out operations in a number of countries as well."[4] Either ownership is held in one country and control in another country or both in one country and the operations in many countries. The corporations have operations and sales extending to various countries with some of them exceeding the Gross National Product of even the advanced developed countries. The strategy of expansion is through private direct investment abroad through setting up of subsidiaries or branch offices or in joint ventures. As most of the companies have reached their limit of expansion in their own countries, the scope for expansion lies in foreign countries. For horizontal expansion, setting up conglomerates and integrating dissimilar activities, they arrange a holding company to have a number of subsidiaries in a number of countries. By vertical integration with forward and backward linkages, expansion takes place through branches and setting up of factories in other countries, for parts, spares, ancillaries, etc. Another method of expansion is re-investment and self-financing of the various diversified activities of the corporation in the existing countries. The transfer of technology, enterprise and sometimes managerial talent also go along with direct foreign investment by these corporations.

Nearly 50 per cent of the MNCs are based in the U.S. and the rest in the UK, France, Japan and West Germany, which are the major industrialised countries in the world. Industry-wise, the concentration of multinationals is in airlines and extractive industries, such as oils, minerals, etc. Now they are spread over a wide variety of industries such as engineering, chemicals, pharmaceuticals, software I.T., media and other services.

3. For detailed discussion, see Sanjay Lall, *The New Multinationals,* John Wiley and Sons, 1983, Chapter on "Multinationals from India."
4. I.L.O."Multinational Enterprises and Social Policy", 1973.

## Rationale of MNCs Domination

The key to the success of the MNCs lies in their broad-based operations, secrecy of their accounts and vast technological research base. They have control of not only the capital but also technology with which they seek investment avenues and markets in other developed and developing countries. The rationale for their expansion is both offensive as to capture new markets and defensive in the sense of retaining their share of the market in the teeth of competition. Their expansion is mostly in fields of minerals, oils and plantations, where foreign investment was welcomed historically in less developed countries. The scale of operations increases and costs per unit go down significantly. Similarly, larger technological transfers permit larger research and development costs, as they are now spread over a larger scale of operations. The establishment of their units in foreign countries is based on the availability of cheaper labour, managerial talent or other inputs or to reduce the transport costs or to expand their market and scale of operations. Secondly, they have the controlling interest in technology as well as capital which enables them to wield political as well as economic power in more than one country. They seek unexploited resources, natural as well as human in the developing countries for exploitation and to capture the markets. Besides, the foreign governments encourage the inflow of foreign direct investment, for the purpose of expansion of economic activity, income and employment. With the increasing tariff barriers and protectionism in most of the developed countries, MNCs have found a method of circumventing them by establishing their own factories, processing units and joint ventures in these countries. They also take advantage of tax-concession in some of the LDCs. They secure benefits of lower costs through technology-sharing, economies of scale, marketing and managerial expansion and a further boost to technological upgradation and R&D. The increasing role of MNCs has both advantages and disadvantages.

In conclusion, it is to the advantage of both the MNCs and their home countries to have their activities expanding in many countries. However, the host countries have both advantages and disadvantages due to flow of investments from the MNCs. The merits are briefly, the promotion of investments, income and employment in the host country, provision of latest technology with a productive capacity at low costs of production, increased competition with the domestic enterprise, and larger world trade which result in better all-around specialisation. The MNCs have also started adapting themselves to the requirements of the LDCs which are their host countries. Restrictions with respect to the direction of investments as well as the quantum, location and capacity and other regulations are generally complied with by them.

❖ ❖ ❖

# GOALS AND GROWTH OF MULTINATIONALS

3

## Emergence and Growth of MNCs

Environmental factors include increasing globalisation and changing business methods. Globalisation is dealt in this chapter and the business methods in the next chapter. Definitionally multinational corporation is one which operates in more than one country. It is engaged in producing and selling in many countries or producing in some countries and selling in the same or other countries. The *modus operandi* is that the parent company in one country would have subsidiaries or joint ventures in a number of other countries. Globalisation leads to growth of MNCs.

**1. Easy Mobility of Factors:** The classical theory of comparative advantage and specialisation of countries in some commodities gave way to more easy mobility of some factors of production in the modern global economy. With time and distance being conquered, communication and spread of information have brought the world closer. The growth of research and technology spread with the mobility of capital across borders aided globalisation. Labour, capital and enterprise become more mobile in search of potential uses and markets to cater to. Natural resources and differences in their endowments among countries no longer stood in the way of factors moving across borders. The endowments of countries in terms of skills of labour, management, technology and know-how and capital have been emphasised in the modern world of interdependence. These are all mobile and moved as between countries, to enjoy the economies of scale, apply latest developments in technology to exploit the untapped natural resources, and bring in the skills and knowledge for application in areas not covered so far or covered inefficiently and in relatively high cost combinations. The freer flow of factors, commodities and services will lower the costs and prices and increase the world welfare.

In the present day dynamic world, financial markets have become global and with that markets for commodities and services have tended to be global. Competition and free market forces have made it imperative for companies to produce in the cheapest markets and sell in the markets where there is a demand for those products at the prices as cheap as competition sets.

**2. Increased Role of Private Enterprise:** There are a number of other factors which explain the emergence of MNCs. The increased emphasis on the private sector and free market forces led to free mobility of finance or capital. Along with capital, ownership, production and distribution also moved across the borders. Some countries imposed barriers to foreign produced goods to come into the local markets. The reaction of the exporting companies is to move the production also into those local markets and along with that distribution. The scarcity of capital and the need to attract foreign funds forced the developing countries to allow the foreign companies to set up joint ventures and participate in equity and management of local companies. Sometimes foreign companies used the route of branches and subsidiaries to market their products locally and sometimes produce and market their products locally. That is how Gillette, Colgate, Zerox, Coca-Cola and a host of other products and name brands became household names in India. They all belong to U.S. multinational corporations.

**3. Trends of Globalisation:** The operations of MNCs will make their production, factor markets and product markets etc. global and multinational. It is globally co-ordinated strategy of allocation of resources, among different markets and countries that differentiates the multinational enterprise from other firms engaged in international trade in products and services. Many MNCs start with export and import business as first step to globalisation. After some familiarity with foreign markets and their capital requirements and potential demand and supply conditions, the foreign company switches from simple exporting to setting up a marketing network, distribution channels and depots for after sales services in the importing countries. This gives them an entry into these importing countries and finally leads to the setting up of a subsidiary for distribution and after sales services. If it has a tie up with a local firm for market penetration it may set up a joint venture.

**4. Seekers of Supplies and Markets:** In fact many multinationals first come to the developing countries as seekers of natural resources as inputs for their products. Many multinational giants in oil like British Petroleum and mining companies in Africa and Latin America and Asia belong to the category of seekers of natural resources, like mines, minerals, oil, etc., which they badly need for their parent countries.

The next category of earliest multinationals are seekers of markets for their products. They promote their brands, develop the market by creating a taste for them and then sell them in these markets. They are diversifying and expanding into various new markets. The bulk of the foreign direct investment after the Second World War was in the form of acquisition of plant and equipment of the local firms. This was in the form of flow of investment from USA to West Germany. Later, West European countries and Japan joined the bandwagon and made foreign investments in America, Africa and Asia.

These market seekers first produce in their home country and sell in the foreign markets. If the tariffs are high and there are other restrictions on their imports they invite the foreign capital for investment. Then multinational corporates start production also in the local markets, through a subsidiary or a joint venture with a local partner who is in this line of business.

**5. Goals of MNCs:** All multinationals seek to minimise costs and maximise profits. They seek to produce in areas where inputs are available cheaply and they bring in technology of theirs along with the capital from the cheapest Euro currency markets to set up production units in many countries and allocate resources through a centralised management strategy in many countries to produce at the cheapest centre and sell in the markets where there is a demand for them at the maximum profit. They need not sell in the country where they produce but where the market for them is located. The objective is wealth maximisation.

The other category of multinationals are those who want to expand their markets and thus, seek entry into other countries, where there is a market. Their globalisation efforts is a sheer commercial motive of profit maximisation through larger scale of production and enjoy economies of scale. Many drug companies have thus expanded in India like Glaxo, Cipla, Hoechst etc. Some of these MNCs have unique products or monopoly products due to their superior know-how and technology through R&D efforts and they want to cash in on them by enlarged markets in developing countries.

**6. Compelling Global Environment:** Thus, multinational operations of many corporates are the result of the circumstances, competition and environment, which force them to start with exports, then enter into joint ventures and lastly set up their own subsidiaries in these markets. Marketing and distribution leads to the setting up of the production units. The circumstances of the company may be such that they have to "expand or die" as the local markets are saturated and they have to seek markets abroad. The geographical endowments of their domestic economy does not have any further opportunities as in the case of oil and the domestic companies like Shell have to expand to oil rich countries. Thus, the natural resources, input availability, markets, need for economies of scale and a host of other external factors force the national companies to become multinational. This starts with exports of goods and services, followed by direct selling to MNCs, which when objected to by the concerned national governments, will lead to overseas production and sale. As a next step, overseas production started in countries with low costs, local skills and abundant labour accompanied by sales in third countries. This means that MNC belongs to USA or Japan but produces its products in India and sells in Africa or Europe or Latin America. Through local production, corporate production and marketing are integrated, sales network is developed and after sales service is ensured. By this means, the technology and capital of the home country is used in coordination with land and labour in the host country to produce some products for sale in host country or in home country or in third countries as the case may be. The need for adjusting to local tastes and conditions is to be satisfied and then local law and regulations are to be followed. Thus, familiarity with local conditions is a necessary condition for success of MNCs for their global operations.

The entry stage strategy varies from company to company and country to country. It may start with franchising or licensing a local firm to sell its products under its brand name for the local market. The return for the MNC is only royalty or franchise fees. This is earliest entry method but with low cash inflow.

Then there are other alternatives for MNCs, namely, direct selling, start a joint venture with a local firm, set up its own subsidiary or a branch incorporated in the host country or acquire local going concern. Each has its own advantages and disadvantages. In India since the economic reforms started in 1992, many FDI* proposals were approved, by the FIPB@. Direct selling firms were prohibited to operate in India at one time. They have either to manufacture the product locally or buy them from local SSI units or enter into a joint venture with a local firm for their manufacture in India. Items purely imported and not manufactured in India cannot be sold by foreign MNCs in India as per prevailing rules. During 1999 new patent law was passed and direct selling of some unique products is now allowed in India. This patent Act as amended in 2004 to conform "made in India" to the requirements of W.T.O. provides for patenting of generics of drugs and brands, made in India.

## Special Features of MNCs

MNCs have a different state of mind. They think globally, plan globally and act globally. In any decision of expansion or diversification they think in terms of where in the world should they set up their next plant. The management thinks globally in deciding the plant size, for the global market. The multinational financial management differs from domestic managements in the following factors:

(1) Seek out its capital needs from low cost markets on an international basis.

(2) Its investment proposals are decided on global basis and decided on simple cost benefit principle but on global basis. The investment opportunities are spread over the whole world and not confined to any single country.

(3) It has a commitment, dedication and perseverance to seek out opportunities in other countries, for joint venture, subsidiaries or branches for integrated production scale, for integrating production to marketing, R&D and for capturing financial opportunities on a global basis. It has no national barriers. It has competence and management skills and financial support to think and act globally.

(4) It is necessary for MNCs to integrate world wide operations. Its expertise lies in identifying its core competence and spread this expertise across nations without any national barriers.

(5) It must have flexible plans, adaptability and quickness in decision. Innovation initiative and competence with a vision are necessary inputs to the global players. They have the best, talented management and put the right person in the right place to operate on an independent basis and show results by which he is judged. Competition is taken as a challenge and they meet this with ease by lowering costs and raising the profit margins. The global operations are planned in a manner that overall total operations result in maximum profits. It is not always necessary that each country units show net profits or that each unit

* FDI is Foreign Direct Investment.

@ FIPB is Foreign Investment Promotion Body a using of the Government of India.

should be self sufficient and profitable, but the total net profits of all units should be maximised and shareholders' wealth is optimised. He has to develop an efficient MIS and R&D efforts.

## Traits of International Financial Manager

The traits of International Financial Manager are different from others. First in the rapidly changing world he is well informed and highly conversant in the core operations of the company. Change is the rule and competition is all pervading and ability of Global Manager lies in his knowledge, competence and his adjustability to change which are necessary to meet challenges of competition.

In making a decision, the Global Manager seeks various alternative countries, sites and locations-where the raw-materials are located and where the markets exist and what are the cost effective methods of relating the inputs to outputs. In the sourcing of inputs he surveys on a global scale the alternative sources and the available markets and plans how to meet them at least cost. Funds are available to him from global financial markets and he has his own internal resources. He has a vision for global operations, split into areas on a geographical basis, anticipates and forecasts the markets where he is operating and understands the trends and is quick to capture the best opportunities available to the company's advantage. His single minded goal is optimisation of the wealth of the shareholders of his company.

The Global Manager has to be well informed of the laws and regulations, social and political systems, habits and customs, and the totality of the economic forces operating in all the countries in which he is operating. In particular the labour problems and political pressures operating in some countries inhibit the progress to globalisation. The Global Manager has to be acquainted with these problems and knows how to deal with them. Many domestic factors of the home country of MNCs oppose these global operations as they export jobs and incomes to the host countries. But the emerging trend is towards global market integration as in the case of U.S.-Canada free trade pact and European Economic community's drive to have a common market. The markets even in developing countries are getting closer by such free trade agreements as in the case of India and Srilanka in 1999 (or SAARC).

The main thrust of a global MNC is the global thinking-the state of mind-spread of its activities and assets in different countries. It is distinguished by agility of penetration into new market segments, seeking out new markets, integrating marketing in one place with manufacture in another place; R&D in yet another place and embracing financing opportunities on a global basis. The Global Manager manages change, anticipates the forthcoming changes and plans for them. The quality of decision making is initial for prospect of survival and growth of MNC. The basic goal of his operations in a global scale of how to maximise the wealth of the shareholders of his company. Some centres may be bad or poor profit earners but the overall operations of all centres are taken into account in accounting for profitability. They have no inhibitions in closing a loss making unit.

## Growth of MNCs

"Twenty years ago there were about 7000 MNCs. Today, this figure stands at over 35000. The top 100 of these commanded a phenomenal $ 3000 billion in assets." Adrian Buckley ("International Capital Budgeting" published by Prentice Hall.) Out of Global 500 MNCs listed by the Time Magazine about 200 are already operating in India and 300 are operating in China. The reason why India lost about 100 global companies' resources is that India's policies are not as welcome as China's. China has better economic growth, stable political system and favourable government policies towards foreign investment, which give an advantage over India. India's tax treatment of foreign investment is such that income is not tax free as in the case of China. India does not give an exit policy for labour and India's reservation of some hundreds of industries to small scale sector stands in the way of attracting foreign investment. In short, China is very liberal and generous to foreign investment unlike India, which explains the larger foreign investment and larger number of MNCs operating in China. Thus, India has lost about 100 MNCs, potentially willing to make foreign investment in India too, but reluctant to do so, due to less generous treatment and less liberal policies of India, red tape and rampant corruption.

It is possible that a change in government policies, its tax treatment of foreign investment income, and reduction of red tape and administrative hassles may encourage more MNCs to operate in India bringing with it, technology, jobs, trading relations and so on.

## Rationale of Growth of MNCs

The MNCs control billions of dollars the world over. Their growth is faster in the last three decades. This was due to growth of private foreign direct investment. There are strategic reasons for growth of direct foreign investment such as need for expansion and diversification and the need for market imperfections, hindrances to free trade and differences in factor endowments, transport costs and government and central bank restrictions in many countries, which also necessitated the big corporations in developed countries to set up subsidiaries or branches or joint ventures etc., in a way to get over the above hurdles.

Maximisation of profits or wealth of the company and minimisation of costs-both manufacturing and selling-are the objectives of the multinationals. They thrive on market imperfections-both structural or natural and man-made. The structural imperfections in markets and the need for market penetration and expansion, transport costs, differences in factor endowments and the need for their exploitation on a world wide basis are the rationale for expansion of MNC operations in these countries. The economies of scale in production, reduction in costs of production and marketing and the need for updating the technology through expenditure on research and development give the rationale for growth of MNCs. The other examples of market imperfections are the uncertainty whether a supplier will deliver the goods promised from abroad, volatility of exchange rates, the costs of negotiating deals as between countries, difficulty of knowing the foreign suppliers and in evaluating their products give advantage to locally placed producers and distributors, which MNCs get if placed locally.

Man-made imperfections are the government restrictions on imports, taxes and subsidies, undeveloped capital markets and monopolistic or oligopolistic markets. There may also be central bank restrictions on foreign exchange flows, exchange rates and controls on banks and foreign exchange markets, etc.

To help augment the operations of MNCs, banks have become multinational. Similarly accounting firms and consultancy firms became multinational like PriceWaterHouse, Arthur Anderson, and Lebrandt which being placed in many nations have acquired the knowledge of local rules, regulations and law, relating to accountancy, audit, etc. Quality and reputation go as hallmarks for their entry into other countries.

*The Reasons for their Growth are:*

(1) Local skills and availability of cheap labour.

(2) Availability of raw-materials and inputs in any productive process.

(3) Availability of markets for their products.

(4) Possible vertical and horizontal integration in the production process.

(5) Availability with them of non-transferable proprietary knowledge, patents, copyrights and technical know-how.

(6) For protecting secrecy, direct investment is preferred to granting a licence or sharing in a Joint Venture.

(7) Foreign direct investment, which leads to the entry of MNCs into a country may be motivated by plentiful natural resources unexploited locally like oil, gas, minerals, and infrastructure and services, as in Asia and Africa.

(8) Complementary resources may be available and natural endowments may differ as between countries, which make the entry of MNCs attractive.

(9) Protecting and exploiting reputations of some firms may make them MNCs, as in the case of Birlas, Tatas and Ambanis.

(10) High level of R&D expenditure and availability of plentiful capital may push some firms to become multinational, like Ranbaxy and Dr. Reddy Labs.

Raymond Vernon has argued that due to drying up of opportunities at home, some corporations have become multinational or go abroad to maintain their rate of growth and for investor wealth maximisation. International investment follows international trade and where market penetration is needed, MNCs will enter in. As per the product life cycle hypothesis, firms come to reach a stage in life cycle when they have to expand abroad due to stagnation of growth at home.

## The Hold of MNCs

MNCs retain their hold in foreign markets by lower costs, better quality, good reputation, larger expenditure on R&D and their secrecy of formulation and product manufacturing process and some monopoly element in their brands, products and product range.

Capital availability is one of the reasons why MNCs move to other countries and retain their hold. In addition to the cause of risk diversification, Robert Alber has suggested that cheaper access of funds to some companies can be reason for companies to move abroad. However, differential cost of capital of companies cannot be a reason according to Edward Graham and Paul Krugman.[1] According to the latter, the majority of the foreign direct investments have been a two-way flow as Japan investing in USA and USA investing in Japan which cannot be explained by differential costs of capital. Secondly, the form of investment (FDI) need not be due to differential costs of capital as the same can take the form of portfolio investment.

Strategic reasons for the FDI are the globalisation of markets, particularly the financial markets that reduced the entry barriers, composition that threatened their market share in the world over, and for avoidance of tariff and quota barriers in some countries. As producing at home and exporting attract these barriers, the alternative of producing in the local markets through FDI is resorted to. Richard E. Caves has argued that FDI route is adopted to overcome the impact of tariffs in the host country and gave a geometrical explanation of the effect of tariffs on direct investments in his book on "Multinational Enterprise and Economic Analysis", Cambridge University press.

## Empirical Evidence

Evaluation of data on direct investments by USA in foreign countries revealed that more investment occurs in countries that have offered investors higher returns. MNCs as opposed to domestic companies (DCs) have some special characteristics relating to the company as such and/or the industry in which the companies are operating. Basically, MNCs are motivated by investor wealth maximisation, larger profits and higher returns on their capital employed. There appears to be some connections between domestic economic activity and the level of foreign investment. The host country should be having high levels of economic activity but with capacity to absorb more capital investment or the host country is not doing well but with potential for growth. The motives and determinants of capital flows are dealt with in later chapters.

Irving Krairs and Robert Lipsey[2] found a number of characteristics which differentiate the MNC from the domestic companies. These are listed in the Table below:

**TABLE 3.1**
**Comparison**

| *MNCs* | *DCs* |
|---|---|
| (1) Larger investment in R&D | Less investment in R&D |
| (2) They have control on cheaper capital | Do not have large excess reserves |
| (3) Access to cheaper funds | No access |
| (4) Rating is higher | Rating is not so high |
| (5) Capital intensive | Not capital intensive |
| (6) International diversification | Domestic diversification |
| (7) Ambitious and expansionist | Less ambitious and less adventurous |
| (8) Lower costs and better quality control and sound financial management. | Not efficient financial management |

1. Graham Edward, M. and Paul R. Krugman, "Foreign Direct Investment in the United States", *Institute of International Economics,* Washington D.C., 1991.
2. I. Krairs and R. Lipsey, "The Location of Overseas Production and Production for Export," *Journal of International Economics,* May 1982.

## MNCs — Problems

MNCs have brought numerous problems with them. By control on huge assets they are a factor to reckon with both politically and economically. They get political influence by their money power through their local contacts. They can manipulate prices and earn huge profits. They can concentrate on the skilled jobs, specialised tasks, leaving the routine and less important work to the local men. They however, involve local alliances, to make the country feel that it is a local firm with their persons manning at various levels of contact with local suppliers or distributors. They can get over many regulations by clever manipulations. They can exploit the local consumers by over pricing and make monopoly profits being motivated by self-interest and high profits. By using the transfer pricing mechanism and other methods, they can manipulate the accounts and reduce the tax liability.

They also use the technique of transnational alliances in different countries, which give them access to foreign markets. By this method, they enter into agreements with local firms to work in co-operation in high technology tasks, and areas of computers, pharmaceuticals, defence materials etc., where direct entry for foreign investment may not be permitted. This method is Joint Venture with local partners as in the case of Modiluft or Modi Zerox. The other methods of entering into foreign markets by MNCs are to set up subsidiaries, and branches for granting marketing/brand franchise to local firms.

## Objectives

The major problem of MNCs is thus, the entry into the foreign markets. But the basic motives for getting access to foreign markets are many and varied.

(1) Economies of scale operate to expand production and trade by MNCs for which they seek markets.

(2) The risk of international exposure being high, they seek diversification of product range and access to different types of markets, both for inputs and outputs.

(3) Their objective is cost minimisation and profit maximisation and this is achieved by seeking inputs where they are cheapest through Business Process Outsourcing; B.P.O. method and manufacturing intermediates and parts in the countries where the wage bills are low. They can secure all the inputs and intermediates from different countries and assemble them in their own country and sell in a number of other countries where there is a demand for the price, which the market can bear.

(4) Different factor endowments in different countries and different levels of technological advances make it possible for MNCs to explore scope for international collaboration and intra-national transactions in trade and aid.

(5) Both the host country and the country of origin will benefit by these international transactions in terms of costs, profits, larger consumption and production and a higher standard of life. But in this process, the problems faced by the MNCs are various risks of political and social constraints, legal and regulatory frameworks, different tax systems, problems of accounting and auditing standards, etc., which are discussed in later chapters.

❖ ❖ ❖

# INTERNATIONAL BUSINESS METHODS

# 4

## Globalisation and MNCs

Increasing globalisation and changing business methods are adjuncts and go together. These are dealt with in this chapter. Organisation and systems are also discussed in this chapter. With the globalisation of markets along with the deregulation and liberalisation the markets have become freer and open to global players-both Indian and foreign. The Indian corporates are thrown open to the winds of change and competition became severe with the foreign MNCs entering the fray along with the Indian MNCs. The markets are widened and foreign inflows and outflows have become freer. Foreign direct investment is encouraged in India along with the Foreign Portfolio Investment. Exports and imports face less restrictions, particularly in quantitative terms. When global players operate in Indian markets and Indian players go global, the first thing they face is more severe *competition* both in costs and quality. After sales service and market research also become crucial for survival. The fittest and strongest survive while the weaker go to the walls. There will be new entries and exits among the corporates. Mergers and acquisition become more common and corporates will try to strengthen their core strengths, shed the fat in other directions and put on weight in the direction where they have some competitive advantages, expertise and special skills.

## Global Winds of Change

With the widening of the markets, for both inputs and outputs, costs of production, sales and marketing costs and other costs undergo changes. The alternatives for both inputs and outputs get widened. This is particularly so in the financial markets and costs of the capital structure and the capital costs will undergo some changes. Both risk and return scenario change. The corporate Treasurers will find new challenges for expansion and diversification and available opportunities will be enlarged.

The globalisation of business has profound effect on

(1) Corporate governance and corporate strategy

(2) Corporate goals and objectives and

(3) Corporate financial strengths and weaknesses

(4) Corporate product markets and input markets both in direction and content.

Many corporate managements are not prepared for these changes, but as it is a matter of survival and survival of the fittest, corporate managements wake up to see the realities of growing competition advantages of financial strength, the importance of cost and quality control to stand up to the competition and to plan for financial resources from a wider spectrum including the international money and capital markets, Euro-markets and a host of alternative sources, now available. The role of financial engineering and reengineering and innovation in financial products, derivatives and other alternatives available to the new breed of corporate managers has altered the whole financial scenario. Corporate financial structure and the routes open to optimisation of shareholder's wealth have changed. The goal of optimisation of wealth has opened up new challenges and new avenues.

## New Challenges and Opportunities

With globalisation, the shareholders or the owners may become globally spread. Input and output markets become global. Financial Markets are now opened up and they become globalised. The revolution in Information Technology, telecommunications and in electronic media has made the whole world closer and nearer, as distance and time are conquered by these revolutions. These are new tides of the ocean which taken up at the right time will lead on to the new fortunes. Those who are late or weak will not survive the competition. Natural forces now operate, interest rates move freely and exchange rates change more frequently and the whole behaviour of the market becomes more volatile and dynamic. Only those managements who are alert, agile and more skilled can take up these opportunities for expanding the markets, strengthening financially and optimise the shareholders' wealth by quick and prompt changes in policy and action and meet the challenges opened up due to the emerging forces of free market competition and globalisation. Global markets, both for inputs and outputs and financial resources have thrown open many opportunities and challenges. Space and time are no longer constraints due to revolution in technology. Corporate management have to adapt themselves to the new sources of fund flows and interlinkages between markets, at the domestic and international levels. They have to change their strategies and undergo a sea-deep transformation to meet the new challenges and opportunities. They have to come out of the protective shells and face the chill winds of competition on a world wide basis.

## Importance of Global Factors

Scarce capital will flow more efficiently from less productive countries to more productive countries and for less profitable ventures to more profitable ventures and capital can now be sourced from cheapest methods and markets all over the world. There will be a wider base or avenues for securing low cost capital and for restructuring the capital base with least cost combination of instruments and methods. There will be mobility to other factors also, namely, human skills, enterprise and technology.

Besides, the scope for freer exports and imports will increase and costs can be lowered due to comparative cost advantage and exploitation of available low cost alternatives due to different factor endowments and freer flow of capital and technology. Both input costs and output costs can be lowered and freer exports and imports of goods and services will lower costs and increase outputs and consumption.

Both short-term and long-term finance will now be available from both domestic and foreign sources and corporates can source the funds at cheapest sources depending upon the purpose of borrowing, whether for investment or working capital purposes or for consumption. Availability of capital, when needed, provides a guaranteed access and reduces the locking of funds and high costs of borrowing. In addition to normal requirements, the contingency requirements can also be met from these sources through back up lines of credit. Money can be now had for revitalisation of the units, modernisation, expansion and diversification and even for acquisition and mergers as these are some of the methods of financial restructuring. The leveraged buy outs and diversification into related and unrelated areas will be a means of financial and technological strengthening which is so necessary for new scenario of global markets.

## Cheaper Sourcing of Funds

Corporates require both debt and equity and various combinations of debt and equity and their need is dependent on the purpose, state of growth of the company and the market conditions. Group activities, joint ventures, acquisitions and divestments of some divisions or lines of activity, shedding the fat in some directions and putting on weight in other directions will be the order of the day in emerging corporate world.

The requirements for multicurrency loans, bridge loans, flexi-rate loans and guarantees and limits for drawal in different currencies will all be available in global markets. In fact, the global markets will produce new financial products as the demand emerges. The depth and width of the markets will expand so fast, that there will be no need which cannot be met by global financial markets.

Those who supply funds in the global markets are those who have excess funds either through balance of payments surpluses of countries or free flow of capital funds across borders. Major innovations are taking place in covering and repackaging of risks, and technology upgradation makes it possible to produce anything for which a need arises. The global scenario expands both demand and supply factors in all cross border markets.

In the present day scenario, the official lendable resources of world bodies like IBRD and International Monetary Fund (IMF) have declined sharply. Soft loans from multilateral agencies have dried up. Supranational bodies lending for commercial purposes like IFC, Asian Development Bank ADB, etc., have reduced access to the traditional sources of funds, namely, USA, UK and Japan. In this background, governments find it difficult to secure funds from the traditional sources even for balance of payments purposes. The only source available is the free markets of European commercial banks through the Euro dollar and Euro-currency markets or offshore funds.

Normally, the governments and central banks of the countries find it easy to raise funds in these markets due to the sovereign debt that they seek. But private corporate units find it difficult to raise funds in these markets unless their credit rating is high and they are export-oriented multinational giants like Tatas, Ambanis, Birlas, etc.

## Regulatory and Legal Framework

The operations of borrowing and lending are governed by the law of the country where the lender is situated. The International Court of Justice has of course jurisdiction and both the borrower and lender have to agree to abide by a legal system which is acceptable to both. International Chamber of Commerce and International Court of Justice are the agencies generally relied upon. But more particularly, the documents and agreements between the parties may specify the law of their choice which should govern their contracts and agreements. In the event of breach of contract or disputes between the parties, the mention of an express choice of law is preferred in documents entered into between the parties.

Only the government has the option to approach the International Court of Justice. The government will not take up cases of private parties to this body. Thus, individuals and corporate bodies have no chance to have recourse to the international court and international law. The International Chamber of Commerce however can adjudicate in the event of both the parties agreeing to this procedure. But it is generally incorporated in the agreements that the matters of dispute between the parties to the contract will be settled by a specific process of law or procedure or the courts of the host country, where the MNCs operate.

## Assumption of Perfect Markets

The globalised system of markets and economic activity presupposes the acceptance of the free market forces as opposed to the controlled and planned economic system by a centralised planning process or communistic political system where private enterprise and free market system do not operate. Globalised market system gives prominence to the free market forces leading to allocative efficiency of factors and capital and competitive market conditions, where supply and demand determine the price and costs have to adjust to the price. Cost control and quality control become essential planks for globalised market system. Pricing mechanism operates to allocate resources optimally and efficiently and government will have no role in this process. The information flow is free and costless and securities markets and financial markets operate under pure demand and supply factors and competition brings about the equilibrium price which equates the demand and supply. This *laissez faire* philosophy in the operation of global markets is justified if the markets are efficient and absorb all information quickly. These factors do not operate in real life and markets are not perfect. In such a situation, there is segmental theory which postulates that there are different segments in markets and in each segment demand and supply factors bring about equilibrium and prices and interest rates in each of the segment may differ. The common factors influencing all these segments are inflation or purchasing power, government policies and the available information. But differences start with the changes in expectations of the future demand and supply, future inflation rates and other factors operating on the markets.

## Monopoly and Semi-monopoly Conditions

Whether it is in the goods markets or factor markets, the brand names, promotion, market interference by vested interests, monopoly elements or the government may lead to truncated markets and price differentials exist due to assumed or real differences. In the financial markets, the demand and supply for financial products also suffer from similar imperfections, interference by the Central Bank or the government of the country. Globalised system cannot create perfection in the markets. It can only create greater competition and emphasis on efficiency and productivity. Corporates are put to financial discipline and are exposed to competitive forces. They are compelled to adopt cost effective and efficient methods of utilisation of input factors to optimise the profits by minimising the costs in general and capital costs in particular. Capital structuring, product designing, transfer prices and marketing strategies will all undergo changes in tune with the competition of the multinationals in the field.

## Global Sourcing

One of the characteristics of the MNC's operation is globalisation of sourcing of inputs and financial resources and globalisation of product markets and factor markets. Japanese and U.S. corporates increasingly depended on outside sources, depending on the lowest cost alternatives. For example, Japanese Toyota depended on outsourcing to the extent of 60 to 70% of the total requirements as against 30%-40% for General Motors of the U.S.A. The sourcing pattern followed was the most competitive strategy based on costs and prices relative to quality.

The reasons for offshore purchases are the following:

(1) Price/Cost consideration and quality.

(2) More advanced technology.

(3) More co-operative delivery and consistent attitude.

(4) Counter trade requirements or agreements with subsidiaries, branches, collaborators.

(5) Reduction of use of capital and labour.

Outsourcing has also some disadvantages:[1]

(1) Leads to problems or issues other than those of costs and prices.

(2) Reduces flexibility of own planning.

(3) Customer services and core competencies might suffer.

(4) There might be hidden costs, not evaluated.

(5) Current cost accounting ignores the possible currency exchange rate changes.

Peter F. Drucker, the well-known Management Guru argued that production sharing will be "the most important form of economic integration needed by developed and developing countries alike. In production sharing the resources of developing countries-their abundant labour for traditional jobs-are brought together with the resources of developed countries — their management, their technology, their educated people, their markets and purchasing power".[2]

Substantial part of production sharing takes place among developed countries. But it is more advantageous to developing countries if they are involved. It is a fallout of the growing international sourcing, which is increasing in more recent times leading to more horizontal diversification with less need for vertical integration. About one-third of the world trade is accounted by international sourcing. This leads to the practice of carrying out different stages of manufacturing of a product in several countries. Auto manufacture is an example of this practice, as Indian auto components industry has become suppliers of heavy weights like General Motors, Renault, Fiat etc.

This trend of international sourcing is rising over years with the increasing operations of transnational corporations, who operate in several countries in the globe. This is particularly true of computers, software products, auto industry, high-tech electronic products where final products are multi country products.

## Global Organisational Restructuring

Organisation under globalisation is a dynamic phenomenon, involving integration of organisation theory, organisation functioning, organisation design and performance. The objectives of an economic unit determines the characteristics of the organisation.

Change is the order under globalisation and adaptation of organisation to change is organisational adaptation. Organisational Theory postulates the adaptation of the organisation to the external environment. It is the human behaviour in the organisation that determines the organisational adaptation to the given environment leading to the organisational practice. Organisation theory states what is expected and practice shows what has happened. Organisational performance is explained by the theory and practice.

Organisation, components and activities, are influenced by environment through human behaviour. Organisational adaptation is explained by the Organisational Dynamics Model, which is basically rooted in the dynamics of causation, modification and outcome of human behaviour in organisations.

1. Edward W. Davis, "Global Out Sourcing", *Business Horizon,* July-August, 1992.
2. Peter F. Drucker, "Managing in Turbulent Times" (New Delhi, Allied Publishers), 1981.

**Chart : 4.1**

## Organisation-Design for Globalisation

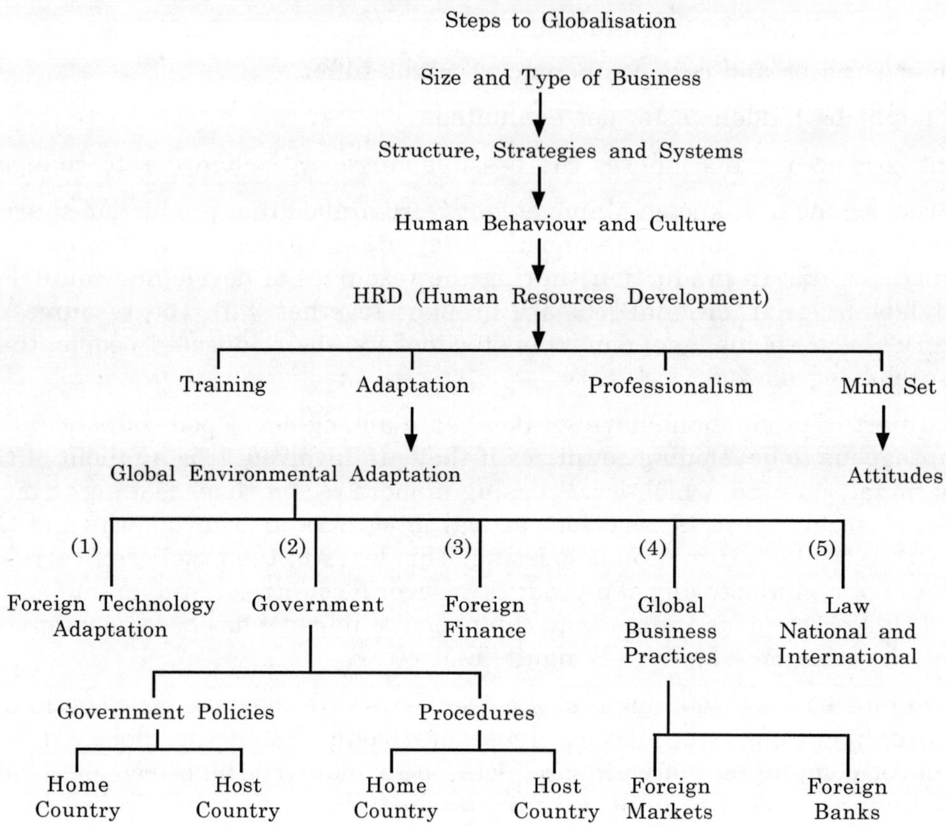


Globalisation involves environmental adaptation and behavioural adaptation of an organisation. Each organisation is evolved on the basis of its culture, tradition and precedents. It can thus, be a partnership culture, family business culture or closely held business culture etc. To this, is added the management goals and ideology and the degree of professionalisation which it has accepted and adopted. As behavioural adaptation is involved, the human resources, their culture preferences and values etc., are involved in the globalisation process. Chart 4.1 presents a design for Globalisation through organisational change

Building Blocks of Globalisation are as follows:

(1) Management Goals, Mission and Process.

(2) Corporate Citizenship, Code of Conduct, Ethics.

(3) Foreign Tie-ups, J.V.s, Alliances, Mergers etc.

(4) Professional Management (Professionalisation).

(5) Technology, Foreign INTERESTS, ADAPTATION.

(6) Foreign Finance, Foreign Markets, Foreign Culture.

(7) Evolution of Global Organisational Structure.

Organisational design for globalisation is set out in the chart above.

## Components of Organisational Change

(1) Management philosophy, objectives, openness and flexibility to change.

(2) Strategies adapted:

*(i)* Innovation, decentralisation, motivation.

*(ii)* New customised and country wise production strategies and inter country co-ordination for overall strategy.

*(iii)* Foreign/global marketing, standardised brands, patents, copyrights, cost effective distribution centres.

*(iv)* Foreign technology adaptation, innovation and inventions, R&D.

*(v)* Globally competent professional management.

*(vi)* Global sourcing, Global finance, cost-effective capital structure etc.

(3) Development of proper Structures:

*(i)* For production at transnational levels.

*(ii)* Optimal mix of production centres.

*(iii)* Optimal mix of marketing centres.

*(iv)* Specialised functions of R&D, global financing and marketing strategies.

(4) *M.I.S.,* sophisticated system of control, audit, co-ordination of accounts and efficient system of collection and dissemination of information on various markets.

(5) Global practices and procedures like international tax planning, adaptation to international legal and regulatory systems and Transfer pricing, transparent accounting and Audit systems.

(6) Human Resources Development, enrichment of staff skills, decentralisation, efficient and quick communication system and promotion of Adaptive skill of the organisation.

## Divisions/Departments (Sub-systems)

Each organisation has its own supporting Departments/Divisions, which are called sub-systems, which are general for all corporates and some of which are specific to globalised environment. These general divisions are normal to all corporates departments like production department, marketing department, collection department, cash department, etc. The sub-systems which are specific to the globalised environment are the following:

Marketing faces international competition and aggressive marketing and tie-ups and alliances are necessary to face this environment and supporting sub-systems for this are supply sources, distribution network, innovative techniques of marketing like telemarketing, website advertisement etc.

Management requires supporting sub-systems of professionalism, strategic planning, corporate governance and a code of ethics. Similarly technology requires both innovation of new productlines and adaptation of foreign technologies. The required sub-system are

HRD, R&D, Personnel and Engineering Departments. Finance function requires international finance sub-division and division of financial services. Human Resources is a sub-system which requires supporting sub-system of Manpower planning, Training, Voluntary Retirement Systems VRS, Motivating and Rewarding sub systems. Accounting and Auditing requires sub-systems of constant dollar accounting, generally accepted principles of accounts, social accounting and accounting as per international standards, transfer pricing etc.

Thus, each sub-system has many supporting sub-systems, which caters to the requirements of adaptation to the exigencies of environment specific to globalisation. Adaptation involves new products, new process and new systems.

## Structure and Systems

Global environment makes it obligatory for Indian corporates to take up externally the restructuring, proper strategy making and quicker adaptation to change and internally take up the sophistication and skill development of human resources and professionalisation of management.

Structure and systems under globalisation face a variety of environmental factors which need adjustment. Thus the typology of turbulence, or conflict situations arise which requires the management to resort to conflict resolving style, dependence on market research, advertisement, forecasting etc. There can be increasing hostility from the consumers/competitors which necessitates standardised output and operations, use of new brands, change in product mix, etc.

Heterogeneity of staff requires participatory management style and technologically complex product mix necessitates sophisticated control, automated, computerised operations and management philosophy has to change to strategic planning, optimisation process and quick adaptation to changes.

Organisational structure is thus a product of environmental factors, both internal and external. Systems and procedures are adjusted flexibly to the dictates of global factors and changes in the global environment. Any change in government policies of parent country or host countries or tax laws of participating countries are for example, the most dynamic environmental factors influencing the management style, systems and procedures.

## Pre-requisites for Globalisation

Management style has to be highly flexible in the global environment. Global players have to adopt strategic planning to meet with the dynamic changes, in the environment that they face. The organisation which enters the global role has to be financially strong, large in size and operations, and good in corporate goals and ethics. They have to take into account foreign interests, through entering into joint ventures, collaborations and marketing tie-up and adoption to technology upgradation. The essential requirement in product strategy is to have large scale operations, many product lines to suit different market segments and aggressive advertisement. Professional management, global sourcing and global finance and global marketing are the planks for good global players.

Organisation has to be in general risk-taking, dynamic, optimising, planning and participative in style of function. There has to be decentralisation of decision-making and accountability of all levels. Entrepreneurial and professional type of management is the *sine qua-non* of success.

Organisation design is to find the best fit type, taking into account the human resources availability, technological and structural factors in the industry and environment in which the organisation is located. The innovation, R&D effort, latest technology absorption and professionalisation of management are the hallmarks to global players. The Indian corporates have to develop these organisational skills and behavioural patterns in management style, philosophy and functioning and in staff skills, attitudes, motivation and reward-punishment systems. Labour problems and trade union activity might stand in the way of free entry and exit policies and hire and fire policy, which are suitable for foreign MNCs. The human resource development should aim at meeting these challenges of conflict situations between management and labour, crisis situations due to poor liquidity by proper crisis management skills. The manpower expertise should be able to meet the emerging situations through proper change management, event management, crisis management and a host of other unforeseen developments as they emerge in the operation and growth of MNCs.

## Business Methods

In the above context, the business methods in the MNCs undergo vast and diverse changes. They face challenges in all directions which may drive them to become more competitive and efficient. Their method is to expand to survive and to enjoy the economies of scale. They strengthen their business by mergers and acquisitions. They are highly cost conscious and go for outsourcing for their inputs or accessories. Many U.S. companies have business processing outside (BPO) in labour efficient and labour cheap countries like China and India. They secure financial inputs for their production from the cheapest sources like LIBOR-related currency markets or international banks or domestic banks.

In the sale of their product mix, they explore the markets where, there is a growing demand and the demand is inelastic and charge prices at what the markets can bear. Some MNCs are unscrupulous and make exorbitant profits by charging heavily much beyond the cost of production. They do not care for the preservation of environment as in the case of Union Carbide in Bhopal or for conservation of nature by discharging effluents and wastages without proper treatment for health care. The MNCs resort to product differentiation, assumed or real quality changes, aggressive sales proforma and brand and patent registration and presentation. Professional and business ethics are set aside and they resort to unscrupulous methods of avoiding taxes, laws and regulations of the host country and meet the corruption and red-tapism in the host country by their own dubious methods.

Ideally, global companies have to observe best corporate governance rules of transparency, full disclosures, social responsibility and business ethics. They may aim at profit maximisation but subject to the constraints of good corporate governance; law, rules and taxation are honoured and customer and investor friendly relations are maintained.

❖ ❖ ❖

# NATURE OF INTERNATIONAL RISK EXPOSURE

# 5

## Introduction

International risks can be broadly classified into those of goods and services and flows of funds which are involved in all international transactions. General character of exposures and risk management are discussed together along with environmental factors. The Corporate Treasurer encounters many types of risks in investment and market operations. In particular the global treasurer faces daily two types of volatility, namely, price and interest rate volatility. The price volatility is managed generally by diversification and adjustment of portfolio Beta to the required risk tolerable in relation to the market Beta. The price fluctuations are wider in the case of equity than in the case of debt. The interest rate changes affect the bond prices more than the equity prices. Generally the higher the interest rate the lower is the bond price and the actual degree of fluctuation depends on the maturity period, coupon rate and expectations. The use of derivative market also helps to hedge against price and interest rate changes. There are many alternative solutions to the problem and the actual strategy depends on the company policy and constraints which the company is faced with.

In the global markets, similarly, he is faced in daily life both interest rate and currency fluctuations. There may be different alternative methods available to the Finance Manager. The actual strategy depends on the guidelines and policy directions given by the top management to the Finance Manager. Some of the hedging policies which may be adopted can be set out here:

(1) Hedge nothing to have the exposures as they are in the hope that downward and upward risks may cancel out and that taking risks would tantamount to higher returns. This policy may lead to management inefficiency in that they fail to take advantage of covering risks before they affect the profitability of the company.

(2) Hedge everything is the opposite of the above policy of hedge nothing. Here, the company is risk averse and this scenario is called low risk-low return option. The company covers all potential risks and foregoes all potential gains by risk taking in preference to the certainties of outcome.

(3) Internal hedging is a strategy of matching the outflows with corresponding inflows both in quantity and timing. This is a difficult exercise as many imponderables influence the inflows and outflows and exact matching of them is next to impossible situation.

(4) Usage of home currency and confining all transactions in rupees would avoid the currency risk. But then the company is not optimising the shareholders' wealth and the opportunities available in global markets are not taken advantage of Confining to deals in domestic currency both in respect of inputs and outputs will lead to no currency exposures which is a "lose-lose" game as opposed to risk taking which may lead to a "win-win" game, as risk is rewarded by return.

(5) Hedge selectively is another option in which calculated risks are taken in currencies, which are more familiar to the operator and which are technically strong. Hedging is to be done in currencies which are weak and take a calculated risk in strong currencies. Thus, if dollar is expected to be strong in the short-run, the operator may leave some exposures in dollars uncovered while the risks in French franc and yen are covered. If in the long-run yen is to appreciate, some long-term contracts in yen may be left uncovered. Most commonly used strategy by global players is this 'hedging selectively.' The parent country's currency is the one in which the MNCs generally take a position or keep exposures open while taking hedge in other currencies.

(6) Matching by leading and lagging. This is the policy of avoiding the risk by matching the currency of price and cost. It is a serious option open to the company. If there are more than one currency in which inputs are secured, then it is better to put all costs in the currency in which major costs are incurred.

All the payments in foreign currencies do not exactly coincide with receipts. Either the amounts are different or currencies are different or the timing may be different. Flexibility of timing is needed to optimise flows by leading and lagging. By the shortening and lengthening of trade credits received or given, one can adjust the timing. The company normally accelerates the collection and conversion of weak currency receivables or delay disbursements in weak currency payables or strong currency receivables as the circumstances may dictate. The treasurer has to take the opportunities that the market offers in respect of acceleration of receipts or payments or delaying them. Time element in risk is discussed in a separate chapter.

## Netting Method

A company uses the netting method-that is netting of the receivables and payables in the same currency for hedging the net position as the exposure. The purpose of multilateral netting is to reduce the exposure and hedging requirements in each of the currencies dealt in. The multinationals will deal with this situation in a manner that each country's subsidiary is a separate entity and risks in the currency of the parent company can be kept open while the currencies of other countries are covered up. Alternatively, multicurrency hedging in various proportions, as desired, can be had in the derivative markets futures and options.

Holding accounts or deposits in other countries in their currencies, other than that of the parent company is considered desirable in all situations when receipts and payments do not tally. Many companies keep U.S. dollar accounts for this purpose. If the payments are in currencies other than dollar, dollars in these accounts can be converted into the desirable currencies and if any receipts have come in currencies other than dollar, they can be quickly converted into dollar for the simple reason that dollar is a strong currency and is unlikely to become weak in the short-run except in deep recession as in 2009. Holding accounts in dollars thus, helps the collection of receivables in any currency and disbursement of payables in foreign currency by conversion into and out of dollars, more easily than in the case of others.

## General Risks

In all international transactions of goods and services, there are many risks from the beginning to the end. Firstly, there is the credit risk arising out of the credit worthiness of the opposite party in another country. That party risk can arise in both export and import trade, due to lack of information and knowledege about the other party. The possibility of default in honouring the contract or agreement, lack of credibility or dishonesty and failures in sticking to standards of quality and quantity of goods, specified in the agreement are possible.

Secondly, there is transit risk in shipping and airways for sending specified goods abroad. There can be accidents, acts of God, war or contingencies in the process of transit, leading to high risks on the parties.

Thirdly, there are risks in banking operations of the parties, due to high costs of borrowing or lending or interest rate and exchange rate fluctuations, the counterparty guarantee and margin payments may go adverse to the party. Time is the essence of the contract but the parties and bank may fail in the timeliness or promptness. Even computer mistakes may lead to transfer failures or in party advices.

Fourthly, there are market risks, in the form of interest rate changes, inflation or purchasing power parities and exchange rate changes. In the output markets, there can be changes in demand or quality standards which lead to some risk exposure. The uncertainties abound in all international transactions, both in flow of goods and services and in the flow of funds. The income and price elasticities of goods in foreign markets may change adversely to the parties.

Fifthly, the government regulations, exchange and trade controls, barriers of tariff and quotas are also risk elements in foreign trade and finance flows. Tax factors and controls on transfers of royalties, dividends etc. are also the risk factors. These are thus, a variety of risks from beginning to end of all international transactions.

# NATURE AND MEASUREMENT OF RISK

## Nature of Risks

The international economic and commercial transactions comprise international trade in merchandise and services and in flow of funds. As referred to, trade transactions are involved in risks arising out of Shipping, transit and credit of the counterparty Shipping, airways or by land (to neighbouring countries) are the modes of transfer of goods. Some services like foreign travel, transportation, banking and insurance have also got risks of accidents, war emergencies, change of national rules and laws, both in respect of exporters and importers. Besides there are contingencies like loss or deterioration in quality and destruction by natural factors. Some of these risks are reduced by insurance, credit rating of parties, etc. referred to later.

The flow of funds across nations have currency risks and foreign exchange risks in addition to interest rate risks and inflation. Loss of currency in physical transfer or loss in transit of credit instruments are examples of risk in currency market. Foreign exchange risks are many and varied in the flow of funds which may take place for transactions hedging and speculation. The risks take the form of interest rate changes, changes in exchange rates, changes in time value of money due to inflation (referred to later).

Speculative and hedging transactions are of short term nature and reversible. These are called hot money flows, which can take place even in convertible currencies on current account. These risks are measurable by movements in short-term currency rates in flows of funds for speculation and volatility in exchange rates, which move even within a day in inter-bank foreign exchange market.

Investment and aid transactions are of two types, foreign direct investment and portfolio investment. These involve risks of medium-term and long-term nature. Currency rates include both for borrowing and lending in international money markets, which are used by MNCs for their working capital and cash management. Call money rates vary even in a day like the exchange rates, which particularly affect the portfolio investment flows.

## Measurement

The risk in currency and exchange rates in medium and long-term rates can be seen from the following Table 1 and the Chart 1. These are real exchange rates and adjusted interest rates. If the nominal rates are taken into account their volatility is much more. The volatility in these rates is a measure of risk.

**TABLE 5.1**
**Real and Exchange Rate Adjusted Interest Rates**

*(Per cent per annum)*

| *Year* | *Real Deposit Rate* | *Real Lending Rate* | *Interest Rate Adjusted Deposit Rate* | *Exchange Rate Adjusted Lending Rate* |
|---|---|---|---|---|
| | *1* | *2* | *3* | *4* |
| 1980-81 | -7.0 | –1.5 | 12.6 | 19.3 |
| 1981-82 | 0.6 | 6.6 | –3.0 | 2.7 |
| 1982-83 | 5.8 | 11.1 | 3.0 | 8.1 |
| 1983-84 | 3.2 | 8.3 | 3.8 | 8.9 |
| 1984-85 | 4.3 | 9.4 | –3.5 | 1.3 |
| 1985-86 | 6.3 | 11.6 | 7.9 | 13.2 |
| 1986-87 | 4.9 | 10.1 | 6.3 | 11.5 |
| 1987-88 | 1.7 | 7.7 | 8.4 | 14.8 |
| 1988-89 | 2.4 | 8.4 | –1.5 | 4.3 |
| 1989-90 | 2.4 | 8.4 | –4.3 | 1.3 |
| 1990-91 | 0.7 | 5.7 | 3.0 | 8.1 |
| 1991-92 | -0.6 | 2.4 | –17.2 | –14.6 |
| 1992-93 | 0.9 | 8.1 | –11.4 | –5.0 |
| 1993-94 | 1.5 | 9.8 | 7.5 | 16.3 |
| 1994-95 | -1.3 | 2.2 | 10.9 | –14.9 |
| 1995-96 | 4.5 | 7.8 | 6.1 | 9.4 |
| 1996-97 | 7.8 | 9.5 | 6.2 | 7.9 |
| 1997-98 | 7.0 | 9.2 | 6.7 | 8.9 |
| 1998-99 | 4.8 | 6.7 | –1.9 | –0.2 |
| 1999-2000 | 6.8 | 8.5 | 7.0 | 8.7 |
| 2000-2001 | 2.4 | 4.1 | 4.1 | 5.8 |
| 2001-2002 | 4.9 | 7.6 | 4.1 | 6.8 |
| 2012-2013 | 5.1 | 9.5 | 1.0 | NA |

*Source:* RBI Report on Currency and Finance.

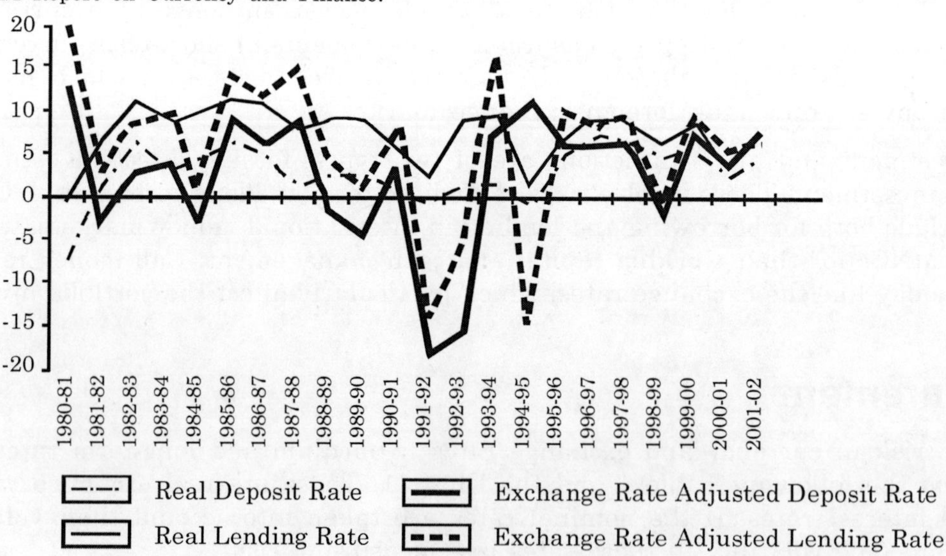


**Chart 1: Real and Exchange Rated Adjusted Interest Rates**

The Table 1 and Chart 1 provide a view of the annual changes in these rates. The daily rates are the most volatile, followed by monthly averages:

The chart 1 presents a picture of volatility in interest rates adjusted by inflation and exchange rate changes, adjusted by deposit rate and lending rate for a long period of 1980-81-2001-02.

The following Table 2 presents the data on the coefficient of variation as a measure of risk in the market. Even though, the data relate to annual changes in exchange rate of Rupee vis-a-vis the U.S. dollar, the dispersion of the rates, indicating the volatility in the market is varying widely. The data are on movements of exchange rate in the form of range of variation, average exchange rate, average of the daily variation in absolute terms. The last column in the Table presents the variation coefficients, which are widely changing. The dates are not material for illustration.

**TABLE 5.2**
**Movements in the Exchange Rate of the Rupee per US Dollar**

| *Year* | *Range* | *Average Exchange Rate* | *Average of the Daily (absolute) Variation* | *Coefficient of Variation (%)* |
|---|---|---|---|---|
| | *1* | *2* | *3* | *4* |
| 1993-94 | 31.21-31.49 | 31.37 | 0.01 | 0.1 |
| 1994-95 | 31.37-31.97 | 31.40 | 0.01 | 0.3 |
| 1995-96 | 31.32-37.95 | 33.45 | 0.10 | 5.8 |
| 1996-97 | 31.14-35.96 | 35.50 | 0.04 | 1.3 |
| 1997-98 | 35.70-40.36 | 37.16 | 0.07 | 4.2 |
| 1998-99 | 39.48-43.42 | 42.07 | 0.05 | 2.1 |
| 1999-2000 | 42.44-43.64 | 43.33 | 0.03 | 0.7 |
| 2000-01 | 43.61-46.89 | 45.68 | 0.04 | 2.3 |
| 2001-02 | 46.58-48.85 | 47.69 | 0.04 | 1.4 |
| 2002-03 | 60.6270-61.5515 | 60.9900 | 0.05 | NA |

Chart 2 provides the same picture of wide fluctuations in the exchange rates, even on an annual basis. These annual rates can be understood to indicate the trend in the movements of exchange rate of rupee as against dollar (U.S.). The variation coefficient was relatively high in the years 1995-96 and 1997-98 due to Asian Currency Crisis following hot money flows.

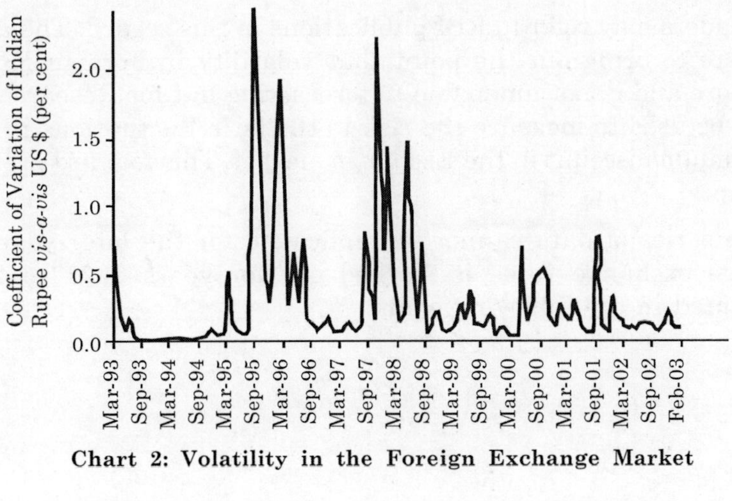


**Chart 2: Volatility in the Foreign Exchange Market**

Chart 3 presents the picture of the same volatility and trend in the exchange rate of the rupee vis-a-vis the major trading currencies of India, during the period 1990-91 to 2002-03, namely, U.S. $, DM, Euro, Japanese Yen and Pound Sterling of U.K.

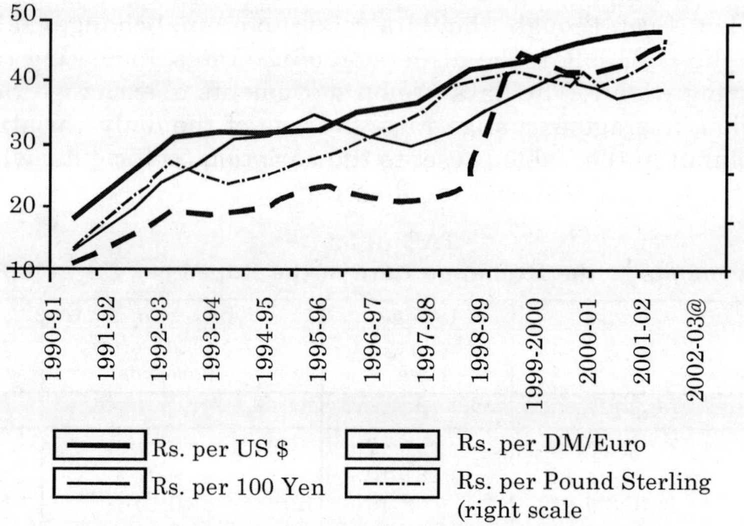


**Chart 3: Indian Rupee *vis-a-vis* Major Currencies**

*Source:* RBI Report on Currency and Finance, 2001-02.

As already mentioned, daily fluctuations are more volatile. The RBI Monthly Bulletin provides the Daily Foreign Exchange rates of rupee in terms of U.S. dollar, Euro, Pound Sterling and Japanese Yen both for purchases and sales separately. Risk can also be measured through forward premia. The volatility in forward rates and spreads between spot rate and forward rate in the form of Forward Premium for one month to six months present a picture of the risk in the exchange market. The date on Forward Premium or discount are presented in the RBI's Handbook of Statistics on the Indian Economy, in the form of daily interbank Forward Premium for 1 month, 3 months and 6 months in percentage form.

Interested readers may refer to RBI publications in this regard. The above Handbook of RBI is used here to bring out the point that volatility in Foreign Exchange rate on a daily basis is more and is not amenable to forecasting but for Research purposes, only the past data can be used to measure the risk in the form fluctuations in daily rates and in the forward premium/discount in the Exchange market. This forward premia is discussed in a separate chapter.

As the above series of data cannot be replicated, for the later years, a new series of data of average exchange rates is worked out for years 2001 to 2009 and their volatility is presented in the following chart.

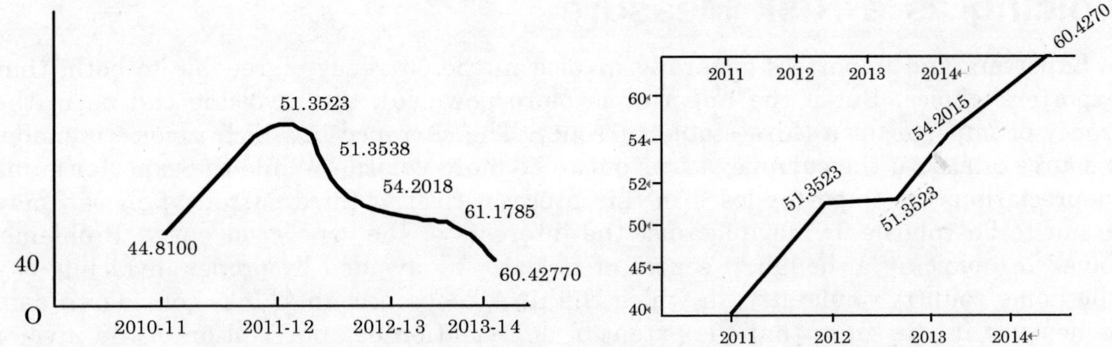


**Chart 4: Volatility in Exchange Rates (Average Rates) 2001-2009.**

*Source:* RBI, Monthly Report, The data has to be redrawn as the earlier rates were introduced.

These are average annual Rates of Exchange which are highly fluctuating, ranging from Rs. 41.2926 for dollar in 2007 to Rs. 51.23 in March 2009, and average of Rs. 49.16 for January to July 2009 (as published in the RBI Annual Report 2008-09)

This rate stood at Rs. 46.68 per US $ as on November 23, 2009.

Similar fluctuation can be seen in the nominal and Real Exchange Rates as presented in the graphs below:

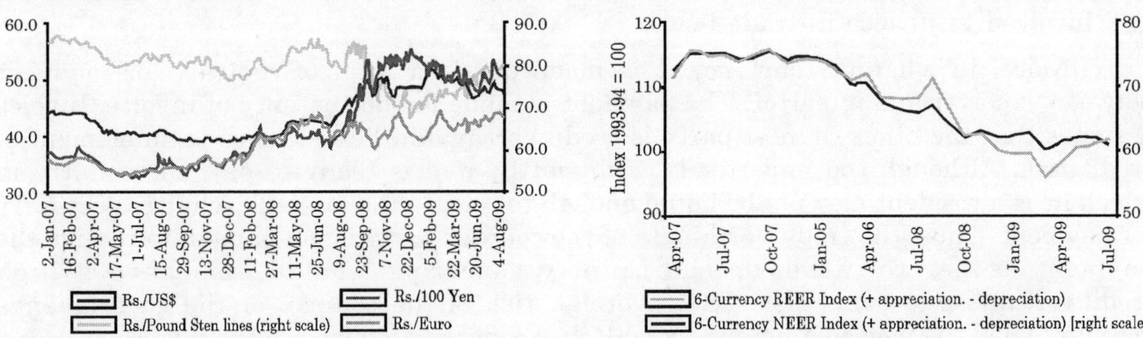


**Chart 5: Nominal and Real Exchange rates of Indian Rupee**

*Source:* RBI, Annual Report 2008-09.

The Chart No. 5, presents the data for Rs. to U.S. dollar, pound sterling, Yen and Euro, in the separate curves in one graph. In the other graph, the Real Exchange rate adjusted for 6-currencies. Who are the major trading partners of India are shown. The indices of 6-currency REER and 6-currency NEER are shown separately in the second graph. Both the graphs present the data for the period 2007 to 2009. They exhibit how volatile these rates are even for the respective months from January 2007 to August 2009, not to speak of the higher daily volatility. The above charts amply exhibit the state of high volatility in exchange rates in India. This necessitates a shrewd and cautions behaviour on the part of the international Financial Manager.

## Invoicing as a Risk Measure

Exporters and importers generally invoice in the currency, agreeable to both, that is exporters' choice. But if the importer is more powerful, the invoicing can be in the currency of importer or a third stable currency. The currency in which invoice is made, in a source of risk, if the currency turns out to be more volatile. While the exporter gains by depreciation, the importer loses in this process. Even a third currency, chosen may turn out to be volatile or move against the interests of the concerned party. Problems, involved in invoicing although, a source of risk can be avoided by proper invoicing, say in the home country's currency, in which the firm keeps accounts. It is considered as a risk measure in the sense that the extent of depreciation or appreciation of the invoice currency cannot be assessed or correctly anticipated.

The risk involved in invoice can be hedged by taking a forward rate agreement with the Banker for the currency in which invoice is made. Invoice, if it is f.o.b. or c.i.f., will decide the transit risk element and will have to be shouldered by either importer or exporter. If the terms of the agreement states clearly whether the exporter or importer bears the transit risks, the concerned party who bears the risk, has to take an insurance like marine insurance policy to hedge the risk of loss in transit, damage, deterioration or destruction by accident, war, natural calamity or fire. Thus, the invoice risk includes the currency risk, transit risk, and time risk. These risks can be hedged by proper resort to forward rate agreements, insurance and an appropriate credit agreement with the banker. Cross currency hedges and multi-currency invoicing are also the avenues of hedging the risk involved in invoice in trade flows.

Invoice, in whatever currency it is made out is a form of contract for payment between exporter and importer. The payment is made in the currency of invoice. Invoice assumes that the other counter party is creditworthy and hence, there is an element of credit risk. Although the importer is creditworthy and is ready to pay, the country in which he is a resident may not be liquid enough to release the foreign exchange necessary for payment. Thus, the creditworthiness of the counter party is not enough to receive the payment as per the invoice. The country concerned should also have a high creditworthiness to avoid risk. The sovereign risk of the country or the government's activity to pay the needed amount is a matter of concern, involved in the invoice exercise. The sudden currency crisis or external payments difficulties of the partner countries are matters of risk. Here, the sovereign risk is country risk, measured generally by country rating which has its own limitations.

## Risks from Global Forces

International Finance Manager is affected by global trade and finance trends. As seen in the year 2004, global external sector imbalances among the G-3 currencies remain a serious threat to the volume and pattern of capital flows into developing countries like India. Studies have shown that the greater volatility in developing countries real exchange rates has been associated with greater misalignment in G-3 currencies, which has adverse effects on trade and finance channels.

Capital flows into India are partly influenced by such global forces and partly by government policies. The major contribution to capital flows are portfolio investments, short-term trade credit and NRI deposits, which are all the outcome of government policy on FDI, pushing the non-debt creating inflows and interest rate policy. The strong fundamentals of the corporate sector induced the portfolio investment to flow in by FFI and FIIs. The Indian forex market was kept relatively stable despite large inflows into Forex reserves, by the RBI sterilisation of liquidity, resulting thereby.

The plus factors for large capital inflows are the relative stability of exchange rate and inflation rate in India in recent years. The current account surplus and balance of payments strength also aided the sentiment, during the period 2001-03. Before that in the eighties and nineties the current deficit persisted due to high trade deficits, leading to the exchange crisis in 1990-91. The problem of structural competitiveness plagued during the period leading to price disadvantage to India as against her trading partners and competitors. Some studies have shown that the trade balance in India is sensitive to exchange rate changes, which imply the need for exchange rate policy to be co-ordinated with the monetary and fiscal policies. The relation of money stock and exchange rate through interest rate is an established fact. The recent empirical evidence of Granger Causality tests between fiscal deficit to GDP ratio and current account deficit to GDP ratio showed that high fiscal deficits in India were reflected in high current account deficit. But this trend could be countermanded by absorption of fiscal deficit by a surplus in domestic saving in private sector.

The risk of volatility of external flows in India has also to be borne in mind. Although, these external inflows help to fill in the gap between domestic investment and savings, these are not an unmixed blessing due to their risk. The Table below shows the trend in volatility, in this respect.

**TABLE 5.3**
**Volatility of External Flows to India**

| | *2010-11 to 2013-14* | *1975-76 to 1989-90* | | *1991-92 to 2002-03* | | *Turnover* |
|---|---|---|---|---|---|---|
| | *Actual (U.S $)* | *CV (per cent) billion)* | *Mean (U.S. $* | *CV (per cent) (U.S. billion)* | *Mean* | *Volatility* |
| Private Transfers | 48903 | 34.2 | 2.1 | 38.7 | 9.8 | 24318 |
| Workers Remittances | 823 | 43.9 | 1.5 | 54.7 | 7.6 | 3364 |
| *Current Account Flows* | | | | | | |
| Services | 252 | 41.2 | 2.7 | 60.7 | 11.6 | 126765 |
| Income | | 42.6 | 0.5 | 66.1 | 1.5 | |
| *Capital Flows* | | | | | | |
| NRI Deposit | 103844 | 101.5 | 0.8 | 62.6 | 1.6 | |
| Foreign Investment | 30983 | - | - | 54.2 | 3.7 | |

C.V. Coefficient of Variation: *Source:* RBI Reports

The above Table evidences the high degree of volatility of both current account flows and capital flows, which result in a high risk element in it. Despite this drawback, capital flows augment domestic savings and boost investment, income and economic growth. The actual impact on real economic variables is an empirical issue. An RBI study was referred in its report, which uses a vector auto regression model (V.A.R.) for the period 1991-2002 in respect of GDP, gross domestic capital formation (proxy for investment), wholesale price index, interest rate, capital flows and exchange rate. An approximate timelag of 2 years is found for a positive shock to capital flows to result in larger investment, higher output in the medium to long-run. The exchange rate appreciated and interest rate declined. It can thus, be concluded that the micro level international finance money has to take a broader view of macro economic and monetary variables affecting all international financial transactions although, its immediate concern is with exchange rates and interest rates in the short-run.

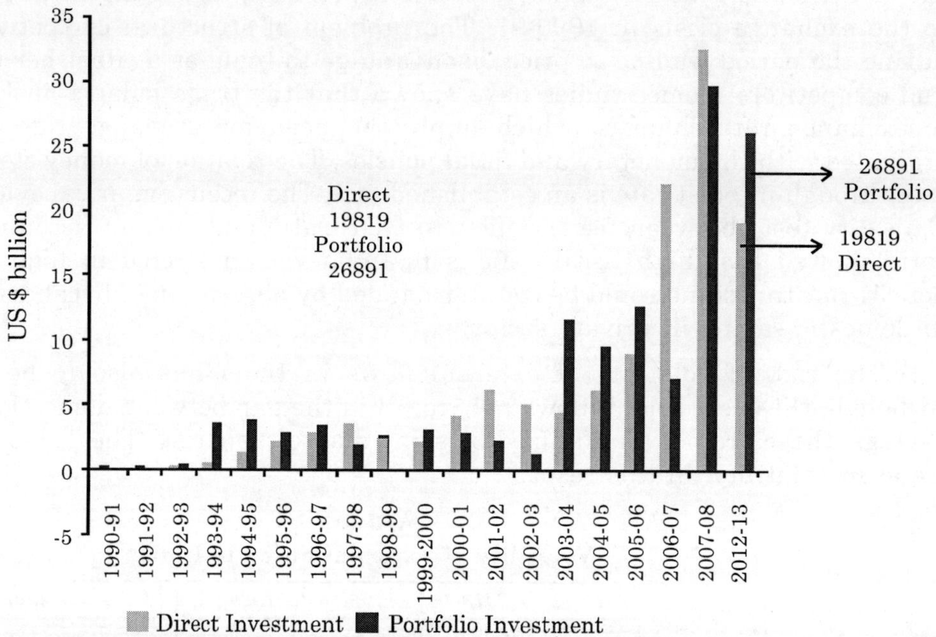


**Chart 6: Volatility in foreign Inflows**

Source: RBI Annual Report 2008-09.

The Chart 6 covers the period of 1990-91 to 2007-08. The volatility of external flows into India is also a well established fact for the operations in the foreign exchange market. This is clearly evidenced by the fact that the above chart 6 shows the ups and downs in both the portfolio investment and direct investment, flowing into India. But there is another fact that has to be noticed namely that they are showing a general rising trend, and a sharp rise during 2004 to 2008 before the global recession started.

## Risks from International Financial Architecture

The weaknesses in the International Finance Architecture are the other sources of risk to international finance manager. What are the constituents of good International Financial Architecture? A well designed infrastructure, effective market discipline and an efficient regulatory and supervisory framework. Unfortunately none of these constituents are fully developed and foolproof in the developing countries particularly in India. A well designed infrastructure requires good telecommunication, efficient shipping and transport system, developed payment and settlement system, proper legal framework, good corporate governance, efficient accounting and auditing standards etc. are required, but some of these basic requirements are inadequate and inefficient. Similarly, effective market discipline requires market integration with "good pass through" effects, well-developed debt and equity markets with a wide variety of instruments for risk diversification, efficient banking and credit system etc., many of which are in the process of developing. A sound regulatory and supervisory system is partially developed, as there are many loopholes in practices and procedures-corruption and red tape etc.

The most important risk element is lack of transparency and predominant role of "news"/"rumours" in the financial architecture, which leads to high speculative fervour and hot money flows across borders. The 1990s saw a series of forex crises, beginning with the fall of the exchange rate mechanism (ERM) in the European Monetary System in 1992-93, Mexican crisis in 1994, the Asian crisis of 1997, of which India was spared, and the Russian and Brazilian crisis of 1998. These crises brought to light the prevailing weakness in the systems, as referred below:

1. The international financial system failed to meet with the increasing demands of expanding trade and finance due to lack of enough resources, efficient and quick actions of surveillance on capital flows and inadequate liquidity to meet emerging crisis situations.

2. The role of expectations on the basis of "news" has increased leading to volatility of capital flows, more risks in the Emerging Market economies due to the market imperfection, impediments to free flow of correct information and inadequate market absorption of information.

3. Higher volatility in trade and capital flows led to large current account deficits, balance of payments imbalances, requiring adequate reserves to act as buffers and insurance for safe tide over of any crisis. India has of course no problem on this account in recent years due to a high level of forex reserves.

4. The experience with the East Asian Crisis has shown the bandwagon effects of spreading from one nation to another and foreign exchange markets of many countries were affected thereby. The international banks in many countries have also been infected with this virus, resulting in losses.

5. Any form of financial crisis imposes severe social costs and the countries take a long time to recover these costs and the financial institutions concerned take a while to offset their losses.

6 The increasing globalisation in many emerging market economies needed speedy adjustment of regulatory systems and existing institutions, both national and international, were found deficient to deal with such situations.

7. It was found that quick monetary and fiscal policy changes were the need of the hour, which was not possible in many developing countries. The surplus and deficit countries were unable and unwilling to make the necessary sacrifices to meet with the challenges thrown up by their liberalisation and globalisation process.

8. International core principles, standards and code of practices were needed to strengthen in the Architecture of International Finance.

The needed reforms to reduce the risks of currency crisis and the weaknesses of the international financial architecture are as follows and are being addressed to by the international and national bodies concerned with international finance.

(1) Ensuring a transparent and stable global system through concerted efforts of all interested parties.

(2) Evolving a process of sharing burden between sovereign debtors and creditors in the event of a crisis.

(3) Strengthening of IMF surveillance system along with the use of new instruments of Supplementary Reserve Facility 1997, and the contingent credit line 1999 in a more liberal manner.

(4) Prudent management of external sector through cautious and discretionary liberalisation process, followed by an effective intervention and surveillance system, efficient use of a mix of monetary and fiscal policies, along with a suitable system of "managed float" of exchange rate.

(5) Insistence on good corporate governance with international accounting and auditing standards, real time gross settlement system and a quick payment system, and adoption of proper risk management by corporates in counter party risk, foreign exchange risk, and other credit and market risks.

(6) Developing liquid and deep markets with transparent practices and procedures with good "pass through" effects to strengthen the financial system.

In the above-mentioned actions there is involvement of international financial institutions, national government and regulatory authorities. So far as the corporates are concerned, they are expected to play an effective role in crisis prevention, by proper estimation and planning the resources needed and mobilisation of those resources in a cost effective manner in the capital markets — domestic and foreign — keeping in mind its impact on the national interests, national debt liability and social costs involved in the process and respect the spillover effects on the home country and third countries through MNC's operation in the financial markets.

The most important contribution that the MNCs are expected to play is the strict observance of good corporate governance, with transparency in their practices, quick dissemination of right information and adoption of internationally accepted standards of accounting and auditing. Their Risk Measurement and Management Practices are to be well-planned and placed in order of precedence and importance of a systematic manner so as to preserve the market discipline and the practices, and procedures of market participants, namely, brokers, bankers, and the concerned financial institutions — domestic and international.

❖ ❖ ❖

# INTERNATIONAL MONETARY SYSTEM

# 6

The International Monetary System is the short-term wing of the international financial system. It encompasses all relations as between the national market systems. I.M.F. is the apex body for this system and acts as a central bank of central banks of the nations.

The establishment of the International Monetary Fund (IMF) in 1945 was a landmark in the international monetary field. Before 1945 there was international monetary disorder, exchange restrictions and a host of other undesirable trade and exchange practices. The need for international monetary co-operation and understanding was felt soon after the war, and the Bretton Woods Conference resulted in the establishment of IMF and the World Bank. Originally 44 member countries met at the Conference and the IMF was set up as per the agreement reached among them in December 1945. It had an original membership of 29 countries and by 2010 rose to cover almost all the countries in the world.

The IMF is governed by a policy-making body, viz., the Board of Governors but the day-to-day affairs are looked into by the Board of Executive Directors consisting of the representatives of 16 elected countries and 6 nominated countries. The Board of Executive Directors meets as often as is necessary to decide on all matters pertaining to the role of the Fund. The Managing Director is the chief executive of the Fund and is appointed by the Board of Executive Directors. It has a secretariat in Washington, U.S.A.

## Objectives of IMF

The IMF is primarily a short-term financial institution-a lender and a borrower-and a central bank of central banks and secondarily, aims at promoting a code of conduct among members for orderly exchange arrangements and international monetary management. The objectives of the Fund as laid down in its Articles may be briefly set out as follows:

(1) To promote international monetary co-operation through consultation and mutual collaboration.

(2) To promote exchange stability and maintain orderly exchange arrangements and avoid competitive exchange depreciation.

(3) To help members with temporary balance of payments difficulties, to tide over them without resort to exchange restrictions.

(4) To promote growth of multilateralism in trade and payments and thus, expand world trade and aid.

(5) To help achieve the balance of payments equilibrium, shorten the duration of disequilibrium and promote orderly international relations.

The main object of the Fund is to promote exchange stability and encourage multilateral trade and payments. It is also a financing institution and has schemes for provision of short-term finance for meeting the balance of payments purposes. It provides international liquidity in tune with the requirements of world trade and fosters the growth of world trade and freer system of payments. Gold was originally the unit of account in which the various currencies were denominated. This was subsequently replaced by Special Drawing Rights (SDRs) which is a standard unit of account whose value is fixed in terms of a basket of currencies. These functions of the Fund are reviewed briefly below:

## IMF's Role of Consultation

In all matters of exchange rate changes, imposition of restrictions on current account, use of discriminatory practices, members are obliged to consult the Fund. Failing this, the members could be ineligible to have recourse to financial resources of the Fund. Such consultations may take the form of supply of economic and financial data to the Fund by the member country. Secondly, the staff of the Fund can call for various types of data from a member country as and when they require on an *ad hoc* basis. Thirdly, the staff teams visit member countries at least once a year for a first-hand study of economic and financial conditions in the member country. At the time of annual general meeting or at the time of negotiating a credit arrangement, representatives of member countries hold consultations and discussions with the Board of Executive Directors. Many times informal consultations also take place between the member's Governor or Executive Director with the IMF staff, particularly at a time when the member country approaches the Fund for a standby arrangement or a credit drawal.

## Sources of Funds — Quotas

Every member country is given a quota in the Fund. These quotas were fixed originally on a formula:

*(i)* 2 per cent of the national income;

*(ii)* 5 per cent of gold and dollar balances;

*(iii)* 10 per cent of average annual imports;

*(iv)* 10 per cent of maximum variation in annual exports.

The sum of the above, increased by the percentage ratios of average annual exports to national income of a member, is used as the basis for fixing the quotas.

Each member's quota was thus, fixed as their initial contribution to the Fund. A member had to contribute its quota to the Fund in the form of gold upto 25 per cent of its quota or 10 per cent of its net gold holdings or U.S. dollars on September 12, 1946, whichever was less and the rest of the quota was payable in member's currency. Since 1980, the clause of 25 per cent of the quota in gold or US dollar was replaced by contribution of SDR and convertible currencies. At the time, gold was valued at $ 35 per fine ounce and India paid $ 27.5 million in gold for a quota of $ 400 million. The quota of India stood at 3056 million SDRs after the 10th General Quota increase in 1995. IMF holds substantial gold reserves which were received as part of members' contribution towards their quotas, and liquid reserves in the form of convertible currencies of member countries.

The total of quotas of 44 nations which gathered at Bretton Woods in 1944 was fixed at $ 8800 million. By end December 1994, the membership rose to 178 with a total of quotas at SDRs 144,620 million after the 9th General Review of quotas made in 1990. The work of Tenth General Review of Quotas was undertaken in 1994-95, and Eleventh quota review was completed in 1998 and a quota increase of 45% was effected in 1999.

## Share Capital of IMF

In January 1999, the increase of share capital or total quota of IMF from SDR 145.6 billion (US $ 204 billion) to SDR 212 billion (US $ 297 billion) took effect, with the consent given by the requisite 85% of the memberships. The Fund's usable resources rose by SDR 45 billion or US. $ 63 billion. India's current quota is SDR 3055.5 million, which comes to about 2.098 per cent of the total IMF quota. This quota is now increased to SDR 4158.2 million which comes to about 1.961 per cent. Thus, in relative terms, the position of India came down considerably in the Fund.

When it was set up, India was among the top five quota holders. Now it has been pushed down to 13th position in the list. The current top countries are U.S.A. Japan, Germany, Francc, U.K., Italy, Saudi Arabia, Canada, Russia, Netherlands, China, Belgium and India.

The increase of IMF quotas has been effected by conventional calculations for determining the quotas of countries, referred to earlier. But, if economic strength of a country is determined by relative purchasing power parity, it is understood that China would be number two or three and India number five or six.

## Other Sources of Funds

The IMF has, in addition to member's quotas, other sources of funds. In 1962 IMF concluded a General Agreement to Borrow (GAB) under which IMF could borrow from the participating members (Group of Ten Developed Countries) specified amounts of their currencies. The amounts which the Ten Countries (Belgium, Canada, France, West Germany, Italy, Japan, Netherlands, Sweden, U.K. and USA) undertook to provide was set in the agreement. Interest and service charges were payable on such loans in agreed terms (upto 5 years) in gold, later replaced by SDR. The IMF borrowed not only from above countries but also from others such as Saudi Arabia on similar terms. The IMF can also acquire any member's currency, as desired , in exchange for the gold, which it holds. India, now being a creditor country, IMF can borrow rupees from it at any time, if there is a demand for Indian rupees.

## Role of Gold in IMF

Since the inception of the IMF, gold used to play a crucial role in the declaration of the quotas of members and in the announcements of their par values. The gold was generally accepted as an international medium of exchange in their international payments and receipts. IMF has adopted the use of gold or dollar as the medium for declaration of par values of members. But slowly gold was replaced by dollar and other convertible currencies in the international dealings.

As dollar got into troubles due to the balance of payments problems of U.S.A., the SMITHSONIAN AGREEMENT in 1971, dollar was stopped for conversion into gold. Subsequently dollar was replaced by the SDRs which is a paper currency for book entries and which is valued in terms of a few selected convertible currencies. Even then Gold continued to play the role of accepted method of payment in international transactions. The member countries contributed their initial quotas in gold up to 25% of the quotas or 10% of their gold holdings at the time of entry into IMF. The rest of 75% was contributed in the currencies of member countries. Since, then gold has come to be held in its vaults. Later on also some members were allowed to repay their dues to the Fund in the form of gold or SDRs.

In 2009 the IMF has come to hold 3,217 tonnes of gold with them. The IMF is now the third largest holder of gold in the world next to the U.S.A. and Germany. France is also a large holder of gold and it has a flair for gold internally as in the case of India. It has used gold for international payments and receipts many times.

The IMF has now decided to sell off 403 tonnes of its gold worth of $ 13 billion for augmenting its lending capacity particularly to the very poor member countries in the background of the on going global recession and incapacity of the USA and other developed countries to lend due to their own balance of payments Deficits and depletion of the lending capacity of the rich developed countries.

The IMF has now 186 members most of which are the poor emerging nations which require the IMF assistance at very concessional terms. The new income method through the sale of gold is designed to provide the FUND with more diverse income sources that are better aligned with the variety of functions performed by the FUND.

The proposal to sell part of the gold worth $ 13 billion which is one-eight of the total gold holdings of the Fund was approved by the Board in April 2009 and was announced in September 2009. This sale proceeds will be used to make long term lending to the very poor countries on much needed concessional terms.

It is reported that India has decided to buy some of this gold from the IMF for diversifying its foreign holdings of reserves from the present pattern mostly held in Treasury bills and bonds of US Federal reserve and in London. The fact is that U.S. economy is itself in deep recession and balance of payments deficits. It is therefore necessary to invest in other avenues. It may be recalled that some of India's gold was mortgaged for borrowing the much needed foreign assistance to tide over its critical balance of payments position during 1990-1991.

## IMF's Lending Operations

As a financial institution, the Fund provides temporary financial assistance for balance of payments purposes in the form of sale of currencies. When a member borrows from the Fund it purchases foreign currencies against its own currency. When it repays loans, it is repurchasing its own currency against foreign currency. The Fund's exchange operations are classified into four categories as follows:

*(1)* Gold Tranche is upto the amount of gold paid by the member towards its quota plus its credit position with the Fund (which is the same thing as other countries' borrowings of its currency). If a country has 25 per cent of its quota in gold, then upto this limit this member can draw upon the Fund automatically. If that country has also a credit position of 10 per cent of its quota as borrowings by other countries, then that country can borrow automatically upto 35 per cent of its quota (gold tranche of 25 per cent plus super gold tranche of 10 per cent).

*(2)* Four Credit Tranches: There are four credit tranches, each equivalent to 25 per cent of its quota. If gold payment is 25 per cent of the quota and the rest of the 75 per cent is paid in own currency, the Fund can hold upto 200 per cent of a member's quota in its currency and credit tranches would aggregate to 100 per cent of quota.

*(3)* Compensatory financing facility was started in February 1963 to provide credit in connection with any shortfalls in export proceeds below some average annual figure. The member was permitted credit upto 50 per cent of the member's quota which was raised in stages to 100 per cent of the quota in 1980.

*(4)* The international buffer stock financing facility was established in June 1969 in respect of any primary commodity that the member country produces. The credit is upto a limit of 50 per cent of its quota for special stocks of sugar, tin, cocoa, etc., under various international commodity agreements.

The above facilities, except in the case of gold tranche which is automatic, are subject to the following conditions:

*(1)* No member should draw in any 12 month period more than 25 per cent of its quota.

*(2)* No member should draw in total beyond a point where the Fund's holdings of the member's currency reaches 200 per cent of its quota which it will have if it has borrowed upto 125 per cent of its quota with a gold subscription of 25 per cent and its own currency upto 75 per cent.

*(3)* The combined drawal under compensatory financing and buffer stock financing should not exceed 75 per cent of the member's quota.

*(4)* Total holding of IMF of any member's currency under all the above facilities should not exceed 275 per cent of the quota of that member, and this condition was waived many times.

These conditionalities can be varied from time to time and exceptions were made many times to the general rules. The conditionality of drawings under various credit tranches and other financial facilities will vary according to the state of the country and the economic and financial policies pursued. Requests for drawings beyond the first credit tranche require substantial justification and the conditions laid down would be more rigorous in terms of policies to be pursued by the member country in fiscal, monetary and foreign exchange fields so as to provide quick corrective programme of action for remedying the balance of payments disequilibrium. These conditions are imposed with a fair degree of flexibility.

## Standby Arrangements

When a member feels that the need for credit might arise during any year, it may enter into standby arrangements with the Fund. This will give an assurance of financial support from the Fund in time of need. This facility was introduced in 1952 to meet a felt need for it although, there was no specific provision for it in the Fund's Articles of Agreement. Since then such facility was frequently used by the members and both the Fund and the members are happy with such prior arrangement in the nature of an overdraft limit. The standby facility is repayable generally in three years, while other types of borrowings are repayable in 3 to 5 years. A member's obligation to repurchase also arises if its exchange reserves rise beyond a limit. The repurchase is made in terms of the currency borrowed or in any convertible currency or a currency which is in demand and the Fund's holdings of it are less than 75 per cent of that country's quota. A member's indebtedness to the IMF can be repaid in three ways:

*(1)* Repurchase with gold and convertible currencies;

*(2)* The drawings of its currency by other countries; and

*(3)* The offset of an earlier creditor position.

## IMF Charges

The schedule of IMF charges on the member's drawings is such that the rate varied with the period for which it is outstanding and the tranche position of the country. For a long time the maximum rate of interest was 5 per cent and now it varied from 5 to 7 per cent. The rates for supplementary financing facility were higher at 10-11.5 per cent or even more, as these rates depended on the rates at which the Fund borrowed from the lender countries and on the money market conditions of the major creditor countries. The margin kept by the IMF is about 0.2 to 0.325 per cent. Since May 1, 1981, IMF had adopted a uniform charge of 7.0 per cent per annum on outstanding borrowings of members from the Fund's own resources and a higher rate for those resources borrowed from outside. The Fund makes a service charge of 0.5 per cent on all purchases other than those in reserve tranche and 0.25 per cent on all standby and extended Fund facilities.

These charges are payable normally in gold or US dollars or SDRs but as in the case of other provisions of the Fund which are operated with flexibility, this may be waived if the nation's external reserves are below half of its quota. Thus, Fund's charges were paid by India in rupees only. These charges are very nominal in view of the fact that Fund does not pay any interest on currencies held by it. Since 1969, IMF was paying about 1½ per cent per annum to a creditor position of a member that is, when its currency held by the Fund fell below 75 per cent of its quota.

## Other Facilities

The oil facility was originally designed in 1974. These funds were lent to countries in balance of payments difficulties due to oil price escalation during 1970-73. Arrangements to borrow SDR 6.9 billion for this Fund from 17 member countries with a strong external payments position were made in 1974. This facility was extended from year to year and by 1982 borrowing members have repaid most of the outstanding debt.

In 1974, the Fund also established an Extended Fund facility to provide special medium-term loans to meet the balance of payments deficits over a longer period and to help correct the structural imbalances in the economy of a member country. This assistance is up to three years and in amounts larger than that permitted by the member's quota.

In August 1975, a Subsidy Account was set up with contributions from 24 members for an amount of SDR 160 million to assist the member countries in balance of payments difficulties due to a rise in oil prices and to provide subsidy to interest payments on the use of resources made available to them through the oil facility. The effective interest rate to borrowing members which include India is 2.7 per cent as against the original rate of 7.7 per cent. The final payment under this Account was completed in August 1983.

In May 1976, a Trust fund was started for providing special balance of payments assistance to developing countries at highly concessional rates. The sources of funds for this Trust are the realisations from the sale proceeds of one-sixth of IMF gold holding, income from investment and loans and proceeds of repayment and donations. Only about

60 member countries (including India) which are developing were eligible for this assistance. The first auction sale of gold by the Fund took place in June 1976.

A Supplementary Financing Facility was established in August 1977 (Wittaveen Facility) with the objective of extending financial assistance to members with large payments difficulties which are larger in relation to their incomes and quotas with the Fund. This is usable by members under a standby or under an extended arrangement for a period of 1 to 3 years. Some 14 member countries agreed to provide SDR 7.8 billion for this facility. The borrowings on this Fund by members were started in May 1979 and IMF has in turn borrowed from the lending members at a rate calculated for each of the six months on the basis of yield on US Government securities of 5-year maturity. A subsidy account was also started in December 1980 for subsidising the interest rate on the borrowings of the low-income developing members under this Wittaveen facility. This facility could not be extended beyond 1982 due to further non-committal of funds by lender-members.

A new Structural Adjustment Facility (SAF) was established in October 1985 and became operative in March 1986 financed out of SDR 2.7 billion that are available during 1985-91 from repayment of Trust Fund loans and interest dues. This facility is confined to the lowest income countries with protracted balance of payments problems needing a structural adjustment programme. This loan carries a rate of ½ of 1 per cent with a grace period of 5 years and subsequent semi-annual repayments extending over five years. The programme of adjustment is expected to be of about three years during which the country's balance of payments position would be strengthened and its debt repayment capacity revived.

Enhanced structural adjustment facility was continued upto 1993 for helping the low income countries, in strengthening their payments position.

Many additional facilities were created from time to time to suit to the changing conditions. Thus, in April 1993, the Fund created a new temporary facility called systemic transformation assistance to members with systemic disruption of economies moving from planned economies to private market-oriented economies. In December 1997 the Fund had set up the supplementary Reserve Facility to provide additional finance to members facing exceptional balance of payments problems due to loss of funds following the loss of market confidence.

## Exchange Rates and Par Values

An important aspect of IMF activities is to maintain orderly exchange arrangements. The exchange rate system set up by the Articles of Agreement was called par value system. Each member is required to express the par value of its currency in terms of gold as a common denominator or in US dollar at a value of $ 35 per fine ounce of gold. Thus, gold was the basis of valuation and exchange rate fluctuations were to be kept within a narrow margin of 1 per cent on either side. While the USA performed this by buying and selling gold for US dollar, other countries did it through an intervention currency, such as US dollar of UK sterling.

The par value can be changed at the initiative of the country but with the concurrence of the IMF. For any change up to 10 per cent in the par value, to make adjustments in the balance of payments, the Fund would not raise any objection. For any change beyond 10 per cent, the country has to justify to the Fund that it would be needed to correct a "fundamental disequilibrium-a concept which has not been defined by the Fund but relates to a structural change in the economies and in cost price parities.

Besides, members are obligated to avoid control on current account except under Article XIV which permits member countries to have such restrictions on a temporary basis. Some members who opted for this clause continue to have these restrictions in some form or the other. Article VIII enjoins on the members to free current transactions from all restrictions which was adopted by the major developed countries in the sixties. About 60 members have accepted Article VIII of the Fund so far and India is one of them since 1994. But a majority of members are still following Article XIV provisions, under which some forms of control on Current Account transactions were permitted.

The stable par value system has broadly served the purpose of larger trade and greater international co-operation. This system continued to prevail up to August 1971 during which time there was international monetary stability and orderly growth in world trade.

So long as the dollar convertibility into gold was maintained, IMF served the purpose and dollar and gold shared the honour of serving as an international medium of exchange. While the surplus countries have not been adjusting their economies, the burden of adjustment fell on the deficit countries. When the US was one of such deficit countries and found it difficult to adjust the domestic economies to the requirements of the IMF system and its role as an international banker, the fixed parity system lost its credibility.

The Bretton Woods system in respect of exchange rates was formally abandoned in August 1971 when convertibility of the US dollar into gold was withdrawn. The continued inflation at home, deficits in balance of payments and persistent pressure on the US dollar by its creditor countries along with speculative attacks on the dollar particularly in Euro-currency market, led to the suspension of its convertibility. The US abandoned its obligation to buy and sell gold in international settlements since August 1971. This was followed by a system of floating rates and a temporary regime of central rates and wider margins since December 1971.

The Smithsonian Agreement of December 1971 put back the broken pieces of the system together into a new shape, based on: (i) A realignment of currency value against the dollar with a small devaluation of $ (revaluation of gold $ 38 = 1 fine ounce) and (ii) A return to fixed parity system by December 1971. But this system was short-lived and UK sterling was the first to abandon the fixed parity system in June 1972, followed by others in favour of a floating system of exchange rates. In February 1973, there was a further devaluation of dollar by 10 per cent in terms of gold in the midst of rampant speculation in dollar. A Committee of Twenty and subsequently the Interim Committee took up to formulate in 1972 a package of reforms in the international monetary system concerning exchange rates, role of gold, SDRs etc. After years of deliberation, they agreed on the following measures, in 1978:

# International Monetary Reforms

In respect of exchange rates it was agreed that the floating exchange system which was a *fait accompli* should be legalised. But members are still under an obligation to collaborate with the Fund to ensure orderly exchange arrangements and promote a system of stable exchange rates. It was also provided that countries may return to a stable but adjustable par value system at a future date. Meanwhile, floating rates with a wider band of fluctuations of 2.25 per cent on either side which was prevailing since the Smithsonian Agreement would continue.

A new concept of "international surveillance of the exchange rate systems" was developed and accepted as a new approach to the exchange rate systems. Of the 149 members in the fund, as at the end of December 1986, there were about 14 countries independently floating, 8 countries in a joint float and 32 countries linked to the US dollar, 14 to the French franc, 12 to SDR, 31 to a currency basket and the rest linked to other currencies. The fixed parity system had disappeared completely.

As regards gold, it would no longer function as an international unit of value or medium of exchange for the purpose of the Fund. The official price for gold is abolished and obligatory payments and receipts in gold between the fund and members were withdrawn. Members are free, however, to deal in gold among themselves, SDR will be the unit and medium of exchange in future. The existing gold stocks of the Fund are to be disposed of by returning to members half of their original contributions and by selling the other half in the market through auctions and to use the proceeds for the Trust Fund. Provisions are made for greater use and resort to SDRs, referred to later.

Two amendments were made to the Articles of Agreement, in connection with the reforms.

Firstly, in 1969 an amendment was made to create a system of SDRs which will be referred to later.

Secondly, Articles were amended in 1978 to introduce reforms in the international monetary system referred to earlier.

The principle of surveillance of the Fund over the members' exchange rate systems was embodied in the Second Amendment. So also was the abandonment of gold as an international unit of account or a medium of exchange for which SDR is redesigned.

Surveillance involves the following principles:

*(1)* A member shall avoid manipulating exchange rates to its advantage or prevent effective balance of payments adjustment.

*(2)* A member shall intervene in the exchange market if necessary to counter disorderly conditions.

*(3)* Members should take into account the interests of other members of the Fund in their intervention policy.

Members are free to choose their exchange rate arrangements except to maintain values in terms of SDR and co-operate with the Fund in the orderly exchange arrangements. India is now under a "managed floating rate system", referred to later.

## International Liquidity

International liquidity is defined to include all the assets gold and currencies that are freely and unconditionally usable in meeting the balance of payments deficits and other international obligations of countries. Gold has for long served as a unit of account, measure of value and medium of exchange. In the narrow official sense, the liquid assets used to meet balance of payments deficit by governments or monetary authorities include gold, convertible foreign exchange assets and reserve position with the IMF. In a sense, all owned and potential borrowings should be included as liquidity. These potential borrowings are vast and the scope for them is expanding with the passage of time. Besides, in a wider sense, all currencies and currency deposits and credits, actual and potential are part of the liquidity whether available to the governments and monetary authority or private parties. But since reserves held by private parties are not available to monetary authorities for meeting balance of payments requirements, only gold, official reserves, gold tranche and super-gold tranche (creditor position) with the IMF are considered as freely usable liquid assets by the authorities. Gold and super-gold tranche positions are drawable without conditions like the current account position with banks. SDRs which have been created by the IMF since 1969 are also included as liquid assets. In a narrow sense, thus, the official foreign exchange assets include gold, foreign currency deposits and investments in currencies which are freely convertible if that country has accepted Article VIII of the IMF Articles of Agreement, whereby no current account restrictions are used. India has accepted this position in March 1994.

## Need for Reserves

With the growth of world trade and payments, the need for reserves increases to meet the payments and deficit requirements. Just as in the case of domestic cash requirements for transactions, precautionary and speculative motives, international reserves also serve these three motives. Under a system of fixed par values adopted by the IMF and operative upto 1971, intervention in the markets to maintain the exchange rates stable used to require a large volume of liquid assets by the authorities. However, under the system of floating rates with a wider band of fluctuations, a larger need for reserves exists for various reasons.

Firstly, the larger the balance of payments deficits, the larger is the need for reserves, and these deficits are growing.

Secondly, then existing exchange rate system called "managed float" requires a larger official intervention which depends on the official holding of reserves.

Thirdly, the IMF has put an obligation on members to return to the fixed par value system as and when conditions permit, for which a comfortable stock of reserves is necessary.

Fourthly, increasing deficits in balance of payments of non-oil producing countries in more recent years require to be financed by reserves.

Fifthly, a large number of poor countries have their exchange rates pegged to a currency or basket of currencies for which central bank's intervention in the market is necessary, particularly when their deficits are growing. The demand for reserves for precautionary motives emerges out of the need for contingencies and to maintain their credit standing. The speculative demand for reserves may not be felt in a country where all exchange dealings are strictly controlled and supervised by the authorities.

## Composition and Level

The official reserve composition of India in 1971 and the latest position are presented below:

**Table 6.1**

*(Rs. crores)*

| | *End March 1971* | *End March 1981* | *Jan. 1994* | *Dec. 1999* | *June 2002* | *March 2004* | *June* 2009 | *End March* 2013 |
|---|---|---|---|---|---|---|---|---|
| Gold* | 182 | 226 | 12,665 | 12,790 | 16,272 | 18,966 | 46,914 | 1,397 |
| Foreign Exchange Assets | 438 | 4,822 | 61,440 | 1,39,134 | 2,67,333 | 4,77,165 | 12,16,345 | 14,126 |
| SDR Units | 112 | 497 | 233 | 18 | 47 | 10 | 2 | 235 |
| Total | 732 | 5,545 | 74,338 | 1,51,942 | 2,83,652 | 4,96,141 | 12,69,235 | 15,884 |

* Valued at London market price.
*Source:* RBI Annual Reports. In 2009, total includes also the Reserve Tranche Position with IMF.

Historically, the role of gold was taken by the US dollar and UK sterling in interwar and post-war periods and was replaced by SDR in the seventies. Gold is now completely replaced by SDR in the international monetary system.

## Adequacy of Reserves

The currency composition of foreign exchange has also undergone substantial changes since 1975. The role of the US dollar was replaced partly by other currencies such as Deutsche Market, DM, Swiss franc and Japanese yen and partly by SDR.

If reserves are important, the adequacy of reserves of international liquidity is equally important. Firstly, adequacy of reserves may be judged by the relationship of reserves to imports, secondly, by the rate of growth of world trade of that county as compared to the rate of growth of reserves and thirdly, by the magnitude of balance of payments deficit today as against a base year. Reserves as percentage of imports for all countries stood at 85 per cent in 1950 but declined to 38 per cent by 1966. By 1970 when SDR allocation started the inadequacy of reserves in relation to imports was glaring.

The adequacy of reserves is also assessed sometimes with reference to the degree of fluctuations in exports earnings. The symptoms of inadequacy include increased restrictions on current account transactions such as imports, efforts to curtail foreign aid, depreciation of currency and greater reliance on trade credits etc. With increased access to international capital markets, more recently by creditworthy countries like India, the question of adequacy of reserves became less important to them, because our reserves are more than our external debt.

India's foreign exchange reserves are more than adequate and it has repaid all its borrowings from the IMF. It has now a surfeit of reserves at US $ 298 billions as at mid-November 2010 and is now discouraging further inflow of reserves.

## Problems of Liquidity

The basic problems of international liquidity are as follows:

**1. Inadequacy of Growth:** Compared to the growth of world trade and increased deficits in balance of payments or judged by any other criteria, the inadequacy of reserves was felt more in the sixties and seventies than before. This was the justification for the creation of SDRs by the IMF.

**2. Unsatisfactory Distribution of Reserves – Inadequacy of Reserves:** The bulk of the reserves, namely, around 60 per cent, was held by the developed world and more recently by the combined groups of developed countries and oil-producing developing countries. The poor developing countries and non-oil producing countries are left with inadequate reserves.

**3. Unsatisfactory Composition of Reserves: The** proportion of gold to total reserves in 1952 was 68 per cent which fell to 53 per cent in 1968 and further to 23 per cent in 1973. Since then gold was completely replaced in official transactions by the SDRs. Gold, however, continued to play an important role with some countries because of its intrinsic worth, despite its demonetisation by IMF in 1973. Gold was revalued in terms of the US dollar from $ 35 to $ 38 per fine ounce in 1971 and again to $ 42.2 per fine ounce in February 1973.

Most of the reserve assets are held in U.S. dollar followed by pound sterling. Official holdings of reserve of assets including reserve position in IMF, SDR, foreign exchanges and gold stood at 1600 billion SDR at end March 2000.

## Augmentation of Liquidity

The methods of augmenting the liquidity adopted by the Fund are the quota increase, borrowing from members under GAB and creation of SDRs. Increase in quotas of all members with the IMF would improve global liquidity as their borrowing operations could simultaneously increase. Normally, quota reviews are held at intervals of not more than 5 years. Then the Fund would consider the growth of world economies, growth of international transactions and world trade and judge the adequacy of existing international liquidity. The quotas of members would determine their existing subscriptions to the Fund, their drawing rights on the Fund under both regular and special facilities and their share of allocation of SDRs and their voting power in the Fund.

So far eleven quota increases took place in the past. The eighth General Review of quotas made in 1984 raised the total quotas with the Fund by 47.5 per cent to 90 billion. Under the ninth quota increase, in 1990, total quotas increased further by 51.7% to SDR 136.7 billion. Even so, the ratio of Fund quotas to world imports is still lower at 4 per cent at present as compared to 9 per cent in 1970 and 12 per cent in 1965. Such general increases in quotas had taken place earlier in addition to some special increases of quotas of a few members whose currencies were supposed to be lower than the general requirements.

## Special Drawing Rights (SDR)

The Special Drawing Rights (SDRs) are another source of augmenting international liquidity. This is an asset specially intended to take the place of gold and as such called paper gold. Each SDR is equal to 0.88671 gms of fine gold, equivalent to one US dollar prior to devaluation in 1971. The value of SDR was changed with the devaluation of dollar in 1971 and 1973. During 1974 to 1980 the value of SDR was fixed on a daily basis as a weighed average value of a basket of 16 currencies of countries with more than 1 per cent of world trade. In 1981 these 16 were replaced by 5 major currencies, namely, US $, DM, UK £, French franc and yen.

These reserve assets have been created by the Fund since 1969 as and when required as part of the long-term strategy of augmenting world liquidity to keep pace with the requirements of a growing world economy and world trade. The actual allocation of SDRs to members would depend on the then quotas with the Fund. The acceptability of the SDR as an international liquid asset would depend upon the unconditional acceptance of this asset by the members of the Fund. The Fund members have been given the option to join the SDR scheme and those who have joined are bound to abide by the rules of unconditional acceptance for international payments, conversion into reserve currencies, payment and receipt of interest etc.

SDR accounts are kept separate from the General Account of the Fund. The SDR is like a coupon or a credit facility which can be exchanged for reserve currency as needed by the user and approved by the Fund. The governments of the countries are holders of the SDR and their accounts in SDRs are maintained by the Fund through book entries. If a member wants to use the SDR, it requests the Fund to designate another member to accept them in exchange for a reserve currency to use in international payments and the latter member is obliged to accept as designated by the Fund. This would then tantamount to a credit granted by the latter member to the former for which an interest rate of 1½ per cent is paid to the creditor by the debtor through the Fund. In this sense, SDRs are better than gold as no interest was received on gold. In order to encourage acceptability of these SDRs, a member country may be required to hold in all 300 per cent of the cumulative allocations – 100 per cent representing the original allocation and 200 per cent representing the part received from others as designated by the Fund. These SDRs are the liability of the member borrowing currencies in exchange for SDRs and not of the Fund which keeps only the accounts with a surveillance over the operations. The members are not expected to transfer SDRs for changing the composition of its international reserves. The Fund may also acquire SDRs in the process of its operations on General Account as the members may repurchase in SDRs or pay interest or service charges in SDRs. Further, with a view to put a limit on the use of this facility by deficit countries, the principle of "reconstitution" is laid down under which a member's net use of SDRs must be such that the average of its daily holdings over a five year period should be not less than 30 per cent (reduced to 15 per cent and later removed altogether) implying thereby, that it could use only 70 per cent of the allocation on average. This puts an obligation on the members using SDRs to repurchase them also.

## SDR Allocation

Starting with January 1970, SDRs were allotted to all member countries of the IMF who accepted the SDR scheme. The first SDR allocations were made during each of the years 1970-72 totalling SDR 9.3 billion. Further allocations were made for each of the years during 1979-81, totalling SDR 12 billion. The cumulative allocations since the beginning of the scheme were SDR 21,433 million. Such cumulative allocations amounted to only 5-7 per cent of the total world reserves other than gold. In timing of the allocations, the Fund kept in view the global need to supplement the existing reserve assets. Since then, in September 1997, a special one time allocation of SDR 21.4 billion was made which raised all participants' cumulative allocations to a common bench mark ratio of 29.3157 per cent of the quotas based on the Ninth General Review.

The SDRs cannot be used directly as reserves as they have to be converted into reserves of one or other currency before use for payments. They can be used by official agencies and for designated purposes only. These are not money as such but are comparable to near money or credit instruments. The fact that interest is payable on SDRs used by the debtors to the creditors would indicate that the SDRs are credit facilities.

## Uses

Countries have made considerable use of these facilities since their first allocation in 1970. These transfers were partly designations by the IMF or by voluntary agreements among the members or in transactions with the Fund by members and partly in transactions by other international bodies who are holders of SDRs. Since then gold has been replaced by SDR in the Fund's transactions as well as in the international transactions of members. The SDRs cannot, however, be exchanged for gold or for changing the composition of reserves of a country.

There are charges payable for use of SDRs. The charge for a creditor position in SDRs with the Fund is paid to the member holding excess SDRs than allocated. This charge of 1½ per cent was raised to 5 per cent in June 1974. Subsequently, the interest rate on borrowings in SDRs is determined quarterly by reference to a combined market interest which is weighed average rate on specified short-term instruments in the money markets of the same five countries in whose currencies the SDR value is determined, namely, the USA, West Germany, UK, France and Japan. The interest rates in the money markets of these five countries are weighted according to the same weights as used for SDR valuation. The IMF rate of remuneration to creditor countries was fixed in terms of SDR interest rate. The DM of Germany and French franc were replaced by Euro in 2000, and SDR is now a basket four currencies ($, £, yen, Euro).

SDRs can also be used in swap arrangements and in forward operations, as a unit of account or measure of value or a means of payment. The SDR is used as a currency peg by some countries and as security or pledge. The Asian Currency Union and a number of international and inter-regional bodies were using SDRs in the above applications.

## SDRs of India

India was allocated SDRs in the name of the Government of India since January 1970. These SDRs do not enter into the accounts of the RBI. During 1979-81, India was given further allocations on the basis of its quota with the Fund beginning with January 1979. India had a total allocation of about SDR 681 million during 1970-81.

India has used the SDRs in a very active manner since their inception and as at end March 2009, SDRs stood at Rs. 6 crores. SDR was used by India for payment of interest and repurchases from the Fund. India has also accepted them under the "Designation" Plans of the Fund. India has very comfortable exchange reserve position now due to economic reforms effected since July 1991.

## India's IMF Net Position

India actively participated in IMF operations since 1947 when they were started. India has drawn IMF credits under most of its schemes. Any country can count as its reserves its IMF position in gold and super-gold tranches. Similarly, its repurchase obligations with the IMF are to be deducted from its official gross reserves. It is in this context that India's IMF position becomes relevant. India's repurchase obligations were nil in 1970-71, when it had repaid Rs. 154 crores due to IMF. But India had a major drawal of about Rs. 815 crores in August 1980 under two credits, namely, Rs. 540 crores from the Special Trust Fund and Rs. 275 crores from the compensatory financing facility. Our gold tranche position was about 25 per cent of the quota which stood at 2207 million SDRs taking into account the 8th General Quota increase granted in January 1984. India has drawn into its credit tranches and stand-by credit arrangement, Extended Fund Facility, also the compensatory and contingency financing facility, oil facility and special Trust Fund facility. In June 2002, we had a reserve position in the IMF at $ 651 million and outstanding use of IMF credit (net) stood at nil SDR. Our net debt position to IMF was zero as at end June 2003. Our foreign exchange reserves stood at US $ 252 billion at end March 2009 which were roughly more than the import bill for any recent year, except in 2009.

## Additional SDRs

SDRs allocation to India was increased in 1997 by an additional 240 million SDRs due to special one time SDR allocation amounting to 21.4 billion. The principle of equitable share of cumulative SDR allocation to member countries as against the earlier principle of allocation as a ratio of quotas benefited India. As against the earlier share of 22%, it has now got 29%, which secured for India an additional 240 million SDR in 1997.

Besides in the 11th General Quota Review, the present quota funds would be increased by 45%, in which India will also benefit. The total of IMF quotas will be increased and 75% of the overall increase will be distributed in proportion to the present quotas of member countries, as against the earlier proportion of 60%. India stood to gain in this respect also.

IMF quote increase was approved in September 2008, through additional SDR allocation. India's quota was thus increased from 4158 million SDR to 5821 million SDRs. India's proportion of total IMF quotas was increased from 1.91% to 2.44%, as a consequence as at end 2008.

❖ ❖ ❖

# PART II

## MANAGEMENT OF EXCHANGE AND INTEREST RATE EXPOSURE

# DETERMINATION OF EXCHANGE RATES

7

## What is Exchange Rate?

There is a price for every thing, whether it is goods, services, finance or money. Just like interest rate is the price for borrowing money or ready cash, or credit, exchange rate is the price of any currency in terms of other currencies. Each nation state has its own currency and is valid and acceptable in that state or nation. If one nation has to pay to any other nation, the currency of the former has to be exchanged for the latter. In the similar manner, the residents of one nation pay to any other nation. They have to convert their currency into the currency of the receiving country. Then the rate of conversion of the currency unit of one country into the currency units of any other country is called the exchange rate.

The exchange rate is fixed by the government of the country in controlled economies and under strict trade and exchange control. But in a free country, it is determined by the intrinsic worth of the currency called Gustav Cassel Theory referred to later. It is also influenced by the following factors:

1. Interest rates in the respective countries.
2. Terms of purchase, spot or forward.
3. Riskiness of the country and the political system.
4. The degree of control in the foreign exchange market and the government interference.

Determination of exchange rates also depends on the policy of the Central Bank of the country and the system on which exchange rate is based such as "managed float", "free float", "controlled rates" etc. The exchange rate varies from the segment of the market, namely, whether it is the RBI rate, for its liquidity adjustment facility or for the RBI operations in its repurchase agreement (REPOs) or in its open market operations. Presently, RBI purchases and sells spot and forward dollars at its officially declared rate called Reference Rate. Besides, FEDA* (Foreign Exchange Dealers Association) has been fixing its own daily exchange rate for inter-bank operations. Based on those rates, the banks are free to fix their own rates for dollars or for other currencies, or for the cross currency rates. These rates for inter-market are different from what the banks quote to the public for their operations with them. Their purchase price is different from the sale price. The rate quoted by them differs depending on the riskiness of the debts and the period of time involved in actual delivery. For this purpose, an element of interest rate is also included in the exchange rate quoted by banks.

## Speculation

More important than the transactions demand for foreign currencies, there is a large segment of international flows of funds for hedging and speculation, for which the exchange rate quoted will be different. The RBI publishes data on the real effective exchange rate (REER) based on the six country trade based weighted average (base 2007-08 = 100) and nominal effective exchange rate for the same six country trade weighted average. RBI also publishes the REER and NEER of 36 country bilateral weights with base 1993-94 = 100, in its Monthly Bulletins (RBI Bulletins).

Speculation and expectations play an important part in the determination of the exchange rate. The speculative transactions are quickly reversed and for short-term from a day to a few days. The RBI keeps a surveillance on the speculative deals and operates on a daily basis to give direction to the rupee rate fluctuations. The expectations are about the forward premium or discount, interest rate variations and country's intrinsic strength on the external front, particularly in competitive strength, export and import trends and in trade in services and in the trends in financial markets, on capital account.

## Exchange Rate Mechanism

As in the case of any commodity, there is a price for any purchase or sale of a currency. Such a price in the exchange market is called the exchange rate. This is defined as the number of units of one currency that will be exchanged for a unit of another currency. The exchange rate of any currency can be expressed in two ways: one in terms of the number of foreign currency units against a given unit of domestic currency (thus, Rs. 100 = £ 1.4734 as indirect method) and the other in terms of the number of domestic currency units against a given unit of foreign currency (thus, £ 1 = Rs. 48.0350) as direct method (at end Nov. 2009) or $ 1 = Rs. 61.785 in 2013 given for illustration.

It is pertinent to ask what factors normally determine the exchange rate in the market. *Prima facie,* if the market is free and rates are allowed to fluctuate, the exchange rate would depend on the supply of and demand for a currency. Thus, taking dollars vis-a-vis rupees, the rate is determined by the demand for dollars and supply of dollars in relation to the rupee. Those who demand dollars are primarily importers from the USA to India who have to pay the US exporters in dollars. Similarly, those who supply dollars are primarily the exporters to USA who are paid in dollars by importers in USA.

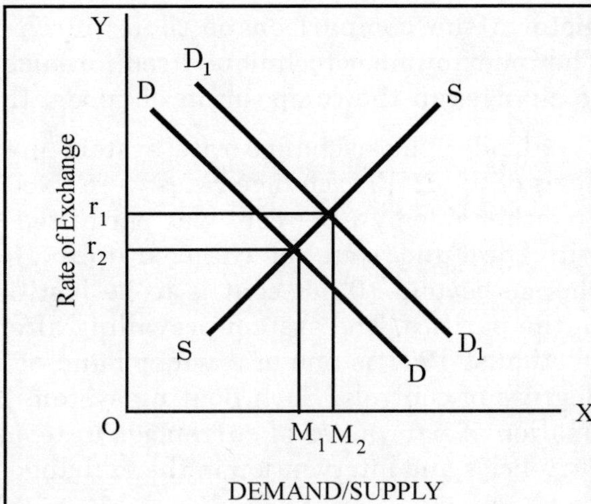

**Fig. 7.1**

The rate of exchange is determined at any moment by the forces of demand for and supply of a currency which in turn depends on the demand for and supply of commodities and services as between India and the USA. They also depend on arbitrage and interest rate speculation, currency speculation and short-term capital flows if these are permitted. This can be represented diagrammatically shown in Fig. 7.1.

Given the supply (SS), if the demand increases from DD to $D_1D_1$ the rate will rise from $r_1$ to $r_2$ and *vice versa*. A rise in the rate for rupee means more foreign currency units are given for a given unit of domestic currency, or vice versa.

## Gustav's Theory

The basic factors which determine the exchange rates are the intrinsic purchasing power of the currencies in their own domestic economies. In the era of paper currencies, which are not backed by gold or gold exchange standard, currencies of different countries are not based on their intrinsic worth in terms of gold, but in terms of what Prof. Gustav Cassel, the renowned classical economist, called the Purchasing Power Parity Theory. According to this theory, exchange rates are determined by what each unit of a currency can buy in terms of real goods and services in its own country. The rate of exchange is the amount of currency which would buy the equivalent basket of goods and services in both the countries. Such an exercise in real world is based on comparison at two periods of time, with one year as the basis of comparison, but no absolute comparison between two currencies is possible as the pattern of goods and services produced varies from country to country. It is assumed that the base year prices in both the countries are at equilibrium and the exchange ratio at that time represents the ratio of their purchasing powers. Thus, if the base period exchange rate is 1:1 a doubling of prices in the domestic economy of B with A's price remaining constant, would lead to a new exchange rate of 1:2. This ratio would set the bounds or limits to day-to-day fluctuations in the exchange rates based on the supply or demand forces for each currency.

## Limitations

This theory of Gustav is criticised on the ground that the quality of goods and services in both the countries is not the same and that a comparison of them is not realistic. The markets are not free due to trade and payment restrictions such as tariffs, quotas etc. Besides the base period exchange rate may not be the equilibrium rate which distorts the comparison of their purchasing power parities at the current period. The index number technique used for such comparison is also criticised as defective due to changes in the composition of goods, their qualities over period of time, etc.

Under the exchange rate system prevailing in the world, before 1971, under the aegis of the IMF, exchange rates were fixed in terms of gold or US dollar and a fluctuation on either side by 1 per cent was permitted. Any changes in exchange rate parity, as fixed with the Fund, could be changed up to 10 per cent by consultation with the Fund. Any change beyond 10 per cent is to be justified on grounds of fundamental disequilibrium in the parities. The system prevailing after the breakdown of the Bretton Woods system in August 1971 is one of a wider band of margins and floating currencies with varying degrees of controls. Such floating system favoured stable but adjustable par values and fixation of par values of currencies in terms of SDR which is represented by a basket of currencies and intervention in the exchange markets in terms of a multi-currency approach.

## Spot and Forward Rates

If an importer is paying on receipt of documents, then he can buy dollars spot and the bank sells him spot dollars. But if the importer agrees to pay three or six months hence, his demand for dollars might arise only after three or six months hence. These dollars are called forward dollars and the market is the forward market. The existence of a forward market provides cover or hedge against fluctuations in exchange rates. This exchange risk falls on the banks who are buying or selling dollars forward. The banks in turn can pass on the risk to the central bank of the country or to a foreign bank at another centre.

Just as banks are buying and selling spot, they also do business in forward currencies. Corresponding to the spot rate of exchange, there is a forward rate for various periods. If any bank succeeds in matching forward purchases with forward sales of the same currency, it avoids "taking a position" and assumes no risk. If they do not match, the bank may have an uncovered position which it may cover with another bank which has a contrary position. If it fails to cover with a bank, it may still do so with the central bank of the country or with a correspondent bank abroad. If a bank takes a position uncovered, it may take a calculated risk in the hope that the rate may move in its favour or it has failed to secure a proper cover in which case it would adjust uncovered position against a spot deal or against a future sale or purchase.

Currencies purchased or sold in forward would be subject to the influences of interest rates at home and abroad. A forward currency will be at premium (higher than the spot expressed in foreign currency per domestic unit quoted as Rs. 100 = $ 4.7555), as at end June 1991; later rates were quoted as $ 1 = Rs. 48.03501 in June 1993, and $ 1 = Rs. 48.3501 at end March 2009, or $ 1 = Rs. 61.1785 at the end of Dec. 2013. If interest rates abroad are higher than at home. The premium or discount will depend on interest rates and expectations of interest rates and exchange rates. Forward premia for U.S. dollar is around 5 per cent per annum at end December, 1999 and around 3.45 per cent per annum at end March 2008 and 2.87 per cent per annum of end July 2009, and 7.2% in May 2012.

Speculation and hedging operations are taking place in free markets to take advantage of interest rate and exchange rate differentials. In the case of India, such hedging and speculation are not possible as banks are not allowed to take position in any currency beyond the minimum working balances to be kept in various centres. In a free foreign exchange market, short-term capital flows take place to take advantage of interest rate differentials and will be quickly reversed, leading to instability in the exchange rates. One-sided speculation is also very destabilising which generally the central bank of a country would not allow unchecked. Controls on capital account, particularly to counter such destabilising short-term flows, are in tune with the spirit of the International Monetary Fund. Speculation on a limited scale and if it is on both sides of purchase and sale, is healthy and welcome to keep the balance in the market and absorb the excesses of demand/supply of currencies in the foreign exchange market.

## Arbitrage

When foreign exchange markets are free to fluctuate, the exchange rate of a currency should be the same in almost all the centres. Thus, if the dollar rate per sterling is different in New York and Frankfurt, then funds would flow in either direction to take advantage of the rate differential. It is, however, possible that slight differentials might be still there due to carrying costs of moving funds from one place to another. Such operations in terms of movements of funds from one centre to another are called arbitrage operations.

Such operations can take place only if there are no exchange controls in both the countries and if funds are free to move. Thus, if either New York or Frankfurt is subject to exchange restrictions involving central bank supervision of funds inflow and outflow and ban on free movements, arbitrage cannot take place and differentials in rates between two countries might exist.

Arbitrage is not limited to two centres or two currencies alone. Three-point and multi-point arbitrage can also take place if the respective currencies are free. Thus, in a three-point arbitrage, the dollar-sterling rate and the dollar-franc rate are considered and the cross rate between sterling and franc should be in conformity with the above two rates. Otherwise, three-point arbitrage can take place by moving funds from dollar to franc and franc to sterling and back to dollar from sterling. Suppose the dollar-sterling rate is £ 1 = $ 2.80 and franc 350 = $ 1 and £ =1020 francs. Starting with $ 100, one can buy up pounds, move from pounds to francs and thence to dollars back, making a gain of about $ 5 per $ 100 in the above example. Thus, arbitrage can take place as between centres or currencies at more than two centres and currencies at a time. Such arbitrage operations may be for gain in exchange rate differential or in interest rate differential as between centres. The former are called currency arbitrage and the latter interest arbitrage. An operation of simultaneous purchase and sale in each of the two markets to take advantage of interest differential is called interest arbitrage. Such deals are put through by swaps or forward deals.

The operations in the foreign exchange market are exposed to a number of risks which are difficult to foresee and forecast. These risks may be credit risks arising out of lending to a foreign borrower whose credit rating is not known for certainty. Secondly, there may be currency risks of trading in a currency whose stability and strength is known to fluctuate. Thirdly, there are country risks involved in lending to a country whose political and economic strength is weak and is uncertain. Fourthly, there are risks of fluctuating interest rates in various currencies in the inter-bank market and anticipations may sometimes go wrong. Fifthly, there are risks of illiquidity due to mismatch between current assets and current liabilities with the result there may be sudden need for borrowing and difficulties may arise in securing funds at short notice. Lastly, the dealers sometimes take risks by exceeding the limits of prudent trading in a currency with the result that they may find it difficult to cover the transactions and incur losses in such a position. Such risks are more marked in international lending and borrowing and in foreign exchange and currency markets. Further details of risk are discussed in a separate chapter.

For a country like India, with a wide network of controls, arbitrage operations are not possible. Indian rupee was insulated from world free currency markets as the banks' operations in India were strictly controlled and monitored by the Reserve Bank of India, until 1992, when the trend to freely convertible rupees was started. As capital account controls are still prevailing, most hot money flows are controlled. But arbitrage and exchange risk cover are possible for current transfers.

# INDIAN FOREIGN EXCHANGE RATES

In India there are 92 commercial and co-operative banks who are authorised to deal in foreign exchange and are called as Authorised Dealers and are eligible to operate in the foreign exchange market. However, not all co-operative banks are authorised to deal in foreign exchange. These banks cover their open positions in currencies in London through their correspondents or branches abroad or in India in the inter-bank market. However, banks finance thousands of crores of foreign trade, and put through crores of foreign remittances and a host of other purchases and sales. In the process of such purchases and sales directly with the public, the authorised dealers would have various currencies which they try to dispose of by matching demand with supply in the inter-bank market. It is only the unmatched net requirements that are purchased from the RBI, or excesses sold to the RBI. These are some authorised broker firms in foreign exchange.

## Exchange Dealers

The foreign department of every bank draws up a position sheet for each currency daily in which purchases and sales of the currency are recorded. As the banks generally avoid taking any exchange risk by keeping uncovered balance and are not permitted to do so under the previous regulations, they try to cover their position by the end of the day. When the purchases exceed sales, the credit balance is plus (or long) and overbought. This is to be covered by equal sales of that currency. When the sales exceed purchases, the debit balance is minus, short or oversold position and is to be covered by equivalent purchases. These sales and purchases would include both spot and forward, import bills or export bills negotiated or purchased, clean sales or purchases (other than through bills, namely, by TT, MT, cheques, drafts), BC sales, etc.

Before entering into the inter-bank market, the banker decides how much to cover and what is the outstanding balance position in his books. Banks operate in the inter-bank market through the foreign exchange brokers. In every important market centre, some brokers operate in these dealings. The banker keeps some minimum balances in his Nostro account to meet the customer needs as they accrue. *The more exactly he synchronises the delivery dates of his purchases and sales, the greater is his profit. The finer the rates he quotes, the better is his position. The better he foresees the trends in exchange rates and interest rates in various centres, the more efficient he is and the better is his profitability.*

In the inter-bank market, banks put through the dealings of purchase and sale of currency through authorised brokers. Brokers in each centre are in contact with other centres in India and in foreign countries for effecting matching transactions in various currencies. In all centres, export bills, import bills and various remittances are daily purchased and sold by banks. Imports give rise to payments abroad and purchase of foreign currencies. As the bulk of the imports in India is on government account and the SBI keeps the account of the public sector undertakings and of the government, the SBI enters the foreign exchange market mostly as a buyer of foreign currencies. Exports are more concentrated in the private sector, in which all banks are involved in varying degrees. Hence, sales of foreign currencies in the exchange market are more evenly spread among the banks in India. Many times, brokers cannot match in the local centres for odd currencies like Austrian shilling or Nigerian naira or Libyan dinar, which are to be put through in a more sophisticated market like London or Singapore.

In India, some financial centres are more developed than others in the foreign exchange market. Thus, Mumbai, Kolkata and Chennai are more developed than others. Some of the foreign exchange transactions being seasonal, the markets are also seasonal.

## RBI and Exchange Market

The RBI operates in the market as the last recourse agency. The RBI purchases and sells sterling spot and buys and sells forward sterling up to six months but since June 1966, forward sales have been stopped. Since the abandonment of convertibility of the US dollars in 1971, the forward cover for a longer period was felt necessary due to greater exchange risks and it was provided by the RBI up to 9 months at a rate of £ 0.005 per month fixed extendable up to one year in total, at a nominal charge of £ 0.0075 per month for the extended period.

The other currencies in which the RBI started operations during the seventies were dollars, D.M. and yen. The RBI started purchases spot and forward dollars from July and August 1966 respectively and with brief interruptions from August 1971 to October 1972 and February 1973 to September 1973, the RBI continued to purchase spot and forward dollars. Similar purchases of DM and of yen were started from March and May 1974 respectively. The period of forward cover was up to three months initially but was extended up to six months from September 1975. Thus, the RBI provided cover for 4 currencies which are our major trading partners, namely, sterling, dollar, DM and yen. The Bank purchased and sold spot £ buys forward sterling and bought dollar, DM and yen both spot and forward.

Thus, the RBI was operating in four major currencies, namely, UK £, US $, Japanese yen and DM. Early in 1987, the RBI has started selling spot US dollars with the result that it used to buy and sell two currencies, UK £ and US$, in addition to its purchases of DM and Japanese yen. It has also adopted recently the practice of changing the rates quoted by it in the course of the day if the conditions in that market warranted it. The RBI used to quote both the spot and forward rates in the currencies it transacts with the banks and in ACU[1] on a daily basis.

The RBI was providing cover for a fairly long period of up to 10 years in respect of long-term contracts for engineering exports and construction projects. Since November 1975, the RBI has also offered the cover to (ADs Authorised Dealers) against exchange rate fluctuation in respect of deposits received in foreign currency from non-residents. Most of the facilities which the RBI offers are intended for exporters in terms of cover or purchase and sale. This is justified in view of the national importance attached to exports. But they have not offered similar facilities for importers for two reasons.

Firstly, the bulk of the imports into India is by the government or public sector agencies who do not need such facilities.

Secondly, the inter-bank market is designed to develop to provide cover as and when needed by the importers in this regard. The RBI is maintaining itself as a last resort institution of foreign exchange as in domestic finance. The policy of RBI in this regard is very flexible and designed to promote self-reliance by banks and greater resort to the inter-bank market.

The RBI has, however, responded to emerging situation in the foreign exchange market quickly and promptly. Since rupee convertibility was launched in March 1992, RBI is publishing a reference rate around which it operates in the market to stabilise the rate of exchange of rupee in terms of US dollar. RBI operates in the Forex Market both directly and indirectly and tries to stabilise and influence the market, through its operations in dollar and Euro.

## Exchange Rate System in India

India was a formal member of the sterling area from September 1939 to June 1972, during which period the external value of the rupee (exchange rate) was kept stable in terms of sterling. Since the establishment of IMF, of which India was a founder member, the external value of the rupee was declared in terms of gold and US dollar (Re. 1 = 0.268601 grams of fine gold or Re. 1 = US \$ 0.3022) and its value was maintained stable in terms of £ by purchases and sales of sterling by the RBI (the sterling rupee rate was Re. 1 = 1 S. 6d). Rupee was devalued twice, namely, in September 1949 by 30.5 per cent and in June 1966 by 36.5 per cent to maintain parity with £. Since June 1966, the new rate has been Re. 1 = 13.3 US cents. This link with sterling which was maintained by keeping the rupee stable in terms of sterling and using the sterling as an intervention currency was justified on the ground that the bulk of India's trade was either with the sterling area or was denominated in sterling and that India's foreign interests lie with sterling which was considered at that time a stable and strong reserve currency.

With the breakdown of the Bretton Woods system in August 1971, and the floatations of various major currencies, the Indian rupee was temporarily kept pegged to the US dollar at Rs. 7.5 per US \$ 1, and this rate was kept stable by intervention in the market

1. Asian currency unit, which is now replaced by SDR, referre to in another chapter.

by purchases and sales of sterling. Rupee-dollar peg was used to determine the rupee-sterling rate. This position continued up to December 1971, when under the Smithsonian agreement, the exchange rate of sterling was fixed in terms of US dollar and the rupee was again linked to sterling thereafter. This sterling link proved short-lived up to June 1972 when sterling and other major currencies started floating. Between June 1972 and September 1975, rupee was kept stable in terms of sterling but was allowed to fluctuate against all other currencies. During this period, rupee was effectively devalued against all major currencies other than £ by as much as 18-20 per cent. Since the effect of such depreciation was not favourable to India with her inelastic supplies of export goods and growing debt burden, along with the rising import bill, India decided to delink itself with £ completely in September 1975. Since then, the external value of rupee was determined by the market value, as quoted in London, of a basket of currencies. The currencies included in the basket and the relative currency weights as well as the method of compilation of the exchange rate were kept confidential. Since then the rupee valuation has been based on a mix of international currencies with which India has trade relations and this has resulted in changes in its value very frequently and a net depreciation in terms of sterling. Since September 1975, the value of rupee has been maintained stable within a wider margin of 2.25 per cent on either side. A middle rate, as between selling and buying rates, is fixed in terms of sterling which continued to be an intervention currency. The cross rates for the rupee against other currencies are calculated and fixed by banks in terms of the cross quotations in London. Whenever there is a change in the market value of the rates of the currencies in the basket by more than $2^1/_4$ per cent against the standard unit of account, namely, SDR, the rupee-sterling rate is altered suitably. The external value of rupee was kept relatively stable within the permitted band of 5 per cent on either side of the middle rate. Minor fluctuations on either side evidence the fact that India does not need the support of any currency, namely, sterling or dollar. But there was, however, a net depreciation in terms of sterling. The wisdom of using the sterling as an intervention currency was doubted and advocates were not wanting in demanding the use of dollar for the purpose, at that time.



## Floating vs. Fixed Exchange Rates

In the post-Smithsonian era, the currencies have been on various types of floating systems due to the abandonment of the convertibility of US dollar. Single float, joint float, managed float etc., are examples of such floats. The system of fixed exchange parities (par values) was given decent burial following the breakdown of the Bretton Woods system in August 1971.

Floating rate is a rate which is allowed to fluctuate freely according to supply and demand Forces. Such float is a free float if no intervention takes place by the Central Bank of the country. In the real world, some degree of intervention exists which leads to a managed float. Such managed floats are either single or joint. Dollar, sterling and yen were floating with varying degrees of intervention within a band of 2.25 per cent on either side and they are single floats. The European Common Market countries (West Germany, France, Belgium, Netherlands, Luxemburg and Ireland, Denmark and Sweeden) are under a joint float within a narrow band called “Snake in the Tunnel. The new IMF policy is to keep relatively stable exchange rates within a wider band of fluctuations.

Indian rupee is kept relatively stable with the help of a basket of currencies, up to July 1991, when the rupee was devalued and LERMS (Limited Exchange Rate Management System) was adopted later.

## Advantage of Basket Currencies

With the existing system of exchange controls in India, a free floating rupee was out of question in the eighties. The rupee is not strong enough to withstand the speculative onslaughts. Our trade would have suffered. Alternatives left to the monetary authorities in India were, therefore, to link it with $ or £ or a combination of some major currencies like the SDR. Since both $ and £ were having their own problems, the choice has fallen on a basket of currencies but unlike the 16 major currencies in the case of the SDR, at that time only 5 major currencies having good trade connections with India in 1975 were chosen in its basket. The SDR valuation would have been unrealistic for India as some of the currencies represented in SDR have no relations with India's trade. The basis of SDR valuation was itself changed to a bag of five currencies in 1981. It was felt that it would be advantageous for India to link the rupee to a mix of currencies properly weighted as this would give greater stability and more certainty so that India's trade and investment abroad would not suffer. The import bill and debt servicing burden are heavy for India and it would be necessary to have relative stability in the exchange rate. The fact that moderate depreciation took place in effect as against $, DM etc., would have probably helped our export trader in particular.

With the initiation of economic and financial reforms, in July 1991, far reaching changes were introduced in the foreign exchange policy and exchange rate management. Foreign Exchange Regulation Act, FERA was diluted and banks have been allowed greater freedom of lending and their deposit and lending rates have also been freed to a large extent. Foreign exchange release is mostly left to the banks, for many purposes, subject to an upper limit for each purpose. Rupee was made partially convertible first in 1992 followed by full convertibility on trade account in 1993 and thereafter full convertibility on current account, inclusive of invisible account in 1994. The era of decontrol on foreign exchange has started with these reforms. We have now a System of Exchange rate management adopted by the RBI since 1994, and the FERA was replaced by Foreign Exchange Management Act, FEMA in the year 2000.

## RBI Policy Applied to Banks

RBI continued to delegate more powers to ADs in dealing in the forex market and in effecting receipts and payments.

RBI has been publishing the Reference Rate of rupee against dollar on a daily basis. The RBI is dealing in the buying and selling of rupee for the dollar only, the both spot and forward. On the basis of the RBI's Refinance rate, Foreign Exchange Dealers Association of India (FEDAI) is giving the rates for banks, but banks are free to adjust their rates depending upon their currency positions. RBI gives the reference rates for the rupee against US dollar and Euro currency at present.

Examples of RBI and FEDAI Rates are given below for U.S. dollar.

**Table 7.1**

*$ 1 = in Rupees*

| | *RBI Rates* | *FEDAI Rates* |
|---|---|---|
| March 4, 1994 | 31.3800 | 31.3790 |
| March 3, 1995 | 31.5725 | 31.5659 |
| June 30, 1995 | 31.3940 | 31.3940 |
| July 1997 (End) | 35.7100 | 35.7150 |
| May 1999 (End) | 42.8400 | 42.8500 |
| December 1999 (End) | 43.4900 | 43.5100 |
| February 2004 | 45.2600 | 45.2600 |
| March 2004 | 43.3900 | 43.4300 |
| March 2009 | 50.9500 | 50.9400 |
| November 2009 | 48.0400 | 48.0350 |
| March end of 2014 | 60.0998 | 60.0998 |

*Source:* RBI Bulletin

In the forward exchange market, RBI allowed free functioning following the current account convertibility of the rupee since March 1994, particularly after deregulation of lending rates in October 1994. The swap premia seemed to adjust to real interest rates, i.e., interest rates adjusted for inflation rates. Another factor affecting the swap premia is the call money rates in the respective countries.

RBI has been persuading banks to develop forward market in India by dealings with inter-bank and in foreign market. There is however need to develop foreign exchange derivatives for providing hedge through forward contracts, swaps and cross currency options. It is possible to develop rupee based options if international quotes for rupee are available which is not the case at present.

## Currency Deals

Right now, the quotations are called direct quotes. The principle the banker follows is to give two way quotes-based on "give less and take more." The spread between the buying and selling rates is the banks' profit. The interest component for any period is shown separately from the currency position. The spread depends on the cable cost, brokerage cost and administrative cost leaving only a small margin of profit to the banker.

If the quotation is $ 1 = Rs. 35.750 – 35.780, then the banker is prepared to buy dollars at Rs. 35.750 and sell dollars at Rs. 35.780. Here the principle is buy low and sell high. Let us take a quote of $ to pounds say pound = $ 1.5200 – 10, the quoting bank wants to sell sterling at $ 1.5210 and buy at $ 1.5200. The price of dollar to D.M. at $ 1.5810/20 means that for every dollar, the quoting bank will pay 1.5810 DM and would receive 1.5820 DM for dollar. In the quotation, the bank always wants to gain.

## Trading by Banks

In some banks, the dealing rooms are also located at Chennai and Bangalore. In fact foreign banks concentrate their deals mostly in Mumbai, while SBI has its Central Dealing room at Kolkata. The largest component of inter-bank market operations is concentrated in Mumbai.

**Table 7.2: SPOT Trading Operations**

This bank has classified the trading operations as shown below:

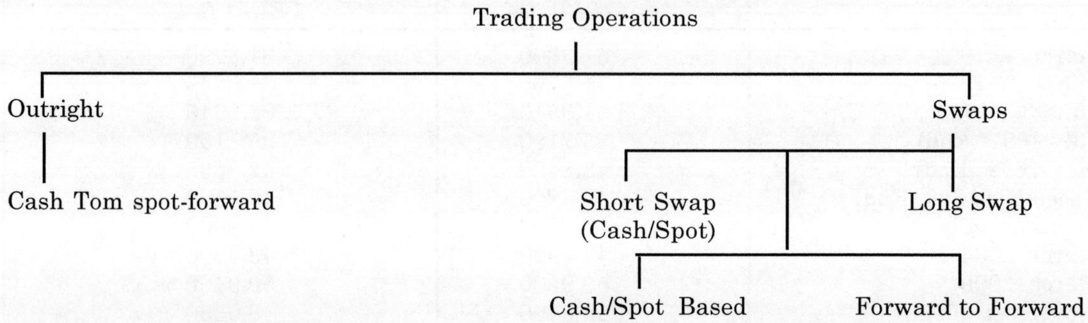


Tom means Tomorrow here. Spot is settled on the same day (cash), value tomorrow (tom) and forward (beyond spot date); spot deals are less risky while forwards are more risky. The forwards may be for a few months, say 1 to 6 months.

Spot trading has two types of deals:

**1. In and Out Trading:** The number of deals are many but the profit/loss in each is minimal. Minimal exposure and minimum risk is involved in this.

**2. Position Trading:** There will be fewer deals with large exposure being held for some time for profit to be booked.

The portfolio dealer in foreign currency has to go in for a judicious mix of these two strategies. Examples of these two strategies of the trader in Mumbai is given below. For in and out trading the exposure, pound 1 million.

1 million pounds bought @ 1.5270, sold 1.5272 profit: 2 pips

1 million pound bought @ 1.5274, sold 1,5277, profit: 3 pips

and so on; he made 10 deals, each with a profit of 1 to 3 pips. For 10 transactions of 1 million pound, he has made a profit of say 20 pips, exposure is only 1 million pound total.

In position trading, the trader takes a big exposure say of $ 5 million hoping DM will improve against dollar. He sells $ 3 million first at DM 1.5840 and if the trend assumed is correct, he sells another $ 2 million at DM 1.5780. When the DM rose to 1.5700, he sells all the DM for dollars back to make profit on his total position. Say the average sale price of dollars is 1.5780 and now purchase price is 1.5700. He made a profit of 80 points for dollar, which is a large amount, for deals involving millions of dollars.

# Exchange Rates Quotations

Daily Financial Press gives TT rates of various currencies in terms of rupees TT means Telegraphic Transfers which is next best means and quickest method of transferring funds from one currency to another currency. It is next to physical delivery of currency on spot. The rates for TT buying and selling for major currencies in the world are given in terms of rupees for each of the foreign currency units. The margin between buying and selling rate is the profit to the wholesaler. Exchange rates for currency or cash and cheques are also available in the daily press. Forward premium for one month or three or six months are also published, by the RBI, in their hand book of statistics.

London Inter Bank Offer Rates (LIBOR) for one month, 3 months and 6 months for various currencies are also given. These are the interest rates for deposits kept in those currencies in the Euro-Currency market, for the respective maturities. The last column gives the values of each currency in terms of U.S. dollar, which will be useful to calculate the cross-currency rates for the rupee as we know the rupee rate in terms of dollar and dollar rates in terms of each of the other currencies, we can work out by crossing, the rupee values of the other currencies (see Daily ET for illustrations).

## Cross Currency Deals

Dealings in Forex market depend on the availability of rupee funds as also the foreign funds. Therefore, the surplus funds or floating funds of the banks are used for the dealing *vis-a-vis* the foreign currencies.

In India, premium or discount depends on the demand and supply position and not much on the interest rates. Movements in the spot currency rates also influence the forward premium or discount. Suppose, a large import payment in dollars is due 3 months hence, the premium for 3 months is higher than 6 months premium because of demand and supply factors, although in terms of interest rate gain, 6 months premium should be higher than 3 months premium as per normal interest rate structure.

Let us take a simple crude example:

Suppose the pound rupees rates are as follows:

| | *$ - Rs.* | *Rs. - pound* | *pound - $* |
|---|---|---|---|
| Spot | 31.25-28 | 47.50-53 | 1.5260-70 |
| 1 month | 15-20 points | 13-16 points | 36-32 points |

Suppose you have a deficit in pound, what is the best way to cover it? Rupee is at discount over pound. If we buy pound or sell pound, we receive less (13 paise). Instead of going directly to sterling, if we go through $ - rupee route and $ to pound, on one $, we gain 15 paise by this method. We bought spot $ at 31.28 and sold one month forward at 31.43 (discount added 31.28 + 15). Then take the pound - $ forwards 36-32 pound is at a discount and dollar at premium. Here we sell spot dollar at 1.5270 and bought one month forward dollar at 1.5234 (36 points deducted from spot rate 1.5270 – 36).

Combining the above two deals we bought $ at 31.28 and sold at £ = 1.5270 to acquire pound. The spot £ is at Rs. 47.7645 = (31.28 × 1.5270). We sold forward $ at 31.43 and bought forward $ at 1.5234 for one pound. We sold one month forward pound at 47.8804 Rs. = (31.43 × 1.5234). Thus, we bought spot pound for Rs. 47.7645. We sold one month forward pound at Rs. 47.8804. We gained 12 paise in this swap deal, whereas we would have lost in direct deal as the rupee was at a discount on pound.

## Cross Rates in Forex Market

The rates of exchange as between any foreign currencies, other than the domestic currency as quoted in the domestic forex market are the cross rates. To give an example, if a dollar is quoted at Rs. 45.36 spot, on a day in Mumbai, it is an indirect market quotation in the domestic market. Leaving aside rupee-dollar rate, the rates for US dollar as against other currencies, say pound sterling, Euro, Japanese yen and Australian dollar are called cross rates.

Given below are two tables, showing the spot rates of rupees for buying and selling foreign currencies and travellers' cheques in foreign currencies in one Table and cross currency rates for U.S. dollar, Australian dollar, Canadian dollar, pound, sterling, Japanese yen, Euro, etc. against each other, called cross currency rates in another table.

In Indian forex market if the U.S. dollar to rupee is given as \$ 1 = Rs. 45.36, then the buying rates will be lower than this and selling rate of banks will be higher than this in respect of both for currency notes and travellers cheque. This is because, the rate of \$1 = Rs. 45.36 as the inter-bank rate, etc. which banks can buy dollars, but they add or substract their own margins when they deal with the public. The principle of "Buy low and sell high" is followed in these quotations. Thus, \$1 = Rs. 44.40 is the banks' buying rate and Rs. 45.90 is the banks' selling rate. The buying and selling rates of banks vary from bank to bank, depending on their costs and margins fixed for the purpose, whether they deal in currency notes or travellers cheques. There is again a margin which differs between currency notes and travellers cheques. The principle underlying these transactions is that the bank stands to gain both in buying and selling foreign currencies. The bank's buying rate is the selling rate for the public and vice versa and the quotations given are the bank's own rates to the public sales and purchases of foreign currencies. The currency in which banks deal in India is the U.S. dollar, as this is the currency in which the RBI makes open market operations and the RBI gives its reference rate in dollar and Euro.

## Cross Currency Deals in India

**Table 7.3: Forex Market**

Buying and selling rates of leading foreign currencies and traveller's cheques in the local market

| | *Currency Notes* | | *Travellers Cheques* | | | *Currency Notes* | | *Travellers Cheques* | |
|---|---|---|---|---|---|---|---|---|---|
| *Currency* | *Buying* | *Selling* | *Buying* | *Selling* | *Currency* | *Buying* | *Selling* | *Buying* | *Selling* |
| British Pound | 79.40 | 82.40 | 80.00 | 81.95 | Australian Dollar | 30.55 | 32.80 | 31.10 | 32.50 |
| US Dollar | 44.40 | 45.90 | 44.70 | 45.70 | Singapore Dollar | 25.00 | 27.30 | 25.80 | 26.75 |
| Euro | 52.80 | 55.30 | 53.60 | 55.00 | Saudi Riyal | 11.40 | 12.55 | Not Available | |
| Swiss Francs | 33.60 | 36.05 | 34.85 | 35.90 | Hong Kong Dollar | 5.40 | 6.00 | No TCs | |
| Canadian Dollar | 31.00 | 34.10 | 32.45 | 33.40 | UAE Dirham | 11.70 | 12.90 | No TCs | |
| Japanese Yen (100) | 37.95 | 41.10 | 39.50 | 40.55 | Kuwaiti Dinar | 144.80 | 158.65 | No TCs | |

*Source:* Canara Bank Foreign Department (September 2008)

**Table 7.4: Cross Currency Rates**

| *Country* | *INR* | *USD* | *AUD* | *GBP* | *CAD* | *JPY* | *SGD* | *CHF* | *AED* | *EUR* |
|---|---|---|---|---|---|---|---|---|---|---|
| US | 46.3412 | – | 1.0779 | 0.5990 | 1.0462 | 87.1700 | 1.3806 | 0.9988 | 3.6730 | 0.6627 |
| Australia | 42.9845 | 1.0781 | – | 0.5557 | 0.9707 | 80.8700 | 1.2808 | 0.9266 | 3.4075 | 0.6149 |
| Britain | 77.3539 | 1.6693 | 1.7993 | – | 1.7465 | 145.5100 | 2.3047 | 1.6674 | 6.1317 | 1.1063 |
| Canada | 44.2830 | 0.9558 | 1.0302 | 0.5726 | – | 83.3100 | 1.3192 | 0.9547 | – | 0.6334 |
| Japan | 0.5317 | 0.0115 | 1.2365 | 0.6872 | 1.2002 | – | 1.5838 | 1.1459 | 4.2139 | 0.7603 |
| Singapore | 33.5666 | 0.7243 | 0.7807 | 0.4339 | 0.7580 | 63.1400 | – | 0.7235 | – | 0.4800 |
| Switzerland | 46.3882 | 1.0011 | 1.0791 | 0.5997 | 1.0474 | 87.2700 | 1.3821 | – | 3.6772 | 0.6635 |
| UAE | 12.6154 | 0.2722 | 0.2935 | – | – | 23.7300 | 0.3759 | – | – | 0.1804 |
| Euroland | 69.9165 | 1.5089 | 1.6263 | 0.9039 | 1.5787 | 131.5200 | 2.0832 | 1.5072 | 5.5422 | – |

**Exchange Rates**

| *Exchange Rates* | *TT Buy* | *Bill Buy* | *TT Sell* | *Bill Sell* | *TC Buy* | *CCY Buy* | *TC Sell* | *CCY Sell* |
|---|---|---|---|---|---|---|---|---|
| Australian Dollar | 42.4825 | 42.3975 | 43.2750 | 43.3625 | 42.0500 | 41.8500 | 43.7500 | 43.9500 |
| British Pound | 76.0475 | 75.8950 | 77.4500 | 77.6025 | 75.2500 | 74.9000 | 78.2500 | 78.6500 |
| Canadian Dollar | 43.8075 | 43.7200 | 44.6250 | 44.7125 | 43.3500 | 43.1500 | 45.1000 | 45.3000 |
| Danish Krone | 9.2550 | 9.2350 | 9.4450 | 9.4650 | 9.1500 | 9.1000 | 9.5500 | 9.6000 |
| Euro | 69.0425 | 68.9025 | 70.3175 | 70.4550 | 68.3500 | 68.0000 | 71.0500 | 71.4000 |
| Hong Kong Dollar | 5.8975 | 5.8850 | 6.0250 | 6.0375 | 5.800 | 5.800 | 6.1000 | 6.1500 |
| Japanese Yen (*100) | 52.5125 | 52.4075 | 53.4875 | 53.5950 | 51.9500 | 51.7000 | 54.0500 | 54.3000 |
| New Zealand Dollar | 33.2775 | 33.2125 | 33.9050 | 33.9725 | 32.9500 | 32.7500 | 34.2500 | 34.4500 |
| Singapore Dollar | 33.1475 | 33.0800 | 33.7700 | 33.8375 | 32.8000 | 32.6500 | 34.1500 | 34.3000 |
| Swedish Krona | 6.6175 | 6.6050 | 6.7625 | 6.7750 | 6.5500 | 6.500 | 6.8500 | 6.9000 |
| Swiss Franc | 45.6875 | 45.5950 | 46.5400 | 46.6325 | 45.2000 | 45.0000 | 47.0000 | 47.2500 |
| UAE Dirham | 12.3225 | 12.2975 | 12.8425 | 12.8675 | 12.2000 | 12.1000 | 13.0000 | 13.0500 |
| US Dollar | 45.9175 | 45.8250 | 46.3325 | 46.4250 | 45.4500 | 45.2000 | 46.8000 | 47.0500 |

As in Dec. 2009/ET, Dec. 3, 2009.

The cross currency rates are very handy for banks dealing in the currency markets. These are published on a daily basis by the FEDA (Federation of Exchange Dealers Association). The turnover of trade in the inter-bank market is nearly five times higher than in the trade with the public, that is called merchant trade. Cross currency rates are useful for international merchant transactions for imports and exports and current account transfers. For hedge purposes, cross rates are used in respect of future receipts and payments in foreign currencies other than dollar. Forward rate agreements and forward margins, futures trading in currencies are facilitated by cross currency rates. For foreign currency borrowings and lending and funds transfers, these rates come in handy. Capital transfers for working capital, investments both of direct and portfolio nature are aided by these cross rates. Thus, the merchant transactions hedge and speculative deals are all facilitated by the cross rate.

While the rupee depreciated during 1993 to 2003 by 35% against U.S. dollar, its depreciation in terms of other currencies varied, say by 37% against pound sterling, 27% against Japanese yen and so on. In this scenario, the cross rates as between U.S. dollar and sterling, yen etc. are bound to change and these differences give chance for arbitrage transactions. Arbitrage refers to buying in one market, say yen and selling in another market, say Euro or sterling. If dollar is appreciated against rupee, it may be worth while sometimes to buy UK pounds with rupees and move from pound to dollars in a time frame. These are arbitrage transactions which bring about parity as between exchange rates of varying currencies and put them in conformity with the prevailing rates in all currencies in the forex market. If any currency is cheaper relatively, move to it before we move to a dearer currency. A stable currency is preferred to a more volatile currency.

# FORECASTING EXCHANGE RATES

# 8

## Introduction

All international transactions are exposed to some risks. These transactions can be merchandise trade or invisibles, current account flow of funds or capital account flow of funds. Risk can arise in commodity markets, financial markets, or transit periods, due to value of time. Even transactions in merchandise trade and invisibles involve payments and receipts in currencies and lead to foreign exchange exposures. As there are risk exposures in all international transactions, there is need for risk management. As most of these exposures are in foreign exchange market, exchange rates and interest rate changes are more important risks to be managed.

One of the methods of managing exchange rate risk is forecasting the exchange rate. Any forecast is based on some variables and subjective factors. The forecast itself may involve uncertainty as it may go wrong or the actual may be off the forecast. Besides, forecast has many limitations. The choice of variables or the forecasting model may go wrong. The base year may be incorrect level to compare the levels. There can be statistical mistakes or errors of the model chosen.

The mathematical modelling is not attempted here, but the likely variables influencing the exchange rate can be indicated. Gustav Cassel's theory states that exchange rates as between two currencies vary with the purchasing power parity of these currencies in the domestic markets. This theory is discussed in the detail in the following pages.

There are many other factors, other than purchasing power parities, which influence the exchange rates.

Firstly, the fundamentals of the economy, the GDP growth rate, export-import growth rates and their relative importance to the GDP, trade and current account deficits in the respective countries are to be compared.

Secondly, interest rate changes in the levels in the concerned countries are to be taken into account in the forecast of the exchange rate.

Thirdly, the levels of exchange controls, tariff and non-tariff barriers to trade, tax rates in the respective countries are the other factors which influence exchange rates. Some factors are non-quantifiable and subjective.

Fourthly, there are a number of variables like speculation, government interference in trade and forex exchange and anticipations of their changes which are not foreseeable and predictable.

Fifthly, subjective factors like anticipation in interest rates, inflation, exchange rates, etc. influence the actual exchange rate.

Sixthly, the total transactions demand for and supply of foreign exchange, as reflected in the expected export and import trade in merchandise goods and services are given in the Central Government Budget for the coming year, which can be used as proxies to forecast the exchange rates in the medium and long run.

Lastly, the speculative and hedge demand for a currency cannot be predicted and they are the major causes of exchange rate volatility in short-term.

In this scenario the flow of funds as between two countries in any time period cannot be predicted. The day-to-day volatility of exchange rate is a major risk factor, which cannot be solved by forecasting the exchange rate. This is particularly true for the freely convertible currencies, atleast convertible on current account and liberalised and privatised system of the economy.

The forecasting technique through mathematical models is outside the scope of this book. But the above discussion on the factors influencing the exchange rates which are so numerous, should make it clear that forecasting of the exchange rates in the short-run is not a feasible proposition and is not a risk reduction method. Risk exposure will be there even with forecasts of exchange rates. However, forecasting is a tool of analyses for medium-term movements in exchange rates.

## Interest Parity

In forecasting the exchange rates, the only reliable indicator is interest rates in domestic country and the respective foreign country. Two key parity conditions are covered interest parity (CIP) and uncovered interest parity (UIP). These provide roughly a measurement of the extent of risk through identification, integration and efficiency of the market. According to CIP condition, the forward premium/discount should equal the interest rate differential between domestic and foreign rates.

Available empirical evidence, as provided by the studies of the RBI, shows that the interest differential, measured as the difference between 3 month treasury bill yields in U.S. and India are positively correlated with the forward premia for a period 1993-2003, but the operation of CIP is not validated, on account of many deficiencies like the market imperfections or statistical errors in the model. This subject is discussed also in the section on Forward Market, later in the book and in a separate chapter.

Basically, foreign exchange involves no physical exchange of currencies except in small denominations when travellers and tourists carry them across national borders, but through exchange of credit instruments or book entries in the books of banks in various centres. The banks are linked together by phone, cable, electronic telex, post or other means of communication. The transactions are put through directly by the banks or through the brokers located at various centres where these transactions are concentrated like Mumbai, Kolkata, Chennai, etc. All the dealer banks in foreign exchange in India have an association called Foreign Exchange Dealers' Association of India.

## Traditional Model

As in the case of any commodity, there is a price for any purchase or sale of a currency. Such a price in the exchange market is called the exchange rate. This is defined as the number of units of one currency that will be exchanged for a unit of another currency. The exchange rate of any currency can be expressed in two ways-one in terms of the number of foreign currency units against a given unit of domestic currency (thus, Rs. 100 = £ 1.4734 as Indirect method) and the other in terms of the number of domestic currency units against a given unit of foreign currency (thus, £ 1 = Rs. 75.60 as direct method) as at end June 2003 and in 2012 84.6955 (average) Rupees in units of foreign currency. The fundamental forces which determine the exchange rate are the prices of goods and services and purchasing parity theory, referred to earlier.

It is pertinent to ask what factors normally determine the exchange rate in the market. *Prima facie,* if the market is free and rates are allowed to fluctuate, the exchange rate would depend on the supply of and demand for a currency which is a function of economic fundamentals.

Thus, taking dollars *vis-a-vis* rupees, the rate is determined by the demand for dollars and supply of dollars in relation to the rupee. Those who demand dollars are primarily importers from the USA to India who have to pay the US exporters in dollars. Similarly, those who supply dollars are primarily the exporters to USA who are paid in dollars by importers in USA.

The rate of exchange is determined at any moment by the forces of demand for and supply of a currency which in turn depends on the demand for and supply of commodities and services as between India and the USA. They also depend on arbitrage and interest rate speculation, currency speculation and short-term capital flows if these are permitted. This has been referred to in an earlier chapter.

## Modern Forecasting Models

There are two types of forecasting models, namely, monetarist models and portfolio models. The monetarist models are current account monetary model and capital account monetary model. While current account model takes for granted that PPP theory holds and that there is only one asset, money for which demand and supply determines the exchange rate. The variables chosen in the model include money supply and real income as exogenous and autonomous. We have already seen that these variables are interrelated. Besides, nominal interest rate is also associated with exchange rate changes. Thus, the model postulates that the exchange rate is a function of changes in money supply, real incomes and nominal interest rates in both the countries, namely, A and B, for which the exchange rate is estimated. Thus, if money supply in A increases, it increases *inter alia,* the demand for B currency and A currency depreciates. Similarly, if the money supply increases in A, it leads to fall in *real income,* which leads to the same effect on exchange rate, that is, the depreciation of A currency. If the nominal rate rises, there will be lower demand for real balances, due to expectations of depreciation, causing actual depreciation of A currency.

The capital account monetary model, considers not only money supply and real incomes changes and nominal interest rates, but inflationary expectations as well. This is similar to Frankel[1] Model about the long-term forecast of exchange rates, taking all the fundamentals of the economy into account. Not only money need, incomes and interest rates, but expected inflation rates play an important role to bring about equilibrium in balance of payments. The demand for all assets, money and their supply play a role in the model.

This leads us to the portfolio balance models. Risk return analyses and portfolio theory holds good for this model. This model takes not only money but all assets, domestic and foreign as substitutes and the portfolio holdings are studied. All the assets are assessed in terms of risks and return and these include foreign assets as well.

The expected return for a foreign asset depends not only on the expected return in domestic currency but on the expected exchange rate as well. The change in the supply of foreign assets and domestic assets affects the returns in domestic currency but trigger expectation of future movements in exchange rates. These expectations on future exchange rate will induce changes in the spot rate as well. In this model, the reduction in money supply domestically results in appreciation in its currency, through reduction in prices and inflationary expectations but increases domestic interest rate, which causes domestic demand for bonds to increase vis-a-vis foreign bonds, to maintain asset allocation equilibrium. This also causes appreciation of "A" currency.

Similar changes in real income bring about higher savings and greater increase in demand for domestic bonds than foreign bonds. As a result, domestic interest rates fall causing investors to switch from domestic bonds to foreign bonds, which depreciates the domestic currency.

The nominal interest rate, real income and money supply, along with inflation rates, thus, are the variables taken to forecast the exchange rates. But expectations of

1. Frankel: "On the Mark:A Theory of Floating Exchange Rates"-AER.1979.

interest rate changes and exchange rate changes play a greater role in the model. Thus, the portfolio model is more comprehensive than the monetary models. But the limitations of those models are that they are not easy to test and verify empirically. The data on money supply, incomes, interest rates may be available, but the difficulties lies with expected changes in inflation rates and exchange rates, which have their impact on the spot rate. Besides, there are wide variety of money stock and income variables and it is not certain which variables will fit in best. Similarly, inflation can be measured by various indices, namely, wholesale price, cost of living index, wage index, etc. There are a number of statistical pitfalls in the choice of variables and the base years. It is not clear from any sound empirical testing whether the relation is linear, logarithmic or semi logarithmic. It can thus be concluded that forecasting of short-term exchange rate is not practical from these models, particularly because of the role of expectations and lack of efficient markets.

## Limitations

There is also problem of the choice of real variables and their specifications. The economic and political factors and expectations which play a vital role in the determination of exchange rate cannot be quantified as most of them are subjective factors. To get out of these problems, some analysts depend on the forecasting method of trend analysis of the past exchange trends to project for the immediate future. Some use the technical analysis, which is prevalent in the analysis of stock prices in the stock market. They make use of the cyclical and trend movements in the past data to derive the future trend or reversal of the trend. They can at best arrive at appreciation or depreciation in exchange market and indicate the direction of the movement.

Another factor that is considered is the purpose of the forecasting. If it is for hedge, the forward rate, vis-a-vis the spot rate for various periods quoted, the LIBOR and its expected changes and forward margins for the exchange rates and interest rates for various relevant periods are adequate. It is not adequate if it is for trading for profits in the currencies by the foreign exchange trader in a bank or a finance manager for capital movements of a speculative nature. If it is a non-financial company, the target for hedging is the cash flows and if it is a finance company, the value added concept is used for hedging. The objective in either case is the maximisation of profits and optimising of net wealth of the company.

A trader in forex market needs the forecast of direction of movement as well as the magnitude of movement. A few basis points, say 2 to 5 points make a lot of difference to total gain or loss when he is dealing in millions of dollars a day. As the forecasting by the help of fundamentals is difficult for a day or a few days, the trader depends on the help of professional research bodies or his own experience and intuition. In the practical field, forecasting of exchange rate is not a feasible proposition except for the indication of direction from the rate in the forward market and margins, as between time periods of one to six months or more but less than one year.

An example of practical hedging is given below for export and import trader.

## Risk in Export Markets

If the invoices are in local currency the depreciation of the currency is a risk to be hedged. Exchange and trade controls in the countries concerned is another risk, for which correct information flow is necessary. Political risks of the foreign country to be expected are to be covered by Foreign Investment Guarantee by the foreign government. The rating of country risks from international credit rating agencies are available. Sudden changes in tastes and preferences of consumers in foreign countries can be taken care by market research and planning. The risks of transport, shipping and airways are to be insured and thus hedged.

Risk in export marketing depends on the proportion of export sales to total sales, the nature of the product mix and elasticity of demand for the product. If export sales are a small proportion of total sales, the MNC may keep its prices unchanged in the hope of keeping its market share but if competition dictates, it may even lower prices to hold its share in the market. If the product is produced to the requirements of the client, the price is not disturbed. If the product is a consumer good and product mix can be changed at short notice, product differentiation will be introduced and price is maintained.

An MNC can use its foreign subsidiary as an export platform and will benefit by local currency devaluation. Devaluation benefits exports and import substitutes. The income and price elasticities of goods exported will determine the extent of gains. Export sales and the impact of exchange risk on it will depend also on its ability to shift production and change the product mix, market shifts and changing of the sources of inputs, among countries.

Finally, the actual impact of a currency change on a firm depends on whether the exchange rate change is fully offset by differences in inflation rates or whether the real exchange rates and relative price changes are different. In the latter case only there will be real effect of exchange risk on export sales of a firm.

## Hedging in Import Trade

If import is on f.o.b. (free on board) basis the importer has to take care of costs of cargo insurance and freight (c.i.f.) and get an insurance to cover them. The importer has to pay in the currency of the exporter leading to an exchange rate risk. This can be hedged, if his payment liability is denominated in local currency say rupees. If this is not possible, the payable amount in exporter's currency, say dollars can be hedged by entering into a Forward Rate Agreement or buy dollars in futures market. Generally, the importer gets the banker to enter into a Forward Contract, which includes, the cost of time element, interest rate and exchange rate risk.

## Government Controls on Trade

Forecasting is affected by many subjective factors like expectations and changes in government policy and control on trade and forex market. In this section controls on trade are discussed. Due to liberalisation of trade policy, tariff and non-tariff barriers are brought down. So is the case with many members of W.T.O.

Both exporters and importers have to investigate first whether the commodity they wish to export or import requires a licence under any law for the time being in force. Under the Import and Export Control Act of 1947, the Central Government is empowered to prohibit, restrict or otherwise control imports and exports. Under this Act, the Import Control Order (1955) was passed and Schedule I to this order contains the list of articles subject to control which cannot be imported except with a licence. The commodities on Open General Licence (OGL) can be imported without a licence. The rationale for licensing is to keep exports and imports in conformity with the current government policy.

Imports and exports of gold, silver, currency notes, coins etc., are prohibited, except with prior permission of the RBI, as they are subject to FEMA rules. The current regulations with respect to imports and exports are found in the latest Hand Book on Import Policy and Export Policy respectively. Under the Imports and Exports Control Order 1977 and rules made thereunder, all exporters require a licence for specified commodities. Export control extends to all commodities included in Schedule I to the Export Control Order 1977 or as announced from time to time in the exim policy. The regulations of the government on trade are very few and importance of licensing was cut drastically due to economic reforms since 1992.

## Licensing Policy

Generally, licensing policy is framed on the basis of a foreign exchange budget prepared periodically by the government. The budget is based on the expected export earnings and other inward exchange receipts. After allocating for expenditure on debt servicing and maintenance of our embassies and other expenditures abroad, the balance is allocated among different users of imports. The requirements of food, fertilisers, petroleum and its products get priority allotment and they are all in public sector. The following agencies get allotment:

Public sector undertakings

The Iron and Steel Controller

Ministry of Finance for private sector.

EPCG* Scheme is extended to all sectors without threshold limit. Duty draw back, pass book scheme for exporters is also continued. Duty free replenishment certificate scheme is announced for more than 500 products. Sector specific initiatives for EOUs and EPZs in gems, jewellery, biotech, pharma products, leather, garments, silk and granites is planned. The policy aims at a boost to e-commerce, electronic filing of forms and capital goods imports are subject to only 5% duty. There was no SIL from 2000-01. There was major rationalisation of export promotion schemes in the following year and it changed from time to time.

## Indian Shipping and Other Infrastructure

Another development in India's foreign trade is the increased role of Indian shipping and Indian insurance in carrying our trade. Insurance is a hedge for risks in transit shipping and accidents like fire, damage, etc.

Indian shipping has grown vastly from 0.39 million Gross Registered Tonnage-GRT to about 7 million GRT over the period 1950 to 1999 and there was also a high degree of diversification of her fleet. The seventies has witnessed the maximum increase in tonnage (3.73 million GRT). By 1992, the shipping capacity of India has increased to 5.91 million GRT, with ships numbering about 422 and this increased to 480 ships in 2004. Of this, public sector shipping companies owned a tonnage accounting for about 56 per cent of the country's tonnage. This was made possible by the availability of deferred payment facilities and foreign lines of credit. The Shipping Development Fund set up in 1958 by the government aided the industry which was later aided by OSCICI in the process of expansion. The public sector shipping companies provided effective competition to private sector companies with the result that shipping has grown on healthy lines. The Indian share in world shipping ranged from 1 per cent to 2 per cent but Indian ships could carry about 50 per cent of Indian cargo which fell steeply more recently. There was stiff competition from non-conference foreign lines and inadequate container carrying facilities in Indian ships, stood in the way of further expansion.

The government has kept a goal of carrying 50 per cent of our trade by Indian ships and the actual achievement was much less. The export policy resolution of the government aims at further encouragement to Indian shipping: "Among the inadequacies of the existing infrastructure for exports, that of shipping needs to be emphasised. The government proposes to intensify its efforts to expand the national merchant marine fleet, to start new services and to strengthen existing ones, as may be necessary for the development of our trade." The Eighth plan tonnage target is 7 million GRT which may not be achieved due to severe competition and finance problems. The 9th plan target is 9 million GRT which was increased further in Tenth Plan. The government also proposes to secure fair treatment for our export cargo and to provide improved shipping opportunities for it. Methods for the handling of export cargo in our ports have also been improved. The total cargo handled by Indian ports was increasing with improved handling facilities at ports. Our cargo handling capacity at ports was reported to be about 153 million tonnes at end 1991 and has increased further due to Navi Mumbai Port and better facilities at Visakhapatnam port.

In view of the rising cost of shipping, India would be losing foreign exchange if its trade is carried on in foreign ships. The loss is put at $ 4.4 billion in an year. It is understood that the ratio of freight costs of f.o.b. value of exports varied from 5 to 20 per cent.

## Problems of Indian Shipping and Banking

The main problems are dwindling Indian fleet strength and decreasing share of Indian ships in India's foreign trade. Indian shipping despite our vast ocean coast has never been in a good shape. The government has not given enough thought to developing Indian shipping industry, as fast as the overseas trade.

During 1999-2003 world trade was in recession and Baltic Freight index and Baltic Handy Index are down to their lowest levels. With no immediate prospects of improvement, Indian shipping is also at its worst phase. Neglect of the interests of Indian shipping by the government taxation policy and lack of non-resident status to its earnings, outgo of manpower and problems of depreciation of vessels are some of the reasons for the poor shape of the Shipping Industry.

During the period of 1980 to 2003, Gross Registered Tonnage (GRT) rose from 5.54 million to 6.43 million (a rise of 22.2 per cent, as compared to a rise by several times of foreign trade). The share of India's ships in foreign trade of the country declined during the recent past. The control on shipping including public sector shipping companies rests with the government.

Like shipping, banking is also an infrastructure for foreign trade and finance, controlled by the governments. All Indian banks have entered foreign trade business in a big way. ADs in India have increased from 76 in 1975 to 92 by 2004 and representative offices of Indian banks and branches are present abroad. Correspondingly 32 foreign banks have about 293 branches and 43 representative offices in India. Recently, with liberalisation and globalisation of banking many foreign banks were permitted to open branches in India. Three deposit-taking companies were set up in Hong Kong by Indian banks and there were also two banking subsidiaries wholly owned by Indian banks operating abroad and some foreign branches, loss making, were asked to close down.

India can increasingly share in international currency markets through its foreign branch network of banks. Government has recently strengthened the capital base of nationalised banks with foreign branch network so as to enable them to improve their image abroad and facilitate their larger participation in foreign currency markets. Indian banks can also compete more efficiently with foreign banks at home and abroad by improving their expertise and efficiency. At present, only the SBI and a few other nationalised banks such as Bank of India and Bank of Baroda are able to operate in Euro and Asian currency markets as they have the largest network of offices abroad. Banking is controlled by the RBI and the government.

The government has allowed the IDBI to borrow in the international capital markets syndicated by the Lloyds Bank International and SBI. In addition to existing 24 private sector scheduled banks, many more private sector banks were licensed since 1992. The ICICI has also concluded arrangement for a floating rate note issues to augment its foreign currency resources for lending to the private sector. The IDBI and other financial institutions are now permitted to enter the Euro-currency and Euro-bond markets. A number of private and public companies are also encouraged to raise funds from non-residents and since 1992 to borrow abroad through GDRs and ADRs and FCCBs.

## Marine Insurance

The government's policy was throughout for encouraging marine insurance to be covered by Indian companies. As in the case of shipping, increasing proportion of insurance coverage has come into Indian hands after independence and more so after nationalisation of general insurance.

Marine insurance is intended to protect the interests of the shippers in international trade against the perils of sea, including fire, acts of piracy, stranding of ships, collision or other accidents. There are various risks involved in handling the cargo or in the process of transfer of goods through various hands, namely, forwarding agents, freight brokers, the shipping agents, charterers, clearing agents and the like. But basically three parties are involved in any shipping business, namely, the shipper of the goods (exporters), the shipping company and the consignee (importer). The insurance policy covers risk generally from the point of handing over the goods to an agent of the consignee or to the port of destination. Insurance business in this line is governed by the provisions of Marine Insurance Act of 1963. In actual practice, insurance in the world over is in the "Lloyds form", and various clauses known as "Institute clauses" are attached to it. These clauses define the scope of the coverage available generally from insurers.

The hazards of insurance have increased in recent years due to increase in size of ships, unsatisfactory conditions in various ports and lowering standards of conduct by human agents in handling of cargo, etc. Oil tankers and bulk carriers involve larger risk elements. Sometimes, frauds are committed on the insurers by collusion between shippers and shipping companies. Reasonable precaution has to be taken by the exporters and importers against frauds by shipping companies. The International Chamber of Commerce at Paris has issued a publication "Guide to Prevention of Maritime Frauds" which would help in this regard.

## Recent Exim Policy

The recent thrust of Exim Policy is to boost service exports, such as in the fields of health, hospitality and entertainment. All service exports with a minimum foreign exchange earnings of Rs. 10 lakhs were allowed duty free imports to the extent of 5% of their exports from the year 2003-04.

Agro-exports and food-processing are the other area of focus. Some exports like paddy, sugar etc. are allowed duty free. Exports of autos and auto parts textiles, gems and jewellery have received a boost. Imports of secondhand capital goods of more than 10 years old have been made easier, by waiving the "actual user condition."

Procedures have been simplified and special incentives were provided to EPCG and DEPB Schemes. The export performance criteria was dispensed with in favour of criteria of net foreign exchange earner. In general, all service exporters can import 10% of their overseas sales at zero duty. Export obligations under EPCG Scheme were cut to a quarter of current levels. Sales to SEZs from DTA was to be treated as export, while sales to DTA from SEZ to be exempt from special additional duty (SAD). Sales from domestic market to special economic zones (SEZ Units) would be entitled to duty entitlement pass book (DEPB), duty drawback benefits and free from central sales tax. All these tax and non-tax sops will cost the exchequer about Rs.30,000 crores in a year.

Now that all quantitative restrictions are removed, the future thrust of exim policy is only on export promotion. Exports in 2002-03 have grown by 17%, while it was a decline of 2% in 2001-02. The exports from India now constitute only 0.7% of total world trade, while it aims to expand to 1% of total world trade. More recently the export growth rate was around 12%.

Exim policy for the Tenth Plan period 2002-07 was announced in March 2002. The policy was oriented to growth of trade to 1% of world trade by 2007. For this purpose, the growth rate of India's trade should be 12% per annum or more. The objective of the policy was to make it a vital part of the growth of the economy, employment and poverty alleviation. The growth rate of 9% of the economy would be possible if both industry, and agriculture contribute through maximisation of exports. The international environment being dynamic, the exim policy has to be adjusted annually to the tune of changing conditions. In this context, the latest policy shift has been to the growth of service exports and export of agro-based products in the coming years. Sector wise, the export thrust has been given to texitles, garments, auto parts, gems and jewellery, drugs and chemicals. Export houses, EOUs, EPZs and SEZs are given greater freedom and incentives by reducing the transaction costs and hassles of administrative machinery of the government and by simplification of procedures.

In the area of service exports, I.T. software exports, has been given the prime importance of growth boosters. Besides, exports of health services tourism, entertainment, media etc. are the other thrust areas of policy, which got some incentive scheme in the exim policy. These incentives are in the form of duty free imports and other tax concessions and augmentation of the flow of credit and finance to these sectors.

In the area of agriculture and allied products, the policy identified thrust areas as horticulture —flowers, fruits and vegetables and dairy and marine products. The measures were intended to help their growth of exports and include the association of corporates with Agri Export Zones, modification of norms for fixing the Duty Exemption Pass Book (DEPB) rates for some inputs and output of agriculture, promotion of special zones with some tax and bank finance schemes, development of towns of export excellence or industrial cluster towns (Ludhiana for woollen knit wear, Tirupur for hosiery etc.) and special strategic packages for export status holders and diversification of markets into North America and Latin America. The policy includes measures for administrative simplification and some modifications of Traditional Export Promotion Schemes. Quality control and brand schemes are to be encouraged by the central and state governments through modernisation and upgradation of test houses and by setting up of machinery to investigate complaints by DGFT.

The exim policy for the Tenth Plan has continued the earlier schemes like Duty Exemption Pass Book (DEPB) scheme, Duty Free Replenishment Certificate (DFRC), Advance licences, Export Promotion Capital Goods Scheme (EPCG), Export Oriented Units (EOU), Special Economic Zones (SEZ) etc. There was a greater emphasis on promotion of trade to Latin American countries such as Argentina, Brazil, Chile etc., through bilateral trade agreements and to African countries, where India has diplomatic missions. These schemes contain emphasis on promotion of exports and imports of India to these regions. The Focus Latin American Countries (LAC) scheme was launched in 1997 and the Focus Africa Scheme was launched in 2002. The trade to these countries stood at around 7-10% of India's total trade.

All the above factors are non-quantifiable and constitute a hurdle to any forecasting model for exchange rate. The trade policy and trade conditions in the international context are a major force in the international financial transactions, as the export and import trade in merchandise and invisibles constitute the bulk of the economic and commercial transactions, dealt within the foreign exchange market. The transactions demand for foreign exchange in the merchant market segment of the foreign exchange market constitute a major factor influencing the exchange rate. The above factors lead to market imperfection which results in difficulties of forecasting the exchange rate.

## Current Account and Exchange Rate

In forecasting, the exchange rate, the short-term variables are different from those of long-term variables. Among the latter, mention has to be made of the trade balance and current account deficit. They are positively related both in theory and practice. Empirical evidence from a study on 'J' curve hypothesis by Bahmani-Oskoee and Brooks (1999) and by Kulkarni-Bhatia (2002) showed that the hypothesis holds good in the U.S., in the long-run. The 'J' curve empirical evidence is mixed both for and against the hypothesis. The hypothesis states that there is a significant effect of the real exchange rate on the trade balance.

The 'S' curve hypothesis postulates that there is a symmetric shape of the curve relating the real exchange rate with the trade balance. They are negatively related with current and future movements but positively related with the past movements (Backus 1994). These movements give the 'S' curve shape. In the Indian context, studies have found that the trade balance is sensitive to exchange rate changes. There is a bi-directional causality relation between trade balance and real exchange rate. After depreciation of a currency, there is a tendency for trade balance to worsen first and then improve.

The causality between current account deficit to GDP ratio and nominal exchange rate shock shows a 'J' curve response during the short and medium-term. Thereafter the response function shows a downward trend ('S' curve hypothesis), in the Indian context. This was presented by a study of RBI for data of 1951-2002 by taking CAD/GDP ratio on the one hand and nominal and real exchange rates on the other. This shows the acceptance of 'J' curve hypothesis to the Indian conditions.

(*Source:* RBI Report on Currency and Finance, 2002-03)

❖ ❖ ❖

# BALANCE OF PAYMENTS (EQUILIBRIUM vs. DISEQUILIBRIUM)

# 9

Foreign Exchange market and exchange rates are intricately connected with the position and trends in balance of payments of a country. So it is imperative that we should set out here a discussion on balance of payments. No country is self-sufficient and the interdependence of countries is reflected in international economic and commercial transactions. An economic transaction is an exchange of value or transfer of a title for a goods or an asset. A commercial transaction is an exchange of goods or service for money which will result in payment in currency or monetary assets leading to financial flows. The resource flows from one country to another due to purchase and sale of financial claims are referred to as financial transactions. The international exchange of goods for goods, goods for services or services for services or goods and services for money are all referred to as international economic and commercial transactions. Besides, there are flows of funds on capital account for working capital (short-term funds) or for investment (long-term funds).

## Definition

Balance of payments of a country is a "systematic record of all economic and commercial transactions between the residents of the reporting country and residents of foreign countries". This account is for a period of time, normally one year. These transactions are as between residents of one country with those of other countries. Residents are to be differentiated from nationals and are normally resident in the reporting country for a greater part of the year. A national is a citizen of a state and may be a resident in his own nation or outside. On the other hand, diplomats, military personnel, temporary migratory workers and branches of domestic companies abroad are regarded as residents of the country, where they come from rather than where they reside because they are not subject to the control of national authorities of the country where they reside. Balance of payments refers to the transactions between the residents of one country with another, rather than as between nationals of two countries. The basic idea is that balance of payments should record economic and commercial transactions flowing from one geographical region to another, constituting the nation states with the domestic incomes and output subject to the control of national authorities. Such records may help the government of the reporting country to measure the flows of goods and services or resource flows from their country to others and *vice versa*. Monetary authorities of the reporting country should know the receipts and payments as between the reporting country and others so as to assess the impact of such flows on domestic money supply and on the savings of the economy. Besides, economists would like to study from these data the impact of foreign transactions on national income of the reporting country—their impact on current income and expenditure (current account) and on assets and liabilities of the country (capital side).



The monetary and fiscal policies and foreign exchange policy would be formulated or reformulated on the basis of these data. It would thus, be seen that the balance of payments data are very useful from the point of view of formulation and operation of the domestic economic policy and foreign exchange Policy for the international bodies like IMF.

## Accounting of Balance of Payments

Balance of payments is kept on a double entry book-keeping system with credits and debits of equal size. For every transaction, there is a corresponding entry on both the credit and debit sides. Thus, if exports are made, there will be a credit for outflow of goods on Current Account and a corresponding entry of debit for claim on a foreign company or country or increase in foreign assets or claims on foreigners. Similarly, imports will appear as a debit item for the inflow of goods and the credit item for being paid out is shown by increase in foreign liabilities, reduction of foreign assets or outflow of funds or claims on us. Thus, for every credit/debit entry on Current Account, there is a corresponding entry on Capital Account to match the former. In case of unilateral transfers such as gifts, donations etc., there is no corresponding payment or change in assets or liabilities. The contraentry is donations or gifts on the debit side and for the credit, it is the flow of goods from out of the country. It is not always possible to match all debits with credits due to differences in sources and timing of events. A discrepancy might then arise necessitating a balancing entry, namely, errors and omissions.

## Sources of Compilation

In the case of countries which do not have exchange controls, statistical recording of balance of payments data is done by the government with the help of their Statistical Office which in turn depends upon a host of private and government agencies, banks, companies, etc. Each member country of the IMF is compiling these data for onward transmission to the Fund and for their own records and use. In view of the crucial importance of these data for policy-making, planning etc., compilation and timely availability of these data are considered to be of utmost importance.

The usual sources of compilation for any country are the government agencies and the monetary authority of the country. These data are collected either on a statutory basis or a voluntary basis from various private and government agencies, airways, ports, etc., banks and financial institutions. Where exchange controls operate, these data are more easily available with the agencies entrusted with the operation of exchange controls such as the monetary authority of the country, the government and the banks.

A few limitations in compilation of balance of payments may be noticed here:

(1) Not all transactions are reported through official channels, particularly where there are no exchange and trade restrictions.

(2) A time-lag between an actual transaction and its reporting is possible so that the balance of payments do not properly record the transactions during the period.

(3) There could be under-invoicing or over-invoicing of goods and services so that they do not represent the true value of gain or loss to the country.

(4) Not sufficient details of all transactions are available in some cases as, for example, in remittances, short-term capital inflows or outflows, gifts, samples, etc., particularly in respect of services or invisible items.

The errors and omissions will be a major component of balance of payments if such limitations are substantial and it is always possible that debits and credits do not tally during any period of time.

## Components of Balance of Payments

The major classes of transactions recorded in the balance of payments are current account and capital account transactions. On the current account, only transactions of current nature resulting in incomes or expenditure and not leading to asset formation are recorded. There are four sub-categories under this head, namely: (i) Transactions of merchandise or visible items of goods, namely, exports including re-exports and imports, (ii) Transactions on invisible account, namely, foreign travel, transportation, banking, insurance and other services, interest, dividends, royalties, Government Embassy expenditures, etc., (iii) Unilateral transfers like gifts, donations, charities, etc., (iv) Non-monetary gold movements. All the above items can take place on private account or government account and may be subject to government restrictions or controls, if any. Gold is a special category as it can be used both as a commodity and as an international medium of exchange or money. Domestic transactions of gold, namely, sale of gold by residents to monetary authorities are also recorded in the balance of payments, as they affect gold holdings and international reserves of the country. Gold is held as part of international reserves of countries.

**Growth Rates of companies**

| Exports | Imports |
|---|---|
| Rates of Growth of Exports | Rates of Growth of Imports |
| 2013-14 – 11.5 | 2013-14 – 11.3 |
| 2014-15 – 11.5 | 2014-15 – 10.2 |
| 2015-16 – 11.4 | 2015-16 – 11.3, 10.2, 10 } Import Growth |

The capital account transactions are short-term capital inflows and outflows for private purposes, official purposes or banking purposes. Private flows of capital include private company remittances for working capital purposes to subsidiaries or branches of foreign companies or short-term loans, grants, etc., from foreign banks, international financial institutions, foreign government etc. These short-term flows may be for investment purposes or speculation on private account or for compensatory purposes on government account. These can also be banking funds for short-term purposes.

There are also long-term capital movements which may again be private or governmental. The private flows include loans and advances granted to private parties (buyers' credit), investment in shares, bonds, debentures, etc., by Indians abroad or by foreigners in India, investment in joint ventures, consultancy, turnkey projects, deferred payment credits, etc. Such flows on official account also take place through governments or governmental agencies or financial institutions in India through lines of credit, foreign government loans, credits, grants etc., for private long-term purposes.

The capital account reflects the changes in foreign assets and liabilities of the country and affects its creditor/debtor position. An excess of foreign assets over foreign liabilities indicates a net creditor position and *vice versa.* Net changes in current account are reflected by a corresponding and opposite change in the capital account, changing the foreign assets and liabilities position of the country. Current account is like an income and expenditure statement with surplus or deficit in it transferred to capital account which is like a balance sheet. If all these accounts do not tally, errors and omissions are added to balance the corresponding column of balance of payments. In an economic sense, a country has a surplus or deficit in its balance of payments, when its transactions other than those merely financing the real transactions are not in balance. Those merely financing are said to be "below the line" while others are "above the line." The selection of items below the line is generally decided by each country, depending upon its requirements for economic policy in the short run and long run. The various concepts used by countries at present are discussed later in the chapter.

In a statistical sense, errors and omissions is a balancing entry to correct any discrepancy between total credits and debits after including all the items in the balance of payments. The balancing item is derived on a net basis so that net current account balance together with "errors and omissions" would equal the net opposite position in the capital account. Suppose the net surplus (credit) on current account is Rs. 60 crores and the net debit on capital account is Rs. 40 crores, the errors and omissions would be Rs. 20 crores (+).

The size and magnitude of errors may reflect the sophistication in the reporting system rather than the reliability of the data conceptually. These errors being random, variables should reflect movements on both debits and credits (plus or minus) over the long run. A consistent positive sign would indicate that receipts are understated or payments overstated and *vice versa.*

The last item on balance of payments other than "errors and omission" is the movement in foreign exchange reserves of the country normally shown in capital account. These reserves are in foreign currencies, foreign assets, investments and balances held abroad, or gold of the government, and official monetary agencies like the Central Bank.

## Balance of Payments Data

As referred to earlier, there are continuous interactions between the domestic sectors and foreign sectors in every country. The movements in the balance of payments influence the savings and investments in the economy and the national income and expenditure of the Country. These data are useful to estimate and plan for the following:

(1) Savings gap.

(2) Foreign exchange gap.

(3) Investment outlays.

Firstly each of the sectors has some savings and investments and while some are net savers, others are net investors. In India, the foreign sector has been a net saver for some time in the past and this promotes investment by other sectors of the economy. Such investment helps the growth of incomes and employment in the economy.

Secondly besides, these inflows relieve the balance of payments constraint (or foreign exchange gap) of the developing country due to the absence of adequate import capacity, or the inadequacy of foreign exchange reserves would stand in the way of growth of income and employment of these countries.

Thirdly, such inflows would promote markets, specialisation and larger production in the world, as a whole. These data are thus useful for formulation of savings and investment policy, planning the growth of the economy, internal monetary policy, fiscal policy and more directly, the foreign exchange policy. The trends in balance of payments would have repercussions on the internal and international monetary scene and influences the foreign exchange, monetary and fiscal policies of the country and the overall growth of the economy. In particular, the trade deficit or surplus could indicate the comparative and competitive strength or weakness of the economy vis-a-vis the trading partners. The cost and quality aspects, productivity and efficiency of factors etc. are reflected.

## Mechanism of Adjustment

When entries are made on a double-entry basis, credits and debits must tally. In this sense, balance of payments must always balance. But it is only in an accounting sense. In an economic sense, what we need to know is the mechanism of adjustment. How are the forces operating towards balancing of inflows and outflows of a country when there can be larger export than imports (a positive trade balance) or a larger invisible exports over imports (or a positive invisible trade balance) or a larger current account balance? Normally, a deficit in current account will be made good (if not due to statistical errors or omissions) by the outflow of monetary gold, short-term credits or a loss of foreign exchange assets or increase foreign exchange liabilities. If the short-term credits and inflows of funds are autonomous and not induced for financing a deficit on other accounts, then these will be a part of regular balance of payments. Leaving aside such deliberate efforts at balancing due to induced flow of funds, the mechanism of adjustment works automatically through: *(a)* Price changes, and *(b)* Income changes or both.

## Price Mechanism

In international trade, price mechanism works through price elasticities of demand and supply. Under the classical assumption of perfect competition at home, factor mobility internally and constant factor proportions, elasticities are high and a small price change may correct a deficit or surplus in balance of payments. Here, price is used in the micro sense of price of a goods or macro sense of prices of all goods and services. International trade takes place due to excess supply at home and excess demand abroad for any product. If these excess supply schedules are price-elastic, small changes in them may bring about quick adjustment, because a small fall in price for example, may increase the demand for or reduce the supply of and clear the market for the good. Elasticity is measured by $\frac{\Delta S/S}{\Delta P/P}$ or $\frac{\Delta D/D}{\Delta P/P}$ in respect of supply and demand — responsiveness of supply/demand to a small change in price.

In real world, these elasticities are low, particularly for a developing country like India, whose production structure is based mainly on agriculture. For price mechanism to work effectively the relevant elasticities should be high. Marshall-Lerner condition for improvement in balance of trade and payment as a result of changes in price is as follows. "The sum of elasticities of demand-the demand at home for a country's imports and the demand abroad for its export-must be greater than one." Depreciation or lowering of the price of a currency in international transactions would then improve the balance of payments. Depreciation or devaluation would mean a lowering of the domestic price in terms of foreign currencies. Devaluation can improve the balance of payments, if the relative elasticities of supply of and demand for goods entering into the international markets are high. Besides, the deficits in balance of payments should not be high or chronic.

The above analysis of the effect of price change suffers from limitations of unrealistic assumptions of perfect competition and constancy of other conditions and is based on partial equilibrium analysis. If the sum of elasticities is less than one, appreciation of currency (or re-valuation) may improve the trade balance. Revaluation means an increase in the price of one currency in terms of another currency. Besides there will be simultaneous income effects — effect on domestic incomes and foreign repercussion of such price changes which may promote or thwart the price effect.

## Income Adjustment

If we start with Hume's law of no foreign savings, an increase in exports will increase income at home which in turn would lead to larger imports which would balance the trade and payments. The amount by which an initial increase in exports would lead to an increase in income is called foreign trade multiplier-equal to 1/MPM where MPM is marginal propensity to import. This is the automatic adjustment process through income changes over a period of time. This thesis follows from the postulation that $Y = C + X - M^*$; Income, Y = consumption, C + exports, X – imports, M where no savings exist But if savings also exist, the increase in exports will be balanced by increase in imports and in savings, provided that investment is unchanged. In this case the multiplier is 1/MPM + MPS where MPS is marginal propensity to save. The foreign trade multiplier expresses the change in income caused by a change in exports or investments/savings in an open economy in which income spills over into imports. The above formulation is based on simple assumptions. If complex formulations are necessary, the final outcome would be indeterminate if

(1) Price and income effects operate simultaneously as in the real world, and

(2) If there is a significant effect from a change in imports on income abroad which again produces a substantial change on its exports, which is said to be the foreign repercussion effect-an income change at home producing income changes abroad and thus on domestic incomes again.

If the accelerator is also at work at home, then an increase in exports would lead to an increase in investment and to further rise in income. If the foreign effects are also operating then the original increase in exports may produce a larger increase in imports and lead to an unfavourable balance of trade or the effect would be indeterminate.

## Absorption Approach of Alexander

Adjustment in balance of payments may take place due to "redistribution effect" or "money illusion effect" or "demonstration effect." An important mode of adjustment is the income redistribution. If import prices rise due to depreciation or for other reasons, the cost of living of the classes consuming imports would rise and profits may be made in the foreign trade sector, particularly exports which might lead to lower absorption of imports resulting in adjustment in the balance of payments. A decline in consumption or a decline in investment may lead to a readjustment of balance of payments according to S.S. Alexander.[1]

If there is money illusion, called the Pigou effect, with a constant money supply and increase in prices and money incomes, there will be larger savings and investment and lower consumption to keep up savings. Thus, lower consumption and lower absorption might lead to lower imports and to balance the deficit in balance of payments. If there

---

*Sources:*

1. S.S. Alexander, "Effect of a Devaluation on a Trade Balance", in AER, *Readings in International Economics.*

is less than full employment, a rise in prices leads to a larger production, larger income leading to larger savings and investment. Thus, income changes consequent on foreign trade changes would lead to an adjustment in the balance of payments. It should be conceded that these adjustments are possible in flexible economies with free competition and free flow of economic forces which are non-existent in the real world. Adjustment in the balance of payments is also possible through the demonstration effect on production and consumption at home emanating from abroad. Thus, larger exports might induce larger imports through the demonstration effect. It is also possible that larger imports facilitate larger exports through its effect on production and expenditure on goods and on savings and investment at home.

## Elasticity Approach Vs. Absorption Approach

The elasticity approach postulates that foreign trade changes operate through price and terms of trade changes in a way that income and spending would adjust to trade. On the other hand, the absorption approach works through savings and investment which will determine expenditure and incomes and the trade would adjust to these changes. A deficit in balance of payments would mean that domestic expenditure is more than domestic output. Adjustment would have to work by increasing the level of income to equal to expenditure and domestic investment to domestic savings and foreign savings (X – M). In the short run, elasticity approach may be more suitable while in the long-run income expenditure adjustments are possible and absorption approach may appear to be more apt. In the real world, such simplified approaches may not be appropriate. What happens is a mileu of all forces, including price and income effects, investment and savings changes and a host of other factors operate on balance of payments. Adjustment in the balance of payments on the general equilibrium model takes place through a complete set of forces emanating from all sectors of the economy, including domestic and foreign, and a combination of both the approaches is thus relevant.

## General Equilibrium Approaches

The balance of payments disequilibrium may be a monetary phenomenon or real phenomenon or the result of structural maladjustments. In the first case, disequilibrium is the result of difference between aggregate receipts and payments, which is to be made good by monetary adjustments, namely, credit creation or destruction — changes in 'M' or 'V' (Money Stock or Velocity). The deficit may reflect a "stock" decision or "flow" decision of economic units. The stock decision refers to the community's preference for foreign assets and money as against domestic assets and money. Then direct controls would have to be resorted to. In a flow concept, the reference is to excess payments over receipts which can be corrected by expenditure-reduction policy or expenditure-switching policy. The former leads to anti-inflationary policy and the latter to selective monetary and fiscal policies or controls. Expenditure reduction or increased output or both can be aimed at with expenditure switching from foreign to domestic goods and services.

If balance of payments deficit is due to real factors, then increase in output and income or adjustment in the production structure is necessary. So was the case of India which has persistent balance of payments imbalances to be corrected by economic reforms since 1991. Structural maladjustment is a possible reason for real factors operating adversely on the balance of payments. In that event, long-run structural changes in the economy and in production patterns have to be effected. Devaluation and controls might help only as temporary expedients for adjustment in the balance of payments in such cases. The economic and financial reforms initiated since July 1991 have improved the balance of payments position of India.

## Measurement of Deficits

The total of credits and debits in current and capital accounts may not always balance. There can be surplus or deficit which is made good by a corresponding balancing entry, namely, official financing items. These items may be gold, use of IMF assistance or drawal on the country's foreign exchange reserves.

For purposes of economic analysis and policy formulation, there are various types of balances arising out of credits and debits in the balance of payments. A few of such concepts of balances may be set out as: *(a)* Trade Balance; *(b)* Current A/c Balance; *(c)* Basic Balance; *(d)* Balance in regular transactions; and *(e)* Balance settled by official transactions.

**(a) Trade Balance: ($X + M = 0$):** It is the most widely used concept where X is exports and M is imports on merchandise account as the relevant data are the earliest to be available for any period and easy to comprehend and handle. Trade balance is the balance of exports and imports of merchandise goods. It is useful for analysis of flow of goods, sector-wise, and in input-output tables. Price and income elasticities are more easily analysed in terms of merchandise trade balance-exports and imports. But these data are not useful for further analysis in foreign exchange budget or in money supply analysis or in national income analysis.

**(b) Current Account Balance: $X + M + X^1 + M^1 = 0$:** where $X^1$ is exports on invisible trade account and $M^1$ is imports on the same account.

Exports and imports of both goods and services are considered in this concept and it is a combination of balance on merchandise account plus balance on invisible trade account. A total outstanding balance on the current account is made good by contra balance on short-term and long-term capital flows, excluding errors and omissions. This concept is useful for national income analysis. If $X + M + X^1 + M^1 > 0$, meaning that if the current account balance is positive, the country is gaining from the rest of the world and it stimulates domestic national income if there is unemployment or under-employment of resources. If this positive balance adds to foreign exchange reserves, money supply increases and produces an inflationary impact in the short run. If the foreign savings are productively invested, income, output and employment will be increased under conditions of less than full employment. If all countries aim at a positive current account balance, it will lead to a scramble, undercutting etc. If some have a positive balance, there must be others with a negative balance as all cannot have a positive balance. But this concept is not very useful for some purposes such as foreign exchange budgeting.

**(c) Basic Balance ($X + M + X^1 + M^1 + LTC$) = STC where STC is Short-term Capital and LTC is Long-term Capital:** This concept was propagated by economists like Ragner Nurkse for the purposes of economic analysis. It assumes that current account balance and long-term capital flows are autonomous and they are counter-balanced by short-term capital flows which are generally induced. There may, however be short-term flows which are autonomous and motivated by investment or speculative gains. The concept helps the analysis of transfer problem in international payments. Thus, if autonomous receipts and payments leave a negative balance, it is to be counter-balanced or financed by short-term inflow in the form of gold, international currencies or credits. This would involve exchange of currencies or credit instruments in the foreign exchange market.

This concept is useful in national income analysis, foreign exchange budgeting, funds flow analysis etc. Besides by the basic balance concept, equilibrium in the balance of payments can be judged and the pressure on the exchange market and the extent of the transfer problem can be analysed. Briefly, transfer problem relates to the difficulty of exchanging one currency against another. If one currency is more in supply in the Exchange market, its value depreciates. So on top of the country's difficulty of finding resources for transfer, the transfer itself would lead to depreciation of currency due to the difficulty of proper matching of currencies.

**(d) Balance of Regular Transactions:** This concept is a finer version of the Basic Balance in that all short-term capital (STC) is not used for balancing purposes. A part of it is STC(d) or autonomous and domestic and a part of it is STC(f) or induced and foreign. This latter part would be considered as liquid funds whose conversion would create a problem in the foreign exchange markets.

$$X + M + X^1 + M^1 + LTC + STC(d) = STC(f).$$

In the above equation, STC(f) is the liquidity in the international markets which will create problems of transfer and lead to disturbances in international markets, particularly when countries do not have enough gold to enable conversion of foreign funds into gold at the will of the surplus country. When a country is a banker and a trader like the USA or UK, it will have a liquidity crisis due to a run on their currencies. So what is relevant for them is a concept which will include only induced official flows of funds, as on such occasions, private flows cannot be depended upon. Thus, some STC(f) may flow on private account for interest rate gains or speculation or for working capital purposes. Hence, the need for a concept which distinguishes private and official capital flows is felt particularly in countries which are international bankers and traders. Thus, a balance settled by official short-term capital flows has been formulated.

**(e) Balance Settled by Official Transactions:** The induced flow of funds to finance the balance of payments deficits is further split up into official and private. Thus, STC(f) is of two components-private and official-STC(fp) and STC(fo). STC(fo) is short-term capital on account of official agencies or monetary authorities of the country. This reflects the official funds flowing in or out to balance the balance of payments. These are induced funds as opposed to autonomous flows which are again both official and private. Of the induced flows, it is only officially induced flows which are taken to represent deficit in the balance of payments. These flows include both monetary gold movements and international currency flows. The above distinction between official and private flows under short-term foreign capital flows was spearheaded by a former IMF Chief Mr. M. Bernstein. This distinction is also in tune with the original distinction made by the IMF in its first Balance of Payments Year Book of 1949 between autonomous or private transactions, on the one hand, and official or compensatory movements, on the other. This type of classification has been used by the IMF to measure the disequilibrium in the balance of payments for the purpose of change of par values or imposition of control on trade and payments.

For a country like India, the concept of basic balance is adequate to measure the balance of payment disequilibrium. But there are a number of trader-banker countries at international level like the USA, UK, West Germany or Japan whose currencies serve as international liquidity or reserve currencies. As in domestic banking, the concepts of solvency, liquidity and safety apply to international banking. Countries whose currencies constitute reserve assets in international liquidity may have to observe better caution against run on their currencies which may lead to non-conversion of such currencies into gold. In these cases, disequilibrium in balance of payments should be measured by short-term official foreign capital which is induced to be of a compensatory nature and not by short-term foreign capital which includes both private and government flows.

In the present scenario most of the countries are in "managed float", where some form of intervention by the Central Banks is permitted. When some Asian countries liberalised both current account and capital account in the nineties, there was a currency crisis in 1997 due to sudden reversals of flows-outflow of speculative funds. The need for caution on capital account controls was observed by the Reserve Bank of India. Even in the foreign exchange market, Reserve Bank interferes selectively to prevent undue fluctuations in the value of the rupee as against the major foreign currencies and against dollar in particular.

## India's Balance of Payments

In India, balance of payments compilation, concepts and techniques are almost similar to those followed by the International Monetary Fund (IMF). These are codified by the Fund in their Balance of Payments Manual given to member countries for their reference and guidance. Although, the details of items and the mode of presentation may differ from country to country, the broad framework does not differ as between the member countries who submit periodically their balance of payments accounts to the Fund for their consolidation, assessment and/or publication.

The usual classification of the accounts into current and capital items-the former of income nature and the latter of capital nature-is followed by India also. The items shown above the line are considered to be of autonomous nature and those below the line, of a financing nature. The concept of surplus or deficit as followed by the Ministry of Finance is the sum total of items shown below the line, namely: (1) IMF Net, (2) SDR Net, and (3) changes in the country's foreign exchange reserves. The rest of the items of current and capital nature appear above the line. In the presentation of data by the RBI, reserves and monetary gold appear as balancing items, leaving aside "errors and omissions."

In India, balance of payments in the past were showing consistent deficits which were designed to finance the plan expenditure. Thus, our imbalance in balance of payments is not really of a short-term disequilibrium nature but of a structural nature. Massive doses of foreign aid (official loans, grants and commodity assistance) have been used for financing a sizeable part of our import requirements for planned investment. So, the measurement of the deficit is being made in terms of drawal on induced foreign official resources (loans and grants), borrowings from IMF and use of foreign exchange reserves.

## Sectoral Breakdowns

India's balance of payments data are presented in a way as to be amenable to sectoral analysis. The details of short-term and long-term nature under both government and private sectors are presented separately. Thus, the contributions to the foreign sector represented by the balance of payments from the government, business and financial sectors are available from these data. In current account, imports and exports are given as credits and debits. Under the category of invisibles, government and credit receipts and expenditure and government remittances-inflows and outflows-and other items to the extent possible, are presented for the government and the private business sector. The transfer payments and receipts are presented separately for governments and private sector. Balance of payments data are published both in rupee and U.S. dollar terms. Quarterly data for the recent years and current account data are given in RBI's monthly Bulletin

Appendix I presents the proforma, in which India's balance of payments is presented. Credits relate to inflows or receipts while debits relate to outflows or payments. Since exports relate to the inflow of funds, these are credits while imports relate to debits. Sometimes, receipts are shown as disbursements and payments are shown as amortisation in the presentation of data.

The details on capital account are also available but not published now in terms of the government (official), private and banking sectors. Private sector represents the business and household sectors in India and primarily the former while the banking sector represents the flows of the financial sector. The data on capital account is presented under broad heads of FDI, portfolio investment, loans and banking capital (*Source:* RBI Bulletins). The government and private sector flows may be of both short-term and long-term nature and are presented as Foreign Investment, Loans and Banking Sector. Loans include External Assistance, Commercial Borrowings and short-term capital flow. These details are given in Capital Account. The data also include Rupee Debt Service and other capital. Errors and omissions are shown as part of the balance of payments while the rest are shown as financing arrangements. But banking sector flows are definitionally of short-term nature and the amounts involved are also small. The banks are now permitted under the existing liberalised exchange rules to keep some amounts abroad and bring funds from abroad for their own business. Banks can, normally keep minimum working balances abroad and loans and overdrafts can be secured from abroad upto a limit without the RBI's prior permission. Banking capital excludes payments and receipts on behalf of the RBI and presented as assets and liabilities. Private loans include foreign, private and official loans received by the private sector in India, either through the government financial institutions or through private sector banks and financial institutions. Since 1992, private and government companies have been permitted to borrow directly from abroad as ECB, ADRs, GDRs etc. Government loans are official credits received from foreign governments or government bodies, foreign central banks or other financial institutions abroad. Foreign direct and portfolio investment is permitted and so is Indian investment abroad albeit on a limited scale.

## Sources of Data

In India, the Reserve Bank of India is the sole agency responsible for the compilation of balance of payments data. The RBI in turn collects these data from various sources, namely, banks, corporate units, government bodies and Indian government missions abroad, etc., and from the surveys conducted by them. As exchange control authority, the RBI gets some data from the banks who are authorised dealers in foreign exchange, from customs and trade authorities who are in charge of import and export licences under the Trade Control Act and from the government and government agencies, including the Ministry of Finance in respect of investment capital flows, joint ventures, etc., and in respect of their receipts and expenditures abroad. Airways, oil companies, shipping companies and post offices also provide information to the RBI on the inflows and outflows of funds. In respect of service payments and receipts, investment income, remittances etc., companies in the private sector and branches of foreign companies provide the necessary information. The Reserve Bank conducts surveys and collects data directly on private investment and foreign collaborations to collect data on joint ventures, deferred payments and other modes of flow of private capital. The Ministry of Finance provides all the data on capital flows of government account and on account of corporate sector on the basis of their approvals for foreign borrowings and for investment proposals in India. The Post and Telegraphs operate the exchange control in respect of some imports, exports and remittances etc. They are also a source of information for balance of payments data.

Authorised dealers, who are agents of the RBI in the implementation of exchange regulations, report to the RBI regularly their transactions with the public-all receipts and payments and transactions of sale or purchase of currencies. Besides, Customs send the export-import licences data as reported in the Trade Control Returns submitted by exporters/importers. These are also routed through the ADs. The transactions of the government and some private sector undertakings, which are put through the government agencies abroad such as the Indian High Commissioner, India Supply Mission, and embassies abroad, report the relevant particulars about these to the RBI on a monthly basis. Particulars relating to external assistance received or given are obtained from the Ministry of Finance in the form of monthly statements.

There is still a deficiency in the balance of payments compilation due to the inadequate coverage of private capital movements, which are not on a cash basis. The bulk of the foreign capital flows in the private sector is in the form of retained earnings. The data relating to them are collected through a survey designed for this purpose on a quarterly basis from branches/or subsidiaries of foreign companies. Such details are collected from 1963-64 onwards.

Transactions in imports were also refined as to reflect imports on f.o.b. basis instead of c.i.f. and incorporate i.f. elements in insurance and transportation. Deferred payment exports and imports are split up year-wise for changes in foreign assets and liabilities and entries are made in the balance of payments to reflect these changes.

## Role of Services in Balance of Payments

In more recent years, trade in services has come into greater focus for many reasons. Firstly, the comparative advantage for trade in goods has reached a limit in respect of many developing countries while the need for imports and exchange earnings continued to grow. It is in this context that these developing countries have to divert their attention to the promotion of services sector in international trade. Secondly, the growth of transport and communications and shortening of distance and other barriers due to technological breakthrough, international trade in services such as labour, consultancy, education, professional services, personal services etc., has grown. Thirdly, some of the non-trade services became tradable and trading in services has increased due to growing restrictions on trade in goods in many countries. Fourthly, revolution in technology, growth in software services, biotechnology, media communications, knowledge based services etc. led to larger trade in services.

Some of the services have become internationally tradable due to the growing role of transnational companies and technological revolution in the dimensions of time and space. These services can be classified under the following heads:

*(i)* Those in which the producer moves to the consumer, such as Indian labourers working in Gulf countries or international chain of hotels serving in foreign countries (Hilton Group).

*(ii)* Those in which consumer moves to the producer such as tourists or students, patients seeking treatment etc., visiting foreign countries for the services.

*(iii)* Those in which either producer or consumer moves to others such as dancers and singers, artists, scientists visiting abroad for performances or lecturers or foreigners visiting our country to hear them or learning from them.

*(iv)* Those in which neither the producer nor the consumer moves out such as in banking, insurance or technology transfers, but information flows, etc.

As regards the quantum of world trade in services, the value of trade has grown enormously during the last two decades. Here the term "services" is defined to include all current account items other than merchandise trade and pure transfer payments. At present trade in services is about one-third to one-half of the value of the merchandise exports or imports. It is also interesting to note that this trade in services is more concentrated in industrialised developed countries than the trade in merchandise items, and it will take a long time before developing countries can capture any important segment of the world trade in this respect.

## Non-resident Inflows

Under invisibles, a substantial inflow took place in recent years in non-official flows into India. Since 1982, the government has been encouraging these inflows through higher rates of interest on non-resident rupee accounts with banks than on domestic deposits, the RBI has kept SLR on them lower at 25 per cent as against the normal requirement against domestic deposits at 31.5 per cent. Such deposits were exempt for wealth tax purposes and interest income exempt for income tax purposes. The rates of interest on foreign currency non-resident accounts were, however, kept lower than on Indian deposits due to lower interest rates in the markets abroad for foreign currencies. The aggregate inflow of funds on all non-resident accounts during 2008-09 was $ 4.3 billion which was almost three times that of the amount five years ago. The NRI inflows slowed down recently and RBI has also discouraged these inflows due to our excess reserve position now.

## Foreign Exchange Reserves

The components of India's foreign exchange reserves which are used for financing our foreign trade are as follows:

(1) RBI balances held abroad.

(2) RBI foreign investments.

(3) Gold held by the RBI.

(4) Balances held abroad by Government agencies.

(5) Balances held abroad by authorised dealers.

Upto 1950-51, a bulk of our foreign reserves was held as sterling balance. In 1950-51 our reserves (including gold) stood at Rs. 1029 crores. During the First Plan, reserves financed nearly 37 per cent of the deficit and they fell to Rs. 902 crores by end of this period. During the Second Plan, about 25 per cent of the deficit was financed by reserves, which stood at a low level of Rs. 304 crores. By the end of Third Plan the reserves touched the lowest level of Rs. 298 crores.

After the devaluation of the rupee in 1966, there was a distinct change in the trends in balance of payments. By the time the Fourth Plan was started in 1969-70, our reserves stood at Rs. 728 crores (excluding SDRs). During the seventies, reserves were built up considerably, following some improvement in trade balance and substantial inflows of funds on invisible trade account and remittances from abroad. Our reserves including gold increased from Rs. 764 crores at end 1973-74 (end of Fourth Plan) to Rs. 5388 cores by end 1979-80 (excluding SDRs). There has been a deterioration in our payments position since then and our reserves including gold stood at Rs. 3660 crores at end December 1982 but improved again to Rs. 7,170 crores by end February 1987 and stood at Rs. 9,926 crores in June 1991 and rose to Rs. 3,38,349 crores at end December. 2002, and to Rs. 4,90,129 crores at end March 2004. These reserves were Rs. 12,69,235 crores in June 2009. These data include Indian's Reserve Tranche position with the IMF, gold, SDRs and foreign currency assets.

The gold component of our reserves rose from Rs. 117.8 crores in 1950-51 to Rs. 182.5 crores in 1966-67 due to revaluation of gold from Rs. 53.58 per 10 grams in 1996 to Rs. 84.39 per 10 grams thereafter. The quantity of gold holdings was augmented by Rs. 5.3 crores each in January 1977, December 1977 and December 1978 and by Rs. 5.2 crores in December 1979 due to restitution of gold by the IMF to India. The increase in gold value in June 1978 was due to purchase of gold under a non-competitive bid at IMF gold auction. At end March 1981, gold held by the RBI was valued at Rs. 224.7 crores and at end December 1981 at Rs. 225.6 crores. There was fresh acquisition of gold by

RBI from Central Government in 1984-85 by Rs. 20.25 crores and in 1985-86 by Rs. 28.50 crores with the result that gold stocks with RBI stood at Rs. 46,914 crores at end June 2009 and Rs. 1,288.22 billion at end March 2014.

SDRs are a new international reserve asset created since January 1970 by the IMF to supplement the traditional international reserves in the form of gold and convertible currencies. The expansion of world trade has turned out to be larger than the growth of newly-mined gold. So the expansion of international liquidity needed to be augmented to facilitate the growth of world trade. Accordingly, Special Drawing Rights (SDRs) were created, each equivalent to 0.888671 gram of fine gold. These were allocated to member countries on the basis of the member's original quotas with the Fund. The first allocation was done in January 1970 and India's share was SDRs 126 million. This was followed by an allocation of SDRs 101 million in January 1971 and SDRs 100 million in January 1972. The restitution and use of the SDRs is controlled by the IMF through a formula and India has been using them since their inception. From time to time SDRs were allotted to India and the allocation in January 1981 was to the extent of SDR 117 million as compared to SDR 119 million in January 1979 and a similar amount in January 1980. The outstanding amount on SDR account of India stood at a high of 306 million dollars in December 1985 but fell to 197.6 million dollars at end January 1987 and stood at a low of US $ 10 million at end December. 2002; the holdings of SDRs by India has declined further later on, due to our repayments abroad. But by end March 2010 they stood at a high of 3297 million SDRs and 26,820 million in March 2014.

## Foreign Assistance

External assistance utilised during the First Plan was only Rs. 221 crores. But the role of external assistance had increased during the Second and Third Plans to Rs. 1446 crores and Rs. 2805 crores respectively (inclusive of PL 480 and 665 Assistance). During the three years of annual plans (1967-69), external assistance utilised was Rs. 3228 crores and during the Fourth Plan (1969-70 to 1973-74), the corresponding amount was Rs. 4184 crores. In the next five years external assistance utilised had gone up further to Rs. 7309 crores (1974-75 to 1978-79). External aid in the Sixth Plan was about Rs. 11000 crores which was the largest amount used in any plan period. Grants and PL 480 and 665 assistance ceased from 1971-72. Grants proportion has come down to 9-10% of the total external assistance, which has dried down due to problems in creditor countries. Net assistance after repayments and service payments are excluded, has become negative.

In the Sixth Plan period (1980-81 to 1984-85) the objective of self-reliance was pursued more vigorously and the proportion of external assistance to total outlay was brought down to about 8 per cent. In the Seventh Plan period (1985-86 to 1989-90) the corresponding proportion did not exceed 10 per cent. The annual debt burden due to repayment of principal and interest was estimated by the Planning Commission (Ninth Five Year Plan Document) at around 18-20 per cent of the current account receipts and stood at 18.3% in 2004. After 1990-91 the policy was one of free market economy and free trade. The external debt to GDP ratio was 20% at end March 2004 and stood at 22% in 2009 debt-service ratio was 18.3% in 2004, and declined to 4.6% in 2009.

India's external debt declined from $ 99 billion at end March 1995 to $ 92.2 billion at end March 1996 and stood at $ 104 billion at end March 2004, and $ 230 billion at end march 2009 which was not considered a heavy burden in terms of the debt servicing ratio and low percentage of short-term debt (21.5%) and a large component of concessional aid (18.2%). Foreign reserves also reached a peak of US $ 270 billion in March 2010 and US $ 8304 billion in March 2014.

India has repaid some external loans which are of high cost in the present services of low interest cost. Repayments are more in excess of inflow of loans in more recent years with the result that there was a net outflow on account of external assistance. Our foreign exchange position has been comfortable and further inflow of funds due to External Commercial Borrowings and due to NRI funds are now discouraged by India, since 2000. As regards The IMF, we are in a creditor position, having repaid all our debt to it.

# APPENDIX

### The Proforma in which India's Balance of Payments are Presented by the Reserve Bank of India

| | Credit | Debit | Net |
|---|---|---|---|
| *A. Current Account* | | | |
| I. Merchandise | | | |
| II. Invisibles | | | |
| (A) Services | | | |
| 1. Travel | | | |
| 2. Transportation | | | |
| 3. Insurance | | | |
| 4. Government not Included Elsewhere | | | |
| 5. Miscellaneous | | | |
| (B) Transfer Receipts/Payments | | | |
| (i) Official | | | |
| (ii) Private | | | |
| (C) Investment Income | | | |
| **Total Current Account (I + II)** | | | |
| *B. Capital Account* | | | |
| 1. Foreign Investment (a + b) | | | |
| (a) In India | | | |
| Direct | | | |
| Portfolio | | | |
| (b) Abroad | | | |
| 2. Loans | | | |
| (a) External Assistance | | | |
| 1. By India | | | |
| 2. To India | | | |
| (b) Commercial Borrowings (Medium-term and long-term) | | | |
| 1. By India | | | |
| 2. To India | | | |
| (c) Short-term Capital Flow | | | |
| To India | | | |
| 3. Banking Capital | | | |
| (a) Commercial Banks | | | |
| (i) Assets | | | |
| (ii) Liabilities | | | |
| (iii) Non-Resident deposits | | | |
| (b) Other | | | |
| 4. Rupee Debt Service | | | |
| 5. Other Capital | | | |
| **Total Capital Account (1 + 2 + 3 + 4 + 5 )** | | | |
| *C. Errors and Omissions* | | | |
| *D. Over all Balance (Total)* | | | |
| *E. Monetary Movements* | | | |
| (i) IMF | | | |
| (ii) Foreign Exchange Reserves. | | | |

❖❖❖

Balance of Payments (Equilibrium Vs. Disequilibrium)

# INTERNATIONAL TRADE FLOWS

# 10

## India's Trade Philosophy

International trade flows include both exports and imports of goods and services. Trade policy is an important adjunct of the foreign exchange policy. Trade, aid and exchange policies are interrelated with international politico-economic relations. International trade is basically a reflection, firstly, of the structure and trends in world production. But more importantly international political forces, regional affinities and socio-economic factors play a vital role in deciding the pattern of aid and trade. In a developing country, trade depends on aid and the composition and direction of trade are dictated by aid flows to some extent. Aid was necessary to pay for growing imports, in a state of inadequate growth of exports. Planned investment could not be maintained without a minimum component of imports, despite the existence of a wide network of controls. It would thus be vital to promote exports to pay for imports which are themselves growing due to increasing costs and growing requirements of investment. Exports also pay for debt servicing, namely, repayment of old debts and payment of interest, etc. In a country whose exchange reserves are exiguous and exports can meet only part of the requirements of imports and debt servicing liabilities, aid continues to play an important role. In fact, a prudent country has to plan to build up the exchange reserves by a deliberate export strategy to boost export surplus.

The objectives of trade policy in India may be broadly set out as follows:

*(1)* To promote exports, necessary to pay for imports;

*(2)* To allow imports which would facilitate planned investment and increased utilisation of capacity, and promote growth.

*(3)* Trade liberalisation and move towards globalisation.

*(4)* To make foreign trade a dynamic agent for faster economic growth in India.

## Importance of Trade Transactions

The role of foreign trade in the national economy can be judged by the proportion of foreign trade to national income. As a proportion of national income, exports were about 8 per cent in 1951-52 which fell to 4.4 per cent in 1971-72 but rose again to around 8 per cent in the seventies and eighties due to faster growth of exports. Imports as a percentage of national income have also declined from 10.7 per cent in 1951-52 to 4.9 per cent in 1971-72 but stood at 9-10 per cent in the seventies. In 2003-04 exports as a percentage of national income stood at 10 per cent while the corresponding percentage for imports was 13 per cent. These data should be compared with that, in 2009, when exports to GDP was 15.0% and imports to GDP was 25% of GDP.

Exports to GDP was 20% and imports to GDP was 29% in 2014. The gap is made good by invisible trade.

Firstly, India is less dependent on the world economy than many other developing countries.

Secondly, India's exports did not grow adequately to keep its share in world trade due to the vast domestic market at home and inward-looking growth of the economy.

Thirdly, world exports grew much faster than those of India due to the larger share in the growth by developed countries and a few oil rich countries. India's share in world trade fell from 2.2 per cent in 1950 to 0.6 per cent in 1970 and further declined during eighties and nineties to around 0.5%. Although it is undesirable to have a declining share of world trade from the point of international importance of a country, it is not *ipso facto* an adverse development for two reasons.

Firstly, the pattern of growth of Indian economy, is not export-oriented.

Secondly, the larger the size of a country, the smaller is its share in world trade. Today India's share in world trade is slightly less than one percent of GDP.

## Changes in Demand

Trade pattern, direction and quantum depend on the demand and supply factors. If there is a shift in the offer on demand curve due to, say, an increase in Indian demand for US wheat, it will no doubt result in improved terms of trade for USA but it is doubtful whether it will lead to a higher level of welfare. The reason is the presence of many indeterminates and subjective factors. The USA may move to a higher indifference curve because India would now be offering a larger quantity of cloth for a given unit of American wheat due to a rise in its demand for wheat. Similarly, technological progress may shift the offer curve to the left, in the sense that more wheat can now be offered by USA for the same amount of Indian cloth. The resulting change in the terms of trade may not necessarily improve the level of welfare in USA due to trade taking place. The ability of a country to improve the terms of trade will depend on its size of the share in the world trade and relative elasticities of supply and demand for internationally-traded goods.

## Trade Gains

Trade results in gains in consumption and welfare and leads to greater specialisation and production. Trade also produces effects on income distribution. Larger production and consumption do not necessarily lead to greater welfare of all the sections of the people. In some countries trade may increase wages, while in others the returns to capital may rise. The export sector and merchant community may gain at the expense of producers or other sections of the population. If the gains to the former sections are larger than those to the latter, the former should be able to compensate the latter to conclude that the welfare of the community as a whole has increased. Introduction of distributional effects of trade on a nation would alter the conclusions arrived at through production and consumption effects of trade. Thus, trade is expected to alter savings and investment in such a way so as to promote the growth of economy if the gains to those benefitted are greater than the losses to others. Gains and losses would also depend on the relative average propensities and marginal propensities to consume and save, of the respective sections of the community.

## Generalised Trade Theory

The theory of international trade has been generalised by Prof. Gray to include the role of multinational corporations (MNC). Traditional theories depend on the comparative cost theory and different resource endowments of different countries and their international immobility. Once these assumptions are invalidated by the MNCs through trade and private foreign direct investment, we have to introduce other variables and trade barriers for the purpose of trade theory.

If the resources are specific and immobile but their services are transferable through MNCs we have a theory of foreign direct investment through MNCs. What Prof. Gray[1] has done is to link international trade with international production and foreign direct investment. Harry Johnson and Bertil Ohlin had introduced the various trade barriers and locational factors into the theory of international trade. The specific barriers to trade incorporated into the trade theory were: (1) Transportation costs; (2) Psychic distance factors; and (3) Government policy variables like tariffs and subsidies.

The orthodox theory is based on the multi-factor and multi-commodity approach to the factor proportions theory and emphasises gains from trade through larger consumption and greater specialisation in production in line with the comparative cost theory. The change needed for the Generalised Theory is to incorporate factors like specific goods used as inputs and firm-specific factors of production and product-specific inputs, and

1. Prof. H. Peter Gray: "A Generalised Theory of International Trade" and "Towards a Unified Theory of International Trade, International Production and Direct Foreign Investment" (The Macmillan Press, 1976).

integrate the theory of international production with world trade and foreign direct investment. John H. Dunning's approach in his eclectic theory of "Trade Location of Economic Activity and MNC" involved three sets of determinants of international production, namely *viz.*, ownership-specific advantages of enterprises of one nationality over those of another, internationalisation of incentives and location specific advantages. Gray's theory adopts Dunning's approach and takes into account the transferability of proprietary technology and other specific natural resources or endowments of some countries into others through the MNCs. Knowledge-know-how, R&D, different levels of technology and country specific factors have been the base for Modern Trade Theory.

The short-run analysis assumes constant global factoral supplies. These supplies are distributed among countries so as to maximise international production and to achieve the lowest costs of production, thanks to the foreign direct investment and the activities of MNCs. The new international allocation of resources could maximise the rates of return to factors of production which are both internationally mobile and immobile and product specific factors are spread out across borders so as to optimise international production. A proper allocation of resource inputs to maximise production and to determine the optimum pattern of trade across national boundaries is simultaneously determined to set an equilibrium according to this theory. Any disturbance in factoral inputs in production and resource allocation would change the pattern of production internationally and thus of trade accordingly.

The proprietary technology, know-how and product specific capital may not allow substitution of such factors in the input-mix of a product. This would then result in a quasi-rent payable to that specific factor. The MNCs would achieve the maximum feasible net value added and quasi-rent for their specific factors by achieving optimum geographical distribution of their assets and their sales and earnings. The MNCs may use such factors and distribute the products or services involving the use of such inputs among nations so as to lower costs of production through better specialisation and increased scales of production. The MNCs may transfer such specific factors of production or their services from one country to another if such relocation would lower the costs and enable the company to make their goods available in the market at a price lower than any other source of supply, namely, through trade or through import substitution measures in the domestic economy.

The only countervailing factors to be considered from the point of the LDCs are the alternatives to foreign direct investment, namely, imports through trade or domestic production in substitution of products available through the MNCs. As quasi-rent or the monopoly element of the MNCs is not desirable for promoting strict competition in any economy, MNCs are not prima facie desirable unless the other alternatives are not feasible in the existing set-up. It is in this context that the role of MNCs in international division of labour and in trade has to be carefully assessed in respect of the LDCs.

In the Modern Theory of International Trade, the changes necessitated by introduction of multinationals and foreign direct investment are: *(i)* The assumptions for a two-country and two-commodity model are to be changed; *(ii)* There are five categories of inputs, viz., capital, land, skilled labour and unskilled labour, enterprise and technology, some of which are firm specific and some product specific; *(iii)* The principal resource endowments, tastes and production functions are supposed to be known and fixed and trade is balanced by means of free exchange rates; *(iv)* There is mobility of knowledge, IT and enterprise as well as funds; *(v)* The basis of trade is the availability of technology transfers and enjoyment of economies of scale.

The international transfer of resources and factors of production wherever possible is in substitution for international trade for goods and services. Such migration can be in respect of product specific factors, or firm specific technology and can either be trade creating or trade supplementary or trade diverting. The factors for and against any proposal for foreign direct investment are complex and each case is to be studied separately. Given the assumption that the MNC could make a direct investment and transfer their proprietary specific inputs and product specific inputs to another country, this could create markets and expand trade on a global basis which could be in the interests of the host country or not depending on the alternatives available to the host country.

If the potential for investment by MNC exists through expected higher quasi-rents in the host country, the short-term equilibrium is disturbed and foreign direct investment takes place. A reverse position can be visualised when foreign direct investment will leave the country due to changes in the pattern of costs and prices or of demand to lower the quasi-rents.

The effects of impediments to trade through commercial policies, transportation costs and other psychological barriers would get reflected in the pattern of costs and prices of foreign goods versus domestic goods. The ranking of importable goods in the domestic country and of exportable goods in the foreign country would change. Psychic distance impediments to trade would get reflected through changes in cost and prices of tradable commodities.

The generalised theory of international trade would also incorporate the location specific factors through foreign direct investments by MNCs as also country specific and product specific factors of production. The final outcome of international trade would depend upon the changes introduced in the production patterns in the two countries under consideration and in the costs and prices including the factor prices in the respective countries and a host of other factors and including tastes, habits, technological levels etc.

The exports and imports of merchandise items and invisible service items depend as seen above on the demand and supply of these items in the respective countries. These money flows internationally involve the transfers of purchasing powers or foreign exchange. This has two aspects — one on the domestic level by losing money or gaining money and another at the international exchange by the burden of transfer of exchange of currencies. These effects are seen in the financial field involving domestic and foreign currencies.

## Dynamics of Transactions in Trade

The transactions in finance are the reflection of the transactions in goods and services. International Trade is thus an important constituent of the study of International Financial Management. Demand and supply elasticities in respect of exports and imports relative to prices and incomes of the countries play a vital role in the volume of international trade flows. Merchandise trade constitutes the bulk of total flows on current account.

Trade leads to greater welfare of trading nations and promotes the growth of production and consumption through greater specialisation and lower costs and prices. Historically economic growth of some countries was led by exports due to larger markets and larger production and consequential industrial and commercial revolution. In more recent years, however, barring a few smaller nation-states like Taiwan and Korea or oil producing, developing countries in the Middle East, trade was not a major propellant to growth. But the basic proposition remains that growth can be led by exports or exports will expand with growth and that they are interrelated. Theoretically, what is the mechanism that links them? How economic growth influences trade or is influenced by trade will be discussed here. Static theories were based on assumptions of constancy of tastes, factors of production and technology, perfect markets, etc.

In dynamic trade conditions equilibrium would change under the following conditions:

*(i)* Changes in factor endowment such as population growth or capital growth, etc.

*(ii)* Technological growth or technological changes.

*(iii)* Structural changes in the economy due to growth of the industries, changes in tastes and habits, etc.

Some dynamic factors of growth are discussed below:

## Effect of Tastes

Changes in tastes would introduce changes in the available supplies for trade, pattern of consumption and relative costs and prices of commodities and factors. Nurkse spoke of the "demonstration effect" of trade on tastes and how the demand for goods and services would change with changes in tastes. The indifference curve map would change with changes in tastes and habits and resultant changes in trade may lead to a new equilibrium in production and consumption. Change in tastes may sometimes increase or decrease trade, alter the composition of trade and production structures, etc. The possible degree of disequilibrium from changes in tastes is unpredictable and uncertain.

## Changes in Factor Endowments

While labour and capital may expand, land may not change except in a sense that its uses can grow due to technological changes or to the discovery of new mines or minerals. The changes in factor endowments would influence the production possibility curve. A uniform growth of all factors might push the curve outward evenly while the disparate growth in factors with no other changes in the economy can lead to more exports or less imports depending upon the sector in which the expanding factors are used more. Such growth in factors might lead to export-biased growth if expanding factors are used more in the export sector or import-biased growth in the economy if expanding factors are used more in the import sector or is neutral to both if the goods using the factors expanding in the economy are only for domestic consumption. Not only the quantity of trade might change, but the terms of trade, namely, the ratio of export price to import price, might alter due to changes in costs and prices of goods produced. It is possible that a bias in production due to the growth of factors might be offset by bias in consumption at home or abroad or by changes in cost-price parities.

## Technology Changes

Technological growth can be neutral or export-biased or import-biased on the same lines. If it is neutral only productivity and efficiency might increase, leading to lower costs and prices. Terms of trade will deteriorate for that country. A neutral technological growth is as good as an even growth of all factors of production. An export-biased technological growth will augment the abundant factor and further expand the exports. An import-biased growth in technology will augment the scarce factor in the country and promote the import competing goods resulting in import-biased growth. In between such possibilities, there are a host of combinations of growth of technology resulting in growth of the economies. Technological changes may also result in the production of new goods or services which have a market abroad, and it is possible that old goods may be changed in form and content. These changes take place continuously with the result that pattern, quality and direction trade flows changes in a continuous fashion in the real world. Such changes may result in trade taking place in fashion unrelated to factor endowments at least in the short run. These dynamic factors lead to changes in Trade pattern, direction, quantity and quality etc.

## Trade and Growth in LDCs

Whether the LDCs gain by trade in terms of growth under present-day conditions in controversial. R. Prebisch and a host of other economists have maintained that conditions conducive to growth by trade are not present today due to disadvantages suffered by the LDCs.

(1) Firstly, their terms of trade move adverse to them due to inelasticities in their supply of exportable goods and in foreign demand for their goods.

(2) Their export earnings are unstable due to their greater dependence on a few agricultural products for export which are demand-inelastic abroad. The supply of such products fluctuate widely due to the vagaries of monsoon as they are agricultural products.

(3) The demand for foreign products of LDCs are elastic, while foreign demand for their products is inelastic, leading to a situation adverse to the LDCs in terms of both income and price elasticities.

(4) The tariff and non-tariff barriers of developed countries stand in the way of the export markets of the LDCs.

(5) The high cost price parities in the LDCs due to lower productivity put the LDCs in a disadvantageous position.

(6) The multinationals and monopolistic firms abroad keep out the products of the LDCs in the international markets.

In view of such disadvantages, the LDCs tend to rely on import competing goods or on domestic markets while developed countries could have export-led growth.

## Linkage — Forward and Backward

The traditional links between trade and growth can be set out in terms of: *(i)* Expansion of markets or opening of new markets, *(ii)* Larger production of export goods and *(iii)* Specialisation in selected lines of production leading to lower costs, prices, etc. These would lead to the forces which will increase the output, incomes and employment. The process by which one product stimulates the production of others is called "linkage" by A.O. Hirschman. Both forward and backward linkage operate to promote growth of production. While forward linkages lead to industries which utilise this product as input, backward linkages promote industries which provide ancillaries and inputs to this product. Besides, there is a possibility of growth in terms of "demonstration effect" through a multiplier process. The growth of some industries would accelerate the growth process in general and stimulate the growth of others as in the case of plantations in the LDCs and oil in the Middle East. Such linkages produce changes in production, consumption and distribution in the economy.

## National Income and Trade (Exports)

Trade affects national product and income through changes in production for export markets. In the national income identity in macro terms, domestic product + net inflows from abroad would equal national product. In an open economy National Income = Consumption + Investment + (Exports -Import denoted by Sf or If.)

$$\text{or } Y = C + I + (X - M)$$

In a static situation trade would increase income through larger exports than imports leading to higher foreign savings (X – M) = If. In a dynamic situation, these savings are invested leading to a further rise in incomes and output of the nation. Such a rise depends on the foreign trade multiplier and accelerator. It is foreign saving or investment denoted by Sf or If).

$$\text{Investment} = \text{Domestic Savings} + \text{Foreign Savings.}$$

$$I = Sd + Sf$$

If leads to Y by a multiple of original If, over a period of time, which is called the foreign trade multiplier. Incomes will increase not only by a multiple of domestic investment but of foreign investment also, (X – M).

In general equilibrium models, we have to take both income equation and balance of payments equation and a simultaneous solution is to be sought for both. Balance of payments or trade equation will increase income, which in turn leads to greater investment at home (Id) and greater exports (x) resulting in an accelerator effect on incomes. In the income equation, investments increase income due to operation of the multiplier. Rise in incomes would lead to greater investments and further income growth through the accelerator in operation. Here investment is made a function of increments in income.

Both the multiplier and accelerator operate in respect of the foreign sector's impact on the domestic economy.

## Imports and Growth

Yet another aspect of the impact of foreign trade is through imports acting as a propeller to growth. Imports of both consumption and capital goods influence the goods market and the factor market and through them, the expenditure and income growth in the economy.[2]

It was shown in the author's model how imports promote growth of capital formation in the LDCs and thus, of income and output. Consumption imports add to the goods market and investment imports to the factor market and propel both larger consumption and greater investment, provided imports are used productively and import control channelises the flows into those avenues with growth potential in terms of utilisation of capacity or greater production in the economy.

It would thus, be seen that growth of income via foreign trade sector is both feasible and realistic whether conceived in an accounting sense or in a conceptual sense. Both exports and imports have a role to play to promote the economic development, incomes and employment in the country. In the dynamics of the real world, continuous interactions between the foreign sector and domestic sector take place to lead to greater interdependence, mutual benefit and all-round growth of the economies. In this chapter, we explain the concepts of terms of trade which has a wide application in international trade theory.

## Terms of Trade

Terms of trade are the relation between the prices of exports and imports. To express this relation, various formulae and variants are used. Gross barter terms of trade are quantity of imports (Qm) dividend by quantity of exports (Qx) – $\frac{Qm}{Qx}$ .Net barter terms of trade are price of exports (Px) divided by price of imports (Pm) – $\frac{Px}{Pm}$. These terms were used originally by Taussig and Viner.

A higher price paid for imports, export price remaining constant, would mean adverse terms in the sense that more will have to be paid for imports in terms of exports. If a larger quantity of exports are required to be sent for a given quantity of imports, it is again adverse to the country. This is represented by gross barter terms of trade $\frac{Qm}{Qx}$.

These concepts do not measure strictly the welfare from foreign trade. Suppose a country has a high export price relative to import price but cannot export much, it cannot obviously increase its welfare. Similarly, a country may have a high capacity to import

2. V.A. Avadhani, *Imports and Capital Formation in Underdeveloped Countries,* Sudhir Publications, 1979.

but its foreign trade is negligible relative to its income, then the country cannot gain much. Besides one has to consider the productivity gains also. Suppose technology is of neutral type and uniform productivity gains are secured, then terms of trade may worsen but it does not mean that its welfare is reduced; it is only sharing some of its productivity gains with its customers. Taking productivity into account the concept of "single factoral terms of trade" is used in the form of an expression $\frac{Px}{Pm}$ multiplied by Zx, where Zx stands for productivity in exports. In actual practice, Zx, can be represented by an index number over the base period in terms of output per worker. In a similar way, double factoral terms of trade are represented by $\frac{Px}{Pm} \times \frac{Zx}{Zm}$ where Zm is productivity of foreign factors in the import sector. Single factoral terms of trade are more relevant as we are interested in knowing what our factors can earn in terms of goods and not knowing what our factor services can command in terms of services of foreign factors.

Terms of trade have been deteriorating secularly for the developing countries, as demonstrated by economists like R. Prebisch. The reasons for such secular deterioration of terms of trade of a developing economy are to be sought in the structural features, nature of the export products, tariff and other barriers by developed countries and a host of other factors.

Some other concepts used in this connections are merchandise terms of trade, invisible account terms of trade or current account terms of trade. In actual practice, what is lost in terms of trade on merchandise account may be gained on the invisible trade account. So current account terms of trade are a more comprehensive term for measurement of exchange terms.

Inclusion of transport cost can create a problem as exports are on f.o.b. (free on board) and imports are on c.i.f. (cost, insurance and freight). If a country carries a part of its exports and also a part of its imports, then the above is not a good measure of exchange terms. In the case of a rise/fall in the costs of transport, real changes in the import and export prices and quantities are not reflected by the above formalities. Transport costs, therefore, create problems in the measurement of terms of trade. Inclusion of i.f. in imports and exclusion of them in exports are ideal only if each country is carrying its own imports and have its own ships or aircraft and none of the exports is so carried. Thus, although, the terms of trade broadly reflect the gains from trade or welfare, they are not an exact measure which can be depended upon in all circumstances.

## Conclusion

At the international level, the transaction demand for money has various factors, involving the markets for goods and services as well as financial markets, comprising money and monetary assets and their transfers across national borders. At the global level, these effects are very prominent in the present day world due to liberalisation in trade, WTO measures and globalisation trends. As trade is an adjunct to aid and investment, money flows on both current account and capital account have to be considered. The risks, which are part of these transactions are to be managed effectively by a global player.

# INTEREST RATES PARITY

# 11

Interest rate parity is based on the levels of purchasing power in two or more countries. They are the basis for determination of exchange rate.

The object of this chapter is to examine the conceptual and operational aspects of interest rate parity. The importance of this policy can be better appreciated in the background of a conceptual discussion on the mechanism of its operations and its significance to the economy. It would thus, be apt to start with the role of interest rates in the economy.

## Role of Interest Income

Conceptually, interest is a return to the capital as a factor of production. According to the traditional theory, interest is paid for abstaining from present consumption leading to savings. Savings is the basis of investment and capital formation. At the macro level, capital is a major factor of production to which interest is a reward or income just as wages, profits, rents, etc., are rewards to the other factors of production.

*Inter alia,* investment is a function of interest rate, and the quantum and directional flow of investment determine income. More scientifically, the impact of interest rate is both on savings and investments in the economy. In other words, the borrowings as well as lending are influenced by the interest rates. The costs of production which depend upon the production function also include the credit costs, as credit is an input in the productive process.

In the macro sense, interest rate and interest income have a vital role in the economy, as capital, for which it is a reward, plays a significant part in the growth dynamics of the country. Capital formation and capital accumulation are very much dependent upon the level and rate of savings and investment in the economy. Thus, interest is not a simple monetary phenomenon; it is the product of interaction of the monetary system with the real system.

The savings and investment in the economy which are influenced by the interest rates are the real economic variables. The incomes and expenditures of the various sectors of the economy result in excess savings or excess investment in each of the sectors. The sectors having excess savings provide them to those with excess investment. It is these savings and investment activities of the real sector which are influenced and facilitated by the flow of funds from the financial system. Here, both domestic as well as international forces operate if the economies are open.

## Role of Interest Rates

Interest rate has diverse roles in the economy such as a reward to capital which is a factor of production, a return to saving and a cost to investment and an instrument of monetary policy for credit control. The role of interest rate mechanism in India has been the subject of controversy. In fact, even in theory, there has been a controversy from the days of Lord Keynes about the role of interest rates in the economy. In this background, it is relevant to examine the role of interest rates in India. Do interest rates influence mobilisation of savings? Do they have an allocative role in the distribution of savings as between different instruments? How far the interest rates influence deposits of banks and shift as between deposits of various maturities? These and other aspects of interest rates are relevant for policy makers.

At the macro level, interest is a reward to the capital which is a factor of production. In the developing economy, capital formation and capital accumulation are of vital importance to economic development. Interest rates influence both savings and investment in the economy and serve a vital role for the mobilisation of savings. Besides, interest rate has a role in the allocation of investment funds as between different uses. Thus, in addition to influencing their cost, and availability of funds from the supply side, interest rates also influence the quantum of investments from the demand side and thus determine the income and employment in the economy, and can influence the allocation of investment funds.

Interest rate is a price for borrowing money or monetary assets. Despite the common belief that savings in India are interest-insensitive, our study has shown that while the overall household sector savings are mildly influenced by interest rates, household sector savings in the form of bank deposits are highly sensitive to interest rates. It would, therefore, appear that interest rates have a positive role in the savings mobilisation, particularly with regard to savings in the form of bank deposits. In addition to interest rates, personal disposable income, per capita income, the ratio of non-agricultural income to agricultural income and the population coverage per bank office have been found to be significantly influencing household savings in bank deposits, as revealed in our research studies.

Interest rates have also a significant role in the investment process in India. Our empirical tests have shown that domestic capital formation in India is a function of GDP, MEC[1] and the cost of capital.

The costs of borrowing from banks to the corporate sector are not high, constituting as they do only about 5 per cent of the total value of production in respect of large and medium public limited companies, as revealed by the Company Finance Studies of the RBI.

## Theories of Interest Rate

The classical view of interest rate can be expressed as the loanable funds theory which postulates that interest rate is determined by the supply of and demand for loanable funds. These loanable funds are in the present-day parlance the IOUs of financial institutions. The demand for and supply of these funds will determine the interest rate.

When Keynes considered the interest rate as a monetary phenomenon, he took money as an asset with an opportunity cost, namely, the return on short-term bonds. Under the partial equilibrium approach, one can assume that the forces in the real economic system remain constant and analyse the financial factors which explain the interest rates. Under this theory, interest rate is determined by the relative supply of and demand for liquidity or money in the economy which is a function of the financial system. Keynes' motives for the demand for liquidity are well-known, namely, the transactions, precautionary and speculative motives. The last motive has been renamed as an asset motive by the neoclassical economists.

The nominal interest rates according to the neo-classical theories depended also on the expectations of the public and the rate of inflation in the economy. According to Irving Fisher, for example, interest rate is also a function of inflation as the nominal rate is affected by the expected rate of inflation. The Gibson-Wicksell proposition that interest rates and wholesale prices move together in the long-run has been found to be empirically valid but the linkage coefficient is less than unity in India. This is so if only the organised financial sector is considered. During periods of inflation, the gap between the rates in the organised financial system and those in the unorganised system widen sharply although, the linkages are weak. Funds flow from the organised to the unorganised sector and *vice versa* which influence rates in both the sectors.

The maturity pattern of debt is an important factor for interest rate determination. The maturity pattern is particularly relevant in the gilt-edged market, small savings schemes and deposit and lending rates of banks. The longer the maturity, the larger is the risk and hence the risk premium. Time value of money is discussed in a later chapter. The prime criterion to be looked into is the extent of liquidity premium that public is prepared to pay on money *vis-a-vis* near money assets. The public are concerned with the real rate of return as the nominal interest paid can be eroded by the degree of inflation. The flow of savings and availability of funds would depend on positive real

1. Marginal efficiency of capital represented by the Return on Investment (ROI).

rates in the first place. Money has no return and to hold on to money has an opportunity cost as the alternatives to money have returns.

## Factors Influencing Interest Rates

Savings flow into various physical and financial assets. Financial assets are future claims on money like bank deposits, UTI units, shares, debentures, etc. These are in the form of IOUs. These financial assets have a structure of interest rates which should be rationally based on the degree of risk of ownership, uncertainty of return, period of maturity and a host of other factors.

The factors which influence interest rates on various financial investments are the nature of the instrument, maturity period, risk, tax status, marketability and liquidity. These are discussed below:

(1) The return on ownership capital should be higher than on loan capital, as the risk of the former is greater than that of the latter.

(2) Difference in maturity periods would influence the extent of the risk taken during the period when the lender is out of funds for varying periods of time. Ordinarily, the longer the period, the higher is the interest rate.

(3) The degree of default risks or uncertainty of return would also determine the interest rates. Such risks are nil or negligible in the case of government bonds while they are higher in the case of private debt or private ownership securities or company deposits. The rate is to be higher on those which have a higher risk.

(4) The tax provisions on the financial instruments or incentives or disincentives in the form of taxes on interest income or tax concessions would also influence the demand for different types of financial assets. Thus the effective rate on some postal certificates are higher due to tax concessions which would increase the effective take home rates.

(5) Another factor is the marketability of financial instruments with facilities for discounting or re-discounting and/or ready saleability which thus imparts liquidity and/or ready saleability. Liquidity means convertibility of assets into cash as and when required without loss of time or money. The more is the liquidity, the less is the rate of interest.

The normal pattern of yields is that the short-term rates are lower than the long-term rates and under normal expectations, the yields on ownership capital (risk taking ventures) would be higher than on loan capital. Besides the interest rates on government bonds which are less risky would also be lower than those on private securities of similar maturity. It is also true that the interest rates on some securities subject to special incentives or tax concessions may be lower than on comparable other instruments. Similarly, the financial instruments which have a good marketability like units of the Unit Trust of India or the shares quoted on the stock exchange may have lower rates than those which are not so marketable and/or not quoted on the stock exchanges. It would thus, be seen that a number of cognisable factors operate on the determination of interest rates. In India even now the rates are partly fixed by the government and the Reserve Bank of India, but the above basic principles of interest rate determination hold good. The existing term structure in India is a by-product of administrative fiat and exigencies of monetary and credit policies.

**Table 11.1**

These Factors are in Brief

| Risk of Ownership or Debt | Maturity Period | Variability or Uncertainty of Returns | Tax Status | Marketability & Liquidity | Safety |
|---|---|---|---|---|---|

These are drawbacks inherent in any system of partially controlled market forces with some rates fixed by the government, some rates by the Reserve Bank and a few left to the market forces. The multiplicity of controls and the agencies controlling have made the interest rate system in India complicated and distorted. This complex system prevailing even in the organised markets is made more difficult to comprehend by the generally uncontrollable interest rates charged in the unorganised and primitive markets in India. The deficiencies and anomalies in the present system of partially administered rates in India are ably brought out by the Sukhamoy Chakravarthy Committee (RBI, 1985).

Most of the interest rates in India are controlled and administratively fixed. It would, therefore, be difficult to isolate the free market forces which influence the interest rates in India. So far, interest rate policy has been used as a support to other instruments of monetary policy in India. Even under these controlled conditions, the basic postulates that interest rates are influenced by the money, liquidity and the rates of inflation etc. hold good particularly in uncontrolled unorganised market. But where there exists some correspondence, the linkages are weak statistically.

## Bank Rate and Refinance Rates

In the organised sector of the financial system for which data are available, interest rate policy is set by the actions of the Central Bank as its discount rate (*viz.*, Bank rate is the leader of interest rates). In India, the bank rate is the discount rate at which the central bank of the country makes advances to the commercial and cooperative banks against eligible assets. Section 49 of the RBI Act defines Bank Rate as the standard rate at which the Bank is prepared to buy and discount bill of exchange or other commercial paper eligible for purchase under the Act. In view of the limited role of the money market and bill market in India, the Bank rate is not the real leader among the interest rates. Under Section 17 of the RBI Act, the Reserve Bank provides refinance through various windows at different rates. It is these refinance rates which are the discount rates of the central bank in India.

The weighted average rate of interest on these various types of refinance would be the effective rate of discount by the RBI. This is different from the bank rate. The multiplicity of rates is necessitated by the social obligations of the banking system and the nature of our financial system.

## Nominal and Real Interest Rates

Nominal interest rates refer to interest rates denominated in money terms. Examples are the coupon rates on government bonds or bank deposit and lending rates. Real interest rates are the nominal rates adjusted for the inflation rate or purchasing power of money. Thus to give an example, if the banks' deposit rate for one year deposits is 6%, at present, and the inflation rate per annum is 5% on average basis, then the real interest rate is only 1%. Generally interest rates being compensation for saving or obstaining from the present consumption, they should be well above inflation rates to encourage savings, which is the basis for capital. Saving lead to investment which forms the basis for capital formation in the economy. Capital is a factor of production and is necessary for economic growth.

As referred to earlier, interest rate is a function of demand and supply of loanable funds or money. The equilibrium rate under free market conditions is the rate which equates the demand with supply. Leaving aside this general postulate of equilibrium condition, there are some fundamentals in the economy which influence interest rates. An attempt is made below to specify these fundamental variables which influence interest rates.

## Nodal Factors Influencing Interest Rates

Firstly, money supply or growth in money stock is a major factor influencing interest rate as it increases expenditure and the demand for money and also increases the supply of money. A new equilibrium rate of interest emerges due to changes in money stock.

Secondly, real income influences the interest rate, through rise in expenditure and the demand for money or real balances grow in the portfolio of the public. Real income changes occur due to changes in national product and changes in prices and changes in the distribution of national product among savers, dissavers and investors. Thus, savings and investment may both change due to above factors leading to changes in interest rates, as supply and demand for money changes as a consequence.

Thirdly, purchasing power of money or inflation influences the interest rates through changes in the value of money. If inflation rate goes up, it leads to a rise in interest rate to compensate the savers by raising the return to money funds to induce savers to have incentive and willingness to save through maintaining the real rate of return to them. It is a well-known fact that interest rate is a price for money or saving through abstaining from present consumption.

Fourthly, time factor of waiting for a future consumption by abstaining the present consumption is also factor influencing interest rate. The rate varies for the period of lending as in the case of deposit rates for various periods of time. Time has value and is a risk factor and has to be compensated. Thus, long-term lending or long-term bonds carry a higher coupon rate than short-term instruments. Detailed discussion on time factor is presented in a separate chapter.

Fifthly, interest rates vary with the risk factor involved in lending or parting with money. If the borrower is less creditworthy, there is more risk and a higher rate is warranted. If there is less risk due to high credit rating, the borrowing is generally at

LIBOR (London Inter Bank Offer Rate) or a few points above it. Thus, the companies with high credit rating in the country with rating above investment grade, find it easier and cheaper to borrow in the international markets. The interest charged to high credit rated firms is lower than the rate charged to low credit rated firms in general.

The above factors of money income, inflation, time and risk are the basic fundamental factors in the economy influencing the interest rates. Leaving aside time and risk factors, which get ingrained in the quantum change in the rates, depending on the period of maturity and the nature of the instrument of borrowing, the interest rate is a function of money stock, real income and inflation rate in the economy.

## Interest Rate Parity

This leads us to the international relation of interest rates in countries represented by the theory of international purchasing power parity. This theory states that assuming free market for interest rates and free flow of capital across countries, the interest rates for the same period and same risk element are brought to parity. If the rate is high in country A, the capital from country 'B' will flow into country A, then the rate in country B will rise bringing the interest parity as between A and B countries, to maintain equilibrium condition.

The international interest parity postulates that, under condition of free capital mobility, the interest rates across countries will be on parity due to capital movement across borders and flexibility of interest rates in the respective countries. The assumptions are clear that the interest rates are flexible and there is a free competitive market for capital in each country and that there is free mobility of capital across countries.

## Limitations of PPP Theory

The PPP theory is discussed in various sections of the book, as and when it has some relevance. The theory however suffers from various loopholes and weaknesses. Firstly, the above assumptions of free markets for goods, money and capital domestically and internationally are not practical. There are no perfect markets and the Market Efficiency Theory holds good only in its weak form in reality. Secondly, almost all countries, including those on full convertibility resort to control on indiscriminate flows of capital across borders due to the possible speculative element in it, which destabilise the balance of payments equilibrium. There are a variety of instruments with varying rates of interest and theory does not specify which rates will go for international parity, lastly the variables which influence interest rate, like money, income etc. cannot be correctly specified but the theory is empirically testable.

## Interest Rate Risk

The normal tools used for Interest Rate Risk management are FRAs, Financial Futures, Interest Rate Swaps, Interest Rate Options, caps, collars and floors, etc. The problem is that there is risk of rising interest cost for the company due to the fluctuating rate clause in its loan agreement. The basis for fluctuating rate may be LIBOR plus or Treasury Bill rate plus, or Treasury Bond rate plus, etc. The company would like this interest commitment fixed in foreign currency to be paid at a future date in order to reduce its risk. This can be done by a swap from floating rate basis, to fixed rate basis or enter into a Forward Rate agreement with a bank or a forward to forward transaction. A forward to forward deal to hedge interest rate exposure involves that he borrows 6 months from now and lends for 3 months in the same currency, if he has to cover a borrowing requirement arising in 3 months from now.

The realignment of the futures and cash market is not perfect and the yield difference due to this imperfection is called the 'basis.' Take an example. The price of 3 month LIBOR on spot is say 91.875. But the futures contract is say 91.650. The difference between the spot market and futures market is 91.87-91.65 = .22 basis points.

A company with 'BBB' rating has an exposure to interest rate via floating rate basis. It goes to the bank to hedge its exposure. The bank can borrow from the market on prime terms, as it has a 'AAA' rating. The company wants a loan for 5 years and it has to pay for it at $13^3/_4$% to raise $ 25 million, from the market. The company needs a fixed interest cost to hedge against possible increase in LIBOR.

The Bank is approached to provide fixed interest loan for 3 years. The company is unable to get finer rates from the market due to its low rating. The cost of converting the floating rate exposure to fixed rate is 14% as the bank is able to reduce its cost of issue by 1/4% by receiving LIBOR funds from the market. The rate for the bank is LIBOR + 1/4 and the rate for the company is LIBOR + 3/4. If the bank borrows, from the market, it is cheaper by 1/2%. The bank thus borrows from the market on Floating Rate Note basis for 6 months at a time, renewable, while the company got the loan from the bank at a fixed rate basis for a 5 year period, at $12^3/_4$%. It is still cheaper than the rate ($13^3/_4$%) at which it can borrow from the market. For the bank, it works out to a borrowing at 121/4% – leading a margin of 1/2% for hedge charge. On floating rate basis, it is related to the LIBOR, which works out to $12^1/_4$% p.a. on a fixed rate basis.

If a company XYZ has entered into a contract for a period costing $ 200 million and if it wants to protect itself from rising interest rates or hedge against fluctuating interest rates in the future, it has the following courses of action:

(1) XYZ can borrow $ 200 million right now and deposit the amount at floating rates maturing at various periods coinciding with the needed inflows of the company.

(2) Borrow floating rate funds for the period of the contract and swap the floating interest rate into fixed rate payment.

(3) Buy financial future contracts if the contract is to start after a period say 3 months.

(4) Enter into forward borrowing 3 months hence.

(5) Enter into a Forward Rate Agreement.

There are thus, many ways by which a company can hedge future uncertain flows into certain flows, either for receipts or payments.

## RBI Guidelines on Risk Management in Banks

The RBI issued some guidelines on asset liability management by banks earlier in April 1999 and in October 1999, they issued guidelines on risk management by banks. These two sets of guidelines are expected to be integrated by the coordination of the activities of Asset Liability Management Committee and credit policy committee for management of credit and market risks, in the banks. This has relevance for the corporates for their own operations.

The Board of Directors have the primary responsibility for laying down risk parameters and establishing a risk management and control system. The implementation of integrated risk management could be assigned to a management committee to top executives that report to the Board. The bank should constitute a high level credit policy committee to deal with issues relating to management and control for credit risk of the bank, as a whole. There should be an independent Credit Risk Management Department to enforce and monitor the due compliance of the risk parameters and observe the prudential limits set by the Board.

The RBI guidelines cover management of credit, market interest rate and operational risk, which, among others, are the following:

(1) The management of credit risk should receive the prime attention of the top management.

(2) Loan policy should cover the methodology of measurement of, monitoring and control of credit risk and keep the market risk in mind.

(3) They should evolve comprehensive risk rating system that serves as a single point indicator of diverse risk factors of counterparties in relation to credit and investment decisions.

(4) They should integrate the credit risk management into a comprehensive package of asset liability management.

(5) Banks have to evaluate the portfolio quality on an ongoing basis rather than at the time of balance sheet finalisation.

(6) As regards to the off-balance sheet exposure, the current and potential credit exposures have to be measured on a daily basis.

(7) Banks have to take a centralised overview of the aggregate exposure on other banks and the counter party and country risks and develop ready reckoners for measuring, monitoring and control of these risks.

(8) To manage liquidity risks, banks have been asked to consider putting in place prudential limits on inter-bank borrowings, call fundings, purchased funds, core deposits to core assets, off balance sheet commitments, swap funds, etc.

(9) Banks have been asked to evaluate liquidity profile under bank specific and market crisis scenarios and prepare plans to meet any worst crisis scenarios.

(10) Banks have to move over to "value at risk" and duration approaches for measurement of interest rate risk.

(11) They have to adopt international standards on providing explicit capital cushion for the market risks to which banks are exposed.

(12) Banks have to adopt proper standards for measurement of operational risk due to vast increase in variety and volume of transactions, and attempt at monitoring and control of that rise.

(13) Banks operating in international markets have been asked to develop by March 31, 2001, suitable methodologies for estimating and maintaining economic capital.

(14) Banks should identify the gaps in the existing risk management system and practices and take measures to filling up the gaps and strengthen the total risk management system on an efficient basis and adopt policies and strategies to comply in full the guidelines given by the RBI in this regard. They should review the policies and practices on a half-yearly basis.

As banks differ in their risk exposures, the type of services rendered and the extent of investment operations, no uniform rules can be applied and each individual bank should have its own system of risk management techniques and methods of monitoring and control of risk.

There are multinational banks and corporates in India, to which the above guidelines become relevant to hedge operations in the market.

## Role of Banks

Besides, banks were asked to strengthen their concurrent audit control systems. Banks have to deal only with Triple (AAA) Rated parties and counter party guarantee risk has to be limited by identifying the credit quality and potential risk. The interest rate sensitivity of assets or investments held by banks has to be assessed. The risk of multicurrency and multimarket portfolio of banks have to be minimised by diversification and observe prudential norms of risk management. The emphasis is on keeping the duration short and risk tolerance limits set by the Board of Management of the bank have to be strictly observed in exposure to currency or interest risks. Each bank has to choose instruments with least interest rate risk to be kept in its portfolio and cover that risk by hedging in the inter-bank market in India or abroad. The banks are encouraged to enter forward rate agreements or interest rate swaps to control the risk element to the limit tolerable by the bank.

The covered interest parity (CIP) condition is one where forward premia remains stable and reflects the genuine hedge demands of banks forward rate covers. The domestic liquidity conditions and external currency demand and supply conditions will reach a reasonable equilibrium level, as reflected by the volatility and turnover in the foreign exchange market. The spot and forward rates and interest rate parities are in consonance with genuine transactions demand and supply conditions. The interest parity effect is seen in this equilibrating process between the spot and forward rates (or premium or forward rates) and in the domestic inter-bank market and foreign exchange inter-bank market.

The operations of RBI can help this process of equilibrating the interest rate parities and exchange rate parities. The inter-bank markets give indication of excesses, to be absorbed by the RBI. Thus, management of foreign exchange market-exchange rate and interest rate parities are the responsibility of banks and the RBI.

We discuss below different types of interest rates in India and their level and structure.

## Money Market Rates

Next to the Bank rate, the other short-term rates of significance are the Treasury Bills rates and Call Money rate. The 91-day Treasury Bill rate has remained frozen for years at 4.6% but from January 1993, this rate was freed. This is because there is no market for Treasury Bills in India and the instrument is used for the purpose of financing government expenditure. As such this rate has no significance for the general structure of interest rates. Treasury bills of 182 days sold on auction basis since 1987 bear higher rates which are more realistic and market-oriented.

As regards call money rate, it has no doubt some relevance to the money market conditions, as the stringency or otherwise of the banks' funds is reflected in this market. The ceiling rate was fixed at 10% in April 1980 but was removed in May 1989. Since, then the rates fluctuated daily depending on the demand and supply conditions.

## Rates in Gilt-edged Market

In the government securities market, interest rates are set by the government in the form of coupon rates. The yields on these securities are also influenced by the RBI through their purchase and sale operations in the market. In India, there is a captive market in the government securities as the banks are required to invest a proportion of their funds in government securities and other approved trustee securities as fixed by the statutory liquidity ratio (SLR). Similarly, the non-bank financial institutions, provident funds, trusts etc. are also required to invest a proportion of their funds by law in the government securities. From the point of view of risk, these securities are least risky and if the return is to be positive in real terms, the yield has to be higher than the actual inflation rate in the economy. The yields are also related to the maturity period and a differential is maintained as between the Centre and States and government guaranteed bonds. As part of reforms in gilt-edged markets their rates of interest are decided through auction system. Only a few are sold on a fixed rate system.

The auctioning system of 182 days of Treasury bills was extended to Treasury bills of 364 days since April 1992. This has become an additional money market instrument between 91 day Treasury bill and dated government security. The Discount and Finance House of India Ltd. was allowed to operate in government securities since April 1992 in addition to their operations in Money Market instruments like Treasury bills and Commercial paper and the inter-bank call market.

## Private and Government Bond Rates

Earlier there used to be a gap between the return on public debt vis-a-vis the return on the private debt. The interest rates on debentures and company deposits and preference shares are substantially higher at around 14-15 per cent as against the yield of 7 to 8 per cent which one might get on government debt. This anomaly dissuades one from entering the government securities market. So there was a need for two types of adjustments is gilt-edged market; firstly, the long end of the spectrum has to be made more attractive, consistent with the expected rate of inflation. Secondly, the yields on government securities should be attractive vis-a-vis yields on private securities, which is reflected in gaps and reverse gaps. A gap is positive if the risk is rewarded. If is a reverse gap, there is risk aversion in the economy which has to be corrected.

These adjustments were made over the decade of the eighties with result that the gap between them was narrower at around 2 percentage points. The coupon rates offered in the gilt-edged market during the last few years have been jacked up to bring them to realistic levels of the expected rate of inflation. Besides, this has improved the earnings of banks and made them more attractive to banks and non-bank investors. In more recent years the interest rates in general have been lowered and related to inflation rates due to flexible interest rate policy.

## Rates of Borrowings and Lending by Banks

In view of the limited role of the interest rate policy in India and the weak linkages as between the various segments in the market, it has become necessary for the RBI to resort to direct controls on banks' lending and borrowing rates. Minimum lending rates of scheduled commercial banks were first fixed in 1960 and the maximum lending rates in 1964. Similarly, interest rates on deposits have been fixed by the Reserve Bank of India since September 1969. The control encompasses most categories of borrowers and different maturities of deposits.

The Reserve Bank of India derives its authority to fix interest rates of banks under Sections 21 and 35 (A) of the B.R. Act. These provisions have been used by the Reserve Bank in a flexible manner since 1960.

The rationale of direct controls on interest rates may be briefly set out here. Firstly, in view of the weak linkages between the bank rate and/or refinance rate of the RBI with other money market rates, the effectiveness of monetary and credit policy can only be ensured by the direct fixation of various categories of interest rates. Secondly, the banking structure of India is such that there is uneven competition amongst the banks, namely, as between the weaker and smaller banks and dominant bigger banks. It is, therefore, necessary that competition in matters of interest rates has to be regulated by the Reserve Bank. Thirdly, with the acceptance of social obligations by the banking system following the nationalisation of banks in 1969, the multiplicity of lending rates has become necessary to encourage lending to priority sectors, neglected segments of the economy and backward classes of people. The geographical and sectorial credit gaps have to be filled in through price and non-price incentives. Lastly, the developmental needs of the country have to be met at the lowest possible costs by the banking system through bank credit to government, borrowings through bonds, Treasury bills, etc. This has also necessitated the differential interest rate system in India.

The Sukhmoy Chakrabarty Committee (1985) has opined that the administered interest rate system has adverse effects on the financial system and the economy due to the complexity introduced by it. The number of administered rates were brought down since then.

The same policy of fixing the interest rates was followed for the co-operative banks as well. However, in respect of co-operative credit societies, the RBI has permitted the payment of additional interest of 1/4 to 1 per cent per annum on deposits over and above those allowed for commercial banks. Similarly, the RBI stipulation on lending rates were also made applicable to co-operative banks.

The data on interest rates prevailing on term credit by banks and the IDBI show that they are generally kept lower to facilitate long-term investment in capital assets by borrowers and promote capital formation in the corporate sector. These rates are varying from 12 to 15%. The bank lending rates were freed from control of RBI in October 1990. There is no minimum lending rates for limits above Rs. 2 lakhs. The controls on deposit rates are removed for reduced to those above one year since 1996-97, and many controls on banks' interest rates were removed or reduced since then.

## Interest Rates on Small Savings

Interest rates on saving deposits, cumulative time deposits and other categories of deposits in post offices and banks are fixed from time to time by the government in consultation with the Reserve Bank. Some rates are marginally higher than those offered by commercial and co-operative banks in order to attract the small savers and to encourage the flow of savings into the government sector. Similarly, interest rates on various categories of national savings certificates, social security certificates etc. are fixed higher, as they are for lumpsum investments and meant for small savers. These are now lowered in stages and are related to inflation rates since 2000 AD.

Since 1975, the Government of India has been encouraging the inflow of foreign currency funds and Non-Resident Deposit Accounts. The FCNR deposits scheme was introduced in November 1975 for non-Resident Indians to keep their accounts in time deposits of one to five year duration in US $ and pound sterling with remittances from abroad. Till March 1982, interest rates under, FCNR deposits were the same as those applicable to domestic deposits. However, from March 1982, the deposits under Non-resident External (NRE), Rupee Accounts were offered at 2% higher interest rates than those on domestic deposits.

Interest rates under FCNR accounts continued to be higher than those offered in international currency markets on European deposits but there is no cover for exchange fluctuations. The incentive of additional interest has attracted the non-resident funds in India judged by the net inflow in the past, although it is no longer true now, due to fluctuating rupee rate, the rates offered on FCNR and NRNR accounts are now freed by RBI and are fixed by banks, but are related to LIBOR.

## Export Credit Interest

Interest rates on export credits have been subject to a ceiling with a view to encouraging exports from India. These rates have been uniformly lower than those applicable to domestic creditors. Term credits and those on deferred payments arrangements are kept still further lower. The ceiling rates on export credit stood at a range of 9% to 12% depending upon the nature of goods and period of credit in the nineties. While the interest rate on their deferred payments is at present 8.6%, the credits by Exim Bank are given at 8.5%. Banks have been asked to provide at least 12% of their total advances to exports and to reduce the interest rate by one percentage point but the philosophy of subsidised credit to exports was given up in 2000. In 2004, the export credit rates were lower than bank prime lending rates by 2.5 percentage points. The PLR was left free to be decided by banks.

There are some rates which were raised while others lowered. The ceiling of 10% on call money rate was removed in May 1989. Similarly, in October 1990, the banks were given freedom to charge rates for lending at their own discretion in respect of non-priority sector advances. The government policy of lending at concessional rates to priority sectors like agriculture, SSIs, weaker sections of society etc., however, continued to be operative; but the slabs are brought down from 4 to 3. Most of the interest rates are now free from controls.

New Treasury bills of 182 days were sold on an auction basis since 1986-87 and their interest rates are determined by the market forces. The short-term deposit rates varied from 9 to 12% at that time but came down to 4-6% by 2005. The yields on government securities were raised over the period in a significant way so as to make them attractive to investors and to bring them nearer to the free market rates. The recent liberalisation of interest rate policy in respect of banks' lending rates is also in tune with the policy of financial deregulation followed by the government and recommended by the Committee, to review the working of Monetary Policy (Chakrabarty Committee 1985). The term lending rate was for the purpose of encouraging long-term investment raised to 15.5% only while the other rates were raised more. But the rate of rise was neither consistent throughout nor was it offsetting the fall in the value of money through inflation. In fact, the rate payable on company deposit was lowered to 14% over the decade along with a similar cut in the rate on debt capital of debentures and on ownership capital of preference shares. The only significant rise in interest rates is seen in the case of those on government securities as they were kept at artificially lower rates for a long time and hence, the need for readjustment in an upward direction. The rate on company deposits was 15% as of June 1998 and the rate on debentures was freed from controls in 1992. Since 1998, the interest rates were lowered and a flexible interest rate policy was followed since then.

The level and structure of interest rates in India is thus a product of *ad hoc* policies pursued from time to time. The rates do not reflect the true value of capital risk element and the maturity period of the instrument. The free market forces are not operating in India. Only in limited spheres is the liberalisation process implemented and that too on an *ad hoc* basis. While some controlled rates still continue some free market rates are now available. Similarly, the changes in rates are affected to suit the changing conditions in the economy and in tune with the monetary policy.

Thus, in India the structure of interest rates is complicated and administered by the government although, there is some liberalisation in this policy in recent years. The level in interest rates does not reflect the true market forces or the scarcity value of capital or the depreciation in the value of money as measured by inflation.

## Level of Interest Rates

Leaving aside the basic postulate that there are many factors influencing interest rates in general as reflected above, we have to note that in some countries like India, the interest rates are fixed by the government or by the central bank of the country (RBI). In such cases, the level and structures of interest rates will be determined by the policy of the government and the RBI and not by the market forces of supply and demand. The traditional theories do not apply in India.

Talking of the economy in macro terms, according to the traditional theory, the level of interest rate is determined by the supply and demand for money or loanable funds. The larger the available funds for lending, the lower is the interest rate. Similarly, the larger the demand for funds, higher is the interest rate. The level of interest rate, therefore, depends on the demand and supply pressures in the market. Looked at from different angle, if there are more borrowers than lenders, interest rates would be high. On the other hand, if there are more lenders than borrowers, interest rates will be lower.

Assuming free market forces where demand and supply pressures determine the interest rates, the level of interest rates can be depicted as shown in the following Figure. If MN is the available supply of money or funds, then the amount of demand for funds will determine the level of interest rates. Thus, when $D_1$ - $D_1$ is the demand curve for funds, the interest rate will be $R_1$ and if the demand increases to $D_2$ - $D_2$, the interest rate will rise to $R_2$. Similarly, if the demand falls to $D_6$ - $D_0$ the interest rate will also fall to $R_0$ as shown in Fig. 11.1.

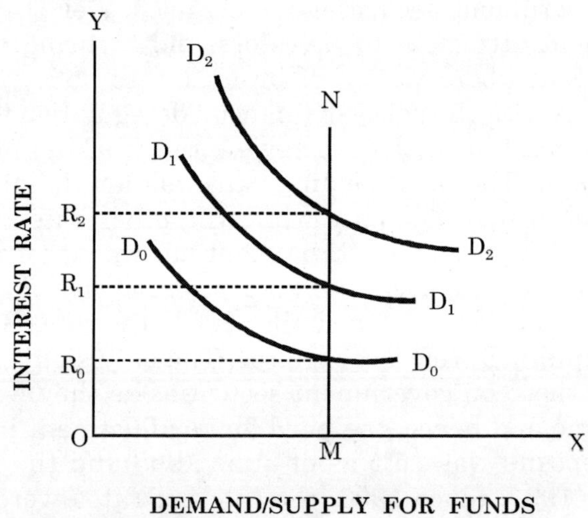


**Fig. 11.1 Determination of Interest Rate**

## Structure of Interest Rates

Leaving aside the time factor, the increase in risk in respect of banks' lending rates and the longer period involved in such lending have been reflected in the higher level of interest rates on them. As compared with the call money rates or Treasury bill rates, which are for short periods, the interest rates on debentures. PSU bonds and term-lending rates by banks are higher due to the higher risk involved. Thus, risk, maturity period, the safety and certainty of funds, etc. would influence the relative levels of interest rates and the structure of rates as seen from Table below which also, represents the data on the structure of rates. There are various types of instruments with varying rates of interest rates in India. These rates will depend on the characteristics of the instruments like ownership risk, variability of return, maturity period, safety, marketability, etc. The data clearly brings out the upward and downward shifts in the structure of rates depending upon the level of risk, time period of maturity and other features of the financial instruments involved.

The bank rate rose, as also the banks' borrowing and lending rates and yields on government securities, etc. But the rate on company deposits and the term-lending rate of banks and FIs stood at around 14-15% during the recent part. Now all interest rates are flexible and vary depending on the inflation rate and the rate of yield on gilted securities.

The Table below presents the data on interest rates, maturitywise to illustrate the influence of time risk and credit risk on interest rate parity. As the purpose is for illustration, the date of the data is not relevant. This reflects also the structure of interest rates in the domestic field. Similarly the case with the foreign countries, each with its structure of interest parity starting in the LIBOR, LIBID etc. The Bank Rate is now kept at 6% and the other rates vary with market forces.

**TABLE 11.2**

**Structure of Interest Rates in India**

| *(Structurally arranged)* | *2013-14* | *March 2009* | *at end March 2004 (in %)* |
|---|---|---|---|
| Inter-bank call rate | 9 | 4.17 | 4.34 |
| 91 day Treasury Bill | 8.20 | 6.96% | 4.24 |
| 364 day Treasury Bill | 8.30 | 7.19% | 4.31 |
| Certificate of Deposit by banks | 9.0 | 7.53% | 4.86 |
| Commercial Paper by companies | 9.5 | 9.79% | 4.70 – 6.50 |
| Banks' Deposit Rates | 8.75 – 9.05 | 3.25% – 8.0% | 4.00 – 5.50 |
| Banks' Prime Lending Rate | 10 – 10.5 | 11.5% – 12.5% | 10.25 – 11.00 |
| Yield on Govt. securities | 7.40 – 9.40 | 6.59% | 5.00 – 6.00 |
| Corporate Debt/Debentures | 10.5 – 11 | 14% – 15% | 12.00 |

*Source*: RBI Annual Reports

In addition, the LIBOR are to be compared with MIBOR. Mumbai Inter Bank offer Rate. Inter-bank call rates are comparable to MIBOR and detailed discussion is made on LIBOR in another chapter. In the Table, compare the rates on Treasury bills (T.B.) of 91 days to those of 364 days. Here, the credit risk remains the same as the borrowing agency is the same, namely, the union government. Time risk is rewarded by a larger return. The rate on 364 day T.B. is more than that on 91 day T.B. Similarly compare the rate on certificates of deposit by banks to that of Commercial Paper. Here the time period being kept constant, the credit risk is changed. Commercial Paper being issued by corporates is having larger credit risk than that issued by banks. So the rate on Commercial Paper is more on average than that on Certificate of Deposit. Government paper being more creditworthy, it will have a lower rate than that of corporates. The above Table throws light on interest parity and the impact of time risk and credit risk on the rates in India. What is true in the case of India is also true in the case of all the foreign countries. In inter-country comparisons for the purpose of interest rate parity, one has to bear in mind the time element and credit risk of interest rates countrywise for the purposes of comparison. Thus, the 91 day Treasury bill in India can be compared with the 91 day Treasury bills of the U.S. Even here, the sovereign risk of government may vary. These constitute the limitations on the international interest parity theory.

The structure of interest rates has changed over time as between, say 1980 and 2004. Generally the level of interest rate has increased over time to reflect the increased cost of rising funds and degree of inflation which erodes the value of money. The interest rates were brought down since 1996-97, to boost the sagging economy. By March 2009, they were generally higher than in 2004.

In India, many of these interest rates are fixed by the government. The banks' deposits and lending rates and those of financial institutions are fixed by the RBI, while the rates on P.O. instruments, PSU and those on government securities are all fixed by the Government in consultation with the RBI.

The rationale of regulating interest rates in India is given as follows:

*(i)* It keeps the interest cost low for the government borrowings and their investment.

*(ii)* It promotes the socio-economic objectives of providing cheaper finance to weaker sections and priority sectors of the economy.

# Reforms

Certain adjustments may be necessary to remove the deficiencies in the interest rate structure. Firstly, interest rates in the Indian economy are to be positive in real terms so as to promote real savings in the economy. This point has been emphasised by the Sukhmoy Chakrabarty Committee. The implementation of this suggestion involves a projection of the expected rate of inflation and ensuring that the basic or the minimum rates are marginally above the average inflation rate. Secondly, the short-term money markets, namely, bill market, discount market and call money market, are to be further developed and broadbased. Thirdly, in the gilt-edged market, the government and the public sector bodies should be provided finance in the forms of Treasury bills or of government securities and/or loans and advances at positive real rates. This would ensure that the government gets its funds at the scarcity value of capital and curtail the Reserve Bank credit to the government to the minimum.

It was felt necessary to rationalise call money rates to reflect the scarcity of inter-bank funds or stringency in the resources of the banks. Thus, the existing ceiling of 10% was removed in May 1989. The need for a ceiling was eliminated when the supply of funds was augmented by allowing non-bank financial institutions also to operate in the market, such as IDBI, IFC, and even MFS etc.

In the government securities market, the interest rate reforms were already started earlier and coupon rates were adjusted in an upward direction to reflect the scarcity value of the capital in India and to improve the attractiveness of the government bonds with the primary savers and financial intermediaries. These reforms are to be carried forward to rationalise the term structure of the interest rates. The short-term debt which is of a low proportion has to be increased and long-term debt is to be reduced. The gaps between these short and the long-term yields and the gap on government debt *vis-a-vis* the private debt should be rational. Between the venture (ownership) yield and debt yields, there is a reverse gap discouraging the flow of funds to the risk market.

The existing framework of controls on bank lending and borrowing operations has been based on some justification. The reforms were in the form of reducing the various tiers of interest rate to a minimum of three or less both at the lending and borrowing ends. Interest rates on special categories like term credit, export credit, etc. may be kept out of this normal spectrum of interest rates by funding the concessionalities on them either by the government or the Reserve Bank. The fiscal and tax benefits should be kept out of the purview of these savings instruments.

## Recent Deregulation Measures

Following the recommendations of the High Level Committee on Financial System (of Shri M. Narasimham, November 1991), some measures of deregulation were initiated in the banking and monetary system. The SLR on an incremental basis stood at 25% in 1995 and the incremental CRR of 10% was discontinued. The Committee's recommendations on capital adequacy norms, prudential norms of income recognition and provisioning for bad debts are also being implemented in stages. The recommendations aimed at improving the functional autonomy of banks and financial institutions and enhance competition, efficiency and profitability.

Interest rates are being increasingly left to market forces. In August 1991, interest rates on debentures and P.S.U. bonds were freed from all restrictions. The system of ceiling rates for term lending institutions was replaced by a system of minimum rate of 13-15%. The ceiling rate on fixed deposits of companies was raised to 15% in January, 1992, but lowered to 12% in stages by 2004.

The banks have been given greater autonomy in their lending operations and rates of interest charged subjected to a ceiling on deposit rates at 12%. New financial instruments such as Participation Certificates, Commercial Paper, Certificates of Deposits, Money Market Mutual Funds and Non-Resident (Non-repatriable) Rupee Deposit Scheme are being promoted at the market related interest rates.

New guidelines were issued in June 1992 and again in 1997 for non-bank financial institutions. The maximum interest rate payable is 15% at monthly or quarterly interests, on a compounding basis. As in the case of shares, deposits can be accepted in joint names, not exceeding three with or without either or survivor etc.

This maximum was lowered in stages to 12% as referred to earlier. Premature repayment is permitted without penalty in the event of death of the depositor to surviving holder or the legal heirs of the deceased.

In respect of Hire Purchase and Equipment leasing companies which enjoy separate limits and conditions, it has been decided that if a company is engaged in hire purchase finance and equipment leasing activities, its business in both these lines will be taken together in determining its classification.

# THE YIELDS OF DIFFERENT TYPES

**1. Current Yield:** Another facet of interest rate is the return on capital invested or yields. Hence, a brief description of yields is relevant here. Yield is interest rate on a financial asset.

The concept of yield relates on investment made in any security or financial instrument. Yields may be classified into different types on the securities. In the case of equities, the yield refers to the current yield, which means the return on investment made at the present juncture. The yield is derived by dividing the Dividend + Capital appreciation by the purchase price of share. In the case of debentures and government securities, they are having coupon rates. Normally, the coupon rate is the rate of interest payable on a face value of Rs. 100. It is not related to the market price or the purchase price. The current yield in the case of these fixed income securities is annual interest divided by current price or purchase price of the security. Thus, if 6% 1998 government loan was purchased at Rs. 95, the current yield is = 6/95 × 100, which gives 6.3% as current yield.

**2. Redemption Yield:** Redemption yield refers to yield to maturity. It is the average rate of return involving the return in the form of interest as well as appreciation or depreciation of capital over the period remaining to maturity. Thus for working out the redemption yield for a government bond or a debenture, the following steps are to be taken:

1. Compute the capital gain (or loss) if it is held up to the maturity date. If the purchase price is Rs. 95 and its face value is Rs. 100, the amount realised will be Rs. 100 involving a capital appreciation of Rs. 5 at the time of maturity.
2. Allocate a capital gain for the remaining part of the maturity or life of the security. Thus, if the security has five year maturity, an appreciation of Rs. 5 is to be distributed equally among all the 5 years, which means that there will be an appreciation of one rupee per year.
3. This annual appreciation is to be added to the annual interest rate paid on the security. If the coupon rate is 6%, an income distribution of Rs. 6 per annum is available and this is to be added to rupee one per annum as capital appreciation.
4. As a next step, add the redemption proceeds at the time of maturity and the purchase price and divide it by 2 which gives the average cost of holding the security.
5. Then divide the total return of investment, namely (6 + 1) by the average holding cost, arrived at above. In the example, the average cost of holding is (100 + 95) divided by 2 is equal to Rs. 97.5. Then the redemption yield is arrived at by dividing the total return by the average cost of holding, namely, Rs. 7/97.5 = 7.2%.

It will thus be seen that the redemption yield is slightly different from other concepts. The redemption yield gives the actual return on investment in the form of Interest or Dividend + Capital Appreciation or Depreciation. The formula for deriving redemption yield is as follows:

$$V = \sum_{n=1}^{n} \frac{I_n}{(1+i)^n} + \frac{P_N}{(1+i)^N}$$

Where *V* is the value of the bond, *I* is the interest amount paid in absolute terms, *i* is the rate of interest or yield required to be derived, $P_N$, is the face value at maturity and *N* is the number of years to maturity.

**3. Holding Period Yield (HPY):** Where redemption yield is not relevant, holding period yield (HPY) is used. Holding period yield brings out the possibility of purchase and the sale of a security during the period of its maturity without waiting until the date of maturity. Thus one can buy a 13.5% debenture of Reliance Petro at Rs. 80 against its face value of Rs. 100. It could be sold at Rs. 85 after a year, without waiting up to the time of maturity, say after 5 years. In this case, the holding period yield is relevant. The investor has purchased at Rs. 80 and sold at Rs. 85 after a year. The holding period is one year and the yield is interest at 13.5% that he receives during the year + an appreciation of Rs. 5 for holding it over the year, which gives a total of 18.5%. The formula for the holding period yield is as follows: The return (18.5) is divided by the purchase price (Rs. 80) which gives the holding period yield (23.1%).

$$\text{The formula is HPY} = \frac{(P_t - P_o) + 1}{P_o}$$

where *I* is the interest payment, $P_o$ is price at the beginning of the holding period and $P_t$ is price at the end of the holding period.

**Real Yield:** Real yield is a different concept which takes into account the depreciation in the value of money. Thus as opposed to nominal yield, which is the coupon rate as, for example, 6%, the real yield is adjusted for depreciation in the value of the rupee, namely, an increase in the prices of goods and services. If the price increase is represented by Wholesale Price Index (WPI), then the nominal yield is deflated by the rise in WPI over the period considered. Thus, the nominal yield of 6% if deflated by the rise in prices of, say 10% will give a negative yield of 4%. Thus the concept of real yield presents the picture of the return in terms of goods and services and purchasing power of the return.

**4. Net Yield:** The above concept of yields present the picture of general yields common to any investor, irrespective of his status such as tax status or type such as an individual or institutions, etc. As such, they are gross yields — yields prior to tax payment. The net yield is that after payment of tax. As tax liability varies from individual to individual or company to company, the general tax deduction rate can be applied, say 10% or 20% of the gross yield to arrive at the net yield. Interest and dividend incomes are paid without deduction of tax at source for amounts up to Rs. 2,500 per annum. These tax factors become relevant for net incomes, and for tax payees.

**5. Maturity and Yields:** Yields vary depending not only on the type of security and interest rate, coupon rate but on the maturity of the security. Thus, the yields are higher, longer is the maturity. This is particularly true of government securities, which are issued with varying maturities.

**6. Yield Curve:** If yields on any security are available on a cross section basis, a yield curve can be drawn to serve for comparative purposes or for indicating the trends and for forecasting purposes. The yield curve is mainly useful in the government securities market where yields differ mainly on the basis of maturity. It depicts the relationship of time periods to yields, referred to earlier.

## Effects on Trade

International trade depends to a large extent on trade credit or bank credit, which has a cost in the form of interest rate and risk coverage. In some countries export credit is kept cheaper comparable to foreign countries so as to make export goods competitive. Interest cost is also included in exchange rate quoted by banks for the transit period or intervening period between the purchase of the credit instrument and time of realisation of proceeds. Even cheques and DDs have a time period of realisation or a gross period for which interest cost is included in the exchange rate. Trade in goods and services involve some time periods and credit instruments which carry with them an interest cost.

## Effects on Funds Flows

International short-term funds flow in and out depending on the level of interest rates and expected exchange rates in the respective countries. Some of those short-term funds, are for speculative purposes. These funds may go out also as quickly as they come thus causing currency crises. So controls on capital flows are adopted by most of the countries although they are allowed on current account convertibility.

## Effect on Exchange Market

As a concomitant of the above flow of funds, foreign exchange market becomes volatile and there will be liquidity problem. The equilibrium between demand and supply for foreign currency *vis-a-vis* domestic currency gets disturbed and genuine trade transactions and investment flows, aid and loan flows will be adversely effected. The external disequilibrium leads to compensating borrowing from IMF or from foreign banks and governments. These developments discourage foreign direct investment and portfolio investment in the affected country.

## Interest Parity International

Internationally, interest rates are a potent weapon of influencing the flows of capital across borders. The money market interest rates of LIBOR. LIBID etc. are fairly representative of cost of borrowing funds from international banks, across borders The Euro rates or dollar rates are the cost of borrowing Euro in E.U. countries or in Euro denomination or in terms of dollars. These rates are highly competitive and vary by a few basis points from one another. The major players in this market are international banks operating in highly free environment, free from any governmental controls. Borrowing and lending takes place in Euro currencies or freely convertible currencies.

Interest rate parity refers to the parity of these rates with the purchasing powers in the respective countries. The cost of borrowing should reflect the reward for risk of loss of liquidity and for saving. Interest rates and purchasing power are related and are next door neighbours. Both help the determination of exchange rates and the interest rate is the price of borrowing or losing purchasing power by the lender and exchange rate is the price of currency for borrowing and lending. The theories of Gustav Cassel are discussed in more detail in other chapters. They reflect the cost of borrowing funds in the form of cash, currency or credit domestically or internationally.

In India, we have partially controlled rates both in respect of interest rates and exchange rates. Domestic interest rates being higher than the interest rates in U.S., U.K., E.U., etc. funds flow in to take advantage of higher interest rates. This is possible if the risk of foreign exchange market, and of exchange rate changes are less or nil. Interest rates influence the economic transactions both nationally and internationally. If capital funds are free to flow across borders, international interest parity holds because domestic interest and foreign interest are brought to parity by free market forces of competition, efficiency and productivity, through capital flows.

Not only trade in merchandise goods but in services will be hit by recurrent foreign exchange problems of volatility and speculative attacks on the currency. The market imperfection stand in the way of achieving the interest rate parity among countries.

## Effects on Balance of Payments

The trade deficit or current account deficit leads to depletion of foreign exchange assets or increase in foreign liabilities. The foreign exchange crisis will also result in the depletion of foreign exchange reserves. For a country with scant foreign exchange reserves, these developments result in a heavy burden of costly borrowing from abroad and lowering of currency and credit rating. The country risk will also increase for foreign investment flows and aid flows. The huge balance of payment deficits lead to repercussions in monetary and fiscal problems and liquidity problems in the domestic economy. This will also influence the rate of growth of the economy, fiscal deficit and heavy debt burden and the external strength of the economy deteriorates. Sometimes inflation and standard of living of the people and employment problems are created by these above developments, further weakening the domestic economic strength. All these results from interest disparities, and volatility in exchange rates lead to destabilising speculative capital flows, and weakening external strength of the economies.

More discussion on the interest rate parity is available in the next chapter on International Fisher Effect.

❖❖❖

# INTERNATIONAL FISHER EFFECT — PARITY RELATIONS

# 12

## Introduction

International Financial System involves many types of transactions as between independent nations, with their own currency systems. The trade in commodities and services is one such type of transactions. These transactions have a two way movement of goods, and services on the one hand and corresponding movement of means of payments and receipts in the respective currencies. The movement of currencies, does not mean their physical movement but book entries in the respective currencies in the form of credits and debits. These movements of currencies are in the foreign exchange market and credit and debits involve the exchange rate-the rates at which one unit of domestic currency is exchanged for one or more units of foreign currency. The mechanics of this exchange and the operations in the exchange market are referred to in the chapter on foreign exchange market. The determination of exchange rates is also discussed in another chapter. In the present chapter, the discussion is confined to transactions in international markets-namely, merchandise trade and trade in services (invisibles) and corresponding capital flows.

These above items come under the broad umbrella of current account of balance of payments and refer to the transactions nature of international relations. There are also corresponding flow of funds on capital account of Balance of Payments. The International Fisher effect is the impact of these transactions on the International Financial Management through exchange rates, interest rates and inflation rates in the respective countries.

There are various types of demand for money, namely, for transactions on day-to-day basis, precautionary purposes for special occasions, needed for occasional and unforeseen demand, such as for accidents, unplanned payments or other incidentals and lastly for storing for future, namely, for asset or wealth creating purposes. The transactions demand constitutes the bulk of the demand for money and currency. In the international parlance it is called the international demand and supply of foreign exchange.

## Basis of International Fisher Effect

The effect of trade transactions, at international level, involving both exports and imports is felt on the exchange rate and interest rate. In India, transactions of this nature account for 60-80% of the total balance on current account of balance of payments. During the recent years, exports and imports of merchandise nature account for about Rs. 6 lakh crores. This transaction effect has various components. Firstly, this involves the exchange of one currency against one another, encompassing currency risks and exchange rate risks. This has to be covered by hedging and forward purchase or sale of currencies in the foreign exchange market. As in the case of foreign exchange market, the credit risks and market risk are also involved. These risks are to be managed by credit rating and adoption of risk reduction techniques such as diversification and trading in futures and options, referred to in later chapters.

Trade in services is called the Invisible Account of Balance of Payments under current account transactions. Trade in services is increasing in importance in the last decade all over the world and in India due to revolution in Information Technology, Telecommunication, Tourism, Transportation and Multi Media etc. In some countries, where trade constitutes a significant part of GDP, the demand for exchange risk cover is very prominent and has to be tackled by various governmental and non-governmental measures and risk reduction techniques. The international Fisher effect is felt through the purchasing parity theory and interest rate parity.



## Purchasing Power Parity (PPP)

Any firm aims at maximising the wealth of the shareholders, for which it minimises the risk and optimises the return. In all international financial operations, a higher risk element is involved than in its domestic operations. The difference is due to foreign currency and foreign exchange variables involved. These are reflected in the interest rate differential in the two trading partners as well their exchange rate differential. Both are related through the purchasing power parity.

Gustav Cassel's purchasing power parity theory states that the differential between the inflation rates in the domestic and foreign centres determines the exchange rate between these two countries. The inflation rate determines the purchasing power of a given basket of goods and services in a country. The same basket of goods and services can be purchased by the foreign currency in a different ratio. In other words, if two units of the domestic currency can purchase a given basket of real goods and services in country 'A', only one unit of foreign currency can purchase the same basket in the concerned foreign country 'B', then the purchasing parity ratio is 2:1, and foreign exchange rate will be in the same ratio, say, 2 units of country 'A' is equal to one unit of foreign currency of 'B.' Exchange rate is thus, a function of purchasing power or inflation which also determines the interest rate. Both interest rate and inflation are the functions of money supply in each country.

Given the money supply exogenously, it is the demand for it that determines the interest rate or the price of money. Exchange rate is the price of foreign currency, while the interest rate is the price for domestic currency. According to Monetarist Theory, money matters, unlike the classical theory which postulates that money is neutral and is only an intermediary for exchange of real goods and services. According to Monetarists, money is an asset and like other assets in the economy, it is an independent variable in the demand function of the public. The household has its own utility maximisation function in which, income, savings, investment, domestic money and foreign money are all variables, *inter alia,* which influence the decision on the portfolio held by the household public. In this process of maximising utility or welfare, substitution takes place for a little more foreign currency vis-a-vis the domestic currency asset, if the return is higher on the foreign currency asset. Thus, if interest rates are higher in foreign currency than in domestic currency and if money or funds are free to move across borders, then capital flows take place to take advantage of interest rate differential. This may bring about the equity of interest rates in both countries under equilibrium conditions and perfect market efficiency. This is the basis for international interest parity theory under perfectly free market conditions, and prices should reflect fully the available information, speculation is free and unbiased leaving no scope for excess return from speculation. Then the exchange rate should truly reflect the inflations in both the countries and forward premium in the exchange market should reflect the interest rate differential between the two countries 'A' and 'B.'

The above discussion leads to the postulation of the theory that the interest rate differential in two periods in a country is a function of money supply differentials, real income differentials, inflation rate differentials in the same period. There may be other factors like saving consumption investment which influence also the interest rate differentials.

## Exchange Market Efficiency vs. Interest Parity

Foreign exchange market efficiency is usually examined through the twin parity conditions-covered and uncovered interest parity. According to Covered Interest Parity Condition (CIP), forward premia or discount in the exchange market should equal interest rate differential between home currency and foreign currency assets. The Uncovered Interest Parity Condition (UIP) states that the currency with higher interest rate is expected to depreciate as in the case of India vis-a-vis US dollar. These postulates help the measurement of the risk element in the market and the degree of market integration and efficiency. This has also policy implications justifying the intervention of the Central Bank or the government in the administered changes in the interest rates or in open market operations in the Forex market.

Available empirical evidence proves the validity of the CIP in advanced economies. But the basic assumption of market efficiency, free capital flows for arbitration and speculation and in respect of assets of similar materials and similar risk profile hold good. But the validity of UIP is doubtful due to time varying risk premium and deviations from the rational expectations. In India many steps have been initiated to improve market efficiency and integration of sub-markets into the Forex market. But forward premia have trailed below the interest rate differential in more recent years. Besides, there was appreciation of Indian rupee for some time during 2003 and 2004, despite higher interest rates in India than in the U.S. There are many reasons why this has happened. There may be other factors influencing exchange rates and exchange returns due to wrong inferences and expectations. These are not predictable variables due to market imperfection. In the medium term, forward premia and interest rate differential move together. In the short-term, deviations from the CIP are due to demand and supply mismatches and are found on a few occasions. The UIP was however, disproved by empirical evidence due to its assumption that expectations are rational and the expected exchange rate is expected to reflect the actual exchange rate, which are not realistic.

In the following chart shown are the forward premia of 3 months and interest differential of 3 months Treasury Bills in India and U.S. In some periods forward premia trailed below the interest differential but the overall trend is that they moved in tandem evidencing the partial validity of CIP.

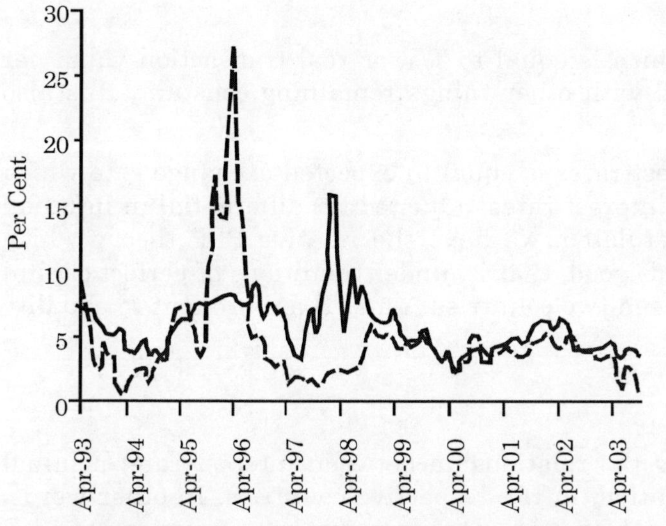


Chart on: Forward Premia 12.1

*Source:* RBI Report.

In the recent years, the coefficient of interest differential has been more stable, indicating the increasing market integration and efficiency of external markets. In the graph shown here, the forward premia and interest rate differentials moved together closely in the recent years.

Similar studies done by RBI for the period 1996 to 2003 in respect of UIP, showed that with the actual exchange rate as the dependent variable, the coefficient of interest differential turned out to be positive, but insignificant as against a prior expectation of unity. The residuals in all estimated equations turned out to be serially correlated, indicating the market inefficiency. These results are in tune with the results of other international studies. (RBI: Report in Currency and Finance, 2002-03).

## Fisher's Equation and PPP Theory

The interest parity condition combined with the purchasing power parity theory will lead us to a relationship between expected change in exchange rate and the expected inflation differential between the two countries 'A' and 'B'. The proportional change in exchange rate between rupee and dollar is equal to the proportional change in the inflation rates between U.S. and India. The Fisher equation is a relationship between nominal interest rate and real interest rate on the one hand and expected rate of inflation on the other hand. Put in other words, the nominal interest rate deflated by the inflation rate leads to the real interest rate in any country.

For the purposes of interest parity theory the Monetarist Theory postulation is relevant and this implies that real money balance is any financial asset like other assets say, real income and are substitutable with other real variables. Fisher' equation of exchange gives us

Money Supply × Velocity of Circulation = Price × Transactions

$$(M) \times (V) = (P) \times (T)$$

$$MV = PT$$

M/P is equal to real balances, which is equal to T/V or real transaction value per unit of transactions. If M is increased with other things remaining constant, P is also increased.

The differential in nominal interest rates is equal to expected exchange rate which in turn is equal to differential in real interest rates, adjusted for differential in inflation rates in any two countries. Thus, postulated, we have the relative PPP theory which implies that Fisher's open relation holds good, that is, under conditions of perfect capital mobility, real rates of interest as between two countries A and B are brought to equality for equilibrium conditions.

## Fisher Effect

The international Fisher effect is the relationship between interest rate, nominal and real and the expected rate of inflation, in the respective countries. In other words, it means that the differential in nominal interest rates between two countries A and B is equal to the difference between real interest rates in A and B, adjusted by the difference in inflation rate in the two countries. The interest rate adjusted for inflation rates reflect the exchange rate, as per the PPP theory. The expressed changes in exchange rates, say forward rate as compared to spot rate is a function of interest rate differential as between the respective countries 'A' and 'B.'

Interest parity is the relation between the interest rates in currency markets to their exchange rates-spot and forward. There is a close correlation between the forward margin and interest differential. In this context it has to be understood that exchange rate changes between A and B are a function of the interest differential adjusted for inflation. The current spot rate of exchange between A and B is determined by the expected future spot rate and interest rate differential. In terms of appreciation and depreciation of exchange rate of rupee against dollar, one can say that the rupee depreciates to the extent of differential in inflation rates between India and U.S. In actual practice it was found that this does not happen exactly atleast in the short-run. Indian rupee is appreciating and depreciating on a daily or monthly basis, despite the fact that the differential between inflation rate in India (at 4 to 5%) and in the U.S. (at 1 to 2%) over the last few years. For some time during 2001 to 2003, rupee steadily appreciated against dollar, despite higher inflation rates in India than in the U.S. In 2002-03 itself rupee appreciated by 2.3% over U.S. dollar, despite stable inflation rates in both the countries.

The above discussion leads one to conclude that PPP holds good only in the long run, and that the quantity of money supply and real incomes in the two countries have influence on the exchange rates. Increase in money supply depreciated the exchange rate and increase in real income leads to an appreciation in exchange rates. These conclusions are supported by current account monetary models and capital account monetary models. These models take into account the demand for money, not only for transactions, for trade, for current account flow of funds, but also for capital account flow of funds, which reflect the demand for foreign money for hedge and speculative purposes in addition to genuine precautionary and investment objectives. The flow equilibrium models dictate the matching of demand and supply of foreign funds for transaction purposes. The asset approach to equilibrium needs that market as a whole is prepared to hold the given stocks of assets in the respective countries. The Frankel model of exchange rate determination is similar to capital account monetary model in which real stock of balances is brought to equality with demand for real balances and assets held in both the currencies.



## Interest Parity

The above discussion leads to some relevant conclusions that in the long run the interest parity and Fisher conditions hold good. They assume that there is a stable demand function for currency in each country and that the expectations play a more important role in the short run, which lead to exchange rate changes to move above or below the equilibrium points, set by the PPP theory. Thus, as per the PPP theory interest rate and exchange rate are all related conceptually, if not empirically. The PPP theory in fact depends on the inflation rate in the domestic economy as compared to that in foreign country. If all these propositions hold good and the demand for money is for all purposes, namely, for trade transactions in goods and services, hedging, investment and speculation, they bring about equilibrium in balance of payment taking both the current account and capital account together, assuming fully flexible exchange rates, floating interest rates and that there is no money illusion implying thereby, that public are interested in real balances.

## Fisher Open Relation

We have seen that under conditions of perfect capital mobility across countries, the real interest rates among them will be equalised. The Fisher equation relates the difference between interest rates in two countries to the difference in their real interest rates, adjusted by the expected rate of inflation. In other words, the real interest rates in two trading partners is equal to the nominal rates, adjusted for the rates of inflation, in those two countries A and B. In this relation, we can evolve the real rates of interest parity among countries, given the nominal rates in A and B and expected inflation rates in them. This equality of real rates of interest among countries is valid given the assumption of free and unfettered capital movements across countries. This is called the Fisher open position.

## Covered Interest Parity (CIP)

The forward rate in the nth year ahead is adjusted to the rate which is related to the future interest rate in country A adjusted to future interest rate in country B. The differential in interest rates between country 'A' and country 'B' is related to the difference between forward rate and spot rate, called forward margin. Thus, interest rate differential between two countries A and B is equal to forward margin. This is called covered interest parity.

## Uncovered Interest Parity (UIP)

It is an equilibrium condition under which returns on two assets in country A and country B respectively are equal, if perfect capital mobility holds and this relation is dependent on forward rate differential with the spot rate at a future date (the nth period). There is no causal relationship between returns on assets in two currencies and the expected exchange rates; as it is a theoretical proposition for equilibrium condition. Expected exchange rate movements are dependent on expected interest rates on the same assets, denominated in two currencies of A and B.

## Forward Margins and Parity Theory

Forward market depends *inter alia* on the demand and supply for forward dollars. There are interrelations between spot market and forward market and expectations play an important role in the market. As in the spot market, there are two segments, namely, merchant transactions and inter-bank transactions.

Forward market exists for most commodities like gold, silver, oil, etc. as also for currencies as in the case of Forex market. There is a forward market in the form of futures, options, etc. in the case of stocks and shares in equity and debt instruments, as well as in the gilted market. Interest rates vary with the maturities of the instrument in the money market, capital market and gilt-edged market, which lead to futures market for all these instruments, for hedge operations.

In this section, attention is paid only to the forward market in foreign exchange. In India, the RBI manages a floating rate for the rupee against dollar which requires its operations and intervention both in the spot and forward markets. RBI operations are confined to the interbank segment to influence the supply and demand conditions with a view to maintain orderly and stability conditions. But rupee is allowed to freely find its own level of appreciation or depreciation, depending on market conditions and free flow of funds, subject to some limits.

Spot rate and forward rate are related by what is called margin, which may be positive (premium) or negative (discount). Excess demand conditions lead to premium while excess supply conditions result in a discount. Here reference may be made to the theoretical proposition of interest parity in the determination of forward rate as against spot rate. The Reserve Bank's empirical study in this respect is published in its annual report for 2002-03, the main findings of which are set out in this section.

During greater part of 2002-03, there was appreciation in the value of rupee vis-a-vis dollar, due to improved sentiment, following fall in oil prices, and rising level of our forex reserves. The dollar was depreciating against all currencies, due to weakness in the economic fundamentals in the U.S. and a partial reflection of this is seen in rupee appreciation.

## Testing of Interest Parity

The covered interest parity condition (CIP) would suggest that forward rates reflect the differential between domestic and foreign interest rates. The covered parity condition and interest parity condition provide a measurement of the extent of market efficiency. Taken together they suggest that the forward premia or discounts are an appropriate predictor of future spot rate. The uncovered parity (UIP) condition lays down that the expected change in exchange rate should equal the interest rate differential. Empirical evidence is divided and does not support unequivocally the above postulates, particularly with respect to the short-term forward rates, due to sudden shifts in risk perception and expectations that are the basis for hot money flow. The market perfections are also violated by government and Central Bank interventions in the forex market.

In this context, the empirical study made by RBI for the period 1993-2003 may be referred to. In this study the interest differential between 3 month Treasury Bill yields for India and the U.S. is found to be positively related to forward premia, but the operation of CIP is not validated due to imprecision in the estimated coefficients and the presence of correlated errors. As regards UIP, the results reject outright the hypothesis. The residuals in all estimated equations turned out to be serially correlated, indicating inefficiency of markets. This evidence is reported to have been corroborated by other international studies as well.

One had to admit that theoretically as well as empirically. This results in forward market, both forward premia and interest differentials tend to move together in the long-run. It means that the expected future spot rate is related to spot rate at present and a number of other factors including interest rates domestic and foreign. The markets are not generally efficient and perfect integration of the various segments is not present, particularly in India. The policy injunction of these findings is that the RBI should selectively intervene to ensure orderly condition in the market. The rumours and speculative flows should be corrected by the RBI. The weak market efficiency holds good and this gives a valid reason for the government or RBI rules and regulations.

## Inter-Relations Among Parities

It will be seen from the above discussion that PPP theory, exchange rates, inflation rate and interest rates in any two countries are related. Exchange rate differential leads to movements across borders and tries to equate the returns on capital, namely, interest rates. Inflation, which is a rise in prices, wholesale or retail, influences purchasing power and cost of living and through them the prices of goods and services are affected and the real incomes of the people. Interest rates are a function of money supply and real incomes. But they are affected by the inflation and rise or fall in prices, under conditions of free and competitive markets. Real exchange rates are nominal rates adjusted for inflation rates in the two trading partners under free foreign exchange market conditions. The PPP theory relates the exchange rates to the purchasing powers in the two countries, as reflected in change in retail and wholesale prices in the two trading partners, namely, inflation in the respective countries. Interest, being the price for money or capital is influencing the exchange rate; if the capital is free to flow across borders, it flows freely to high interest countries from low interest countries and thus, equates the interest rates across borders.

Interest rates parity postulates equality in interest rates among two trading partners, if the capital flows across them freely under competitive conditions. Fisher effect shows the relationship between nominal interest and real interest rates in two countries, on the one hand and inflation rates in the two countries on the other. Indirectly it signifies the relation of inflation rate in two countries to their respective interest rates. Exchange rates in turn are influenced by the inflation and interest rates in the domestic markets vis-a-vis the foreign markets. This proves international parity relationships as between interest rate parity, purchasing power parity and Fisher effects.

❖ ❖ ❖

# TIME FACTOR IN INTERNATIONAL RISKS

# 13

## Introduction

It was already referred that time factor is an important part of risk in international financial management. Time period is involved in all international economic and commercial transactions. Time is taken between shipment of goods and the receipt of money from abroad. Time is involved in transit of goods and credit instruments. From the time of sanctioning of loan to its utilisation there is a lag. So is the case with the Bills of Exchange. Even if it is a sight bill, which is payable on sight, a grace period is normally granted to the importer. If it is a usance bill, a time period is given to importer to the extent usually of 90 days. If a bill for collection is given to the banker he normally takes a week to 10 days to credit the account of the exporter. Even now, with the electronic transfer of funds, a couple of days of grace is given to the banker except in some cases of real time gross settlement system adopted by some banks (RTGS). There is thus, a time element involved in all international transactions. Even in cases of fund transfer on current transactions or foreign investment or inter-firm transfers, there is a time element between credit receipt and the corresponding entries of banks. Time is all embracing in international portfolio investments and investment managements by corporates. Reference to the time element in the form of duration is discussed separately in the chapter of Risk Reduction and Diversification.

Why is time, so important even if it seeps through all international transactions? It is because time is valuable in money forms. One minute lost cannot be replaced and time has innumerable alternatives and expensive to lose. Time has value. It cannot be reverted or retraced. Future is uncertain and hence constitutes an element of risk management. People prefer present consumption to future consumption and today's money to tomorrow's money, because tomorrow is uncertain, and people avoid risk and prefer the present to the future.

Time element, constituting a risk taken needs to be rewarded. Thus, time gets value for many reasons. It is neither reversible nor replaceable. People prefer a bird in hand to two in bush and avoid risk but time has a risk component. Time is also important because of uncertainty of future and public preference for avoidance of risk. Inflation, rise in prices in future will reduce the value of money. Time preference for money is reflected in all economic activities. Today's consumption and income is preferred to that of tomorrow. That is the reason why money can be borrowed at an interest rate which varies with the time period. That is also the reason why savings or abstaining from present consumption for the future requires to be rewarded by a return, which is called interest rate. Time is invaluable as it cannot be replaced or reversed. It has alternative uses, which is the reason why there is a saying "Do it today what you can do tomorrow, if it has to be done." This time preference for the present is reflected in the higher yields on financial securities of the medium-term and long-term than for short-term. That is the reason why the rates in the call money segment is the inter-bank market are the lowest followed by rates on longer duration assets like C.D., C.P., and bills discounted. That is also the reason why there is a premium on forward rates in the term money market and forex market. One might argue that there is a possibility of long-term yields being lower sometimes and forward exchange rates are quoted at a discount. This is true if the anticipation or expectations of the market operators of the future are such and speculation plays a more important role in the market or the government keeps the long-term rates lower deliberately by its own interference and controls, and if it has to keep its interest burden on debt at lower level for the purposes of fiscal discipline and reduced expenditure on current account.

## Time Preference for Money

We prefer today's money to that of tomorrow due to our pressing needs for consumption and cost of abstinence from the present consumption, fall in the value of money of tomorrow due to inflation and possible use of money when exchanged for tomorrow's money. Thus, when we lend money, we forego all the advantages of liquidity, ready usability, pressing needs, safety, etc. We abstain from present consumption when lent to somebody or invested. All these, will lead to what is called the time preference for money. To compensate for that future money will have to be discounted to the present time, because both are not the same. Future money has to be more say 120, if the present money is Rs. 100, taking a discount factor of 20%. Normally future is discounted and present is compounded.

Tomorrow's money or money a year hence has to be discounted to the present day by a discount rate suitable as a reward for the above sacrifices. This is called discounting, used for cash flows or dividends to be received in future and to be calculated for the present.

Similarly an investment of today, if it is to be returned after a year or so, today's money has to be compounded by a discount rate to equate to the future funds likely to be available in return. This is called compounding. Compounding and discounting are thus, two major methods of analysing the time value of money.

## Applications

In purchase or sale of a share, bond, or debenture, the price we pay has to be compared to the value of future flows in terms of dividends or interest and future price realised. The principle of buy low and sell high to be applied after an analysis of the present value of future flows of dividends, bonus, visible rights etc., as compared, to the present price paid for it.

To give an example, the future value to be estimated at present for cash flow over three years is shown below:

**Table 13.1: Future Value of a Single Cash Flow**

| *Year* | *(PV) Principal at the beginning* | *(V) Interest 10%* | *(FV) Principal at the end* |
|---|---|---|---|
| 1 | 1000 | 100 | 1100 |
| 2 | 1100 | 110 | 1210 |
| 3 | 1210 | 121 | 1331 |

FV = PV $(1 + r)^n$, FV is future value, PV is present value and 'r' is rate of interest.

# SINKING FUND FACTOR

$$FVA = A\left[\frac{(1+r)^n - 1}{r}\right]$$

$$A = FV\left[\frac{r}{(1+r)^n - 1}\right]$$

where $\gamma$ is required discount rate.

**Table 13.2: Future Value of an Annuity @ 10%**

| *1* | *2* | *3* | *4* | *5* | |
|---|---|---|---|---|---|
| 1000 | 1100 | 1210 | 1331 | 1464 | $(1 + r)^4$ |
| | 1000 | 1100 | 1210 | 1331 | $(1 + r)^3$ |
| | | 1000 | 1100 | 1210 | $(1 + r)^2$ |
| | | | 1000 | 1100 | $(1 + r)^1$ |
| | | | | 1000 | $(1 + r)^0$ |
| | | | | 6105 | |

Time Factor in International Risks

$$A = (1 + r)^{n-1} + (1 + r)^{n-2} + (1 + r)^{n-3} + (1 + r)^{n-4} + - + (1 + r)^{n-n}$$

$$A\left[\frac{(1+r)^n - 1}{r}\right]$$

# FUTURE VALUES

$$F = A\left[\frac{(1+r)^n - 1}{r}\right]$$

$$A = F\left[\frac{(1+r)^n - 1}{r}\right]$$

$$= F\left[\frac{r}{(1+r)^n - 1}\right] \times \frac{1}{FVIFA\,(r,n)}$$

(FVIFA) Future Value Interest Factor for Annuity and (PVIFA) Present Value Interest Factor for Annuity are given in Tables, specially meant for Portfolio Management books.

**Table 13.3: Present Value of Annuity**

Here is an example of present value of an annuity at 10%, payable after 3 years.

| *0* | *1* | *2* | *3* | |
|---|---|---|---|---|
| 901.1 | 1000 | | | $\frac{1000}{(1+0.1)^1}$ |
| 826.4 | 901.1 | 1000 | | $\frac{1000}{(1+0.1)^2}$ |
| 751.3 | 828.4 | 901.1 | 1000 | $\frac{1000}{(1+0.1)^3}$ |
| 2478.8 | | | | |

$$PVA = A\left[\frac{(1+r)^n - 1}{r\,(1-r)^n}\right]$$

$$FVA = A\left[\frac{(1+r)^n - 1}{r}\right]$$

$$PV = FV\,\frac{1}{(1-r)^n}$$

$$PVA = A\left[\frac{(1+r)^n - 1}{r}\right]\left[\frac{1}{(1+r)^n}\right]$$

# SHORTER COMPOUNDING PERIOD

If interest is credited quarterly @ 12% per annum (3% per quarter)

**Table 13.4**

| *Quarter* | *Balance at the Beginning* | *Interest* | *Bal. at the end Rs.* |
|---|---|---|---|
| 1 | 1000 | 30 | 1030 |
| 2 | 1030 | 30.90 | 1060.90 |
| 3 | 1060.90 | 31.827 | 1092.727 |
| 4 | 1092.727 | 32.782 | 1125.51 |

Effective rate of interest = 12.551%

The formula is given below:

$$r = \left(1+\frac{k}{m}\right)^{m-1}$$

$$FV = PV\left(1+\frac{k}{m}\right)^{m \times n}$$

Where K = Nominal rate of interest

m = Number of times compounding is done during a year

n = Number of years for which compounding is done

# BOND VALUATION

Features of a Bond, given the following variables:

Par Value

Coupon rate of interest

Maturity Period

Par value Rs. 1000

Coupon rate 12%

Maturity Period 5 years

Required Rate of Return 10%, 12%, 15%

At 12%

Rs. 120 × PVIFA (12%, 5) + 1000 × PVIF (12%, 5)

= 432.5 + 567.5 = Rs. 1000

At 10%

Rs. 120 × 3.791 + Rs. 1000 × 0.621

= 454.90 + 621.02 = Rs. 1075.92

At 15%

Rs. 120 × 3.352 + Rs. 1000 × 0.497

= 402.24 + 497.00 = Rs. 899.24

If the Maturity Period is 3 Years

At 12% Rs. 120 × 2.402 + Rs. 1000 × 0.712 = Rs. 1000

At 10% Rs. 120 × 2.487 + Rs. 1000 × 0.751 = Rs. 1049.44

At 15% Rs. 120 × 2.283 + Rs. 1000 × 0.658 = Rs. 931.96

# YIELD TO MATURITY

$$\frac{\text{Interest} + (\text{Par Value} - \text{Present Price})/n}{\text{Par Value} + \text{Present Price}/2}$$

# EQUITY VALUATION

Dividend Capitalisation Approach

Present value of the dividends expected D (1 + K)

\+ Present value of the resale price expected P (1 + K)

= Value of an Equity share

Basic assumptions:

1. Dividends are paid annually (D)
2. The first dividend is paid one year after the equity share is brought.

Single Period Valuation Model is presented for a simple example.

$$P_o = \frac{D_1}{(1+k)} + \frac{P_1}{(1+k)}$$

If the price is expected to grow at the rate 'g'

$P_1 = P_o\ (1 + g)$

$$P_o = \frac{D_t}{(1+k)} + \frac{P_o(1+k)}{(1+k)}$$

$$P_o = \frac{D_t}{k-g}$$

Where 'K' is the required rate of interest, and "g" is the growth rate.

## Management of Time Risk

In all the operations of MNCs, the time element is there involving risk — whether it is in operations of exports or imports, or transfer of working capital funds through banks or in capital investment flows. In the interest parity theory, time element is there in forward margins, which are equated to interest differentials as between two countries. Time is there in collecting, negotiating and discounting foreign trade bills by banks. The term structure of interest rates depends on the time factor, reflecting the role of time in money market. So is the case in capital and stock market, where security valuation is done by discounting the future cash inflows into Present Asset Value (NPV). In capital budgeting, the NPV is used for project evaluation. In foreign investment a valuation of stock, expected future returns are considered in the context of expected exchange rate depreciation or appreciation, which are all products of time element. In the Forex market and Foreign currency markets forward premia or discount depend on expected interest changes. The expected future or forward rate depends, *inter alia,* on the expected spot rate at a future time say 3 to 6 months hence.

The forecast of exchange rate depends on various variables like money stock, real income, inflation rates with various time lags. Time factor plays an important role in all Forex deals and currency deals through varying margins for the future. The portfolio foreign investment involves time in the form of duration in the portfolio. The risk return scenario changes with time. The use of time element is all pervasive in all international transactions in trade and finance.

Time risk is managed through insurance, hedge and other tools of risk management. Time element is internalised in the operational risk exposure. In portfolio investments and management time is dealt with the other risks in it in the form of riskless and risky assets of various durations. Equity and debt have different risks partly due to time and credit risks, and partly due to inherent nature of instruments. Country rating, credit rating and instrument rating are all relevant to a time period and vary with the periods considered in the time frame. Thus, it can be concluded that directly or indirectly time risk is inherent in all deals and has to be provided for.

❖ ❖ ❖

# PART III

# MANAGEMENT OF RISKS IN INTERNATIONAL TRANSACTIONS

# FOREIGN EXCHANGE MARKETS

14

## Functions

Foreign Exchange as a subject deals with the means and methods by which rights to income and wealth in one country's currency are converted into similar rights in terms of another country's currency. It involves the investigation of the methods by which the currency of one country is exchanged for that of another, the cause which renders such exchange necessary, the forms in which exchange may take place and the ratios or equivalent values at which such exchanges are effected.

Such exchange may be in the form of one currency to another or of conversion of credit instruments denominated in different currencies such as cheques, drafts, airmail transfers, fax and telegraphic transfers, cable transfers, bills of exchange, trade bills, bankers' bill or any promissory notes. It is through these instruments and foreign currency accounts of banks that the banks are able to effect such exchange of currencies or claims to currencies. Electronic funds transfer at the international level is the recent addition of currency transfers.

Every exchange of goods and services is having a corresponding exchange of remittances involving two currencies, as depicted in Chart below:

**Chart 14.1**

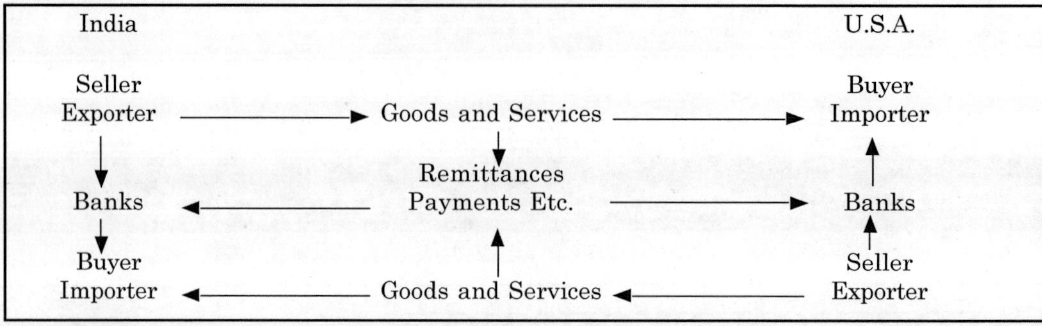


No currency will be physically exchanged except in small amounts by tourists and travellers as it is not legal tender in any country other than in the issuing country. So exchanges take place through book entries and/or through credit instruments by banks. The instruments through which exchange of currencies take place are Telegraphic Transfers (TTs), Mail Transfers (MT), Demand Drafts (DDs), cheques, Bill of Exchange, etc. In the absence of banks, the buyer-importer who has to pay in dollars has to hunt for an exporter-seller who received an equivalent amount of dollars from the foreign importer. Banks facilitate such transactions by acting as intermediaries between buyers and sellers or importers and exporters.

## International Financial System and Forex Market

One of the important components of the international financial system is the foreign exchange market. The various commercial and financial transactions as between countries result in receipts and payments as between them. The items of balance of payments leading to receipts and payments are trade, travel, transportation, royalties, fees, investment income, unilateral transfers, short-term and long-term capital receipts and payments etc. Such receipts and payment involve exchange of one currency for another. Thus, rupee is a legal tender in India, but an exporter in UK will have no use for these rupees. He, therefore, wishes to receive from the importer in India only in pounds sterling. Then the importer will have to convert such rupees into pounds in that transaction. The foreign exchange market provides facilities for such operations. The demand for goods and services from one country to another is the basis for demand for currencies in the exchange market. Such merchandise and invisible trade items constitute nearly 70-80 per cent of the total transactions in the market. Conversion of currencies is also necessary for short-term capital flows or long-term investment in financial or physical assets of another country. It will thus, be seen that the services of the exchange market are necessary not only for trade transactions but for any financial receipts or payments as between countries. Any receipt and payment of foreign cash, coins, claims in currencies or credit instrument involve a foreign exchange transaction.

## Foreign Sector and Forex Market

Each economy has a foreign sector representing that economy's external transactions. All such external transactions are either economic and commercial or financial transactions.

These result in receipts into and payments out of the domestic economy. Such receipts and payments involve exchange of domestic currency as against all foreign currencies of countries with which domestic economy has dealings. Such exchange transactions are put through in the exchange market for that currency. For each nation, therefore, there is an exchange market for that country's currency, *vis-a-vis* other currencies. These national foreign exchange markets are components of the international financial system.

There is thus, as for any other currency, a market for the rupee. If an Indian bank buys dollars, it will pay rupees for dollars and if it sells, dollars, it will receive rupees for dollars. The origin of these transactions is an export or an import, transactions in an export or an import in goods of services, inward or outward remittances or any similar transactions between Indian residents and foreign residents. An exporter in India receives dollars from say, USA and he surrenders the bill of exchange along with other documents to his bank. The bank would have brought that currency from the exporter. The bank has since been on the look-out for selling those dollars in the foreign exchange market for those in need of dollars. Let us say an importer in India importing from the USA is in need of dollars to cover up his position from the former bank.

Thus, basically demand for and supply of foreign currencies arises from exporters or importers or the public having some receipts from or payments to foreign countries. These receipts or payments may give rise to foreign credit instruments which the banks buy or sell at specified rates. There are different rates for buying and selling in which an interest element is included and quoted by the banks if the bill or promissory note or any instrument of exchange is not a demand or sight bill but a usance note involving some period to run to maturity for payment. Even in the case of sight bills, some grace period of 2 days and transit period of 10 to 20 days are allowed as fixed by the Foreign Exchange Dealers' Association, depending upon the place on which it is drawn and interest element for these periods is also included in the rate quoted by banks.

Banks generally cover up these positions in currencies by corresponding purchases or sales from other banks. Such a market as between banks is called inter-bank market. There are reputed brokers who act as intermediaries for banks in these transactions.

## Bank's Purchase and Sale

Every foreign exchange transaction involves a two-way conversion — a purchase and a sale. Conversion of rupees into dollars involves purchase of dollars and sale of rupee or *vice versa* depending upon the angle from which we are looking. If it is looked at from the country having rupees (India), then the transaction looks as follows:

(i) Sale of rupees for dollars (import) — conversion of home currency into foreign currency.

(ii) Purchase of rupees for dollars (exporter) conversion of foreign currency into home currency.

As an Indian banker has to keep his accounts in rupees, he buys and sells foreign currencies like any commodity for money (Indian rupee).

# Instruments of Credit Traded

In addition of conversion of foreign currency notes and cash for domestic currency notes/coin, a number of instruments of credit are used for effecting conversion of one currency into another. These instruments are discussed below.

**(1) Telegraphic Transfers (TT):** A TT is a transfer of money by telegram or cable or telex or fax from one centre to another in a foreign country. It is a method used by banks with their own codes and correspondent relations with banks abroad for transaction of funds. As it involves the payment of funds on the same day, it is the quickest means of transaction of funds. As there is no loss of interest or capital risk in this mode, it enjoys the best rate for the value of receipts.

**(2) Mail Transfers (MT):** It is an order to pay cash to a third party sent by mail by a bank to its correspondent or branch abroad. It is issued in duplicate-one to the party buying it and the other to the banker-correspondent or agent abroad. The amount is paid by the agent bank to the third party mentioned therein in the transferee country by its own cheque or by crediting the party's account. As the payment is made after the mail advice is received at the other end, which will take a few days, the rate charged to the purchaser is cheaper to the extent of the interest gain to the seller bank. MT rates are cheaper than TT rates.

**(3) Drafts and Cheques:** Draft is a pay order issued by a bank on its own branch or correspondent bank abroad. It is payable on sight but there is always a time lapse in the transit or in post between the payment by the purchaser of the draft to his bank and the receipt of the money by the seller in the foreign centre. As in the case of MT, there is risk of loss of the draft in transit, delay in effecting payment to the beneficiary and loss of interest during the intervening period. The rate charged by the bank for this is less advantageous to the buyer of the draft than in other modes.

**(4) Bills of Exchange:** It is an unconditional written order, addressed by one person to another, requiring the person to whom it is addressed to pay a certain sum on demand or within a specified date. If it is payabale on demand, it is a sight bill and if it is payable after a period, it is a long bill or a usance bill. Such bills can be banker bills or trade bills. Banks bills are drawn on a bank abroad. While the bank bills carry better rates due to their greater security, the trade bills on private parties may not fetch good rates. Sight bills are paid on sight but allow a transit period of 10 to 20 days on which interest is lost. In the case of usance bills, the purchase price is adjusted on the basis of maturity date of the bill for the interest lost, adjusted in the rate quoted for such a bill.

# Foreign Exchange Market Components

There are three major components of this market, depending upon the level at which transactions are put through:

Firstly, transactions between the public and the market or banks at the base level involve receipts from any payments to the public or purchases from and sales to public.

Secondly, transactions as between the banks dealing in foreign exchange involving conversion of currencies taking place in the same centre or as between centres in the same country (inter-bank market) or as between countries involving the correspondent or agent banks abroad or branches of the domestic banks abroad.

Thirdly, transactions between banks and central bank involving purchase and sale of foreign currencies for cover or final disposal of excess foreign balances. The central banks may in turn deal with the foreign central banks or foreign governments.

Basically, the above exchanges involve no physical exchange of currencies except in small denominations when travellers and tourists carry across national borders, but through exchange of credit instruments or book entries in the books of banks in various centres. The banks are linked together by phone, cable, telex, post or other means of communication. The transactions are put through directly by the banks or through the brokers located at various centres where these transactions are concentrated like Mumbai, Kolkata, Chennai, etc. All the dealer banks in foreign exchange in India have an Association called Foreign Exchange Dealers' Association of India.

## Participants

The participants in the exchange market are classified broadly into RBI, the central bank of the country, the bank authorities to deal in foreign exchange and the public. The public includes the exporters, importers, money changers, international money brokers, and all those who have dealings abroad, such as companies with branches, subscribers abroad, and those who have to pay or receive remittances to and from foreign countries.

RBI operates in the market as a regulator and stabiliser of the market. It may operate directly or through authorised dealers in the market. In essence, it absorbs excess of supply and demand for foreign currencies. The operations may take the form of open market operations or liquidity adjustment facility or stabilisation of the market. The inter-bank foreign exchange operations have their impact on the domestic inter-bank money market, which is sought to be regulated by the RBI through Repo or Reverse Repo operations. The foreign exchange inflows, if they are in excess of demand are sterilised by the RBI through the various instruments at its command.

The banks also operate in the market through their trade in the inter-bank market or through their customers with demand and supply of foreign currencies. They try to match their outstanding position in any currency with other banks, for hedge purposes. They trade in foreign currencies through purchase and sales in acceptable currencies, like dollar, sterling, Euro and yen. The banks provide credit to exports – post-shipment or pre-shipment. They buy and negotiate their foreign bills of exchange, provide letters of credit, guarantees, or collect the proceeds from the banks abroad through their correspondents, agents and counter parties abroad.

There are also other participants in the market such as money changers, authorised to buy and sell foreign currency, and brokers who deal with authorised dealers as intermediaries.

## Spot and Forward Rates

If an importer is paying on receipt of documents, then he can buy dollars spot and the bank sells him spot dollars. But if the importer agrees to pay three or six months hence, his demand for dollars might arise only after three or six months hence. These dollars are called forward dollars and the market is the forward market. The existence of a forward market provides cover or hedge against fluctuations in exchange rates. This exchange risk falls on the banks who are buying or selling dollars forward. The banks in turn can pass on the risk to the central bank of the country or to a foreign bank at another centre.

Just as banks are buying and selling spot, they also do business in forward currencies. Corresponding to the spot rate of exchange, there is a forward rate for various periods. If any bank succeeds in matching forward purchases with forward sales of the same currency, it avoids -taking a position- and assumes no risk. If they do not match, the bank may have an uncovered position which it may cover with another bank which has a contrary position. If it fails to cover with a bank, it may still do so with the central bank of the country or with a correspondent bank abroad. If a bank takes a position uncovered against a spot deal or against a future sale or purchase, it takes the risk of gain or loss.

Currencies purchased or sold in forward would be subject to the influence of interest rates at home and abroad. A forward currency will be at premium (higher than the spot expressed in foreign currency per domestic unit quoted at Rs. 100 = $ 4.7555), as at end June 1991. Later rates were quoted as $ 1 = Rs. 31.3283 in June 1993, and $ 1 = Rs. 31.2100 in January 1995, and $ 1 = Rs. 48.04 at end November 2004 and Rs. 48.04 in November 2009 1 $ = Rs. 63.36 in Dec. 2014. The premium or discount will depend on interest rates and expectations of interest rates and exchange rates. Forward premia for U.S. dollar turned into discount as on end March 2009. Quotations are given upto 6 months forward on a daily basis, as so many basis points above spot rate in foreign exchange market, as premium or discount.

## Speculation

Speculation and hedging operations are taking place in free markets to take advantage of interest rate and exchange rate differentials. In the case of India, such hedging and speculation are possible to a limited extent, due to continued capital account controls and banks are not allowed to take position in any currency beyond the minimum working balances to be kept in various centres. In a free foreign exchange market, short-term capital flows take place to the advantage of interest rate differentials and will be quickly reversed, leading to instability in the exchange rates. One-sided speculation is also very destabilising which generally the central bank of a country would not allow unchecked. Controls on capital account, particularly to counter such destabilising short-term flows, are in tune with the spirit of the International Monetary Fund. Speculation on a limited scale and if it is on both sides of purchase and sale is healthy and welcome to keep the balance in the market and absorb the excesses of demand/supply of currencies in the foreign exchange market.

## Arbitrage Profits

When foreign exchange markets are free to fluctuate, the exchange rate of a currency should be the same in almost all the centres. Thus, if the dollar rate per sterling is different in New York and Frankfurt, then funds would flow in either direction to take advantage of the rate differential. It is, however, possible that slight differentials might be still there due to carrying costs of moving funds from one place to another. Such operations in terms of movements of funds from one centre to another are called arbitrage operations.

Such operations can take place only if there are no exchange controls in both the countries and if funds are free to move. Thus, if either New York or Frankfurt is subject to exchange restrictions involving central bank supervision of funds inflow and outflow and ban on free movements, arbitrage cannot take place and differentials in rates between two countries might exist.

Arbitrage is not limited to two centres or two currencies alone. Three-point and multi-point arbitrage can also take place if the respective currencies are free. Thus, in a three-point arbitrage, the dollar-sterling rate and the dollar-franc rate are considered and the cross rate between sterling and franc should be in conformity with the above two rates. Otherwise, three-point arbitrage can take place by moving funds from dollar to franc and franc to sterling and back to dollar from sterling. Suppose the dollar-sterling rate is £ 1 = $ 2.80 and franc 350 = $ 1 and £ = 1020 francs. Starting with $ 100, one can buy up pounds, move from pounds to francs and then to dollars back, making a gain of about $ 5 per $ 100 in the above example. Thus, arbitrage can take place as between centers or currencies at more than two centers and currencies at a time. Such arbitrage operations may be for gain in exchange rate differential or in interest rate differential as between centres. The former are called currency arbitrage and the latter interest arbitrage. An operation of simultaneous purchase and sale in each of the two markets to take advantage of interest differential is called interest arbitrage. Such deals are put through swaps or forward deals.

The operations in the foreign exchange market are exposed to a number of risks which are difficult to foresee and forecast. These risks may be credit risks arising out of lending to a foreign borrower whose credit rating is not known for certainty. Secondly, there may be currency risks of trading in a currency whose political and economic strength is weak and is uncertain. Thirdly, there are risks of fluctuating interest rates in various currencies in the inter-bank market and anticipations may sometimes go wrong. Fourthly, there are risks of illiquidity due to mismatch between current assets and current liabilities with the result there may be sudden need for borrowing and difficulties may arise in securing funds at short notice. Lastly, the dealers sometimes take risks by exceeding the limits of prudent trading in a currency with the result that they may find it difficult to cover the transactions and incur losses in such a position. Such risks are more marked in international lending and borrowing and in foreign exchange and currency markets. Further details of risk are discussed in a separate chapter.

For a country like India, with a wide network of controls, arbitrage operations were not possible. Indian rupee was insulated from world free currency markets as the banks' operations in India were strictly controlled and monitored by the Reserve Bank of India, until 1992, when spot tend to freely convertible rupee was started.

# INDIAN FOREIGN EXCHANGE MARKET

In India there are many commercial and co-operative banks who are authorised to deal in foreign exchange called Authorised Dealers and are eligible to operate in the foreign exchange market. However, not all co-operative banks are authorised to deal in foreign exchange. These banks cover their open positions in currencies in London, through their correspondents or branches abroad or in India in the inter-bank market. There are no published figures as thousands of crores of foreign trade, are put through and crores of foreign remittances and a host of other purchases and sale take place except through the balance of payments data. In the process of such purchases and sales directly with the public, the authorised dealers would have various currencies which they try to dispose of by matching demand with supply in the inter-bank market. It is only the unmatched net requirements that are purchased from the RBI, or excess sold to the RBI. The data on turnover in foreign exchange market both merchant and inter-bank and RBI operations of purchase and sale on a daily basis are now published in the RBI monthly bulletins.

The foreign department of every bank draws up a position sheet for each currency daily in which purchases and sales of the currency are recorded. As the banks generally avoid taking any exchange risk by keeping uncovered balance and are not permitted to do so under the previous regulations, they try to cover their position by the end of the day. When the purchases exceed sales, the credit balance is plus (or long) and overbrought. This is to be covered by equal sales of that currency. When the sales exceed purchases, the debit balance is minus, short or oversold position and is to be covered by equivalent purchases. These sales and purchases would include both spot and forward, import bills or export bills negotiated or purchased, clear sales or purchases (other than through bills, namely, by TT, MT, cheques, drafts) BC sales and OD sales etc.

Before entering into the inter-bank market, the banker decides how much to cover and what is the outstanding balance position in his books. Banks operate in the inter-bank market through the foreign exchange brokers. In every important market centre, some brokers operate in these dealings. The banker keeps some minimum balances in all his Nostro accounts to meet the customer needs as they accrue. The more exactly he synchronises the delivery dates of his purchases and sales, the greater is his profit. The finer the rates he quotes, the better is his position. The better he foresees the trends in exchange rates and interest rates in various centres, the more efficient he is and the better is his profitability.

In the inter-bank market, banks put through the dealings of purchase and sale of currency through authorised brokers. Brokers in each centre are in contact with other centres in India and in foreign countries for effecting matching transactions in various currencies. In all centres, export bills, import bills and various remittances are daily purchased and sold by banks. Imports give rise to payments abroad and purchase for foreign currencies. As the bulk of the imports in India is on government account and the SBI keeps the account of the public sector undertakings and of the government, the SBI enters the foreign exchange market mostly as a buyer of foreign currencies. Exports are more concentrated in the private sector, in which all banks are involved in varying degrees. Hence, sales of foreign currencies in the exchange market are more evenly spread among the banks in India. Many times, brokers cannot match in the local centres for odd currencies like Austrian Shilling or Nigerian naira or Libyan dinar, which are to be put through in a more sophisticated market like London or Singapore.

In India, some financial centres are more developed than others in the foreign exchange market. Thus, Mumbai, Kolkata and Chennai are more developed than others. Some of the foreign exchange transactions being seasonal, the markets are also seasonal.

## RBI and Exchange Market

The RBI operates in the market as the last recourse agency. The RBI purchases and sells sterling spot and buys and sells forward sterling upto six months but since June 1966, forward sales have been stopped. Since the abandonment of convertibility of the US dollars in 1971, the forward cover for a longer period was felt necessary due to greater exchange risks and it was provided by the RBI normally at 0.0005 and for the extended period of 9 months at a rate of 0.0075 per month for the extended period.

The other currencies in which the RBI started operations during the seventies are dollars, D.M. and yen. The RBI started purchases spot and forward dollars from July and August 1966 respectively, and with brief interruptions from August 1971 to October 1972 and February 1973, the RBI continued to purchase spot and forward dollars. Similar purchase of DM and of yen were started from March and May 1974 respectively. The period of forward cover was upto three months initially but was extended upto six months from September 1975. Thus, the RBI provided cover for 4 currencies which are our major trading partners, namely, sterling dollar, Euro and yen. The Bank purchased and sold spot, and bought forward Sterling and bought dollar, Euro and yen both spot and forward. As from early 2005, the RBI gives reference rates only in U.S. dollar and Euro at which it is prepared do its operations. But RBI did open market operations in dollar both spot and forward upto 2004 and thereafter only on spot.

The RBI was operating by buying in four major currencies, namely, UK £, US $, Japanese yen and DM. Early in 1987, the RBI has started selling spot US dollars with the result that it used to buying and selling two currencies, UK £ and U.S. $, in addition to its purchases of DM and Japanese yen. It has also adopted recently the practice of changing the rates quoted by it in the course of the day if the conditions in the market warranted it. The RBI used to quote both the spot and forward rates in the currencies it transacts with the banks on a daily basis.

The RBI was providing cover for a fairly long period of upto 10 years in respect of long-term contracts for engineering exports and construction projects. Since November 1975, the RBI has also offered the cover to ADs against exchange rate fluctuations in respect of deposits received in foreign currency from non-residents. Most of the facilities which the RBI offers are intended for exporters in terms of cover or purchase and sale. This is justified in view of the national importance attached to exports and inflow of funds. But they have not offered similar facilities for importers for two reasons. Firstly, the bulk of the imports into India is by the government or public sector agencies who do not need such facilities. Secondly, the inter-bank market is designed to develop to provide cover as a last resort institution in foreign exchange as in domestic finance. The policy of RBI in this regard is very flexible and designed to promote self-reliance by banks and greater resort to the inter-bank market. The RBI has, however, responded to emerging situation in the foreign exchange market quickly and promptly. Since rupee convertibility was launched in March 1992, RBI was publishing a reference rate around which it operates in the market to stabilise the rate of exchange of rupee in terms of U.S. dollar.

## Mismatch — Need for Matching

In export and import deals and other purchase and sale deals, the dealer gets short dollar purchase 1,000 million — not covered; forward dollar sale 2,000 million — not matched. If the purchases and sales of the same currency and of the same maturity are done on the same day, they are said to be matched. Otherwise matching is to be done through inter-bank deals or with foreign branches and foreign correspondents abroad, so that open position is minimal. The uncovered open position in any currency overnight should not exceed a limit as per the banks' own guidelines. The cover can be done through swap — spot to forward or forward to forward. However, risk matching or risk reduction can also be adopted by the dealers through any derivative products.

When you expect premium to go up or swap differentials to rise, pay now and receive later — sell now and buy later. When you expect premium to come down in any currency, buy now and sell later.

## Forex Management

If we have extra Nostro funds, keep them in call market, in that currency and earn some interest abroad. If German interest rate (6%) is higher than in US rate of 4%, buy DM spot and keep in the call market at the higher rate of 6%, in Frankfurt and convert back to dollar by selling forward DM one month to three months hence. Here the currency rate expectations play a major role. If the DM is becoming dearer and its interest rate (6%), higher than in New York (4%) then the above operation in funds management will earn profit. Such operations should maximise profits with minimum risk.

Similarly, payments are due to come to India in dollars three months hence, from US. Three months later dollars will be in demand. So buy spot dollar and keep earning interest in Europe at 6% more than in US and sell them to those needing dollars three months hence.

There are a host of other methods of gaining in Forex market due to interest rate differentials and expectations regarding them and exchange rate changes and their expectations or cross rate differentials in exchange rates.

## Currency Derivatives

One of the methods of risk coverage by the Treasury Manager is the use of derivatives, either in the foreign bond market or in the Forex market. The risk in the cash market can be hedged in the derivative market. An example of such deals in the Forex Market is the forward contract to cover the risk of currency fluctuations in the spot contract. Swaps and options are other examples of risk covering instruments. Detailed discussion is provided under Risk Management sections of this book.

## Forward Contracts

Forward contract is a contract for delivery of foreign currency at a specified future date at a fixed exchange rate. Only genuine trade and invisible transactions can be covered in India, as per the RBI guidelines. These forward contracts for foreign currency can be delivered at a fixed date or within a specified range of dates and penalty provisions may be laid down for breach of contract by either party. These depend on the terms of the approved contracts, usage and practice.

## Swaps

A swap is a deal in which a bank buys a specified foreign currency and sells the same at different maturity dates, like simultaneous purchase of dollar on spot and sale of forward dollars of the same amount. Here, the risk is possible due to adverse movement in exchange rate which is covered by prior fixing of the rates. Forward to forward deal is the purchase of two months dollars, followed by a sale of three months dollars. Swap deals are used as a tool to cover arbitrage operations, namely, buy in Frankfurt and sell in London of the same currency (dollars); swaps are also required to cover a mismatch in Forex deliveries to the genuine clients of the bank. Use of swaps or even Repos for speculative purposes are not permitted by the RBI. Arbitrage of risk cover or genuine matching of demand with supply are permitted by RBI. Repos are repurchase agreements, which have been referred to later.

## Options

Currency options are contracts with a right to buy or sell a stated currency without any obligation, at a fixed rate on a future date. If the future rate moves against expected line the holder of the option can exercise the right to buy or sell. The traders can hedge their deals in the option market referred to later in the book.

## Futures

While forward contracts can be entered into by any parties outside the stock exchange or in any organised system, the futures contracts are regulated by a proper authority with fixed terms, involving an obligation to buy and sell or give and take delivery. Delivery is compulsory in forwards and not in futures. Contract is an agreement to buy or sell a foreign currency at a fixed amount at a stated price or rate at a specified future time. The obligations rest on both the parties and their deals are regulated and supervised by a properly constituted authority. But holder of an option can exercise the right to buy or sell. For this right to cover the risk, the party has to pay a price called premium. Under the American options, the customer can exercise the options at any time during the currency of the contract but under the European contract, the option has to be exercised only at a specified date mentioned. As it is only a right, but no obligation, it need not be based on genuine transactions and no delivery may be there and may lead to speculation.

## Sodhani Committee Report (1995)

This Committee has come out with two reports, one on the details on various schemes and incentives available to NRIs and the other for development of active exchange market system. The major recommendation are set out below:

NRI investments are not freely flowing in due to the following constraints, which have to be removed, namely, administrative red tape, tax hurdles, government interference, rampant corruption, infrastructure and inadequate access to bank credit by NRIs. The time taken for allotment of new issues to NRIs is very long; despatch of certificates or statements should be faster and there should be quick transfer of shares from one to other and for payment of dividends etc. The issue of shares to NRIs by Company is to be left free without prior permission of these holdings as per the committee's recommendations.

NRIs should be free to buy not only in new issues but from existing shares from Indians directly. Only the ADs should have the powers to scrutinise and effect the payments. There should be no lock-in period for shares in sick units acquired by NRIs, OCBs – the Overseas Corporate Bodies and they should be brought in on par with all FFIs. Most of these recommendations are implemented in stages since October 1996.

As regard the measures for the development of Forex Market, the following are given as a few examples:

(1) To increase the number of participants by inclusion of companies, and merchant exporters.

(2) To allow the ADs to lend and invest or borrow abroad and to allow them to keep cross currency positions abroad.

(3) To allow developments of modern products and derivatives such as future, options etc.

(4) To develop proper accounting practices and disclosure standards for such operations.

(5) Companies and exporters can keep funds abroad and take positions.

(6) The RBI and tax authorities should clearly bring down their requirements and relax their controls and formalities regarding the abolition of withholding tax on derivative transactions.

(7) Legal and regulatory framework should be simplified and even reduced.

(8) Risk management techniques should be expanded and developed through the introduction of futures and other derivative products.

(9) RBI's attitude should change from regulatory angle to development angle.

Although, the wording of the Sodhani's report is different from the words used above, the substance of the Report's recommendations is set out here. The most important pre-requisite for developments of the Forex Market in India is the reduction of controls and restrictions, delegation of more powers to ADs and expertise in RBI and banks to be improved and banks to be empowered to deal with risk management techniques and for development of derivative markets. The government and tax authorities should be either liberal or free such foreign transactions with a withholding tax of not more than 10% as applicable to FFIs in some respects at present. The treatment given to NRIs by banks has to be improved and OCBs and NRIs should be treated on par which is now implemented. The role of the Treasury Manager in banks and companies, therefore, becomes critical, needing a multi disciplinary expertise, in the Forex market, as it is more volatile and complicated by national and international factors. The turnover in the Forex Market rose from $ 465228 to $ 989401 over the period of 2011-12 to 2013-14 (3 years).

## Forward Rate Agreement (FRA)

Major foreign banks are offering FRAs to depositors and borrowers. Here the bank guarantees the depositor or borrower the difference between the agreed rate and the LIBOR. If the six month LIBOR under the FRA is say 9% but the actual rate happens to be 10%, the difference will be reimbursed by the bank to the customer with a premium or price. If the actual rate of LIBOR is 8%, the customer will have to pay 1% to the bank. Under the agreement this is a type of hedge measure provided by the bank.

## Forward and Future Contracts

The difference between forward contracts and future contracts is as follows:

In forward contracts, the delivery is compulsory but not in futures. In forward contracts the amount and maturity periods are flexible but in futures it is organised trading in the Exchange with standard contracts, standard maturity dates and contract trading is regulated by the authorities through down payment margins and other margins which are marked to market. Forward contracts are traded over the counter telex, telegram etc. These can be contracts for various amounts and periods of maturity, say, one month to 12 months.

## Currency and Interest Rate Swaps

Swap is simultaneous sale and purchase of identified amounts of one currency against another for different maturities, for different interest rates (from fixed rate to LIBOR and *vice versa*). It is a finance transaction in which two parties agree to exchange streams of payments or cash flows over time. There are three main types of swaps: (1) Coupon Swaps. Fixed for floating rates. (2) Basis swaps — exchange of one bench mark for another — say from LIBOR to Treasury Bill rate. (3) Cross Currency Swaps — flows from one currency to another.

## Interest Rate Futures

If interest rates are freely fluctuating the traders and bankers can cover their position by buying an interest rate future at say one to three months. Normally, futures beyond three months are rare and are negotiated for any particular need. For broken periods of say 10 days to 15 days charges will be high. Trading in futures are for specified periods and these are regulated by a competent authority like SEBI and RBI. The need for future arises, when the trader has borrowed at floating rates and he desires to limit his commitments by a fixed amount by buying a future for the period when his liability becomes due. Bankers and companies who have some liabilities in future enter into these transactions. This facility of hedge through futures is now allowed in inter-bank money and gilted markets.

❖ ❖ ❖

# GOVERNMENT INFLUENCE ON EXCHANGE RATE

# 15

## Introduction

Controls on foreign exchange dealings involving foreign receipts and payments are an adjunct to the controls on foreign trade. These controls were first resorted to during the Second World War for the purpose of conserving limited foreign exchange reserves and mobilising them for war effort. The war-time controls were put on a statutory basis soon after the war by the Foreign Exchange Act of 1947, in India. This Act was replaced by a more comprehensive legislation "Foreign Exchange Regulation Act of 1973" (FERA) incorporating wider powers of control to the RBI and better enforcement through Inspecting Officers and Enforcement Directorate with a view of plugging all the loopholes or leakages noticed in its working since 1947. But the basic framework of controls remains the same under the new Act as under the old. As a member of the IMF, India is under an obligation to collaborate with the Fund to ensure orderly exchange arrangements and to promote stable exchange rate. Although, current account controls are not permitted by the Fund, India secured their permission under Article XIV to keep these controls as transitional measure. In March 1992 limited convertibility of rupee was launched and on the basis of experience gained, full convertibility of rupee on trade account was announced in March 1993, followed by full convertibility of rupee on current account since March 1994. Now India is under article VIII of IMF Articles of agreement. The Foreign Exchange Management Act has replaced Foreign Exchange Regulation Act in 1999.

## RBI as the Exchange Control Authority

Government of India has entrusted the regulation of foreign exchange and foreign currency markets to RBI, as much as domestic currency market. One of the important central banking functions of the RBI is maintenance of external value of the rupee. As such it has been given the custody of foreign exchange reserves and sole agency for administration of exchange controls in India. All receipts and payments in and out of India require general or special permission of the RBI. The dealings in foreign exchange and foreign securities in India, payments to person resident outside and export and import of currency notes, bullion or precious stones etc., are subjected to general or special permission of RBI or are prohibited. The administration of controls is carried on by the RBI with the help of ADs, and money-changers.

The types of transactions which are controlled by the RBI and the government are in general, those having international financial implications and include *inter alia* the following important items. Many of them are liberalised and some of them withdrawn since 1991 economic reforms.

(1) Purchase and sale of and other dealings in foreign exchange and maintenance of balances at foreign centres by residents.

(2) Procedure for realisation of proceeds of exports of goods and services.

(3) Payments to non-residents or to their accounts in India for imports and others.

(4) Transfer of securities as between residents and non-residents and acquisition and holding of foreign securities.

(5) Foreign travel (with or without foreign exchange).

(6) Export and import of currency, cheques, drafts, travellers' cheques and other financial instruments, securities, gold, jewelleries, etc.

(7) Trading, commercial and industrial activities in India of foreign firms and companies (including branches of foreign firms and companies) and foreign nationals as well as acquisition of business undertakings or holding of shares in Indian companies by such firms, companies and persons.

(8) Appointment of non-residents and foreign nationals and companies as agents or as technical and management advisers in India.

(9) Employment, profession etc., undertaken in India by foreign nationals.

(10) Acquisition, holding and disposal of immovable property in India by foreign nationals and companies.

(11) Acquisition, holding and disposal of immovable property outside India by persons resident in India.

## Authorised Dealers (ADs)

Authorised dealers are the scheduled commercial and some co-operative banks who are authorised by the RBI to deal in foreign exchange which include all scheduled commercial and some co-operative banks at present. The regulations under the FERA governing the banks are contained in the Exchange Control Manual and in the various circulars and notifications issued thereunder, by the RBI. The ADs can deal in foreign currencies and for that purpose open and maintain accounts abroad in such currencies, approve applications from the residents for purchase of foreign currencies and maintain rupee accounts in the names of non-residents and pass debits and credits to such accounts. The ADs can deal directly with the public and the RBI with the ADs in putting through these transactions.

The ADs have an association called Foreign Exchange Dealers' Association (FEDA) which fixes the rates for dealing in sterling with rupee on the basis on RBI's declared rates for buying and selling and the middle rates. The ADs are free to quote their own rates for other currencies on the basis of cross rates quoted in London as between sterling and other currencies and on the basis of RBI's buying rates for D.M., the US dollar and yen. The RBI buys and sells sterling under Section 40 without limit while it buys only £$DM and yen under Section 17 (3) of the RBI Act. The RBI used the Pound Sterling as its intervention currency for keeping the exchange rate of the rupee stable for a long time. The RBI has also started selling US $ from February 1987. Since 1992, RBI is quoting a Reference Rate in terms of US $ and intervenes in the market to stabilise the rupee in terms of dollar.

As agent of the RBI, the ADs have to scrutinise applications from the public and implement the rules and regulations of exchange control under power delegated to them by the RBI. They have to satisfy themselves that all receipts and payments are in accordance with the Exchange Control Manual. It is obligatory for ADs under Section 74 of FERA to comply with all general or special directions and instructions given by the RBI. They can keep Non-Resident Accounts (your account with us and our account with you) and operate on them subject to the overall control and reporting to RBI. They can deal in permitted methods of receipts and payments, keep minimum working balances in foreign centres, operate in the inter-bank market and maintain a square or near square position in each currency which means that their purchases (spot and forward) and sales should be matched as far as possible.

## Money Changers

Money changers are authorised by the RBI to deal in foreign currencies and coins. Restricted money-changers can only purchase while others can do both purchases and sales in foreign currencies and coins. Some hotels, firms and establishments etc., have been given licences by the RBI to act as money-changers.

## Permitted Method

All exporters have to get a code number from the RBI for which an application in form CNX has to be made in duplicate. This code number has to be quoted in all subsequent correspondence with banks and RBI. The inward remittances are freely permitted except that they are to be reported to the RBI. The export receipts are to be declared in the prescribed form and should represent the full export value of the goods and the transactions should be put through the ADs. The method of receipt should be in permitted currencies (listed in the Exchange Control Manual) and in approved forms. The proceeds should normally be realised within six months and in the case of Pakistan and Afghanistan within three months (extended to six months in October 1985), except in the case of exports of engineering goods under deferred payment arrangements when permission is generally given for extended periods of receipt. Trade discounts and agency commissions are permitted normally upto 5 per cent of the invoice value.

The object of control in respect of exports is to ensure that the export earnings are duly and promptly repatriated back to India in full, within the stipulated time and in the currency of the importing country or a convertible currency. No under-invoicing or over-invoicing or any measure to earn foreign exchange, with a view to keeping it abroad is permitted. Blanket range permits and exchange release for sales promotion are permitted up to certain limits. Exporters are now permitted to keep some part of their earnings abroad.

The prescribed methods of receipt and payment are as follows:

**(a) External Group Countries:** Include all countries who are not in Group 'B' – Bilateral Group. Export receipt should be in the currency of importing country or of any country in this Group. Import payment from India should be in rupees to the account of the resident of the exporting country or of any country in this Group.

**(b) Bilateral Group Countries:** Include Czechoslovakia, East Germany, Poland, Rumania and Russia. Any receipts or payments in respect of these countries should be in non-convertible rupees or as per the relative agreement on which ADs are advised from time to time.

In respect of Nepal and Bhutan, the receipts and payments are to be effected in rupees without reference to the Exchange Control formalities.

## Other Receipts

All receipts whether current or capital are to be channelised through ADs. Any unauthorised use of foreign exchange is not permitted. The foreign exchange earned should be repatriated home at the earliest possible time through the ADs into the official channels. The purpose of remittance and the beneficiary of remittance and other details are to be recorded and reported to the RBI by the ADs. All inward remittances for investment of foreign capital in India should be made to the Ministry of Commerce and Industry, while those for repatriation after such clearance are to be made to the RBI. All flows on current account are now free while those on capital account are liberalised, but subject to control by RBI and Government, Ministry of Finance.

## Payment for Imports

Authorised dealers are permitted to open letters of credit or make remittances abroad for imports, if they are covered by import licences or are under OGL. If the goods are covered under deferred payment terms, prior approval of RBI is also necessary for opening of letters of credit or giving a bank guarantee. The method of payment should be in terms of permitted currencies and advance payments require prior approval of RBI and are granted in respect of engineering goods or capital goods. Payment to bilateral account countries should be in non-convertible rupees, as per the relative trade agreements. Payments are freely allowed and at free market rates of exchange since March 1992.

## Other Payments

Payments for travel, education, medical treatment, etc., are permitted as per scales laid down by the RBI from time to time, depending upon the purpose and the country of visit. These payment restrictions are advised to the ADs from time to time and have been fairly liberalised more recently due to comfortable foreign exchange position of India. Remittances of freight, profits, dividends, insurance etc., are permitted to actual beneficiaries abroad. Family remittances of foreign nationals are permitted but not of Indian nationals or Indian residents for maintenance of their families abroad. Similarly, transfer of assets by Indian nationals emigrating abroad is also not allowed except in small quantities or in special circumstances. Some of these items of flows of funds on current account are now freed for residents to remit funds abroad.

All applications for transfer of funds for investment abroad are to be made to the Ministry of Commerce and Industry for clearance first and then to the Ministry of Finance and RBI. These are now granted freely in view of comfortable foreign exchange position and liberalised policy. An automatic route for flow of funds for investment abroad is allowed to exporters and foreign exchange earners subject to some limits.

## Delegation to ADs

ADs have been delegated some powers to approve and to make remittances for dividends, profits, subscription to magazines, membership fees, correspondence course fees, examination fees, etc., up to prescribed limits without reference to the RBI. Similarly, remittances out of income for family maintenance abroad for non-nationals are permitted upto some limits. Payments for samples for trade and laboratory testing upto some limits of value are permitted by the ADs. But prior permission is required in case of reduction in proceeds over invoice value, change in terms of sale or penalties, quality claims or any other deductions in invoice value. Since 1992, FERA was diluted very much and many controls were removed.

## Forward Covers

Exchange control permits ADs to enter into forward sales and purchases with customers for genuine trade transactions provided they are in permitted currencies and in prescribed methods and corresponding foreign country's exchange control does not prohibit such transactions. The ADs can in turn cover them in an inter-bank market in India or abroad or with the RBI. The AD has to satisfy himself that the importer has an import licence with an exchange control copy, except when the imported goods are on OGL. The customer must have also entered into a purchase contract, opened a letter of credit or produced other documentary evidence in that direction. Banks can normally enter into sale contracts upto six months except in the case of deferred payment imports in which case RBI's permission for long periods is secured. Where an export is made on consignment basis, a forward sale is given only after shipment is effected and upto the extent of the value declared in the shipping bill. The contract should be based on the value expected to be received minus agency commission. Any extension of contract beyond six months normally requires prior permission of RBI. Cancellation of forward contracts should also be referred to RBI for approval. The RBI has introduced many changes in December 1995 to expand the spectrum of forward cover facilities such as for overseas projects, contracts, commissioning charges, consultancy fees, cross currency imports etc. Banks are now permitted to cover such risks in foreign markets. In 1994-95, RBI has permitted banks and companies to trade freely in the forward market and stopped giving the cover and without prior permission of RBI forward contracts on interest rates are also permitted.

## Securities

There are no restrictions on import of securities, Indian or foreign. Export of securities is prohibited except with the prior approval of the RBI. Similarly, issue and transfer of securities to non-residents require the general or special permission of the RBI as also the Foreign Investment Board of the Ministry of Industrial Development. Indian residents require prior permission to hold foreign securities or export or send out of India, Indian securities. Now these transfers are freely permitted and both direct and portfolio investments are now permitted by NRIs, FFIs and FIIs.

## Foreign Currency Accounts

The RBI has granted general permission to persons resident but not domiciled in India to maintain and operate foreign currency accounts. Such of the accounts of residents as existed before 1947 were continued but fresh credits to such accounts are to be approved by RBI beforehand. Normally, residents of India are not permitted to open or maintain such accounts in foreign currency abroad except those permitted in connection with technical collaboration or joint collaboration agreements. More recently banks and export earners are permitted to keep some amounts abroad for their immediate or short-term requirement. Indians who are resident outside India had to close such accounts when they return to India on a permanent basis, but it is not necessary at present due to recent liberalisations.

## Non-resident Accounts

The terms resident and non-resident have been defined in the Foreign Exchange Regulation Act of 1973. A non-resident is one who resides outside India for the whole or a substantial part of the year, Indians who are working abroad, and offices and branches abroad of Indian or foreign companies in India (excluding residents of Nepal and Bhutan). Two types of non-resident accounts are clearly discernible:

(1) Private non-resident accounts (of individuals, firms, companies and organisations).

(2) Non-resident bank accounts.

The private non-resident accounts are again of three categories:

(1) Ordinary non-resident (rupee) accounts (NRO) are opened without reference to RBI in respect of non-Indians and Indians residing abroad but holding a passport of a country other than that of India with funds from abroad but others require prior permission of RBI.

(2) National Defence Remittance Scheme Special Accounts were opened during 1965-66 with the rupee proceeds of inward remittance received under the NDR scheme from non-resident Indians abroad. These funds are not repatriable from India under any circumstances but can be converted into rupee accounts and used in India, if the circumstances of the account holder warranted it.

(3) Non-resident (External) Accounts Rules 1970 permit the opening of such accounts (FCNR) in the names of persons of Indian origin or Indian nationality but resident abroad provided the funds are transferred into India from abroad through banking channels. Such funds can be paid back in foreign currency for repayment of principal and interest without prior approval of the RBI after the maturity of fixed deposits. Non-resident (ordinary) accounts can be converted into non-resident (external) accounts or transfers from one to the other are permitted. The operation on these accounts are no longer subject to earlier controls.

In more recent years, foreign investment in India is encouraged. Non-residents of Indian origin are given liberal facilities for investment in shares, debentures and units of the UTI., both on repatriation basis and non-repatriation basis. There are provisions for non-resident investment in new issues up to 40 per cent to 74 per cent in the case of some industries and even 100 per cent in respect of a few priority industries such as hospitals and hotels, which are foreign exchange-earners and in sick units. Funds have thus flown in through the non-resident accounts for remittances and investment. Foreign investment in Indian Companies is now permitted up to 49% to 51% of equity capital.

The operating Non-resident Deposit categories in 2009 are as follows:

(1) Foreign Currency Non-Resident (Banks) Scheme-This is for banks' borrowing abroad [FCNR (B)].

(2) FCNR (A) Scheme was discontinued with only outflows of maturing deposits.

(3) Non-Resident Non-repatriable Rupee deposits [NR (NR) RD] scheme has facility for repatriation of interest amount only and not principal. This not been phased out

(4) NR(E) RA is deposits in foreign currencies by foreign individuals and institutions or NRIs, when has now become NRO Accounts.

The total outstanding balances on these accounts stood at $ U.S. 17,895 million at end March 1996 and at $ U.S. 25,151 million at end March 2002 and U.S. $ 32,266 million at end March 2004, and U.S. $ 41, 554 million at end March 2009 and $ 1,03,844 million at end 2014.

## Non-resident (Bank) Accounts

All accounts kept in India by foreign banking companies including foreign branches of Indian banks, are designated non-resident bank accounts. ADs can open accounts in Indian rupees for their correspondents, branches, agents, etc., abroad subject to the advice of the RBI. The operations (credits and debits) on these accounts have to be reported to the RBI. They have the same implication as operation in foreign currency accounts kept by Indian banks abroad with their agents, correspondents and branches. The operations on these accounts are freely allowed now.

## Loans and Overdrafts

ADs can grant temporary loans and overdrafts to their agents. Correspondents and branches etc., abroad other than from bilateral group without prior approval of RBI up to a limit. They can also receive similar financial assistance from abroad. Such facilities are for current operations and of working capital nature and not for investment in term capital and loans to private parties. Such operations are to be reported to the RBI. ADs can also lend to NRIs out of their NRI accounts now.

## Blocked Accounts

An account is blocked if operations on it are not permitted without the prior approval of the RBI. Any account of a person, firm or company, resident abroad may be opened as blocked or may be declared as blocked by the RBI under the Exchange Control Rules. Thus, assets in India, including bank accounts and securities etc., of Indians emigrating to foreign countries, are set out as blocked accounts. Balances in blocked accounts can, however, be invested with RBI's permission in fixed deposits with banks, or other approved categories of shares, debentures, etc. The rules governing the blocked accounts are laid down in the Exchange Control Manual and have been liberalised more recently allowing more liberal use of these funds for local payments or investments by accounts having less than Rs. 50,000. The operations on such accounts are normally governed by rules of the RBI and subject to scrutiny of RBI and to be reported to it in Form A-4. Blocked accounts have disappeared with the liberalisation in FERA and permission given to free use of all such funds, since 1992-93.

# LIBERALISATION OF EXCHANGE CONTROL

Since 1992, deregulation and liberalisation were pursued by the government and the RBI in respect of foreign exchange and exchange controls. The basic framework of controls remained, except for liberalisation in some directions; rupee was freed on trade account in 1993 and on current account in 1994. Consequential and supplemental to these measures the RBI has diluted many provisions in FERA, and operates the FEMA provisions, since 2000.

ADs were given more powers, through delegation of authority in respect of both Trade Account and Invisibles Account. ADs were allowed to export surplus stocks of foreign currency notes and coins, keep balances and short-term investment abroad for their working requirements. The ceiling of Rs. 15 crores, imposed in 1995, on AD's over night position was removed, in January 1996. ADs can use their discretion in releasing foreign exchange for foreign travel for business seminars, conferences, medical treatment and studies. Banks have to maintain Tier I capital funds at 5% of foreign exchange open position.

Exporters were permitted to keep Exchange Earner Foreign Currency accounts, abroad (EEFC) to utilise them for all purposes connected with trade promotion and other current account purposes. ADs were given freedom to fix their own Aggregate Gap Limit (AGL) for more efficient management of their assets and liabilities. They were also allowed, if they have the expertise, to initiate positions overseas in cross currency dealings. They can give forward cover to overseas investors on account of dividends due or returns on foreign investment in India or to shipping companies in respect of foreign collections.

ADs are allowed to offer hedges, interest rate swaps, currency swaps, caps/collars, and forward rate agreements to corporates, without prior permission of RBI or government. RBI has been providing single window clearance under fast track within 21 days for proposals of joint ventures and foreign investment in Indian companies upto a limit.

Interbank deals account for about 80-85% of total transactions in Forex market and the RBI has initiated the process of setting up clearing house facilities for settlement and clearance for the operations of ADs. The RBI has set up a Market Intelligence cell to study and monitor the developments in Forex Market, on a daily basis.

# CAPITAL ACCOUNT LIBERALISATION

Throughout nineties, the role assigned to foreign capital is guided by considerations of financing a level of current account deficit that is sustainable by other economic criteria. The capital account convertibility is to be a slow process, subject to many prior conditions to be achieved. There has been a policy shift in favour of non-debt capital flows into India in the nineties.

India is following a gradualist approach to capital account liberalisation, as it is fraught with dangers to the economy. So FDI and foreign portfolio investment are being encouraged. Many developing countries have liberalised capital controls in the seventies and eighties but had faced many banking problems and have reversed. These liberalisations complete sequencing of many prior developments and macroeconomic stabilisation programmes are necessary for successful experiment of freeing of capital account.

The main recommendations of the committee on capital account convertibility are being implemented in stages, as follows:

(1) Fiscal Consolidation-Gross fiscal deficit to be brought down by stages to 3.5% of GDP.

(2) Mandated rate of inflation to be 3 to 5% per annum.

(3) Strengthening of the financial system-flexible interest rate regime to be deregulated-CRR to be brought down to 3%. Statutory limit-Gross NPAs of

banks to be brought down to 5% and 100% marked to market valuation of investments.

(4) Best practices for Forex risk management.

(5) Banks to follow international accounting norms and disclosure norms.

(6) Capital prescription to be stipulated to market risks.

(7) Debt service ratio to be brought down to 20%.

(8) Adequate foreign exchange reserves to cover not less than 6 months imports.

## Recent Liberalisation Measures

Exporters are permitted to extend trade related loans/credit to overseas importers out of their exchange earners foreign currency balances (EEFC). Advance remittance facilities for import of goods without bank guarantee were liberalised. Indian companies are allowed to retain abroad funds raised through ADRs/GDRs. They are also permitted to acquire property outside India for their business purposes and their offices abroad. Traders are allowed to hedge their foreign exchange exposures without any limit. There was further simplification of procedures in foreign exchange transactions and in the banks' reporting system.

Indian residents and companies and the mutual funds are permitted to invest in certain listed companies abroad. Banks are allowed to invest their unimpaired Tier I capital in overseas money market or debt instruments. Funds raised through FCNR (B) route or ADRs and GDRs are allowed to invest abroad in CDs/TBs and other money market instruments, pending their targeted utilisation.

Residents are allowed to open Resident Foreign Currency (RFC) accounts without limits. They can remit foreign exchange for acquisition of foreign securities under Employees Stock Option Scheme (ESOP). They can acquire ADRs/GDRs and sell them for foreign currency by way of credit to their EEFC/RFC domestic accounts or their rupee accounts at their discretion. ADs can issue international credit cards, to their customers.

As regards foreign investment in India FIIs are allowed to hedge the market value of their entire investment in equity at any time. ADs are authorised to offer forward contracts to non-residents/FIIs to hedge their investments made in India. Foreign banks in India are allowed to hedge their Tier I capital in Indian books without any restrictions. NRIs and PIOs are permitted to remit upto US $ 1 million a year out of their NRO accounts for specified purposes.

## Sodhani Committee Recommendations

Following the recommendations of this committee the RBI implemented the following measures:

(1) General permission for sale of shares, required under Portfolio Investment Scheme given to NRIs was extended to OCBs.

(2) NRIs and not OCBs have been permitted to invest in MMMFs, set up for money market operations in India.

(3) General permission to NRIs for subscribing to Articles of Association of Indian Companies engaged in industrial activities to cover other companies engaged in other permissible activities.

(4) Granting of housing loans to NRI staff of Indian companies.

(5) ADs are permitted to remit sale proceeds of shares kept under pledge for liquidation of loan outstandings.

(6) General permission for crediting interest on delayed refunds of share application money.

(7) Extending the scope of safe custody of securities on behalf of NRIs to institutional custodians.

In short, consideration was given to NRIs for more liberal treatment of their repatriation and operations of them under Portfolio Management. Funds mobilised by banks through the NRI deposits (FCNRA, EFFC and NRERA) can be invested abroad by banks in short-term investment, in addition to their lending at home.

ADs can effect remittance up to U.S. $ 10,000 or its equivalent for importers to settle disputes abroad on trade account. Hotels and airline companies are allowed to receive payment in Indian rupees from foreign tourists without insisting on their encashment certificates.

Software exports were permitted since September 1995 without receipt of advance payment and software exports are put on par with any other exports. Since October 1995, RBI has stopped announcing dollar buying and selling rates, but specific quotes are given for a deal with RBI, by any AD. Since November 1995, ADs are allowed to provide U.S. $ 5,000 or less in any year to close relatives abroad for their maintenance by any resident Indian if the beneficiary abroad is a permanent resident abroad and has insufficient income and unable to return to India. Authorised dealers are permitted since February 1996, to effect remittances towards import of designs and drawings, up to Rs. 25 lakhs on production of suppliers' invoice postal wrappings and exchange control copy of Bill of Entry as documentary evidence in support of import.

Norms for investment abroad were eased in May 1997. Indian companies are now allowed to freely invest in overseas market up to $ 15 million raised through GDR or EEFC without RBI prior permission, provided they are invested in overseas projects. Corporates are allowed since June 1997 to raise funds abroad up to $ 15 million as short-term finance useful for even rupee expenditure on their projects, if they are export earners and EOCG licence holders. Other corporates are allowed to rise up to $ 3 million for their foreign currency requirements or for their rupee expenditure. These limits were raised later on. Residents can invest abroad upto U.S. $ 25,000 in listed companies or for specified purposes.

## Exchange Rate Management

Since 1994, when the rupee was declared convertible, Exchange control in the strict sense was not operated. What the RBI did is better called Exchange Rate Management (ERM). FERA was replaced by FEMA.

The RBI policy in this regard was guided by market conditions, current account deficit, and capital inflows/outflows. Excess demand and supply pressures of rupee versus dollar were absorbed by RBI intervention. The rupee value was maintained within a narrow range between Rs. 36 to 40 per U.S. $ at end December 1997 and at around Rs. 44 in 1999 to 2004. The RBI had to maintain a delicate balance between price stability or control of inflation and the required exchange rate stability. Even at Rs. 36, per U.S. dollar, rupee depreciated by about 15% during the Eighth Plan period (1992-97). From March 1993, there was a temporary appreciation of the rupee due to the adoption of convertibility on trade account followed by convertibility on current account in March 1994. In 2003-04, the dollar was around Rs. 45-46, but stood at Rs. 44 in February 2005.

There was relative stability of the rupee during 1994-95 and up to September 1995; in 1995-96, the RBI allowed the rate to fall from Rs. 31 to Rs. 35 and started supporting it between Rs. 35 and 36. It has stabilised around Rs. 36 by May-June 1996. The RBI intervention in the Forex market since October 1995 helped the rupee rate to remain around Rs. 35-36, until November 1997 when it fell to Rs. 39. It has purchased dollars, when there are larger inflows into the country and also sold when there is large demand for dollars, from its foreign exchange assets. The exchange rate has since fallen to Rs. 47-48 per US dollar at end March 2003 and at end of September 2009 and Rs. 63.36 at end 2014. Excluding gold and SDRs, India's foreign currency assets rose from a low of $ 29 billions in March 1991 to a peak of U.S. $ 75 billion in December 2002 U.S. $ 264 billion early in October, 2009 and $ 2,76,359 million at end 2014. This sharp rise in exchange reserves was due to foreign confidence in Indian economy and large foreign inflows of funds from abroad. This enabled India to repay some of its high cost foreign debt obligations and the RBI to intervene in the Forex market to stabilise the rupee, which is necessary for sustained growth of our exports.

## RBI on Exchange Control Norms

On June 9, 1999, the Reserve Bank of India has announced the relaxation of exchange control guidelines. There is now more freedom for remittances-for commission on exports, by shipping companies to protection and indemnity clubs and on investments by NRIs and OCBs.

In addition, the RBI has given general permission for several transactions.

Authorised dealers (ADs) have been allowed to remit casual gifts up to $ 1,000 per calendar year to the corporate clients and other applicants to relatives and friends abroad.

ADs are allowed to make remittances up to $ 250 or its equivalent per transaction in respect of post parcel imports without insisting on the parcel receipt.

ADs may also allow remittances towards import of drawings and designs received by e-mail or fax, subject to production of documents prescribed for software imports.

ADs have been allowed to remit commission on exports within the prescribed limit of 12.5 per cent of the invoice value, even in cases where the amount of commission has not been declared on export declaration forms.

Foreign embassies, missions and diplomats, who could earlier open foreign currency accounts only with the main offices of the State Bank of India have been allowed to open foreign currency accounts with any bank with an AD status, subject to the accounts being funded by inward remittance in convertible currencies.

ADs can allow remittances by shipping companies which are their constituents towards subscription to protection and indemnity (P & I) clubs in accordance with the approval granted to shipping companies by the government under the General Insurance Business (Nationalisation) Act, 1972.

Exim Bank can directly receive, consider and approve project export proposals up to a value of Rs. 100 crores, provided all facilities required for the execution of such contracts are provided by it.

ADs have also been empowered to allow remittances by recognised international, national and state level sports organisations towards prize, sponsorship money for sports events up to $ 100,000 in each case as against $ 25,000 earlier.

Credit card issuers can issue rupee credit cards valid in India, Nepal and Bhutan. These may be issued to non-resident Indians (NRIs) and Persons of Indian Origin (PIOs) also. Remittance from India will, however, not be allowed in settlement of bills in the event of use of such cards in other countries.

Indian residents are now allowed to hold international credit cards (ICC) provided by overseas organisations subject to the condition that the liabilities arising from the use of such cards in India as well as outside India are met by the organisation issuing the card, without any remittance from India.

ADs and full-fledged money changers need not submit a copy of the letter from the applicant giving particulars like name and address while applying for exchange under basic travel quota (BTQ), along with a statement in form FLM 8.

ADs can now renew the general permission granted by the RBI not only to NRIs but also to Overseas Corporate Bodies (OCBs) under the Portfolio Investment Scheme. The permission may be renewed for a period of five years at a time.

Domestic mutual funds have been given general permission to issue units or any other similar instrument under the schemes floated by them to NRIs, PIOs and OCBs on non-repatriation or repatriation basis, subject to SEBI approval.

Proprietorship concerns or a firm in India have been given general permission to accept deposits from NRIs and PIOs on non-repatriation basis. Indian companies (including non-banking finance companies registered with the Reserve Bank) also have the general permission to accept deposits from NRIs, PIO and OCBs on a non-repatriation benefits, subject to certain conditions.

Domestic ATOs have been given general permission to issue shares or convertible debentures upto 100 per cent of paid-up capital to NRIs, PIO and OCBs subject to certain conditions.

NRIs and PIOs have been given general permission to transfer, by way of gifting any rupee security, shares, bonds or debentures of a company registered in India held by them to a registered charitable trust or organisation.

Resident individuals, proprietorship concerns and partnership firms can now avail interest-free loans from NRIs and PIOs on a non-repatriation basis.

Non-resident PIOs have been given general permission to transfer immovable property held by them in India to relatives and registered charitable trusts or organisations by way of a gift.

Non-resident holders have been exempted from the operation of provision of Section 29(1) (b) of FERA 1973 to acquire the underlying shares released by Indian custodians of ADRs and GDRs upon the surrender of these. General permission has also been given to the company or depository concerned under Section 19(4) of FERA 1973 for entering an address outside India in its register or books in respect of such shares.

NRIs, PIOs and OCBs have been given general exemption for the sale and transfer of shares, bonds or debentures of Indian companies through stock exchanges in cases where such transfers are made in favour in Indian citizens, PIO or in favour of a company or body incorporated under any law in force in India.

Since 2004, there was further liberalisation under current and capital accounts. Foreign banks in India are permitted to remit their net profit after tax in the normal course of business. The Indian corporates can issue equity to foreign entities against ECBs, fees and royalties etc. payable by them which convert debt into equity. General permission was given to foreign corporates to establish their own units to branches in SEZs in India to undertake manufacturing and service activities. Resident corporates can now invest abroad in JV/WOS upto 100% of their net worth.

Indian corporates can avail of ECBs upto US $ 500 million with some limits, for loans upto 3 years and 5 years respectively. They can invest and disinvest abroad in JV/WOS, upto a limit. Resident corporates and ADs can hedge their investments abroad through forward option contract. Multinational banks like IFC, ADB, etc. are permitted to float rupee bonds, and purchase government dated securities. Thus, these liberalisations are spread widely in both current and capital account with some safeguards.

The mutual funds, registered with SEBI, were given more liberal foreign investment in listed securities abroad. The foreign investment limit in credit information companies was raised to 49%. The ECB regulations were further liberalized in 2008, in respect of borrowers of infrastructure sector, in particular. The period of realization of export proceeds of goods and software was increased from 6 months to 12 months. It will be seen that such liberalizations were gradually introduced for both current and capital account transactions.

❖ ❖ ❖

# EXCHANGE RATE RISK MANAGEMENT

# 16

## Economic Exposure

The most vital risk exposure in international transactions is the economic exposure. The economic policies, privatisation, liberalisation and government rules and regulations, the fundamentals and growth prospects of the country are the major concern of any exchange rate system.

With the Indian rupee being convertible, since March 1994, the risks in the foreign exchange market have become more pronounced and the need to take risk or protect oneself from these risks has become evident. Many countries have already made their currencies convertible and some are in the process of doing so. In the context of such scenario of free foreign exchange markets, uncertainty of currency rates and their volatility has made it imperative for the dealers in foreign exchange to expose themselves to the risk. Risk is inherent in the foreign dealings due to the following reasons:

1. Trade across countries involve dealings with parties-exporter or importer-who are unknown and whose creditworthiness is uncertain.
2. Foreign dealings also involve countries whose credibility and creditworthiness is not certain.

Many countries are having political and economic problems, racial, and communal riots or other disturbances and there is no certainty about their economic and financial policies and their willingness and capacity to repay the loans or service them, through their exports and inward remittances. Fundamentals in the economy may be in doubt and inflation and other problems of the country, such as unemployment, poverty, low rates of growth or no growth in the economies etc., may be plaguing the country, when they may default in their external obligations, as in the case of some African and Latin American countries. Their capacity to borrow on commercial lines will be then poor and they depend on donations, gifts and concessional aid from governments and international bodies. They are not able to service and repay the debts to foreigners. Country rating is one of the measures of economic risk exposure of a country. All the important economic variables are taken into account in measuring the country rating (referred to another chapter).

Exchange risk is due to fluctuations in the rate of exchange in conversion of one currency into another and likely changes in interest rates which might effect the forward rates. Forward cover of any currency which the banks provide will take into account the possible changes in interest rates, inflation rates and the intrinsic strength of country and the currency. Exchange risk will basically depend on the economic strength of the country and its foreign exchange reserves, as the volatility of the exchange rate depends on them.

## Strength of Currency

Exchange risk depends on the strength or weakness of currency which in turn is a reflection of the degree of strength of the economy. Thus, a country whose productivity is low and its competitive strength in international markets is poor, cannot export enough of the domestic products abroad and its foreign exchange earnings will be poor. Such a country will have a weak currency and its rate of exchange will be uncertain.

A strong country like U.S.A. or Japan will have good export performance resulting in trade surplus and good inflow of foreign funds for investment because of its high productivity, low costs of production, latest technology and good investment climate, leading to high rates of growth of output, employment and income. So economy, its strength and its rate of growth and its competitive strength along with a host of other factors will influence the currency rates. The exchange risk is thus, dependent upon an array of economic and extra economic factors which will lead to an unpredictable rate of exchange. The risk and uncertainty of exchange rate is a multi-dimensional phenomenon and requires an expert to fend and manage the risks involved. Genuine trade and investment require a stable and fixed exchange rate which is not possible in free and competitive world, where trade and receipts and payments abroad are all free and market determined. There is thus need for risk management for all dealings in foreign exchange, particularly so for exporters and importers.

## Exchange Risk Defined

Exchange risk simply means that the rate at which a currency is exchanged for another currency may be uncertain and volatile and the amount that an exporter receives in domestic currency or an importer has to pay in terms of domestic currency will be unpredictable and uncertain. Similarly, if funds are transmitted from one country to another, the amounts to be sent or to be received will not be certain, if exchange rates are not fixed. But in the present global economy, free market forces operate to determine the exchange rates depending upon the supply and demand for the currency. This will lead to fluctuating rates, which may result in profits or losses to the holders of foreign currency.

The fluctuating rates result in uncertainty and risk, which will have to be managed by the genuine traders and investors in foreign countries and dealers in foreign exchange and banks. Under free market forces operating, no individual dealer in foreign exchange can influence its price, but the supply and demand pressures for any currency in total lead to its appreciation or depreciation. The totality of receipts either for exports or inward remittances or inflows of funds will decide the supply pressure while the demand for foreign currency emanate from those who have to make payments outside for imports, outward remittances or outflow of funds etc. Such demand and supply pressures influence the exchange rates on a daily and hourly basis and from time to time and lead to uncertainty, in exchange rates.

## Factors Affecting Exchange Rates

Foreign exchange rates, being freely determined, the following factors influence the exchange rates and enhance the risk in particular.

1. Hot money flows as between countries and currencies will take place to take advantage of short-term economic and political factors or disturbances or fears of such developments leading to changes in currency rates and interest rates.

2. Speculative attacks on currencies in anticipation of exchange rate changes and interest rate changes through short-term flows of funds due to rumours "news" and expectations.

3. Exchange rate volatility emerges out of erratic fund flows as between countries, short-term flows of funds in either direction and inflows of funds followed by immediate reversals, etc.

4. Freely fluctuating exchange rates across countries do sometimes lead to erratic movements of rates on either side, unless countervailed by Central Bank of the country to off-set such excesses.

5. Present international monetary system under the IMF imposes the burden of adjustment on the deficit countries to change their exchange rates rather than on the surplus countries. In the absence of adjustment on both sides, balance of payments adjustment is delayed and partial with the result that exchange rates remain uncertain and fluctuating and sometimes even unpredictable.

6. Limited powers of IMF to discipline the surplus countries also lead to partial adjustment or lack of adjustment as between currencies of countries with the result that currency rates may fluctuate very widely and requires Central Bank intervention to stabilise the rates.

Basically exchange rates as between two currencies should reflect the true fundamentals of the concerned countries, such as domestic purchasing powers, relative strength or weakness of the economies in terms of their productive power and trends in output, employment and income. In the absence of stabilised and equilibrated rates, the actual prevailing rates may fluctuate widely which will lead to uncertainty and risk. In order to avoid such destabilising fluctuations in rates, many developing countries maintain exchange and trade controls to reduce such risk and promote trade and investment in their own countries.

India has also moved to current account convertibility in March 1994, with the result that rupee exchange rate is now freely fluctuating in either direction. But to reduce undue fluctuations the RBI has been announcing a reference rate for rupee in terms of dollars and the Foreign Exchange Dealers Association (FEDA) has been fixing the major currency rates in terms of rupees for banks to adopt them to the extent possible, as warranted by the foreign funds position. Even so, the risk and uncertainty is not eliminated in the foreign exchange market in India. It is still the demand and supply pressures on rupee that determines its exchange rate. The RBI is intervening to see that the fall of rupee is slow and even to prevent undue fluctuations due to hedge deals and speculation. During the early years of 21st century, exchange reserves were built up and many foreign debts of the government to IMF and other agencies were paid off. The RBI is in a better position to stabilise the market and prevent speculation.

## Types of Risk in General

The risks in foreign exchange market in India are of the following nature and include transactions in both trade and non-trade items of balance of payments:

1. Risk of credit worthiness of the other party in trade in concerned countries.
2. Risk of credit control and exchange control rules in countries.
3. Risk of economic and political policy changes in the other country.
4. Risk of interest rate changes in the respective countries.
5. Risk of loss of goods shipped in transit or theft, damage, or destruction.
6. Risk of market changes in the concerned countries or changes in the costs or in duties or levies imposed by the trading partners on others.
7. Risk of war or epidemics, or riots or any untoward events affecting trading relations as between the trading partners.
8. Risk and uncertainty of exchange rates of one currency against another due to changing expectations.
9. Risk and uncertainty due to change in forward rates for the currency following the changes in interest rates as between countries.
10. Risk of changes in cross currency rates for any unpredictable changes in the currency markets and in foreign exchange markets.

Foreign exchange markets are very sensitive and volatile as they are influenced by all and sundry developments in economic, political, social and financial factors among the countries. Events across borders and domestic and international forces operate on the markets to force volatility in rates and attendant risks in the exchange markets.

## Exchange Rate Management in India

The rupee was devalued twice in July 1991 and the depreciation of the rupee continued in the free market thereafter. The rupee dollar rate was Rs. 17.1274 in March 1990 which fell to Rs. 32.6456 in February 1993, and thereafter it stabilised around Rs. 31.3727 since March 1994 when current account convertibility was introduced by the government. Since then the rupee depreciated slowly and reached Rs. 48 per dollar at one time and is stabilised around Rs. 45-46 by mid 2004 and stood at around Rs. 48-49 per dollar in the first half of 2009 and Rs. 63,600 by end 2014.

After the structural reforms undertaken since July 1991, the rupee exchange rate management assumed all the importance and attention from the RBI and the government. The Liberalised Exchange Rate Management System (LERMS) introduced in March 1992 is a step in that direction of a freely convertible rupee at a future date. Under this system, rupee can be freely converted with a free market rate up to 60% of exports, while official rate still prevailed for the 40% or rest of the exports. This system helped to stabilise the rupee and the official rate remained unchanged except for a downward adjustment of 1.12% in the rate effected on December 4,1992. The market determined rate also remained stable and the spread between the official rate and the market rate also remained in a narrow range except for short and extraordinary periods.

The experiment with limited convertibility was successful and the government was emboldened to launch the full convertibility on trade account in March 1993. Since then there was unification of the dual exchange rate into a single floating rate which imparted considerable strength to the rupee. Now the external value of the rupee is determined by market forces fully. As this is on the trade account, it only meant that the ADs did not have to surrender to the RBI the exchange proceeds at fixed rate as before. The exporters can sell their earnings at the free market rates to the banks as the importers have to buy the same from banks at the prevailing market rates from time to time.

Since mid-January, 1995, the RBI has banned the rollover of forward contracts, and as a step in the direction of liberalisation, allowed the customers to book forward contracts in any permitted currency. Now the companies will have to book forward contracts matching with their foreign exchange exposure. This facility to hedge in any currency will permit the corporates to take positions in currencies and develop the foreign exchange market and the forward market in particular.

## Full Convertibility of Rupee

As referred to earlier the convertibility on trade account was launched on March 1993 and exports have become convertible at free market rates up to 100% of them. The experiment on convertibility on trade account proved a success in the sense that no untoward fluctuations in the rupee rate were noticed during 1993-94 with the result that the government has announced in March 1994 the full convertibility on current account also which means that all invisible receipts and payments have to be effected at market related rates. Thus, not only trade items but all invisible items or services are paid and received at the free market rates since March 1994.

In the Budget 1994-95, the Government of India have also announced a package of further measures to promote and facilitate exports. Exporters are allowed to retain 25% of the foreign exchange earned in dollar denominated accounts abroad. Export Oriented Units (EOUs) are permitted to retain up to 50% of their exchange earnings in dollar terms abroad. These measures would help reduce conversion costs in payments abroad for their import requirements and other services payments. These measures were further liberalised later.

The foreign exchange receipts and payments are now freer than before under all current account items, particularly for travel, tourism, medical expenses and education. The Government have introduced amendments to the FERA to do away with many controls on foreign investments in India, inflow of foreign technology, employment etc. India is now on a path of full convertibility of the rupee on both current and capital account. Preparatory to that, foreign investment in equity of Indian companies is permitted up to 51%. Much of this investment which requires to be cleared by the Government, Ministry of Finance, Investment Division has been flowing into priority sector industries. Foreign direct portfolio investment has been freely allowed without limit and foreign financial institutions and foreign security firms have been permitted by the SEBI to operate in the Indian stock and capital markets.

## Multilateral Investment Guarantee Agency (MIGA)

The MIGA is an international agency set up in 1988 for the purpose of promoting and encouraging the flow of foreign direct investment. It offers investment insurance and advisory services for foreign direct investment in developing countries. It provides protection to international investors against losses arising out of non-commercial risk of currency transfers, expropriation, war and civil disturbances. It provides promotional and advisory role to Governments in framing and implementing foreign investment policy. India signed the MIGA convention in 1992 and with this the member countries who signed this convention increased to 85. India has also opened up bilateral negotiations for extending the investment guarantee with other countries for promoting the foreign direct investment in India. Thus, it has entered into bilateral guarantees with many countries, including the U.S.A. Russia, among others. This is intended to reduce risks in foreign Investments.

## FERA Liberalisation

FERA companies which are companies incorporated in India but in which non-resident interest is more than 40% have now got freedom from many restrictive provisions under Sections 26 (7), 28, 29 and 31 of FERA.

FERA companies are now permitted to do the following:

(1) To borrow money or accept deposits from persons resident in India.

(2) To acquire an undertaking, carry on any trade, commerce or industry, or purchase shares of any company.

(3) To allow trade marks of theirs to be used by any person or company.

(4) To accept any appointment as agent or technical or management advisers.

(5) To acquire, hold, transfer any immovable property in India.

## Trade and Exchange Risk

In dealing with international currencies, risk is inherent in both trade and finance. These risks arise out of dealings as between countries:

(1) In terms of exchange of goods for money.

(2) In terms of sale of services and payment thereof in foreign currencies.

(3) Lending and borrowing in foreign currencies.

(4) Capital inflows and outflows from foreign countries.

Risks arise out of all these transactions and due to unpredictable market related forces which determine the supply and demand pressures on foreign currencies and speculative forces. Demand and supply for currencies emanate from corresponding demand and supply for goods and services and needed receipts and payments to and from abroad. Arbitrage and speculative demands for currencies lead to inflows and outflows which are reversible and these create more uncertainty and volatility in the market.

The instruments involved in foreign trade and in foreign exchange dealings have also a component of risk in them. Briefly, these instruments are:

(1) Currency dealt with in small quantities and involve loss or theft or cheating for counterfeit notes, etc.

(2) MT, TT, DD, cheques, etc. – risk is in transit loss, time in transit and delays involved, etc.

(3) Commercial and trade bills: bills of exchange and other foreign trade bills and documents have risks involved in the parties, drawer, drawee, banker and the goods involved in these bills.

Sight bills have a grace period during which payment can be delayed. Usance bills have a period to maturity of 30 to 180 days usually. These bills and documents are given to banks for collection or for outright purchase, which are again full of risks. The risks arise out of defective documents, time for waiting, problems with goods in transit, shipping or airfreight, etc., party risk and country risk and risk of default or non-payment. Besides, there is the currency risk during the conversion of foreign currency into domestic currency and *vice versa*.

The exporters and importers have to bear some risks. Some risks like party, country and currency risks are passed on to the banks, ECGC and Exim Bank. Insurance agencies cover some risks like those in transit time, shipping and airfreight, etc. Banks in turn pass on some risks to Central Bank of the country, or cover them with foreign correspondents, international markets or inter-bank market.

## Exchange Rate and Currency Risk

Exchange rate is determined by free flow of demand and supply forces for one currency against another. Receipts and payments on trade account, for services and capital flows would influence the demand and supply forces which are in turn determined by the following factors:

(1) Relative quantum of exports and imports and other remittances;

(2) Cost and price differences in goods and services as well as their quality;

(3) Relative purchasing power parity of domestic currency *vis-a-vis* foreign currency;

(4) Interest rates at home and abroad; and

(5) Inflation rates at home and abroad.

Spot rate is decided by the demand and supply pressures, which are influenced by the above factors. Besides, the demand for a currency is also influenced by the hedge and speculative forces. The forward rates are at discount or at premium depending on the current interest rates and expectations about them, present rates of exchange and expectations about their movements, future arbitrage and hedge deals and short-term speculative flows of funds etc. Some discussion on forward rates is also found later in the chapter.

## Types of Exchange Rates

The exchange risk depends on the type of rate. In this context, it is relevant to know the types of rates which are common in the foreign exchange market. The major types are set out below:

(1) *Spot Rate:* The rate for immediate exchange of currency or receipts. Thus, the rate for exchange of currency notes, TTs, MTs, cheques, and DDs which are clean and unaccompanied by documents is called the spot rate;

(2) *Short Rates:* The rates for short periods of 30 to 90 days;

(3) *Long Rates:* The rates for long periods of 90 days and above;

(4) *Telquel Rates:* the rates for broken periods of 15 days or 45 days etc.

The risk varies with the rate dealt with. The longer the period of rate, the larger is the risk The Telquel rates are generally higher than for rounded periods of one/2/3 months due to more administrative work. Short rates for those with documents carry higher risk than clean credits or instruments, for the same reason. Similarly, the forward rates are having more risk than spot rates.

Risk also varies with the country and the currency, in which the instruments are drawn. The political and economic factors, stability or otherwise of the political system and economic policies and a host of non-economic factors play a role in deciding the risk.

Forward rate is generally at a premium due to larger risk involved in it. It is assumed here that the rate is quoted in direct method say $ 1:1.58 D.M. The forward premium will indicate the larger number of D.M. per dollar to be given in each transaction.

Applying the principle of "buy high and sell low" for the indirect method of quotation, as in the case of rupee, the forward rate for the rupee will be at a premium in the sense that more rupees are to be given for a dollar. Take an example. Say $ 1: Rs. 31.2100 for TT buying spot. The forward premium for one month is 10 points which means that the rate will be $ 1: Rs. 31.2110 for one month forward and so on. That means that you have to give more, say Rs. 31.2110 for buying a dollar forward, one month as against Rs. 31.2100 for spot buying. If you are selling dollars, you will only get Rs. 31.2090 for dollar forward.

## Arbitrage and Speculation

In addition to the financing of the genuine trade and payments on merchandise and invisible trade account, banks do finance capital flows of both short-term and long-term. Funds move in and out for hedging and speculation as between currencies. While sometimes the hedging transactions help to stabilise the rates, the same cannot be said of the speculative flows of short-term nature. The excesses of such flows destabilise the exchange market and lead to violent fluctuations in exchange rates. The greater the volatility, the larger is the risk in foreign exchange market and premiums on forwards will go up abnormally. Arbitrage is dealing in foreign exchange to take advantage of the difference in cross rates as between centres or currencies or as between quotations in two or more centres. Thus, if dollars are cheap in one centre and dear in another centre, arbitrage takes place to buy in the cheap centre and sell in dear centre with the result the rate quotations will tend to get equalised as between centres. Thus, to an extent, arbitrage has a stabilising influence on the foreign exchange market.

## Risk in Foreign Trade and Finance

There are different types of exchange risks in the foreign exchange market which are set out briefly below, even at the risk of repetition.

**(1) Credit Risk of Customer:** Credit rating by international banks and international credit rating agencies will help reducing this risk. In India, ECGC and banks do take this risk for the exporters.

**(2) Country Risk:** This is different slightly from the currency risk and arises out of the policies of economic and political nature and their external payments position and their export earnings to service the foreign creditors, convertibility or otherwise of their currencies, etc.

**(3) Currency Risk:** This risk arises out of the volatility or otherwise of the currency and its strength or weakness in terms of other currencies and interest rates and relative degrees of inflation in the respective countries which influence the exchange rates. It also depends on the hot money flows and speculative short-term flows as between countries which will destabilise the exchange rates. The currency risk is generally covered by banks on the guarantee of the ECGC. The country risk may be covered by the ECGC in some cases or by the Exim Bank.

**(4) Market Risk:** Risks of commodities, their quality and the change of government policies of taxation etc., are borne by the exporters or the ECGC in some cases. It will thus be seen that some risks cannot be avoided or passed on by the exporters and in fact many more risks are to be borne by the importers than by the exporters, as the government policy in India wants to encourage the exports from the country.

**(5)** Interest rate and exchange rate volatility were already referred to in many chapters.

## Coverage of Risks

In India both exporters and importers face risks of foreign exchange market, referred to above, but risk coverage to exporters is more than to importers. The reason is that the Indian government has to enable exporters to compete effectively with their foreign counterparts, where exporters get many facilities, particularly credit at low rates of interest and lower tax rates.

The RBI cannot impose controls in foreign exchange market as hitherto as FEMA has been liberalised but it has been entering the market to stabilise the rate and it has been announcing a reference rate for its operations, to stabilise the market. FEDA is fixing the rate for major currencies around which banks are free to operate in the Indian foreign exchange market. Banks continue to cover the currency risk and Exim Bank provides the credit and country risk cover for long duration export contracts. ECGC extends the risk coverage by insurance -country and party credit insurance-for banks to lend to parties of unknown credit rating. But banks and firms are allowed to keep funds abroad and take risk in currencies and even trade in foreign currency markets. They can hedge, swap currencies, enter into arbitrage deals, secure/provide cover abroad, and even take open positions in currencies. Options and futures are also open to banks and firms to cover their risks and trade in the markets. These terms are explained in other chapters.

## Market Makers in Foreign Exchange Market

A market maker is one who takes the risk and gives a two way quotation for any currency-bid and offer rates-and deals in given currencies. As the RBI deals only in dollars, the banks who act as market makers, which are generally foreign banks, concentrate deals in dollar to yen etc. The market makers are generally prone to take positions or hold uncovered currency holdings in strong currencies such as dollar, yen or Euro as their rate fluctuations are minimal and risk is lower. The risk manager in a company or in a bank, plans his holdings of uncovered currencies into a diversified portfolio, to reduce risk and maximise returns. He may invest in short-term assets or money market instruments of countries whose currencies are strong. Such currencies are unlikely to fluctuate violently and are stable, but returns may be lower, due to lower interest rates. The risk manager has a trade off between risk and return. If he takes a higher risk, he gets higher returns.

A market maker has to forecast not only the currency rates but the interest rates in the respective countries, which will influence the forward rates. He may cover the risk in some currencies but keep open positions in others. He takes calculated risks to maximise his returns. Leaving the uncovered positions, he may cover by the following methods:

(1) Swap forward to spot,

(2) Swap forward of one maturity to another maturity,

(3) Swap one currency against another of same maturity or a different maturity,

(4) Buy spot for future liability,

(5) Buy strong currency and sell weak currency,

(6) Buy forward of one maturity against sale of another maturity or of another currency and a host of other techniques. Derivative products for hedging and risk coverage like those of options swaps, caps, collars are to being developed in India.

Market makers in foreign exchange market are authorised dealers, and the Reserve Bank in the case of India. In well developed markets, the Central Bank, intervention is minimal and the market making is left to reputed foreign exchange dealers and international banks.

## Measurement of Risk

As referred to earlier, the risk in exchange rate lies in the volatility in the rate particularly in the short-run. The daily rates quoted, for example, by the FEDAI, in March 2004 ranged from a low 45.2900 to a high of 43.4300 rupees per dollar. The average exchange rate for 2002 was Rs. 48.5993 per dollar. It has depreciated from Rs. 22.689 per dollar in 1991 before reforms were started to Rs. 48.5993 in 2002. On a monthly basis (averages), the rupee appreciated by 2.3% against dollar in 2002-03. The average exchange rate for April 2002 was Rs. 48.92 and reached a peak of Rs. 49.00 in May 2002 but strengthened thereafter to Rs. 46.23 for the month of July 2003. The rupee appreciated during 2003-04 reaching Rs. 43.43 per dollar by end March 2004, but reached a low of Rs. 45 during November 2004, and felt further to Rs. 48-49 in 2009.

The above data are given for illustration of volatility in yearly averages, monthly and daily averages. But this conceals greater volatility in daily quotations — intra-day and inter-day volatility and only calculation of coefficient of variation of these data shows the actual measurement of risk in exchange rate. As such measurement and data of coefficient of variation was already presented in another chapter, no further attempt is made in the direction. For interested readers, the availability of data may be given here. The daily variations of spot of rates and monthly variations of REER and NEER (with 36 country weights and base of 1993-94 = 100 and with 6 country weights and Base of 1991-92 = 100, 1993-94 = 100 and 2008-09 = 100) are published in the RBI monthly bulletins. Monthly average of spot exchange rates are published in RBI Annual Reports and monthly averages of spot rates and forward margins are also available in the "Handbook of Statistics of the Indian Economy", published by the RBI yearly. The data on daily Forward Margins are also available in this publication.

# RISK IN FORWARD MARKET

As referred to earlier forward exchange rates are more risky than spot rates. These refer to rates which are quoted for the currencies of delivery in one month to six months ahead. During 1991 to 1994 the exchange markets were undergoing many changes due to the ongoing reforms in India.

During major part of 1994 following the full convertibility of rupee on Current Account, forward markets turned more volatile and listless conditions prevailed in the spot market. Again in September to December 1995, the Forex market was very volatile and rupees depreciated to Rs. 36 per US $. During August 1997 to February 1998, again the exchange rate was very volatile due to the Asian currency crisis and rupee depreciated to Rs. 42 per dollar by July 1998 and stood at around Rs. 44 per dollar in March 2000, and Rs. 46.3 in July 2003, and Rs. 48.04 at end September 2009.

The forward exchange market is generally influenced by many factors, in addition to spot market conditions, like:

(i) Perception regarding U.S. dollar rate and Indian Non-resident rupee exchange rate against dollar and in general currency markets.

(ii) Current position and forecast of domestic and foreign money market conditions. Expectation of forthcoming short-term rates in the months ahead.

(iii) Arbitrage, hedge and speculative deals effecting the market.

(iv) Currency risk manager's strategies of the proportion of forward cover effected to total exposures.

Forward market cover was as high as 18% in 1992 just at the time of introduction of partial convertibility of the rupee in February 1992 but fell to less than 10% by February 1994, when the rupee gained in strength.

The exporters and importers are able to cover their forward risk with the banks for their receipts and payments, but in times of currency stability such covers are less in demand and the traders chose to take some risk themselves. Similarly, the currency risk manager will also keep some open positions. Since January 1995 firms are allowed to trade in currencies and in forward exchange as referred to earlier. The currency risks of short-term of 3 to 6 months are generally lower. The currency risks, involved in medium and long-term foreign exchange exposures of companies are unpredictable and difficult to cover. But these risks are high in India at present. The earlier practice of covering such risks by Exim Bank and ECGC will have to be turned into developing a long and medium-term forward market. Now banks as well as firms can keep foreign currencies abroad and trade with the attendant risks. The RBI policy is to encourage a well developed forward market in foreign exchange.

The factors of interest rates and money market conditions are important determinants of forward market. The banks started covering their positions of exposure under FCNR Scheme, when the market was volatile. The market was more stable in 1994-95, but turned volatile again in the latter half of 1995-96.

The risk of currency manager is higher or lower depending on a host of factors. The proportion of risk covered by him to total exposure will depend on his perception of money market rates in India and abroad and volatility of the currency market and number of financial and non-financial factors. When the U.S. dollar interest rates are high, exporters prefer to keep their earnings abroad. If the rupee — dollar rate is stable, exporters can take a view on the future exchange rate and lock-in a forward to forward Swap arrangement with banks to obtain a better cover on their receivables. The forward market is however, illiquid beyond 6 months as the banks find it difficult to foresee the coming trends.

The risk that the currency manager takes will vary from manager to manager depending upon the conditions in the money market and currency market. He generally covers his risk by taking forward to forward cover by adopting appropriate swap techniques and calculated risk management through diversification and proper investment strategies. The currencies in which he takes a position should be stable as U.S. dollar or Euro or yen. The same can be said of the currencies held abroad by firms and companies in India.

Hedge cover of exchange risk for the trader is common. Besides, banks resort to currency swaps, options and futures in foreign currencies to cover their exchange risk. The risk manager generally keeps an open position only in strong currencies, which are likely to be less volatile. Highly volatile currencies are generally less traded, and their risk is invariably covered. But the cover rates are higher. The terms of hedge, swaps and options as applied to foreign exchange markets are explained in other chapters.

The recent attempts of the RBI to develop a rupee exchange market and a forward exchange market were already referred to. The companies are in a position to trade in the market and take position in currencies which need not be in the currency in which their foreign trade contract lies. They can keep foreign exchange earned abroad and trade in the currencies permitted by the RBI. The exporters are permitted to keep 100% of their earnings abroad in EEFC Account for use of their import payment and other current account deals. Units in EO zones and in SEZ are also allowed the facility. The foreign currency option and futures market is also expected to be developed well due to the measures taken recently by the RBI, as also the forward exchange market and interest rate futures market.

## Portfolio Management in Foreign Assets

Banks keep their foreign funds in various forms: cash on hand, balances with other banks, deposits with banks of various maturities, foreign government bonds, Treasury bills, short-term commercial bills and Treasury paper etc. These assets are of various maturities and risks. The maturities may vary from ready cash in foreign currencies to various durations of short and medium nature.

Management of the above assets involve the same principles of risk and return, as applicable to domestic assets. Risk is more in foreign assets than in domestic assets. The foreign currency and funds managers have to plan to maximise the returns and minimise the risk through proper diversification into country and currency combinations and the use of Beta for long-term assets. The currency manager has to choose a proper coverage of risk and reduce his risk in currency positions, through various options open to the trader in foreign exchange market.

In general, the principles of portfolio management in domestic market will apply to management of foreign assets as well. The special risk to be covered in the foreign markets is referred to in later chapters. Both investment and trading are involved in portfolio management.

## Investment and Trading

Investment is purchase of securities or any financial instrument or claims of money. Companies keep some investments in short-term, some in medium-term and also in long-term assets. The investment and trading activities should be distinguished. As cash is required at short notice, investments in Treasury bills, bills of exchange, Commercial Paper or other short-term credit instruments is necessary. Inter-corporate deposits or investments for a few days to a few months in UTI units, PSU bonds etc. are examples of medium-term investments. Long-term investments are in equity shares, debentures, bonds, etc. including those in its subsidiary companies.

Trading is investment and disinvestment in above categories for the purpose of making capital gains or appreciation. Speculation is such trading for short-term gains. When some manufacturing companies are not making adequate profits, the finance manager will try to find alternatives of raising income. The funds manager or treasury manager will be given a role of profit generating centre in funds management or in Treasury function in such cases. Some manufacturing companies combine manufacture with trading. Normally, manufacturing companies do not actively trade but keep investments of both short-term and long-term nature in the portfolio, to enable the company to improve its profits and generate cash at short notice from the existing investment portfolio.

Basically, Treasury function involves both investment and trading. Taking open position in trading in stock market and in trading in Forex market are examples of active trading, which is also called speculation. Investment aims at long-term gains and take less risk while speculation is trading for short-term gain and most risky. Both investment and trading expertise is necessary for Treasury Manager to operate in those markets. But trading involves knowledge of financial engineering and reengineering as referred to below.

## Financial Engineering (Derivative Markets)

Treasury Manager has to be conversant with financial engineering as a means of financing and as a mode of risk management. Financial Engineering is a multidisciplinary approach to the management of risk and return in Treasury Management or Portfolio Management. This involves the use of derivative financial products to decompose the standard financial transactions into their elements and then synthesise them into innovative cross structures to suit the requirements of the parties and preference of investors and the issuers.

Financial Engineering is thus, the by-product of several factors which have grown in importance in recent years, namely-

(1) Development of many financial new products and OTC (over the counter) derivatives.

(2) Revolution in Information Technology.

(3) Financial deregulation and liberalisation.

(4) Increasing volatility of the markets and need for risk coverage.

(5) Growing sophistication of risk management techniques and their application to financial field.

(6) Application of scientific and advanced management techniques.

## Financial Engineering Involves

(i) Multi-disciplinary discipline comprising engineers, mechanics and scientists.

(ii) Adoption of derivative products like swaps, repos and option and futures, options on futures, and futures on option and various combinations of them.

(iii) Decomposition into elements and recomposition of elements and

(iv) Synthesis of new elements.

## Recent Innovations Introduced through Engineering and Reengineering

**Balance Sheet-Price risk transfers:**

(i) Adjustable rate mortgages.

(ii) Floating rate notes.

(iii) Back-to-back loans.

**Credit Transfers (examples)**

Loan Swaps.

Asset Sales without recourse.

Securitised assets.

Transferable loan contracts.

**Liquidity Enhancing Transfers (examples)**

Securitised assets instruments.

Securitised debt instruments.

Swap accounts.

**Credit Enhancing Transfers (examples)**

Junk Bonds.

Zero Coupon Bonds.

Money Market Mutual Funds.

Capital Index Bonds.

**Equity Participating Financing (examples)**

PCD, FDC, and convertibles, warrants, loyalty coupon etc.

**Off Balance Sheet Instruments (examples)**

Future, Options, Loan caps, Swaps, Repos, Forward Rate Contracts.

**Letters of Credit (examples)**

Note Insurance Facilities, Guarantees, Sureties, Contingent liabilities.

# INTEREST RATE RISK MEASURES

Currency risk is closely related to interest rate risk, as referred to earlier.

## Gap or Mismatch Risk

This gap will rise when assets and liabilities will fall due to repricing at different times. A floating rate issue will reduce the risk to zero, as there is no gap or time for repricing. Mismatched repricing the periods of assets and liabilities is a form of risk.

## Net Interest Position Risk

If a bank has more assets, on which interest is earned than liabilities on which it pays interest then the bank has net interest position which leads to risk. But, when interest rates rise, the bank positive net interest position will gain.

## Basis Risk

Interest rate of any two instruments will not change by the same degree or percentage. Besides, borrowing rate and lending rate will not change in the same degree or proportion, which causes risk. This is the change in interest rates by basis points which will vary from instrument to instrument. The differences in basis point changes will lead to an additional risk. Thus rates on deposits of some maturities will change while some lending rates only are changed as in the case of banks in India in recent years.

## Repayment or Withdrawal Risk

If interest rates fall, there is a possibility of some borrowers repaying the high interest loans and if interest rates rise on deposits, old deposits may be withdrawn and new deposits are kept at high interest rates. As interest rates rise and fall, the banks are exposed to some degree of risk as customers exercise the embedded options, inherent in their deposits and loan contracts. The larger the interest rate changes in quantum and more frequent these changes are, the greater will be the risk to the bank.

## Yield and Price Changes

With change in interest rates, yields and price of fixed income securities change in inverse relation. Prices fall when yields rise and *vice versa.* A bank having a large component of long-term loans, a rise in yield will lead to fall in prices and hence depreciation and loss of capital value. Yields curve risk arises when the yield curve varies as between different securities and of differing maturities. Changes in yields result in price changes and such frequent changes upset the planning for income and profits. Price risk along with reinvestment risk should be looked into. The difference in the timing of interest cash flows for investment between assets and liabilities may create a further risk.

## How to Cope with Interest?

Obviously it is better for the bank or corporate to manage its balance sheet items to have less interest sensitive assets and liabilities. They have to resort to floating rate liabilities and flexi-debt instruments. Bankers can also vary the gap in tune with interest rate changes on the basis of forecasts.

The portfolio composition should be constantly reviewed and changed in tune with the change in interest rates. The one method of doing it is to get the duration of its loans to match with the duration of deposit or match the cash inflows with outflows as exactly as possible.

The banks have to reduce asset sensitivity, after maximising the discretionary funds.

Extend investment portfolio maturities, increase short-term deposits and borrowings to suit to lending or investment pattern, increase fixed rate lending of long-term or adjustable rate loans.

The banks have to reduce sensitivity of liabilities.

Increase longer term deposits and borrow on flexi-rate basis and but sell fixed rate loans.

More recently banks and Financial Institutions are opting for flexible rate loans or loans adjustable to basic deposit rate of one year and above. Banks can adopt strategies like matching long-term assets by equity owned funds and match repriceable assets with similar repriceable liabilities and resort to options, futures and various combinations of them to hedge interest rate risk by swaps for principal as well as flows of interests to improve the quality of assets and reduce the NPAs (Non-performing Assets). What was discussed here in relation to banks is equally relevant to MNCs.

## Asset Liability Management (ALM)

Asset liability management can be defined as the process of adjusting liabilities to meet loans and asset demand, liquidity needs and safety requirements. It should take care to ensure the following:

(i) an active management of liabilities or deposits.

(ii) ensuring the units profitability.

(iii) securing the long-term operating viability.

ALM is management of funds wherein the discretionary elements are properly used, by increase or decrease of the interest sensitive funds. It should ensure that interest rates are competitive on both liabilities and assets. Besides regulatory factors should be favourable to enable the company to change the composition of assets and liabilities. These factors require a good secondary market, interest rate deregulation, and competitive market free scenario.

## Instruments for ALM

1. Use of CDs and active primary and secondary market in them; the interest rates on them are freed.
2. Another instrument for use, where interest rates are freed is call and notice money which banks can use and larger use of term money market.
3. Since 1988, inter-bank participations certificates are used for adjusting liabilities with flexibility of rates offered and minimum costs and maximum return.
4. Float or liability in the process of collection or cash and credit in the course of collection.
5. Refinance from parent company or RBI and IDBI etc.

Banks' discretionary funds should be maximum in order to enable them to make proper ALM. Bank wise data showed that SBI and its associate banks are having maximum discretionary funds.

## Objectives of ALM

1. To maximise the income, and control risk exposure.
2. Liquidity should be ensured and the spread between return and costs should be maximum.
3. Bank interest income minus interest expense should be termed as gap which should be maximised.

## Spread Management

RBI will fix a minimum rate or maximum rate on deposits and loans and subject them to these guidelines. The banks should have a large component of interest sensitive assets and liabilities which is possible with big size banks. If a small bank has predominantly retail deposit mix of fixed rates, it needs to aim at fixed rate earning assets and maintain as much spread as possible between return and costs.

Disintermediation reduces the low cost funds, bank's deregulation of interest rates, puts pressure on banks and spreads may be reduced. Liquidity pressures due to deregulation and disintermediation can be managed effectively by big sized banks. Interest sensitivity is measured by changes in interest rate on the concerned assets or liability divided by the change in RBI refinance rate. GAP = RSA – RSL, where RSA is the rate sensitive asset and RSL is rate sensitive liability.

## Traditional Gap Management

Banks first fix the length of the plan horizon, of say 3 months, then the estimates of return and risk for pursuing various alternative programmes of borrowing and lending should be set and finally the bank chooses that programme with a stable net interest income. The gap is the excess of interest sensitive assets over interest sensitive liabilities; incremental gap is worked out by talking one year, dividend into quarters and maximum insulation of net interest income is achieved by making the incremental gap equal to zero. Under the traditional approach, banks would have their net interest income immunised from interest rate changes. Some banks are MNCs and all the analysis here is applicable to corporates as well.

Examples of interest sensitive assets are short-term investments in securities, Treasury bills, CP and CD etc.

Examples of interest liabilities are instruments of CDs and ICD and volatile call money, notice money term deposits, short-term debts are all rate sensitive.

## Rate Adjusted Gap

Different parts of assets and liabilities will respond differently to change in interest rates. Each asset and liability item of balance sheet should be multiplied by its corresponding rate change ratio, namely, RSA/RSL. After those adjustments if the rate adjusted gap is zero, then interest income of a company is considered to be fully immunised to market rate changes.

Maturity mismatches can be offset by lengthening or shortening either assets or liabilities. Liquidity problem can arise at any point in the period. Hence, it is necessary to be prepared to adjust continuously both the assets and liabilities.

Liquidity needs of companies arise due to:

1. Meeting the contingent liabilities.
2. Non-receipt of expected funds inflows.
3. Non-renewal of borrowings or withdrawal of funds.
4. Profits may change either in investment or in other items of balance sheet.

The source of illiquidity may arise from any one or more items both in assets and liabilities. Companies should be prepared to adjust on both sides of the balance sheet, to plan for proper risk management.

❖ ❖ ❖

# HEDGING IN DERIVATIVE MARKETS (FUTURES AND OPTIONS)

# 17

One of the measures of risk management is to operate in derivative markets, futures, options, swaps etc. The derivative markets are for those assets or instruments, which are synthetic financial products derived from the real assets or stocks or commodities. These new financial products have combinations of features of the existing real products and can be traded separately independent of the instruments or stocks, from which they are derived.

The major derivative products have been classified as options, futures and hybrids, which are all widely used in developed countries and in some developing countries. These products are increasingly becoming popular and traded volumes in these products are increasing, year after year.

## Why Derivative Markets?

In emerging markets, there is a greater need for these markets for risk reduction from the high volatility of financial markets. Portfolio managers, particularly FFIs may face market risks, commodity price risks and foreign exchange risks that can be properly controlled through the prudent use of these derivatives for hedging. Increasing globalisation and operations of foreigners in domestic markets make it necessary to develop certain facilities like hedging which in developed countries, they are used to.

The domestic markets will improve asset diversification, deepen the financial structure and promote the sophistication of the markets through the route of the derivative markets, offshore markets etc. These new financial products deepen the structure and promote the superior allocation of resources so as to maximise return and minimise risk and ultimately to better capital formation and higher economic growth.

Absence of derivative markets make the domestic firms less competitive locally and globally and the domestic markets less attractive and imperfect. There will be unfilled gaps in the financial structure. Increased inter linkages of markets due to globalisation make it necessary to promote the derivatives, which lead to sophistication of these markets by filling up the gaps.

## Pitfalls

The experience of developed countries with the derivative markets was not all that rosy. Without adequate safeguards trading has been taking place, in these markets with a speculative objective, with the result that there are instances of spectacular debacles in the derivative markets. There were failures of Barings Bank, and Metall Geslschaft due to speculative over exposures and financial difficulties of Orange County and Bankers' Trust due to operations in these markets without proper comprehension of the risks involved.

In view of such failures or difficulties, what is wanted is education of the pitfalls of trading in derivative markets and provision of training facilities for traders and investors alike.

## Role of Regulator

Too much regulation and too little regulation are both bad in respect of these markets. Too much regulation will have a throttling effect and prevent the entry and growth of the market. Too little regulation will lead to lack of enough protection to investors and fear of failures in the market.

The role of regulator has many objectives. The purpose of regulation is to protect the interests of investors, infuse confidence in the market and prevent unfair trade practices. Next regulatory objective is to promote smooth functioning of the market and prevent undue speculation and trade defaults.

Regulatory role of the market has its impact in many ways, namely, through the throttling effect on growth, minimising incentive to gaming and abuse, and promoting a healthy growth. It is now well accepted that only optimal level of regulation promotes a healthy market. This is particularly relevant to developing countries and emerging markets. The control effect operates through imposition of margins and prevention of over speculation and leading to gaming failures of the dealers and traders.

## Trading in Derivatives

Trading on healthy lines necessitate adequate disclosures of open positions of traders, and trading by companies, and proper reporting. Disclosure of the covered positions, open positions, volume of trade and net losses and gains etc. would help the market to grow in right directions. The disclosures are to the investors by all the players in the market and the companies and to the regulators for enforcing proper controls, and margins and by imposing trade restrictions. All the trading firms should have their own internal controls and by observing standards of capital adequacy and prudential norms, real hedging purpose can be served. A well capitalised clearing house improves the confidence in the market. The regulators and the exchange authorities have to impose and implement an optimal level of controls.

## Problems

One of the major problems of these derivative markets is over speculation which has to be controlled by a right degree of regulation. Developing countries like to promote them in a meticulous manner, through education, training and with all necessary infrastructure. A right degree of regulation with a fair degree of self regulation of the exchange authority and trading and dealer members. Derivative market depends on the observance of the rules of the game, like disclosures and transparency, maintenance of capital adequacy standards and avoidance of monopoly positions (undue long positions) and unfair trading practices.

The regulation of these markets is an important factor, as the confidence of investors is to be build in these markets. Market integrity and investor confidence are the major issues to be dealt with in earnest for promotion of the market. This confidence is dependent on the right degree of regulatory rules, exchange procedures and by member actions. Trades in the derivative markets unlike in the primary markets or cash markets have zero sum consequences which means that for every deal the gain of one is the loss of another. The losses are therefore inherent in the market operations itself.

Although, some degree of speculation is necessary and tolerated in any of these markets, a strict control through margins on these deals is necessary. This market is also sensitive to rumours and trading positions of numbers. It has to be nebulously protected from these problems to promote its growth.

## Currency Futures and Options

The best examples of derivative markets are currency futures and options in U.S. and other developed countries. Futures contracts in currencies are contracts tradeable and contracts for specific quantities of given currencies, the exchange rate being fixed at the time that contract is entered into and delivery dates set by the controlling authority. The International Money Market Division of Chicago Mercantile Exchange (IMM) sets the terms of the contracts and contract specifications. The currencies in which they are available relate to most convertible currencies.

Although, the volume of futures market is still smaller than the forward market it is growing at a rapid pace. Inter-bank call market and international money market are all parts of the foreign exchange market. Here, the traders charge commission which may work out to 0.05% of the value of the contract. There will be a bid-ask spreads as in the Euro-currency markets. Deals are struck by brokers on the trading floor and trading on telephone and telex is much less. In India, options in currencies have become tradeable from July 2003. Earlier, only forward contracts were permitted for hedge and risk management.

## Futures and Forwards

The futures have standardised specifications and trading takes place in an organised market. As contract sizes and maturities are standardised, all participants in the market are familiar with them and trading is well organised. The smaller size of a futures contract and freedom to liquidate the contract at any time before its maturity will differentiate them from the forward contracts.

Forward contracts are private deals, mostly confined to between any two parties who can sign a type of contract they agree on. The amounts involved and maturities and other terms are specific to the individuals/parties concerned. They are not standardised as in the futures contracts.

In IMM, contract lots are all fixed and terms standardised. The trading volumes are large as default risk is eliminated. In contrast, private deals are forward contracts as between two specific parties and run the risk of default. As it is a contract, the law of contract will apply for any defaults or violation of the terms of the contract.

Futures trading is organised on a regular basis with a clearing house and default risks are reduced. Profits and losses of futures contracts are settled at the end of each day on a daily settlement basis with a practice called marking to the market. Every day, futures investors must pay for any losses and receive any gains from the day's price movements. This process of marking to the market on a daily basis goes on until the maturity date. A forward contract is not settled on a daily basis but at the time of maturity. Futures contracts are closed by taking delivery or with an off-setting trade. A long position in D.M., can be offset by a sale of a futures contracts of a like amount. The distinction between forward and futures contracts can be seen below

| *Forward Contracts* | *Future Contracts* |
|---|---|
| 1. Traded on phone or telex. | Traded in a competitive arena. |
| 2. Self Regulating. | Regulated by an authority like the Exchange. |
| 3. Tailor made sizes. | Standardised sizes. |
| 4. Delivery on any date and as per the requirements of the party. | Delivery on specific dates fixed before hand. |
| 5. Settlements on the due date. | Settlement on a daily basis |
| 6. Margins are not required. | Margins are required. |
| 7. Credit risk is borne by each party to the contract. | The clearing house is the counter party which reduces risk. |

In forward contracts, more than 90% of all contracts are settled by delivery. On the other hand less than 1% of all futures are settled by delivery. The quotes are in European style in forward contracts (local currency units per U.S. dollar). Futures contracts are quoted in American style (dollars per foreign currency unit). The transaction costs are based on bid — and ask spread in forward contracts; the same are based on brokerage fees for buy and sell orders for futures contracts.

An example of contract specifications of foreign currency futures is given below in Table 17.1, for illustrating, although the data is outdated.

**TABLE 17.1**

| *Contract Currencies* | *British Pound* | *Canadian Dollar* | *D.M.* | *French Franc* | *Japan Yen* |
|---|---|---|---|---|---|
| Contract Sizes | £ 62,500 | C$ 100,000 | DM 1,25,000 | ff 250,000 | Y 12,500,000 |
| Margin Requirements<br>Initial | $ 2000 | $ 700 | $ 14000 | $ 700 | $ 1700 |
| Maintenance | 1500 | 500 | 1000 | 500 | 1300 |
| Minimum Price<br>Change | .0002<br>(2 pts) | .0001<br>(1 pt) | .0001<br>(1 pt) | .00005<br>(5 pts) | .00005<br>(1 pt) |
| Value of one point | $ 6.25 | 10 | 12.5 | 2.5 | 12.5 |
| Months traded | January, March, April, June, July, Sept., October, December month. | | | | |
| Last day of trading | Third Wednesday of the delivery month. | | | | |

*Source:* Chicago Mercantile Exchange Publications.

Both forward contracts and futures contracts, have their own advantages and disadvantages. Futures do not offer any sizes and any currency that we desire to have. They offer a well organised mechanism for speculation and hedge in currencies. It offers a risk-free contract, with freedom to liquidate the contract at any time before the maturity. It is only by chance that corporate clients will get future contracts to their exact requirements. If forward contracts are entered into they can have size maturity and other specifications to their requirements. But these contracts carry a great risk which has to be covered again in futures market.

There is a regular arbitrage between the forwards offered by banks and IMM contracts offered by Chicago Mercantile Exchange. In practice the arbitrage operations bring about parity in terms offered or price of these contracts in forwards and futures. They will bid up futures price and bid down the forward price and approximate equality is brought about. Because of these arbitrage operations on a daily basis regularly, the futures and forwards prices do not differ significantly.

## Currency Options

Currency futures and forwards protect the holder against the risk of adverse exchange rate changes, but they also deny him the possibility of windfall gains. One can hedge against the risk of a possible loss, but the risk taking itself might reward the risk taker.

**How to use the option**

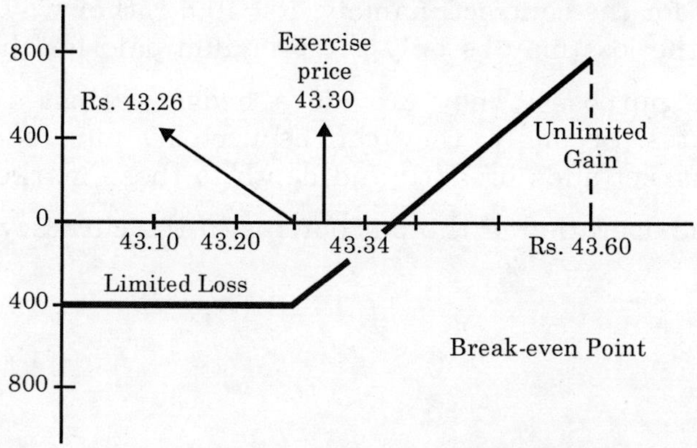


Examine the following graph. U.S. dollars 10,000 contract size option premium Re. 0.04 per dollar
Exercise Price = 43.30 Rs. per $
Spot Price = 43.30 Rs. per $

**Chart 17.1**

An option would be profitable to exercise in certain situations when the option is in the money at the current exchange rate. As applied to currencies, call options give a right but no obligation to buy while put options give a right but no obligation to sell the contracted currencies at the exercise price. The option can be exercised at any time up to the expiration date under the American type of option, while the same can be exercised at the expiration date only under the European type of option.

If an Indian importer has to pay three months hence $ 10,000 to U.S. exporter, he has purchased an option at a price (Premium) of dollars 0.04 per dollar or $ 400 for $ 10,000, contracted for. In this case he has hedged his currency risk for his payment due in U.S. $. If by chance the spot price at the time of his payment is Rs. 43.60 per $ he is in the money. He would exercise this option and buy $ 10,000 at the option exercise price of Rs. 43.30, when the spot price is 43.60, a gain of $ 3000, which more than offsets the premium of $ 400 that he paid. If at the time of payment, the spot price is less than Rs. 43.30 the option is out of money and he will not exercise the option; he will buy the required dollars from the spot market and his loss on the contract is $ 400 only. The importer will exercise the option only when the spot price is more than Rs. 43.34 per dollar inclusive of the premium paid for option ($ 0.04) (spot 43.30 + 0.04 = 43.34). (See the chart 17.1 above)

The reverse is the case of put option. The exercise price and premium paid may remain the same. Here, the exporter wants to sell his $ 10,000 due to be received at the end of 3 months. The put option would be "in-the-money" at any price of Rs. 43.26 or less. Break-even point is Rs. 43.26. At any price of Rs. 43.34 and above, the option would be out-of-money. If the spot price at the time of expiration date and the date of receipt of dollars, is Rs. 43.10, he will exercise the option and sell $ 10,000 to writer of the option at Rs. 43.30. That means that he will receive Rs. 4,33,000, but if he has sold in the spot market at that time, he would have received only Rs. 4,31,000. His notional gain is the difference between the above two figures, adjusted for the premium price paid for the put option. This means that he would have gained Rs. 2,000 minus Rs. 400, viz., Rs. 1,600 in the options contract. If on the other hand, the spot price has gone upto Rs. 43.60 he would not exercise his option but sell in the market and get Rs. 4,36,000 instead of Rs.

4,33,000, which he would have got under the option. From this gain, he would have to deduct the option premium paid for the contract, namely, Rs. 400. Either way, he does not lose but may gain, if at all, the loss may be only the premium paid for the option.

Currency options serve two purposes. They provide a hedge against a possible adverse moment of exchange rates. Secondly, they can be used by pure speculators whose presence in the options market adds breadth and depth to those markets.

The chart below presents the operation of the put options in the currency market.

Contract size = $ 10,000

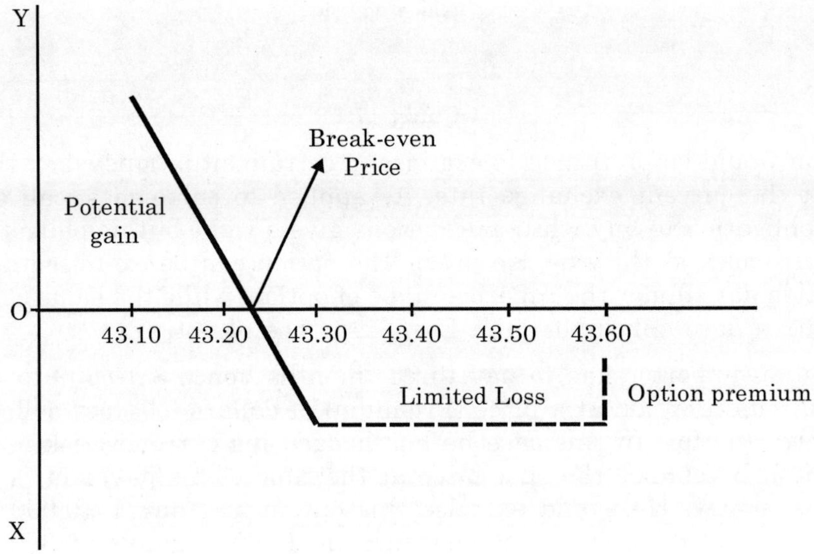


**Chart 17.2**

Option premium = Re. 0.04 per dollar

Exercise price = Rs. 43.30 per dollar

Premium paid Rs. 400 for the contract

The option holder's profit, net of the option premium paid is higher, the larger is the fall in the spot rate. If the spot rate rises above the exercise price, the option becomes valueless as he would better sell in the spot market after that, where he would get a higher price than at the exercise price.

The main users of currency options for genuine hedge are traders -exporters and importers. Many MNC affiliates buy these options if they want to be certain of how much to receive or pay in the future when the exchange rates may be uncertain. Investors or bidders for overseas firms or joint ventures or takeovers, whose requirement for funds, comes on the acceptance of bids, buy call and put options which are safer hedges than the futures and forwards. Many speculators find it better to operate in the options market where they can get better returns than in the futures and forwards.

## Differences between Futures and Options

Futures hedge offers the closest offset to the loss due to the decline in rupee value. With rapidly rising exchange rates, the company would benefit most from hedging with a long position in an option market as opposed to a futures contract. Conversely with rapidly falling exchange rates, the company would benefit most from hedging with a futures contract. Each of them, namely, futures and options have their advantages and disadvantages and each has a role in providing product differentiation in the financial markets. They deepen and widen the market and improve the liquidity and volumes in the market.

## Market Structure

Options are traded in an organised Exchange or over the counter market OTC. Exchange traded options are listed options which are standardised contracts with predetermined exercise price, standard maturities-upto 12 months each maturing in every month in most convertible currencies, which are major trading currencies of the world. Traded options are available in major exchanges like Amsterdam, Chicago and Montreal since 1983. They have grown in volume year after year.

OTC options are contracts whose specification is generally negotiated as to amount, exercise price and rights and expiration. OTC currency options are traded by commercial and investment banks in many world financial centres. The branches of international banks in major financial centres are willing to write these options against the currency of the home country as per the demand for them. The principles governing traded options are the same as those of OTC options. American types of options are widely used and options in major international currencies are available for corporates from the multinational banks operating in Euro-markets and international capital markets and having subsidiary branches in many countries.

OTC options market has two segments, namely, wholesale segment for inter bank deals and retail segment for non-bank customers. The inter-bank market in currency option is similar to the inter-bank market in spot and forward exchange. Banks provide the needed currency options to customers in retail market and cover them up in the wholesale-inter-bank market. Many MNCs and affiliates turn to the banks for hedges through options in order to find precisely the terms that match their needs. It is this retail market which is most useful to the multinational corporations. But the writers are also the multinational banks in respect of OTC options. Unlike in the spot and forward exchange, the options market exposes the writers to more risk and there is an asymmetry between the demand and supply in the option market. In India, forward rate agreements and hedging in futures are allowed in the inter-bank market, which has access to Clearing Corporation of India Ltd. (CCIL).

## Futures Options

These are options written on futures contracts. Here, the option gives the right to buy or sell the standard futures contracts, in a currency rather than the currency itself. When exercised, the holder receives a short or long position in a currency futures contract that expires one week after expiration of the option contract. The future contract is delivered exactly like the delivery of a currency, if the option is exercised. If it is not exercised, trading is done on a daily basis and profit or loss is booked from time to time. The introduction of the futures options has been hailed as an important landmark in the development of the financial markets and provides the traders, investors and speculators a wider variety of instruments to reduce the risks, or take risks for speculative instinct. This wide variety of instruments has improved the breadth and depth of the financial markets in the world over.

## Risk Management in India

RBI has announced its intention of developing interest rate swaps and forward markets for currencies. Forward rate agreements are also being provided by banks. Strips and asset backed securities have a greater role to play and a beginning has been made in India for residential mortgages and auto loans. Strips are explained later and these are all derivative markets.

Credit swaps offer advantage of hedging risk and some institutions like IDFC can take over credit risks and banks can lend against guarantee of other banks.

Active use of derivatives require the existence of term money market for 6 months to one year, which the RBI is trying to promote. Freeing of interest rates, in the money market, deregulation of term deposit rates and lending rates, freedom given to banks to determine their own rates of penalty for premature withdrawals, exemption of inter-bank liabilities from the CRR and SLR requirements are some of the steps that the RBI has taken for banks to develop their own methods of risk management. Interest rate hedge by swaps are already allowed in India since 2003.

Banks have to develop the system of ALM or asset liability management by identifying mismatches for various periods of time. Some banks can quote bid and offer rates for various periods of term money to initiate the growth of this market. FRAs (Forward Rate Agreements) and Interest Rate Swaps (IRS) would provide good hedges against interest rate risk. The development of forward currency market would also provide hedge against currency fluctuations. Derivative markets, short selling options and futures etc. are the next steps which the banks should be encouraged to adopt as techniques of risk management as much as corporates in India.

# MANAGING FINANCIAL RISKS IN INDIA

**Table 17.2**

I. Domestic risks are depicted below:

| Credit Risk | Market Risk | Interest Rate Risk | Liquidity Risk |
|---|---|---|---|

II. Foreign Risks (Unique to Foreign Markets)

| Currency Risk (Or Exchange Risk Volatility) | Interest Rate Variability |
|---|---|

## Methods of Meeting these Risks

(1) Insurance for credit risks.

(2) Asset liability matching or exposure liability to be matched by asset changes.

(3) Matching the inflows with outflows for liquidity risk management or use of Repos.

(4) Hedging the risk such as interest rate risk or currency risk.

(5) Use of derivative products like options, futures, forwards, swaps, switches etc.

## Repos

Repos are repurchase agreements involving sale and repurchase. Currently banks, and primary dealers (PDs) can create liquidity through Repos. Repos in the PSU bonds and corporate bonds have not grown but only in government securities. Repos are used by RBI to control liquidity in the economy. Repos protects from risk of illiquidity.

## Short Positions

Short positions are prohibited or restricted by the RBI and SEBI, in the debt market. But once the short sale is allowed atleast by PDs they can hedge the position without having to offload the securities in the market.

**P. L. R.:** Banks fix PLRs-one for short-term advances and the other for term loans. Now the banks are free to fix their own rates. Suppose there are no fixed PLR and banks offer floating deposit rates and accordingly change the PLR as per the deposit rate changes, then the asset liability mismatches will be less.

**R. U. F.:** Revolving underwriting facilities is to be provided by banks to corporates. This will increase the fee based income for banks and allow corporates to raise short-term funds through Commercial Paper and other methods.

## Asset Based Securitisation

The securitisation of assets is not popular in India. The book debts of a bank or a company can be converted into securities and sold off to a third party which will increase the cash flow to this company. This will remove the fluctuating stock of receivables from the company. It will be removing from the balance sheet these assets, some of which may be of doubtful character and thereby balance sheet will look healthier. Securitisation replaces receivables with funds. This will lead to better management of credit risk and asset backed securitisation enables originators to remove market risk from the interest rate mismatches by transferring it to investors, who may be institutions and FIs.

Prohibitive stamp duties and lukewarm participation of investors and lack of secondary market in them and inadequate foreclosure laws have hindered the growth of this market in India. Asset backed securitisation has great scope in India, if there are no hurdles to its growth and there is a secondary market in them. Now, there are signs of developing securitisation market in India, and some FIs have securitised their mortgaged loans and other doubtful assets into tradeable securities. The asset reconstruction companies were set up to help the securitisation of book debts and promote the market in them.

## Strips

The strips are separated instruments for interest payments as against principal amounts. This is particularly relevant to government bonds and corporate bonds. A ten year gilted bond is strippable for example into 20 half-yearly coupons for interest, separate from that of repayment of principal. Strips facilitate a risk-free zero, coupon yield curve, which can be used for pricing other instruments.

If strips have fixed interest coupon it has no reinvestment risk and the investor could get desired pattern of cash flows with certainty. Another major advantage of strips is that it helps development of a zero coupon, risk-free yield curve. This could act as a benchmark for pricing of derivative instruments. Strips also offer banks a trading instrument for Duration management.

A market for strips is yet to be developed in India. The gilted securities have no uniformity of dates for payment of coupon interest. There is no standardisation of strips for trading. The infrastructure in the form of clearing and settlement is yet to be developed, for the strips to be traded on a standardised basis. If the coupons fall due on fixed dates in a year and an auction system is developed with a proper cut off yield, the prices of strips are determined and strips become eligible for trading.

## Credit Risk Management

The traditional methods of credit risk management are operational limits to loans, loan provisioning, portfolio diversification and collateralisation. The more innovative methods are loan securitisation and capitalised derivatives, which are available internationally to manage credit risk.

Credit derivatives have flexibility and reduce costs. They allow banks to hedge the credit risk of a loan without having to assign the loan and with no deterioration in customer relationship.

Credit Derivatives fall into two categories-swap based and option based.

The swap based versions include the credit swaps, basket credit swaps and total return swaps. The option based versions include spread options and sovereign risk options.

Credit swaps allow to take over the credit risk without having to grant loan. Banks with resources may not have the risk appetite. Hence, international banks can guarantee and take the risk while the funding can be done by a domestic bank. The present practice of the bank is that if it is appraising and taking the risk it should also grant the loan. But risk of credit and granting of credit can now be dissociated and credit risk can be guaranteed or insured.

## Interest Rate Risk Exposure

RBI has suggested that the traditional gap analysis-gap in maturities of assets and liabilities is a suitable method to measure interest rate risk. Moreover, there are some interest sensitive assets and liabilities. A positive gap indicates that more assets than liabilities will reprice in a given time period. A negative gap indicates that more liabilities than assets will reprice in a given time period. Rate sensitivity is more in short-term instruments than in longer term instruments. Duration analysis can be added to gap analysis to get better insight into the interest rate exposure of an institution.

There are two methods that banks can use for meeting this gap in assets and liabilities-Direct restructuring of balance sheet items and the use of synthetic instruments, like swaps, futures, options etc. As balance sheet restructuring is difficult in the short run, banks have to have recourse to synthetic methods to the asset-liability gap management. Forward rate agreements and interest rate swaps are more frequently used. It is reported that the interest rate hedging was already allowed by the banks and F.I.s in 2003.

Forward rate agreements (FRAs) allow a borrower or lender to lock-in an interest rate for a period in the future, which thus, effectively extends the maturity of its assets and liabilities. It is an off balance sheet contract between two parties say the bank and customer, wherein one party, agrees on the start date that on a specified future date (settlement date) that party will lodge a notional deposit with the other for a specified sum of money, for a specified period of time at a specified rate of interest.

FRAs are products which banks can market to their corporate customer as part of their cash management services. The bank is left with an open interest rate position that it can close with an FRA in the inter-bank market. The customer is protected from an upward movement in interest rate by the process.

If gap analysis shows that in a particular period risk sensitive assets (RSA) are greater than the risk sensitive liabilities (RSL) and the bank expects downward movement in interest rate, it can sell FRA for an amount equal to (RSA — RSL) corresponding to the time period. If interest rates fall the squeeze in net interest income will be approximately compensated by FRA. On the other hand, if the RSL > RSA and the bank expects the interest rates to rise, the bank will buy FRA for an amount equal to (RSL — RSA).

By using FRA, the bank can lock-in its costs. The bank can sell FRAs when the loan demand does not pick up, in order to lock-in a targeted return. It may buy FRAs if it is funding longer term loans by rolling over the shorter term liabilities. In a number of situations the banks can buy FRAs to match the maturities of its assets and liabilities from an interest rate perspective.

## Interest Rate Swaps (IRS)

The interest rate swaps are over the counter contracts between two counter parties for exchanging interest payments for a specified period, based on a given principal amount. The principal amount remains unchanged but the flows of interest payments are exchanged, say from floating rate to fixed rate and so on and only cash flows are exchanged and not the principal.

IRS has the following advantages:

(1) Banks use swap transaction for trading and hedging purposes.

(2) Banks can act as intermediary for arranging IRS as between two other parties.

(3) Banks can use swaps as an integral part of their management of interest risk.

(4) Alter the cost of the existing borrowing from fixed to floating rate and vice versa.

(5) Convert the rate of return on asset from uncertainty to certainty.

(6) Generate profits or avoid losses from interest rate fluctuations.

(7) Banks can use swap deals to hedge existing assets and liabilities.

(8) Depending upon the interest rate expectations, the bank may use swap transactions to hedge to avoid losses and to adjust the duration of assets and liabilities.

The bank uses prudential norms and sets limits for unmatched positions. The capital to be maintained under capital adequacy norms will be decided by risk exposure and hence the need for cover on such exposures. Prudential norms are required to determine the extent of leverage used. Tax implications of swap payments and receipts are also to be looked into, depending whether it is interest income or other income.

What has been stated above in respect of banks is applicable to all MNCs and banks only respond to all the operations of MNCs with others or FIs. In the above paras banks' position was discussed, as most of them are MNCs and corporates use banks as intermediaries for risk coverage operation in most cases.

❖ ❖ ❖

# HEDGING IN SWAP MARKET

# 18

Swaps are useful for interest rate risk management and a detailed discussion on them is attempted. Swaps and switches are derivatives and synthetic markets among the financial markets. These can be seen in gilt-edged markets, money market, Forex market, interest rate and currency markets. These are derived from the existing instruments through exchange of one instrument for the other. Swap is defined as an exchange contract between two parties for two instruments of different yields, interest rates and currencies. Switch is also similar to swap. In gilt-edged market, banks and FIs, exchange one loan of a definite maturity and yield for another of different maturity and yield. The asset portfolio is adjusted from time to time for changes in yield, liquidity and maturity and in the process, banks require a short-term loan of two or three years when they have too many loans maturing between 5 to 10 years but less of those between 1 to 5 years. Switch is not exchange of a security for cash but an exchange of one security for another both in the spot market.

Swap is an agreement for exchanging of forward dollars for spot dollars and *vice versa* or of floating rate instrument for a fixed rate instrument. Swap is of different varieties say coupon swaps, basis swaps and currency swaps from one currency to another. It can also be an exchange of forward for spot currency. Some swaps will hedge both interest rate risk and currency risks.

Swaps and switches reduce the risks, and costs involved. They are hedge instruments, used as risk management instruments. They widen the market, increase depth and width of the market and sophistication of operations in the financial markets.

## Motivation for Swaps

The need for swaps arose out of felt needs of corporates to hedge the underlying risk and uncertainty of financial outlays and outflows. The risks may arise out of trade in merchandise items or invisible items of balance of payments. Even in capital account, foreign borrowings require both interest rate risk coverage and currency risk coverage.

In respect of domestic financial markets also all the risks mentioned above are there except for the currency risk. The swaps in the domestic markets are required for risk coverage in interest rate changes, yield adjustments, timings of inflows and of outflows to be synchronised, asset liability matching, and adjustments for duration of the portfolio. In trading in the financial markets, particularly in the gilted market, yield and price differences as between loans attract swaps. Swaps from fixed interest to floating interest rate loans is an example to adjust the yield pattern. Similarly portfolio adjustments require the change of the portfolio composition to tune the expected inflows to come at the timings of expected outlays. This is called portfolio duration adjustments.

Risk and uncertainty hedge is also an objective of swaps. For example, risk hedging can be done by a swap between floating rate loan and fixed interest loan and for shifting the basis of interest rate fixation from LIBOR based (as LIBOR plus) to one based on Treasury Bill rate or a government bond or Bank Rate. Lastly, there are two basic objectives, namely, income and capital gains in addition to hedge against risk. Swaps will enable the parties to the contract to exchange the principals at maturity at the current spot rate or predetermined exchange rate or swaps of coupon rates only are also possible. Some swaps and switches are used for tax saving purposes or for effecting capital losses to offset earlier capital gains liable to taxes.

## Economic Advantages of Swaps

Swaps provide real economic advantages to both the parties to the swap. Otherwise swap will not take place. If arbitrage functions fully and the markets are perfectly efficient, there will be no advantage in swaps. But imperfections in the markets do exist leading to differential in risk-return characteristics. The impediments to perfect markets exist in the form of legal restrictions on spot and forward deals, different perceptions of risk and credit worthiness of two parties, tax differentials, etc.

A U.S. MNC operating in Germany wanted to hold dollars although, D.M. was more stable than dollars at that time, because the operator was more familiar with U.S. dollar than with D.M. Both parties received a cost advantage because they borrowed initially in the market where it had a comparative advantage and then swapped for its preferred currency and interest rate liability.

Currency swaps save in costs, promote liquidity and depth in the markets and/or provide a hedge to the risk that the party is exposed to Currency swaps are used to help financing the long-term requirements of funds for the projects of MNCs. In many foreign countries, long-term capital forward foreign exchange markets are absent and not well developed. In this scenario swaps are useful as special purpose vehicles for meeting the financial needs of MNCs and for providing liquidity to these markets. Imperfections and absence of perfect arbitrage system help the growth of the swap markets.

## Currency Swaps

A swap contract can be entered in two or more currencies, involving two or more parties. More often than not, banks are intermediaries between two parties to the swap. An MNC, say Suzuki has borrowed in Japanese yen at a fixed rate. It wants dollars for its operation in India. It can swap its exchange risk by entering into a contract for giving dollars at a floating rate or fixed rate, for yen, it has got at a fixed rate. If it wants both exchange risk hedge and interest rate hedge, Suzuki might surrender its yen loan at a floating rate to a dollar loan at a fixed rate. Many banks- domestic and international- arrange these swaps for a charge or commission. If they do not wish to take the risk themselves they can cover it in the inter-bank market.

Currency swap is a contract or agreement and is not a loan by itself. Currency swap gives to the parties the right to offset, namely, a non-payment of principal or interest with corresponding non-payment in the other currency. In currency swap there is always an exchange of principal amounts at maturity, based on the original amounts of currency at the pre-determined exchange rate. This means that a swap contract behaves like a long dated forward exchange contract, where the forward rate is the current spot rate. Forward rates of a currency are a function of spot rates and expected interest rate differentials, according to interest rate parity theory. The differences in forward exchange rates between say U.S. dollar and German D.M. is due to differences in interest rates between USA and Germany. If a swap in interest rates is taken between D.M. and US dollars, it will automatically protect from the changes in forward rates.

## Debt-equity Swaps

This is something similar to exchange of debt for equity of the domestic companies. Financial institutions are given the right to convert their loans given to a company into equity of that company, if it has failed in repayment of instalment of debt and interest payment. This right is used very infrequently and under same conditions, when the management is recalcitrant and proved inefficient and company will go into further red, if things are not set right.

The LDC debt equity swaps relate to the debt of the domestic corporates given by international banks. Six major debtor nations, namely, Chile, Brazil, Mexico, Venezuela, Argentina and Philippines have initiated these debt-equity swaps.

During the eighties, many Latin American countries were in a debt trap unable to repay their loans to MNCs and international banks. Then the European and U.S. banks found a way of settling their debt at a discount which ranged from 20% to 50%. These debts are sold in the secondary market comprising of big commercial banks, investment banks and even MNCs, as junk bonds.

Sometimes an international bank acts as an intermediary for sale of this discounted debt in the secondary market. Suppose the Nissan Motors, an MNC operating in Mexico wanted to invest an additional $ 60 million to expand its truck factory. Citi Corp offered to get a debt equity swaps for Nissan. Citi Corp. combed the area and observed all the formalities and got a debt of $ 70 million to be given in the form of peso for an equivalent of $ 60 million-a write off of $ 10 million. The Citi Corp. gave Nissan $ 60 million in pesos for an equivalent U.S. dollars of $ 40 million, of which $ 2 million is taken away by the Citi Corp. as its fees for the deal.

Debt swaps allow investors to acquire the domestic country's currency more cheaply than official exchange rate allows. The domestic currency is given for investment in the country as equity in investment in exchange for the debt in foreign currency due by that country. The foreign currency debt is discounted by 10-50% and sold to a foreign bank in the secondary market and equivalent amount of local currency is given to the MNC, for the surrender of dollars by the MNC. This is done at a highly discounted price. In the above example Nissan paid only $ 40 million to acquire $ 60 million worth of pesos of Mexico for investment as equity in the subsidiary of Nissan in Mexico.

MNCs get a cheaper method of financing their operations in a developing country through debt equity swaps. A firm buys a country's dollar debt in the secondary loan market at a discount and swaps it into equity in the local market. The major international banks like American Express or City Corp. do the intermediation for the sale of debt in the secondary market at a discount in dollars. These dollars are sold to MNCs, who want dollars to invest as equity in those countries. It benefits both the giver and the taker. The Mexico government got $ 70 million loan paid off for $ 60 million a gain to the Mexican Government. The debt is repaid. The purchasing MNC buys these dollars for conversion to local currency of the indebted country for the operations of its subsidiaries, at a rate cheaper than the official exchange rate.

## Nature of Swaps

A swap in international parlance is an agreement between two or more counter parties to exchange the obligations arising from two or more debt instruments. These swaps are restructuring agreements of obligations from any of the debt instruments. Assume that parent company A (USA) has a subsidiary in UK called A (UK). Similarly there is a parent company B (UK) which has a subsidiary in USA, B (USA). The parent company A (USA) wants to invest in its subsidiary in U.K. and needs sterling for this purpose. And B (UK) wants to send funds to its subsidiary in USA called B (USA) and requires dollars for this purpose. Then with or without the help of an international bank to act as an intermediary, the parties can enter into a swap deal of the loans in sterling and dollar; without US company sending sterling to its UK subsidiary, B (UK) provides dollars to B (USA). These transactions can be shown in the following chart as flow of funds or swaps of loans.

SWAP OF FUNDS

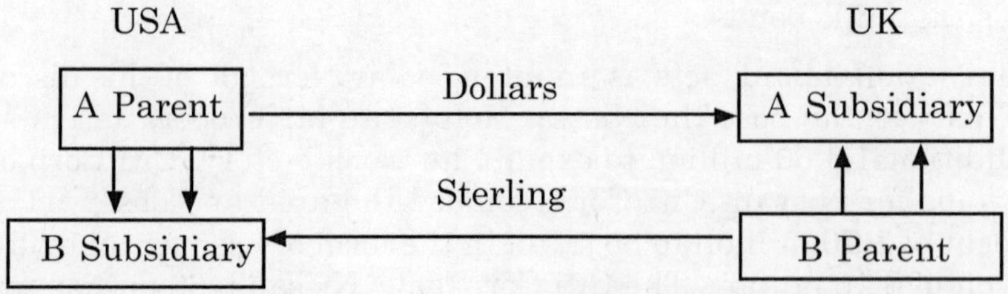


**Chart : 18 A**

In the above chart A parent has to borrow sterling as a loan and B parent has to borrow dollars as a loan. These loans can be swapped so that A parent gives dollars to B subsidiary and B parent gives sterling to A subsidiary as shown below:

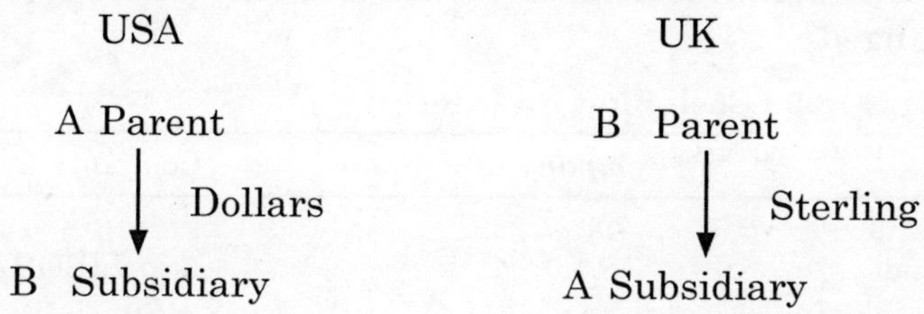


**Chart : 18 B**

## Types of Swaps

There are different types of Swaps, namely:

1. Interest Rate Swaps
2. Fixed Rate Currency Swaps
3. Cross Currency Interest Rate Swaps
4. Basis Swaps

## Interest Rate Swaps

Suppose a party has an obligation to pay a fixed rate of interest on a bond and another party has a floating rate debt instrument. If these parties exchange their interest obligations, then the principal amount remains with the original parties. The principal amount should be the same in the case of both the parties. The principal amount is not swapped, as it is in the same currency and for the same amount. Only interest rate payments are swapped, to suit their requirements and preferences.

Both the parties should gain, otherwise they will not agree to the swap. The gain will be in the form of lower costs. Consider Party A and B as shown in the following chart:

**TABLE 18.1**

| | *Credit Rating* | *Cost of Fixed Rate Funds (P.A.)* | *Cost of Floating Rate Funds* |
|---|---|---|---|
| Party A | AAA | 7.5% | 6 M Libor + 0.25 |
| Party B | BBB | 9.0 % | 6 M Libor + 0.75 |
| Comparative Advantage of A over B | | 1.5 | 0.50 |

A is rated Tripple A and cost of funds is lower for A than for B. These two parties enter into an agreement of interest rate swap. A borrows fixed rate and lends floating rate to B and B borrows floating rate and lends fixed rate. This should be a win-win situation when both parties stand to gain. For B company to do a swap, its cost of funds should be lower, below what it would have to pay, if it had to directly enter the market. 6M refers to six months libor.

The principal amount remains with the original parties and only the cash flows due to interest payments are exchanged.

**TABLE 18.2 : Cash Flow on Interest**

| | *Company A* | *Company B* |
|---|---|---|
| A borrows directly fixed rate funds | 7.5% | - |
| B borrows directly floating rate funds | | - 6 m LIBOR + 0.75 |
| A pays B floating rate interest at only Libor | - 6m Libor | + 6 m Libor |
| B pays A fixed rate interest at 8% | + 8.0% | - 8.0% |

Company 'A' borrows at fixed rate and pays 7.5%, but pays to B Libor + 0; 'B' company borrows at floating rate and has to pay 6M Libor + 0.75 but pays to A fixed interest at 8%. Here B got rid of the uncertainty of floating rate and hence, reduced the risk. A takes the risk but gets the funds at lower rate than it can get directly in the market, i.e., Libor + 0.25. The gain for each of the parties is as follows:

**TABLE 18.3**

| | *Company A* | *Company B* |
|---|---|---|
| Overall cost of funds (as shown in the above chart) | 6 m Libor -0.50 | 8.75 |
| Comparable direct Cost of funding | 6 m Libor + 0.25 | 9.00 |
| Gain | +0.75 | +0.25 |

The gain is there for both the parties, but the gain is more for the company A than company B due to its higher credit rating and its lower cost of borrowing.

## Fixed Rate Currency Swaps

Fixed Rate Currency Swaps are transactions between two parties with fixed rate interest liabilities but in different currencies. Each exchange takes its fixed rate interest liability in one currency for fixed rate interest liability in another currency. For this exchange to be effected the initial exchange rate at which the principal and fixed interest payments are to be exchanged and the subsequent exchange rate at maturity when the principal amounts have to be reexchanged are to be agreed upon. Whether the actual exchange takes place physically or it is done on a notional basis, it has to be agreed upon what are the principal amounts due at maturity and the interest amounts to be paid as per schedule. This will result in an effective transformation of debt raised in one currency into a stream of flows of fixed amounts in another currency. To be more specific A has a natural advantage of borrowing in Swiss franc, while he needs the U.S. dollars. There is another party 'B', who has borrowed in dollars and this stream of dollar payments can be swapped to 'A', in exchange for a flow of Swiss franc payments to 'B.' If B does not have inflows of Swiss franc; he has to hedge these payments through the forward exchange market. These deals are put through reputed international bankers.

The advantages are obvious: One prefers a currency in which he wants the loan and he wants a hedge so that he knows how much funds he has to set apart periodically. Lastly these swaps provide major cost savings. The swap enables the counter parties to arbitrage to have access to markets in which they are strong or have a preference. Each gets the currency which he wants and the market to deal in which he has relative strength of advantage. Unless both parties to the swap stand to gain such swap does not take place. It has to satisfy the relative preferences of each party.

## Cross Currency Interest Rate Swap

The cross currency interest rate swap is a swap of both the currency and the interest rate. A company has borrowed through a US dollar denominated fixed coupon rate bond; but the company's requirement is a D.M. denominated floating rate bond to be used for its German subsidiary. His fixed rate U.S. dollar bond is now exchanged for the floating rate D.M. denominated bond. This can be assigned through an intermediary or a bank. This should be suitable and gainful to both the parties.

The currency swap market has grown rapidly, due to the growth of local capital market and the respective Euro-currency market in a wide range of currencies. The most frequently used currencies are U.S. $, Japanese yen, German D.M., pound sterling, Canadian dollar, Swiss franc etc. More recent currency to be used is Euro.

## Multilegged Swap

In this swap market there are more than two parties and notably an intermediary bank of international operations. The bank acts as a counter party to each company and takes the risk for each company and is rewarded by a return for taking the risk. The bank provides company with what it wants, say floating rate interest bond in D.M. and takes its fixed rate interest bond in U.S. $. Similarly, for another party, it takes its floating rate interest bond in Swiss francs in return for its fixed interest bond in U.S. $. This process goes on and this may lead to the bank having uncovered risks while the companies are all hedged by the cover facilities provided by the bank. This is called Multilegged Swap.

## Basis Swaps

This is a swap of interest rate basis from one of floating on U.S. Treasury bill rate to that of LIBOR or from that of floating on Commercial Paper to U.S. Treasury bond rate etc. This refers to the basis on which the floating rate is linked. Basis Swaps also apply to cross currency swaps, where interest is on a floating rate basis in each currency.

## Interest Rate Swaps in India

Despite the halting progress of the convertibility of the rupee, the deregulation of domestic interest rates is progressing steadily. Until 1994, the RBI set the rates at which banks borrowed money and lent and the spread between them is their profit. Since 1994, the RBI has been dismantling the controlled interest rate structure. Banks can now set their own borrowing and lending rates. The only remnants of regulation is the interest rates on savings accounts and on deposits of 1 to 15 days. Similarly on the lending side, the left over controls are on the lendings below Rs. 2 lakhs, export credit and loans for housing and to weaker sections. The banks are still controlled for monetary control purposes by the CRR and SLR.

The RBI has asked the banks to set up a system under which they will be forced to recognise their cash flows and interest rate risk exposures through the asset-liability management process. The banks will now have to grapple with interest rate and liquidity risks. The interest rate swap is one instrument through which anybody can hedge risk of interest rates. Banks are already taking credit risks, which they try to reduce by better appraisal, greater care in lending and emphasis on quality lending which will reduce the bad and doubtful debts. On top of this, the flexible interest rate policy and fluctuating rates have forced banks and all players in the financial markets to run for a cover for interest rate risk.

An Interest Rate Swap (IRS) is a transaction between two parties, whereby, there is a notional exchange of and re-exchange of flows of interest and /or principal. It involves the receipt and payment of interest during the life of the swap. This exchange may involve one from fixed rate to floating rate interest payments and *vice versa.* Similarly one can hedge the rise in interest rate. One can also go short on interest rates, if he expects a fall in rates. Once the bank can hedge on interest rates they are sure of the payments and they can accordingly adjust the receipts through the lending rates. The transaction in IRS market will not attract CRR and SLR.

There is no inter-bank term money market now due to the CRR and SLR provisions. This market will help the growth of debt and derivative markets in India. RBI has allowed banks to develop IRS market in India, and has been encouraging term money market.

Banks will have to seggregate the credit risk and interest rate risk. Interest rate risks will have to be eliminated in risk management. In making any financing decision, it is now easier to come to a conclusion on credit risk that they can take and credit policy they should adopt.

IRS will reduce the spreads between banks' lending and borrowing rates and between bid and offer rates in gilts trading. The benefits that follow from this derivative market are many to both bank and non-bank participants in financial markets. IRS will develop the debt market and impart liquidity to NCD market.

One example of the benefits of this derivative market can be given by the low cost of flexible mortgage loans that the Americans enjoy. These are available to them because of a large market in mortgage backed securities and the existence of a sophisticated interest rate derivative market, there.

Accounting and documentation treatment and removal of stamp duty on such contracts of IRS will have to be accepted for IRS to grow in India. Standard futures and options contracts will have to be allowed and developed. Otherwise, IRS will grow only so far as the forward exchange market has grown.

## Interest Rate and Currency Swaps

Corporates use the interest rate and currency swaps as special financing vehicles for reducing costs and risks in financing their foreign investments. In the deregulated and free markets, there are wide fluctuations in currency rates and interest rates. Swap has led to a refinement of risk management technique which in turn led to MNCs greater involvement in the international capital market.

An interest rate swap is an agreement between two parties to exchange interest payments in a foreign currency for a specific maturity upon notional amount. This notional amount is the principal against which interest is calculated and which does not change hands. The main types of swaps are coupon swaps and basis swaps. The coupon swaps refer to the exchange of payments of interest from a floating rate basis to a fixed rate basis, and *vice versa.* The basis swap refers to one wherein two parties exchange floating interest rate payments, based on two different reference rates, one say on Treasury bond and the other on Treasury bill or on Libor.

A floating rate loan can be 50 basis points on the LIBOR rate. The basis point is 0.01% of the quoted rate. The swap is as between A and B.

**TABLE 18.4**

| *A* | *B* |
|---|---|
| Fixed rate is 13.25<br>Libor = 11.35<br>11.35 + .50 = 11.85<br>Net lock-in spread<br>1.40 | Libor+0.50<br>is the floating rate<br><br>differences is<br>13.25 – 11.85 = 1.40 |
| Fixed rate payment is 13.25<br>Floating Rate Payment Libor + 0.50; 11.35 + .50 = 11.85 | |

This is only an example and the actual rates are much lower now.

If LIBOR goes up to 13.00, then 13.00 + .50 = 13.50 will be payable by him instead of 13.25.

The hedge is set at an upper limit of LIBOR.

The banks will be counter party to provide this hedge by swap to the exporters and importers, traders and manufacturers and to any debtors in general. The banks take the risk and cover it up in the inter-bank market. In the swap segment in the currency market forward premia ranged from 4% to 7% during the years 2001-2003, reaching a peak at about 7% in March 2002.

## Advantages

Interest Swaps reduce the risk when they are acting as a hedge. They also reduce costs. When different parties have different credit rating, their cost of borrowing is accordingly decided. The differences in terms of borrowing in different markets arise due to the risk and creditworthiness of the borrowing party. Party A is having a low rating (BBB) and cannot secure at floating rate market at the rate of LIBOR. But a bank with a high credit rating (of AAA) can borrow at LIBOR. B (the Bank) then borrows at LIBOR and swaps with 'A' who borrowed in a fixed rate of 12.5% or at LIBOR + 0.50. When the LIBOR is 11% and the swap is at 11.5%, then there is no gain to A, as he can borrow at LIBOR + 0.50. If the swap is at 11.25%, and he can borrow at 11.50%, then 'A' stands to gain and reduces his cost by 0.25%. If one has to borrow at fixed rate of 12.50%, but he can borrow floating rate of 11.50% and swaps for a fixed rate of anything from 11.50% to 11.75%, he gains in costs.

'B' also gains as he has borrowed at 11.00% from the floating rate and exchanged it for 11.75%, which is still lower than what he can borrow from the fixed rate market (12.50%).

## RBI Scheme of Interest Rate Swaps

Scheduled commercial banks, excluding the RRBs, primary dealers (PDs) and all India financial institutions (FIs) are free to undertake interest rate swaps. The purposes for which they can undertake swaps as a financial product are for trading, hedge or balance sheet management or for market making. They can offer these products to corporates who wish to hedge the loans on their books. Once these institutions undertake these transactions on a regular basis they have to inform the RBI.

These transactions for hedging and trading have to be recorded separately. Those for hedging purposes shall be accounted for on an accrual basis. Those for trading purposes should be marked to the market (value at the ruling market price). The fees or income and expenses relating to swaps should be recognised in the income and expenditure statement at the time of settlement.

The participants should have to maintain the capital adequacy norms in the case of banks and FIs, in respect of these assets. The PDs have to maintain additional capital at 12% of risk weighted assets towards credit risk on interest rate contracts. They have to disclose all the details in their balance sheets on the outstanding contracts, their notional principal amount, nature and terms, etc., including information on credit and market risk and accounting practices adopted for swaps.

The fair value is the estimated amount that they would pay or receive to terminate the swap. There are no restrictions on the size or tenor of any interest rate swap. The RBI wants the market to develop and did not lay down any benchmark interest rates like money market or debt market rates.

## Repos and RBI

Repos are repurchase agreements and constitute segment of short-term financial market, open to all companies and banks for cover of rate risk and liquidity risk. Repos are an useful instrument of managing interest rate risk. There are arbitrage operations as domestic call money market and foreign exchange market. There are interlinkages among all market segments and RBI operates in this market to control the volatility in the call money and Forex inter-bank money.

The interlinkages as between these markets is through arbitrage operation to absorb the excesses or fill in the shortfalls in the Forex liquidity and in call money due to operations of MNCs and domestic companies with the banks. The Repos can be done in

Treasury bills and gilt-edged securities, which are normally the accepted channels of investment for short-term money or excess cash. MNCs can also benefit from the facility through their bankers.

There are two components of this market, namely, the operations of the corporates and banks among themselves or with foreign banks. The second component has great potential for risk management by the MNCs and is still to develop. The RBI aims at the control of liquidity and through that the interest rates in the domestic market and foreign exchange market. The volatility of foreign exchange rates caused by excess supply or demand for foreign currencies can also be controlled by Repos in approved securities, according to norms of the RBI.

Reverse repos are purchases with an agreement to sell, while Repos are sales with an agreement to buy back at a later date, say one day to 14 days. These operations facilitate risk management by adjustment of the portfolio for yield or interest rate, maturity and duration of instruments held in the portfolio of banks, both foreign and domestic. These operations help the funds flows of MNCs as a sequential or follow up step, at the international level as well.

## Spot and Forward Rates

If an importer is paying on receipt of documents, then he can buy dollars spot and the bank sells him spot dollars. But if the importer agrees to pay three or six months hence, his demand for dollars might arise only after three or six months hence. These dollars are called forward dollars and the market is the forward market. The existence of a forward market provides cover or hedge against fluctuations in exchange rates. This exchange risk falls on the banks who are buying or selling dollars forward. The banks in turn can pass on the risk to the Central Bank of the country or to a foreign bank at another centre.

Just as banks are buying and selling spot, they also do business in forward currencies. Corresponding to the spot rate of exchange, there is a forward rate for various periods. If any bank succeeds in matching forward purchases with forward sales of the same currency, it avoids "taking a position" and assumes no risk. If they do not match, the bank may have an uncovered position which it may cover with another bank which has a contrary position. If it fails to cover with a bank, it may still do so with the Central Bank of the country or with a correspondent bank abroad. If a bank takes a position uncovered, it may take a calculated risk in the hope that the rate may move in its favour or it has failed to secure a proper cover in which case it would adjust uncovered position against a spot deal or against a future sale or purchase.

Currencies purchased or sold in forward would be subject to the influences of interest rates at home and abroad. A forward currency will be at premium higher than the spot expressed in foreign currency per domestic unit quoted as Rs. 100 = $ 4.7555, as at end June 1991. Later rates were quoted as $ 1 = Rs. 31.3283 in June 1993, and $ 1 = 44.75 at end November 2004 and Rs. 48.04 at end September 2009. The premium or discount will depend on interest rates and expectations of interest rates and exchange rates. Forward premia for U.S. dollar was around 5 per cent per annum at end December, 1999, and dipped to 2-3% by May 2004, and stood at 2.57% for six months forward at end July 2009 and 8.95% in March 2014 and 7.93% in May 2014.

## Speculation

Speculation and hedging operations are taking place in free markets to take advantage of interest rate and exchange rate differentials. In the case of India, such hedging and speculation are not possible as banks are not allowed to take position in any currency beyond the minimum working balances to be kept in various centres. In a free foreign exchange market, short-term capital flows take place to take advantage of interest rate differentials and will be quickly reversed, leading to instability in the exchange rates. One-sided speculation is also very destabilising which generally the Central Bank of a country would not allow unchecked. Controls on capital account, particularly to counter such destabilising short-term flows, are in tune with the spirit of The International Monetary Fund. Speculation on a limited scale and if it is on both sides of purchase and sale is healthy and welcome to keep the balance in the market and absorb the excesses of demand/supply of currencies in the foreign exchange market.

## Arbitrage

When foreign exchange markets are free to fluctuate, the exchange rate of a currency should be the same in almost all the centres. Thus if the dollar rate per sterling is different in New York and Frankfurt, then funds would flow in either direction to take advantage of the rate differential. It is, however, possible that slight differentials might be still there due to carrying costs of moving funds from one place to another. Such operations in terms of movements of funds from one centre to another are called arbitrage operations.

Such operations can take place only if there are no exchange controls in both the countries and if funds are free to move. Thus, if either New York or Frankfurt is subject to exchange restrictions involving Central Bank supervision of funds inflow and outflow and ban on free movements, arbitrage cannot take place and differentials in rates between two countries might exist.

Arbitrage is not limited to two centres or two currencies alone. Three-point and multi-point arbitrage can also take place if the respective currencies are free. Thus, in a three-point arbitrage, the dollar-sterling rate and the dollar-franc rate are considered and the cross rate between sterling and franc should be in conformity with the above two rates. Otherwise, three-point arbitrage can take place by moving funds from dollar to franc and franc to sterling and back to dollar from sterling. Suppose the dollar-sterling rate is £ 1 = $ 2.80 and franc 350 = $ 1 and £ = 1020 francs. Starting with $ 100, one can buy up pounds, move from pounds to francs and thence to dollars back, making a gain of about $ 5 per $ 100 in the above example. Thus, arbitrage can take place as between centres or currencies at more than two centres and currencies at a time. Such arbitrage operations may be for gain in exchange rate differential or in interest rate differential as between centres. The former are called currency arbitrage and the latter interest arbitrage. An operation of simultaneous purchase and sale in each of the two markets to take advantage of interest differential is called interest arbitrage. Such deals are put through by swaps or forward deals.

The operations in the foreign exchange market are exposed to a number of risks which are difficult to foresee and forecast.

Firstly these risks may be credit risks arising out of lending to a foreign borrower whose credit rating is not known for certainty.

Secondly, there may be currency risks of trading in a currency whose stability and strength is known to fluctuate.

Thirdly, there are country risks involved in lending to a country whose political and economic strength is weak and is uncertain.

Fourthly, there are risks of fluctuating interest rates in various currencies in the inter-bank market and anticipations may sometimes go wrong.

Fifthly, there are risks of illiquidity due to mismatch between current assets and current liabilities with the result there may be a sudden need for borrowing and difficulties may arise in securing funds at short notice.

Lastly, the dealers sometimes take risks by exceeding the limits of prudent trading in a currency with the result that they may find it difficult to cover the transactions and incur losses in such a position. Such risks are more marked in international lending and borrowing and in foreign exchange and currency markets.

## Hedging and Speculation

Hedging of a transaction exposure is covering up the exposure by a suitable method of avoiding the risk arising out of currency or interest rate changes differing from the contractually fixed positions. Hedging for protection from the uncovered position to covered position, is different from speculation. Speculation refers to taking risk with uncovered position, hoping to gain from the change. The hedge requires a transaction to start with, while speculation does not need any transaction, to take up open positions, such as buying a currency like dollar with the hope that it will appreciate for selling at a profit. Similarly, one can make a deposit in Euro at a higher rate and gain interest advantage over dollar which has a lower interest rate, starting with dollars in the currency markets.

Hedging of a transaction may take place in different forms, like passive approach or active approach, depending on the nature of the exposure. To give an example, invoice currency exposure may be left unhedged, if the currency is expected to be stable or controlled. This is passive hedging. Active hedging refers to buy forward, the currency in which it is invoiced. Hedging of a series of transactions, say bills receivables and payable in U.S. dollars on netting basis, can be done covering all the exports and imports of the firm or its receipt and payments in dollar. When there are different methods of hedging, like futures, options etc., the cost of hedging has to be taken into account in choosing the right hedge.

Sometimes the amount of currency to be received is fixed in terms of home currency but timing of it is uncertain due to time involved in transit of the goods shifted. Then the hedge can be effected by buying option to be settled in a period of time say in 3 to 4 months option forward for delivery of 3 to 4 months. A forward to forward contract can be entered as a swap of selling a foreign currency and buying the same amount at a later date, and *vice-versa.*

Hedging can be of varying amounts or varying time periods, depending on the transactions, exports, imports, remittances, inflows or outflows, etc. It can be in Forex market, currency market by forwards, futures, etc.

Speculation refers to taking positions deliberately with a view to book profit by changes in exchange rate or interest rate. Speculation takes the risk and it is a high risk and high reward scenario. One way of looking at it is that not hedging a position in a currency or interest rate exposure is speculation. Another way of looking at it is to take deliberate position, to profit from it. The speculator may gain or lose, depending on the future changes. A speculator can trade in currencies, buy one currency, dollar in the hope of its appreciation and sell these dollars after appreciation into rupees back. Suppose, Euro interest rates are higher than in dollar, keep a Euro deposit of three to six months and sell these Euro back for dollar and speculator gains if the dollar does not appreciate during the period.

Speculation in futures market and in option market is more patent example of pure speculation. A trader in currencies takes open position in futures, as they are having intermediate cash flows or one can buy or sell them at any time before maturity. A position in futures can be liquidated before maturity of the contract while forwards have fixed tenure. A pure speculator operates in the options market where put and call options can be combined and he can take open position and take limited risk many times. There is thus basic difference between hedging and speculation and international finance manager should be clear in his choice of dealing with the exposures in the transactions that he undertakes in the course of his business.

❖ ❖ ❖

# OPERATIONAL EXPOSURE — RISK MANAGEMENT

# 19

## What is Operational Exposure?

Any corporate operating in international economic and commercial transactions is exposed to the risk of changes in exchange rates, currency rates and inflation rates in the respective countries. These rates are interrelated in the sense that the inflation and cost of living influences the interest rates, which in turn influences the exchange rates. Reference was already made to how exchange rates are determined and the influence of purchasing power parity as between any countries on their exchange rates. Inflation rates also influence the interest rates as the latter are a cost or return on monetary funds and the former influences the time value of money and is influenced by it.

Exchange rates influence the firm's assets, liabilities and all its financial statements. Their effect is felt on input costs, output mix, and the cash flows of the firm. In a sense, the transactions and transaction exposures from flows of funds or the flow of goods and services lead to accounting exposures resulting in changes in financial statements, income and expenditure statements, and balance sheets. The net effect of these operations exposures of exchange rates is on cash flows and on net profits after taxes.

All operational decisions of the firm, namely, the input-output mix, input sourcing, product/market mix, financing and investment decisions are all influenced by exchange rate if they operate in more than one country and one currency. The impact of exchange rate changes can be both direct and indirect. The impact is direct on input sourcing, inter-branch transfers, and cost of production. The impact is indirect if the firm is dependent on another firm importing from abroad for its inputs or output mix. Inputs include financial inputs, which can be sourced from local currency sources or foreign sources depending on their relative costs and accessibility. Direct impact is felt on costs and prices of the firm and indirect impact is felt through income effects of customers and suppliers who depend on foreign sourcing. An exporter of domestic goods with domestic inputs only will have a different impact from that of an exporter, with an import content from abroad. An exporter or importer with domestic sourcing of inputs will have different impact from that of on an exporter or importer with foreign sourcing or a mix of domestic and foreign agencies. If a firm has production facility in the same country as the input sources, like Japanese Toyota setting up a manufacturing unit in India, then the determination and denomination of operations will be in the same currency, avoiding the operational exposure. But MNCs operate in relative low cost currencies, while their inputs are secured in other low cost currencies. Thus, the American software company may go for B.P.O. in China or India for low wage labour expertise but production is in the home country and exports to EU and other countries.

Lowering or raising of costs may occur for MNC due to operations exposure, leading to price changes of the output. If the market for output is inelastic, price can be raised or kept unchanged. If the demand and the market for the output is highly competitive, the MNC firm has to sell at the set price and change the composition of output or lower the costs of inputs. The exposure effect on the firm depends on the market structure — highly competitive oligopolistic or monopolistic — and on the classification of demand and supply. The firm affected by the exchange rate change can raise the price of the product for sources if it has a monopoly as in the OPEC countries or Airlines Services. The firm facing inelastic demand can also set the prices but not in a country with a set of domestic suppliers and a high degree of competition. There are also a host of other factors affecting the operational exposure and the firm's reaction to it. The labour cost and trade union activity, wage flexibility, hire and fire policy, tariffs, taxes and government regulation etc. in the host countries would also affect the firm's decisions in this regard.

## Nominal and Real Exchange Rates

As referred to earlier the exchange rates, interest rates and the purchasing power of currencies are all auto-correlated. Their influences need to be understood on the operations of the firm. Exchange rates influence the costs and cash flows of the firm, which in turn lead to price changes. The price changes lead to income changes of shareholders and of the public in general, which in turn has repercussions effect on the purchases from abroad. The income effects on the respective countries result in demand changes of consumers which again lead to further price effects and further income effects and so on. To break this cycle, exposure effects are to be offset by corresponding policy changes by the firm. The micro decisions of the firms operating abroad have thus both price and income effects at the macro level. The final net result becomes indeterminate and unmeasurable. The reactions of the firm to these changes in exchange rates have to be studied separately.

In this context, nominal and real exchange rates have to be distinguished. Nominal rates are those as quoted by the banks in the respective countries in nominal currencies.

The real exchange rates are those which are adjusted by interest rates in the respective countries and by the trade weights, according to the volumes of trade as between the countries. References may be made to real effective exchange rate (REER) and nominal effective exchange rate (NEER) as published by the RBI in their monthly bulletins. There are two series — one with 6 country trade based weights and the other with 36 country bilateral weights. The REER indices are adjusted for the wholesale price index (WPI). Both NEER and REER are in the form of indices, with base 1985 = 100 in respect of 36 country bilateral weights and with different bases of 1993-94 = 100 and 2008-09 = 100 for 6 country trade based weights. For the methodology of calculation and for the data, the reader can refer to RBI Bulletin and the July 1998 issue of the bulletin in particular.

## Nature of the Exposure

The operations exposures to exchange rates whether nominal or real, are in the form of the changes in the costs and cash flows in particular. They influence all physical and financial transactions as goods, services and flow of funds are all influenced by exchange rates and interest rates. The relative cost of goods, services, financial inputs and other inputs are influenced, if they are involved in foreign sources and foreign currencies. Even if the inputs of a firm may appear to be from domestic sources, in reality, these inputs may have some import content from abroad. Besides some firms access foreign funds for working capital (accounts payable) or investment (long-term debt or equity), affecting, the income expenditure account and balance sheet.

The impact is felt on the costs, price and quality of output and input mix and output mix. The production function, being inflexible, in the short run, there are some adjustments which are not open to the firm like changing production function or output mix. The firm has flexibility only in respect of pricing if the market conditions permit and quantity of sales as between different countries, if opportunities are given. The costs and prices affect sales of the firm and the expected and final cash inflows or net profit after tax. As the firm's objective is maximisation of shareholders' wealth, it will only try to increase the cash inflows and will not accept a fall in it. To obviate the fall in inflows, the firm reacts by changing the invoicing currency into home country's currency.

If a currency appreciates, it will discourage exports and inflow of funds. If it depreciates, it will discourage imports and encourage exports. In the quotations of rupee which is indirect method, as so many rupees for dollar or sterling, depreciation means giving more rupees for dollar or sterling. Appreciation of the rupees means forgoing less rupees for dollar or sterling or any other currency.

## Quality and Price Factors

The effects on price and quality depend on many factors. The more important factors are as follows:

**1. Geographical Coverage of the Market:** The market can be a big or small market and integrated market or segmented market and the market share of the firm may be small or big. The impact is more if it is geographically a big market and is a segmented market, where product or brand differentiation, apparent or real, is possible.

**2. Demand and Supply Elasticities in the Market:** Whether in the input market or output market elasticities are low or high depend on the nature of the product or service and tastes and preferences of consumers or users of services. If the product is inelastic in demand, the price changes can be effected more easily. But if the elasticities are high or the demand is elastic, competition will be significant and the firm has to sell at the set prices. Then the firm has to make adjustment in costs and input sources.

**3. Availability of Substitutes:** If the output of the firm has domestic substitutes in the foreign market or from other countries, then the price and quality changes are difficult to implement. For example petroleum and diesel have no effective substitutes for the automobile industry and this led the OPEC countries to change the quantities and prices of crude petrol in terms of dollars, as they wish.

**4. Dominance of Producer or Consumer:** If the firm is the dominant producer of the product it can influence and set the price for others to follow. On the other hand, if the consumer or the firm using it as input is the dominant part of the market it can influence the demand and makes it difficult for the supplier to change the price and quantity. The firm producing the product has little to choose except to cater to the need of the user or the consumer at the quantity and price set for it.

**5. Degree of Competition and Interference:** If the market is free and competitive, either for inputs or outputs, price is determined by the market forces and the foreign firm can sell its products at around the market price. If the market is of varying degrees of oligopoly and market interference by the governmental agencies in quality and price is prevalent, then the impact of the exposure varies with the capacity of the firm to adjust to the market requirements as set by the government as in the case of some pharmaceuticals in India.

**6. Currency Composition of Input and Output:** The impact of the exposure on the firm's operations depends on the nature of currencies for inputs or outputs. If all inputs are of domestic origin but all outputs are sold in foreign currencies, then the nature of the impact depends on the nature of currencies, whether they are depreciating, or appreciating, or relatively stable, freely fluctuating or managed floats etc.

## Firm's Reaction

The MNCs firm will generally source from the cheapest source for inputs and sells at prices at which the market can bear. The variable costs are to be covered generally, but the operating margin will vary with the sale price. There is supposed to be a relation of market integration to the coverage of variable costs; the higher the competition, the higher is the risk of exposure of the market. Similarly the more is the coverage of variable costs, in addition to fiscal costs, the more is the risk, given the *ceteris* condition. Currency mismatch of input and output markets is the vital factor affecting the exposure of the firm. If both the inputs and outputs are denominated in the same currency, the operational exposure is minimal. This is true only in the case of domestic companies or the subsidiaries of the parent company, set up and registered in a foreign country where inputs are available or output is sold there only. The example is the British Oil Companies, exploring and refining oil in India and selling back in India only. So is the case with some foreign subsidiaries, like Glaxo in pharmaceutical industry in India.

## Transaction Effect

There are thus many forces that operate in the operational exposure of the firm. Many MNCs have burnt their fingers without proper coverage of the risks during the currency crisis of many countries in eighties and nineties and in particular dollar depreciation and Asian currency crisis in the nineties, following the opening of their currency with full convertibility. India was wiser in this respect that it opted for a slow opening of the country with only Current Account Convertibility in 1994 but with varying degrees of capital account controls. The result is that India and China are thus today favoured destinations for MNCs to invest and trade.

The cost and price effects of the operational exposure are also dependent on the degree of inflation at home and in the trading partners. Inflation affects the purchasing power party and exchange rates, if completely left free to operate. But with varying degrees of market interference by the government and regulatory bodies, the impact of conversion effect in respect of exposed currencies is rather accentuated by the "pass through" effect, which percolates from market to market and through the whole set of operations in the input and output markets. All these currency operations and their effects emanate from the "transactions effect" during physical purchase of goods and services as inputs and the sale of the outputs in other markets. Transaction effects lead to conversion effects and the risks in the commodity markets are perpetuated by the risks in the financial markets.

Exchange rate changes lead to complications of demand changes for the products in question through changes in prices, incomes and expenditure of people, and through changes in interest rates, cost of living etc. These changes in cost of living lead to trade union demands and wage increases and employment changes. For example, in the US the appreciation of dollar led to rise in import prices and cost of living resulting in an uptrend in unemployment and interest rates were lowered in late nineties. There are thus complex interrelations of exchange rate changes in the economy and the firm.

# POLITICO ECONOMIC RISKS AND OPERATIONAL EXPOSURE

One of the initial points to consider is the country risk that the MNC firm faces which are dealt with in a later chapter. It is in the form of political risks of confiscation of investments. There are controls on location and sectoral investments, caps on the levels of investment, exchange controls and limit on transfer of funds or royalties or profits, etc., trade controls in the form of tariff barriers and quotas for exports. Controls of the government in any field of the operations of the MNCs are not welcome. At present, many controls of the governments have been liberalised as members of W.T.O. and the government policies have been maintained as stable with bilateral investment guarantees between countries and liberal policies are pursued by most developing countries in Asia, opening up avenues for trade and investment by foreign countries. Both foreign direct investment and portfolio investments are permitted freely. Exchange controls on current account have been abolished in India and foreign exchange market is freed for free inflows and outflows. Country ratings which helps the MNC firms to decide to enter a country or not are available by international standard rating companies like Moodys and Standard and Poor.

Economic risks are changes in economic policies, taxation of a discriminating nature. Controls of industrial policy changes, quality controls and distribution and advertisement restrictions may also hinder the entry of foreign firms into a country. As adjunct to these controls, social responsibilities and corporate good governance norms may sometimes be inhibitive. But presently, business ethics, social responsibilities and good corporate governance are observed by all MNCs and there should be no difficulties on this account. There are social inhibition of some communities in a society against foreign goods particularly in respect of consumer goods, as happened in India in sixties and seventies with regard to entry of Pepsi, Coco-Cola, burgers and pizzas, etc. Since 1992 economic reforms in India, all these hurdles were swept away and the socio-political risks are therefore almost nil or negligible. There may still be some problems of terrorism, aggressive trade union activity, controls on free pricing as in the case of pharmaceuticals, etc. The country risks are also covered in another chapter.

## Measurement and Management

Measurement of the operational exposure would be difficult with such sets of complex relations of the micro actions of the firm on macro variables and *vice versa*. Even if an attempt is made, as some researches and authors have done, they would be undependable and unrealistic. In practice, it is to be admitted that measurement is not a way to the management of the operational exposure. Yet some authors have used statistical technique of regression of exchange rate changes on the rate of change of firm's cash flows.

**TABLE 19.1**

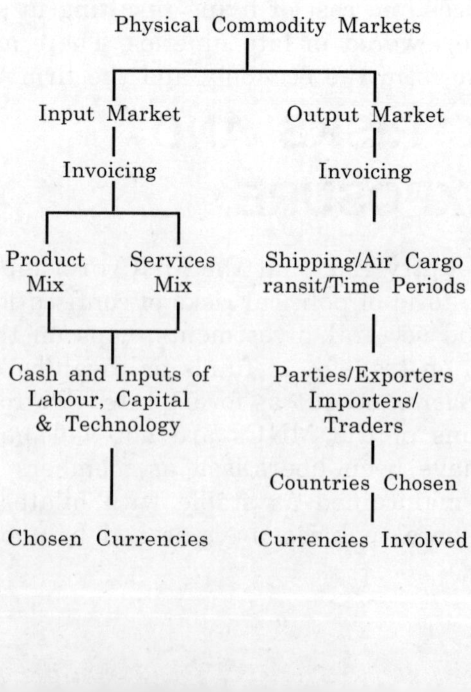


**TABLE 19.2**

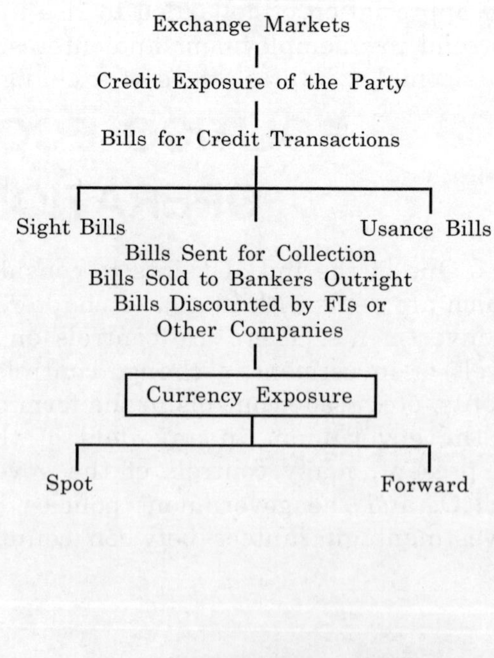

Firstly, the assumption of linear relationship is not acceptable and without going into the complex multivariate models, it should be stated that there is no continuous series of data on some macro economic changes which influence exchange rates as these are *ad hoc* and depend on government policies and there are many imperfections and interferences in the markets in the respective countries.

Secondly, there are a multitude of factors, which influence cash flows, other than exchange rates. There is no theoretical justification for a unique relation between a firm's cash flows and the exchange rate changes.

Thirdly, other factors influencing the cash flows do not remain constant and unchanged to assume any linear relationship between exchange rates and cash inflows of a firm.

In this context, it is better to study the methods of covering exchange rate exposure instead of any measurement. To start with, the exposure is classified into those of two markets.

## Proper Invoicing

Management of operational exposure can be, in effect started with right invoicing in a currency which is stable or in home currency. Shipping or air transport risk are insurable and do not constitute a major exposure. Time involved in transit or in bills or credit instruments is generally accounted for in the quoted exchange rates spot or Forward in the form of interest component.

## Need for Proper Sourcing

Firms generally plan their capital budgets to take into account the input sourcing; labour (wages), capital (interest rate) and technology (input-output matrix) and the problems involved therein. They plan to resort to outsourcing in respect of inputs and spare parts. They set up subsidiaries or joint ventures to avoid problems with local labour, laws and rules and regulations. Accounting risk is also covered by sourcing all inputs in one currency which has the market potential for the output sales. This is not always possible, as generally a firm faces a scenario of many sources of input and many outlets for sale of output increasing many currency baskets. In such a case, accounts payable and accounts receivable may be matched in each of the currencies, concerned in transactions, to reduce the operational exposure.

In the case of counter party exposure in another country, the exporter/importer gets the credit information from its banker or Exim bank in India, out of their own sources. In some cases, the credit information on the counter party can be got at some cost and time involved in the process. This will then cost the exporter/importer additional charges. Bills of credit and other credit instruments, whether usance or sight bills have an element of time involved whose cost is included in the exchange rate, quoted by the bank. These transactions as also transactions of funds flows, borrowing funds in the currency markets etc. involve the cost of interest rate risk in addition to exchange rate risk for the MNC firm, operating in any country.

## Hedging Risk Exposure

Hedging of the operational risk is thus possible in all its operations. Firms take them in the normal course, as part of their activities. Forward rate agreements and interest rate hedges through swaps and futures are possible. Forward premium over the spot rate includes the charges for interest rate differential between the countries, for which the exchange rates are quoted and also the cost of interest involved for time period of the forward contract or forward rate. The data on forward premium are available in the publication of the Handbook of statistics on the Indian economy, and reference is made to this in another chapter. Forward rate may be also at a discount if the future is more certain and better than the spot in the expectation of the traders. It can thus be seen that in the exchange market, all the risks of operations are amenable to hedge cover.

In the commodity markets also, there are futures market for many agricultural product and the risk involved in these commodities can be hedged in the future market. Many banks in India are being permitted to operate in the commodity futures as in the case of interest rates and exchange rates. In the case of manufacturers or intermediate products the trade contracts entered into between the exporter and importer specify the quality, quantity and other requirements. There is no risk involved, if the terms of the contract of agreement are adhered to by the firms.

It will thus, be seen that firms do not take seriously the operational risk exposure, as the risks can be covered for or hedged. A prudent firm foresees these risks and provides for them in their short-term plans. Operationally and empirically there is not much evidence to suggest that MNCs are inhibited by the operational exposure in any country.

But these risks have a cost and risk coverage drains the cash flows. The firm's profitability is affected thereby. But the short-term plans can take care of these costs and accounting for the risks and returns can be effected.

## Cost and Time in Hedging

It is only in the long run that some adjustments in product mix or market mix can be made. Technological changes take time and involve costs. So is the case of foreign long-term capital investments. It is in this context that the choice of foreign branches or a subsidiary or joint ventures has to be made for operations. Mergers and acquisitions have presently become very common in the global context.

Pricing, costing, input sourcing, change of product and market mix require, of course, a good degree of flexibility in the firm's operations. If the demand for any product is highly elastic, the firm has to shift to near substitute product which is less elastic. The shift of product lines, change in the composition of the output, changing the brand name, advertisement and sales promotion may help in some respects. In the case of input sources, there can be greater flexibility in some lines, but in the case of many natural resources like oil, petroleum, minerals, the choice may be limited. If the exchange rate fluctuations are very high in some countries, the firm can shift to sources with less fluctuations although it may involve higher costs. There is a trade-off as between costs of exchange rate changes and costs of shifting input sources. There is a greater degree of freedom in shifting the sources of financial inputs — short-term funds sourcing and borrowing in the international currency markets at the present juncture. This, of course, assumes the current account convertibility of the currencies covered.

More difficult is the changes in location of production and input-output matrix, or changes in composition of inputs and output, as they involve technological changes or R and D efforts. MNCs spend a considerable amount of their profit on the research and upgradation of technology. This requires a long-term strategy.

## Matching of Currencies

The best way to hedge the operational exposure is the matching of input and output sourcing currencies. In other words, the firm has to arrange input sourcing in the currencies where outlets for output are also available. The matching of revenues and costs can be done by outsourcing or B.P.O. in countries with low cost efficient labour which have also good geographical coverage of the market. Many U.S. firms are outsourcing in India and China for their software and hardware components of the electronic goods. Globalisation of corporate activity is based on this ground, also that inter-firm trade will be free, and funds transfer and outsourcing will be easier.

Matching of revenue and costs is the need of the MNC firms, which they may secure through globalisation of operations and matching of the input and output sourcing currencies. It is easier said than done, in view of the difficulties of time involved, efforts to be taken and costs of the changes to be effected. There is a trade-off in the reduction of costs of operational exposure with the reduction of operational revenue or net cash inflow.

## Impact of Taxation

Here, the effects of taxation in the respective countries, economies or diseconomies of scale and a host of other factors are considered, but assumed to be favourable to the MNC. Besides, in view of the difficulties of forecasting or foreseeing the currency risk profiles and operational rigidity many firms do not attempt at assessment and quantification of their operational risks. They take for granted that their existence is real and they are a part and parcel of their operations. Even bigger MNCs have not been found to make any conscious effort at tracing these risks, quantification and making planned efforts at reducing them. But in practice they are found to be using financial hedges, forward rate agreements, swaps, futures, options, etc. which are discussed in other chapters. The impact of taxation is reduced by transfer pricing and reinvestment policies.

## Short and Long-term Effects

Distinction should be drawn between short-term risks and long-term risks. Short-term operational risks include the impact of exchange rate changes and interest rate changes in costs, selling price and quantity of output and similar changes in inputs. These are hedged normally by the firm through the operations in the commodity markets and outsourcing at least indirectly through their bankers. There are commodity futures markets, where hedging is possible and financial derivative markets where bankers operate for transactions hedging of the exporters and importers. In this context it should be admitted that this is possible only with some bankers and with bigger MNC firms, who can operate in the domestic and foreign short-term financial markets, namely, domestic money market and Forex market, of course, through their bankers who have contacts abroad and are authorised to deal in foreign exchange.

In this context, it should be clearly set out here that the operational exposure is a combination of two effects, namely, conversion effect and competitive effect. The conversion effect involves the change of foreign currency inflows into home currency inflows, which is hedged by covering up in forward exchange markets and futures and proper invoicing. The competitive effect is the impact of exchange rate changes on changes in prices and quantity. This is similar to the transactions exposure which is difficult to measure and quantify. The nature of the impact will depend on many considerations including the structure of the markets for inputs and outputs. These output and quantity changes depend on foreign inflation and domestic inflation, nominal exchange rate changes and the corresponding real effective rate changes. The macro factors of inflation, wage flexibility, labour union activity and income effects have their impact on the micro-variables of the firm. Similarly, the micro factors of the firm have their repercussions on the macro variables.

The long-term exposures refer to changes in the firm's location, production technology and product mix and market mix. The long-term effects are covered by mergers and acquisitions, changes in patents, brand names and product lines. The extent of coverage depends on the flexibility and management ability to withstand the rigours of these changes.

## Micro and Macro Effects

Exchange rate, interest rate and inflation which effect the firm are macro variables which influence the micro variables of the firm in the form of costs, prices and quantum of inputs and outputs. The macro changes have their impact on the firm's operational exposure both short-term and long-term in nature, which have been referred to above. But in the same way, the micro operational aspects of the firm leave their impact on macro factors, through for example their effects on wages, paid to labour, employment and unemployment, the extent of their borrowings from domestic and foreign sources, which will affect the interest rates, the cost of living of the people through their price effects and their income effects. The price effects have effects on incomes of people and this in turn have their effects on demand for their products and have further repercussions on micro operations of firms. There is thus, a circular relationship of micro and macro variables of the MNCs and the economy.

## Conclusion

The chapter has set out the nature of the firm's exposure to operations from the foreign exchange and currency markets. Attempts made to measure and quantify these exposures have partial effects. Short-term effects are generally covered by financial and operational hedges. The long-term effects are supposed to make changes with firm's basic fundamentals. Operational exposure is generally taken for granted by many firms and they are taken care in the normal course of their activity.

# MEASUREMENT OF POLITICO-ECONOMIC RISKS (COUNTRY RISK MANAGEMENT)

# 20

## Introduction

MNCs operate in many countries and some of them are developing and not so developed. Many of them have their own problems of political instability, lack of continuity in policies and undependability of the bureaucracy and corruption at all levels and too many controls. These controls take the form of credit and monetary controls, fiscal and financial controls and foreign exchange controls. For MNCs to operate in production and marketing in such countries is highly risky as these will jeopardise the basic objectives of MNCs, namely, maximisation of profits, minimisation of costs and the optimisation of their shareholders' wealth.

The interests of MNCs lie in free trade, free markets, private enterprise, free and unfettered investment opportunities, uncontrolled and liberalised procedures and practices for investment, production and marketing and not only to make profits but to repatriate them back to their home country. MNCs invest in other countries for diversification and reduction of risk, expansion and larger assets for growth and increased profits and larger shareholders' wealth. If these objectives of MNCs are frustrated by countries, there is no point in investing or trading in these countries. Herein lies the importance of country risk for MNCs, viz., the sovereign risk of the government, political and social risk, economic risks and credit and market risks etc., of the host countries.

In the international borrowing and lending as well, the country risk is relevant as the debt service and repayment capacity of each of the country varies. The factors to be looked into are not only the repayment capacity of the company borrowing, but that of the country in allowing conversion of their currency for repayment to foreigners through an internationally accepted convertible currency like dollar, sterling or yen. Here again the country risk is relevant for the MNCs to trade and invest in other countries.

## Why Risk Rating?

In international borrowing, the risk of a country varies depending upon a number of factors. As in the case of internal borrowing by companies the risk of a company is rated, so in international borrowing, risk of country is also rated. The risk arises out of factors such as large existing debt, high debt service ratio, poor export and foreign exchange earnings and reserves etc. The risk is of default or delay in payment of interest and repayment of principal.

The company's borrowing and repaying capacity in international markets depends not only on the company's credit rating, its debt equity ratio, its leverage, current ratio and its earning potential and debt servicing capacity, but also on the country's sovereign debt servicing capacity, as the company's payments in rupees have to be converted into convertible currencies like dollar and this depends on that country's ability to earn foreign exchange and maintain the convertibility of the currency. The country's risk is the potential inability of the country to repay debts in foreign currencies due to poor exports and low foreign exchange earnings and the extent of the changes in the exchange rate of the domestic currency or depreciation or appreciation which will change the amount of rupees to be given for a given amount of foreign currency to be paid to the lender.

## Cost and Availability of Foreign Funds

There are two factors involved in the country risk-one is the cost and the other is availability of foreign exchange to convert rupees into dollars. The greatest risk is the default of the country to repay the international debt or even to pay the interest instalments as it happened in the case of some Latin American countries like Mexico. Some countries ask for rescheduling of debts which tantamounts to default only.

## Debt Burden of Countries

International banks who are the major lenders across borders face this problem of sovereign debt reschedule as the borrowing country is unable to service or repay the debt as per the normal repayment schedule. During seventies, the oil surpluses of the OPEC countries were used to lend to the Latin American Countries. Due to high inflation rates in the debtor countries, and their continued deficits in balance of payments due to the restrictive trade policies of developed countries and due to fall in commodity prices which are export products of developing countries, in early eighties, interest rates in international markets rose fast and debt servicing burden became explosive. Many Latin American developing countries including Mexico witnessed increasing hardship and Mexico declared moratorium on its debts.

In fact, lending banks have to infuse fresh funds to keep the debt burdened countries going. Their debts are scheduled and sometimes more funds are provided to tide over their balance of payments crisis. The lenders were kept at the mercy of the debtors and this led to some drying up of funds in the eighties. The book debts and bad debts of these countries were securitised as junk bonds and sold at heavy discounts in international markets, thus, raising the interest rates.

Thus the interest rate charged on international lending depends on the country-rating. The tools of country risk assessment have come to be used widely. The internationally reputed agencies like Moodys and Standard and Poor have been doing this job of country-rating with the help of a highly efficient expert research staff with them for this purpose.

## Credit Risk and Country Risk

There are two components of risk which international lending involves, namely, Credit Risk and Country Risk. In the case of a corporate borrower, its credit rating has to go together with country risk rating. Credit Risk depends on the risk of the borrowing company's ability to meet its debt service obligations, represented in the risk of Business, Financial Risk, Market Risk, Labour problems, restrictions on dividend distribution, fluctuations in profits and a host of other company related problems. Country Risk is reflected in the Balance of Payments Position-export earning capacity of the country, its GDP growth and inflation rate and existing infrastructure and regulatory framework etc.

To influence the Country Risk, there are both quantifiable and qualitative aspects of the country. The quantifiable factors are given weightage by the rating agency, according to their perception of the importance of each of these factors. Both these factors are referred to below for illustration. These are included in the analyst's assessment, in general to the extent that they are quantifiable and form part of the statistical and econometric models built by the rating agency for risk rating. Those which cannot be quantified but are invariably considered are political stability, socio-political factors, stability of economic and financial policies, extent of restrictions or freedom in the economy, relations with other countries, nature of the political and economic system and many more such factors. Some models are built taking these factors and quantification of these factors, including some qualitative factors like political risk, which is very important to be omitted in any model for assessment of the country risk.

## Quantifiable Factors

The quantifiable factors which are invariably taken into account in all rating exercises are listed here and some quantifiable weight is also given to them in the exercises conducted by the credit rating agencies.

(1) *GNP and rate of growth of GNP:* This indicates the economic activity, its stability and the rate of growth of this indicator, shows the progress, maturity of the system and the strength of the economy to withstand the vicissitudes of nature of business cycle fluctuations.

(2) *Sectorial growth of the economy:* say that of agriculture, industry and services. The more balanced is the sectorial distribution, the better is the country in its growth prospects.

(3) *Infrastructural Industries:* social and economic infrastructure, etc., which creates the right basis for economic growth to be sustained.

(4) *Population growth* is a relevant variable for a developing country and high density countries like India and China, whose population constitutes a significant proportion of world population. Population growth rate decides the per capita product and income and the potential for the growth of standard of living. The population and its expenditure pattern decides the market pattern, depth and width of the market and potential for growth.

(5) *Savings and Investment growth rates:* Savings as a proportion of GDP and similarly investment as a proportion of GDP throw light on the extent of domestic savings which can finance investment and the extent of the dependence on the foreign funds for the domestic investment in the country. A country which depends more on foreign funds is more susceptible to instability and fluctuations in investment and growth of the economy.

## External Debt and Debt Service Ratio

External debt involves two types of debt burden-one of finding rupee resources and second exchanging the rupees for foreign currency. In exchanging, the foreign exchange market will witness the selling pressure and rupee may depreciate in the process. External debt burden is measured by its proportion to GDP and debt servicing burden is measured by the interest payment and any repayment instalments of debt divided by the foreign exchange earnings. If the debt service ratio is as high as 100% as in the case of some Latin American countries, then rescheduling of debt is done and it is a high risk and default scenario. This position is also seen in some African countries like Libya, Nigeria, etc.

Composition of debt is equally important. If the bulk of the debt is of shorter nature, this is more risky than when the bulk of the debt is of long-term nature. The softer debt structure which means a larger proportion of softer debt at low rates is less risky than a large proportion of commercial debt which is generally at higher interest rates. Similarly if loans are from IDA, World Bank and IMF, these are least burdensome and hence, less risky. Multilateral debt and untied debt is least risky as compared to bilateral and tied debt. The stable exchange earnings and lower debt service ratio will lead to lower risk of the country.

## Balance of Payments Position

To assess the impact of balance of payments, one has to study the structure of trade, payments, inflows and outflows. The lower is the elasticity of exports which happens in the case of most agricultural and primary products, the volatility of exchange earnings is more. Similarly, the poor elasticity of imports will lead to larger import payments. This is the case of imports of essential raw-materials, oil, food stuffs etc. Not only the elasticity of supply is poor but the elasticity of demand in importing countries is high, which makes the primary commodity exports, very volatile and poor export earners. The terms of trade move against such countries which depend upon primary exports.

Export structure and import structure will reveal the vulnerability of balance of payments going against the country leading to volatility of exchange earnings. The higher the volatility of exports the more risky is the country. The other factors to be considered are the Current Account and Trade Account deficits and whether they are in manageable limits. The high risk countries will have perpetual trade deficits and even current account deficits. The questions to be asked of any basket of exports are how diversified they are and about quality of exports -how much value added components have they got and how much is high value and low bulk exports. The question of technology imports and the absorption of technology and the extent of royalty payments are also considered. If imports are to be paid in hard currency like dollar, then the level of foreign exchange earnings of the country is important.

## Foreign Exchange Reserves

These are the total of gold, foreign currencies and foreign exchange assets of the Reserve Bank and the government, which are available for meeting the deficits in balance of payments. If the country has Current Account convertibility as in the case of India, these reserves are also used to support the value of the rupee and offset undue fluctuations in the value of the rupee. So a high level of reserves, say equivalent to 12-month imports is a safe reserve position, but if the reserves are just adequate to meet 3 to 6 month imports, that is a high risk scenario. At that moment, the country's reserve position with the IMF that is available, channels of borrowing from the IMF, available SDRs, potential credit lines open etc., are taken into account. If the country has limited reserves and they have borrowed heavily from the IMF and the unused limits are nil then that country is a high risk country.

## Structural Imbalances

If a country has structural imbalances and a chronic balance of payments deficit on current account, accompanying the high fiscal deficit, these are symptoms of high risk scenario. Similarly the structural reforms may be going on but current account deficit and fiscal deficits continued to be high which may lead to stagnation in growth rate and high inflation in the country. These are danger symptoms for creditworthiness of a country. India for example had a current account deficit of more than 2% of GDP and fiscal deficit was as high as 8% of GDP early in the nineties, which made India borrow from the IMF for structural reforms. Although, fiscal deficit is kept at levels of about 5 to 6%, in 1998 and 1999 they were considered to be high by analysts. The gross fiscal deficit is expected to be brought down in stages to less than 4%. But the stagnancy in exports growth in 1997-98 and 1998-99 led to continued Current Account deficits and balance of payments situation was rated to be pecarious. Then the Moody's rating of India fell below the Investment Grade (BBB). The external deficit continued to be high and fiscal deficit at 6% during 2000-03 and although it came down later, went up again to 6-7% during 2008 to 2010.

The highest rating is Triple AAA for countries like U.S.A. and Japan based on the economy's strength and balance of payments position. The minimum investment grade is Triple BBB for Moodys and Standard and Poor. The reason for downgrading India's rating in 1998 and 1999 was due to Pokhran Nuclear Blast in May 1998 followed by economic sanctions by USA, Japan etc. on India and stoppage of all aid and loans from them accompanied by poor export performance and continued high fiscal deficit of the government

## Proportion of External Trade to World Trade

Aggregate debt has to be considered in relation to external earnings If debt is not more than 2 to 3 times the external earnings, then the country is reasonably above board so far as its external solvency is concerned. In this context, the proportion of external trade to world trade is significant. If a country is not dependent on external trade for its growth and domestic market is large, as in the case of India, the question of external solvency cannot be judged by external earnings or external trade. But this indicator is relevant for countries like Malaysia, Australia, Mexico etc., which have an export-led growth, and depended on foreign funds for investment to a large extent. In India, its foreign trade is less than 1% of world trade and foreign funds inflow constitute 10% or less of the total domestic investment.

India's external debt, both short-term and long-term was referred to in an earlier chapter. Of this, short-term debt is only 4%. External debt as percentage of GDP is 22% and its debt service ratio is 4.6% in 2009. India's export earnings are insignificant in relation to GDP (10%). India's external debt is two times the export earnings, which is not relatively high either. India's foreign exchange reserves including SDRs and gold stood at US $ 265 billion as at end June 2009 which accounts for about 13 months of imports of the country.

Long-term debt and softer loans constitute less burden on the country than short-term debt and commercial loans. In India long-term debt constitute 80% and so is the composition of softer loans (18%). Our commercial loans stood at about 18% of the gross total outstanding borrowing. The above data show that the debt burden of India would not be significant in the long-run. Yet the current account deficit at around 2% to 3% in relation to GDP may create balance of payments problems. This deficit persisted from 2004 onwards.

## Maturity Pattern of Debt

The composition of debt maturity-wise will indicate the short-term and medium and long-term components. The quantum of debt which is of short-term is one which has maturity of less than one year. If a country has a high short-term debt, this may lead to difficulties of repayment, if there are sudden slumps in earnings. Normally, the short-term debt should not exceed 4 months' imports. The higher the ratio, the greater is the risk and vulnerability to crisis of confidence. Normally, trade related debts are of maturities of 3 months to 6 months, at the maximum level. If thus, imports financed by debts is one-third of the total, this is equivalent to 4 months' imports.

## Liquid Reserves

Among the factors looked into for credit rating of a country is the level of liquid reserves which is also called foreign exchange deficit at any point of time. Payments outside is mainly due to imports and hence the level of reserves is measured in terms of imports. India's foreign exchange assets are now equivalent to 13 months imports as referred to earlier. This is considered a comfortable level to infuse confidence to foreign creditors and lenders. Reserves can also be related to current account deficit plus maturing debt which indicates the short-term financing requirements. The liquidity gap ratio is thus the financing requirement (current account deficit plus maturing debt) as a ratio of export earning and gold is also part of foreign exchange reserves.

But gold held with RBI and the government can be taken as official holdings of foreign exchange available to meet foreign trade deficit or foreign payments. In India there are large holdings of private gold stocks but prima facie, they are not available for official use immediately. There are times when gold was pledged by India to secure loans from international bodies, as in the case of 1990-91, when we had severe balance of payments problems. There is a method of swaps between gold and Forex reserves (foreign exchange) and private gold holdings can be collected through such schemes as gold bonds or gold linked deposits etc. India has adopted all these methods at some time or other.

## Weightage to Factors

All the above factors are given some weightage points to arrive at the total weighted average level of confidence or of risk of a country. The above quantitative factors may be given a total of 70 or 80 points and the rest 20 or 30 points can be given to qualitative factors.

Country's internal political stability is one single important factor for risk weightage. Socio-economic factors, like poverty and illiteracy, levels of education for the country are also to be looked into. Global geopolitical groupism like the NATO and the country's external relationships also count. Cold war and border tensions like Indo-Pakistan Conflict, government policies, regulatory or liberalised regimes, corruption, nature of bureaucracy and systems and procedures with respect to foreign investment in domestic economy, etc. are also important qualitative factors.

## Investment Grade

Investment by International Fund Managers is diversified into many emerging markets. To facilitate such investment, some quantitative indices and categorisation into investment grades and non-investment grades or ranking of countries in the order of riskiness are used. The International Finance Corporation, which invests in private sector of the developing countries uses these methods of country ranking. Some indexes are also compiled by Research Groups of Morgan Stanley and Baring Brothers, which are used for investment by country and regional funds. Most of these indexes give a good proportion of weightage to political risk, which includes policy changes, restrictive or liberal regimes, exchange and trade controls and international goodwill for the country etc. The Baring Emerging Market Index covers 12 countries, 6 for Asia and over 200 scrips which are not significantly correlated with each other. The markets in the emerging countries are analysed for their depth, liquidity, floating stock, delivery and settlement time and a host of other factors.

## Indexing Method

This indexing method and quantification of qualitative factors like socio-political factors are bound to have their own limitations. The broad classification of index as investment grade, or more or less etc. has some merit. The Investment Grade of Triple BBB of Standard and Poor or Moodys etc. influences the terms of lending and interest spread over LIBOR by international banks to the countries in question.

One survey of grading of information on countries by leading international bankers is compiled by the "Institutional Investor."

Bankers are asked in this survey to grade each country on a scale of zero to 100, with 100 representing the state of least chance of default or lowest risk. The sample includes 75 to 100 banks with international exposure. The opinions of bankers are then weighted as per the importance of banks in their exposure to international business.

## Limitations of Grading

These rankings and weightages are all subjective. Whether they are from Moodys or Standard and Poor or from Institutional Investor, some element of bias will percolate. Bankers in particular have their own order of preferences. They are not without political and social bias. It is not strictly appropriate to compare countries in different stages of growth and under different economic and political systems. International Fund Managers have to keep these limitations in mind and have to use their own analysis of markets in developing countries before they can channel their funds into these markets.

Merchant International Group (MIG), a London based strategic research and corporate intelligence company specialises in rating countries in terms of "Grey Area Dynamics" (GAD). The GADs are invisible risks in investment in emerging countries. These relate to such factors as red tape, corruption in government and public life, parallel economy, unorganised sector and its importance, nature of bureaucracy, policies and procedures, product diversion, cheating and frauds, legal safeguards and many more.

## MIG Grading

MIG's Rating and Information System is useful to investing countries and companies. GAD forms the basis on which MIG assists the countries and companies with strategies of entry, exit, joint ventures, mergers and acquisitions in emerging countries in the world for global investment.

MIG holds a copyright on the term 'GAD.' MIG charter is quite different from internationally reputed rating agencies like Moody's or Standard and Poor, which will focus entirely on sovereign risks. There will be significant differences as between the ratings of these different agencies. The extent of the dependence on them by international investor groups also varies. U.S. based Moody's has down graded India's rating after the

Pokhran Nuclear Tests in May 1998 into something less than the investment grade. But surprisingly soon after, the India Resurgent Bonds, issued by India in August 1998 to foreigners and NRIs was a thumping success, garnering about US dollar 4 billion.

The MIG has been assisting the British corporates and investment groups. It tracks regularly 40 emerging markets around the world and has been tracking India since it went in for liberalisation since 1992. It helps even Indian companies in joint ventures, mergers and acquisitions etc.

MIG has given India, in February 1999, a seventh rank and considers India better off than Indonesia, Russia, Colombia, Belarus and Ukraine. India is given 76 points and is put in the top 10 risky countries in the world (see Table below).

**TABLE 20.1**

| *Country* | *Points* | *Criteria* |
|---|---|---|
| Pakistan | 92 | Bureaucracy |
| Indonesia | 84.5 | Corruption |
| Russia | 83.5 | Counterfeiting and Fraud |
| Colombia | 81.5 | Cultural Integration |
| Belarus | 80 | Legal Safeguards |
| Ukrarine | 77 | Organised Crime |
| India | 76 | Parallel Trading and Product Diversion |
| Algeria | 76 | Unfair Competition |
| Vietnam | 73 | Extremism |

*Source:* ET

## Credit Rating of Debt Investments

A rating agency like Standard and Poor has an international reputation for rating. It has wide network of research staff, experts in diverse fields and specialise in rating of the country's sovereign risk, credit risks of companies and instruments.

Major factors influencing the rating are the following:

(1) Likelihood of default — capacity and willingness of the issuer for timely payment of interest and repayment of principal in accordance with the terms and conditions.

(2) Nature and provisions of the obligations and whether secured or unsecured debt, guaranteed by a third party, senior debt or subordinate debt, etc.

(3) Protection accorded to the creditors in the events of liquidation, merger, reorganisation etc.

(4) The type of analysis and rating exercises done by the credit rating agency is to see that long-term and short-term debt are rated separately. Instruments are rated and not the companies as a whole. Any company desiring to raise debt in international market has to get a rating from an international agency.

## Credit Rating Exercises

(1) Fundamental analysis of the company, industry in which the company is operating and the economy to which it belongs.

(2) Financial risks, Business Risks and Market Risk are to be evaluated. Purchasing power risks and interest rate risks are assessed.

(3) On the spot evaluation of the company's operations by visit to the plants, interviews with the top executives of the company, its trade unions, dealers, suppliers, customers, etc. on a confidential basis and examine the potential for latent risks.

## Standard and Poor

**Table 20.2**

Rating grades for debt of long and short-term nature are given below for illustration:

| *Long-term debt Bonds/Debentures* | | *Short-term debt Commercial Paper* | |
|---|---|---|---|
| AAA | : Extremely safe | (Ps) or A1+ | : extremely safe |
| AA | : Very safe | $A_1$ | : Safe |
| A | : Safe | $A_2$ | : Satisfactory |
| BBB | : Adequate | $A_3$ | : Adequate |
| BB | : Moderately speculative | B | : Speculative |
| B | : Speculative grades | C | : Doubtful |
| CCC | : Highly speculative | D | : In default |
| CC | : Prone to bankruptcy | | |
| C | : Failed to repay | | |
| D | : In default | | |

*Moody's Investor Services*

| *Long-term Debt* | | *Commercial Paper* | |
|---|---|---|---|
| Aaa | : Best quality | $P_1$ | : Superior Safety |
| Aa | : High quality | $P_2$ | : Strong ability |
| A | : Upper Medium grade | $P_3$ | : Adequately safe |
| Baa | : Medium grade | Anything above $P_3$ are prone to default | |
| Ba | : Speculative grade | | |
| B | : Lacking Desirable features or Inadequate safety | | |
| Caa | : Poor Standing | | |
| Ca | : High Speculative elements | | |
| C | : Lowest Quality class | | |

## Nature of Country Risk

Country risk is a broader term than either the political risk or sovereign risk. The latter terms refer mostly the government and the semi-government bodies or government backed bodies. The former term is all pervasive including the political risk, economic risk and the social risk, as well as risks faced by the private sector investments. Various agencies are there for rating the country risks. Some countries are regularly rated and the rating published in the order from the lowest risk to the highest risk by Euro-money publication. Euro-money country rating system is explained below.

## Methods of Reducing Country Risk

(1) Keeping secret of their formulations like Coke.

(2) Control over the crucial operations in the hands of the technicians of MNC and not locals.

(3) Getting brand names registered in their name and preventing others from using the same.

(4) Probability of expropriation is reduced by the government guarantee of foreign investment which is given by the Government of India by signing the agreement of MIG (Multinational Investment Guarantee) and with bilateral agreements with some countries.

(5) Entering into joint ventures with local partners.

(6) By using the local funds and local employment the fear of expropriation can be reduced.

(7) By taking appropriate cover operations for foreign exchange risk and interest rate risk.

(8) By purchasing investment insurance provided in some countries (say from Oversees Investment Corporation and Exim Bank in the U.S.A.).

## Euromoney's Country Risk Rating

One of the well-known evaluators of the country risk is *Euromoney*, a monthly Magazine that produces periodically a ranking of country risks. Euromoney has regular consultants who give the ratings for each of the factors mentioned below:

| | *Percentage weight* |
|---|---|
| (1) Analytical Indicators | 50% |
| (2) Credit Indicators | 30% |
| (3) Market Indicators | 20% |

Analytical indicators comprise of the economic growth and Political risk which takes into account political stability and political philosophy and social set up of the country. Credit indicators include debt serving capacity, foreign exchange reserves, foreign debt in relation to GNP and debt servicing ratio and current account deficit of the balance of payments of the country.

Risk evaluators take into account defaults of debt or their rescheduling and credit rating. Market indicators mostly reflect the state of the financial markets — how easy is the access to bank, and to other short-term sources of finance, strength and depth of the capital market and access to long-term funds from F.I.s and the capital market and lastly the interest rates, yields, discount rates and forfeiting discount. Large insurance premiums for cargo freight, shipping etc. indicate large perceived risks. Some of the factors taken into account show overlapping among the factors.

*Source:* Country-Risk-Methodology, *Euromoney Issue,* Sept. 1994.

❖ ❖ ❖

# MANAGEMENT OF INTERNATIONAL TRANSACTIONS EXPOSURE

# 21

## Introduction

International transactions in trade and economic and commercial transactions as between nations result in many risks of which the foreign exchange risks are most prominent. The corporates which are more directly affected are the MNCs, as all their operations are involved in inter-country trade, aid and investment. These operations involve transfers of currencies across nations, receipts and payments in foreign currencies. Their inputs and intermediates come from one or more countries, manufacturing or assembling in another country or countries and distribution or marketing in another set of countries. They have branches, agencies or subsidiaries in all these sets of countries. They obviously face international risk exposures of the following types.

They have currency exposure due to change in exchange rates arising out of reporting and consolidation of accounts, or due to converting financial statements from the host country to that of the parent country's currency. Due to exchange rate changes, there is need for translation and restatement of the assets, liabilities, revenue and expenses-gains or losses etc. that are denominated in foreign currencies into the currency of the home country of the parent company. There is risk exposure in such restatements of accounts, as the exchange rate at the time of purchase or sale may be different from that at the time of transfer of funds. The preparation of statement in local currency of the host country is necessary for the purposes of compliance with government rules and taxation of that country. The parent company has to compile its own statements in the home country's currency for complying with home country rules, regulations and laws. All MNCs and global operators face the risks of change in exchange rates, government policies on foreign exchange trade and transfer of funds and in the rates of taxation. These risks are neither exactly measurable nor avoidable for them. They have only to learn how to manage them in a way that their take home profits or cash flows are positive and investors' interests and wealth are protected and enhanced. Wealth maximisation being their objective, the operations have to comply and manage the international transactions risks.

The accounting risks can be stated as translation risks. In the context, it is pertinent to note here, that there are four major methods of translation, namely, current and non-current method, monetary and non-monetary method, temporal method and current rate method. All the above risks, referred to earlier due to currency or exchange rate changes are reflected in the company's balance sheet, income-expenditure statement and all other cash flow and financial statements.

The company has to decide which foreign currency assets and liabilities are to be translated at the post change exchange rate and which will be kept at the pre-change exchange rate. While the former are exposed the latter are not exposed. The translation exposure is the difference between exposed assets and exposed liabilities.

## Translation Methods

The four principal translation methods are briefly explained below:

**(1) Current/Non-current Methods:** Under this method the current assets and liabilities are translated into home country's currency from that of the host country at the current exchange rate. But the non-current assets and liabilities are translated at the historical exchange rate or the rate at which assets were acquired and liabilities were incurred.

**(2) Monetary and Non-monetary Method:** Under this method, monetary items like cash, accounts receivable, payables, etc. which are all claims on money or money itself are translated at the current rate, while non-monetary items such as inventory, fixed assets, long-term investments are translated at historical rates.

**(3) Temporal Method:** This is more or less similar to monetary/non-monetary method, except for that in temporal method, inventory is translated at historical rate but can be translated at current rate, if the inventory is shown in the balance sheet at the market prices. In temporal method, the theoretical basis is the approach to evaluating cost either on historical or market price basis. Those which are carried to the balance sheet at market prices, are valued at current rate.

**(4) Current Rate Method:** In this method, all balance sheet and income items are translated at current rate except the fixed assets. This is simple and was recommended by the Institute of Chartered Accountants of England and Wales and Scotland. Under this method, if a firm's foreign currency denominated assets exceed liabilities, a devaluation must result in a loss and a revaluation in a gain.

## Managing Accounting Exposure

The management of accounting exposure including both translation and transaction exposure requires the use of hedging process. Regardless of what happens to the future exchange rate movements, hedging locks-in the home currency of the parent company, the values which are subject to currency exposure.

Hedging is a method of managing a particular currency exposure, including both the translation and transaction exposure. Translation exposure arises when currency value changes and the accountant's entries have to show gains or losses. The values of current assets and current liabilities and non-current assets and liabilities may undergo changes. There is also a transaction exposure due to effecting of a transaction, namely, sale, purchase, borrowing and lending.

Hedging cannot provide protection against expected rate changes. Hedging is to protect a company against unexpected exchange rate changes. Firms cope with anticipated currency changes through the use of forward contracts, borrowing locally and adjusting their present and credit sales, etc.

Forward contracts are entered in the forward market where forward rates are the unbiased estimates to the future spot rates. As per the International Fisher Effect, given the assumption of perfect markets and no government controls, the exchange rates and interest rates adjust to the changes in purchasing power parities as between the countries. In a way, the inflation rates and currency rates move in sympathy due to their interrelations, following the international Fisher effect. It is found empirically that gains and losses on debt in currencies are offset by corresponding rate changes. Interest rates are generally lower in hard currencies and higher in soft currencies. In real world there are various barriers that obstruct the equalisation of real interest rates.

Forward rates depend on the expected future spot rates and any persistent differences among them would provide profitable opportunities for speculation. However, the differences referred to above will bring in buying and selling forward, which would bring about equality between hedging costs and expected currency changes.

The other hedging methods are adjusting their pricing and credit policies. These will benefit only in the short-run due to time lag in information flows. No firm can thus, gain continuously by these short-term adjustments. The real value of factoring currency rate change expectations into its pricing and credit policy changes is to prevent others from profiting at its expense.

## Centralisation and Decentralisation

In the field of currency risk management, there are arguments both for and against centralisation of policy decisions. In decentralised system, each affiliate takes decisions to optimise its own financial and exposure positions. In the process, some will end with both positive and negative exposures, in the same currency. These positions may net out to increase the total exposure of the corporate entity of the MNC.

The centralisation policy would allow an overall view of all exposures by taking the net position of all affiliates in each currency. The Head Office can weigh the costs and benefits of each hedging process and take the after tax benefit accruing to the parent company for each policy decision.

But this centralisation policy leaves the local affiliates with no initiative and no chance to benefit from the local knowledge and the opportunities available for hedging locally, which may sometimes be cheaper than what the parent company can do. In sum, each MNC follows its own policy of the mix of the centralisation and decentralisation.

## Managing Translation Exposure

The MNCs have the following methods open to them for managing the translation exposure:

(1) Adjusting funds flows.

(2) Entering into forward contracts.

(3) Netting of the exposure.

The methods of entering into use of forward contracts for protecting against risk exposure and the advantages of netting the exposure, currency wise, by the parent company are referred to already. The funds flow adjustment is a strategy, which a local office has to adopt.

Hedging cannot provide any protection against expected rate changes as referred to earlier, but only against unexpected rate changes. Forward contracts can provide hedge against expected rate changes. Besides, exchange rate movements have to be generally in sympathy with inflation rate changes, according to the Fisher effect. But the government controls and market imperfections preclude any equalisation of real interest rates.

The other hedging methods, which are in the nature of adjustments in pricing and credit decisions can be profitable, so long as some are informed more than others. This will therefore, be a hedging tool upto a point, when these dealings are with less knowledgeable people. In general to the extent that governments do not permit interest rates and forward rates to fully adjust to market expectations, a firm with access to these financial instruments like hedging can gain from currency changes. Forward rates try to adjust to expected spot rates in future and to the extent that they do not adjust accordingly and there are differences between forward and future spot rates they will provide profitable scope for speculation.

The MNC may use netting method to hedge their total risk that is netting the receivables and payables in each currency. Each subsidiary is treated as a separate unit for hedging in their currency while currency of the parent company can be kept open and unhedged. Holding accounts or deposits in other countries in their currencies, other than that of the parent company is considered desirable in all situations when receipts and payments do not tally. Many companies keep U.S. dollar accounts for this purpose. If the payments are in currencies other than dollar, dollars in these accounts can be converted into the desirable currencies and if any receipts have come in currencies other than dollar, they can be quickly converted into dollar for the simple reason that dollar is a strong currency and is unlikely to become weak in the short-run. Holding accounts in dollars thus, helps the collection of receivables in any currency and disbursement of payables in foreign currency by conversion into and out of dollars, more easily than in the case of others.

## Enterprise Risk Management

Enterprise Risk Management (ERM) is defined as the system and procedures, designed to deal with multiple types of risks that an enterprise faces, namely, credit risk, market risk and operational risks; these arise in its dealings in different asset classes that they have to deal with, namely, currencies, time zones and instruments like equity or debt. The objective of ERM process is to obtain all relevant information and analyse data so that uncertainty is turned into quantifiable risk and adopt software and hardware (technology) suitable to manage these risks. The tripod of tools for ERM consists of Data Information, Analytics and technology, which is necessary to manage the risks. These tools are applicable to all enterprises, whether they are private, public or joint and irrespective of the nature of ownership and type of activity.

Risk dimension or depth has to be assessed and top management has to give guidelines for management of risk in each of the directions of operations that the enterprise is involved. Risk management encompasses tools for offensive and defensive approaches. Value at Risk (VAR) is an estimate of maximum loss that will be incurred in a portfolio, given a level of confidence and parameters within which the market will behave in a given time period.

The process of Risk Management Framework is explained through the following chart.

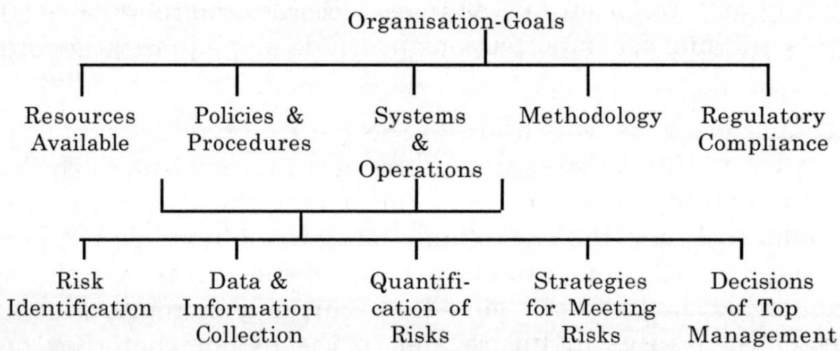


**Chart 21.1**

## Exchange Rate Management

Domestic and foreign sectors are closely interlinked through exports, imports and flows of funds across borders. Market participants hold portfolios of both domestic and foreign monies. Domestic money supply, interest rates and exchange rates are all linked together and money and monetary policy impinge on the exchange rate policy and *vice versa*. If money supply rises, interest rates fall and exchange rate would depreciate.

Excess Money Pressures (EMP) in the exchange market are caused by domestic excess money and falling interest rates. The Monetary Conditions Index (MCI) is nowadays employed as the operating target for monetary policy to work. It is more easily computable version of EMP. EMP would indicate the extent of exchange market pressures on account of monetary disequilibria. If exchange rate is managed, as in India, there is some degree of intervention by the RBI in the market, which is measured by the net change in foreign exchange assets (NFA). MCI would indicate the monetary conditions prevailing at a point of time, in relation to some base period conditions. A decline in MCI indicates a tightening of monetary conditions while a rise in MCI reflects easing of monetary conditions. MCI depends on the interest rates and exchange rates and the weightage given to each of them depends on the prevailing conditions in the economy.

Exchange rate volatility is high in times of monetary disequilibrium and interest rates are not in tune with the money market conditions. The linking factor between domestic market equilibrium and exchange market equilibrium is interest rate. Hedging, speculation and host of other factors influence the exchange market, causing its disequilibrium and this percolates to the domestic market conditions, leading to monetary policy changes. Interest rates, exchange rates and money market conditions must be in equilibrium for stability in the markets.

Balance of payments crisis affects the exchange rates. The rupee was very volatile during 1990-91, due to balance of payments pressures leading to depreciation of rupee by 18% in July 1991. The *de facto* administrated regime of exchange rate based on a basket of currencies prevailing since 1975 was replaced in 1992 by a dual exchange rate system under which 60% of the exchange earnings were transacted at free market rate and 40% of all current receipts were exchanged at RBI fixed exchange rates. This dual rate system tantamounted to a depreciation of rupee by 11% and implied simultaneous use of monetary policy and exchange restrictions. In March 1993, rupee was made convertible in all trade account transactions and the dual exchange rate system was abandoned.

Inflows of funds under the Foreign Exchange (Immunities) Scheme and the India Development Bonds in October 1991, combined with some easing of monetary conditions led to the MCI edging up and from August 1992 to February 1993; the EMP turned negative and downward pressures on exchange rate continued. After 1993 budget presentation and convertibility of the rupee on Trade Account, capital inflows bulged the RBI foreign exchange reserves and there were net purchases of dollar from March 1993 to March 1995, reflecting an effort of the RBI to prevent an appreciation of the rupee.

A marginal weakening of the rupee was allowed in August 1995. Downward pressures were intensified during 1995 September to 1996 February A similar downward pressure on rupee was noticed from September 1997 to January 1998; the easing of monetary policy and interventionist policy of RBI helped the exchange market to regain the stability, although, exchange rate of the rupee fell steeply during this period and reached a low of Rs. 45 per dollar at one stage. These episodes testify to the inter-market pressures and risks resulting therefrom.

## External Hedging

The following are the external methods, followed for hedging purposes:

*Currency Forwards:* This is a forward contract in a foreign currency -say one to 9 months, with forward premiums and discounts which in turn depend on the interest rate differentials.

Example: U.S. to Italian Lira

| Spot | Buying | Selling | |
|---|---|---|---|
| $ = Lira | 1798 | 1796 | |
| Forward | | Buying | Selling |
| 1 Month | 8 dis. | 1806 | 1804 |
| 3 Month | 18 disc. | 1816 | 1814 |

If we take lira to U.S. dollar or rupees to U.S. dollar, they are at discount. If we take dollars to lira or rupees, the rate will be a premium on the spot rate. If we quote the rate as so many dollars per Rs. 100, then the forward rate is at a premium. If we quote rate as so many rupees per dollar, then the forward rate is at a discount. Here the U.S. currency is at a premium due to its strength, inherent due to strength of the economy and not necessarily due to higher interest rates in U.S.A. than in India. But inflation adjusted real rates are to be taken into account, to compare the two currencies. In India, capital flows on capital account are restricted and controlled; there is however free flow on Current Account. Even so, the forward premiums or discounts are influenced by the demand and supply of the forward currencies and the relative strengths of the currencies. Interest rates do not play any significant role as there are no deposit arbitrage opportunities.

The depth of the forward market is limited in India and the RBI is encouraging it to grow atleast as between the banks. These forward contract facilities are not available in less traded currencies and of broken periods. The most forward contracts entered into are upto 12 months or less. The rates quoted are not finer rates and banks depend upon the cross currency quotations, given by the FEDA. The forward contracts of longer periods of more than 12 months are not generally available except in special cases. Besides there is no free currency borrowing or deposits abroad by Indian nationals or companies. Banks can do these transactions upto certain limits as approved by the Boards of the Banks concerned, as per the RBI policy guidelines.

## Currency Borrowings and Deposits

If a company has receivables in foreign currencies for a customer in 12 months and the receivables are in U.S. dollars and our costs are in pound sterling then we would sell the dollars forward for 12 months against spot buying. Alternatively, we can borrow Euro dollars for 12 months to be repaid out of receipts from the customers at the end of 12 months. The tax and accounting considerations and forward premiums decide the method used by this company. If the interest rates are higher by 5% in pound sterling than in Euro dollar, then there will be a gain of 5% on forward dollars sold as against the spot rate.

There is flexibility in currency borrowings because there can be flexibility in periods of time and easy repayment schedules, variable interest rates and rollover facilities. But these facilities are available to highly creditworthy customers or companies with high credit rating. A company with excess liquidity is unlikely to borrow as that would increase its gearing. Similarly companies which are already heavily geared and reached their borrowing limits are unlikely to resort to this method.

## Currency Futures

If a company wants to hedge a future currency payment at present, it can neutralise the exposure by buying a currency future. That will transfer the risk to somebody else, say the writer of the future contract. In this case, he gains only if the currency movement is in the direction of expected movement. Thus if the payment is in dollar and dollar is appreciating against rupee, he can buy a future contract in dollars, three months hence or 6 months hence, when the payment is due. But in this case, if the dollar depreciates, against his expectation, he foregoes any windfall gains. He is sure of his commitment and this contract has helped him to hedge a future uncertain movement of a dollar to a fixed and certain account in terms of dollars.

## Currency Options

Unlike the currency futures, option does not entail any outright payment but the premium or price of option is to be paid. These will cover the downside risk but at the same time allow one to gain from a favourable movement of rates. If the MNC has operations in UK and Germany and sterling is expected to decline and D.M. to appreciate, the company may sell sterling option and buy D.M. option to remain hedged when sterling declines. If the sterling had actually strengthened instead of weakening, then the option would be abandoned and the sterling would be sold in the market with the cost being the option premium paid. The currency options are resorted as hedge by importers to pay funds abroad at a future date and a host of other purposes such as speculation in currency markets.

## Exposure Hedging

When an MNC is consolidating its balance sheet with those of its subsidiaries in foreign currencies, then some exposures arise during the conversion, such as-

(1) subsidiary is undercapitalised and its borrowing in local currency is increased.

(2) subsidiaries may be asked to pay dividends in excess of retained earnings.

(3) subsidiaries may use local capital to repay the parent company equity and loans.

(4) subsidiaries hold assets in parent company's currency.

In India, these measures of the subsidiaries are not allowed as per the FERA provisions. The above internal methods of hedging are resorted to in countries, where they are permitted by law, or are not prohibited. The external methods of hedging by parent company for the operations of subsidiary are:

(1) Match the net worth of subsidiary, i.e., currency assets through borrowings in the same currency, with a view to match assets in a currency by equal liabilities in the same currency.

(2) If currency finance is raised for the subsidiary in domestic currency, keeping an equivalent domestic deposit would hedge the currency exposure of the company.

(3) If borrowing is resorted to in the currency of the host country, then sufficient currency income is necessary to service it.

(4) Treatment of intangible assets and subsequent write-offs must be in the same currency, so that the question of currency exposure does not arise in respect of these assets.

(5) Tax and accounting treatment of the parent and subsidiaries have to be coordinated without the need for a hedge.

Translation exposures, if they are large, are difficult to hedge as they require huge premiums to be paid. Besides, hedges for longer periods than one year are difficult and costly. Then the solution that the parent company adopts is in the nature of cost optimisation in the first stage and restructuring and reorganisation of productions structures and sourcing of raw-materials and other inputs in the next stage. In the last stage the parent company may switch production base for the high cost to low cost location with greater comparative advantage. A foreign MNC may choose to produce, say in India, as a low cost centre for securing of input resources and sell outside India in high cost countries. India thus provides only berth for production base in this case, which is provided in the Free Trade Zones.

## Forward Market Hedge

The affiliates in many countries have alternative hedging techniques like using forward contracts, price adjustment clauses to be included in contracts of sale, borrowing and lending, using currency option clauses, borrowing and lending in the parent home currency etc. Transaction exposure can also be eliminated by invoicing all the transactions in the parent home currency.

In forward market hedge, a company that is long in a foreign currency will sell the foreign currency forward for the period that matches the inflows with outflows in future. Similarly a company which is short in a foreign currency will buy the currency forward. The object is to fix in a strong currency, like dollar, the future currency inflow to match with the expected outflows.

A money market hedge is a simultaneous borrowing and lending activity in two different currencies, so as to lock-in for a specified period in terms of dollars of a foreign currency cash inflow and outflow. To give an example, suppose a German company borrows D.M. to repay a fixed amount of D.M. 25 million of principal with interest at the end of one year. D.M. may depreciate against dollar by end of one year and the interest rates in Germany and in U.S. are 15% and 10% respectively. German firm will borrow in D.M. = 25 m at \$1 = 1.15 D.M. giving D.M. 21.74 million for one year and convert into dollars and invest the equivalent dollar 8.7 million in the short-term market for one year (conversion rate 2.50). At the end of one year the company will receive 8.7 × 1.10 = 9.57 million from dollar investment. The company will sell spot dollars to buy back D.M. 1.15 × 21.74 = D.M. 25 million to pay back the loan.

There will be loss or gain depending on the \$ to D.M. rate.

If the dollar rate in terms of D.M. falls from 2.50 to 2.66 by the end of one year, the dollar investment at the end of one year gives \$ 9.57 million when converted into D.M. will yield 25.456 D.M., of which D.M. 25 million will be used to payback the principal and interest borrowed. The gain or loss will depend on the exact currency rate changes over the period.

Basic Hedging Techniques are listed below:

**TABLE 21.1**

| *Techniques used in Depreciation* | *Techniques used in Appreciation* |
|---|---|
| 1. Keep current assets in foreign currency | Keep current assets in local currency |
| 2. Keep current liabilities in local currency | Keep liabilities in foreign currency |
| 3. Sell local currency forward | Buy local currency forward |
| 4. Tighten local credit policy | Loosen the local credit terms |
| 5. Borrow locally | Reduce local borrowing |
| 6. Delay collection of hard currency receivables | Speed up the collection of soft currency receivables |
| 7. Delay payments on bills payable | Speed up payments on bills payable |
| 8. Invoice exports in foreign currency and imports in local currency | Reverse the process to be followed |
| 9. Speed up fees, dividends etc. payable to parent company and interest and other payments to affiliates | Delay payments to parent and subsidiaries |
| 10. Delay collection of inter-affiliate accounts receivable | Speed up the recollection of inter-subsidiary accounts receivable |

## Hedging Economic Exposures

Economic exposures have been defined as the extent to which currency and price changes effect the firm's income-expenditure sheet and balance sheet.

Basically risks of MNCs are due to currency and inflation rate changes, leaving aside the interest rate changes. If these changes are mutually adjusting perfectly and simultaneously, the risk in market is adjusted automatically. But due to prevailing imperfections in the market, risks do arise and they have to be hedged. Even speculation enters the market depending upon the expected changes in currency rates -spot and forward.

Due to the close association of the currency rate fluctuations with inflation rate changes, we have to measure the exposure properly by using the inflation adjusted or real exchange rates. Due to constant changes in prices, the firm's balance sheet of each quarter is likely to change and become incomparable with the past quarterly results. The impact of economic exposures can be reduced by presenting inflation adjusted balance sheet data in constant dollars.

The above impact on the firm depends on a great number of variables including the location of its major markets, and its competitors. Price elasticities of supply and demand, input substitution and adjustments in output input matrix, flexibility in cost and pricing, local currency financing and a host of other variables relating to the firm are affected by inflation. Currency volatility which is a risk factor is closely associated with interest rate changes also, the risk of which is to be hedged as was referred to earlier.

## Managing Economic Exposures

There are two types of economic exposure, namely, short-term and long-term. Currency risks affect the MNC's subsidiaries in almost all the foreign countries, in all facets of their operations. The short-run exposures require local affiliates' action in hedging and using flexible policies of product mix, pricing and adoption of market segmentation approach. Both in terms of currency changes and price changes the affiliates have to adopt a flexible policy. But in the long run, the parent company as a whole has to plan to involve the Finance Manager with all other top level functionaries in evolving and operating strategies to hedge against these currency risks. They have to be anticipatory and pro-active rather than reactive to any changes in currency and prices.

All the top level executives are to be involved in the exchange risk management. A committee of top level officers, co-ordinated by the Finance Manager is held responsible to plan and act so as to offset the forthcoming currency changes and incorporate hedges in their planning strategies and in their own decisions.

The currency induced changes affect the prices of outputs as well as inputs bought and sold in foreign countries. They will also affect the levels of borrowing and lending in different currencies differently. These changes in turn impinge on the corporate costs and revenue and profit margins. The degree of impact depends upon the firm's international trade, its market share and competitive environment and the degree of operational flexibility. To the extent that currency changes affect different firms differently, their relative competitive power can be affected adversely.

Firstly, the firms can offset some impacts through making necessary production and marketing strategy changes. There has to be changes in production strategy and corresponding marketing strategies for long-term adjustments. To currency appreciation and depreciation, the firms generally use the expected real exchange rates, instead of nominal exchange rates. The trend series of nominal exchange rates and real exchange rates are published regularly in the RBI publications.

## Use of Real Effective Rates

An illustrative table of nominal effective exchange rates and real effective exchange rates and corresponding Inter Bank Forward premia for 3 months and 6 months is presented below:

**TABLE 21.2**

*(Base : 1993-94 = 100)*

| *Years* | *Trade based weights (36 country weights) (Annual Average Indices)* | | | *Monthly averages Forward premia* | |
|---|---|---|---|---|---|
| *Months* | *REER* | *NEER* | | *(3 month)* | *(6 month) (in per cent per annum)* |
| | | | 2005 | | |
| 1997 | 100.40 | 91.85 | April | 1.96 | 1.76 |
| | | | Dec | 1.51 | 1.07 |
| | | | 2007 | | |
| 2002 | 98.90 | 90.08 | April | 6.91 | 5.93 |
| | | | Dec | 1.64 | 1.70 |
| | | | 2009 | | |
| 2007 | 104.10 | 92.58 | April | 3.34 | 2.82 |
| 2008 | 97.87 | 88.35 | July | 2.57 | 2.43 |
| 2013 | 107.03 | 75.53 | May | 8.30 | 7.93 |
| | | | 2014 | | |

*Source:* RBI Bulletins and Handbook of Statistics.
Note: Market based exchange rate system was introduced in March, 1993.

The Table shows that the higher the depreciation of the currency, the higher will be the forward premium. The higher depreciation is a reflection of the higher inflation rates and increase in prices and there will be consequential positive relation between the Trade weighted exchange rates and the forward exchange rate premium.

## Pro-active Strategies

The Table below presents some of the proactive marketing and production strategies that an MNC can follow to offset the impact of currency changes.

**TABLE 21.3**

| | *Production Initiatives* | *Marketing Initiatives* |
|---|---|---|
| (1) | Production Input Mix | Product output strategy of Marketing |
| (2) | Product Sourcing | Market selection and segmentation of market to maintain growth of sales |
| (3) | Plant location | Product differentiation and pricing differentiation Distribution network strategy |
| (4) | Cost reduction and increased productivity | Promotional sales strategy and aggressive brand promotion |

The final objective of the firm being maintaining and promoting its market share, its first priority is to maintain its competitive ability and to improve it. Then plan to maintain its market share and if possible increase it. For instance, if the currency change is expected to be short-term the firm may not change its price to keep its market share intact. A longer term and permanent shift in currency rates may need raising the foreign prices, keeping the domestic prices intact. It may bear temporary loss or reduced profits and reduction in sales.

## Components of Economic Exposure

MNC will have an additional advantage of shifting production from one country where currency depreciation is more to another country affiliate where depreciation is less. It can shift production and marketing values for one country to another country to maintain total all country affiliates' position intact or unchanged. Production and marketing will increase in the centre, where depreciation is less and there are tax advantages and decrease in another centre where the depreciation is more and tax burden is heavy.

Economic exposure can be separated into two components — transactions exposure and operating exposure. Transactions exposure stems for the gains or losses on foreign currency denominated sales, contractual obligations etc. Its impact is felt mainly on the cash flow statements and profitability. Operating exposure is a longer term exposure to currency risks impacting on firm's costs and revenues and hence operating cash flows. The cost and price competitiveness will be changed. It may involve fresh investment to new product development, new brands with product differentiation, foreign supply contacts and distribution channels. The firm has to change its product lines, marketing strategy and promotion.

Transaction exposure arises only if the commitments lead to foreign currency denominated sales or purchases or enter into other contractual obligations in foreign currencies. This impact is due to the change in the nominal exchange rate. Admittedly, any change in the nominal exchange rate, accompanied by an equal change in price level should have no effects on relative competitive position of domestic firm *vis-à-vis* the foreign firms or competitors.

The assumption implied in the above analysis is that inflation, involving a rise in prices of say 10% does not change the relative prices involved in the inflation and all the goods rise by the same percentage. If then the exchange rate also depreciates by 10% then the relative export competitiveness of MNC and others will not change. Again so long as the contracts are entered into, not in nominal terms but only in real terms; the company should avoid contracts, fixed in foreign currency terms — then there will be no exchange risk but there will be only price or inflation risk.

## Factors Influencing Sensitivity

Sensitivity of a firm to economic exposure comprising the transaction exposure and operational exposure depends on the following factors:

(1) Price elasticity of demand for the firm's product.

(2) Firm's ability to shift the mix of input to inflation or exchange risk (substitutability).

(3) Firm's ability to differentiate the product.

(4) Price flexibility in tune with cost flexibility.

(5) The proportion of local currency financing relative to the foreign sources.

(6) Location of its major markets and its competitors and their behaviour towards the price and product change/flexibility.

(7) Extent to which inflation offsets the change in exchange rate.

(8) The long run effects of exchange rates are less due to the compensating measures that can be taken.

To sum up, the exchange risk is easy to identify; it is difficult to measure quantitatively the practical impact of this on the firm's cash flows.

## Integrated Strategy

As seen earlier, the total economic exposure comprise of two components, namely, short-run transactions exposure and long-run operational exposure. The strategy of MNC is for tracing the management of foreign exchange risk in terms of —

(1) Production Initiatives

(2) Marketing Initiatives

(3) Financial Management Strategies.

The short-run transactions exposure can be covered by denominating currency contracts in terms of the currency of the parent country (say the dollar); this will protect the earnings of the parent company as a whole in terms of its own currency.

In the case of long-term economic exposure, on the company's operations, it should not be the Finance Manager's concern alone; it should involve the Production and Marketing Manager as well as the top executives of the company as a whole, who should form a committee to chalk out pro-active strategy to meet the economic exposures. It is the general responsibility to be shared by not only the local affiliate but the parent company's whole management team. In such an integrated approach, the following flexible changes are to be kept in mind:

(1) Local management should be fed with the forecasts of inflation and exchange rate changes.

(2) To identify and highlight the areas which will be hit by the competitive exposure.

(3) Operating and financial managers should be given a free hand to meet these exposures, as and when affected.

It is necessary to estimate the degree of risk exposed and take up counter balancing measures in the overall strategy laid down by the Risk Management Team.

*(i)* Market selection and shifts in the marketing outlets.

*(ii)* Shifts in the production mix in tune with the changes in market selection.

*(iii)* To make necessary price adjustments through presumably introducing brand changes and trademark changes.

*(iv)* Promotional strategy should be geared up to the new pattern of production mix and marketing strategy.

(v) Shifting production locations among the plants of affiliates to take advantage of the exchange rate changes.

(vi) Shifting production capacity without changing the production location.

(vii) Changing the input mix through R&D results and changing the sourcing of inputs.

(viii) Raising the total productivity by reducing costs and increasing margins or even maintaining the margins.

The strategic marketing and production strategies referred to above should be followed by the Finance Manager's strategy of matching the asset liability mismatch. The changes in cash inflows should be offset by corresponding changes in outflows currency-wise. This should relate to the whole parent corporation and not to any single affiliate, which will contribute to the total MNC strategic plan to meet the economic exposure of exchange rate changes.

❖ ❖ ❖

# PART IV

# MANAGEMENT OF INTERNATIONAL BUSINESS OPERATIONS AND PRACTICES

# OPERATIONAL STRATEGIES OF MNCs

# 22

## Introduction

The tone of this chapter is confined to selective adaptative models in respect of business organisation and finance. These adaptative models relate to Five Mega 'M's

**LADDER TO GLOBALISATION**

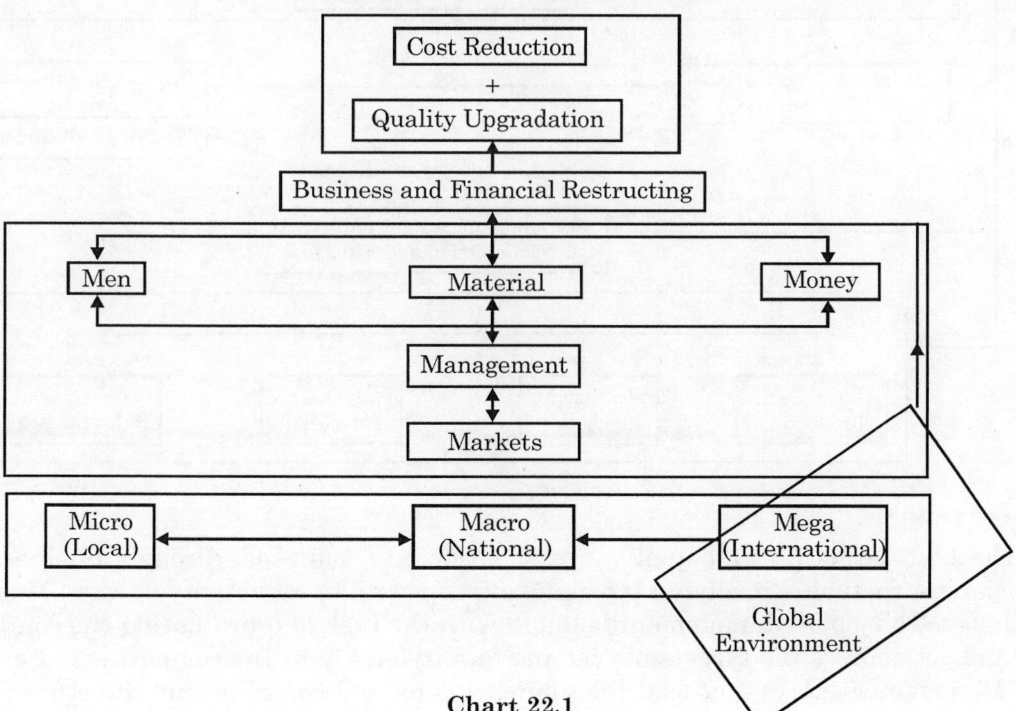


**Chart 22.1**

which matter to any organisation, namely, Men, Money, Materials, Markets and Management. Of these Five 'M's, which are 'Panchabhootas', constituting the totality of the organisational Universe, the vitals are, namely, 'Vayu' or breath giving life blood is Money or Finance. Restructuring is the buzz word which connects these two major planks of Business and Finance, which can elevate any economic unit to the global playground. The Business and Financial Restructuring is the theme of this Chapter.

## Strategy to Globalisation

The above conceptual chart is designed to impart an intuitive vision into the broad contours of this Chapter.

As the chart shows, the ladder to globalisation is steep and painful involving difficult cost reduction process with simultaneous steps towards quality upgradation, reaching global standards, where prices are given and competition is tough. Cost targeting is set by the market prices of the competitors in the global scenario and the quality is standardised to reach top ranking among the global players. The following chart shows steps in this direction:

**STRATEGY FOR GLOBALISATION**

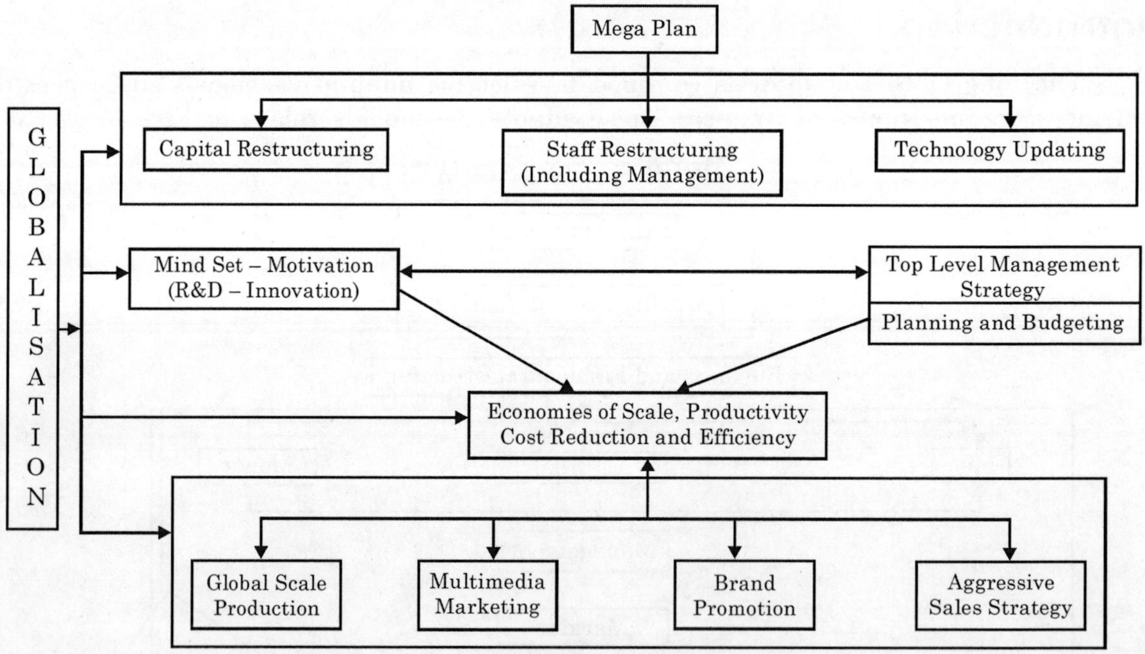


**Chart 22.2**

The cost targeting and quality upgradation are achieved through Business and Financial restructuring involving economy, efficiency and productivity of Men, Materials and Money. The job of Management is tough with the task of coordinating the conflicting goals and yet achieve the targets in cost and quality and fight the competitors at a global level. Management plays a crucial role in developing and co-ordinating the other factors men, money and materials to suit the product to market requirements. The Management requires a Mega Plan for Metamorphic transformation of the Business Organisation and effective financial restructuring.

Before describing the above chart on Mega Plan, it is apt to set out the aims of Management in this regard. The Mega Plan is a strategic Management plan to adapt the operations of economic unit to emerging economic, financial and international forces and other environmental factors. The major goal for the corporate unit is to come out as a global player making a dent on the market and maximise the wealth of the shareholders. The Management aims at:

*(i)* Meeting the competition in costs and prices in the global scenario.

*(ii)* Reaching the international standards in quality and secure brand names worth the name, and

*(iii)* Capture good chunk of the world markets, in addition to domestic market.

The Mega Plan for the above objectives involves the restructuring at a multi-dimensional level, namely, for capital employed, staff, technology and management strategies. The move to multi-nationalism encompasses changes in all the levels and mix of production, multimedia marketing, brand promotion, marketing strategies and distribution channels. The HRD component involves changes in motivation, R&D innovation and suitable top management strategy.

The management strategies have to be reshaped in the following directions:

(1) Economies of scale, cost reduction, efficiency in production process.

(2) Organisational restructuring involving men, materials and management, suitable for global production.

(3) Calibrating to globalisation through Foreign Direct Investment (FDI), capital flow and capital restructuring.

(4) Latest Technology Absorption and Modernisation.

(5) Cost Reduction and Quality Controls, leading to efficiency.

(6) Aggressive sales strategy, Multimedia marketing, Brand Promotion and Trademarks and patent rights.

(7) Financial strengthening through mergers, joint ventures and acquisitions.

## Organisational Change

Economic and financial reforms since 1991 have brought about some changes with an impact on corporate governance, namely:

(1) Increased domestic competition due to liberalisation and deregulation in the industrial and financial sectors of the economy.

(2) Opening up of the economy and globalisation leading to increased international competition.

(3) Devaluation of the rupee and freeing of the rupee on the current account leading to risks of the companies on the foreign front.

The stakeholders in the corporate performance are the investors, employees, customers, creditors and the government, whose interests predominate in influencing the corporate governance. The organisational and structural changes, needed for the strategic management for the given change in environmental factors are part of the total change in corporate governance. The organisational changes encompass the totality of changes starting from the composition and decision making process of the Board of Directors to the lowest level of a section or unit of the company's factory. They start with a SWOT analysis of the corporate organisation and lead to all needed structural, procedural changes, closures, mergers, acquisitions of other business divisions or units, demergers, spin offs, or divestments like that of Lakmi Machine divesting granite and floriculture business and Reliance Industries giving up stock broking business. Organisational restructuring involves changes in management tools and techniques, policies of control and administration and structures, systems and procedures such as decentralisation, delayering, product or market segment-based divisionalisation, changes in accountability, internal audit, quality and cost control systems reporting and disclosure method and practices etc.

## Corporate Governance

The Cadbury Committee Report on Corporate Governance in U.K. American Law institute's Researches into Regulatory practices in U.S.A. and CII's Draft Code of ethics in India have all aimed at improving the corporate governance in tune with the changing conditions at the national and international levels. As objective of corporate governance is to maximise the shareholders' wealth, and satisfy the requirements and interests of all the stakeholders in the company, it is closely related to the organisational and structural changes needed for globalisation and other ongoing economic and financial changes in the country. Corporate restructuring is also closely connected with all physical and financial changes in its operations, expansion, contractions, changes in structure, ownership and control, reorientation of policies for efficiency, cost and quality controls, productivity and profitability needed for achieving better objectives of all stakeholders of the company, referred to above. These changes are brought about as a result of responses of the management to the environmental challenges, posed by privatisation, liberalisation and globalisation, initiated by economic reforms. Changes in corporate governance is yet another aspect. Clause 49 of the Listing Agreement of the Stock Exchanges was made compulsory by the SEBI for all listed companies, imposing observance of good corporate governance of international standards from January 2006.

Management has to follow a policy of constant adjustment in planned strategies to changes in factors affecting the company. Strategic changes are no doubt the result of the internal dynamism of the organisation and perspectives of the management but are brought about importantly by the changing environment. Strategies aim at the corporate goals in the long-run, but changes in strategies are sometimes necessitated by growth of MNCs, international competition and the need for improving the quality to acceptable standards. All this requires a reorientation of management tools and strategies and adoption of strategic planning. There is need for transparency and proper disclosures, adoption of international standards of accounting and auditing and timely redressal of investor grievances, and accountability at all level of management of the organisation.

Most strategic policy changes would focus on internal aspects of the company, namely, intrinsic strengths and weaknesses, weeding out inefficient and weak divisions and strengthening of the core areas' competencies in the organisation, such as improving the quality of staff, productivity, capacity utilisation, etc. External aspects such as alliances, external support, collaboration and partnerships are the other lines of attack of the corporate managements. The immediate concern will no doubt be the costs and profit of the corporate unit to maximise the shareholders' wealth and promote an image building process to the public, government and other external agents.

In addition to profits and maximisation of wealth, the long run interests of the company lay in observance of laws of the land, social costs and benefits, pollution control, conservation of energy and preservation of ecological balance etc., which are social responsibilities of the company. The objectives of a global company are also achieved by better disclosures, transparency, international standards of accounting and, reporting, accountability and decentralisation and a sense of dynamism in management. All these involve observance of good business ethics and good corporate governance.

In sum, organisational restructuring encompasses changes in strategic planning, management perspectives, policy changes, structural changes in organisation and administration, systems and procedures etc. These aim at improving the internal strengths and competencies, quality, costs and profits etc. and adaptation of policies to suit to competition, globalisation and international factors.

## Role of FDI in Investment and Production

Both at macro level and micro level, the role of foreign direct investment is to accelerate the process of capital formation and production. The level of total production and production abroad through joint ventures, subsidiaries and affiliates or subcontractors is an indication of the adaptation of domestic corporates to the needs of globalisation. Similarly, one can look at globalisation as internationalisation of corporate strategies, their observance of the rules of global corporate governance, code of ethics, internationally accepted accounting standards and their commitment to meet competition across borders etc. These trends operate in both directions, viz., the Indian corporates operating abroad as MNCs, through their overseas joint ventures and affiliates and the foreign MNCs operating in India through their subsidiaries, branches and affiliates.

There is another related indicator of the corporate strategy towards globalisation, namely, through exports of goods and services produced at home, exports of patents, copy rights and technology related products. The ratio of exports to domestic production is a flow concept which measures the trend to globalisation. In this case, the corporate governance is to be adapted to a vigorous export penetrating strategy. Thus, the globalisation of business here means not only a shift in capital and tangible assets but also a shift in output of goods and services and in all needed inputs and intangible assets like management expertise and technological know-how, etc.

The other indicator of globalisation is a stock concept measured by proportion of fixed assets in the domestic economy financed by foreign investment or foreign finance inflow. Here, the corporate strategy of financing the capital structure and related issues become prominent at the micro-level.

Measured by either flow concept or stock concept, globalisation rate grew faster in the post-reform (1991) era than before. But the globalisation rate is much lower in India than some of the developing countries like China, not to speak of developed countries. Each of the corporate units as well as the corporates at the specific industry level have to evolve a strategy for the level of FDI which can be easily absorbed without creating problems of over-globalisation and to avoid immiserisation. Exporters of capital can then plan their export of tangible and intangible assets along with a corporate strategy for export of goods and services across borders, without saturation in any of the markets.

India's share in Foreign Direct Investment flows to developing countries during 1991-99 rose no doubt but still constituted hardly 2.5% of the total or even less. Besides total foreign investment as a proportion of total national investment in India constitutes less than 5%. There is a vast potential for Indian corporates to attract foreign equity and technology into Indian Corporate capital structure. The government policy is of course to encourage foreign inflows on a selective basis, but the actual inflows are less than 20 to 25% of the government clearances and approvals. This indicates that the Indian Corporate governance is still not tuned to the quick and full absorption of foreign funds and foreign technology. There is much to be desired at the individual corporate level for a proper corporate strategy suitable to globalisation rate at the level of both investment in fixed stock (both tangible and intangible) and at the level of export of goods and services. The Reserve Bank studies show that net foreign inflow is in fact negative on the revenue account in respect of many large and medium scale industrial units, indicating insufficient export thrust in their strategies. So is the case with the absorption of foreign investment funds by the Indian Corporates. These are the two areas where the management efficiency has to be improved and effective corporate strategy needs to be implemented. There are no doubt some hurdles for better absorption of FDI in India due to government controls, trade and fiscal policies and taxation. There are other problems of red tape and corruption in bureaucracy and administrative machinery.

## Technology Adaptation

Technology is a vital input in the process of economic growth. Innovations and inventions have brought about Industrial Revolution. As the technological developments and progress is uneven as between the countries, and there is concentration of R&D activity in developed world with 94% of the total expenditure incurred there, corporates find compelling reasons for promotion of transfer of technology. There are areas where foreign technology is needed and other areas where indigenous technology is more relevant and cheaper. As such the government policy is to encourage inflow of technology in selected areas and indigenous technology in other areas.

Adaptation of foreign technology to Indian conditions is another area of concern, as absorption is more important than importation of foreign technology. The constraints to the use of foreign technology is the availability of free foreign exchange to pay for it, absorption capacity in the host country and the problems of adaptation arising out of environmental factors, infrastructural constraints and structural deficiencies.

The latest technology for cost saving purposes is a specific requirement of any industry to remain competitive. This goes by the name of upgradation and modernisation of technology. It is in this context that the types of technology that have to be adapted by the host country require special mention.

The following Table presents these relations in Chart 22.3

**GLOBALISATION AND TECHNOLOGY**

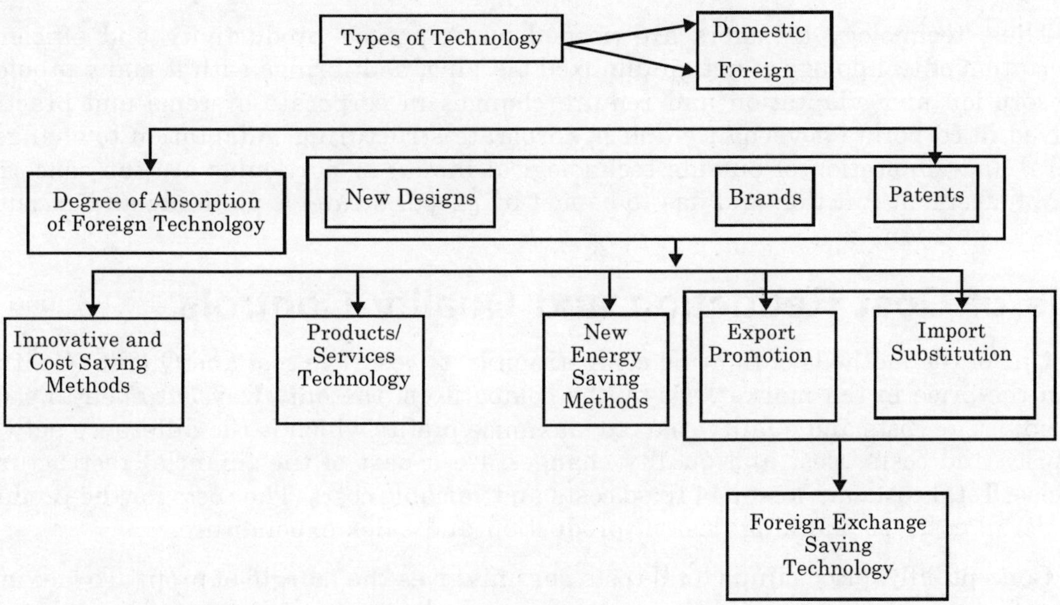


**Chart 22.3**

In the above chart, foreign technology has the problems of absorption and adaptation and in some cases leads to substitution by indigenous technology. New designs, brand names and patent rights are some of the forms that technology flows in and these should encourage innovation, cost savings methods of energy and foreign exchange savings. Export promotion, import substitution and saving in foreign exchange are the ultimate objectives. In the interim period, foreign technology plays a catalytic role.

The absorption of each of these types gives rise to specific problems to be met by proper corporate strategy. Some of them give rise to labour problems, some to input shortages and the others to specific skill requirements. Some technologies imported will produce negative effects such as disincentives for local entrepreneurs to develop indigenous technologies, redeployment or unemployment of labour, emergence of new competition in domestic markets, obsolescence, wage disparities and staff unrest. More importantly there will be resistance to any change and organisational restructuring become more difficult. It is therefore, not a simple matter to engraft foreign technology into Indian soil where management practices and procedures differ. It will lead to many labour and managerial problems, connected with employment, labour practices, social and political unrest and work environment. Resolving these issues are the subject of technology absorption, which requires the attention of top management and organisational restructuring.

Easy adaptation to change is the first requirement of any efficient management, but how easily can they carry with them the whole team of middle and lower level management and workforce is a matter to be attended to in strategic planning. Attitudinal changes, systems changes and a host of other changes are needed for adaptation to new technology, and upgradation or modernisation of technology. Technology adaptation is a difficult and painful process, requiring high managerial skills and organisational changes.

Thus, technology transfers are needed for improved productivity and efficiency. Importation of technology is not an unmixed blessing, as it brings with it many problems of absorption and adaptation and require changes in corporate systems and practices involved in corporate governance and in corporate structuring. Adaptation to change in general and adaptation of outside technological inputs in particular are the concern of Top Management function and has to be met by proper strategic planning and execution of the Mega Plan.

## Role of Cost Reduction and Quality Controls

One of the methods of fighting competition is to resort to cost and Quality Controls. Given the price in the market, set by the competitors, the only way left open to a unit is to adjust its costs and quality so as to maximise profits which is the difference between the price and costs. Cost and quality changes are a part of the financial restructuring exercise. Total costs are a sum of fixed costs and variable costs. The costs for the producer include all costs of planning design, production and sales expenditure.

Conceptually, price minus total costs per unit gives the margin of profit. To maximise the profits, given the price, the objective of any productive unit is to minimise the costs per unit. In the scheme of price led costing, sales are determined by demand and price, and the concept of target costing is developed. In this approach, costs are examined from the start of planning and design itself and upto the stage of production, marketing, distribution and sales. The customer determined price and his preferred quality are the targets for cost and quality management.

Target Cost Management (TCM) is a scientific technique to establish a cost target along with a breakdown of it and to achieve it, the unit adopts latest technologies possible to reach production specification for the designed costs and include in it the life cycle costs, namely, development, design, manufacturing, distribution, sales, usage and waste disposal costs. It should however be noted that evolving and achieving a target cost is the joint endeavour of a cross functional team and may encompass the whole organisational effort.

Target costing is different from standard costing. While the latter focuses on internal factors, with waste within allowable limits and meeting the specifications within tolerable limits of the standards set by industry, the former concentrates on the external factors, leading to the demand, quality and specifications, at a zero defect approach, design or reinvent a specification and quality, suited to the customer through the team work of the organisation and the competitive environment. TCM is a strategic planning technique from conception to cremation of a product synthesising the external market information with the internal cost information. In the era of globalisation and growing multi-nationalisation of trade and industry, strategic management involving target costing and internationally accepted Quality Standards, is a must for meeting the competitive forces and yet maintain the profit margins, if not to increase them. For this purpose, various forms of restructuring of the corporate unit may be needed, namely, Business restructuring, financial restructuring, organisational restructuring and even Technological restructuring.

## Role of Brands and Trademarks

In the internationally competitive environment each unit and each product of each unit has to be distinct and unique to stand above the troubled waters. For this purpose, strategic planning should encompass a scheme of product uniqueness, aggressive marketing through a worldwide network and after sales service to maintain its image and market share. In the global context, many product markets, brands and trademarks are designed and patented and sales are made through aggressive thrust of advertisement. In the consumers' mind, the product is known by the brand like Colgate or PEPSODENT and not as toothpaste of any company. Advertisement has to establish the uniqueness of the quality and product and superiority of it over its rivals. This brand sale is one of the marketing strategies particularly suitable to consumer products in a globalised context. For decades, the advertisement of Horlicks as product used nationally and internationally is another example in brand name promotion.

Brand names and trade marks are strategies in the marketing, relative to target costing in manufacture. Assam Tea or Darjeeling Tea is not only a generic sales name, but is also a product in manufacturing. There are hosts of such examples on the Indian Corporate scene itself, not to speak of such products, in developed countries. Indian corporates have much to learn in this respect from their counterparts and foreign MNCs, operating in India.

Both in respect of quality standardisation or upgradation, and cost reduction, Indian corporates have to pursue aggressively production and sales strategies to beat the competition, for which their factorial efficiencies, labour and capital productivity and their average and marginal costing have to be comparable with those internationally operating giants. The tools of strategic planning, for environmental adaptation are thus necessary, from inception of product to its cremation and waste disposal.

## Financial Strengthening

Corporate reorganisation and structuring may also aim at financial strengthening. Any restructuring should lead to additional cashflow, reduce costs and increased profits. In this respect, financial restructuring may have different facets, as shown on next page:

It will be seen from the chart 22.4 that financial restructuring has two aspects, namely, internal and external. The tools of internal restructure are changes in capital structure to take advantage of low cost financing (Capital Productivity), labour redeployment to improve labour productivity (HRD) and changes in technology and

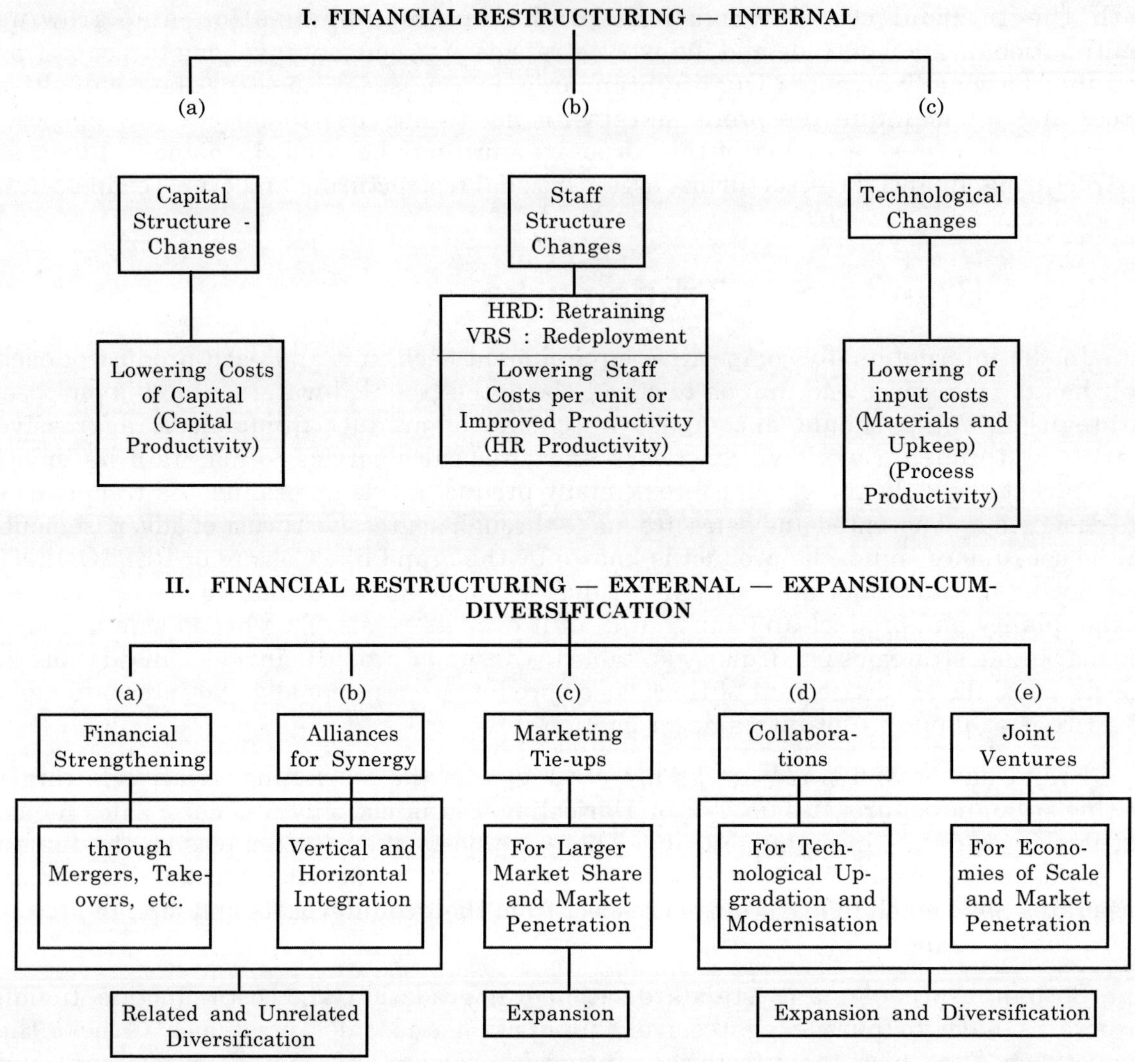


**Chart 22.4**

practices to lower the manufacturing costs and marketing costs, both domestically and internationally (process productivity).

Financial restructuring through external means includes such methods as mergers, acquisitions (and takeovers), strategic alliances, collaborations, marketing tie-ups and joint ventures. Some of these methods are pure strategic tools for financial strengthening, namely, vertical and horizontal integration, economies of scale, marketing strategies for market penetration. All these tools are actively used by many foreign companies of Western developed countries. MNCs now operating in India have also been resorting to financial strengthening, vertical and horizontal integration, market penetration, modernisation and expansion and to lower the costs to remain competitive in the global environment. The Indian corporates have begun to adapt these strategies forced by sheer competitive pressures and as a method of survival of the fittest.

An example of merger for convenience is that of Roussel India Ltd. with Hoechst M. Roussel. The losses of Roussel India would now be covered up by profits of Hoechst M. Roussel (HMR). Another example of loss making unit seeking saviours is that of Kalyani Seamless. Tisco took over the marketing of Kalyani Seamless Tubes and pipes through an agreement, as it has shut down its own unit for tubes. India Cements took over Rasi Cements and ICICI, the I.T.C. Classic to consolidate their respective strengths. An example of strategic alliance for globalisation is the agreement between Kotak Mahindra Capital Co (KMCC) and Goldman Sachs to strengthen their respective positions in the Indian market, namely, investment banking on the one hand and stock broking on the other.

## Mergers and Acquisitions

In the context of stiff competition from MNCs who have free access to both manufacturing and trading activity in India, Indian Corporates have to meet this challenge by improving efficiency and productivity. Besides, their technical upgradation should be the main plank for facing foreign competition.

To meet this competition and to be able to operate on level playing ground with MNCs and foreign companies, Indian corporates can strengthen themselves by mergers and acquisition to augment their resource base, achieve economies of scale and increase their asset size, and scale of operations.

Mergers can be friendly takeovers, like the parent companies merging its subsidiaries with it and achieve vertical and horizontal integration. Reliances Industries has adopted this method to become a large Indian MNC. Sometimes, bail out takeover is made to merge with sick and non-viable undertakings. The examples of horizontal diversification and acquisition are those of ITC, Birla Jute etc.

Mergers can also be arranged marriages particularly arranged by the B.I.F.R. in the case of many sick and non-viable units. Hostile takeovers are controlled by SEBI's Rules for takeovers, clauses 40A and B of Listing, Agreement and Company Law Provisions.

Examples of mergers of group companies are Nav Bharat Ferro taking over of Nav Chrome and Rasi Cements taking over of Rasi Ceramics and Indian Cements taking over Rasi Cements. Hindustan Lever has effected a number of group mergers. Gujarat Ambuja got BIFR nod to acquire the ailing Modi Cement.

Mergers among banks are also common and this has been recommended by Narasimham Committee Report. SBI has taken over a number of small sick banks. The new Bank of India was merged with Punjab National Bank. The RBI has permitted many such mergers in the last decade.

The Corporates have to build global capacities in the present scenario. The financially weak companies have all to fear. From 1995 onwards there were a number of mergers and takeovers. Some of them are for consolidation, like the merger of the East Coast Breweries and Distilleries and Sica Distilleries into Shaw Wallace.

Some weak companies sold off some of their divisions in the case of Allwyn Refrigerators to Voltas. Duphar International sold its brand Crocin to the Smithkline-Beecham. PLCI Ajay Piramal Group has taken over Nicholas Laboratories and so is the case of Sumitra Pharmaceuticals with Roche Products etc.

## Consolidation

The objective of consolidation is achieved by agreements with competitors and related companies. Thus, DSP and Merill Lynch have had a joint venture in financial services. ICICI is in strategic alliance with South Indian Bank, to share business interests and strategies. French automobile major Renault has been planning strategic alliance with ailing Pal-peugeut Ltd. Modiluft is in strategic alliance with British Airways. Swiss air and Air India have planned to share capacity etc.

## Global Joint Ventures Abroad

With the permission given for mutual funds to invest abroad, UTI has announced its plans to go abroad. Many export, oriented companies are also planning to operate abroad. Bharati Global will be the first Indian company to set and operate telecom services outside India, particularly in Seychelles. Ispat of Laxmi Mutual group has launched a new production unit in Mexico and got this company listed in New YORK. Joint Ventures abroad may also increase. Currently as the RBI has freed the A.Ds from prior RBI permission for releasing funds for joint ventures abroad, subject to some limits, Indian Companies have to become global as in the case of Dabur India and Ranbaxy which have set up units in UK, Mexico, China and a number of other countries. Dr. Reddy Labs has also planned for expansion in the USA.

The Indian giants have to compete with similar giants abroad. Things are however not that easy for the average Indian Corporates. They have the threat of foreign competition and fear of building global capacities, in terms of technology, quality, cost and marketing strategies etc. The Indian laws, taxation and government procedures and a host of other environmental problems stand as hurdles for the Indian companies to go global. Only the fittest and the strong companies can succeed in competing effectively abroad and become global players. Financial strengthening and business restructuring are thus the need of the hour. In sum, each organisation has to adopt a plan unique to itself to meet the global challenges. The opportunities particularly for those with export market and export potential are vast. Each of the corporates has to plan its own strategies suitable to its structure, culture, tradition and environment. But the opening of the economy of India and with foreign players actively engaged in Indian markets, both in product markets and financial markets has opened up challenges to Indian Corporates to meet the foreign MNCs on equal terms and at the same time expand abroad to play in the foreign markets. The chapter covered a gamut of tools and techniques in business restructuring and financial strengthening of the Indian Corporates to become global players and meet the challenge of global players in India.

❖ ❖ ❖

# MANAGEMENT OF MULTINATIONAL OPERATIONS

23

## Traditional Theory

With the increasing role of MNCs, in the world economy, the traditional theories of Trade and Investment have been restated. The contribution of MNCs to the economies in which they operate are felt in many areas, as shown below:

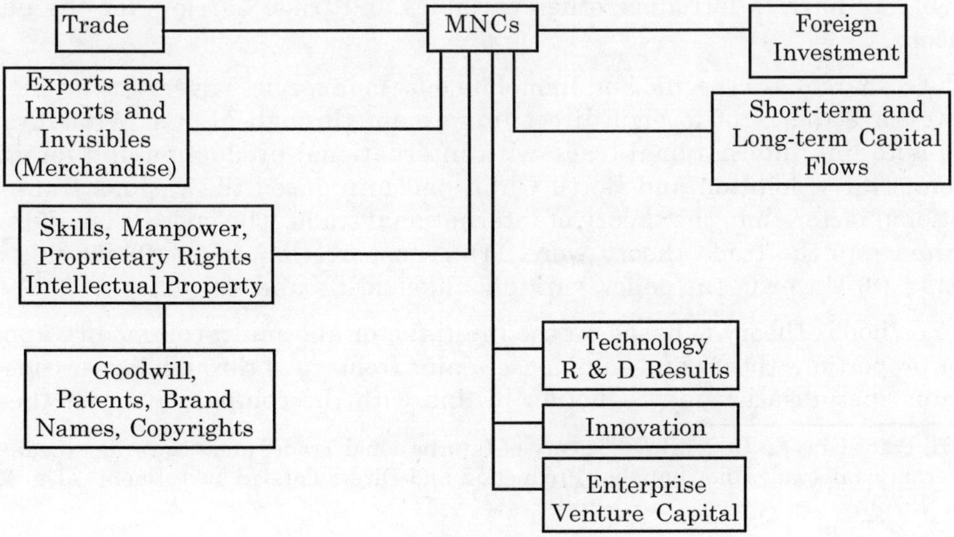


**Chart 23.1**

Factoral immobility and commodity mobility which have been assumed by the traditional theory do not hold good now. Except land, all the other factors are mobile. Differences in natural endowments are now evened out by bringing in the co-operating factors into areas which are immobile like infrastructure, mining oil, energy etc. by MNCs. The scarcities of some factors and abundance of others are smoothened out, across borders by MNCs.

Basically, they reduce costs by conquering time and space. The whole globe is for them one unit, wherein distance and communications and other barriers to trade and investment are got over and bridged. Transportation costs, government policy variables, taxes, tariffs, trade and exchange controls are no longer barriers to the MNCs as they know how to get over them. Information Revolution has opened up the national borders.

Perfect markets do not exist; various degrees of semi-monopoly conditions exist and private enterprise and competitive forces co-exist with such semi-monopoly conditions in both factor and commodity markets. Financial markets have got interlinked more closely across borders. The weaker are taken over or cease to exist and the stronger survives.

The strengths of MNCs are in respect of their control over capital, , technology R&D, skills and information technology (MIS). The theories of Trade and Foreign Investment across borders have been reformulated to incorporate the above factors relating to MNCs. A more generalised theory of trade is formulated and movement of capital funds have found new channels in search of profits and where direct entry is banned, indirect entries through joint ventures and technology penetration have become now possible and common.

## Generalised Trade Theory

The theory of international trade has been generalised by Prof. Gray to include the role of multinational corporations (MNCs). Traditional theories depend on the different resources endowments of different countries and their international immobility. Once these assumptions are invalidated by the MNCs through trade and private foreign direct investment, we have to introduce other variables and trade barriers for the purpose of trade theory.

If the resources are specific and immobile but their services are transferable through MNCs, we have theory of foreign direct investment through MNCs. What Prof. Gray[1] has done is to link international trade with international production and foreign direct investment. Harry Johnson and Bertil Ohlin had introduced the various trade barriers and locational factors into the theory of international trade. The specific barriers to trade incorporated into the trade theory were: (1) Transportation costs; (2) Psychic distance factors; and (3) Government policy variables like tariffs and subsidies.

The orthodox theory is based on the multi-factor and multi-commodity approach to the factor proportions theory and emphasises gains from trade through larger consumption and greater specialisation in production in line with the comparative cost theory. The

1. Prof. H. Peter Gray "A Generalised Theory of International Trade" and "Towards a Unified Theory of International Trade, International Production and Direct Foreign Investment" (The Macmillan Press, 1976).

change needed for the Generalised Theory is to incorporate factors like specific goods used as inputs and firm-specific factors of production and product-specific inputs, and integrate the theory of international production with world trade and foreign direct investment. John H. Dunning's approach in his eclectic theory of "Trade Location of Economic Activity and MNC" involved three sets of determinants of international production, viz., ownership-specific advantages of enterprises of one nationality over those of another, internationalisation of incentives and location specific advantages. Gray's theory adopts Dunning's approach and takes into account the transferability of proprietary technology and other specific natural resources or endowments of some countries into others through the MNCs. The modern theory has integrated trade with Aid and investment and takes into account technology differences and product specific and country specific factors and market imperfection.

The short-run analysis assumes constant global factoral supplies. These supplies are distributed among countries so as to maximise international production and to achieve the lowest costs of production, thanks to the foreign direct investment and the activities of MNCs. The new international allocation of resources could maximise the rates of return to factors of production which are both internationally mobile and immobile and products specific factors are spread out across borders so as to optimise international production. A proper allocation of resource inputs to maximise production and to achieve optimum pattern of trade across national boundaries is simultaneously determined to set an equilibrium according to this theory. Any disturbance in factoral inputs in production and resources allocation would change the pattern of production internationally and thus, of trade accordingly.

The proprietary technology, know-how and product specific capital may not allow substitution of such factors in the input-mix of a product. This would then result in a quasi-rent payable to that specific factor. The MNCs would achieve the maximum feasible net value added and quasi-rent for their specific factors by achieving optimum geographical distribution of their assets and their sales and earnings. The MNCs may use such factors and distribute the products or services involving the use of such inputs among nations so as to lower costs of production through better specialisation and increased scale of production. The MNCs may transfer such specific factors of production or their services from one country to another if such relocation would lower the costs and enable the company to make their goods available in the market at a price lower than any other sources of supply, namely, through trade or through import substitution measures in the domestic economy.

The only countervailing factors to be considered from the point of the LDCs are the alternatives to foreign direct investment, namely, imports through trade or domestic production in substitution of products available through the MNCs. A quasi-rent or the monopoly element of the MNCs is not desirable for promoting strict competition in any economy; MNCs are not prima facie desirable unless the other alternatives are not feasible in the existing set-up. It is in this context that the role of MNCs in international division of labour and in trade has to be carefully assessed in respect of the LDCs.

In the Modern Theory of International Trade, the changes necessitated by introduction of multinationals and foreign direct investment are: *(i)* The assumptions for a two-country and two-commodity model are to be changed; *(ii)* There are five categories of inputs, viz., capital, land, skilled labour and unskilled labour, enterprise and technology, some of which are firm specific and some product specific; *(iii)* The principal resource endowments, tastes and production functions are supposed to be known and fixed and trade balanced by means of free exchange rates.

The international transfer of resources and factors of production wherever, possible is in substitution of international trade for goods and services. Such migration can be in respect of product specific factors, or firm specific technology and can either be trade creating or trade supplementary or trade diverting. The factors for and against any proposal for foreign direct investment are complex and each case is to be studied separately, given the assumption that the MNC could make a direct investment and transfer its proprietary specific inputs and products specific inputs to another country. This could create markets and expand trade on a global basis which could be in the interests of the host country or not depending on the alternatives available to the host country.

If the potential for investment by MNC exists through expected higher quasi-rents in the host country, the short-term equilibrium is disturbed and foreign direct investment takes place. A reverse position can be visualised when foreign direct investment will leave the country due to changes in the pattern of costs and prices or of demand to lower the quasi-rents. The factor specific and commodity specific factors have to be paid quasi-rent in the host country.

The effects of impediments to trade through commercial policies, transportation costs and other psychological barriers would get reflected in the pattern of costs and prices of foreign goods versus domestic goods. The ranking of importable goods in the domestic country and of exportable goods in the foreign country would change. Psychic-distance impediments to trade would get reflected through changes in cost and prices of tradable commodities.

The generalised theory of international trade would also incorporate the location specific factors through foreign direct investments by MNCs as also country specific and product specific factors of production. The final outcome of international trade would depend upon the changes introduced in the production patterns in the two countries under consideration and in the costs and prices, including the factor prices in the respective countries and a host of other factors including tastes, habits, technological levels etc.

## Multinational Corporations (MNCs)[2]

The role of multinational corporations in the pattern of world production and trade has been increasing over the decades. As estimated by the Brandt Commission, they now control about one-third of the world production and the intra-national branch transfers of these MNCs would work out to about one-fourth of the world sales. The bulk of private investment is accounted for by the MNCs. The induction of latest technology and exploitation of the natural resources in the developing countries may be mainly due to the enterprise of multinational corporations. The oligopoly situation in their operations can be gleaned from the concentration of their productive capacity in the big 50 MNCs.

2. For detailed discussion, see Sanjaya Lall, *The New Multinationals,* John Wiley and Sons, 1983, Chapter on "Multinationals from India."

## Definition[3]

By definition, a multinational corporation is an enterprise which has "managerial headquarters located in one country while the enterprise carries out operations in a number of countries as well." Either ownership is held in one country and control in another country or both in one country and the operations in many countries. These corporations have operations and sales extending to various countries with some of them exceeding the Gross National Product of even the advanced developed countries. The strategy of expansion is through private direct investment abroad through setting up of subsidiaries or branch offices or joint ventures. As most of the companies have reached their limit of expansion in their own countries, the scope of expansion lies in foreign countries. For horizontal expansion, setting up conglomerates and integrating dissimilar activities, they arrange a holding company to have a number of subsidiaries in a number of countries. By vertical integration with forward and backward linkages, expansion takes place through branches and setting up of factories in other countries, for parts, spares, ancillaries, etc. Another method of expansion is re-investment and self-financing of the various diversified activities of the corporation in the existing countries. The transfer of technology, enterprise and sometimes managerial talent also go along with direct foreign investment by these corporations.

Nearly 50 per cent of the MNCs are based in the U.S. and the rest in the UK, France, Japan and West Germany, which are the major industrialised countries in the world. Industry-wise, the concentration of multinationals is in airlines and extractive industries, such as oils, minerals, drugs and software.

## Rationale of the Dominance of MNCs

The key to the success of the MNCs lies in their broad-based operations, secrecy of their accounts and vast technological research base. They have control of not only the capital but also technology with which they seek investment avenues and markets in other developed and developing countries.

Firstly the rationale for their expansion is both offensive as to capture new markets and defensive in the sense of retaining their share of the market in the teeth of competition. Their expansion is mostly in fields of minerals, oils and plantations, where foreign investment was welcomed historically. The scale of operations increases and costs per unit go down significantly. Similarly, larger technological transfers permit larger research and development costs, as they are now spread over a large scale of operations. The establishment of their units in foreign countries is based on the availability of cheaper labour, managerial talent or other inputs or to reduce the transport costs or to expand their market and scale of operations.

Secondly, they have the controlling interest in technology as well as capital which enables them to wield political as well as economic power in more than one country. They seek unexploited resources, natural as well as human in the developing countries for exploitation and to capture the markets. Besides, the foreign governments encourage the

3. I.L.O.,"Multinational Enterprises and Social Policy", 1973.

inflow of foreign direct investment, for the purpose of expansion of economic activity, income and employment in their economies.

With the increasing tariff barriers and protectionism in most of the developed countries, MNCs have found a method of circumventing them by establishing their own factories, processing units and joint ventures in these countries. They also take advantage of tax-concession and low labour costs in some of the LDCs. They secure benefits of lower costs through technology-sharing, economies of scale, marketing and managerial expansion and a further boost to technological upgradation and R&D.

## Merits and Demerits

Admittedly, it is to the advantage of both the MNCs and their home countries to have their activities expanding in many countries. However, the host countries have both advantages and disadvantages due to flow of investments from the MNCs. The merits are briefly, the promotion of investments, income and employment in the host country, provision of latest technology with a productive capacity at low costs of production, increased competition with the domestic enterprise, and larger world trade which result in better all-round specialisation. The MNCs have also started adapting themselves to the requirements of the LDCs which are their host countries. Restrictions with respect to the direction of investments as well as the quantum, location as well as the capacity and other regulations are generally complied by them in the host countries. The multinationals spread their activities not only in Emerging Market economics but in developed countries as well.

There are also disadvantages in the operations of the MNCs. Motivated by profit, they exploit natural resources as in the case of oil resources without replenishment, undermine the national interest by charging exorbitant prices unrelated to costs, ignore all standards of quality, health precaution and pollution control which they could not do in their own home countries. They could manipulate their accounts through transfer price mechanism and avoid showing excess profits and escape from the tax net. They have the money power with the result they wield their influence on political and administrative system of the governments of the host countries. Many of the MNCs are reported to be unscrupulous to violate all cannons of equity and justice and promote their own self-interest through expansion of their activities and making super-profits.

## Re-assessment of the MNCs' Role

In more recent years, the role of MNCs has been accepted as inescapable. They have an important part to play in the transfer of private resources for investment and technologies which very few developing countries can afford to miss. The vast natural resources and the underdeveloped nature of the technologies in many LDCs require the services of MNCs. The governments of the host countries have also regulated their inflows and outflows and the pattern of their operations. Many countries have now established their own multinational corporations albeit on a small-scale, as in the case of India, in the field of banking, hotel services and consultancy services. Besides, in the future, the smaller-sized multinationals are going to capture the market of the vast growing multinationals as the latter are getting unwieldy. Even in India L&T, Tatas and

Ambanis, among others have become MNCs. This development is taking place in both developed and developing countries, although, MNCs have readjusted their future role on a different pattern from that in the past. A new category of multinational corporations is coming up from the LDCs to reap the monopolistic advantages and higher benefits from technological intensity and advanced marketing techniques.[4]

The motives of foreign investment would continue to dominate in the future world and the need for capital and advanced research technology is indispensable for the growth of the poorer countries as Asia and Africa. The MNCs bring in certain definite advantages to both the host countries as well as home countries referred to earlier. They increase employment, expand the flow of goods and services and improve the living standard of the people across the world. Thus, had it not been for the MNCs, the developing countries would not have been able to acquire these inputs necessary for development and this assures the continuance of the importance of the MNCs in the future world pattern of production and trade.

The liberalised policy of foreign flows into Indian industries and dilution of FERA, encouraging MNC to operate and expand in India are promoting the competition and make our economy more competitive and efficient.

The multinational corporations have revolutionised the system of world production and sales. Their activities have brought to question the traditional trade theory, based on comparative costs and locational advantage. The transnational company may produce at one corner of the world and supply the finished goods at another corner of the world at a cost lower than that when produced locally with its traditional comparative cost advantage and locational superiority.

The growth of MNC activities has changed the patterns of trade based on skill endowments and transport cost. Some more recent theories such as "Neo-technology" and "Neo-factor proportions theories" base their explanation of trade patterns on market imperfections, differences in technology, skill levels, economies of scale and product differentiation. These take into account the role of MNCs and technological dynamism in LDCs. Professor Gray generalised theory also incorporates the effects of MNC's operations on world production and trade.

## Impact of MNCs' Operations

The operations of MNCs on a global scale have both advantages and disadvantages. But the advantages to the world are more than the disadvantages which are to be taken as the necessary evils. The disadvantages are briefly the greater concentration of wealth, increase in financial power and with the greater political clout, weeding out of the weaker and smaller ones in competition, exploitation of natural resources, without adequate replenishment, exploitation of labour with their free exit and entry policies etc. These are all more acutely felt in underdeveloped and developing countries with less than full employment and with a large component of poor, illiterate and weaker sections, and large unemployment.

4. Sanjaya Lall, *The New Multinationals,* John Wiley and Sons, 1983.

The advantages are more pronounced. They bring in scarce capital and other scare resources like skills, technology and R&D. They increase outputs, lower costs and raise profits and increase the shareholders' wealth. There will be a qualitative improvement in outputs, sales strategies, after sales services. The consumers would benefit by a wider range of goods, better standardised quality, raise in standard of living of the people in general. The producers are forced to improve the quality and lower the costs in competition with the others. Markets are penetrated and increased. R&D results and technologies including the latest ones would be available. Overall investment will rise leading to growth in output, employment and income in the long run. The distributional effects of income may however turn out to be adverse.

The operations of MNCs increase with the reduction of barriers to trade and investment. The benefits of larger world trade, larger incomes, lower costs and prices due to economies of scale follow from their operations. Their impact on the goods and services markets is improvement in quality, reduction in costs and better services. Their impact on the factor markets is to increase their mobility and increase their rewards by improving their skills and better utilisation of them. Their impact on the financial markets is far superior, as capital mobility will be increased and its scarcity factor is reduced. The cost of capital is lowered and the advantages of capital gearing, access to cheaper foreign funds and better capital structuring are the results. The overall productivity and profitability of capital will be increased.

## Growth Theories

Theoretically, the MNC operations impact on all the markets, as shown below:

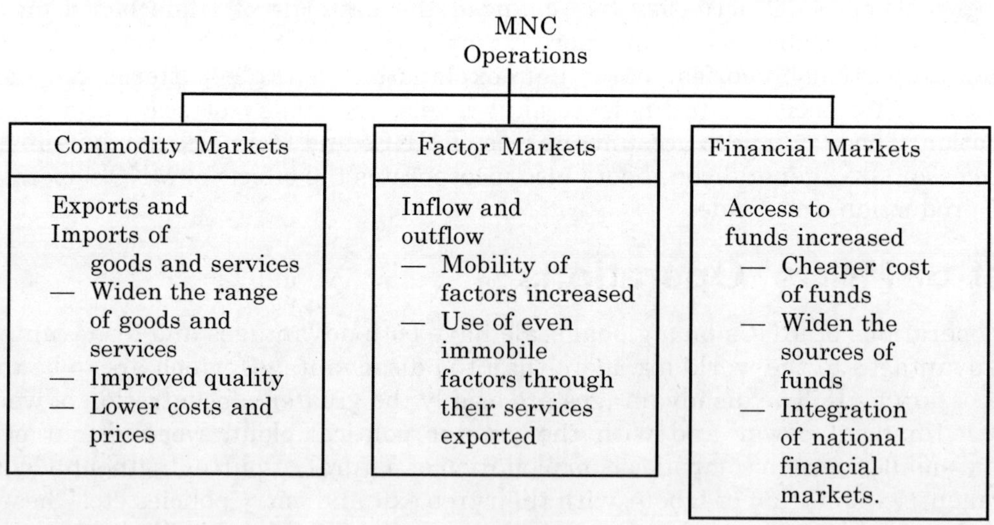


**Chart 23.2**

An analysis of the contribution of the MNCs to the concerned countries shows the following factors at work:

**(1) Complementary effect:** They bring in resources which complement the domestic resources and promote output and income.

**(2) Supplementary effect:** They augment resources, which are not adequate and utilise the unutilised or under-utilised resources more effectively.

Critics argue that the above effects should be seen in the context of their negative role of supplanting the domestic resources and their exploitation. This possibility is there, which can be safeguarded by a proper policy, but in most cases, supplanting will arise, if the domestic resources are inefficiently used and are not competitive or technologically outdated.

**(3) Bottleneck relieving effect:** The foreign trade and foreign investment promoted by MNCs can relieve some shortages of critical inputs like foreign exchange resources, up-to-date technology, etc.

**(4) Augmentation effect:** The range of commodities and services available domestically can be increased and widened, improve quality and after sales services, useful to consumers and public.

**(5) R&D effect:** MNCs spend more on R&D and their results may lower costs and prices and widen the range of goods.

**(6) Savings and Investment effect:** The operations of MNCs augment savings and investment at home through the following:

(a) Foreign investment multiplier ($\Delta I$), increase in investment leading to a multiple increase in income ($\Delta Y$).

(b) Foreign Trade Multiplier, operating through exports and imports on the domestic production and income by a multiple increase in exports, consequent on the role of MNCs.

The above effects are seen in the growth of economic development of some countries, increase in world output and income as also in world trade. Increase in output arises out of all the above effects and in particular by their gap filling role in trade and investment. Foreign trade in both goods and services may increase; technology and skills flow in either direction. Under-utilised or unutilised resources are effectively used and better allocative efficiency may be achieved. The growth in global business will bring out the potential of the domestic MNCs to expand and diversify into global players. Efficiency and productivity being the watch words, increase in competition and the free play of market forces achieve wider horizons of productive activity, profitability and rise in standards of living of the people in the world in general.

Empirically, some studies (RBI) have shown a positive correlation between growth of GDP and foreign capital inflow. Since 1992, FDI and portfolio investment by FII in India has grown fast and this might have helped the growth of income, employment and exports. It was estimated that nearly 18% of corporate market capitalisation is now owned by FIIs and nearly one-half of manufacturing output has been exported in 2003-04. These facts evidence the positive impact of MNCs role in the Indian economy.

❖ ❖ ❖

# MANAGEMENT OF GLOBAL BUSINESS PRACTICES

# 24

Business management, whether it is global or domestic, involves an efficient management of assets and liabilities of the firm in a way that the return on assets minus the costs involved in liabilities is maximised and that there is no mismatch between the maturity pattern of assets and liabilities.

Any firm manages its business in a way that its short-term liquidity and long-term solvency are ensured and that it is in a position to meet its obligations as and when they arise and maintain its creditworthiness in the eyes of creditors, investors and public. It has also to increase its profits and profitability.

Besides, any firm is faced with three major decisions in its business operations and policy, namely, investment decision, financing decision and dividend decision. Each of these decisions have an impact on the value of the firm. The basic objective of the firm is to maximise its wealth and the shareholders' value of their equity shares. To raise this value, and achieve the above objective of profit maximisation, the firm has to maximise the returns, minimise the risk, consistent with its level of operations and given the constraints that it has to face from the environment and government policies.

These constraints are more and problems galore in the case of global players. Their objectives are the same but the choices and alternatives are more varied and strategies that they adopt are different and their tools and techniques are more diverse and complex. But the principles involved in corporate financial management of the global players do not change from those of the domestic corporate players.

## Current Asset Management

Short-term capital requirements of MNCs are discussed in this chapter. The management of working capital by MNCs is in principle similar to that of any domestic corporate. The differences between them arise due to *(a)* Wider options for short-term financing, *(b)* Wider options for short-term investment of surplus funds and *(c)* Impact of the taxes, currency fluctuations and exchange controls.

Short-term current assets include Cash, Marketable Securities, Accounts Receivable and Inventories. The objectives of working capital management are to ensure the solvency of the company and to maximise the return or minimise the cost by optimum utilisation of funds. Money Manager or Treasurer is faced with a larger number of constraints due to exchange control regulations and lack of free and uncontrolled funds flow across borders. He has to be informed of all the controls and regulations on the flow of funds and investments abroad. At times of recession when the Money Manager has to scramble for funds and plan for inflows and outflows, he finds that they are controlled by the governments of the concerned countries. The MNCs have to face exchange rate fluctuations when he borrows from abroad or when he wants to keep short-term funds abroad.

## Cash Budgeting

Prudent financial management involves the economy in cash, optimum utilisation of surplus funds and maximisation of return and if there is a deficit, borrow at least cost option open to him, including funds inflow from affiliates abroad or from Euro-markets or other markets abroad. MNCs have wider options and larger access to funds from affiliates in other countries, better credit rating, lower cost of borrowing abroad and better opportunities of investing abroad. The need to keep idle cash is less in the case of global corporates as they have access to the funds from affiliates spread over many countries. The total pool of funds, to which they have access is greater. Even if that is not adequate they can borrow from anywhere in the world at cheaper cost unlike the domestic counterparts.

The cash planning and budgeting of the MNCs is often centralised at head office or parent company. They have relations with a number of international banks due to their worldwide network of affiliates. Due to these reasons they do not have to keep excess cash in any one centre as they can quickly transfer from the central pool to the deficit centre. Even in the headquarters, they do not have to keep cash excess due to their easy access to bank funds in any of the centres of international banks. Due to a larger pool of resources that they have access to, no single affiliate needs to keep cash in excess of the minimum. They will be able to operate on smaller cash balances than their domestic counterparts. By reducing the need to hold larger current assets they reduce the financing costs and economise on cash and marketable securities.

If headquarters are in charge of overall planning of current assets, they can better perceive problems and opportunities due to their MIS and R&D efforts. They can take a better view of the emerging scene in various countries and plan for inter-country transfers. The head office in view of the sheer size of their transactions get better quotes from the banks for funds and for foreign exchange. Their staff will also have better skills and thus, head office is better equipped to manage cash and current assets of various affiliates. The various affiliates deal with the parent company in the first place and with their approval they may borrow or lend — borrow in case of shortage of capital and lend if they have excess funds with them.

Accelerating the receipts and delaying the payments is the principle adopted by any company. But MNCs have advantage in collection of funds as well transfers within the country and across the borders, due to the facility of electronic transfer of funds (swift network) which has standardised international message formats and employs a dedicated computer network to support funds transfer messages. All international banks have this means of transfer of funds across borders at lower costs and on the basis of same day credits. The chief financial officers of MNCs rely on computers and electronic communication systems, in cash managements.

## Multilateral Netting

The MNCs also use the system of netting payments. There is a continuous inflow of goods and services and outflows also as between the affiliates. The inter-affiliate funds flows are also netted on a daily or a weekly basis and net amount is sent out or received. This saves the transactions costs which vary from 0.25% to 1.5% of the volume transferred. There is thus a case for reducing inter-affiliate funds flow which is done by payments on netting basis. This netting can be done on a bilateral basis as between two affiliates or on a multilateral basis among all branches and affiliates with the parent company. Many research estimates put that companies can eliminate 50% or more of inter-company deals among affiliates through netting method. This will reduce the costs at the rate of 1.5% per dollar netted. An Indian affiliate Smith Kline Beckman reported that their MNC saves annually $ 3,00,000 in foreign exchange transaction costs and bank transfer costs by using a multilateral netting system for intra-affiliate funds transfers within the system.

## Marketable Securities

The ideal way of managing the cash balances is to get the exact matching of cash outflows by corresponding inflows both in terms of timing and quantum of such flows. To do this, the Finance Manager has to forecast as realistically as possible the inflows and outflows by past experience and expertise. There is need to estimate the minimum cash position for the coming period, after taking into account the impact of cost inflation and anticipated currency changes on future cash flows.

To achieve the exact matching of cash flows the Finance Manager has to invest in a series of Money Market instruments in various centres so that as and when they mature they will take care of the cash outflows. This is the job of the parent company as they have the expertise and R&D facility. Given the transactions costs, they maintain an appropriate investment mix in different instruments of money in different currencies and countries. These instruments are set out below along with their characteristics and they are all short-term money market instruments open to MNCs. The difference between the MNCs and domestic companies is that the former have a wider choice of instruments, currencies and countries. The quantum of funds involved and the expertise to deal with them is also significantly higher.

The MNC will have generally centralised cash management for all its affiliates in different countries, they can have a central cash pool, which may be managed by a single international bank. Precautionary and contingency balances are held by the central pool while the balances required for transactions will be kept to the minimum and held by the affiliates. This will help to smoothen out the surpluses and deficits of affiliates, saves in costs and helps as an insurance against sudden liquidity problems. Investment return out of excess cash is maximised.



## Money Market Instruments (upto one year)

Inter alia, the following are the major avenues for short-term investments of MNCs:

(1) Treasury bills: Issued by the central government of many countries and is a safe and most liquid investment.

(2) Overnight call Money Market: Invest in the inter-bank call market (also called Federal Funds Market in the USA) for a few days say 7 to 14 days, or one to 14 days, as the case may be.

(3) Demand and time deposits with banks: Sometimes demand deposits do not fetch any interest rates and hence funds are kept in time deposits or notice deposits of various time periods, as desired by the company.

(4) Bankers acceptances: These are bills of exchange of highest quality investment grade next to Treasury bills, available in developed markets like the U.S. and U.K.

(5) Commercial paper issued by large public limited companies, negotiable and unsecured promissory notes, available in all major markets.

(6) Deposits with non-bank finance companies which are not negotiable in India, but negotiable in developed countries, and offer higher yields than those of banks.

(7) Certificates of deposits, issued by banks for deposits kept with them, negotiable paper representing the debt of banks, more liquid than straight deposits with banks and NBFCs.

(8) Inter-corporate investments — which offer higher return with more risks for varying periods of time and not negotiable in India but negotiable in developed markets.

## Investment Guidelines

The MNCs will build up a short-term portfolio of investments for meeting their liquidity requirements; the major guidelines are set at below:

(1) Diversification of risk and maximisation of return for a given level of risk.

(2) Review of the portfolio on a daily basis to change the composition and maturity or duration.

(3) If immediate cash flows are necessary, funds are kept in most liquid assets like the Treasury bills and inter-bank call market.

(4) If return is important then invest in high return, high risk investments like the deposits with NBFCs and inter-corporate deposits or investments.

(5) Incremental interest earned in portfolio changes more than compensate for transaction costs and add-on costs for clerical work.

(6) Investments are to be spread in both risky and high return avenues as also in the least risky and liquid assets.

(7) Maturity of the investments should follow the pattern of the outflow of funds, in planning the portfolio.

(8) Generally they prefer investments with a well developed secondary market for ready marketability.

Currency convertibility and free international markets are preferred for such investments. Most of this activity is confined to big international banks through which investment portfolio is built and managed. Very few will prefer to do it themselves as investment expertise is different from the financial management expertise of the Treasurer.

It has to be noted here that it is not always profitable to invest outside the domestic markets and in foreign currencies. If the returns are higher adjusted for possible currency changes, in domestic markets, the parent company may advice the affiliate to invest in local market only. But MNCs have generally centralised cash planning and investment, unlike the domestic companies. Each of the affiliates has to keep the head office informed with their day-to-day cash position. For this an efficient reporting system and a M.I.S. are necessary.

## Cash Planning and Budgeting

The parent company takes the responsibility for an efficient cash management. For this a good reporting system is to be set up with an electronic network. The head office builds up an efficient Management Information System with a two way flow of information from the parent company to the affiliates and *vice versa*.

Like credit planning, cash planning is also attempted by the head office on the basis of reported information from the affiliates on a daily basis. This information contains the balance of cash in the beginning of the day, expected cash inflows and outflows and cash balances at the end of the day. This will enable the head office to know the surplus centres and deficit centres and arrange the flow of funds to the deficit centres from the surplus centres directly. This flow takes place from one affiliate to another instead of crediting the head office first and then head office arranging for the despatch of cash advice to the deficit centres.

The reporting system and information flow helps the head office to build a multinational cash mobilisation system, designed to optimise the use of funds. Through proper planning and budgeting they will avoid the need to borrow from outside the affiliate network, namely, from the banks or the financial institutions.

## Cash Pooling

Each affiliate will have a minimum cash balance to be kept for its transactions purposes. It will prepare a proforma statement for the coming one week on a daily basis, on the daily closing balances, minimum to be kept at each centre and the emerging surplus or deficit. The affiliates each send a projection of their cash budget in the following proforma:

**TABLE 24.1 : Period Covered — Jan. 1 to 7, Centre: India**

**Daily Minimum cash required $ 100 million**

| *Day* | *Receipts* | *Payments* | *Net Balance* |
|---|---|---|---|
| 1 | 150 | 100 | + 50 |
| 2 | 180 | 120 | + 60 |
| 3 | 200 | 140 | + 60 |
| 4 | 210 | 160 | + 50 |
| 5 | 180 | 190 | – 10 |

Saturday and Sunday excluded.

Each centre sends such statements to the head office, which co-ordinates these budgets and takes a net surplus/deficit position on a daily basis which are used for investing in marketable securities, if there is a surplus and for disinvesting if there is a deficit in the overall net position. But as between the affiliates, the head office arranges for inter-affiliate transfers. For each of the centres, the daily cash position is maintained by the head office in the following proforma. All these figures are in a common denominator say dollar for a U.S. parent company and pound for a U.K. parent company and so on.

**TABLE 24.2**

| *Centre of the affiliate* | *Closing Balance* | *Minimum* | *Surplus/ Required deficit* |
|---|---|---|---|
| France | −150 | 100 | −250 |
| Algeria etc. | +100 | 50 | + 50 |

On the basis of the above daily position of each of the affiliates, a five day forecast of all the affiliates is prepared on a daily basis and summed up. This will show the total net surplus or deficit of all the centres. A weekly or a fortnight forecast is sometimes supplemented by monthly forecasts, which will give a meaningful role to portfolio investment and disinvestment in the Money Market by the parent company.

For making these operations meaningful the projections are compared with the actuals by each of the affiliates and their projections are improved from time to time. Hence the basic principles involved are:

(1) Centralised planning for cash requirements.

(2) Economies of scale due to head office operating on behalf of the affiliates.

(3) Lower transactions costs and higher risk adjusted returns on their portfolio.

(4) The portfolio investment and disinvestment operations are mostly confined to short-term instruments with marketability and liquidity.

(5) The main objective is to maintain the solvency and liquidity of each of the affiliates and at the same time maximising the return from the idle cash balances and cash surpluses of the affiliates.

All the principles of planning and budgeting will apply. This requires a system of two way reporting and information flow and an efficient method for forecasting cash needs. There must be a bank for each of affiliates to meet any emergency need for funds locally. All these are co-ordinated by the parent company's head office.

All these require efficient and timely coordination between head office and affiliates. If the firm is a WOS or JV, all these activities are left to the local office to manage with coordination and reporting to the parent company.

## Inventory Management

Principles of inventory management are the same for both the domestic firms and MNCs. If MNCs manufacture the products locally the total affiliate will plan for the inventory. Some MNCs find it difficult to manage the foreign operations from the head office. The local affiliate has strategic advantages such as familiarly with local demand, tastes, habits etc. and keeps its pulse on local developments which the head office cannot do. Sometimes some MNCs prefer offshore production to take advantage of low wages, low overheads, tax holidays and low interest loans. Firms producing abroad have to keep high inventories of raw materials and finished goods which lead to high carrying costs which might offset lower production costs. So it may be preferable to have local production and sales locally when the inventory held can be limited to the minimum required and the company will be in a better position to project its demand and sales better than the parent company.

Inventory Management should also be preferably locally managed rather than organised from the head office of the parent company. This is due to variable transit controls, transportation costs, sudden and unforeseen changes like dock strike, workers' strike, changes in duties and currency values. A local bank is also entrusted with the financing of working capital, if that is cheaper than arranging from the head office. Many international banks have branches in main centres of the world like American Express which will take care of the credit needs of the affiliates in specified centres.

## Accounts Receivables

MNCs, like the domestic companies grant credit to buyers for periods ranging from one month to 6 months. The extent of credit sales depend on the local habits and the industry practices, which the MNCs will have to take into account. Credit sales may be necessary to boost sales or to prevent the competitors to overtake its sales programme and customers.

The MNCs may have to lay down the credit policy of the firm — the extent, quality and quantum of credit sales. In countries with rapid inflation rates, credit terms are to be scrutinised more carefully, as the customers prefer to postpone payments at that time. MNCs make it a policy to change the credit terms depending on the country and the currency. If competition is eroding their sales, they will increase credit sales to keep up their market share. Local affiliates may give preference to credit sales as a mode of raising sales even if it raises the costs, due to the fact that the alternative of spending more on inventory is more disadvantageous and more costly.

Besides Finance Managers and Marketing Managers have to work together to get a trade-off between increasing selling costs to increasing inventory costs. Marketing Department wants to increase sales while the Finance Department wants quicker cash flow. One way of reconciling both these Departments is to increase credit sales but improve collection machinery with incentives for quicker cash inflows. The MNCs invariably follow cost minimising strategies in respect of receivables and payables and inventory management.

MNCs have a higher credit rating and lower cost of credit from bankers. In managing accounts receivables, an optimum credit sales position is taken by each of the affiliates. The head office uses its strategy of controlling credit sales through its own notional interest charge on credit sales made. So if the affiliate can get a better return from credit sales than the interest expense paid to the parent company, it will go on extending the credit to the customers.

Nestle has an Indian subsidiary for the parent U.S. Company. Nestle charges local subsidiary for interest expenses on the net working capital using an internally devised notional rate. The charging of interest item prompts the subsidiary to keep a tight rein on accounts receivables and inventories, because the lower the net working capital used, the lower will be the theoretical interest charge that the subsidiary has to pay to its parent company.

The basic difference of the MNC from that of the domestic company is that some of its accounts receivable may be denominated in foreign currencies. Two key credit decisions for it are the total amount of credit to be extended and the currencies in which the credit sales are to be filled. If some of the currencies or the currency in which the credit sales are denominated depreciates, the gain in sales is offset by depreciation of the currency. The parent company takes this also into account in crediting the subsidiary for its performance. Both inflation and devaluation of the developing countries are the major factors to be looked into in evaluating the bills receivable accounts of the affiliates. The affiliate will have to carefully scrutinise all credit accounts and credit policy. The affiliate of an MNC may have no option but extend credit, as required by customers, if competitors offer them. Then survival in the market comes first. As a next step, if the perception of affiliate on currency depreciation and inflation rate tally, the affiliate has to weigh the credit sales with the discount sales and see which is more favourable. The MNCs have two advantages than their competitors, namely, its cost of funds is lower due to their access to global markets and its access to funds is easier due to their network of operations and contact with international banks. The incremental cost of credit under any change in credit policy has to be assessed against the incremental profits arising out of new policy. This is the calculus that MNCs work out taking the advantage of their easy access to funds and the lower average cost of funds for them. The general principle of accepting any credit policy is to compare the incremental profits and incremental costs arising out of the new credit policy. In the case of MNCs, they have to take into account the possibilities of currency depreciation and inflation if the credits are given in the local currency. These two factors reduce the benefits or gains from credit sales to the MNCs, as their calculations are in an internationally convertible currency, say the U.S. dollar or the currency of the parent company.

## Inventory Optimisation

Inventory of inputs, raw-materials, spare parts or semi-processed goods for MNCs is somewhat different from that domestic company. It may be partly procured from the domestic sources and partly from the parent company or foreign sources. It may also happen that all inventory is procured from domestic sources. Similarly, the inventory of finished goods is fixed at a particular level, by the parent company, and the network of distribution channels is also set out by them.

In the case of raw-materials and work-in-process, they have to be held to facilitate the production. The level of this inventory depends on the level of production and the input-output matrix. The inventory of finished goods is to facilitate the production level and to make sure that goods are available as and when there is a demand. The difference of inventory management in a multinational firm from that of a domestic company is in respect of dealings in foreign countries, in foreign currencies and difficulty of controlling them from a distance. If the supply has to come from foreign sources many imponderables come in the way such as transit problems, customs clearance, import controls, dock strikes or delays, supply disruption and changes in currency values.

There are both advantages and disadvantages in local production in affiliate country *vis-a-vis* production in parent country. But the actual decision depends on the circumstances of each case. If firms are producing abroad they have to keep large stocks of finished goods in the local market. The increased carrying costs due to keeping of larger stocks are offset by lower cost of production of those goods abroad than locally. Some affiliates produce and supply the goods locally however.

In developing countries if futures contracts are available, inventory of raw-materials and inputs can be purchased for various contract periods of say 1 to 6 months coinciding with the time when the inputs have to be purchased on spot. These forward purchases will ensure a hedge mechanism for future uncertainty of price. Similarly, if free conversion of local currency into any convertible currency or the parent country's currency is possible, the excess funds are repatriated back to the hard currency or the parent company. This will facilitate raw-material purchases from anywhere in the world, depending the cheapest source of them.

The factors to be considered are the following:

(1) inflationary rise in prices of parts or raw materials.

(2) currency depreciation during the same period, if the supplies have to come from abroad.

(3) holding costs in the parent company's currency.

(4) interest cost of funds used for inventory holding.

(5) opportunity cost for funds locally.

(6) delivery lead time.

International Fisher effect is seen in the disparities of purchasing power of currencies in which affiliates of the parent company are dealing. This Fisher effect has to be offset by hedge or futures contracts in the concerned commodities whose stocks are held in inventory that is purchase of 3 or 4 months of inventory at today's prices as in the case of Brazil, where the increase in prices and depreciation of currency will have an impact greater than the interest cost of the finance required for holding inventory for the next 3-4 months. Advance purchases of inventory are also justified in cases of long delivery lead items. The principles of economic order quantity and optimal quantity of inventory to be held etc. do not apply exactly to MNCs when they are facing problems of inter-country purchases and sales in the form of inflation and currency depreciation. Under the threat of disruption for supply, the MNCs will face conditions that take the knowledge and execution of an optimal stock policy more critical than for domestic companies. The affiliates generally prefer to holding low cost inventory, to excessive holding in anticipation of supply cut off situations or disruptions in supply. But if multi-country dealings are involved and risks of not holding enough stocks are greater than the risks of holding excess stocks then the affiliates may prefer either a hedge or a futures contract for supplies or excess stockholding, than that optimally required. If the costs of stock-outs or zero stock probability are high; then the additional costs of stock piling of inventory may be offset by the greater risks of stock out and loss of orders. The parent company and the affiliates concerned will be able to decide on these factors and come to a conclusion on the desirable or permitted level of stock piling.

As far as the level of inventory holding is concerned, the normal rules of so many months of inventory as optimal holding does not hold good in the case of MNCs. A number of extra-territorial factors operate on the problem in this case. The currency factors, interest cost, inflation possibilities, possible stock out situation, conditions in relation to foreign suppliers and a host of other factors influence the level of stock holding of the affiliates.

❖ ❖ ❖

# NATURE OF INTERNATIONAL BUSINESS FINANCE — PRACTICES

# 25

## Nature of Business Finance

Global finance is funds and currencies which are globally acceptable. The funds are global in the sense that the demand for and supply of funds comes from any quarter of the globe. The funds are in freely convertible currencies, which provide much needed foreign exchange for many LDCs with balance of payments problems, shortage of domestic capital and inadequate savings to meet with the planned investment targets.

As this book deals with international financial management it is apt to note here that many LDCs have shifted or are shifting to a state of convertibility of domestic currencies. This makes it easy for funds inflows and outflows. Capital becomes mobile internationally, and as it is a scarce factor of production, its free flow across borders assumes considerable importance particularly for LDCs, and for savings, investment and growth of these countries.

Global finance is concerned with the global dimensions of corporate financing, access to global financial markets, institutions and instruments and techniques and their inter linkages. Global financial markets comprise both short, medium and long-term finances and the demand and supply for them. These markets arise from demand and supply for foreign currencies by corporates, firms, individuals, governments and semi-government bodies. As these agencies belong to a nation and it has its own currency, the demand for all other currencies from global markets necessitate conversion of those foreign currencies into domestic currencies. So the global financial markets comprise first and foremost the foreign exchange markets, wherein the rupee is converted into dollars and *vice versa*. There is a demand and supply of these foreign currencies and to exchange these currencies into domestic currency, the foreign exchange market comes into the picture and this is an adjunct to the foreign currency markets. Global financial markets thus comprise Money and Capital Market for convertible currencies and offshore funds and encompass both the foreign currency markets and foreign exchange markets.

There are interlinkages between the domestic money market and foreign money markets and domestic capital market and foreign capital markets through international commercial banks, investment banks and intermediary security firms and dealer firms. These interlinkages are depicted in the following Figure:

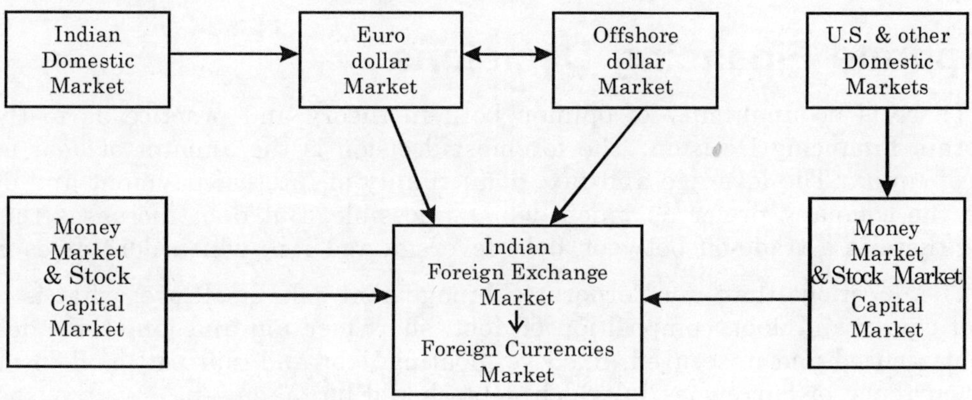


**Fig. 25.1**

## Debt Crisis — Effects on Bank

International banks were the victims of debt default of many governments in the eighties. When loans are given to corporates, they can be forced into liquidation but not so in the case of the governments. The banks have therefore spent time and money to reschedule and recover the money in instalments and some debts were written off. The debt crisis weakened the banks but the banking system did not collapse. The banks have become more cautious and started lending only to countries with market oriented economies and undergoing structural reforms.

The developments in the international debt market gave rise to the new instruments and secondary markets in many instruments such as securitised debt. Debt repaying capacity and foreign exchange earnings and productive use of capital are all taken into account. Sufficient equity capital base is also insisted for debt to be increased. Solutions to Debt Crisis adopted by nations and banks are depicted in Figure on next page:

**Solutions to Debt Crisis**

1. Development of Secondary Market → Diversify the ownership risk among many banks → Reduce the concentration Risk and liquidity risk of the borrowers
2. Reduction of over-lending & Insistence of equity base & Existence of debt servicing capacity
3. Debt absorption capacity of the borrower → Debt Reschedule → Debt write off
4. Economic policy Reforms → Increase in efficiency and productivity of capital

**Fig. 25.2**

## Corporate Financing Decisions

There is no unanimity of opinion both in theory and practice as to the optimal corporate Financing Decision. The foremost decision is the amount of debt for a given level of equity. The leverage and tax deductibility of interest payment and debt would make the company prefer as much debt as possible. But debt increases the risk and hence there is a trade-off between debt leverage and risk which debt gives rise to.

The questions that any Corporate Management asks itself are: what is the proper mix of equity and debt, composition of debt, short-medium and long-term debt, nature of debt secured and unsecured, fixed vs. floating debt and maturity and terms of debt, what currency or currencies in which debt should be taken, etc.

**Role of Heading on Debt Burdens**

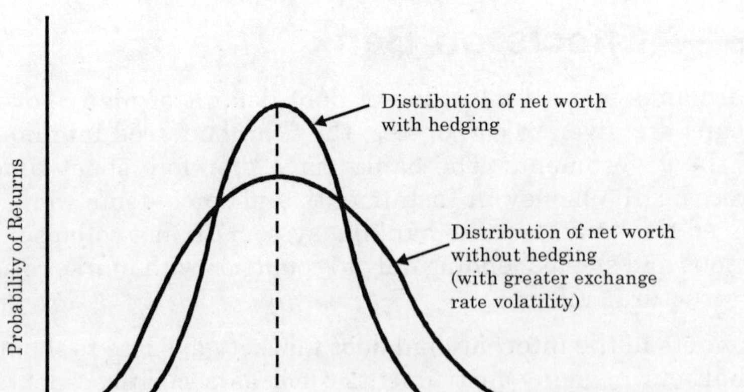


**Fig. 25.3**

The firm should keep its debt at the optimum level. This debt should be self liquidating through the returns that it generates. It should be in currencies in which it earns its export earnings. One should borrow in currencies which are likely to be weakened or depreciated.

The object of Finance Manager is to maximise net worth of the shareholder. Debt increases leverage and also the risk. Hence we can increase the net worth by having leverage of debt and yet hedge the risk of debt servicing. The Figure 25.3 shows the need for hedging which Global Financial Markets provide.

# Alternatives to Debt Financing

(1) Derivatives and Hybrids in financing.

(2) Quasi equity financing debt with equity conversion facility (FCCBs)

(3) Debt with warrants and sweeteners.

The value of the company's shareholdings will increase with the leverage enjoyed by debt but the risk associated with the debt is to be hedged to improve the value of the firm.

The following Fig. 25.4 shows the financing of MNCs.

**Options or Alternatives for MNCs**

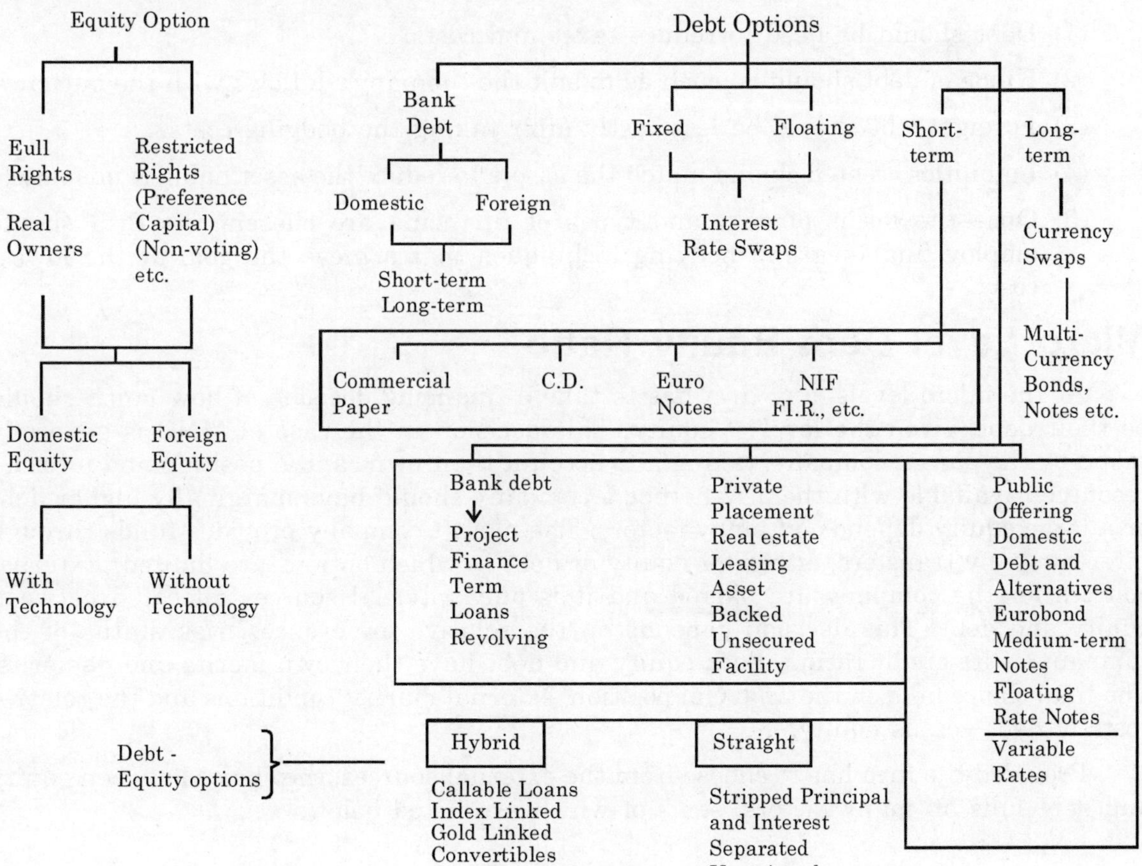


Fig. 25.4

## Capital Structure

The composition of capital structure influences the cost of capital and return and thus the shareholders' value. The composition of debt, its currency, interest rate maturity and other terms of debt are relevant variables to be considered. Hedging of the debt risk reduces the risk of financial stress and even crisis.

The firms have to match the composition of debt to the payment characteristics of assets created so as to minimise the probability of financial distress. It pays a company to deviate from the minimum risk debt composition, if only the firm can beat the market. This means that hedging of the debt risk should be part of the strategy. Swaps, caps and other derivatives play a role in different ways.

(1) To hedge an existing exposure of the company.

(2) Hybrid bonds, when used in conjunction with options and other derivatives can be an effective way of getting cheaper funds by exploiting the market imperfections.

(3) To position the company to gain from a favourable movement in some market variables such as interest rates.

The principles for deciding the capital structure may be set out briefly as follows:

(1) Debt should be used to reduce taxes and costs.

(2) Kinds of debt should be such as to suit the company's inflows with the outflows.

(3) Foreign debt should be less costly after taking the hedging costs.

(4) Liabilities created should match the assets to reduce the asset liability mismatch.

(5) Once the forms of debt and types of financing are chosen, the firm should employ financing and hedging techniques that achieve the goal at the lowest cost.

## Micro Level Debt Equity Ratio

At the micro levels, any firm has to take a financing decision of how much should be their debt, given the level of equity. This decision in the case of MNC is generally taken by the parent company, taking into account their own capital position and internal resources available with them. Whether a company should have marginally higher debt or a large equity depends on many factors. The parent company provides funds through inter-company transfers, either for equity or debt in which options are limited. External sources for the company are barred and it is only internal sources allocated between equity and debt. This decision depends on the relative preferences, risk status of the company or its credit rating. Both equity and debt have their own merits and demerits. The final choice falls on the financial position, external market conditions and the relative costs of debt versus equity.

Provided the firm has to choose from the external sources, the choice between equity and debt falls on many factors, some of which are listed below:

(1) Cost of capital for equity and debt for the firm.

(2) Costs of issue and incidentals, in respect of both.

(3) Total average cost of capital employed before issue and of infusion of new capital and after issue.

(4) The cost of capital has to be seen in the context of expected return on capital and the margin of profit.

(5) The market conditions, in domestic and foreign markets and the expected reception to the proposed issue — whether equity or debt is preferred by investors.

(6) The environmental factors — the actions of the competitors in the industry in particular and in the economy in general.

(7) The government policies of the host country and home country regarding issue and servicing of debt or equity.

(8) Liquidity in the international markets.

## Role of Exchange Market

Global financial system revolves around the foreign exchange market. Domestic currency markets are linked to foreign currency markets through the exchange rates between these currencies. The exchange rates in different countries are a function of purchasing power parities, which in turn depends on the inflation rates. Thus, the foreign exchange market links national interest rates, inflation rates and monetary policies. National interest rates reflect the time value of their respective monies and the forward exchange rates reflect the time value of the exchange rate between two monies. The foreign exchange market links the national interest rates, inflation rates and monetary policies of different countries.

Exchange market is an adjunct of the foreign currency market. Trading in foreign currencies need the exchange market for conversion of foreign currencies into domestic currency. Euro currency market is again a supplement to the domestic money market. Funds flow in and flow out, in which the money markets of different countries partake in the operations.

Euro notes and Euro bonds and a number of new financial instruments are in vogue today in the global financial markets. National markets are linked to international markets through these instruments. These interlinkages are shown in the Fig. 25.5 below. Bankers are the main players and are intermediaries in these operations.

The main users of the global markets are the MNCs, domestic companies, government and government bodies and PSUs. Banks and security dealers and firms are important constituents of these markets. The corporate financial structure is decided on the basis of the available sources both national and global and the major considerations are cost or return and risks. Equity and debt and many variants of these two are selected by the corporates depending on their business, debt servicing capacity, cash inflows and outflows and a host of other factors. The various new derivatives are now available to hedge the risk by the corporates. The choices open are plenty such as flexible bonds, FRN variable rates of interest, multi currency loans, variable maturities and various permutations and combinations of these features. For these instruments, the hedge operations are available in the form of swaps, options, hybrids etc. which are the techniques to reduce the risk of debt.

**INTER-LINKAGES OF DOMESTIC AND FOREIGN MARKETS**

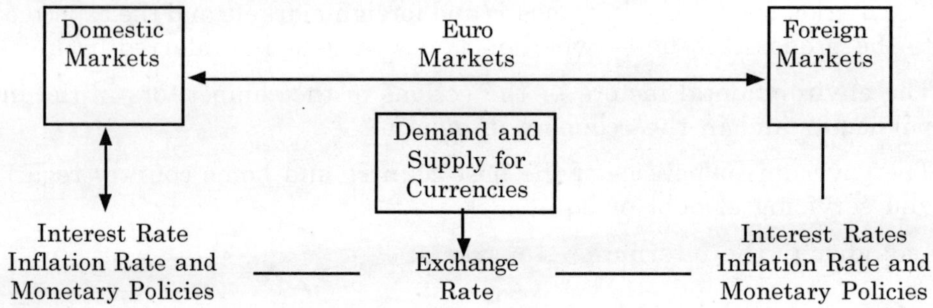


**Fig. 25.5**

In the short end there are commercial papers, adjustable rate preferred stock, Euro-notes, FRN, Euro currency loans in the offshore markets, in addition to the domestic sources.

In the long end of the sources of finance, there are the international lending agencies, regional bodies and corporates. The government to government loans are the preferred methods so far as the government and government bodies are concerned. For the MNCs and corporates the International Financial Corporation, international banks, term loans, revolving credits, various forms of private placement of loans, Euro bonds and public offers are some of the major sources of funds. To avoid the exchange risk, the first preference is for domestic funds and second preference is for soft loans from multilateral and regional development agencies and lastly Euro currency bonds and other variants of Euro loans.

## Innovations

*Why do innovations emerge?* There are many market imperfections that make the total worth of an instrument more than the sum of the parts of that instrument and certain investors, companies and others prefer new instruments for their advantages and new features.

Examples are convertible Euro bond, ADR, GDR, FCCB, etc. Many of the imperfections arise from barriers to international arbitrage, from currency preferences and the different conditions that investors and issuers face in different countries. These instruments arise due to restrictions in the domestic markets, lack of taxes on off shore funds and taxes and high transaction costs in the case of domestic funds.

## Types of Innovations

*(i)* Reduction of transaction and monitoring costs. The callable bonds fall in this category.

*(ii)* Regulation driven innovations. An example is the dollar denominated Euro bond free of withholding tax whereas a Yen denominated bond would have to pay the withholding tax.

*(iii)* Preferred stock pays fixed dividend. In U.S. and U.K. corporations owning shares in other corporations are taxed at a reduced rate. Companies with zero tax liabilities will issue preferred stock instead of straight bonds.

*(iv)* In some cases, splits are possible, that is, interest streams are separated from the principal for trading purposes.

Hybrid securities can be broken down into two components, say in zero coupon funds — forward contracts — and options with call and put options, callable bonds with two components callable and non-callable etc. are all examples of satisfying the preference of investors.

To avoid the effect of market imperfections, the MNCs use swaps, caps, collars and hybrids in their financing programme. Hybrids are the instruments combining the features of two or more financial instruments. These derivatives are used to hedge the existing exposure that the company is subject to and to take advantage of the market imperfection or of interest rate changes. There can be interest rate swaps or currency swaps.

The purposes for which these derivatives are used are hedging, positioning and arbitrage operations. One can hedge a risk by taking a cap, collar for interest rate changes or currency rate changes. Swaps can take shift of risk of fluctuating interest rate to a fixed rate. The use of dual currency bonds or principal in one currency and interest in another currency is based on the expectation that some currencies are risky in the short run but stable in the long run. Use of swaps and forward contracts help cover the risk of currencies' volatility.

Securitisation of mortgages, car loans, credit cards, receivables and other assets with predictable cash flows represent a whole category of segmentation driven innovations.

Structured financing can be arranged for the corporates by the investment bankers or international bankers. Flexibility can be introduced into medium term borrowing by the bank, to suit the requirement of the corporate in terms of currencies, maturities and basis of interest rates. After finding suitables counter parties, swaps and strips can be arranged for the corporates to suit the cash flows. Finally the bank stands willing to buy back securities at a later date to provide liquidity.

## Emerging Scenario

In the present day dynamic world, it is unpredictable as to the number of new instruments that will come up for financing the MNC. Competition will increase and the global financing becomes more frequently used, depending on the taxes and transaction costs. With the global economies changing fast and countries shifting to market oriented and free competitive scenarios, the role of global finance tends to grow. The risk management techniques and coverage of credit and market risks will undergo fast changes. The interrelations between money, bonds, currency, commodity and equity markets are bound to grow. Similarly the role of derivative markets will grow more and in a comprehensive manner. The more the controls on the domestic markets, the more will be the role of the global markets.

The emergence of Euro as a currency commonly used by the European common union participants augur well for a possible unification of many more countries and currencies. The forward exchange markets, cross currency deals and multi-currency transactions will tend to grow. There will be a realignment of currency strengths and the markets for them.

Global finance, in sum, is a dynamic area and frequent changes are bound to take place and the results of financial engineering are bound to be felt. The domestic markets and global markets will be increasingly interlinked and the global finance area will turn out to be wide and deep, which helps the MNCs in their financial needs.

❖ ❖ ❖

# INTER-CORPORATE FUNDS FLOW

# 26

## Introduction

The MNC has the flexibility of funds flowing as between firms and between subsidiaries and the parent company. The transfers can take the form of inputs, including financial inputs followed by corresponding flow of funds. They include inter-company loans, dividends, royalty charges, the timing of which is adjusted to suit the companies after complying with government law and rules. The mechanism of transfer pricing is used for transfer of goods, services as between firms, within the same MNC. The transfers, inter-company, encompass the flows of working capital, equity or debt investment, and technology and know-how transfers, for which a return is envisaged for accounting purposes. These also include the franchise for use of brand/patent name or R&D efforts of the parent company etc.

Between the parent company and affiliation and subsidiaries, there are to and fro movements of real goods and services and financial flows. Each of the trade flows are priced, and the management decision in this regard is based on a host of factors. The management decisions of the parent company are on the following issues and these factors influence the flows, inter-firm:

(1) To determine the optimum debt equity ratio.

(2) To decide the mix of sources for borrowing funds.

(3) To fix the prices of such borrowing in the form of costs.

(4) The extent of borrowing, inter-firm and for outside agencies, including the domestic source of the firm.

(5) To decide on the transfer price for inter-firm transfers and lay down guidelines for transfer pricing, as required generally by the tax authorities in the host countries.

(6) To fix the dividend payments, royalty and other payments.

The above are some of the financial decisions to be initially taken by the finance manager based on the information supplied by the local affiliate or the subsidiary and their own information (MIS) on the various countries, in which they have affiliates and the international markets. Finally these decisions are to be approved by the parent company's Board of Directors and by the local board before their implementation.

The real flows of goods and services among the parent and affiliates are as follows:

*(a)* Market Information system and sharing of it.

*(b)* Sharing of R&D results.

*(c)* Technology Transfers.

*(d)* Right to use patents or brand names.

*(e)* Raw material or intermediate products.

*(f)* Finished goods for assembly or sale.

*(g)* Capital goods, plant, machinery etc.

*(h)* Transfer of skilled personnel and management talent.

Corresponding to these real flows, there are reverse flows of returns to them in financial form. In addition there are funds flows for working capital purposes and capital goods investment in affiliates. To start with some capital investment takes the form of equity for which dividends have to be paid. In addition to equity, there may be loan capital provided by the parent company and inter-company loans or borrowings, which are paid by a return in the form of transfer price or interest on capital borrowed.

For the use of patent, brand names or for technology transfers, there is a return flow of royalties, fees, charges etc. Even for sharing of R&D results, market research results etc., there will be a price. Their prices are all fixed by the parent company as transfer prices. MNC has freedom of selecting the financial channels through which funds should flow and the transfer prices through which these flows should be accounted for in the Balance Sheet and Income Expenditure statements of the subsidiaries and parent company. Many developed countries and USA in particular have strict rules of accounting for the global operations of the MNCs.

## Transfer Pricing

Transfer prices can be used to their advantage and can also be misused, as the MNCs have some freedom subject to the laws of the home country and the host country to select the financial flows and the channels through which they are sent. Transfer of goods and services result in financial flows in the reverse direction at specific transfer prices. The host country and the home country may require the accounts books in both to be kept in a transparent manner with all disclosures and justification of transfer prices. Similarly investment flows can be sent either as debt with terms which are flexible and in currencies, suitable to them or in the form of equity with return in the form of dividends. The return to patents, trademarks or the use of brand names, is in the form of royalty, fees or charges and financial flows in this regard are to be sent as agreed upon. A detailed discussion is given on the subject later in the chapter.

## Timing Flexibility

The leading and lagging of the above flows or inter affiliate trade credit or royalty or fee payments have to be timed according to their convenience and not in a rigid schedule. Subject to the government regulations and law of the land, a firm in the global network has some flexibility as per the mutual convenience of the affiliates and the parent company. This flexibility of timing applies to both real flows of goods and services and financial flows. For example, dividend on equity can be retained or paid to the parent company. So are the royalty and interest payments.

## Use and Misuse of Inter Unit Transfers

Many global players try to maximise the utility of these inter-unit transfers, by timing to their advantage by preponing or postponing the payments. They take advantage of the differences in tax laws and in the loopholes of the laws and regulations. They can misuse these facilities like transfer pricing to the total advantage of group companies.

## Functions of Management

Financial Management has two major functions, namely, financing decision and investment decision, in addition to dividend decision. The MNC has greater choice and more alternatives between internal and external sources of funds. They have easy access to many financial markets and sources in different countries and currencies. In the investment decision, the allocation of funds is done as per the corporate strategy of the group as a whole, but each affiliate has some flexibility in their use. Financing decision will take into account the need to maximise shareholders' wealth and design a capital structure that is a least-cost combination of various types of funds. These two decisions are used to minimise the costs and maximise the returns to shareholders. The risks in various markets are so varied that proper diversification and risk management techniques are to be used.

Unlike domestic companies, the MNCs face greater risks such as exchange risks, inflation risks, tax rates and laws of the lands in different countries, political risks and controls and policy changes. Thus, the financial management of the MNCs is not the same as that of the domestic companies and hence a separate treatment of this subject.

They have to face many more risks as challenges and convert them to their advantage. They have to deal in different countries, with different laws, rules and currencies. The MNCs should have the competency to face these hurdles and move men, money and materials on a global basis. They have opportunities to take advantage of the international diversification or differences in risk scenarios of different countries. In short, the business finance principles remain basically the same, but there are many other differences between MNCs and domestic corporates in their financial management in risk-return scenarios and in the environments that they face. MNCs are superior in strength in two respects, namely, financial resources or control of larger funds and secondly, the technological advantage together with management expertise. They have to face a higher total risk than the domestic corporates. They face a global market place for real goods and financial resources. But the advancement and even revolution in electronic information system through computers and in telecommunications along with revolution in transportation has brought the world together. In specific terms, capital, knowledge, skills and technology and intellectual property rights became more mobile on global basis. Distance and time are conquered with the result that countries are brought together in the world. This led to a global market place and that is where MNCs operate which distinguishes them from domestic corporates.

Arbitrage and market perfections bring about theoretical framework for Market Efficiency Theory and Capital Asset Pricing Model. But in real world there are imperfections and asymmetries. Recent empirical research has shown that there are capital market imperfections and asymmetries in tax regulations in the global financial scenario. The traditional methods of financial management in increasing the value of the firm by the financial decision and investment decision or by manipulation of accounts cannot hold good in global financial management. Here what is needed are the skills, knowledge and information which make the MNC financial management different. The value of the firm in the global scenario can be increased by better skills in diversification of risk and expertise in risk management and application of extra skills to take advantage of market imperfections across borders and asymmetry in tax laws.

| | *MNCs* | *Domestic Corporates* |
|---|---|---|
| (1) Product Market | Wider | Narrower |
| (2) Technology | More update | Less update |
| (3) R & D Expenses | More than 5% | Less than 1% |
| (4) Sources of Finance graphically presented below | Wider by addition of parent transfers and Inter affiliate transfers | narrower |

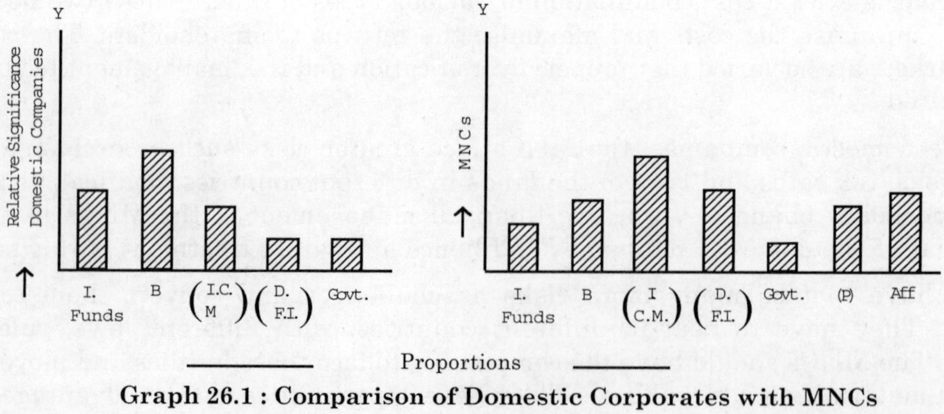


**Graph 26.1 : Comparison of Domestic Corporates with MNCs**

Explanation —

| | |
|---|---|
| I | : Funds: Internally Generated Funds |
| B | : Banks, both Internal & International |
| ICM | : International Capital Markets |
| D.F.I. | : Development Financial Institutions |
| Govt | : In the form of loans, subsidies, incentives and tax rebates |
| P | : Parent transfers and investments |
| Aff | : Affiliate transfers |

(5) Risk : Risk is reduced due to asset diversification and country risk diversification.

(6) Reward : With reduced risk, reward should be lower as per the theory. But in the case of MNCs there will be same reward or higher reward at the same risk level, or lower risk.

| | *MNCs* | *Domestic Corporates* |
|---|---|---|
| (7) Tax Factors | Scope for taking advantage of Tax haven systems greater role for tax planning | Less Scope for planning or tax avoidance |
| (8) Cost Factors graphically presented below | Lower average costs | Higher average costs |

## Cost Curves Comparison

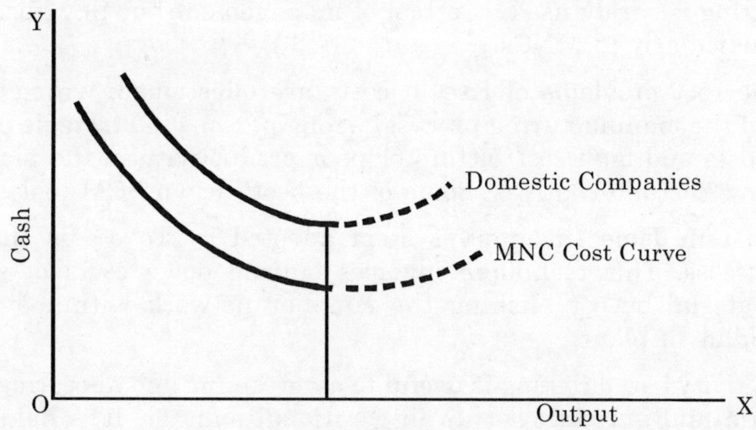


Average Cost Curvs

**Graph 26.2**

Two points to note from the above graph:

*(a)* Average cost curve is definitely lower for the MNC than for the domestic companies due to advantages of economies of scale, wider sources of finance and lower cost of capital employed. Differential factor endowments and natural resources of different countries can be exploited.

*(b)* The gap between them is wider at the optimum point where diseconomies start operating and favourable factors of diversification disappear due to increasing country risks.

## Strategic Cost Management

Quality and cost go together. Given the price and quality standard, maximisation of profits would depend on the extent of cost reduction. Many times rising input prices and demands of labour unions for wage rise lead to rise in costs but, the price is given by the buyer in the buyers' market or by the competitors in a competitive market scenario.

In this context cost reduction exercises assume importance. Many times they lead to human problems or reduction in quality. It is in this scenario that strategic cost management (SCM) has become a crucial tool. SCM is fast emerging as a powerful and effective cost management tool, which can help a company's top management in cost reduction, attain high levels of productivity and the desirable quality at an acceptable price to the consumer.

Cost reduction exercises are generally *ad hoc* and short-term in nature in many companies. But strategic cost management is long-term and sustaining cost reduction. SCM is used when faced with constraints of maintenance of standard quality and when price is given and cannot be raised. Besides when cost reduction is planned and executed as per a strategy and objective, as under SCM, then it will give more effective solution. Under SCM, strategic business decisions are made taking into account various alternatives and their costs and a most feasible alternative with least cost is chosen.

One of the latest marketing techniques is brand warfare. When competing brands emerge price cutting is rarely used as a tool of management but SCM becomes a tool of management, particularly to MNCs.

In SCM, the root problems of rise in costs are questioned: wrong plant location, faulty selection of the manufacturing process, wrong persons in strategic places and high material input costs and high cost factors or poor productivity in the plant and factory and choose the low cost alternatives. Some of the best known SCM tools are as follows:

JITI : Just in Time Inventory system adopted by Toyota is the key to their success. This technique involves cutting down costs of supply of raw-material by establishing the supplier network within a short distance radius of plant.

ABC : Activity based costing is useful to ascertaining and allocating the overheads in a multi-product set up in a rational manner. It is helpful in arriving at a correct product price and to assess process and product costs in a multi-product set up. Activities which generate costs are identified and called cost drivers. Their value addition is assessed for overhead cost allocation in a rational manner based on value addition. Such allocation of costs among various products helps keeping costs low in the products, earmarked for cost cutting. Such multi-product units are mostly seen among the automobiles and the application of SCM is seen in voyager project of Mahindra and Mahindra Ltd. The multi-product units are seen among soaps, detergents washing and clearing materials and among tooth pastes and powders and related products. The examples of MNCs in India, which use cost cutting methods through SCM tools are Colgate, HLL, etc.

The scope of SCM lies not only in reducing manufacturing and marketing costs through proper inventory management but in the entire resource use, namely, of men, money, materials, machines and in process. Strategic decisions based on assessment of alternative costing are basic to the SCM. Its applications are diverse and universal and presently many MNCs, mostly of foreign origin apply this tool for cutting costs in an environment of competition and changing market conditions in the global marketing scenario.

## Ad Expenses of MNCs

The advertising policy of MNCs is indicative of aggressive marketing that is necessary for global marketing strategy. MNCs in India operate mostly in consumer goods both durables and non-durables and food products and beverages, where Ads can more effectively influence the consumers' decisions. On the other hand, the products of many Indian MNCs like Tisco, Reliance and Telco are less influenced by advertisements and Ad strategy is different.

The aggregate expenditure on advertisements by 25 MNCs in India showed in a study by E.T.@ that it increases in recession to make up atleast partially the fall in sales. This is because their long-term policy of marketing influences the advertising expenses. In this study, the Ad expenses are highly correlated with sales figures of MNCs. Thus, the correlation coefficient between sales and advertisement expenses of the sample was as high as 0.990 in 1998-99 and 0.988 in 1997-98. At the individual company level, the relationship between annual sales and advertisement expenditure taken over a longer period of 1994 to 1999 turns out to be strong and positive.

**Spend to Sell**

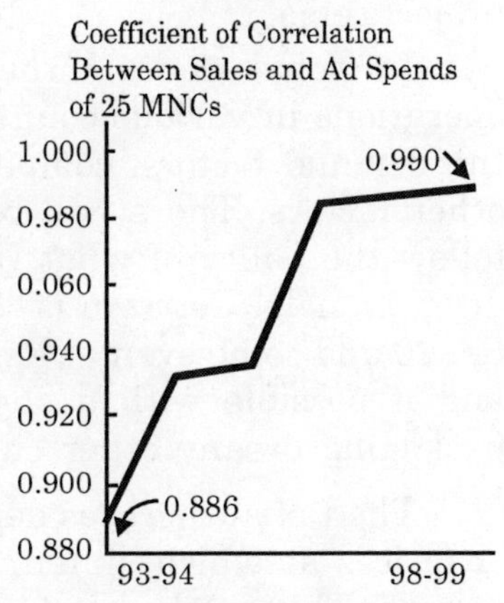


**Graph 26.3**

In times of recession say in 1997-98 and in 1998-99, the Ad expenses of these MNCs, say HLL, Proctor and Gamble and Nestle etc. have increased more sharply to counter the effects of recession. The chart accompanying shows the coefficient of correlation between sales and Ad expenses of 25 MNCs in India between 1994 and 1999.

## Transfer Pricing Mechanism

Transfer price is a notional price at which transactions are effected between different units and different product units of the same company and between the company and its subsidiaries or other related companies within the same management group. It relates to the charges made, when a company supplies goods, services or finance to another within the same family group. This is mainly used for gaining tax advantages.

The tax advantage is by showing higher expenditure and lower profits in the high tax country by the unit with low expenditure and high profits. The unit using the

*Sources*

@ E.T. 25-31, August 1999. (Brand Equity) Spend To Sell.

transfer pricing, made to acquire goods and services at higher cost than warranted by the costs of the same, from its related company would do so to the effect that its expenditure will increase and profits decline.

At the global level, this concept is used more prominently to cover up their real financial position, as tax rates between countries vary many times by a large margin. Foreign companies in India for example pay at the rate of 38% of its net income while similar rates in Mauritius or Luxemburg may be lower than 30%. It is advantageous to use this transfer pricing mechanism for the companies in India related to those in Mauritius to get input transferred to it at higher prices and thereby, show higher expenditure and lower profits. Consequently Indian company pays lower taxes on its profits, while the related company in Mauritius shows higher profits but pays tax at a lower rate which may lead to combined lower net out go on account of taxes for the two companies together. This mechanism is used only when the products are unique and specific to the companies concerned and not commonly traded and both the companies should be closely related through a common share holding or management such as that of two branches of the same holding companies or two subsidiaries or joint venture projects etc.

In global scenario, the parent company is interested in the overall profits of all its operations in various countries. The pricing policy in each country differs depending on the demand factors, competitors, government policies, say the tax rates and a host of other factors. There will be no uniform cost and price formula for them. Mostly they follow the policy of what the market can bear. To give an illustration, an anti-allergic drug, namely, Cetrizen is sold by some MNCs at around Rs. 7 to 10 and some at around Rs. 20 and some even at Rs. 40 per pack of 10 Tablets, but under different brand names and if possible with a slight change in contents either in quantity or quality or in packaging or any other changes.

The tax authorities detect them only if there are obirous and if there is information on prices at which similar transactions have been entered, as between two unrelated parties. This method is further classified into two categories, namely, into comparable uncontrolled price (CUP) and the cost plus (C+) method. In the former case, prices charged on the products or services, similar or the same, as between two independent companies or parties are taken as yardsticks. In the latter case, an arm's length price is determined by applying an appropriate mark-up on the costs incurred. It can thus, be concluded that the normal methods of deterring the abuse of the transfer price mechanism for tax saving or any other purpose such as foreign exchange leakage are through the commonly practised method of trading of the same as between two independent and unrelated parties, if that is possible or cost plus a reasonable mark-up if the cost data are available for comparable companies and products separately and if the standard costs are available for those products. In all other cases, transfer price mechanism can possibly be used or abused and this happens in many cases of MNCs or foreign companies in India.

Normally, the abuse of transfer price mechanism in global finance is to charge high rates for inter-corporate funds lent by the cash rich and more profitable company to cash poor and less profitable company. This high cost transfer of funds will lead to larger expenditure, as interest is an expenditure item in the Income-Expenditure statement or profit allocation statement. The larger expenditure will lead to less profit, so as to reduce or avoid taxes on the corporate incomes.

The areas prone to transfer price mechanism are the import of raw-materials, semi-finished goods for assembling or final product manufacture and intellectual property rights, know-how and technology. As Indian companies depend on the import of foreign technology, the mechanism of transfer pricing and the abuse of it can be resorted to in this area.

## Provisions of Income Tax Act

The following provisions are available in the I.T. Act of 1961 to deal with the transfer pricing abuses by Indian registered companies:

*Section 40A (2):* They can disallow any expenditure made to a related party if it is excessive.

*Section 80 (1) A:* The tax benefits in the form of tax holiday for a number of years, available under this section can be disallowed, if the abuse of transfer pricing is suspected.

*Section 92:* Taxable income can be enhanced, if any transaction as between related companies led to lower profit income of taxable company.

In developed countries, such as in U.S., UK, Canada, Australia and Germany, the corporate units have to maintain detailed accounts of all such transactions with related parties. These extensive records should provide evidence and justification of the charge for the supplies of goods and services made by one to the other among the global corporate units.

In India, as referred to earlier, provisions to deal T.P. mechanism are there in the Act, but they are not implemented effectively and tax payers do not maintain detailed documents and records to disclose the correct information. In the absence of proper disclosures and transparency, the subsidiaries of foreign companies in India and inter connected companies and foreign MNCs resort to T.P. mechanism to reduce or avoid the tax liability, particularly because they do not maintain proper records and accounts. India has started to enforce these provisions, through stricter audit requirements and insistence on proper records. In India, where use of imported technology and components and exported intellectual property rights are becoming significant, use and abuse of the transfer pricing mechanism is possible, and is prevalent. Indian Tax authorities have laid down for records to be kept for transfer prices, under the I.T. Act.

International consensus on the pricing of cross border transactions among related parties has been reached and guidelines are set out by the OECD, which calls on the tax payers and tax authorities to determine and evaluate transfer by adopting the "arms length" principle. Double Taxation Avoidance Agreements as between two countries normally provide adequate safeguards against abuse of transfer pricing by MNCs. Articles of "DT AA" provide for application of Arm's Length Principle between related parties which are defined as those involved in joint participation in management, control of the enterprise or in capital.

U.S.A. and UK for example initiated aggressive policing of the working of the transfer pricing mechanism among their MNCs. Record keeping requirements for U.S. subsidiaries and branches of foreign companies are very strict. Section 482 of the U.S. Internal Revenue Code requires "Contemporaneous Documentation" of pricing policies. Today, extensive documentary evidence is necessary to justify any MNC's transfer pricing in the U.S.A.

So is the case with the UK. The UK Inland Revenue Authorities require companies to maintain records, disclosing the terms of transactions between related companies, including pricing, charges and the mode of working out those terms, as proof of following the principles of "arm's length" pricing.

Such stricter enforcement of rules is necessary for developing countries also. Even China, South Korea, Thailand and some other developing countries provided for stricter enforcement of transfer pricing rules on the basis of "arm's length" principles. The proof of justification of the pricing adopted lies on the tax payer and not on the tax authorities.

In the U.S., the foreign controlled companies are strictly monitored. Foreign controlled corporation coordinated examination program — "Transfer Pricing Audit Guide" calls for identifying the ultimate owners of the fragmented foreign controlled companies. Concerted action which provides benefits to the parties concerned, rather than mere stake in the ownership or control is the basis on which Internal Revenue Service (IRS) launches their investigation on the U.S. Subsidiaries set up by Asian Companies, including Indian companies. But Indian Tax authorities have also recently laid down stricter guidelines for enforcing the proper transfer pricing.

In India, as in UK, the onus of proof of the misuse of transfer pricing mechanism lies on the Tax Department. Records which would help the Tax authorities to conduct an audit are not statutorily required to be maintained in India. As such, the Indian MNCs can get away from close scrutiny of transfer prices used by not keeping proper records in justification of the use of the transfer prices. In UK, to plug this loophole, the rules have been tightened by the Finance Act 1998. The new Rules have thrust the onus of proving the appropriateness of the transfer prices on the tax paying companies. Now the UK companies have to disclose related party transactions and provide proof of the justification of such transfer prices adopted. The same provisions are now provided in the Tax guidelines in India. Most of the developed countries have plugged all loopholes for misusing the transfer prices to avoid taxes, due by the MNCs.

❖ ❖ ❖

# SOURCES OF FUNDS FOR MNCs

# 27

## General Sources

Any private and public limited company or a foreign company can have various sources of funds depending upon the purpose in mind. Normally there are two purposes, namely, long-term and short-term. As per the government and RBI guidelines, short-term funds of working capital nature are financed only from short-term borrowings while the permanent or core part of working capital has to be financed by long-term sources.

The sources can be enumerated as follows:

Working capital is of two components, namely, permanent and temporary. The permanent part is the minimum of current assets or core part of it which has to be kept by all solvent companies. These two parts of working capital and fixed capital assets are shown in the chart below.

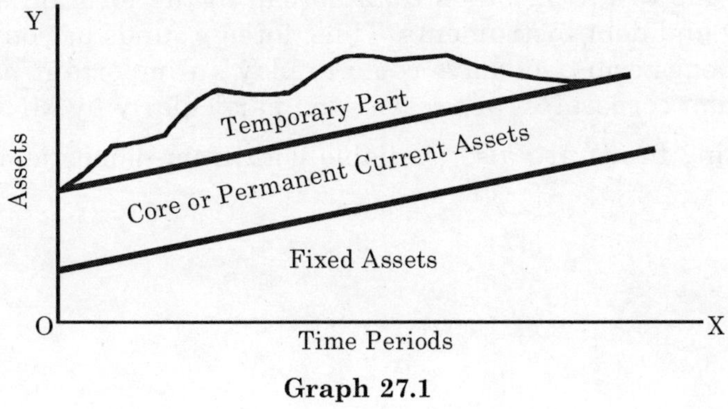


Graph 27.1

*Note:* The requirements are growing in general in the case of fixed assets and core part of current assets in tune with the long-term growth of the company.

(1) External sources (external to the company) Loans and Borrowing from FIs working capital term loans, Deposits, issue of Bonds, etc.

(2) Internal sources — own funds or reserves unpaid dividends, Tax provisions, Depreciation provisions, profits retained, sale of fixed assets.

(3) Foreign sources (Cross border borrowings)
GDRs FCCBs, International banks,
ADRs FCNR, foreign government
Euro currencies etc.

(A) Core part is financed by the any of the above sources:

(B) Temporary part or fluctuating part is financed from the following sources:

(1) Bank Credit

Bank overdraft

Bank cash credits

Bank loans secured and unsecured

(2) Trade credits

(3) Customer Advances

(4) Loans from promoters/directors

(5) Public deposits

(6) Sale of non-current assets etc.

Fixed assets are financed by long-term capital

(1) Equity (2) Preference capital (3) Bonds (4) Debentures (5) Loans and advances and deposits from FIs, GIC and LIC etc. (6) Loans and advances of banks (7) Sale of fixed assets (8) Borrowings from government and from abroad.

Among long-term sources, mention may be made of the following types of both equity and Debt Capital:

(1) Venture capital funds, underwritings and guarantees (2) Rights Issue (3) Bonus Issue (4) Lease finance (5) Foreign GDRs, FCCBs, Flexi Bonds, and (6) foreign currency loans or bonds.

More recently with the opening of the economy and the trend to globalisation, the sources of foreign funds increased due to F.D.I., funds from abroad in the form of NRI and FFI investment in both equity and debt instruments. Thus, foreign funds as source of capital both for short-term and long-term uses have come to play an important part in the sourcing of funds by the Indian corporates, at present and particularly by MNCs.

The following methods of raising funds are also available both from domestic and foreign sources.

# DOMESTIC AND FOREIGN SOURCES

**Table 27.1**

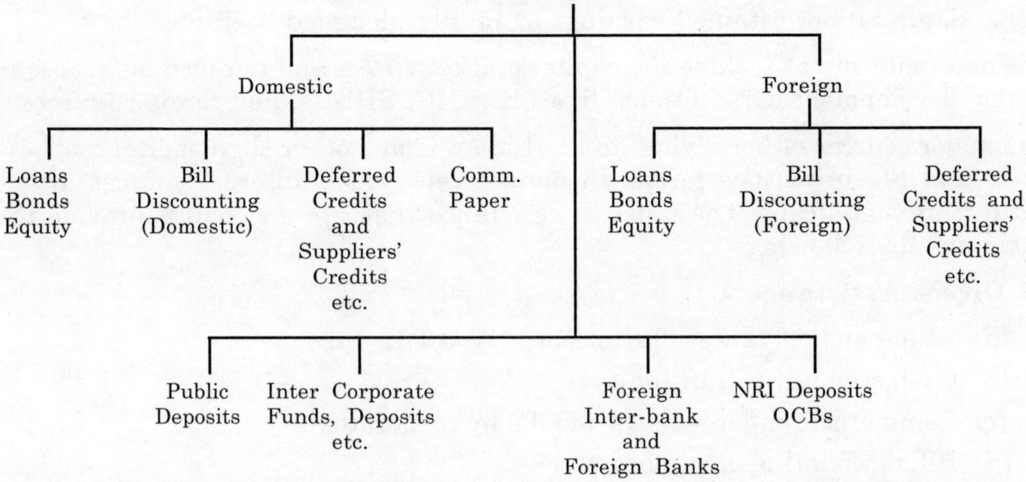


Note that there is an overlapping of short-term funds and long-term funds. Sometimes short-term funds are used for long-term purposes which is more risky. A company which has more debt than it can service easily by earnings flows is a risky venture and more so, if it has a large foreign debt which has to be repaid in foreign exchange. It is also possible that long-term funds are used to finance short-term purposes, but to the extent that these funds are used to finance core part of working capital, it is a welcome development. As an illustration, the following chart 27.1 shows the importance of each of the various sources in the form of their percentages to the total project finance, required by the corporate sector of which MNCs are there as the data relate to large public limited companies

**Chart 27.1 : Sources of Finance and their Relative Importance**

*(in percentage)*

| *Sources* | *1998-99* | | *2002-03* | *2007-08* |
|---|---|---|---|---|
| Indian Equity and preference capital ... | 8.6 | | -2.2 | 17.5 |
| Reserves and Surpluses ... | 8.3 | 13.0 | | 23.8 |
| Depreciation & Provisions | 26.3 | 52.6 | | 12.7 |
| Owned funds | 43.2 | | 63.4 | 54.0 |
| Debt | | | | |
| Bonds and Debentures | 6.9 | — | | |
| Loans from All India FIs | 21.2 | — | | 7.8 |
| Total of long-term debt ... | 28.1 | 3.9 | | 7.8 |
| Banks short-term ... | 11.2 | | | NA |
| LIC / GIC | Neg. | 24.9 | | 20.5 |
| Other deposits, Inter corporate funds, etc. | 3.5 | | | — |
| Others | 14.0 | 7.8 | | 17.7 |
| Borrowed funds | 56.8 | | 36.6 | 46.0 |

*Source:* RBI Bulletin, March, 2000 and April 2004 and August 2009 (Finances of Public Limited Companies)

The RBI publishes data regularly on the corporate finance studies, which they conduct from time to time.

The internal sources are in the form of bonus equity, reserves and surpluses, provisions, depreciation, retained earnings or profits ploughed back etc.

The external sources include the capital market, direct and indirect assistance from FIs, banks, development corporations, like LIC, GIC, SIIDCs, and foreign sources.

The major sources of borrowing to the Indian firms other than capital market are the banks and FIs in various forms. In more recent years, internal sources after the banks are more significant. The types of assistance that FIs and banks provide to the corporates are the following:

**(1) Direct Assistance**

(*a*) Loans and Advances, Term loans, W.C.T.L., etc.

(*b*) Cash credit overdraft limits

(*c*) Commercial paper — issue of CPs by corporates

(*d*) Bill discounting of corporates

(*e*) Export credit finance/Refinance

(*f*) Assistance for new entrepreneurs in the form of loans from Technical Development Fund, or Venture Capital Fund etc.

(*g*) Seed capital assistance in the form of equity

(*h*) Soft loan scheme for assistance to medium and small-scale units etc.

(*i*) Lease finance, H.P. finance, etc.

**(2) Indirect Assistance**

(*a*) Guarantees for or on behalf of the firm

(*b*) Collection of Bills

(*c*) Underwriting of any issues made by firms

(*d*) Investment support to bonds/equity of firms

(*e*) Marketing, export market intelligence, credit information on foreign constituents, etc.

**(3) Foreign Assistance/Loans**

(*a*) Foreign Currency Notes

(*b*) FCCBs

(*c*) Eurobonds

(*d*) Foreign bank loans

(*e*) GDRs, ADRs, IDRs, etc.

(*f*) Joint Ventures in equity participation

(*g*) Technical Assistance

(*h*) FDI upto 51% at present

(*i*) Multilateral and regional development bodies and their assistance, such as from IFC, ADB, etc.

The above sources of finance are both for working capital and for fixed capital purposes. Capital Market sources also provide external funds, for the company in the form of equity, rights, preference capital, bonds, debentures, convertible and non-convertible — both new issues of new companies and new and further issues of existing companies.

## M.N.C. and Global Finance

Multinationals and global operators have more avenues of raising funds than purely domestic companies. International money and capital markets are open to access funds in addition to domestic money and capital markets. The international capital markets which are free for borrowings are USA, UK, Germany and Japan. Controls are most in Japan followed by Germany. Controls are least in USA and UK. Borrowing is most in U.S. dollars (30-40%), followed by sterling and euro and Japanese yen. Control-free markets are Euro-currency markets or offshore funds markets. There are no controls on interest rates, no control on reserves to be kept and no government interference in these funds. The Euro-markets have developed out of felt needs for avenues for surplus dollars or other convertible currencies and the demand for them.

## Capital Markets of Foreign Countries

Funds are raised by the multinationals by various methods in the international capital markets, namely,

(1) Public issue, sale through prospectus or a letter of offer, after getting clearances from the security market regulators.

(2) Bought out deals, where all issue amount is sold to one or more agencies, merchant bankers and financial institutions, who later on sell to the public in retail, at market-related prices or at prices that investors are willing to pay.

(3) Private placement, which is sale through offer of sale to selected parties, institutional agencies and pension funds etc.

(4) Securitised debt: In this case, the book debts of the companies, which may be mortgage finance companies or Housing Finance Companies etc. are sold by securitising the book debts into bonds, which are unsecured and sold to investors at discounts, varying upon the risk involved in these book debts.

(5) Mergers, acquisitions, takeovers of brands, patents, copy rights or demergers of departments, products and processes etc.

If these securitised bonds are of countries like Mexico, whose credit rating is poor and book debts are non-performing assets, then such bonds are called junk bonds, sold at heavy discounts to the public.

Such debts issued in the form of bonds by UK companies are called Bull Dog bonds; if issued by US companies, Yankee bonds and if issued by Japanese companies, Samurai bonds.

The instruments through which the global players borrow are equity or pure debt instruments and more recently by some combination of equity and debt features like ECBs, ADRs and IDRs, FCCBs and PCCBs, callable bonds, partly paid bonds, dual and multiple currency bonds, bonds with attached warrants and loyalty coupons and bonds with call and put options, etc. These instruments are listed and traded in London, New York or Luxemburg.

## Euro-Currency Markets

There is a separate chapter for this market. But for the purpose of enumerating available sources, mention has to be made of these markets, for offshore funds, called by different names such as Euro-bond market, Euro-Currency market, Euro-dollar market, petro-dollar market or Asian dollar market. In these markets, the currencies dealt with are any of the convertible currencies, other than dollar such as pound sterling, D.M. or Japanese yen. The borrowers borrow for various purposes but if it is governments, the borrowings are mostly for meeting the balance of payments deficits and if it is corporates, for working capital term finance, for project expansion, diversification and modernisation etc.

## Money Market

In the short-term money market, the major operators are the commercial banks and investment banks — who along with the primary dealers (or wholesalers) and security firms (broker firms) deal in short-term instruments of money. These may be purchase, discount and trade in bill of exchange, Treasury bills, and Treasury bonds of short duration of less than 12 months. Money at call and short-notice can also be borrowed among banks both Indian and foreign, located in foreign centres. Short-term investments are useful for deployment of excess funds for short duration and disinvest when funds are required again. Leaving aside these traditional instruments a host of new instruments are traded in such money markets, namely, certificates of deposits, factorisation bills, etc.

In this market, corporates can have access to funds or limits and guarantees granted by foreign banks. Floating rate notes and Euro-notes, note issuance facilities are some methods of borrowing short-term, mostly from foreign banks. One can borrow through collateral floaters or inverse coupon floaters which are secured or unsecured loans depending upon the creditworthiness of borrowers.

Banks are the major borrowers and lenders. Sometimes multinationals also borrow short-term through such media as FRNs or note issuance facility which are like granting a limit for borrowing in the short-run. Corporates borrow from a single bank or a syndicate of banks. In the latter case, it is called syndicated loans, which is arranged by the lead banker for large amounts of borrowings by credit worthy borrowers.

## Capital Market

Bonds and debts are the most common form of borrowing in international markets. Equity generally comes in the form of foreign direct investment, joint ventures, acquisitions, etc., which are all subject to the approval of the concerned authorities in the lending and borrowing countries. Where capital account controls on the currency are freed, then these approvals are in the form of reporting to the respective authority.

Bonds have an advantage over equity for leverage, as interest paid on it is an expense item to the company. Similarly companies in the initial stages of production also prefer debt route, due to low cost. Many companies whose equity base is adequate prefer debt route. Bonds can be designed with different features and incentives, such as premium at repayment, or warrants attached for conversion into equity after a period of time and with varying methods of repayments, with or without coupon rates etc.

A number of innovations have been designed in the instruments of debt. Some of the new instruments introduced in the international money and capital markets are the following:

(1) Multi-currency option bonds — with parts of the amounts denominated in different currencies.
(2) Fully convertible bonds like ECCBs, or partly convertible bonds.
(3) Bonds with put and call options — with rights to sell back (put) or right to buy back (call) by the investors and issuers, respectively.
(4) LIBOR or SIBOR related bonds or Treasury note rate related bonds.
(5) Freely floating rate Notes or bonds or Flexi-bonds with changing interest rates depending on inflation rates.
(6) Indexed Bonds, Gold Bonds, Inflation adjusted bonds etc.

Money and capital markets are many times overlapping as banks operate in both these markets and loans of short-term nature can be rolled over into long-term — both in the international capital markets and Euro-currency markets. Many floating rates notes, issued for short-terms varying upto 365 days can be rolled over into medium-term. Similarly, many lines of export credit for short periods are rolled over into medium-term, particularly in respect of capital goods and project exports. So is the case with medium term loans floating into long-term loans.

In the charts below, different types of borrowing and their relative importance are set out in respect of India.

External Sources of Finance for India are the following:
(1) Bilateral Aid from Foreign Governments (around 7%)
(2) Multi Lateral Aid from IMF, World Bank, ADB, etc. (around 10%)
(3) Commercial Borrowing from Foreign Markets (around 52%)
(4) Export Credits or trade credit Offered by Other Countries to India (around 17%)
(5) Miscellaneous Sources (around 11%)
(6) I.M.F. (around 3%), now reduced to zero, due to repayment to IMF.

The percentages in brackets refer to their relative proportion to the total of external sources for India in more recent years, variable from year to year. Thus the most important source of funds is commercial borrowings referred to below: (Table 27.2)

**TABLE 27.2 COMMERCIAL BORROWINGS OF INDIA**

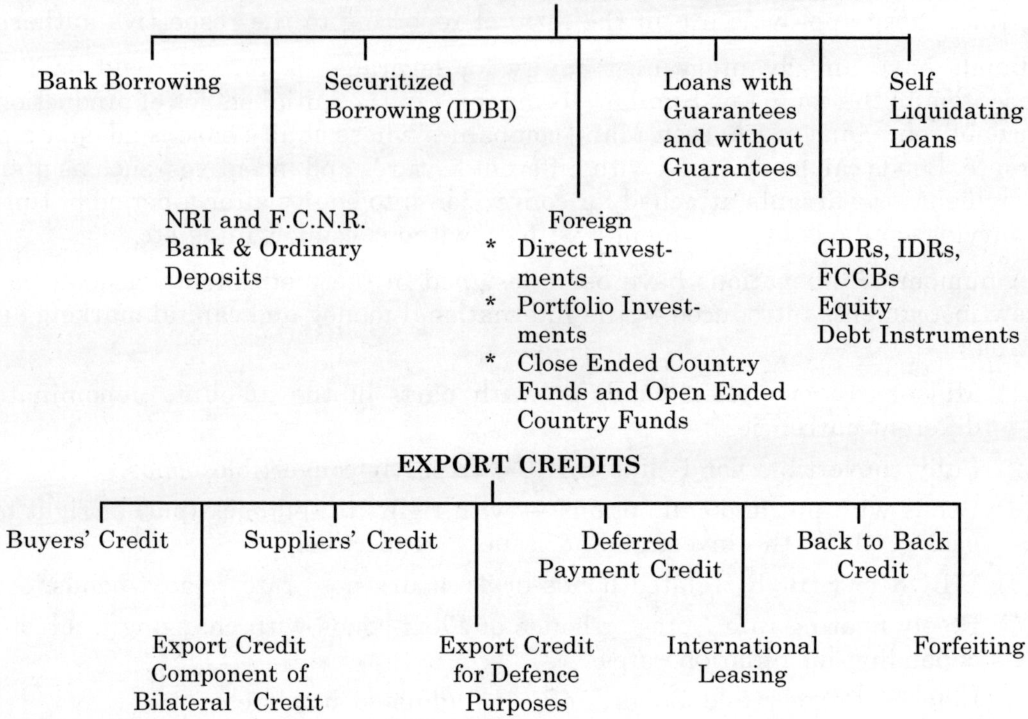


## Cost of Issue

One of the major factors influencing the companies to go for public issues in domestic markets or raise funds abroad or go for short-term borrowings or medium and long-term borrowings is the cost of borrowing. This cost is a relative factor. It includes the cost of raising funds, costs of servicing and repayment of debt or costs in the form of alternative cost. The cost of servicing equity is generally considered zero, but in true sense, the cost of servicing equity includes the costs of alternatives lost for funds in the hands of investors or the company.

The cost of issue guidelines as laid down by the Government for domestic issues are as follows:

(1) For the issue of equity the maximum costs can be mandatory costs plus 5% for issues upto Rs. 5 crores. For issues above Rs. 5 crores this limit is mandatory costs + 2%. The mandatory costs include payment to lead and other managers, underwriters, registrars, bankers, brokers etc. including the cost of listing fees paid to stock exchange. The same guidelines apply for FCBs or equity linked schemes.

(2) For the issue of debt, bonds or debentures the maximum costs can be mandatory costs plus 2% of the issue proceeds for the issue amount upto Rs. 5 crores and mandatory costs plus 1% of the issue proceeds for the amounts above Rs. 5 crores.

In addition to the issue costs, there are costs of servicing and repayment. Debt has the advantage in that the interest costs are treated as expense items and deducted from profit before being taxed. The same is the case of lease rentals paid for lease financing and of the instalment payments for hire purchase which include both current and capital expenses. Current expenses include interest component and capital expenses include instalment of debt repayments. The former is an expense item under current account.

## Buyback of Shares

Early in November 1998, SEBI had announced the guidelines for buyback of shares by companies. The approved modes of buyback are through tender offer, proportionate purchases (reverse of rights), Dutch auction (reverse of book building) and stock market. The prohibited modes of buyback are negotiated deals, spot transactions and private arrangements.

The rights of minority shareholders are protected. Buyback for the purpose of countering a takeover bid is not allowed. Buyback and takeover bids are mutually exclusive. Promoters are debarred from participating if the company is making buyback through the stock market route.

Extensive disclosure requirements are laid down to protect the interests of investors. Promoters have to declare their pre and post buyback holding in the company. The merchant banker has been given the responsibility to ensure that the companies do observe these guidelines. They have to give a "Due Diligence" certificate to the SEBI, and disclosures have to be made to the Stock Exchange where it is listed.

As regards the pricing of shares, the SEBI will not interfere. But it is to be approved by the shareholders in a general body meeting through a special resolution.

Time bound programme for buyback is laid down. An offer of buyback cannot remain open for more than 30 days and within 7 days of the closure of the offer, the shares bought back have to be physically destroyed.

Many of these guidelines are to promote sound corporate governance and prevent the misuse of these arrangements by promoters. The SEBI's role is overall supervision while the actual implementation of these guidelines was left to the merchant banker of the company, who is responsible to the SEBI.

## Limitations

This can be misused by promoters operating through their nominees even in the case of the scheme through the Stock Exchange. The buyback norm of post operation debt equity of 2:1 is unrealistic, as many companies are presently operating at much higher level, permitted by the FIs. Besides industry wise norms of debt-equity ratio change so substantially that an uniform norm is impossible. The SEBI has been asked to relax this norm for the buyback.

Similarly the two year waiting period between the buyback and any other equity issue by the company is also too long. Normally in the interest of transparency one year period is enough to show the effect of buyback operation on Balance Sheet data. The companies will get enough time within one year to factor the buyback details into the Balance Sheet. The government have since revised this norm.

## Advantages

(1) It gives flexibility to companies to reorganise capital structure and lower the average cost of capital.

(2) It improves the earnings per share and optimise the shareholder wealth.

(3) It facilitates the elimination of fractional shareholdings and odd lots.

(4) It maintains the continuation of management control and management stability.

(5) It facilitates the family rearrangements, in the case of family concerns.

(6) It promotes consolidation of the corporate governance, by eliminating the discontented employee shareholders, joint venture shareholders, and others allotted shares under sweat equity scheme or employees stock option scheme.

## Modes of Buyback

(1) Open market purchase — purchase through the Stock Exchange during trading hours.

(2) Buyback scheme to all shareholders on a pro-rata basis.

(3) Through selective purchases through agreement from collaborators and FIs, etc.

(4) Buyback of Employee shares.

(5) Buyback of odd lots or fractional shares.

## Buyback in Global Aspect

Buybacks are very popular in the U.S.A. and other developed countries. Stock prices shoot up on buyback announcements by management. This gives flexibility to MNCs to improve the EPS and shareholder wealth. The companies may buyback from the stock market when its scrip prices are undervalued. A buyback announcement by a company signifies its efforts or restructuring of capital, possible positive effects on the company's operations by confining its operations to areas where it has a comparative cost advantages and divest from non-competitive and unrelated activities. As buyback increases the earnings on net worth and the EPS, MNCs usually take advantage of buyback in countries where their shares are undervalued and there is scope for reorganisation of the business options. Some buybacks lower the cost of subsequent borrowings, while others are tax efficient and surplus funds are used to buyback shares. Reliance had announced buyback of its shares at Rs. 303 per share in April 2000.

The legal framework for buyback varies from country to country and MNCs have to make sure of complying with legal requirements. It helps them to obviate a possible takeover bid or unwanted takeover or destabilisation of management.

For global marketing, production and network of distribution, the global players have to know the legal, regulatory and procedural aspects of anything that they are concerned with, be it mergers, acquisitions or buybacks. As the legal and regulatory framework for each of the countries is different, it is advisable to know the framework for each of the countries.

As stock buybacks is the most popular method of enhancing the shareholder value, the U.S. statistics shows an increase in the amount of authorisations for buyback from nil in 1982 to $ 150 billion in 1996. These buybacks give signalling effects of a positive nature on company's financial position and on its equity price and they have increased in recent years.

If mergers and acquisitions take place they increase the equity stock as well the total capital employed and may lead to either related diversification or unrelated diversification. If the best return lies in the core competency of the firm there is no point of diversification and there is a case for divestment of non-core and inefficient units. There can be an arrangement for buyback which will have the opposite effect of M&A.

## U.S. Law

In view of high rate of use of buyback facility by the U.S. companies, the legal framework of the U.S. may be briefly referred to here. Section 6.31, 6.40 and 8.33 of the Model Business Corporation Act of 1984 expressly authorises a company to buyback its shares. The Board of Directors are empowered to alter the Articles for reducing the authorised capital by the number of shares acquired, if the Articles prohibit the reissue of acquired shares through buyback route.

A company cannot buyback its shares, if the company cannot pay its debts as they become due after buyback. Similarly a company cannot buyback its own shares, if its total assets would be less than its total liabilities plus the amount that would be needed if it is dissolved at that time to satisfy the preferential rights which are superior to equity holders whose shares are bought back. (Section 6.40 of the Model Business Corporation Act 1984). Directors will be liable for any default or violation of any of the above provisions.

## Indian Law

The Companies Act 1956 does not provide for buybacks but the government has amended the Act in 1998 to allow buybacks by Indian companies which apply also to subsidiaries of foreign companies. Buyback is allowed under Section 77A and 77B, newly inserted in the Act.

Buyback can be done out of its free reserves or out of securities premium account or out of the proceeds of an earlier issue. Buyback is permitted, if it is authorised by its articles, and it does not exceed 25% of the total net worth of the company and the ratio of debt to equity after buyback is not more than 2:1. The buyback has to be of shares fully paid up and as per the prevailing SEBI Guidelines. The disclosures have to be fair and full and the acceptable methods of buyback are from open market, from odd lots or from all shareholders on a proportionate basis or from employees' shares purchased under stock option scheme. The other disclosures are all laid down by SEBI in their guidelines.

## Inter-corporate Investments

Early in November 1998, the Central Government has freed from any control of inter corporate investment by both investee and investor companies.

Before November 1998, any company could not lend or invest more than 30% of its N.O.F. without government approval; it could not invest in more than 30% of the stake in another company, under provisions of Section 372(2) of the Companies Act.

The latest government notification provides that the existing Section 370 and 372(2) are replaced by a new Section, which does not specify any limits to either investor or investee company. Only two conditions are laid down:

(1) The approval of the Board would be necessary for investment upto 60% of equity or 100% of free reserves of the company, whichever is more.

(2) A special resolution is necessary for investments and loans exceeding this limit, which the company has already adopted.

In case there are outstanding loans of any FI, it is mandatory for the company to take their approval. This would essentially mean that henceforth, instead of the government, the FIs would be the monitoring agencies, as most companies have some account of loan or other from any one of the various FIs, most of which are government owned and government controlled.

This liberalisation of control on investor and investee company for any intercorporate investments will help the financial restructuring and lowering of cost of capital for domestic companies or MNCs — holding companies and their subsidiaries. This promotes globalisation of companies first by freeing of companies from rigours of Company Law and second by encouraging Intercorporate Investments. The government policy promotes the operations of MNCs for mergers, acquisitions and financial restructuring.

## Euro-commercial Paper

Many times NIFs or Note Insurance Facilities are replaced by Euro-commercial paper which do not have the underwriting facility. Euro-notes or Euro-commercial paper are now more popular and banks are the agents to sell them. These short-term facilities or notes are more popular and less costly and are called Euro-notes. These replaced many times the NIFs. The first part of NIF is the underwritten facility called committed amount. The underwriting banks get the commission but rarely the companies use this facility and when they use, they must be in financial difficulties. The second part of the NIF is uncommitted facility, which is an arrangement to auction off notes, if and when the borrower wishes to raise funds. These are for short periods of 1 to 6 months and are called Euro-notes. The banks which are in the tender panel for issue of these notes will get first priority. The banks keep a margin between borrowing and lending rates of atleast 3 to 5 basis points above the LIBOR.

In recent years a wide variety of instruments have emerged to suit the needs of customers. Multi-currency and multi-tiered loans have become quite common. The customers are given the option of MOF (multiple option facilities). This gives the customers facilities depending on their requirements in the form of Euro-notes of short duration, multi-currency loans, lines of credit in various currencies and with various rates and linked to a basis of Federal Treasury Bill rate or Treasury Bond rate or LIBOR, or LIBID etc. Sometimes a swing line of funds would be available to be used immediately and for temporary purposes. Of all these facilities, the most popular short-term money market instrument is Euro commercial paper, which is cheaper and quicker to raise and flexible provided the borrower company has good credit rating.

Short-term financing refers to the financing of working capital or current assets. MNCs access to short-term funds is more diversified than that of the domestic company. It has access to domestic and foreign money markets, in addition to intra-affiliate and parent company funds. The short-term financing of MNCs poses more complex problems due to many options open to them but with risks of exchange rate changes, different tax rates and regulations of governments of the concerned countries.

## Risks and Costs of Borrowing

The main determinants of the option to be chosen by an affiliate of the MNC are the expected costs, timeliness, and the risks involved in the process.

(1) There are trade-offs between the interest costs and the expected currency changes in currencies. The company has to examine the interest costs in various centres and advantage of interest cost in any centre can be offset by the adverse change in currency of that centre. For example, borrowing in Singapore at 6% may be cheaper than borrowing at 8% in Germany. But if Singapore dollar depreciates more than the German D.M., by 2% or more, then the advantage of borrowing from Singapore is lost and the company may better borrow from Germany.

(2) The element of exchange risk is relative to the company's exposure in that currency. For example, if it is cheaper to borrow from Germany but the affiliate has no exposure in the form of importing from and exporting to that country, then that company's exchange risk is increased by borrowing in that currency.

(3) If the domestic cost of borrowing is cheaper but if that country has possibility of exchange and trade controls, then the parent company will prefer to borrow from external sources which have less possibility of exchange control or political risk attached to that borrowing.

(4) Another factor which influences the option of borrowing is the degree of risk aversion. If the company is very risk averse it may have to pay a high cost to borrow from the best source.

(5) The relative costs of borrowing at various centres net of taking a hedge of exchange risk, determine the source of borrowing for that affiliate, if it has facilities of forward contracts and hedge for its exchange risk.

(6) Lastly there is another factor, namely, tax treatment of exchange gains and losses and interest payments. The tax asymmetries are based on differential treatment of exchange gains and losses on forward contracts or any loan repayment. In comparing relative borrowing costs in different centres for making

a decision on where to borrow, the comparison of costs should be on after tax covered basis.

## Financing Options

The MNCs prefer short-term funds to finance the temporary short fall in Current Assets. Then preference is given to the intra-affiliate transfer of funds. The normal options to the MNC or its subsidiary are: (1) inter-company loans, (2) local currency loans and (3) short-term floating rate notes from Euro markets.

Inter company loans are the first preference for easy sourcing. But interests of the governments of the lending country and borrowing country may differ and government regulations may stand in the way of resorting to inter company loans. The inter-corporate loans are priced through the opportunity cost of funds for lender, adjusting for the prevailing interest rates, tax rates and government regulations and expected exchange rate movement.

## Objectives

MNC's main concern is when, where and in which currencies to borrow short-term. They have various alternatives, as they operate in various countries. For example, Hyundai of South Korea has 62 subsidiaries, spread over the whole world and many U.S. and U.K. companies also have a large number of subsidiaries, joint ventures and alliances.

To the question of when to borrow is decided when the MNC has not got enough intra-affiliate funds and there is need to augment working capital funds. If forward contracts are available, risk can be reduced and MNC borrows in the cheapest source and in any currency which is convertible. Its objective is to minimise the expected cost and minimise expected risk, simultaneously. There is a trade-off between the expected cost and systematic or market related risk and even total risk. A well diversified portfolio of risky assets will reduce some risks while insurance through hedge will reduce other risks. The approach of trading off expected cost and total risk is valid when forward contracts in foreign currencies are available. Otherwise, in practice, the only objective pursued by the MNCs is to select the lowest cost borrowing option with adjustments for currency hedge and for tax payments, if any.

## Local Currency Financing

Most affiliates of MNCs are permitted to borrow their requirements locally in the short-term market and through reputed multinational bank. In borrowing locally, first preference is through a bank which has its parent company or atleast an affiliate in the MNC's own parent country. That will facilitate inter-company transfers and other inflows and outflows of funds and payments.

The local sources are banks, private credit, Commercial paper, bills of exchange or factoring bills. Local sources have some advantages, namely, no risk of currency exposure and no adverse impact of taxes or government regulations. They are also convenient for accounting purposes.

Bank loans are short-term credits for financing the inventory and accounts receivable. They are self liquidating as the cash received due to increase in working capital or repayment of bills can be used to repay bank loans. There are generally credits for short periods of 30 to 90 days. These are mostly unsecured credits and are very flexible so far as the company is concerned.

## Forms of Bank Credit

(1) The firm needs a line of credit to meet its cash flow needs as and when required. When for example there are no private trade credits or suppliers do not provide credit, funds are required at short notice or on a daily basis. Only banks can finance such sudden requirements, through a previously arranged line of credit facility.

(2) Term loans are for fixed periods of 90 days to one year with a flexible schedule of repayment and generally unsecured. The terms of the loan are set out in a promissory note signed by the client company.

(3) Overdrafts on current account of a company are allowed by the bank upto a limit, agreed upon at the beginning. The borrower pays interest on the debt balances in his account on a monthly basis. In India, the cash credits and overdrafts provided by banks which can be diverted for medium-term and long-term financing are discouraged by the RBI.

(4) Revolving credit agreement: This is a line of credit, which when exhausted will be automatically renewed. The bank charges an extra commitment fee on the unused portion of credit line and normal interest rate on the portion utilised. This loan is also secured and is provided to the best and credit worthy customers.

(5) Discounting of Bills, of which factoring bills are a special category of export bills is another method of financing by banks or their subsidiaries. Discounting of trade bills is the most preferred short time financing. The bills are promissory notes signed by the buyer accepting his liability to pay in a specified period of say 90 days or less to the seller or his banker. If the banker of seller or any other banker signs and endorses it, then it becomes bankers' acceptance. Such bankers' acceptances are good bills for discounting and rediscounting whereby the company drawing the bill or the creditor or seller gets his funds in cash. A credit bill is converted into cash at a discount. The discount calculated into a rate per cent per annum is interest rate for that loan.

Effective interest rate is the interest amount paid for the funds received. If it is a straight loan at an interest rate of 12%, then the effective rate is the same as 12%. But if the loan is given on a discount basis and the amount received after discounting is Rs. 95 but the interest is paid at 12%; that means, an amount of Rs. 12% is paid for only Rs. 95 and the effective rate is $(12 \div 95) \times 100 = 12.\ 63\%$.

Many times banks keep some margin money for a loan or insist on a compensating balance with itself. Thus for a loan of Rs. 100, Rs. 20 is kept as the margin and interest rate is 12%. Then usable funds are only Rs. 80 on which Rs. 12 is paid as interest.

The effective interest rate in this case is much higher, namely:

$$= \frac{12}{80} \times 100 = 15\%$$

If interest is prepaid, the usable funds will decline further and effective interest rate is then much higher, namely $= \frac{12}{68} \times 100 = 17.64\%$

## Commercial Paper

An alternative to borrowing from bank is Commercial Paper. It is a promissory note, unsecured, issued by first rated large corporations on a discount basis to institutional investors and to other corporations having surplus funds. In India, it is in a developing stage and a secondary market is not developed well. The terms of the paper, interest rates, maturity and the minimum amount to be issued vary from country to country. If it is sold on a discount basis, the interest rate is automatically decided. But sometimes they carry an interest rate and sold at par. The expense and time involved are less in Commercial Paper than in bank borrowing. Even so, it has to incur costs of a different nature in getting back-up lines of credit from a bank, which is prohibited in India by the RBI, and fees paid to banks for support and rating service fees paid to an agency of rating like CRISIL or ICRA. Credit rating is compulsory in India for all debt instruments both short-term and long-term, if they are issued to public.

The CPs in India are issued at varying rates depending upon the liquidity in the market. In 1999-2000, when the liquidity was easy and rates of interest were lower than the P.L.R. of banks (9-12%) then there was an upsurge of amounts of CPs outstanding. As at end March, 2009, the outstanding amount of C.P. was Rs. 44,171 crores with a range of effective discount rates of 6.4-12.5%

MNCs in India like all big public limited companies with a paid up capital (or net worth) of more than Rs. 4 crores and credit rating of P1 and listed on any Indian stock exchanges can issue Commercial Paper. The maturity period is from 3 to 12 months and minimum amount issued is Rs. 25 lakhs and in multiples of Rs. 5 lakhs. The brokers cannot enter the primary market but allowed in the secondary market. The NRIs are permitted to invest. The issuing company has to bear all issue expenses like commitment charges, stamp duty, etc. Many of the above conditions were liberalised during 2001-04.

## Euro-Notes and Euro-Commercial Paper

Euro notes are short-term paper issued outside the country in dollars, by the corporates and the government. It is a non-bank short-term credit, not underwritten by any agency and comparable to the Commercial Paper in the domestic markets.

They are different from domestic Commercial Paper in that they are of longer maturity and interest rates are adjusted each time the notes are rolled over. The issuers of this paper are rated sometimes and not always. The banks are the buyers of this Euro paper and they may not insist on the rating of the corporations issuing as they are well-known parties or MNCs. Euro-C.P. is actively traded in the secondary market and interest rates are finer than in domestic markets due to large volumes in which Euro-banks trade in them for their surpluses and deficits.

## Costs of Alternative Financing Options

The costs of borrowing through different options are not the same and the least cost option is invariably chosen by the MNCs. The costs are a function of the following factors:

*(i)* Interest rates and effective rates of borrowing, including issue costs.

*(ii)* Tax rates in the parent company's country and affiliate company's country.

*(iii)* Future exchange rates, expected.

If the MNC is of U.S.A. it will look into the dollar cost of the loan. If the loan is denominated in local currency of the affiliate it will have to consider the nominal interest cost plus or minus depreciation of the currency *vis-a-vis* the dollar and after tax interest cost on the loan. The after tax cost is interest cost minus tax gain or loss. This is equal to the dollar value of tax write-off, associated with increased amount of local currency required to repay to dollar principal following the local currency depreciation.

❖ ❖ ❖

# OPERATIONS IN INTERNATIONAL FINANCIAL MARKETS

# 28

MNCs have many sources of finance both for short-term and long-term needs. There are three general sources of funds, namely, internally generated cash, short-term external funds and long-term external funds. External to the company but not necessarily external to the country is the raising of funds from the investors of the company by buying securities in the form of equity or bonds. Instead of selling securities, the companies can borrow from the banks and Financial Institutions (FIs). In selling securities, there are many modes, namely, public issue, or private placement or rights issue to existing shareholders. Privately placed ones are sold directly to a limited number of specialised agencies or investor classes like insurance companies, provident funds, pension funds, etc.

## Financial Disintermediation

The financing pattern of companies differ from country to country. Companies in USA and Europe relied more on internal finance for the bulk of their requirements. The dependence on external funds is about 70% for Japanese companies and 60% in the case of India. The dependence on external sources varies with the business cycle phase, conditions in the markets and a host of other factors. Within the external sources the reliance on debt is more than equity in general and this is natural as debt provides cheaper cost of capital and gives leverage to the company in the form of higher earnings for the equity holders.

The financial deregulation has reduced the intermediation by banks and companies have been encouraged to access funds directly from the market by sale of securities. The cost of accessing from the public and the markets has come down with the increased deregulation globalisation of markets. The financial discipline imposed by banks and their potential threat of interfering with the management has encouraged the companies to go direct to the market. Private placement in particular is cheaper than public sale of securities. Most smaller and medium sized companies have therefore, gone away from banks which reduced their intermediation role.

## Globalisation of Markets

The world has become one interconnected market with the opening up of the economies to foreign funds, technological advances, and conquering of distance and time due to revolution in electronic computing and in telecommunications. The free entry and exit of funds and globalisation of financial markets increased the arbitrage facilities and competition in the markets. The cost of borrowing has come down and financial centres in the world have thrown off their costly regulations.

Increased competition led to increased depth of the markets. Funds borrowed and lent increased multifold into trillions of dollars. This also led to innovations in financial products offered for sale to attract investors. A wide variety of new financial products like ZCB, Flexi-bonds, Gold bonds etc. are being issued with or without special incentives like coupons and warrants attached to them.

Whether international fund flows take place through securitisation and financial markets or through the intermediation of banks and financial institutions depend on the cost of funds, risks attached, and the terms offered. One of the factors influencing these international funds flows is the free flow of information and the cost of collection of information and setting up of MIS.

## Securitisation vs. Intermediation

Whether securitisation or intermediation is cheaper is the main criteria of choice among them. What is cheaper to one company may not be so for another. Securitisation is more suitable for long-term asset formation, while intermediation is more apt for short and medium-term borrowing. This may also take care of the asset liability mismatch among banks, which increases the capital required for the capital adequacy norm to be satisfied.

The main function of financial market is mobilisation of savings, allocation of funds from less profitable to more profitable avenues and shift of purchasing power from savers to investors and from lenders to borrowers. The efficient markets are quick to adjust to all information and provide for free and unfettered competition and risk adjusted returns. This promotes securitisation but does not debar the role of intermediation.

Most major financial markets have developed on the basis of free interflow of funds between borrowers and lenders and savers and investors. If these markets allow the foreigners to enter and exit freely, then they become international markets. The international financial markets have grown due to the non-interference and no regulation from the local governments and economic and political stability and low tax rates or no taxes. These markets required highly sophisticated infrastructure, Telephones, Telex, electronic communication, satellite, Internet access etc.

The most important financial centres are London, New York and Tokyo. More recently well developed domestic financial markets turned into international financial markets as in Germany and France, due to freedom given to foreigners to borrow and lend, mostly through international banks. Some financial centres developed as financial entrepots — channels through which foreign funds pass. Markets such as Switzerland, Hong Kong, Singapore etc. serve this purpose of acting as intermediaries between the non-resident suppliers and non-resident users of funds.

The free access to foreigners requires non-interference from government in financial markets and no restrictions on entry and exit from these markets. International markets developed from domestic markets through dismantling of all restrictions on capital. The multinational banks first start operating and then the multinational corporations with free access promote this market. The basic principle involved is free capital mobility for the international markets to develop and grow.

The MNCs have access to both domestic markets in the countries, where their affiliates are located and the international financial centres, referred to above. In addition they have their own funds in various centres of the world which they are capable of moving to affiliates in need, through inter-corporate transfers. The international markets to which MNCs have access are the Foreign Equity market, Foreign Bond Market and International banks. These markets are discussed below.

## I. Foreign Equity Market

Placing of equity in foreign markets reduced the risk. Besides when large funds are raised by giants like airlines, oil companies etc. domestic markets are too small to raise enough funds. By attracting new shareholders, the company gets demand for its shares from new sources and countries. A company will get international presence by making issues in the foreign markets. It can lower its cost of equity and thereby, increase the market value of the firm.

More recently foreign companies are issuing stock in Europe, Asia and USA while the European and American companies are selling shares in other countries. These offerings are through international equity placements by international syndicates and by international issues. There are a number of advantages of accessing the foreign markets as against domestic markets.

## II. Foreign Bond Market

Foreign bond market is the most important segment tapped by MNCs. The amounts raised in the form of bonds are much more than that raised in the form of equity. The U.S.A. and Switzerland are the major foreign bond markets followed by that in Japan and Luxembourg. Foreign bonds floated in Switzerland, Germany and the Netherlands are subject to a queuing system, where the MNCs have to wait for their turn.

# III. Foreign Bank Market

This market represents that portion of domestic bank loans supplied to foreigners for their use abroad. The importance of foreign banks, particularly Japanese banks as funding sources is a matter well-known by the number of Japanese banks operating in this segment. The largest in terms of assets among the top 10 banking concerns in the world are the Japanese. The high Japanese saving rate is responsible for making the Japanese banks the world's leading bankers who can lend and arrange for loans in the international markets and Euro-markets.

## Euro

An example of free mobility of capital across borders is provided by the European common market. International lending by banks is facilitated by their having one common currency, namely, Euro. From January, 1, 1999 eleven European Union countries, namely, Germany, France, Austria, Belgium, Finland, Ireland, Italy, Luxemburg, the Netherlands, Portugal and Spain, have locked-in their currencies against the new common currency, created, namely, Euro. Britain, Sweden and Denmark although, belong to the same zone, preferred to remain outside the Euro currency for the time being.

The European Union Commission has fixed the following exchange rates for their national currencies *vis-a-vis* the Euro:

1. German Mark — 1.95583
2. French Franc — 6.55957
3. Italian Lire — 1936.27
4. Spanish Pesetas — 166.386
5. Portuguese Escudos — 200.482
6. Finnish Markka — 5.94573
7. Irish Punts — 0.787564
8. Belgium and
9. Luxemburg Francs } 40.3399
10. Dutch Guildersen — 2.20371
11. Austrian Shillingsen — 13.7603

While consumers can still pay for goods and services locally in their respective national currencies, the Euro is used on stock and bond markets and for electronic business transactions as in foreign exchange market and in financial transactions.

There were 15 European countries upto May 2004, when 10 more joined the union and opted to have a common market. The biggest beneficiaries are banks in all countries and international banks in particular.

Indian banks have opened Eurobank accounts with major foreign banks that they deal with. For example, SBI has 14 Nostro accounts in Euro-currencies. It has now opened fresh accounts in Euro with German, French, Italian banks, among other E.U. members, who adopted the new currency — Euro.

# INSTRUMENTS of Issue

## I. Euro-Currency loans Vs. Euro-Bonds

Euro bonds are loans of medium and long-term nature. They may be issued with fixed rate and floating rate forms. But fixed rate forms are preferred if long currency inflows and outflows in the future are to be certain. Euro-currency loans are invariably at floating rate, which enables one to hedge as well as take a risk. If the interest rates decline, they benefit, but they are hurt when interest rates rise, but this is the risk element, which fixed rate loans avoid.

The maturity period is shorter for currency loans which can be rolled over, but Euro bonds shall have longer maturities. The costs of floatation are lower in the case of Euro currency loans than in the case of Euro bonds market. The former will carry a cost of 0.5% of the face value of the bond as the floatation costs. There is flexibility in drawing on the loan in the case of currency notes, while in the case of bond, this must be drawn on a fixed date and also repaid on a fixed date. Besides the speed at which the floating rate notes can be raised is greater than that of the Euro bond.

## II. Note Issuance Facilities

Note Issuance Facilities (NIF) is a low cost substitute for syndicated credits. These are also called the short-term note issuance facility, sold by the large MNCs to the banks and financial institutions. They are like loan commitments and lines of credit given by banks to excellent rated companies and as such called Euro-commerical paper.

Many times, NIFs are short-term unsecured debt, sometimes supported by under writing facilities. The revolving underwriting facility gives long-term continuous access to short-term funds, underwritten by a domestic bank for funds released by an international bank. As NIFs are Commercial Paper, banks are eager to provide them as they do not fatten their loan portfolios, necessitating risk weighted capital adequacy norms to be observed. The note issuance facility is a self liquidating paper issued by high rated companies to banks or a syndicate of banks.

In the Euro-market, next to bonds come the Euro currency notes in importance and then come the short dated Commercial Paper or lines of credit provided by international banks to the corporates. The NIFs are like put options, with a right to the corporates to sell their paper to the bank or a syndicate of banks at a price related to LIBOR, as agreed to beforehand.

## III. FRNs

Floating Rate Notes are similar to Note Issuance Facility. Both are short-term loan facilities and the NIF has a greater drawdown flexibility and greater timing flexibility. The NIF has greater choice of different maturities and different currencies, as per the requirements of their cash outflows. Floating Rate Notes are generally locked-in on one maturity say 3 to 6 months. The FRNs have thus a secondary market which is not there for NIFs.

Unlike the Euro bond market which issues, in the beginning itself Eurobonds at fixed rates, the Floating Rate Notes are issued for shorter periods to less than 12 months as promissory notes with rates of interest floating with LIBOR or SIBOR. Note issuance facilities are different in that they are issued by companies as Commercial Paper for short-term periods with roll over facilities. These are like limits of credit which companies can draw as and when they require the funds. There is no fixed maturity period. These can be repaid much earlier than the period originally fixed or they can be rolled over without making any repayment.

## Debt vs. Equity For MNCs

MNCs generally prefer to keep its original equity investment to the minimum necessary. Subsequently, if they do not want any funds from this affiliate, and there is scope for expansion in their coreline, they will allow the funds to be reinvested as equity. Subsequently, if an affiliate wants funds, they will allow inter-corporate loans to this affiliate. It is easier to take back the funds in the form of interest on loans or royalties on technologies or use of patents and the MNCs prefer to remit funds as loans or allow technology transfers.

Besides loans give leverage to equity of the MNCs already invested. Interest on loans is not tax deductible unlike the dividend payments and hence reduces the total taxes paid by the affiliate. In the home country, the tax authorities also look into the income flows, and if too much funds are coming in the form of interest or royalties they will examine whether the affiliate is under-capitalised and whether MNCs are not substituting loan capital if the affiliate requires equity. They will therefore look into the debt-equity ratio in relation to the business carried on in each of the affiliates. MNCs play safe and keep atleast 50% of the capital required in the form of equity, which will also improve its credit rating in the host country.

Currency devaluation or fears of currency depreciation will make an affiliate designate the invoices in exports in a strong currency and imports in a weak currency. Similarly, if the tax rates are high in a currency, the after tax profits will be lower in that currency and if that currency is also weak and likely to depreciate, that affiliate will move funds to a high interest rate country and strong currency.

## Multinational Financial STRATEGIES of MNC's

The major source of funds for MNCs is their own funds, spread over many countries. The MNCs shift funds across borders easily and quickly and their ability to shift funds and accounting profits is what distinguishes them from domestic corporate finances. Internal financial transactions from among affiliates and parent company per se are inherent in the global strategies of the MNCs. This accompanies their international exchange of goods and services and capital.

The prevailing trade and exchange controls to international transactions, imposed by domestic economies and imperfections in domestic capital markets increase the value and attraction of domestic financial transactions as opposed to international financial transactions. These restrictions maintain artificial values for their currencies and keep the cost of local funds lower than what the free market forces will allow.

Consequent on these imperfections, the ability of MNCs to transfer funds and profits and relocate them from less profitable centres to more profitable centres and less remunerative lines of business to more remunerative lines of business appears limited *prima facie*. They manage to shift profits from units located in high tax nations to lower tax nations. They can also relocate profits from tax paying centres to those with tax losses. By their ability to transfer funds from one affiliate to another, they circumvent exchange control, earn higher risk adjusted yields, reduce their cost of borrowing and adjust the excess funds of some affiliates to those with deficit funds. By such intra-firm adjustments they can defeat the purpose of credit controls and exchange controls in domestic economies. They have the ability to disguise the true profits of any unit by such funds and profit transfers.

The cost-benefit analysis for MNC financial system will be different from that of others. By their capacity to shift funds quickly they save in transfer costs and in cost of borrowing. They use the transfer pricing mechanism, fee and royalty adjustments, inter-corporate loans, dividend and interest adjustments as between affiliates.

Such inter-unit and inter-country flows encounter problems from the policies of national government in the host country and home country. These are: (1) Tax Factors. (2) Tariffs and (3) Exchange Controls. The transfer pricing mechanism is used in a manner to avoid the above hurdles or reduce their impact on the MNCs as a whole. Transfer pricing is also misused to show lower profits of the affiliate and to cover up the true profitability.

The free flow of funds is hindered by the tax factors — tax payments in both the host country and the recipient country. The taxes include corporate taxes on total net income or profits and on dividends declared. Some recipient countries tax foreign source income at a higher rate. But some countries have double taxation avoidance treaties. India and US for example have such an agreement. So the affiliate receiving the profits will be taxed only after taking into account the tax already paid in the host country.

The ways by which MNCs maximise their home country's parent company inflows are set out below.

## I. Transfer Pricing

This subject was already discussed earlier. The transfer price is raised or lowered depending on the tax rates in the host and the recipient countries. If the transfer price is raised, the effect of this is to lower the total taxes paid and raise the consolidated income of the MNC.

Similarly tariffs also affect the transfer pricing policy. If the duty is *ad valorem* on imports, high transfer prices will lead to increased import duties paid. That is why MNCs pressurise their governments to bargain for removal of import restrictions with W.T.O. Low transfer prices may be viewed as tax evasion method in A's country, while B country may see that dumping as revenue foregone. Thus transfer prices have differential impact on different countries depending on their tax and tariff system. Many LDCs have high tariff barriers to protect the local industries. They also impose higher tax rates to regulate the profitability of affiliate firms, MNCs may report low profits by using higher transfer prices from home country to host country, namely, the LDC. Lower reported profits may also help the subsidiary to have better bargaining position with trade unions.

Another factor influencing the transfer price is exchange controls. Some LDCs have restriction on outflow of dividend, royalties, fees, and profits. In such countries, the subsidiary or affiliate will show lower profits and higher expenses. Then other affiliates can sell over-priced goods to this affiliate to show higher expenses by this. This leads to price distortions.

Transfer price adjustments will respond differently to tax hurdles, tariff restrictions and exchange controls. MNC's primary aim is to show larger profits in low tax countries and where trade unions are less powerful. They show lower profits in countries with high tax rates and where trade unions are powerful. Transfer pricing mechanism is also discussed in an earlier chapter.

But there are also disadvantages of misusing the transfer pricing mechanism. They will distort the profitability for true evaluation of management performance. To avoid such misuses, section 482 of U.S. Revenue Code calls for arms length prices — for MNCs to set prices at which a willing buyer and willing unrelated seller would agree to contract a bargain. Many other governments have also similar stipulations on the MNC funds transfer mechanism. So the MNC have started to lay down standard prices for standardised products. But some MNCs have found methods of evading this rule, by having unique products which are not and cannot be standardised, or where there are no unrelated buyers and unrelated sellers. Pricing of rejects, scrap, gifts etc. are also not possible to be standardised. But standard prices or arm-length prices can be set by following methods:

(1) Comparable uncontrolled prices — those fixed or those which rule in a free market in respect of unrelated parties.

(2) Resale price method — a price set for an unrelated party for resale covering resale costs plus a reasonable profit.

(3) Cost plus method — in normal free market conditions, the seller can take his cost and add an appropriate profit to derive the transfer price.

Many times the tax authorities have to approve the accounting practices of MNCs. So the latter prepare the ground well for answering any objections to the transfer price adopted by keeping all the background papers on costs involved as evidence. In practice a combination of methods may be used by the MNC to prove that transfer prices are in fact at arms' length prices.

The transfer pricing mechanism has come under severe criticism from LDCs where the tax authorities have been asked to look carefully into the accounting practices of MNCs. In fact developed countries are also strict in scrutinising accounting practices of MNCs. But the MNCs try to find out loopholes of the existing laws in both LDCs and DCs. One way they adopted to disguise their true profitability and use the transfer pricing policy legally was to set up the reinvoicing centres in the low tax nations.

## II. Role of Reinvocing Centre

Reinvocing Centre acts as the intermediary between two affiliates although, the goods move directly from one affiliate to another. It will receive goods at one price and sell to a local affiliate at a higher price in a currency which leads to higher prices, thereby, the legal hurdles of arms' length pricing in inter-corporate transfer of goods is overcome.

This Reinvoicing Centre, in addition to leading to suspicions, in both the recipient country and the host country, may lead to higher costs of establishment and marketing or sales. Whether in total, the addition of a Reinvoicing Centre adds to the costs more than to the benefits is a matter of decision for the individual MNCs. More recently, these reinvoicing centres are not favoured by MNCs themselves for the reasons specific to each.

MNCs also charge for their services, fees royalties and payments. For technical consultancy and for lending the know-how or trade mark etc., the host country sends regular payments as agreed upon. Unlike the case of goods transfer, the payments for services cannot be standardised and the payments for them are not so restricted as in the case of dividend on equity. The pricing of intangibles like fees and royalties is more difficult and MNCs take advantage of this to rechannel their profits from one centre to another in the form of bloated up payments for consultancy and technology transfers. Due to difficulties of pricing them and the urgent need for technology transfers, the host countries are generally, lenient in allowing such flows of funds for intangibles as between the affiliates. Where exchange controls prevail, initially itself, the MNCs charge higher fees and royalties and maintain them at that level, so as not to raise any suspicion of arbitrary charges or exorbitant charges. MNCs have found this method as a facile conduit for rechanelling and relocation of funds to their best advantage. Another factor to be considered is the interest rates prevailing in the countries having affiliates. In addition to factors like trade and exchange controls, low or high tax rates etc., MNC take into account the prevailing interest rates among the concerned countries for transfer of funds across borders. Higher interest rates *inter alia* attract more funds than low interest rates.

## III. Leading and Lagging

The MNCs have also a choice delaying or accelerating payments and receipts as between the affiliate accounts. This can be done on the terms of invoicing of goods and credit terms allowed. If an affiliate has accounts receivable from B to the extent of $ 100 million for 180 days, it is financing the working capital requirements of B. Similarly, if the terms of payment for supply of goods from one affiliate to another are such, that payments are spread over a period of 6 months, it means that to that extent the working capital financing is done by one to the other.

The extent of leading and lagging of funds flow depends on the opportunity cost of funds to both the receiving company and the sending company. If the cost of funds in B is high, A supplies to B goods in a manner that B gets the supply of cheaper funds. Then there is lagging at B's end. B can reduce outside high cost borrowing, due to this facility. Leading and lagging facilitates the shifting of liquidity to places, where it is most needed and where it is most profitable. This shifting of liquidity is subject to the exchange control regulations and interest rates in the respective countries.

The advantages of leading and lagging are:

(1) Governments do not generally interfere with inter-company accounts for short periods.

(2) Section 482 of the US Revenue Code allows inter-company transfer of accounts upto 6 months interest free.

(3) Not as much regulated as inter-company loans.

(4) No formal note of debt is needed and these leads and lags help the companies in need of low cost finance.

## Means of Transferring Funds by MNC

The major methods by which MNCs transfer funds from one centre to another are:

(1) Dividends, which account for about 50% of the total inflows of the MNCs in the U.S.

(2) Inter company loans of the following types —

(a) Direct loans without any intermediary between the parent company and its affiliates.

(b) Back-to-back loans or linking finance channelled through a bank by parent company to its affiliate or one affiliate to another.

(3) Bills Receivable financing for short-term funds through the involving of purchases from one affiliate to another or parent company to its affiliate giving rise to bills receivable for goods supplied maturing in 30 days to 180 days.

(4) Parallel loans: This is a method of circumventing the exchange control and use of blocked funds. Indian exchange control blocked the funds of Birla who have a subsidiary in Germany and German parent Hoechst has a subsidiary in India. Thus, Birlas finance the subsidiary of Hoechst in India while the latter's parent company finances the Birla's affiliate in Germany. These are synonymous with direct loans, replaced by indirect loans through mutual agreement.

(5) Fees, charges and royalties are sent from the affiliate to parent company subject to exchange control regulations. In countries like India, where there is Current Account Convertibility, such payments of charges, royalties etc. are free to be remitted, subject to the ceiling set by the RBI or the agreement between the collaborators and the Indian affiliate. These remittances including those of dividends are subject to the deduction of tax at source in the originating country.

Financing requirements of affiliates differ and opportunity cost of money among various affiliates will be different. Some have scope for expansion and others nil. Some get funds at cheaper costs outside. A few may have surfeit of funds while others have deficits and need to borrow. The MNCs follow the rule of equalising the surpluses and deficits of its affiliates. The dividend policy will also vary with the cost of funds outside. The parent company can increase the return to the funds by relocating funds from high cost and low profit centres to high profit and low cost centres. The funds may be diverted from centres with high costs of production, low opportunity cost of funds and investment opportunities to those centres with low costs of production, high opportunity cost of funds and large investment opportunities.

The MNCs will take advantage of yield differentials among their affiliates and set a high dividend pay out ratio in centres with low opportunities cost of funds. Generally if profits are not there they will close down the centres with no profits, and if profits are there, they will declare some dividend, which varies as per the conditions referred to above.

Another factor which influences dividend payments, as also any remittances, is the exchange controls prevailing in these countries. If not completely prohibiting the dividend remittances, the exchange controls limit the dividends, either in absolute terms, or as a percentage of total earnings or as a proportion of equity invested. To face such a situation companies located in such countries declare a dividend so as to make out a case of remittances of accumulated dividends later on. In the case of joint ventures, the dividend pay out ratio depends on the ability to pay outs, global factors, local factors and the perception of local partners as to be reasonable payments.

## Designing Global Remittance Strategy

The MNCs have the objectives of maximisation of the wealth of the firm, as a whole. The profit optimisation in each of the affiliates is subject to the environmental constraints, such as taxes, tariffs and exchange controls. The MNCs use these constraints to their advantages. Thus, they move larger profits to centres where taxes are low and show lower profits where taxes are high. Where tariffs are high, instead of exporting goods to that country, they will set up a Joint Venture or a subsidiary there. Similarly, exchange controls, currency strength and weakness influence the decision on debt equity ratio to be maintained and the type of transfer pricing mechanism to be used and the method of remittances to be adopted such as interest on loans or repayment of loans, royalties on patent use or on the know-how supplies. Similarly local credit policy — cost and availability of funds — influence the remittance policy. Remittances are increased from low cost country to high cost country and from countries with fewer credit curbs to those with very large credit curbs.

The remittance policy is designed after taking all the above factors into account and there is no irreversible policy which can be laid down, as conditions might change from time to time. The cost and benefits from each of the remittances may have to be considered. The decisions involve how much money to remit, to which centre, mode of transfer and the timing of transfer etc. The issue boils down to this: Where and how in the world, the funds available can be deployed most profitably.

Internal transfer system of finances for the MNCs depend not only on the external factors referred to above but on a number of internal factors. These include the volume of inter-affiliate funds or surpluses and deficits, the number of countries and their diversity, and the degree of product and service standardisation and the pattern of ownership of foreign affiliates. To the extent of their dependence on inter-affiliate funds their dependence on foreign or external sources will decline. A large volume of inter-affiliate flow of funds is possible with worldwide dispersal of affiliates and interdependence of production activities among the parent and affiliates and among affiliates themselves. Transfer pricing mechanism is used on the basis of the above interdependence of operations and the unique nature of the products, high technology input and high product differentiation.

As plants specialise in different components of production or stages of production intra-affiliate trade increases and with that intra-affiliate financial flows. In this process, 100% ownership of all affiliates improves the process of flow of funds and efficient allocation of funds worldwide, which is not possible where Joint Ventures with local partners are involved in these operations.

In the process of intra-affiliate transfer of funds, the MNCs require a lot of information on the concerned countries and their policies before their strategy can be laid down. The M.I.S. has to be strong and up-to-date for the MNCs to take proper decisions on intra-affiliate transfers. These decisions relate to where and when the funds flow and how they should be used, etc. The pattern of flows takes the form in intra-affiliate trade and use of transfer price mechanism and through leading and lagging, adjustment of the dividend pay outs, relocation of funds on the basis of costs and benefits, opportunity costs and returns and liquidity of these affiliates concerned.

❖❖❖

# PART V

# MANAGEMENT OF SHORT TERM INTERNATIONAL FINANCING

# SHORT-TERM INTERNATIONAL FINANCING

# 29

## Short-term Markets

Mainly commercial banks provide short-term finance. Short-term markets are of two categories. These two categories of short-term finance are:

(1) Currency loans from the domestic banks originating from the country of that currency.

*Example:* Mark loan from domestic banks in Germany.

(2) Short-term loans from Euro-markets — loans in Euro-currency from off shore banks.

*Example:* Dollar loan raised from the London market.

Whether they are domestic banks or offshore banks, they are the source of all short-term finance for MNCs. The Euro-markets are the single longest source of funds, particularly since the seventies, when the currencies deposited from the balance of payments surpluses of countries in the off shore banks began to grow and they are outside the regulatory framework of any Monetary Authority. These are called off shore funds, as they are funds kept with foreign and multinational banks and are not controlled by domestic authorities.

The surpluses of ONGC, STC and G.E. shipping in dollars are credited to their SBI account in London. But as current account funds do not yield any return, the SBI, London is instructed to deposit these funds for short-term of 3 to 6 months or at the most upto 12 months, in a Euro-currency account with Citi Bank in New York. These being short-term deposits, carry interest rates, which are different in different centres.

The Euro-currency market has thus supply coming from the short-term surpluses of dollars and other Convertible Currencies like D.M., Yen, U.K. £ etc. from the governments, companies and exporting firms and even individuals. It is a wholesale market with funds being accepted and lent in large amounts.

The demand comes from those who need funds for short-term shortfalls in income, import payments and working capital purposes. Sometimes even governments borrow for short-term and roll over the loans for medium-term. Bulk of the loans are given for short-term as the deposits are also of short-term nature. The demand and supply factors in each of the currencies determine the interest rates. This market has two components: (a) inter-bank and (b) dealings with the public. Apart from the customer transactions, there is a very active market among banks in these funds. The size of the inter-bank market is much larger constituting about 80% of the total bank claims.

In the inter-bank market, active banks quote two way bids — offers. On the basis of these bid and offer rates the London Inter Bank Bid Rate (LIBID) and the London Inter Bank Offer Rate (LIBOR) have emerged as bench marks for lending and borrowing rates of banks and FIs. These rates change not only from currency to currency but from maturity to maturity.

For illustration some rates quoted in major Euro-currencies are as follows. The rates are varying from day-to-day but the illustration gives rates currency wise and maturity period wise for a day.

| | *1 Month* | *3 Months* | *6 Months* |
|---|---|---|---|
| Euro-dollars | $3\frac{3}{16}-\frac{1}{16}$ | $3\frac{5}{16}-\frac{3}{16}$ | $3\frac{9}{16}-\frac{7}{16}$ |
| UK £ | $6-5\frac{7}{8}$ | $5\frac{15}{16}-\frac{13}{16}$ | $5\frac{7}{16}-\frac{3}{8}$ |
| DM | $7\frac{1}{16}-6\frac{15}{16}$ | $6\frac{15}{16}-\frac{13}{16}$ | $6\frac{3}{4}-\frac{5}{8}$ |
| Yen | $3\frac{1}{4}-\frac{3}{16}$ | $3\frac{1}{4}-\frac{3}{16}$ | $3\frac{1}{8}-\frac{1}{16}$ |

**Table: 29:1**

The LIBID and LIBOR are averages of the leading six international banks dealing in Euro-Currency markets. These are quoted for various major trading currencies in the major markets, *viz.*, London, Frankfurt, New York, etc. and the arbitrage operations bring about uniformity in these rates as between the centres. The margin between the bid and offer rates which is generally of the order of 1/8 gives the trading margin for the bank. The year is taken as 360 days and the calculation of value dates of maturities of receipts and payments of deposits in the Euro-market is the same as in the case of foreign exchange market. A proper value date for a transaction has to be a working day both in the place where the transaction is done and home market of the currency concerned.

## Short-term Loans from Money Market

Major short-term credits availed from the global money markets are export credits and import credits. Export credit is provided by the buyer in foreign countries through the banks to promote exports particularly of capital goods from India or of any other country. Sometimes these credits emanate from the government or government sponsored agency like Exim Bank. Sometimes export credit is clubbed with insurance and bank guarantee, the fees for which are payable by the buyer.

Export credits are again of two types, namely, supplier's credit and buyer's credit. Supplier's credit is granted by the supplier or his bank to the buyer-importer. Deferred payments come in this category and are accompanied by bills of exchange and promissory notes, carrying the bank guarantee. Buyer's credit is granted by the buyer-importer or his bank to the exporter for his short-term requirements. The Exim Bank makes available supplier and buyer's credits and also extends lines of credit to foreign financial institutions to promote exports of capital goods from India.

Importers in India would like to avail of short-term credits from abroad because interest rates for most major currencies are well below the cost of rupee funds. But they will have to face foreign exchange exposure risk. The overall cost of such short-term import credit comprises of:

(1) nominal interest rate in foreign currency,

(2) forward premium, if the foreign exchange risk is to be covered in the forward market,

(3) additional commission to the bank for usance letters of credit as opposed to sight credits as the former involves a time period of waiting,

(4) stamp duty on usance bills, payable normally.

Export credit is thus an important item of short-term credit from the international money market available to corporates.

## Forfeiting

Forfeiting is a commercial source of finance. The claims of the exporter on the buyer are purchased by the forfeiting bank without recourse to him. This is thus, a credit sale converted into cash sale. Banks in London are very active in forfeiting business, both in the primary and secondary market. In India, forfeiting business is in initial stages and there is no secondary market in them.

Forfeiting has grown in the world only in the recent past, and it is another source of external finance to corporates in developing countries. Its importance lies in converting the book debts in foreign currencies into securitised debt, taken over by a bank or its subsidiary, without recourse. Forfeiting is the purchase at a fixed rate of medium-term claims on the foreign buyer. Depending on the credit standing of the importer and the country risk, the importer's bank guarantee is needed on the face of the promissory note or bill of exchange. The credit sales of the export are converted into cash and this is used as working capital or production finance in the cycle of productive operations.

## International Leasing

Cross border leases are now becoming popular. They are an important source of international finance of short and medium-term nature to finance ships, aircraft and capital goods. The asset may be in the ownership of the supplier but its use is with the beneficiary or lessee. This is an off Balance Sheet item and only lease rentals paid half yearly or quarterly are debited to the current account. The lessor may be from one country, the lessee from another country but the finance can be provided by a third country.

The advantages of lease finance depend on the tax benefits in the lessor and lessee countries. The lessor as the owner can provide for capital depreciation which gives a tax advantage. The lessee can write-off the lease rentals as revenue expenses. The lessee is not normally given a purchase option, as it might then become a hire purchase deal rather than lease. The lease agreements provide for the lessee to renew the contract on a nominal rent to protect the lessee's interest in the residual value of leased asset. During the primary lease period, the entire value or atleast 95% of the value of the asset along with the interest on the capital invested is recovered. The lessee will then have the use of asset after that period at a nominal rate.

Many short-term facilities are availed of from the international markets by the government, RBI and commercial and co-operative Banks in India. Government borrows from other governments, multinational and national and regional bodies for its investment and for its balancing of balance of payments of the country. Similarly, if it has surpluses, it invests in short-term instruments in foreign currencies which are convertible and liquid. The RBI keeps its foreign exchange assets in Treasury bills of foreign governments, Treasury bonds, deposits with foreign Central Banks, B.I.S. (Bank for International Settlements) and securities of world bodies and of foreign governments with convertible currencies. The RBI can borrow from IMF or the Central Banks of foreign countries or other multilateral agencies. The domestic commercial and cooperative banks, who are authorised to deal in foreign exchange, called Authorised Dealers, deal with the public for the exchange requirements of the latter and with the banks in the inter-bank markets of domestic and foreign nature for covering operations and hedge and for genuine trade and commercial transactions.

As per the recently liberalised guidelines of RBI, banks can borrow from abroad for temporary short-term requirements upto some limits which are set by the bank's top managements. They can operate in currencies for import-export trade transactions, hedge in currencies covered in the domestic market and borrow from abroad from multinational banks and dealers in Euro-currencies. Banks can also borrow from their branches abroad or correspondents abroad. Similarly, they can invest in short-term instruments abroad upto certain limits or keep deposits with foreign banks and correspondent banks.

## Euro-Market

Euro-market is a market in variable convertible currencies, not necessarily confined to Europe. MNCs and others can borrow cheaply in this Euro-market, than in the international domestic markets. The funds are loaned from short to medium-term in this market. These funds are cheaper for two reasons:

(1) The domestic restrictions on interest rates are not there in this market. The C.D.s are subject to reserve requirements and deposit insurance has to be observed, in the domestic market, which is not there in the Euro-market or offshore funds market.

(2) The Euro-market is a wholesale market with tough competition. With heavy demand and supply pressures, and free forces operating on the market, the emerging interest rates are finer and freer.

Over the years, the Euro market has become the most important form of international lending and borrowing and international banks of high reputation operate here also. This market is essentially short-term as deposits accepted out of trade surpluses are also of short-term in nature. But these short-term note issuance facilities are rolled over into medium-term. Lending medium-term with short-term funds is most risky and more so with quoting fixed interest rates. Therefore, most of the quotations are made for floating rates. Under this system, interest rates charged vary every 3 to 6 months depending upon prevailing inter bank rates. Thus, the basis on which the interest rate is made variable is LIBOR for banks based in Europe and London and US Treasury bill rate or US Treasury bond rate. The spread between the bid and offer rate and between borrowing and lending rate is the bank's profit.

Firstly this spread is very small and narrow at ¼ of one per cent. This spread has widened in recent years due to huge debts written-off in eighties and increased risk in business.

Secondly the imposition of capital adequacy norms on banks in the nineties has led to limitations on the amount of risky lendings that they can make which means costlier funds.



## Syndicated Loans

MNCs require large loans for project finance and for medium-term. Many governments needed funds for meeting Current Account deficits. Some used these funds for working capital or for meeting the budget deficit. Many borrowers use these funds for national development and investment plans.

For such large size loans, no single bank will be in a position to lend or take risk of that order. Hence syndicated loans became popular. The lead bank invites other banks to participate in the loan. Fees payable for syndicated loans include a up-front management fee, commitment fee, agency fees, etc., in addition to other administration expenses. In this, many banks participate in the loan.

Tax shared loans, as in the case of India reduce the cost of borrowing. The Double Taxation Avoidance (DTA) agreements between the borrowing and lending countries, provide for waiver of withholding tax, or tax deduction at source. The lender country will give the lender a tax credit, if a withholding tax of 10% is levied by the borrowing country. The tax shared loans lead to better after tax return to the lender country which the lender shares a part with the borrower by the lower interest rates. Most tax shared loans to India have been from Japan and Western developed countries which have tightened their tax laws.

## International Banking

Traditional banks do financing of foreign trade — exports and imports and arrange for the inflows and outflows of funds on account of the Invisibles on Current Account.

With the drying up of funds to lend by the international capital markets in London and New York, during the post war period, the role of international bankers entered a new phase of filling up the gap of domestic capital markets. The international bankers emerged as international lenders, when the MNCs emerged as the major players in the world economic scenario during the last two decades. Besides, the oil surpluses of OPEC countries found a perch in international banks which they used for lending. Banks located in crucial financial centres participated in funds inflow from OPEC countries which expanded enormously. With this, the growth of Euro-currency markets came into prominence.

After the banking crisis of 1982 which saw many developing countries defaulting in their debt payment, leading to debt crises, new loans dropped drastically. Later offshore banking centres developed as confidence picked up, in London, New York, Frankfurt and Singapore.

Firstly, The present day banking structure is the domestic banks financing exports and imports and normal inflows and outflows under invisibles account of balance of payments.

Secondly, there are foreign banks operating in many domestic centres who have access to world funds and they borrow and lend foreign currencies and arrange foreign credits.

Thirdly, there are full-fledged international bankers who specialise in foreign currencies and Euro-currency markets and have world wide subsidiaries and branch network.

## Capital Adequacy Standards

Under BASEL agreement of 1988, banks must achieve a minimum of 8% risk based ratio of capital for all their domestic and foreign operations by end of 1992. This was raised to 10% recently. This has slowed down a bit the growth of banking operations but banks began to concentrate on profits to meet the capital adequacy norms. Bank's capital is classified into two tiers — Tier I capital consists of shareholders' funds and retained earnings. Tier II capital consists of internationally accepted non-equity items such as hidden reserves, preferred shares and subordinated debt to add to core capital. Tier II can make up only 45% of the bank's capital which makes the core capital of Tier I to account for atleast 40% of risk weighted assets. Under BASEL II agreement standardised method of risk weightage is to be given for maintaining capital adequacy norms, as per the international standards of banking.

Since the nineties there was a tremendous expansion in Japanese banking network in the international banking scene. At present Japanese banks account for the top largest asset based banks in the world. They account for a peak of all cross border bank transactions early in nineties. This was followed by U.S. banks and German banks and British banks, in that order.

## Corresponding Banking

Bank business expansion depends on their overall financial resources, experience with the markets and knowledge of the markets. Possible entry strategies include correspondent banking branch network, local bank, acquisition and representative offices.

Correspondent bank is one located in another country, providing services for another bank outside the country. U.S. banks without branches in some countries had relied on corespondent bank to do business for them for their corporate clients including issuing letters of credit and exchange conversions. Its advantage is low costs when securing the market experience and the business is not adequate to open a branch. Its disadvantage is that service gets a low priority and large-scale business cannot be put through by them, as they give preference to their own customers.

Representative offices are small offices opened up to provide advisory services to banks and customers and to expedite the services of correspondent banks. They become a good source of economic and political intelligence about the local market. These offices are ideal where the value of business does not warrant a full branch and investment in staff but they would like to get contacts with local institutions, government and other agencies and get a feel of the market and understand all the rules and regulations. But the disadvantage of a representative office is that it cannot penetrate into the market, enlarge the business and secure profits beyond the break-even point.

## Foreign Branches

Foreign bank branches offer full-fledged services of all commercial banks borrowing and lending money. The special services relate to cross border loans, syndication of foreign loans, Euro-currency loans and notes, etc.

Firstly, These branches have grown in number in a phenomenal manner due to the growth of domestic customer abroad through MNCs.

Secondly, bank branches make greater contribution to profits through foreign exchange earnings.

Thirdly, the reason for this expansion of foreign branches is their access to foreign money markets, which they secure.

Fourthly, the penetration into markets abroad where normally due to exchange controls prevailing in many LDCs, such entry is not possible.

Lastly, these foreign branches can offer better services to local affiliates through the network that the parent company has set up, through electronic media, fax and quicker transfer of funds.

The disadvantages of the foreign branches are the high initial costs, the time and costs involved in staff training and the loss of correspondent relationships in those countries There will also be difficulties, with conforming to the rules and regulations on the foreign banks by the local Central Bank and the government and the prevailing exchange controls.

## Acquisitions

An alternative to opening branches is to acquire an existing bank there. This will have advantages of the local network of deposit market clients and lending clients, a set of contacts and prestigious goodwill and locational advantages. The disadvantages are poor quality of assets and clients and troubles of staff etc. These are expensive and risky and difficult for the acquisition to work for their benefit. The usual rationale for making the acquisition — the introduction of their synergy is overlooked. The acquiring banks have found that they spend too much energy in making the deal to the exclusion of spending time and money on making the synergy work for their advantage. Many past acquisitions have not worked well, as in the case of Bank of America acquiring in 1983 Banco International in Argentina due to subsequent debt problems of Argentina and the fall of Peso. France's Credit Lyonnais has been obliged to pump in large funds to prop up its Dutch subsidiary.

## Growth of International Banking

International banking grew by leaps and bounds due to growth of foreign trade, expansion of non-funded business of banks and increasing sophistication and growth of financial markets. The growth was particularly marked in the nineties, due to the growth of risk covering mechanisms and derivative markets. There was a large growth of foreign direct investment.

This growth in international banking is more concentrated in major world markets of London, New York, Singapore etc. Many U.S. banks have set up offices in Europe, Hong Kong and Singapore to operate on offshore funds. International banking in Euro-Currency markets has in particular grown enormously. This growth is only constrained a bit due to the capital adequacy norm of 10% of risk weighted assets applied to all banks.

The major developments in International Banking in the nineties are the following:

(1) **Strict Application of Capital Adequacy Norms:** The financial strength of banks is being looked into more carefully by the local governments and MNCs dealing with such banks. With larger capital base, such banks are gaining a competitive advantage in granting underwriting and guarantee facilities and in making advances at lower costs.

(2) **Organisational Strength and HRD:** The Bank should have competitive advantage through its organisational strength, skills of staff and innovative capacity. They must have the competency of analysing the information and provide low cost solution to the corporates as the bank is now rated on the basis of non-banking services, in addition to their normal banking facilities. The banking staff have to be well-trained and innovative in spirit for non-banking

services. The value addition to their services is arranged by the staff skills and bank's organisational strengths.

**(3) Growing Importance of Financial Innovation and Risk Reduction Measures:** Banks operating in financial markets and in foreign currency markets are exposed to a high degree of risks in particular – interest rate and currency rate exposures. The international banks should not only have adequate capital for this but expert trained staff to deal in derivative markets and in techniques of risk reduction and profit maximisation.

**(4) Role of Information Systems:** The challenge to international banker is the explosion in Information Technology. The banks have invested in building up a good MIS, tools of information technology, namely, in the computer aided transfer of funds and instant display of all information on the Internet. Electronic banking, e-mail and Internet banking and high tech banking with facilities for electronic transfer of funds, and for trading in currencies and exchange markets are the need of the hour.

**(5) Transaction Processing Services:** Companies are going global and demanding banking on international and integrated basis. Banks should have the state of art information to take full advantage of the tools of global banking. The transactions processing services such as funds movement, international cash management, lock boxes, collection centres, and global custody are now very profitable businesses and these are demanded by corporate clients. Banks have invested huge sums in acquiring the necessary skills and for equipment infrastructure to maintain their market share of business in the above context.

**(6) Global Fierce Competition:** The survival of the fittest in the highly competitive global banking environment is the order of the day. By end of 2005, top grade banks who could survive these threats and challenges were only a few top high tech and well capitalised banks. Survival will demand that banks would be able to meet all the requirements of MNCs at one window. Banks would have to battle on many fronts such as lending, borrowing, underwriting, leasing, financial advice and risk management services, currency and securities trading, insurance, money management and retail banking and related services. The recent global trend is for universal banking.



## Universal Banking

The latest trend is Universal Banking. Many domestic and international banks are treading towards universal banking which includes all the above-mentioned services and activities. The I.C.I.C.I. has gone for universal banking through a series of acquisitions and mergers and by starting subsidiaries. SBI and IDBI are also in universal banking. Survival in this global competition is through financial strength and human resources skills and technological revolution in all banking services. The weaker ones and smaller ones will not survive except through financial restructuring and gaining strength and skills in the 21st century.

❖❖❖

# OPERATIONS IN INTERNATIONAL MONEY MARKET

# 30

## Introduction

International Money Market is the market for instruments denominated in foreign currencies with maturity of varying periods from one day to one year. It includes borrowing and lending of funds, of short-term nature. It includes internationally traded instruments like Treasury bills, Bank certificates of deposits, Commercial Paper, Bankers' acceptances and Repurchase agreements and other short-term asset backed claims.

This market is critical for MNCs, as it provides much needed liquidity to them. The cash surplus units keep their surplus funds in this market while deficit units borrow from this market for their cash needs, or short-term funds. This market promotes trading in liquid assets. The inter-bank trading of their surpluses and deficits in cash is the important component in it. It promotes operational efficiency in that the spreads between borrowing and lending rates will be as narrow as possible and encourages allocative efficiency that is to channel funds from less profitable to more profitable avenues. As MNCs operate on minimum cash balances, their reliance on this market is more than that of other corporates.

The money market instruments are free from credit risk, as there is a high degree of safety and liquidity for these assets. One important market segment is the Euro-currency market, where bank deposits are issued and traded outside the country that issued the currency. But these are borrowings and lendings in this market for short-periods whose interest rates are linked to LIBOR, SIBOR, etc.

There are other instruments which are also traded in this market. The MNC with subsidiaries in many countries has easy access to these markets in Europe, America or Asia. Floating rate notes, short-term certificates of deposits, Treasury bills, Euro Commercial Paper, Euro notes, Bankers' acceptances and letters of credit and others are all instruments issued and traded in the international money markets. All these instruments differ in risk, cost and liquidity, just like domestic money market instruments.

## Domestic Vs. International Money Market

Domestic money markets differ from international money markets in many respects:

The domestic markets are subject to some controls by the Central Bank. It is a vehicle for transmission of monetary policy and exchange rate policy. The government and the Central Bank uses the money market institutions to influence credit allocation to some favoured sectors such as the government.

On the other hand, international money market is less controlled by national governments. The institutions operating in it developed it on the basis of self regulation. They work on shorter margins and larger volumes and on the basis of the credit worthiness of the parties, and on pure commercial considerations.

## Money Market Instruments

Money kept idle receives no income. It loses its value due to inflation and loss of purchasing power. Money has alternative uses which give a return.

If the Commercial Paper carries no coupon rate, there is no interest rate payable on it. But the yield depends on the face value, purchase price and days to maturity. If the face value is Rs. 100 and purchase price Rs. 98.50 (discounted by Rs. 1.5) and has a period to maturity of 92 days, then the yield on the instrument is

$$= \frac{1.5}{100} \times \frac{360}{92} = 5.87\%$$

If interest payment on a 90 day dollar deposit is 2.5 dollars, then "add-on-yield" is

$$\frac{2.5}{100} \times \frac{360}{90} = 10\%$$

The more common instruments which are available for investment and disinvestment in the money market are the following:

(1) International bank deposits (FD).

(2) Certificates of deposits (CD).

(3) Euro-currency deposits.

(4) Euro-Commercial Paper.

(5) Banker's acceptances.

(6) Bills of Exchange, commercial and trade bills of first class parties.

(7) Treasury bills and Treasury bonds of major international markets say New York, London, Frankfurt, etc.

(8) Corporate bonds, Junk bonds of short-maturities.

(9) Floating rate notes.

(10) Notes Issuance facility.

The interest rate basis is the LIBOR in many cases.

Floating rate notes are to an extent have the features of both bonds and money market instruments, as they can be rolled from short-term periods to medium and long-term periods. They are similar to short-term deposits as their interest risk is variable with some standard basis as LIBOR. All floating rate notes have a coupon rate which is reset in accordance with some formula, such as the following:

(1) There is a reference rate, say the U.S. TB rate or LIBOR, or SIBOR.

(2) The margin is the spread between the coupon rate and the LIBOR, say LIBOR + 2%.

(3) Reference time period, such as 3 months, 6 months, 9 months etc.

(4) Frequency of resetting the rate may be quarterly or half yearly or as per the agreement between the parties.

Coupon payment frequency generally, coincides with the coupon reset periods. Many FRNs have both call and put features or either of them.

## Example of Floating Rate Note

The interest rate on this is reset periodically in relation to a reference rate such as U.S. Treasury bond rate, LIBID, LIBOR, or any other acceptable standard rate. An example of the actual issue by Bank of America is given below.

**Table: 30.1**

| *FRN Terms* | |
|---|---|
| Issuer | Bank of America |
| Amount | $ 400 million |
| Seniority | Subordinated |
| Rating | AA+ |
| Type | Floating |
| Coupon | Semi annual |
| Margin | 6 monthly LIBOR+ 5 basis points |
| Issue date | January 15, 2000 |
| Maturity | January. 15, 2005 |
| Options | Callable at par on any coupon date falling on or after 2001 January 15. |
| Issue price | 100 per cent |

Floating rate notes are a special category with the characteristics of both bonds and money market instruments. The interest rate risk is similar to that on Euro deposits. Many FRNs are medium and long-term bonds in effect as they are rolled over from short-term to medium and long. The methods of pricing and evaluating the return on FRNs reflects the dual characteristics. It is linked to short-term interest rate but with long-term credit risk.

In addition to floating rate note in Euro-currency market, there are a number of other lending type assets for MNCs. These are all of short-term nature.

(1) U.S. Commercial Paper of first class companies with good credit rating.

(2) Euro-Commercial Paper, which is the short-term trade credit instrument in offshore funds. These are also called Euro notes.

(3) Note Issuance Facility also called revolving underwriting facility. Bank or banks underwrite to provide, upto a limit, short-term credit of 3 to 6 months maturity. This potential borrowing facility is generally related to an interest rate such as LIBOR and commitment charge is payable, whether the amount is drawn or not. NIFs have been supplanted in importance by facilities without underwriting commitments, which are called Euro-Commercial Paper facilities. Euro-Commercial paper is issued at short-notice and with odd maturities. The lead bank in this case is a marketing agent.

This facility has two tiers — first tier is the underwritten facility — called committed facility at a rate say LIBOR plus. The underwriting banks receive a fee and the funds will be used when the borrower badly needs the facility.

The second tier is uncommitted facility, which is merely an arrangement to auction off notes, if and when the borrower wishes to raise funds. These notes are auctioned to the bidders and are called Euro notes. For example, a bank may buy Euro notes at a spread of LIBOR (+15 basis points) and resell at LIBOR (+18 basis points) which is a higher price. The bidder with lowest rates get the paper. All the participating banks get a margin of profit on their transactions.

## Bankers' Acceptances

Bankers' acceptances are money market instruments arising from international trade transactions that are financed by banks. It represents an obligation by a specific bank to pay a certain amount on a certain date in future. These are trade bills which become credit worthy by the bank putting its acceptance. It is a liability of the bank, like that of a C.D.

## Letters of Credit

Letters of Credit (L/C) are documents issued by banks in which the bank promises to pay a certain amount on a certain date, if the documents are presented to the bank as specified in the terms of the credit. The bank's liability to pay is a legal commitment, if the conditions of trade documents are fulfilled. Many times, the exporter wants the importer to get the bank's acceptance as surety for payment and for the instrument to be creditworthy. Acceptance means that the bank obliges to pay the face amount upon the due date, when the exporter is expected to receive the funds. The bank collects the funds from the importer along with the interest and a charge for giving its acceptance.

## Stand by Letters of Credit

Stand-by letters of credit are related instruments involving commitment to pay on the part the bank. The stand-by letter of credit is a conditional liability, on the part of the bank, on the happening of an event or production of a document. These are used as a bank guarantee for supporting bids, performance bonds, or advance payment guarantees and other financial commitments. While the letter of credit is unconditional liability and it is payable by the issuer bank on production of some documents, stand-by letters of credit are conditional and comparable to guarantees.

## Euro-Currency Market

Today, international banking is closely tied up with Euro-currency markets. Although international currency markets are discussed in the next chapter it is referred here as it is also a part of the money market operations in the short term. Before the Euro-markets developed, international banking used to mean the transactions between the domestic bank and the foreign banks abroad in foreign currencies. These foreign bank transactions used to be subject to the national laws of the lender bank and borrower bank. Similarly, a national of one country could borrow from the financial institutions of another country subject to the approval of the government and exchange rules of the lending country as also of the borrowing country. Even now, this method of borrowing from foreign financial institutions, banks etc. is open to the nationals of another country in the case of some developed countries.

The Euro-market which developed over the last twenty five years is outside the jurisdiction of any national governments. The offshore funds or external dollars are deposits of dollars kept outside the U.S. with international banks, which they can use for lending and which is outside the jurisdiction of the U.S. Government. Later on, the governments of various countries have recognised these markets and have been using them for borrowing and lending. The U.S. Government has even allowed their banks to keep these offshore funds in any of their centres either in U.S. or outside, with the result that the international market has now become synonymous with Euro-currency market. The word Euro or Asian is not relevant to these markets as all of them are off shore funds denominated in convertible currencies like dollar or £ or D.M.

The domestic money markets are burdened with the Central Bank's regulatory provisions such as CRR and SLR and interest rate floors or ceilings etc. But the Euro-currency markets are free from regulations of the national governments and their Central Banks and have grown by leaps and bounds by sheer forces of competition and demand and supply factors, but devoid of inhibiting controls by national governments.

## Why Euro-Currency Markets Thrive?

The faster growth of this money market is due to many favourable factors:

(1) Lack of government controls on credit allocation and on interest rates.

(2) No taxes and prior commitments.

(3) No need to maintain reserve requirements and other pre-emptions which yield lower rates than the normal commercial rates.

(4) No monopoly elements and free forces of competition operate.

(5) Banks operate on low margins, high turnover and with least formalities.

More important than all the above factors, local money markets have lost their attraction as their controls were tightened due to the problems of the local governments and their own need for funds. This alternative source of funds has therefore, almost lost its significance. The international banks lending to poor developing countries in Latin America have faced difficulties of recovering the loans due to the debt problems of those countries. The loans were later turned into junk bonds with low credit rating.

Euro-currency market provides for the separation of the currency of denomination from the country of jurisdiction. Thus sterling balances dealt outside UK by the international banks and dollar balances traded outside the USA, by international banks are outside the jurisdiction of the country of origin, namely, the UK and USA.

Over time the international bankers have learned to live with the risks associated with the Euro loans to customers of different countries many times without any security. They are now used to deal with these risks, namely, interest rate risk, credit risk, market risk, liquidity risk and many other related risks. To meet with these risks and diversify the risks, they concentrate on high credit rated companies with export earnings to pay in foreign exchange and loan syndication among a number of banks to share the total risk among many banks. The market and interest rate risks are countered by adopting floating rate issues, flexible rate notes and so on.

The international banks dealing in Euro-currency markets learned to operate with low margins, high risks, and in wholesale business. Their costs are low due to lack of national government's interference and their controls.

These markets offer the following instruments, which are referred to earlier.

(1) Federal funds, or inter-bank float money.

(2) Repos or repurchase agreements.

(3) Swaps and switches of principal and interest payments.

(4) Floating rate notes or variable rate notes.

(5) Note issuance facilities.

(6) Commercial Paper and Euro-Commercial Paper.

(7) Certificates of deposits and time deposits.

**Example** (*Source*: Wall Street Journal)

London Inter-bank fixing for a day

| 3 months U.S. dollars | 6 months U.S. dollars |
|---|---|
| Bid $8\frac{1}{4}$, offer $8\frac{3}{8}$, | Bid $8\frac{1}{8}$, offer $8\frac{1}{4}$ |

The point to note is that there is only a tiny margin between bid and offer rates, namely, $^1/_8$ of one per cent. The offer rates are always higher and the margin between the bid and offer rate is as low as $^1/_8$ of one per cent or even lower.

Example of Money Rates (*Source:* Wall Street Journal)

**Prime Rate:** 6%, the base rate on corporate loans posted by the major largest banks.

**Federal Funds Rate:** Reserves traded among commercial banks for overnight use in amounts of $ 1 million or more.

**Call money:** The charge on loans to brokers on collateral and money lent on call basis for overnight to a few days. Banks also can borrow overnight to a few days.

**Bankers' Acceptances:** The rate varies from period to period, say 30 days to 180 days. Negotiable bank-backed business credit instruments typically financing an import order for a well-known customer.

**London Inter Bank Offer Rates (LIBOR):** The average of inter-bank offered rates for dollar deposits in the London market, based on quotations by five major banks.

The other corresponding rate is the bid rate, namely, London Inter Bank Bid Rate (LIBID). The Treasury bill rate, Commercial Paper rate and Certificate of Deposit rate are the other money rates which vary depending on the liquidity position in the market.

## Ancillary Functions of Banks

International banks do not simply accept deposits for the purpose of lending. Their role as intermediaries has no doubt declined, but they now do a number of ancillary and incidental activities. They finance foreign trade and facilitate funds flows across borders. They syndicate foreign loans, arrange for foreign collaborators in equity, loans and technology transfers. They are arrangers, underwriters, and guaranteers and advisers and consultants for bond placement and foreign borrowing. They perform a wide range of services through their own branches and correspondents over many countries. They perform a number of non-funded services.

As finance is becoming global the role of banks in global finance has increased. Arrangement of currency and interest rate swaps, switches, Repos, etc. has widened the scope of bank's operations. The international financial markets are free and highly competitive and banks are the major players in them. Domestic financial markets are closely interlinked with the international financial markets and the interlinkages are through trade and invisibles financing and capital inflows and outflows.

Global financial system has no unique money unit or global money. In January 1999 Euro had emerged as the common currency for European common market. Even so, international financial system involves the exchanges of currencies and borrowing and lending of currencies. Thus, global financial system revolves around the foreign exchange and foreign currency markets. These in turn are influenced by national interest rates, purchasing power parity, inflation rates and monetary policies of the domestic economies which are linked in the global financial system.

## Advantages

Euro-currency markets have a number of advantages over the domestic money markets.

(1) No non-interest bearing reserve requirements.

(2) No regulations that influence credit allocation, and not subject to Exchange control regulations.

(3) No controls on interest rates on deposits or loans.

(4) No stipulation of investments in government or other approved securities.

(5) No taxes and government regulations.

The Euro currency market contains international banks that offer wholesale deposits and loans in a variety of currencies, usually other than that of the country in which the banks are located.

The special features of this market are the following:

(1) Loans of different maturities can be arranged.

(2) Syndication technique is used for international lending. Here, the risk is shared among many banks organised through the Lead Manager or Co-managers.

(3) A direct loan syndicate is a multi lateral loan agreement in which participating banks come to an agreement to advance funds to the borrower. The obligations of the participant banks are several rather than joint.

(4) A participation syndicate on the other hand has a principal and agent relationship. A lead bank or banks executes a loan agreement with the borrower and then forms the syndicate by entering into a participation agreement with other banks. The distinction between this and the earlier one is that in the latter the sub participants are not co-lenders; but in the former, they are co-lenders.

The syndication process has advantages to both the lender and the borrower. It protects the customer from undue influence by any one single lender. It protects the bank from being excessively exposed to the credit risk of any one single customer.

The popularity of syndication loans in the international markets is the result of lack of restrictions. Very large loans and high risks make it virtually a necessity for syndication of loans. The loan agreements governing the syndicated credits are the same as those available from individual banks. Agreements documenting syndicated credits with many participating banks from various countries are the most representative of the unique lending practices that have evolved in the international Money Markets.

## Loan Assignments and Participation

In an assignment, the original lender gets out of the picture by selling all his rights, interest and obligation in a credit facility to the loan buyer. In participation, the lead bank commits itself to the loan and then sells the right to participate in the loans to other banks. But the lead bank's relationship with the borrower remains undeterred. Participation certificates providing evidence of the contract are not negotiable in international market. But in India, the RBI is trying to develop a secondary market for the trading in participation certificates. The distinction between assignment and participation is as follows:

| *Assignment* | *Participation* |
|---|---|
| The borrower acknowledges the assignment. The assignee has direct access to enforcement of rights against borrower. The loan agreement and note is transferred to the assignee at the closing. Novation occurs when the selling bank's note is cancelled and new notes are issued to new and original lenders for adjusted amounts. | The lead bank has the right to participate with other banks. The participants have derivative rights and not direct rights against borrower. Counterparty risk exists for the lead bank, which is responsible for funding for participating shares. The capital rules affect the lead bank. |

The participants are sometimes given limited voting rights and sometimes full voting rights. In full-pass through participation, the lead bank has no unique rights. This bank has to obtain the consent of other participants before waiver or changing any terms of the loan transaction. The lead bank cannot act on anything unilaterally. Just as there is participation granted to some banks, the participants can grant sub-participation to others. This sub-participation is subject to the rights and obligation of the participants and releases funds for other activities.

## Note Issuance Facilities (NIFs)

Note issuance facilities are also called revolving underwriting facilities. These are for medium term from 3 to 10 years. These are loan facility arrangements between a borrower and a group of banks. If the borrower issues short-term paper of 3 to 6 months, in its own name, the agreed banks underwrite or purchase these Euro notes. If the borrower cannot sell them, these banks will step in to purchase or provide stand-by credit upto the level agreed upon at a rate related to LIBOR depending upon the credit rating of the borrower. High quality borrowers can issue Euro notes at around LIBID. The borrowers under NIF are sovereign governments, banks and high credit rated corporates.

## Other Instruments

Of the instruments of money market which the International Finance Manager can have access to, mention should be made of Commercial Paper and certificates of deposit. In the inter-bank market, only banks operate generally and even if they allow corporates, they can only act through banks or FIs. Discussion on Repos, swaps and switches was already presented in other chapters.

As regards Euro Commercial Paper, also called Euro-notes, banks act as agents and they are sold by highly creditworthy, export earning firms of international reputation. They are for short periods of 1 to 6 months. The interest rates are generally related to LIBOR. As the excess funds of other corporate can be invested in them in the domestic markets, the same is bought by banks, and other financial institutions, pension funds etc. in the Euro markets. Sometimes they are replaced by NIFs by banks. These are not underwritten, as the banks know these parties and are high creditworthy units. The

Euro-C.P. is actively traded in the secondary market and banks trade in them for their surpluses and deficits.

The other alternative financing options like certificates of deposits are for higher maturities of 6 months and above. These deposits are kept with banks as term money, from the surpluses of foreign currencies like dollar, pound, DM, etc. earned by the corporates. They are comparable to the term money market operations in the domestic market. The difference is that only offshore funds are dealt with and among international banks.

Thus, there are a number of short-term financing options both for borrowing and lending in the international money markets by the international finance manager. The choice depends on the interest rates, cost involved and the maturity required, and the needs of the company.

❖❖❖

# OPERATIONS IN FOREIGN CURRENCY MARKETS

# 31

Euro-dollar or Euro-currency markets are the international currency markets where currencies are borrowed and lent. Each currency has a demand and a supply in these markets. Thus, dollar deposits outside USA or sterling deposits outside UK are called offshore funds and have a market so long as they are convertible and readily usable in international transactions. Convertible currency is defined as one which is widely accepted in international payments and whose country does not have current account controls under Article VIII of the I.M.F. Agreements. Thus, Euro-currency market is a market principally located in Europe for lending and borrowing the world's most important convertible currencies, namely, dollar, sterling, Euro, yen, etc. On the same basis, the Asian currency market or the African currency market can also be defined.

## International Money and Capital Markets

In general, international money and capital markets are for lending and borrowing moneys or claims to money in various currencies in demand outside the country of origin. By far the most important of such money markets are located in Europe called the Euro-currency markets. Next in importance comes the Asian currency market located in the East. Although, US dollars are most frequently traded in these markets, any internationally convertible currency which has a demand and supply can also be traded.

As in the case of international money markets represented by Euro-currency markets or Asian currency markets, there are international capital markets as well, represented by Euro-bond or Asian-bond markets, which reflect the lendings or borrowings at the long-end of the liquidity spectrum of five years and above. While such international money markets have developed in the fifties, the corresponding capital markets have grown in the sixties.

Both the money and capital markets of this type for off shore funds were of recent vintage when the old sources of funds under the pre-war system of borrowing from the domestic money and capital markets of New York and London etc., had dried up. Domestic money markets in the post-war world were greatly insulated from foreign money markets in most cases due to the prevailing exchange controls in the interest of pursuit of independent domestic monetary policy, but the interactions and effects of one or the other could not be completely ruled out. Trading in these currencies is both for short-term and long-term and in any of the currencies which are convertible. The bonds or certificates can be denominated in any convertible currency in which the borrower and the lender have confidence in terms of the stability of the currency, its future value and intrinsic strength of the economy.

As the short, medium-term and long-term segments are closely interlinked in these markets, all are discussed in this chapter although, briefly.



## Exchange Markets Vs. Currency Markets

The international currency markets are an adjunct of the foreign exchange markets. While in the latter, currencies are exchanged, one for the other, in the former the currencies are borrowed and lent for varying maturities. In the foreign exchange market, one currency is exchanged for another currency at a rate of exchange which is the price in terms of the number of units of one currency exchanged for one unit of any other currency. On the other hand, the price paid for borrowing or lending a currency in the international currency market is the rate of interest. The purpose for which currencies are exchanged in the foreign exchange market or borrowed in the international currency market may be the same, namely, for meeting trade and payment requirements, or for short-term or long-term investment in working capital or fixed capital or for meeting debt or other obligations.

These two markets are interrelated in the sense that operations in the one impinge on the operations in the other and that arbitrage and speculation take place in both and that exchanges of currencies in the exchange market are involved in most or all operations in the international currency markets. When a currency is borrowed, it is possible that this currency is exchanged for another before it is used for payments or a loan may be granted with a multi-currency clause with the result that a number of currencies are borrowed in the same transaction and one is exchanged for the other.

## Origins of the Currency Markets

After the Second World War, a number of European and US banks used to take deposits out of USA to place them in free centres in Europe like London, Zurich, Frankfurt etc. These US dollar deposits with the outside banks were used for short-term lending to the countries in need of dollars for balance of payments purposes or for investment.

Such activity in dollar deposits gathered momentum with the sterling crisis in 1957, which encouraged European and British banks to depend more upon dollars. More particularly, the introduction of non-resident convertibility throughout Western Europe in the early sixties gave a fillip to the use of dollars in the financing of world trade. The imposition of controls in the domestic economies on interest rates on time deposits (Regulation 'Q' in USA) and on free flow of funds across national boundaries and on US banks' lending abroad had added stimulus to the Euro-dollar market. But more importantly, lack of any controls on banks operating in these markets for off shore funds as those imposed on the domestic money markets and absence of any reserve requirements for these international deposits and lendings of the type of domestic deposits enabled these Euro-banks to operate at least cost and at lowest margins. These factors led to highly competitive rates being offered by Euro-banks compared to national banks. Thus, Euro-banks are more competitive and their rates for deposits and lendings are relatively finer as compared to domestic money rates, as the former work on lower margins. Finally, the surplus dollars flowing through persistent deficits in balance of payments of the USA gave lifeblood to this market. The foreign owners of these dollars got a good investment outlet in these markets. The domestic monetary and foreign exchange controls in some countries aided the development of the market for offshore funds.

## Dealers in the Market

International banks or multinational banks and foreign branches of domestic banks, private banks, merchant banks and other banks are the main dealers in this market. In fact, most of the US banks deal in this market. The market is of a wholesale nature, highly flexible and competitive and well-connected in the world over by a wide network of brokers and dealers. London is the focal centre for the Euro-dollars as Singapore is the focal centre for Asian-dollars. There are a number of centres in both West and East, namely, Zurich, Luxembourg, Paris, Tokyo, Hong Kong, Manila, etc. London has grown in importance because of its historical connections with international banks, its link between European and American interests, its expertise in banking field and freedom from controls in their dealings. On a similar basis, Singapore has developed as a centre in the East due to its geographical strategic position in between the London market and Tokyo market. When London is still working, Singapore opens and as such this market provides a link to their dealings, particularly in the inter-bank dealings, with Tokyo or Hong Kong.

Besides, Singapore has other advantages like an excellent telecommunication system, a tradition for free banking, representation for all nationalities, expertise in banking services and positive incentives from the government for its growth in the sixties and seventies.

## Euro-Bond Markets

This is an international market for borrowing capital by any country's governments, corporates and institutions. The centre of activity of borrowing and lending is London and Europe. But borrowers and lenders come from all over the world.

A bond market is a long-term funds market. Banks of multinational character called international banks or investment banks organise those transactions. The supply of deposits in dollar or other convertible currencies come from the exporters with foreign currencies, mostly in dollars and countries with balance of payment surplus with the USA, although, called Euro-dollar, it can be Asian market (Asian dollars), Gulf-market (petro-dollars), etc.

Developed since 1960s, following the huge surpluses of U.S. dollars to countries other than U.S., the reasons for the offshoot of such dollars outside USA, are of the following:

(1) Continued deficits in trade payments of USA.

(2) Use of such surpluses by the owners to lend outside in London and Europe.

(3) Lack of funds in the capital markets of New York and London for the traditional type of borrowing from national capital markets.

(4) Regulation 'Q' in U.S. which controls the interest rates in U.S. time deposits.

It is a telephone and telex market and called the OTC market and thus, depends upon the infrastructure for financial services like telecommunications, telex, phones etc.

While bonds refer to long and medium dated securities and debt, the Euro-currency notes refer to short dated debt of a few months to one year.



## Magnitude of Trade

The magnitude of trade in this market runs into trillions of dollars, particularly in the inter-bank deals. In 1987 the amount of Euro-bonds were 150 billion dollars, while the same in 1964 was 500 million dollars. These are mostly fixed rate issues (60%), warrants, convertibles and floating rate notes or bonds, etc. The borrowers and the issuers of Euro-bond loans are banks and other financial institutions, corporations, governments and some government bodies and supernational organisations. The investors in the bond market are central and commercial banks, government agencies, international financial organisations like ADB, IFC etc. investment and pension funds, insurance, companies and corporations.

## Market Features

(1) Both investors and borrowers are well-known names in the international markets.

(2) These loans are unsecured and no government guarantee either. Only credit worthy borrowers generally approach this market.

(3) Country's credit rating and borrowing party's credit rating are being looked into; ratings by Standard and Poor or Moody's are popular for assessing the creditworthiness of borrower, and the country.

The market is functioning outside the countries and is offshore in nature. No regulation of any national and international nature exists. SROs regulate the investment industry. Thus, the practices in the secondary market trading are based on the rules laid down by Association of International Bond Dealers.

Some parent companies and some foreign governments do guarantee the interest and payment of principal. The interest payment is provided in the agreement itself and stricter controls are exercised in the collection of interest, although these rates are lower than those on national bonds of any country. Many countries notably U.S. and Germany removed the withholding tax to attract bond market to the national level. But Euro-bond market has been kept out of the jurisdiction of any nation.

The maturity period ranges from 5 to 7 years and many Indian companies borrowed in this market in the past. Issues of 10 to 20 years are normally possible and popular issues are for about 5 years. The size of the bond issue varies from a few millions to a few billions of dollars.

These bonds are negotiable and transferable as they have the bearer status. There are no restrictions on transfers, and the right to receive interest and payment of principal is for the bearer of the bond. The bonds are printed on special security printing paper and terms and conditions are printed on the back of the paper. There is also authentication of the individual bonds by the staff of lead manager. The security and safe custody of the bond and avoidance of fake certificates are all the responsibilities of managers to the issue and banks dealing in this market.

## Instruments Issued and Traded

(1) **Fixed Rate Bonds**: Here the company gets a 10% coupon bond for a maturity of 5 years.

(2) **Convertibles:** Issuers of bonds are eligible for conversion into shares of the company after a date, at a fixed conversion price.

(3) **Floating Rate Notes:** This coupon is changed every 3/6 months depending on the LIBOR or any other standard rate, as laid down in the agreement.

(4) **Swaps:** Interest rate swaps — borrowing at a fixed rate but swapping it for floating rate or *vice versa*.

Currency swaps can be depicted as shifting of one bond of dollars into some other currency either at fixed rate or at a floating rate.

**Table 31.1**

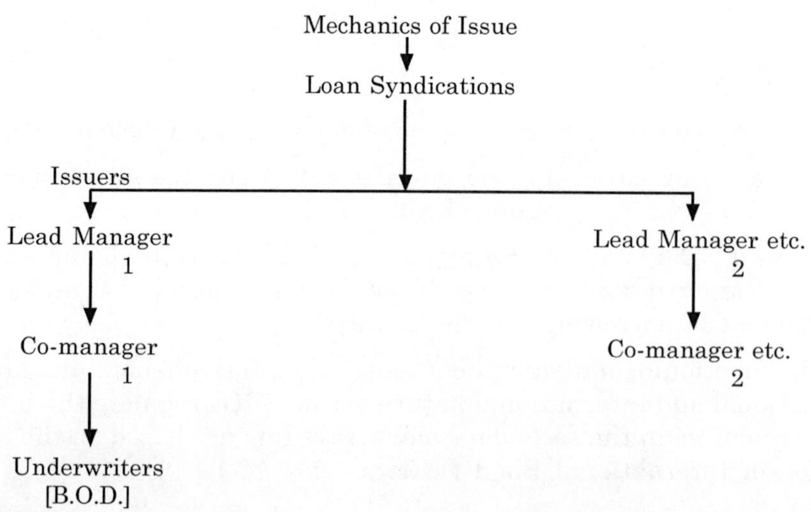

Bought-out Deals (BoD) occur when the lead manager offers to launch the issue at a specified price. There will be trustees and paying agents in different countries and agents are appointed in various commercial centres in different countries.

## Lawyers and Auditors

They are needed for proper documentation of offer circulars and prospectus and preparation of the agreement and signing of the same before the money is released to the borrower-Issue of Tombstone in the press at the end of the issue. The fees are payable to all these parties lead manager, co-manager, underwriter, solicitors, lawyers, auditors etc.

## Euro Bond Clearing and Settlement System

Buyer and seller exchange the notes of what they owe to each other, the buyer of the number of securities and the seller of the money he is due. All the trades are automated and transactions in primary and secondary markets are kept in the form of book keeping entries in the books of traders. Before automation, contract notes were issued to the parties to the trade. They are checked manually and transferred to computer system for matching and confirmations.

**Table 31.2**

ACE System

ACE = Automated Confirmation Entry

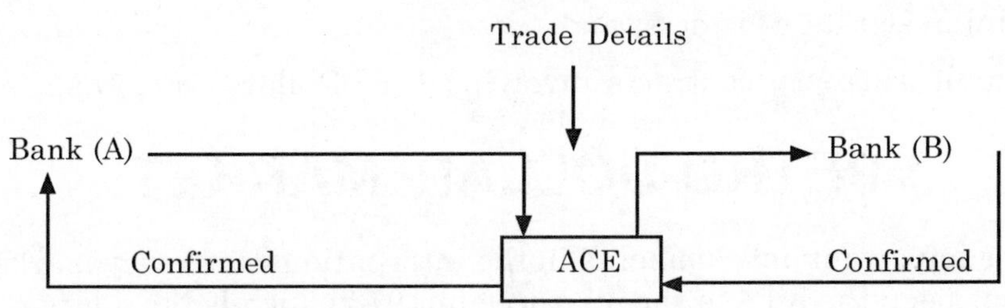


Rules of AIBD or Association of International Bond Dealers and their code of conduct will apply to these entries.

# ASIAN CURRENCY MARKET

Just as Euro-dollars have been popular in the currency markets in the sixties, Asian dollars came into prominence in the seventies. Asian dollars are the same current account surpluses in dollars used in the Asian continent. Singapore has developed as the centre for this market, particularly after 1968.

This market facilitates the use of dollar balances in the Asian continent for balance of payments purposes as well as for investment in development projects. It has imparted greater liquidity to the Asian economies whereby larger trade and larger investment became possible in this region. There was also greater co-operation in economic and financial matters as a result of the Asian dollar market in many centres in the region such as Hong Kong, Sydney and Manila.

Singapore acts as a bridge between the Asian market in Tokyo and Hong Kong and the Western market in London, Paris and Frankfurt. Singapore has both time and location advantages in keeping contact with the Western and Eastern markets. Besides its strategic geographical location, Singapore has the necessary financial infrastructure, expertise and other facilities for developing into an international currency market.

The scheme of market operations and the techniques used by the agents and operators as well as banks in the market are the same either in the Euro-market or the Asian-market. The rates of interest on various maturities, the pattern of financing etc., may vary. The demand and supply forces operated in the Asian zone are different from those in the European zone. The socio-economic factors and the political forces are also different in Asia and the resulting market forces and the operations are, therefore, different. Although, the markets are all interlinked, the Asian dollars are thus, distinguished as a separate entity.

The growth of offshore syndication, offshore funds management and the financial futures are the main developments in the Singapore Asian Dollar market more recently.

The financial futures market resulted in the establishment in 1984 of the Singapore International Monetary Exchange (SIMEX). It started with four contracts traded on SIMEX, namely:

(1) The gold contracts;

(2) The Euro-dollar time deposits;

(3) The interest rate contracts; and

(4) The multi-currency contracts involving U.S. Dollars, yen, D.M., etc.

## PETRO-DOLLAR MARKET

One of the important developments in the international currency markets in the last few decades has been the hike in the oil prices in 1973 which led to a larger flow of funds into these markets. Many petroleum-producing countries have since started accumulating foreign funds due to current account surpluses in their balance of payments. The second price hike in 1979 had also considerably augmented the current account surpluses leading to a larger increase in their foreign assets. These offshore funds of the oil-producing countries have been designated as petroleum dollars and the market in such currencies as a petro-dollar market.

In more recent years, the deregulation of domestic banking and removal of restrictions on the capital accounts of many countries like Switzerland, France and Japan and the repeal of the withholding tax on interest income of non-residents in the USA, Germany and France in 1984 have given a further fillip to the international currency markets and attracted petro-dollars into these markets. There has been an increase in the number of financial instruments, and the methods of floating the instruments have also been diversified. These developments have increased the competitiveness in the international currency markets.

Petro-dollar flowed first into the traditional financial centres as off shore funds such as the USA, West Germany, UK, Japan, and France. In more recent years, Switzerland, Beirut, Singapore and Hong Kong have also attracted these funds in an active manner. The recent removal of restrictions on the capital account in Switzerland and the existence of banks' secrecy and political neutrality aided the development of the international financial centre in Switzerland in the early eighties. The geographical position of this country in the middle of Europe and the well developed banking system in the country have also added attractiveness to this financial centre.

The initial hike in oil prices has resulted in a large inflow of funds into the industrialised countries for investment. Some of the surpluses have been used by the Arab countries to purchase luxury consumer goods and essentials from the international markets. Subsequent flows began to move into the physical assets, dams, railways etc., inside the country and real estate inside and outside these countries. Later, there was investment in short-term or long-term assets of a financial nature. The rest of the current account surpluses have found a place in the international financial centres. These funds were kept with foreign banks or national banks as off shore funds, and have given rise to petro-dollars which are recycled for purposes of relending, investment and use in various developed and developing countries of the world for growth.

The oil-producing countries referred to as "OPEC countries" in the BIS data, include Iraq, Iran, Nigeria, Qatar, UAE, Bahrain, Saudi Arabia, Syria, Oman, Libya, Kuwait, Algeria, Ecuador, Gabon, Indonesia, and Venezuela. The liabilities to oil-producing countries (OPEC) reported by banks to the BIS have increased from 44 billion US dollars in 1974 to 160 billion dollars in a decade. Of this, the share of Swiss banks has been about 14 per cent.

The petro-dollar market started developing since 1974. In addition to the use of the current account surpluses for current consumption and imports, assets have been built abroad by these countries. The use of currencies of these petroleum-producing countries has also been increasing since then. Thus, since 1978, there has been an increase in the share of their currencies in the total identified financial holdings of foreign exchange of the countries from a mere 4.3 per cent in 1978 to 11 per cent at the end of 1984. The second oil price hike in 1979 has given a further boost to the use of their currencies in international financial markets and the increase in their assets abroad. Thus, net assets of the oil-exporting countries rose from US dollars 257 billion at the end of 1979 to US dollars 380 billion at the end of 1983 according to the Bank of England estimates.[1] Of the assets held in industrialised countries, about 60 per cent of the oil-producing countries' assets are held in the UK, USA and Germany and the rest are distributed among the other industrialised countries. These were initially concentrated in liquid assets such as bank deposits and short-term money market instruments and later diversified into long-term investments such as bonds, equities and loans.

European centres like London, Paris, Frankfurt, and Beirut in addition to New York have been the main centres attracting petro-dollars since 1974. Subsequent to the second hike of oil prices in 1979, there has been an increase in financial flows to Asian centres

1. The data for the later years are available in *Bank of England Quarterly Bulletin,* and BIS, International Banking Statistics.

like Singapore, Hong Kong and Tokyo. However, after 1984, the current account surpluses of these oil-producing countries have dwindled due to the consistent fall in oil prices and this resulted in deficits or reduced surpluses of these countries in foreign accounts. The major industrialised countries continue to be the main suppliers of savings to the financial centres.

The petro-dollars like other Euro-currencies affect the volume and geographical pattern of capital flows among countries. These in turn, influence the interest rates in the markets and exchange rates as between the currencies. A larger flow of short-term capital across borders could be destabilising sometimes. On the other hand, a higher degree of capital mobility might have facilitated the functioning of the floating rate system. These funds have also eased the balance of payments pressures of deficit countries like the oil-importing countries. The long-term capital flows on account of Euro-currencies have helped the LDCs in view of the recycling of the petro-dollars for investment and for correcting the balance of payments disequilibria. During the latter half of seventies when petro-dollars flooded the markets, a larger volume of development finance had flowed to the developing countries. A part of these oil surpluses has been multilateralised through regional and international institutions for assistance to the LDCs. IMF oil facility is an example of how petroleum-producing countries aided the oil-importing countries to correct their balance of payments imbalances. Such larger flows of funds for investment in the seventies have in fact given rise to debt repayment problems in respect of LDCs.

## Impact on Exchange Markets

The impact of Euro-currency markets on the foreign exchange markets is multi dimensional. Not only the demand and supply of various currencies are influenced through pressures from the Euro-currency markets but also the exchange rates are altered by speculation and hedging in currencies. Larger international capital mobility due to the operations in the currency markets influences the volume and geographical pattern of capital flows. These flows can be both stabilising and destabilising depending upon the conditions. The geographical asset preferences of nations also influence the exchange rate variations and the role of the financial intermediaries in the currency markets rather than that of the final economic agents became more important. The impact can be either positive or negative or neutral. The impact has to be analysed from the point of view of both sources and uses. As sources, new types of outflow in the form of deposits or investments are possible by lending to Euro-currency markets. This outlet has another dimension in that funds (dollars) can be kept outside the US system. As uses, it is now easier to borrow in dollars as also to obtain dollar credits from banks outside the US. Taking the above points into account, if there is a net capital outflow from the country, the impact on the exchange market is negative. If there is net capital inflow, the effect is positive and in all other cases the impact is neutral.

## Segments of the Market

The business in Euro-dollars starts with the acceptance of dollar deposits of any maturity with fine rates for each maturity. There are two segments in this market, namely, inter-bank and non-bank public. In terms of the number of transactions and amounts involved, bulk of them, namely, about 80 per cent, is accounted for by inter-bank transactions.

Firstly, banks use this market as a buffer-to absorb the excesses of supply and demand-in their transactions of deposits and lendings with the non-bank public.

Secondly, this inter-bank market is a means of adjusting their liquidity position to the requirements.

Thirdly, banks do arbitrage and speculation in the market depending upon their view of how the future movements of interest rates and exchange values of currencies would be. Apart from these, the basic purpose of banks' involvement in the Euro-currency markets is to satisfy the genuine demand for currency in the commercial operations of the borrowers which is the market for non-bank public.

## Sources and Uses



The main sources of funds for the market came from varied groups, individuals, corporations, commercial banks, international institutions, multinationals, the central banks, the governments etc. In view of the controls in the domestic market, many respectable corporations, banks etc., keep their deposits abroad. Thus, a part of the dollar deposits is owned by the US banks and US nationals. Besides the official agencies, governments and central banks also keep their deposits in this market which not only gives an official stamp of approval but an encouragement to the market. Originally, the market had grown without any official favour and as an off-shoot of pure private enterprise. Subsequently, when it reached a state of significant dimensions which no single nation could control, all governments and international institutions began to consider it respectable and partake in its operations. Borrowers and lenders in the market are only banks insofar as the inter-bank segment is concerned. Among the non-bank public, companies in export and import business or in investment business or multinationals in need of funds and governments or central banks for balance of payments purposes figure prominently in the non-bank markets. Among borrowings, bulk of it is for commercial operations by non-bank public and business corporation, and multinational corporates.

The Euro-currency market has no geographical limits or a common market place. Business is done by telex, telephone and other communication systems. Internationally-reputed brokers put through the transactions for the banks. Deposits are secured for the banks operating in the market by the general guarantee of its parent or holding company and in some cases, by its central bank and/or government of the concerned country. Similarly, loans to commercial parties are guaranteed by their respective governments. Deposits and loans to banks are, however, not guaranteed except by the bank's parent companies or their exchange control authorities like the RBI.

The amounts of loans and the periods of maturity vary over a wide range from a few thousands to millions of dollars and from call loans to maturities extending up to 10-15 years. Some of the loans may be syndicated and jointly sponsored by a number of banks. There are also varied interest rates of floating rate notes.

The purposes for which loans are taken from this market are very varied-from balance of payments requirements of governments or monetary authorities to commercial short or long-term investments in the private sector. The market has very little scope for follow-up of the end-use of credits. But terms and payment schedules are tight so that strict financial discipline is imposed on the borrower with penalty clauses. The syndicated loans have a leading bank as the manager, who assesses the worthwhileness of the project financed and insist on a time schedule of drawals and repayments which impose a sense of discipline on the borrower.

## Growth of the Market in Euro-dollars

The Euro-currency market has grown enormously since its inception in 1958. The principal agencies for collection of data on operations in this market are the Bank for International Settlements and the Bank of England. Starting with less than $ 1 billion in 1958, the market has grown to $ 100 billion (net size) by 1972 and further to a few thousand billion late in nineties.[2] The bulk of the rise was accounted by the OPEC and developed countries.

About two-thirds to three-quarters of these funds are in dollars and the rest in various other convertible currencies. In the seventies, the relative importance of non-dollar currencies had increased due to the decline in confidence in dollar and the abandonment of the old Bretton Woods System. The importance of the bond market has also been growing in recent years. Loans of more than 3 years now constitute a larger portion of total loans than before. Loans of shorter duration are rolled over into medium-term loans. Bulk of the loans are in dollars.

## Techniques of Operations

Deposits of currencies are made against a certificate given by the bank. These certificates of deposits are bearer bonds and transferable by endorsement and a market has been developed in them. This is the secondary market which imparts liquidity to the depositors as these certificates can be discounted with the banks dealing in this market.

The loan operations are concluded mostly for short-term duration and if necessary on a revolving basis. Some loans are transacted on a floating interest clause which enables the rate to be varied depending upon the daily interest rates prevailing in the market or on a quarterly or six monthly interest rate review. The long-term loans or bond issues are facilitated by the introduction of revolving credit facility. The increased use of floating rate of interest clause and revolving credit facility and improved performance of the US dollar in the foreign exchange market were responsible for the increase in bond issues in recent years. Multi-currency clause and floating interest rate clauses afford protection to both the borrowers and lenders in the market against a sharp fall or rise in interest rates as well as exchange rates in any currency which influences the Euro-currency market. Basically, short-term funds in the form of deposits are converted into term loans in this market.

Internationally reputed brokers are constantly in touch with the banks dealing in Euro-currencies. Their quotations for borrowing and lending rates of interest in each

2. Total foreign Currency Positions or Liabilities of BIS reporting banks.
*Source: BIS Annual Reports.*

currency are advised to the banks early at the start of the trading hours of the day. These quotations given separately for each of the maturities and for each currency are the starting point for offer and bids in the inter-bank market which is the centre piece of Euro-currency market mechanism and which accounts for 80 per cent of the total transactions in the market. The commercial market consisting of loans to the public-both short and medium-term-is arranged on a syndicated or a consortium basis if the loan is for large amounts. The syndicated loans have become an important segment of the market in more recent years.

In addition to the revolving credit facilities, fixed term facility extending upto 5 or more years has subsequently developed. In such cases, banks are mostly intermediaries taking in deposits for the same maturity as fixed term loans which they are offering to borrowers. Many times banks take a view of the likely trend of interest rate in various currencies before granting such term loans.

Another type of facility granted by banks is standby facility which gives the borrower greater flexibility. Companies in need of funds at a future date can negotiate such a line of standby credit. The borrowers pay a commission of ½ per cent to 1 per cent for such a commitment. These are called the Notes Issuance Facilities (NIFs).

Such large-scale credit arrangements are made possible by banks' operations in the inter-bank market-one bank helping the other banks - or by the syndicated or consortium arrangements among banks. The bulk of growth of the Euro-dollar market must be attributed to the revolving nature of the credits and the gearing ratio on which banks operate.

With the growth of sophistication in operation and rising competition in the market, the margins between the lending and borrowing rates have been reduced considerably in recent years. The margins are anything ¾th per cent to 1½ per cent and in some cases, they are as low as $^3/_8$th per cent to ½ per cent. The fact that these margins are low reflects the efficiency of their operations and the high degree of competition in the markets.

The interest rate in the market is the London Inter-Bank Offer Rate (LIBOR) which is the average of rates offered by the leading banks in the inter-bank market in London. The lending rate is adjusted up to 1/8th of the one per cent of the LIBOR along with a margin to the bank for lending to the non-bank public. The margin or spread depends upon the market conditions of demand and supply and the interest rates in various centres ruling and expectations.

In addition to interest charges, the borrowers have to incur incidental expenses in the form of charges for syndication, management of the issue, negotiation charges, commitment fees, etc. These fees would aggregate to anything from ½ per cent to 3 per cent of the amounts borrowed. The fees which the banks collect also influence the spread they keep between their borrowing and lending rates.

The more recent developments are a lengthening of the maturity period, lowering of margins, growing competition and increased size of loan operations. If the reputation of borrowers is high, no security is taken. Many times it is against a government guarantee and the cases where this security is not taken may be few, mainly accounted for by the reputed multinational corporations. Although, the credit risks are rising and costs of management of the Euro-currency department are growing and inflation is further eroding into their margins, the increasing size of the market and the growth of the deposit and lending operations along with sound banking practices have been responsible for keeping the margins low. The Euro-currency market is thus, developing fast in the international financial scene on healthy competitive lines.

## Importance of the Market

The growth of Euro-currency market has produced far reaching effects on the international financial system and the monetary scene.

Firstly, these floating funds have augmented the official international liquidity and helped the financing of deficits in the balance of payments of countries.

Secondly, these Euro-currency funds are found useful for private corporate investments and for working capital purposes.

Thirdly, the quick and efficient source of funds provided by this market has helped the easing of pressures on the international monetary system, particularly on the dollar and other currencies under strain.

Fourthly, it has provided a channel for profitable investment for excess funds of governments, central banks and business corporations. This market has finally opened up avenues for greater international monetary co-operation and integration.

## India and Foreign Currency Markets

The operation of Indian banks in the international currency markets has been allowed since 1969, particularly in Singapore and Hong Kong. In the seventies, the State Bank of India was permitted to enter the market. Over the past few years, the SBI has raised funds for the public sector units such as the Shipping Corporation of India and later for units in the private sector also (Orissa Aluminium Project). So far loans raised in these markets were well within \$ 50 billion such as for purchase of aircraft by Air India or drilling equipment by ONGC. The SBI has also been instrumental in raising loans for the Birlas for their project in Indonesia and for the TISCO from the US and UK banks. In 1980, a \$ 680 million Euro-dollar loan was raised for the Orissa Aluminium Project. It is thus clear that private parties and banks in India are increasingly allowed to either borrow from this market or operate in this market. The recent decline in flow of funds from IBRD and other world bodies had an added impetus to the growth of these operations. India is borrowing now from these markets through External Commercial Borrowings (ECBs) for the corporates, including MNCs.

Gross capital inflows through ECBs were US \$ 30.4 billion in 2007-08, which fell to US \$ 15.4 billion in 2008-09, due to world wide recession. The outstanding debt due to ECB was US \$ 62.6 billion at end March 2009; this evidenced the importance of ECB in India.

Euro-dollar loans were raised for the Bombay High for its fourth and fifth stages (200 million dollars). For example, the rate at which the loan of \$ 680 million was raised for Orissa Aluminium was at 17 per cent-slightly above the prevailing London Inter-Bank Offer rate of 16.5 per cent. This rate could float up or down depending upon the LIBOR. But even so, it is cheaper than that at which some countries have borrowed (Brazil, for example) namely, at 2 per cent above the LIBOR.

The fact is that we have refrained from resorting to this market for a long time because of its high cost and the commercially-going rate charged therein. In addition to the high cost of borrowing in it, India was deterred from this market because of uncertainty of interest cost due to its variability every six months, under floating interest rate clause and shorter maturities on Euro-loans unsuitable to developmental needs of India. We continued to enjoy until recently the benefit of soft loans from IDA, IBRD and IMF. But now a stage is reached when we have almost exhausted these resources, as their own funds were getting attenuated. Then the only alternative appears to be to allow the private sector to borrow from these markets, compete with their counterparts abroad effectively in both the output markets and input markets as much as in financial markets. When private companies borrow at commercial rates, they have to make enough foreign exchange earnings to pay for the servicing charges on them. The projects must then be of long life but a short gestation period and investment should lead to productive asset creation and enlarge the export potential of the country to repay instalments due on the loans. India has also problems of identifying projects with a short gestation but a long life duration and commercially viable projects. Besides the commercial fees and strict adherence to schedules of repayment etc., were the further deterring factors.

The Indian banks and ICICI have been borrowing in international capital markets and from financial bodies abroad for commercial and industrial purposes. The Government of India has been encouraging more recently the use of Euro-dollar funds in a flexible and yet discretionary manner for commercial enterprises such as Orissa Aluminium. Rastriya Chemicals etc. A number of companies such as Gujarat Narmada Fertilisers, Telco, Tata Power, J.K. Synthetics etc., were able to raise funds from non-residents or foreign capital markets. The government has permitted the IDBI, ICICI and other financial institutions to raise foreign resources through syndicated loans in Euro-currency markets. After making rupee convertible since March 1994 on current account, a number of private sector companies like Reliance and Essar, have been allowed to borrow in these markets abroad. Details of these latest developments are dealt with in a separate chapter.



## International Financial Centre in India

Can India host an international financial centre? What are its repercussion on the domestic economy? The financial centres at Singapore, Hong Kong, London etc., have been evolved historically by natural advantages, convenient locations and deliberate planning. Questions are often asked about the feasibility of developing such centres in India. Efficient manpower and competent bankers, network of communications, computer facilities and other infrastructural facilities are necessary for the development of a financial centre. India has to go ahead further with its reforms to develop such facilities and a set of dedicated secondary markets in broker firms, discount houses, bill market etc., before such a financial centre can be set up.

During the quinquennium 1998 to 2003, many offshore banks were allowed to operate in the Special Economic Zones (SEZs), Free Trade Zones, etc. These banks or branches of Indian and Foreign banks are exempt from exchange control rules and SLR and CRR regulations, so that they are free to operate in the foreign currency and foreign exchange markets abroad. This is a step in the direction of setting up of an offshore market in India.

The other essential pre-requisites are:

(1) Reduction in rigours of exchange restrictions so as to free the current account transactions; this has been done in 1994.

(2) Allow free inflow and outflow of funds at least for genuine investment and not for speculation which was allowed to a limited extent.

(3) Rupee to be strengthened further by greater cost consciousness of producers, greater efficiency and productivity of factors.

(4) Rupee holdings abroad to be liberalised and allowed freer trading in it. It is reported early in 2006 that the rupee papers got circulated freely and accepted in Hong Kong Market, as if it is a free currency.

(5) Necessary fiscal concessions, exemptions and simplification to be made in corporate income-tax, withholding tax on income earned by non-residents etc., which are in the process of being done through on going structural reforms.

(6) The present conditions in 2015-16 indicate a worsening of our balance of payments with a current account deficit of 2.6% of GDP and worse of fiscal position of the Central Government with a gross fiscal deficit of 6% of GDP, both of which are adverse conditions for a free float of the rupee and introduction of an off shore centre in India. Net current account deficit of Balance of Payments stood at 4.7 in 2013.

❖ ❖ ❖

# MANAGEMENT OF CORPORATE FINANCING

# 32

## Wide Range of Sources

The financing policy of MNCs is more complex than that of domestic companies. They have a larger variety of sources to raise funds and the cost benefit analysis of each of the sources is necessary in the choice of financing mix. Here, the costs include the risks of exchange market and difficulties of moving funds across borders due to exchange and trade controls and subsidies. Besides there will be taxes and government controls and guidelines on raising funds from abroad, which all can be encompassed in political risk. The MNCs face the inflation risk also, as most of the developing countries have high degrees of inflation which affects the project costs, rise in input costs and fall in purchasing power of currencies. The MNC financing strategy has to aim at not only minimising costs of finance, reduction of economic exposure, protection from financing risks, currency controls and ensure availability of funds at times of credit squeeze, in all the countries in which its affiliates are operating.

MNC's global financing strategy involves a co-ordination of the financing activities of all affiliates and plan for the whole MNC, at a time, taking into account the economic and political background of each of the affiliates. To achieve a world wide financial structure suitable for the MNC as a whole, they have to minimise expected after tax financing costs, and to reduce riskiness of operating cash flows.

## Minimisation of After Tax Capital Costs

The first choice is to get finance at below the market rate, which is possible, if we buy the debt from the secondary market in countries likely to default (Mexican debt securitised and sold off at a discount).

Interest payments on debt whether extended by the F.I., or the parent company are tax free as interest is a tax deductible item. Minimum holding of equity is necessary in certain countries like India, where promoters have to hold a minimum of 20% of equity. In addition to that, the parent company prefers to give funds in the form of debt to the affiliate.

If the government controls are there on the corporates borrowing from abroad, MNCs will borrow on behalf of the affiliate and lend it to the affiliate at a transfer price. It can circumvent the credit restraint also by sending money from parent company to the affiliate directly. The affiliate's access to the local banks is limited to banks for a portion of working capital. If the local rates are lower, then this facility of working capital is used domestically. The fact that the MNCs have access to international banks and international capital markets, means that they have a wider variety of choice.

## Factors Influencing Global Financing

The factors, which distinguish the MNC Global financing are as follows:

**TABLE 32.1**

| *(1)* | *(2)* | *(3)* |
|---|---|---|
| *Countrywise Taxes and Tax Systems* | *Government Credit and Capital Controls* | *Government Subsidies and Incentives* |
| Differential treatment of dividend income, short-term and long-term capital gains, interest payments fees and royalties. | Regulation of domestic credit markets, influence on yield structure, controls on borrowing abroad, restrictive credit policy. | Incentives to exports and export oriented units. Tax holiday for some investments, accelerated depreciation, and rebate on excise and customs duties etc. |

## Objectives of Strategy

The global financing strategy must reconcile a number of conflicting objectives such as optimising returns and minimising costs reducing economic exposure, providing protection from currency controls and other forms of political risks and ensuring the credit availability in times of credit squeeze.

MNCs are able to exploit fully all domestically available incentives for exports and imports. Besides due to their connections in various countries, they can get on best terms, the suppliers' and buyers' credit which the parent company can organise. For projects involving huge sums, such as those of roads, bridges, ports, airports and electricity and other infrastructural projects, they can line up credit from the multilateral development banks and regional development banks. Besides they can organise the pooling of surpluses of its own affiliates and arrange for internal financing of some projects through inter-corporate and inter-affiliate transfer mechanism.

Financial innovations are another avenue, which MNCs use to raise funds. Sometimes, these innovations can enable the initial issuers to raise money at below market rates. In the financial market, as in the case of product market, marketing concepts and the role of packaging are important. The MNCs, with an in-depth knowledge of marketing, design new financial products such as ZCB, or warrant-linked bonds etc., with attractive incentives that can be sold at attractive prices which will lower the financing costs in the final analysis. MNCs will find that financial innovations are another source of cheaper credit for their operations and expansions in various countries.

## Reduction of Operating Risks

Reduction of Operating Risks is another objective like the reduction in cost of capital. The firm has to show that it is financially sound and viable to inspire confidence in the investors, customers and employees. The company can reduce the risks that it faces in the form of currency fluctuations, sales uncertainty and changing access to funds and political instability. Financing arrangements should be such that they should be viewed as insurance against operating risk.

As regards the exchange risk, the financial inflows in each currency are matched by corresponding outflows. The firm can take up financing opportunities in various currencies in a way that assets are matched by liabilities in each of the currencies. In the case of contractual items, the financial structuring simply involves matching the net positive positions in each currency with borrowings in the same currency with similar maturity.

## Management of Political Risks

As regards political risks, which relate to the exchange controls, blocked accounts and nationalisation or expropriation, the firms should aim at a financial structure with more debt from the parent company rather than equity using local funds for financing and avail of back-to-back and parallel loans, international leasing, where asset ownership lies abroad, local financing, local equity for investment financing and parallel loans will reduce the risk of expropriation. Back-to-back loans are loans given to traders being passed on to manufacturers and parallel loans are such that the parent company in U.S.A. finances the subsidiary of UK parent company in US while the UK parent company finances in local currency the U.S. subsidiary in UK thereby making financing appear to be local financing.

The political risks can also be reduced by financing investment with funds from the host government, semi-government agencies in the host country and from international and regional development agencies. They will go to countries with investment guarantee, given by local government or with a bilateral treaty agreement as between home country and host country.

## Managing Product Risk

As regards the product market risk, some firms can produce against order books where such practice is possible. The risk of demand fluctuations or product-market risk can be reduced by taking advance payments or assured orders or having "take or pay" contracts to have a stable source of supply even at a discount over the market price, to the distributors or wholesalers. Many times, the nature of the product and the trade practices in the product sales determine the market product risks and the methods of hedging them. Some risks have to be invariably taken by all companies, including MNCs.

MNCs have a specific advantage in securing better access to funds and to cheaper funds and having diversified sources. They have good operational flexibility and potential for withstanding all credit and marketing problems. To ward off any wrong signals to the competitors, customers and stock holders, the firm will maintain itself healthy financially with staying power. The firm ensures adequate financial resources and it will maintain substantial unused debt capacity and liquid assets.

Besides, the key element of global financial strategy is to have a broad range of fund sources to lessen its dependence on any one financial market or source. It maintains a fund of financial and economic information for aiding its financial decision-making.

## Warding off Raids

The way that the MNC insures against risk of raids or the competition from others in the field is to maintain excess borrowing capacity. It may borrow more than required and keep the excess over the amount required as a deposit in the inter-corporate market or money market. The cost of this policy of maintaining excess borrowing capacity is the difference between the borrowing rate and the inter-corporate deposit rate. This is the insurance premium, as regarded by the MNC.

Many MNCs borrow from the world major markets and Euro markets to put their name in the minds of major players in the market. Sometimes this diversification of sources helps them to improve their image, credit standing and borrowing potential. Although the local market may offer funds at lower cost, the MNC might prefer to borrow from international markets for two reasons — firstly it will diversify their sources. Secondly that will bring them into limelight with many players in the international markets.

## World Wide Financial Structure

As the MNC is rated as a whole by its stockholders, it will merge the parent company and affiliates in designing the world wide financial structure. The debt equity ratio of the MNC as a whole is perceived to reflect its risk factors. The MNC should have knowledge of costs and benefits of each individual sources of funds; it should have consideration for not only costs but the return on the capital. Thus, minimisation of cost of capital, by taking each subsidiary separately may not be of much help to the MNC as a whole. The world wide debt ratio of the firm is considered by its stockholders. The risk of bankruptcy and the variability of returns are also important for the MNCs as a whole and not only for the affiliates.

On a *prima facie* consideration, the MNC will first decide the appropriate debt equity linked instruments and various types of bonds. The question of borrowing is the next step and even here the emerging debt equity ratio is kept in mind as that is what the stockholders of that company would look into for assessing the risk of the company.

## Foreign Subsidiary — Capital Structure

MNC decides the debt equity ratio for the entire corporation. The next question is the optimal capital structure relevant to the risk of the whole corporation. Should the subsidiary capital structure conform to that of the parent or should it adjust to local capitalisation norms? In practice, the parent company considers that the affiliate having financial structure conforming to parent norms or local norms are not exactly relevant to shareholders' wealth maximisation. Their primary concern is with world wide capital structure as a whole rather than that of any one subsidiary. Then the only option left for the affiliate is to take advantage of the low cost financing available locally to build the capital structure. It will not conform to the debt equity norm of the parent company or of any rigid local norms. It will adjust the capital structure depending on the local conditions to minimise capital costs as much as possible keeping in mind the local political and exchange risks and various alternative sources and their respective after tax costs. Any possible low cost government funds for export oriented units or subsidies on investment etc. will be taken advantage of by the local affiliate, to keep its costs as low as possible.



Each of the subsidiaries as also the parent company follow the cost minimising approach which will allow the affiliates the freedom of approaching the local market in some cases or international markets in other cases or ask the parent company to borrow and lend to them as intra-affiliate transfers. There is no simple and unique solution to each of the affiliates in the combination of sources which will minimise its after tax costs. Both the parent and the subsidiaries will no doubt keep in mind the objectives of cost minimisation on an after tax basis.

In some cases, the foreign units are expected to be financially independent, once the parent's investment in equity is given. The affiliate then depends on local sources and tries to maximise the return and minimise costs in the environment it is put. In other cases, the parent company takes the responsibility for monitoring its financial structure and if need be provide the needed resources by its own borrowing at cheaper rates than the affiliate can do on the premise that parent company cannot allow the risk of the subsidiary to rise beyond a level that it will be prone to default. No parent company can allow its subsidiary to be in financial crisis, as it reflects badly before its own stockholders.

## Parent Company's Guarantee

The credit worthiness of the parent company is much more than that of the affiliates and no parent company can allow an affiliate to be in default. The reasons are obvious that the parent company's credit rating would come down before credit raters and investors and before international bankers. As the parent company has to have continued good relations and high credit worthiness, it follows that parent company stands by its affiliates in times of financial stress.

Some companies argue that their affiliates should be able to stand on their own legs. The protection against expropriation provided by the borrowing of the affiliate itself is lost, if the parent company guarantees this debt. There will be no need in normal times, when the affiliate itself is credit worthy for any guarantee from the parent company. Besides a debt guaranteed by parent company would appear as a contingent liability in its balance sheet, which would affect the parent company's borrowing capacity. So the parent company operates in such a manner that there will be no occasions for financial crisis of the subsidiaries, needing the guarantee.

Guarantee from the parent company has its advantages and disadvantages. In general, parent company's support and guarantee is implicitly understood. But an explicit guarantee is sometimes required for an affiliate which is in financial crisis. This will generate its own adverse effects on the credit worthiness of the parent company. If an explicit guarantee lowers the cost of borrowing then the parent company considers two alternatives — one is to give guarantee to the affiliate to borrow and the other is for the parent company to borrow itself and transfer the funds needed. Whether the latter or the former reduces more the cost of capital for the corporation as a whole is the criterion by which the decision on guarantee will be made.

There were only rare cases when the parent companies allowed the affiliates to go bankrupt, as in the case of Raytheon in Sicily (1968) and Freeport Sulphur in Cuba (1960). But invariably parent companies do not allow their subsidiaries to go bankrupt or lose their credibility lest they lose their own credibility and will not be able to borrow overseas.

The US tax authorities impute an income to the guarantor and levies a tax on it, as their argument is that a valuable service is provided by guaranteeing, and just like a bank guarantee it should be compensated by a fee or charge. The parent company has to weigh the additional cost of tax against the additional benefit of guaranteeing the affiliate.

The parent company consolidates the accounts of all its affiliates with its own accounts, as per the generally accepted accounting principles, in which case the guarantee of the parent company to its own affiliate gets merged in the overall picture. What is loss to the parent is the gain to the subsidiary and vice versa.

## Joint Ventures Vs. Subsidiary

Joint venture accounts are not like that of a wholly owned subsidiary. The debt raised by a Joint Venture firm will not have the same risk impact as the debt raised by the subsidiary. In a Joint Venture, the MNC has limited ownership and control. It is seen on separate lines as an independent unit. The guarantee given to it will not have the same effect on the parent company as that given to a subsidiary. Where the MNC is substantially stronger it may want to own wholly its subsidiary, as in the case of Zerox with Modi, Zerox wanted to buy out the Modi's interests and make it a wholly owned subsidiary, to which Modi has not agreed. Here the interests of the MNC Zerox are different from that of Modi-Zerox.

## International Leasing

This is another method of financing the MNCs in their global operations. If a parent company has affiliates in three countries, namely, Germany, UK and India, Indian affiliate takes a lease of the plant of German affiliate with the financing by UK affiliate for Indian firm, it is an off Balance Sheet item and lease rentals are payable to UK affiliate every six months or every year. It suits the respective countries and their tax system. Here, leasing and borrowing can be considered as two alternatives. UK affiliate is entitled to lease rentals, which is taxable at a lower rate than in Germany. German firm gains in that it could sell its plant to India and gets paid by UK affiliate from its surplus profits. As there are no Capital Account Controls both in UK and Germany these payments and receipts are easy to make. In India where the Current Account flows are free, lease rentals can flow out more easily.

Leasing in the above case is called cross border leasing and can be either operational lease or financial base. The operational lease is that in which the ownership and use of the asset are separated. It covers only part of the useful life of the asset. It can be renewed on period by period basis. Financial lease is one that extends over most of the economic life of the asset and is not non-cancellable. The payments under a financial lease amortise most of the economic life of the asset. In effect the excess period of the economic life in a financial lease over its life cycle lies with the lessee. The lessor's profits come in the form of interest which in the case of the affiliate financing is suitable as it is not taxed at the same rate as dividends in some countries.

Cross border leasing can be used to defer or avoid tax. It can get over the exchange controls which do not allow easily funds outflow for purchase of equipment. The assets can be within network of affiliates and its life is well protected. As regards the vital issues regarding the tax shield, the question to be asked is what is tax status of lease rentals and who gets the ownership of asset and the right for depreciation and investment tax credit.

In a tax-oriented lease, the lessor gets the tax benefits of ownership, and the lessee gets the benefit of lease payments which are expense items in the revenue account. In the case of *financial lease,* lease payments are treated as instalments (like in the case of hire purchase transaction) of the purchase price plus interest, in which case the lease rentals are not fully deductible as paid by the lessee. In this case, the lessee is treated as owner and lessor is taxed on the interest imputed to the lease payment and is not entitled to any tax benefits of ownership.

## Double-Dip Lease

The full advantages of lease can be derived in the case of double-dip lease. Under this, the leasing rules in the two countries concerned are different in that the lessor and lessee countries treat their respective parties as owners and are thus eligible to depreciation and tax credits. In the absence of double dipping, the lessee is entitled to tax deduction for rentals paid. Double dipping is possible with lessees in countries that look into economic realities of the arrangement, say Germany, USA, Japan and the Netherlands, and lessors in countries that characterised leases only on the basis of legal ownership, as in

Switzerland, France and Sweden. The MNCs will take advantage of any loopholes in the legal systems of different countries in which they operate. They can arrange the lease in a manner that tax credit and depreciation benefits are got in both the countries of lessor and lessee. The lessor's country should consider it an operating lease and lessee's country considers it as a financial lease, when both the lessor and lessor would be entitled to tax credits in their respective countries.

The example of double-dipping is that the Dutch airline KLM leased air planes from the US. In this deal, the air planes were registered in both the US and the Netherlands. In the US registry, the company gets the benefit of fast write-offs and investment tax credit. In the Netherlands, the KLM deal is considered a financial lease and as it is registered in the Netherlands, they were allowed the usual write-offs, as if they are the owners.

## Leasing and Tax Planning

MNCs generally keep an international leasing company for inter-affiliate transactions in lease as part of tax planning exercises. This leasing company will be located in an appropriate tax haven country. The MNC should be able to shift income from high tax to low tax jurisdiction or reduce or eliminate withholding tax on lease payments. The MNC should also be able to keep the money within the conglomerate if they adopt the method of having its own leasing company.

Leases are also used where long-term loans are not allowed by the concerned governments. Japan has huge trade surpluses which could not be used for long-term lending due to Japanese Government's restrictions on them. So the Japanese MNCs have entered into the international leasing business with a view to promoting their sales on long-term operating leases and conditional sale leases for high value items like ships, planes, etc.

MNCs can reduce the political risk in politically risky countries by having leased assets there rather than owned assets. Lease assets will have greater chance of recovery by the parent company, in case of nationalisation or expropriation by the countries in this group. Leasing also enables the companies to extract cash with an affiliate in an exchange control country. Lease rentals are more easy to be repatriated than dividends and royalties, under exchange controls.

The international leasing company of an MNC is ideally located in a politically stable country, with stable currency with no exchange controls and with nil or negligible taxes. The MNC will then plan the business of affiliates in such a manner, that profits arise in a low tax-country and that tax deductible returns like depreciation and lease payments arise in high tax countries and that there are no withholding taxes on rents and dividends payable to the parent company by their affiliates and leasing company within the conglomerate.

## Debt Equity Norm in Global Finance

Companies in higher GDP growth rate countries have been found to use a higher debt equity ratio. The comparison of cross border debt equity rates is made difficult due to the different accounting standards, tax rates and bankruptcy laws. Generally the MNCs take the industry norm in the country of operation. The industry norm has to be changed to suit the stage of growth of the company. A company in initial stages of growth depends more on equity, as it enjoys a tax holiday for an initial period of 5 to 10 years and tax advantage of debt may not be there due to lack of adequate taxable income in the initial years. Besides their capacity to debt service will grow as it reaches a profitability stage after the break-even point, when it can raise debt-equity ratio. Finally, the proportion of debt to equity is a matter of choice and management policy and is dependent upon the promoters and management groups. The debt equity ratio also depends in the size of the company, type of ownership, stage of profitability and the size of its operations. Global industry norms have to be looked into. The business risk and financial risks associated with more debt will be less relatively to well diversified MNCs. The extent of leverage depends also in the scale of operations, and the number of countries in which it operates.

The philosophy of minimisation of cost and maximisation of profit remains the same both for the MNCs and domestic companies. But the average cost structure and the shape of the cost curve will be different for global players.

Firstly, their scale of operations is larger and economies of scale operate.

Secondly, their total risk is lower, due to risk in some countries being offset by those in other countries.

Thirdly, their vertical and horizontal integration and diversification will lower their cost curves more than that of domestic companies.



## Factors Influencing the Costs of Capital

(1) Capital structure of equity, debt capital, preference capital, borrowings from FIs and banks, foreign borrowings, issue of hybrid instruments, GDRs, FCCBs, ECBs, etc.

(2) Interest rates on various types of capital, borrowings and foreign capital and costs of issue of each of them.

(3) Business Risks and Financial Risks, associated with various types of capital.

Objective of capital structuring is minimisation of costs and maximisation of profits or net earnings. This can be done by investing in projects with positive net present value, which are projects on which the expected returns are more than the cost of funds. In some cases, even if the expected returns are more than the cost of funds, there will be uncertainty attached to future cash flows. This will make them risky and the riskiness of each project will vary and the higher the risk, the higher is the expectation of return to equity holders.

Financial risk depends on the amount of gearing in the company. The higher the debt the higher is the risk of the company not earning enough to pay the obligated fixed returns on debt borrowed. The chances of lower earnings and rescheduling of debt or interest obligations increase risks. Finally, it may end up in defaults, if profits slump and there is a chance of the company being declared insolvent. These factors and in particular the degree of fluctuations in net earnings has serious implications for the share prices. The volatility of share prices and stock value is directly proportional to the degree of fluctuations in earnings of the company. Thus, gearing is a double edged weapon, it can raise total earnings and earnings per share of equity shareholders through the gearing that it provides and at the same time, raise the riskiness of the company and volatility of share prices and even attract raids on the company by the predators or cash rich companies. It will change credit rating of the company.

## Weighted Average Cost of Capital

The cost of debt for a company depends on the prevailing interest rates for various maturities of debt which may in turn depend on the credit rating of the company and market conditions.

The cost of equity is the dividend payable and is relative to opportunity costs and returns available to that capital. The higher the risk of the company, the higher is the expected return of equityholder. Similarly, if inflation is rising equityholders would demand real returns to be protected or the returns to grow with inflation. The cost of equity is thus, dividend yield plus the expected annual rate of growth of dividends.

Formulating the equations for the cost, we have the cost of equity as CE and is equal to

$$CE = \frac{D}{P} + GD, \text{ where}$$

D is expected dividend per annum.

P is the current share price

GD is expected dividend growth rate

Assume D = Rs. 2 P = Rs. 40 GD = 10%

$$CE = \frac{2}{40} + \frac{10}{100} = \frac{5+10}{100} = 15\%$$

Cost of Debt is similarly formulated as

CD = I (1 – t), where

CD is cost of debt

I is the coupon interest rate

t is the corporate tax rate

Assume I = 12% and t = 40%

$$CD = 0.12\ (1 - 0.4) = 0.12 \times 0.6 = \frac{72}{100} = 7.2\%$$

The weighted average cost is the total of weighted costs of different types of capital. Assume weights for debt as 66% and equity as 34%. $W_1CD + W_2CE = 0.66 \times 7.2\% + 0.34 \times 15\%$ $W_1$ and $W_2$ are weights for debt and equity.

Weighted cost of capital = W = 4.75 + 5.10 = 9.85%.

If the average return on investment is less than 10% then it is a risky venture.

**Model 32:1**

# MNC's Cost of Capital

There are two issues to be examined by an MNC, unlike the domestic corporates. The first question is whether the required rate of return is higher than the cost of capital and second question is whether the required rate of return on foreign projects is higher than on domestic projects, after adjustment for inflation and currency depreciation. Foreign investment proposal cannot be made without the knowledge of the cost of capital. By definition the cost of capital is the minimum risk adjusted return required by the company's stockholders.

There is no single overall cost of capital for the MNCs, in view of investment in varied types of countries abroad, with different degrees of risk. Thus, there are different rates of return (costs of capital) for foreign projects in different countries, which are to be used as measures to decide whether to make the specific investment in a foreign country.

The cost of equity capital of a firm is the minimum rate of return needed to satisfy the equity stockholders of the company. In the conceptual sense, it is the yield covering the time value of money plus a premium for risk. In the accounting sense, the cost of capital is the rate used to capitalise the cash flows, generated from the investments. It is the weighted average rate from the different projects undertaken by the company and in different countries. Thus, the cost of equity capital for the firm as a whole is taken to discount the future equity cash flows to arrive at the value of the equity of the firm. The overall cost of capital is not however, reflective of the required rate of return on individual foreign investments. If the return and capital structure of an investment is expected to be similar to those of the firm's typical investment, the overall cost of equity capital may serve as a proxy for the required return on equity of the project.



# CAPM (Capital Asset Pricing Model)

The firm's overall required rate of return can be estimated by any of the following theoretical models, namely, CAPM and Dividend Equalisation Model. In the CAPM, the equation for the required rate of return ($r_J$) is as follows:

$r_J = r_f + \beta\,(r_m - r_f)$

$r_J$ = equilibrium expected rate of return

$r_f$ = risk free rate of return

$r_m$ = expected return on the market portfolio

$$\beta = \frac{\text{Cov}\,(r_j r_m)}{\sigma^2 (r_m)}$$ (Beta is a measure of systematic risk)

Where Cov $(r_J\ r_m)$ is the covariance between the return on security J and the market portfolio and $\sigma^2\ (r_m)$ is the variance of the returns on the market portfolio.

$(r_m - r_f)$ is the market risk premium and $\beta$ is the systematic risk of the asset and measures the correlation between the returns on a particular asset and the returns on market portfolio.

**Model 32:2**

# Dividend Equalisation Model

The second theoretical framework for the firm's required rate of return is dividend equalisation model, namely:

$P_o = \dfrac{D_i}{K_i - g}$ Where $P_o$ is current market price

$D_i$ = expected dividend

$K_i$ = cost of equity capital or required rate of return on equity

$g$ = rate of growth of dividend

Adjusting the terms in the above equation we have $K_i = \dfrac{D_i}{P_o} + g$

For the firm as a whole these equations are relevant to apply but not for specific investment projects in various foreign countries, where there will be project specific cost of capital or minimum required rates of return.

If a foreign subsidiary is financed with 60% of equity, 30% debt and 10% preferred stock with respective after tax costs of 20%, 6% and 14% then the after tax costs are weighted by the proportions in which they are financed to derive the weighted average cost of capital (WACC).

Thus, WACC= $(0.6 \times 0.2) + (0.3 \times 0.06) + (0.1 \times 0.14)$

$= 0.12 + .018 + .014 = 0.152$

$= 15.2\%$

Take a case when the risk features do not change for the firm, due to the new project undertaken, by the subsidiary and new foreign investment is undertaken in the proportion of 20% as parent company funds, 25% as retained earnings and 55% as new debt by the subsidiary. The cost of parent's equity is 14% and after tax cost of debt is 5% and the firm's current debt ratio is 0.3 then the cost of capital (weighted) is

$$(0.14 \times 0.7 + 0.05 \times 0.3) = 0.113$$

$$= 11.3\%$$

**Model 32:3**

The assumption is that 70% is equity with a required return of 14% and 30% is debt with a required return of 5% (after tax).

If however, the project has a higher risk than the average risk of the parent company, this requires a rate of return of 16% on new equity and 6% on new debt. Based on the incremental tax of 8% on repatriated earnings, the cost of *repatriated earnings* is

$$= 0.16\ (1 - 0.08) = 0.1472 = 14.7\%$$

As regards the LC debt, its rate of interest is 20% with an expected annual devaluation of 7% and the foreign tax rate is 40%.

Then the expected after tax cost of LC debt *(foreign debt)* is as follows:

$$0.20\ (1 - 0.4)\ (1 - 0.07) - 0.07 = 0.042$$
$$= 4.2\%$$

The after tax expected cost to a foreign affiliate of a foreign loan is given by the following formula:

$$r_J\ (1 - d)\ (1 - t) - d$$

$r_J$ = interest rate on foreign currency loan

d = rate of currency devaluation

t = local tax rate.

This formula is used in the above calculation of the after tax cost of debt borrowed locally by the affiliate adjusted for the currency depreciation.

Based on the data, given above, the parent's weighted cost of capital for this project would have been as follows:

$$(0.16 \times .7) + (0.06 \times 0.3) = 0.112 + 0.018$$
$$= 0.130 = 13\%$$

**Model 32:4**

# Use of Beta

Assume that a foreign project has a Beta equal to 1.15 and risk free return is 13% ($r_f$) and the required return on the market is expected to be 21%, then as per the equation of CAPM given earlier, we have the cost of capital, $K_o$:

$$K_o = r_f + \beta\ (r_m - r_f)$$
$$= 0.13 + 1.15\ (0.21 - 0.13)$$
$$= 0.13 + 0.092 = 0.\ 222$$
$$= 22.2\%$$

Here, it is assumed that the foreign project under consideration has similar risk as the whole of the firm's risk.

**Model 32:5**

Foreign projects are generally conceived as devices to reduce the risk and as such it will, if at all, reduce the total risk of the firm and, not increase it. The firm generally invests abroad to diversify the country risks and thus, reduce the total risk of the MNC, as far as possible.

## Risks of MNCs

The two risks that MNCs face in their foreign investments are systematic and unsystematic risks. The latter can be reduced by diversification by the individual investor and they should not affect the discount rate for valuing foreign projects by MNCs. The systematic risk is not diversifiable but the systematic risk of a foreign project particularly in an LDC will be lower than that of its domestic counterpart. The reason is that the economies of LDCs are not closely related to that of the developed countries and their business cycles. Thus, the corporate international diversification through foreign investment should be beneficial to its shareholders, as their risk will be lower and their returns more stable than those of the purely domestic corporates.

Therefore, using the domestic cost of capital to evaluate the overseas investments is likely to understate the benefits of diversification and the reduction of the firm's total risk thereby. By operating in a number of countries, the MNC is able to smoothen the negative swings in some countries with the positive swings in other countries. This will reduce the overall risk for an MNC which is not available for a purely domestic company.

## Empirical Evidence

A study was conducted by Ali Fatemi (Ali M. Fatemi, "Shareholder Benefits from Corporate International Diversification", *Journal of Finance*, December 1984), on effects of foreign operations on the cost of equity capital. This study compared the performance of two carefully constructed stock portfolios — a portfolio of 84 MNCs and a portfolio of 52 purely domestic firms over the period 1976-1980. Despite its own limitations, the study showed that the rates of returns on these two different portfolios are statistically identical. But the returns on the MNC portfolio fluctuate less and their risk is less than that of the purely domestic corporate portfolio. The Betas of the MNC portfolio are definitely lower and more stable than those on the purely domestic portfolios, indicating that corporate international diversification reduces the degree of systematic risk. It was shown that the higher the proportion of international investment, the lower was the Beta. It was found by other studies also that the MNCs do provide some risk reduction for their investors but they are poor substitutes for the international portfolio diversification by the investors themselves. If individual investors diversify their stocks — the domestic scripts with those of international or foreign companies, they would get better diversification. Risks and Diversification are discussed in later chapters also.

❖ ❖ ❖

# CONCEPTUAL BACKDROP OF WORKING CAPITAL

# 33

## Introduction

Basically, management principles influencing the operations of global corporates in respect of all current assets and current liabilities are the same as those of domestic corporates. But what differentiates them is only in respect of practices adopted by these two classes of corporates. The global players are more efficient and cost effective in management of their assets and liabilities, due to sheer forces of competition and survival.

Secondly, the global players have to follow stricter rules of accounting and disclosures so as to be comparable to other global players observing higher international standards. Not only the quantifiable factors are to be revealed but the quality of assets and liabilities have to be disclosed. The generally accepted principles of accounting, in addition to standard accounting practices of internationally reputed chartered accountants and legal firms are used.

Thirdly, the disclosure norms are stricter and the economic implications of any change in accounting practices have to be explained in the financial statements. The responsibility and due diligence rests on the accountants of these transnational corporations who are bound by the laws of the host country as well as the parent country and by the generally accepted International Rules and Regulations adopted by International Court of Justice and used by the International Chamber of Commerce in their contracts and covenants.

Global corporates have to be more transparent and investor friendly than their domestic counterparts. They face greater challenges and opportunities in respect of management of their current assets, cash and liquid assets. Motivated as they are by pure commercial considerations and profits they operate on low cash basis and minimum liquid assets, so as to operate on cost effective principles.

## Management of Cash

Cash is the most liquid of all assets. It is classified as part of current assets. Petty cash represents small amounts of cash maintained to meet the daily disbursements and to conduct current nature business. Petty cash is used for transactions purposes. Petty cash funds are accounted on an imprest basis — viz., a fixed amount is shown in the general ledger say Rs. 1000, which is replenished from time to time when it gets exhausted. At any point of time, the petty cash account should show cash on hand and/or receipts for payments of the amounts, equivalent to the imprest amount of Rs. 1000.

Cash in bank is another component of liquid assets and is part of the current assets. The bank balances as per the records of the bank may differ from the balance of cash indicated in the firm's general ledger as the amount available for withdrawal. If the firm gives a cheque, it shall take a few days to get it debited into the bank. Until that time, the balances as per the bank records will be greater than that of the records of the firm. Similarly, when a cheque is received by the firm, its cash balances will rise but the bank records will not show the rise until the bank realises the cash. In such circumstances periodically when bank statement of account is received the firm reconciles its balance with that of the bank by drawing up a reconciliation statement. A typical reconciliation statement looks as follows: it has to add cheques deposited in transit and substract cheques issued but not yet collected from the bank from outstanding balance as per bank statement to arrive at the balance as per the company books.

## Reconciliation Statement appears as follows:

**Statement 33.:1**

| | | | *(in Rs.)* |
|---|---|---|---|
| Balance as per Bank statement as on 31/12/2016 = | | | 30,120 |
| Add Deposits in transit | 2,000 | | |
| Add bank services charges | 120 | | |
| not yet recorded on books | | 2,120 | |
| | | | 32,240 |
| Deduct | | | |
| Outstanding cheques, not cleared | | | |
| Direct deposit in the bank | 6,000 | | |
| but not yet recorded in books | 4,000 | | |
| | | 10,000 | |
| Balance as per company books of Account | | | 22,240 |

The difference of Rs. 10,000, between the Bank Statement and the company books is thus accounted by this reconciliation statement.

## Non-Current Cash

Not all cash in company's books are cash available to the firm for use. For example, cash held in a sinking fund or special purpose Retirement Fund which are tied to special purposes, cannot be drawn by the firm, when it records its cash in hand and/or cash at bank in its books, these cannot be put as current assets. The above should be put under non-current assets as management has earmarked them for specific non-current purposes. Another example of cash not usable for current purposes is cash kept with the bank. This is the minimum or compensating balances which is to be kept by the firm with the bank for its overdraft facilities or loan or any other borrowing arrangements with the bank in its Current A/c. This is an interest free deposit as cash with the bank but cannot be shown as bank balance for current uses of the firm. As there are withdrawal restrictions, such balances cannot be in truth called current assets although, some firms club them with all other balances of cash with the bank.

The question of compensating balances and their treatment by the firm of this item shows how the letter and spirit of the financial statements may differ. Some assets appear *prima facie* current assets but might finally turn out to be non-current assets. As such a true accountant has to give footnotes of such exceptions to the reader so that, true position of both current and capital accounts is known to the analyst. What is the apparent balance sheet or income statement, and what it is in reality will be known only by such footnotes. Besides another fact that vitiates the presentation is that some cash accruals without actual receipt will be shown as cash and income accrued but not received will be shown as income. This again is very deceptive of the spirit of the balance sheet and income statement as they are not true representations of the actual cash or income position at any point of time.



## Marketable Securities — Valuation

Next to cash, many companies keep liquid assets in the form of short-term marketable securities to meet the liquidity requirements and the need for cash, as and when it arises. All these short-term marketable securities are easily marketable, at short notice or on the same day at the least cost. These securities are for example, Treasury bills, Treasury bonds of less than one year maturity, Commercial Paper, certificates of deposits, bills discounted, inter-corporate investments or notice money and similar short-term very liquid assets. Next to cash these securities provide a cushion of solvency and liquidity of the company. As and when the cash on hand and bank balances get depleted, these short-term instruments are converted into cash. Again when there is surplus cash, they are converted into liquid assets or marketable securities.

These securities have some face value and some market value. Besides the company may have its own original cost of acquisition (or book value). In the books of accounts, these are reported generally, at the original cost with the corresponding market value in brackets. A more accurate way of reporting them is at the current market value rather than the historical cost of acquisition. The reasons for doing this are obvious, namely, these assets are easily marketable and quoted and they can be sold off easily through the broker on the same day as they need cash. If the company wants to follow another alternative, namely, reporting them at "lower of cost or market value", then again a discrepancy arises as between the cost of acquisition or historical cost and the current market value. This discrepancy in the form of gains and losses, both realised and unrealised, is to be reflected in the current account or revenue account.

Conventionally, marketable securities are reported at cost. The increases and decreases in the market value *vis-a-vis* the cost of acquisition are reported only upon the sale of the security. Prudent accounting requires their reporting at the lower of the two above values and the consequent gains and losses are shown in the income statement.

## Receivables and Payables — Valuation

Proper accounting of receivables and payables is a matter of judgement of the accountant, as all receivables may not be realised. Some may lead to bad debts, some to doubtful or difficult to realise and some of delayed receipts. On the basis of past experience of goods returned, cash discounts given for realisation and the percentage of bad debts to total credits given in sales etc., the accountant has to give a fair value of receivables, on the basis of fair value estimation and careful discretion.

The accountant must look into the economic implication of the transactions leading to receivables and payables, rather than a purely mechanistic accounting method. Economic significance becomes important in cases when the sale price on credit sales include some element of interest or penal charges for non-payment of any instalment or delayed payment of an instalment in the case of instalment sales. In such cases the accountant must take a fair sale price and the imputed additional revenue under different heads. This is similar to taking the receivables (credit bills) not at the face value but at the realisable value and the gap between them is accounted in the revenue statement. Recognition of bad and doubtful debts in the total receivables is again a matter of discretion, based on the past experience and the present policies, followed.

On the payables side, account should be taken of the total dues without regard to the possible discounts, if any. But only on the side of receivables, amounts which are realisable should be recognised in the accounts. Losses or bad debts are to be shown as a deduction from revenues. Account should be taken from the past and current practices of the percentages of the total receivables which can be realised, possible allowances, discounts etc. which may be availed of by the customers. Uncollectable and bad debts should be shown as expenditure or losses in the income statement and written-off in the period to which it relates.

## Trend Analysis

Trend Analysis refers to a study of any of the financial and other variables in terms of the year to year changes in percentage terms or in absolute figures over a period of time through time series data in comparison over a base date. These year to year changes can take the form of annual comparison through trend ratios, growth rates or index number changes.

The following Table presents the data in absolute and percentage changes in respect of inventories of XYZ company.

**TABLE 33.1**

| *Year* | *Inventory in Rs. Lakhs* | *Absolute Change* | *Percentage Change* |
|---|---|---|---|
| 2004 | 52.5 | — | — |
| 2005 | 62.0 | +9.5 | + 18.1 |
| 2006 | 70.5 | +8.5 | + 13.7 |
| 2007 | 65.0 | – 5.5 | – 7.8 |
| 2008 | 70.0 | + 5.0 | + 7.6 |
| 2009 | 75.0 | + 5.0 | + 7.1 |

Both negative and positive figures may occur in trends. These can be shown graphically in the form of positive figures above a zero point and negative figures below a zero point. The percentage changes are represented in the Graph.

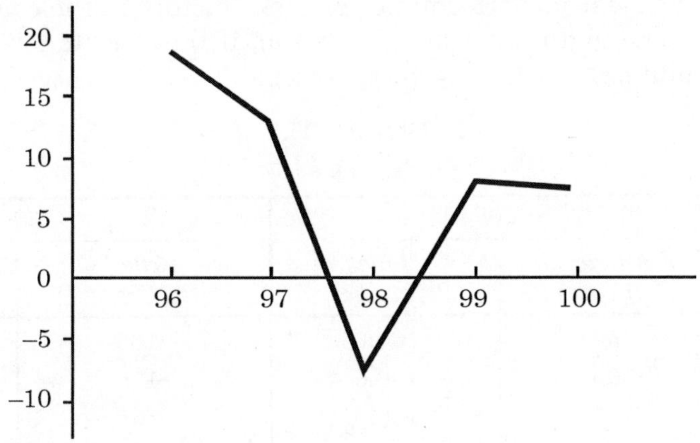


**Graph 33.1**

The inventory control is poor, as the fluctuations are wide, uneven and the levels are high. This company has to give greater attention to Inventory Management.

It will be seen that meaningful conclusions can be drawn if the percentage changes and growth rates are taken, instead of figures in absolute terms. The trends in one series can be meaningfully compared with trends in another series. Thus, trends in sales can be compared with inventory levels or with gross profits and net profits. Here trends in one time period with another time period and trends by one variable with another variable during the same period are possible by this method. These data can throw light for a meaningful analysis of the financial performance of the company and its strengths and weaknesses.

## Comparison Through Index Numbers

We can calculate index numbers for any time series data which show the variations of the variable year by year in a continuous fashion and compare it with a base year.

Comparison of financial variables of a company is possible for a longer period in this method to indicate the secular trends.

To calculate the index numbers, a base year, suitable to the requirements has to be chosen. This can be an year of good performance, or about average performance. Subsequent years' performance can be evaluated in comparison with the base year. The index number for the base period, be it a mouth, a day, or year, has to be taken as 100 and subsequent periods' data has to be deflated by the base year data as the index numbers for each of the later years. Thus, by simply dividing the value of a variable in a particular year by the value of the base year and multiplying the resulting figure with 100, we can arrive at the index number of the later period.

An example will make this clear. Take any time series, say of sales and index numbers can be compiled for them monthwise and comparison can be made of this series with any other year or the next year. Besides, the index numbers of sales can be compared with the index numbers of inventories or Bills Receivables. Such comparison will throw light on the relative performance of these factors in the company's operations. Index numbers are meaningful for the comparison, if they are taken on the actual data rather than on absolute changes or growth rates.

**TABLE 33.2**

**Sales Data**

| | *2003* | | *2004* | |
|---|---|---|---|---|
| *Month* | *Actual Rs. Crores* | *Index Number* | *Actual Rs. Crores* | *Index Number* |
| January | 150 | 100.0 | 165 | 100.0 |
| February | 160 | 106.6 | 170 | 103.0 |
| March | 155 | 103.3 | 165 | 100.0 |
| April | 165 | 110.0 | 175 | 106.0 |
| May | 170 | 113.3 | 180 | 109.0 |
| June | 160 | 106.6 | 170 | 103.0 |
| July | 155 | 103.3 | 160 | 97.0 |
| August | 150 | 100.0 | 165 | 100.0 |
| September | 145 | 96.6 | 160 | 97.0 |
| October | 150 | 100.0 | 165 | 100.0 |
| November | 155 | 103.3 | 170 | 103.0 |
| December | 160 | 106.6 | 180 | 109.1 |

It will be seen from the Table that performance in 2004 was a deterioration over 2003 in many months. Similar data can be compiled for a number of years, year-wise. Such series can be compared with those of inventories or net profits, compiled year-wise with the same base year, for comparability.

## Trend Ratios

Trend Ratios are a device to compare two related variables in corporate performance such as sales and receivables, net profits to capital employed and current assets to current liabilities. The related two or more variables can be set out in the form of index numbers with the same base period and their relative movements over a period will reveal favourable or unfavourable trends. Thus, to illustrate the variables of sales, inventories and receivables may be taken and their movements in relationship can be examined through Trend ratios. The data may be set out as follows:

**TABLE 33.3**
**Trend Ratios**

| Month | *Absolute Figures (in Rs. Cr.)* | | | *Index Numbers* | | |
|---|---|---|---|---|---|---|
| | *Sales* | *Inventories* | *Receivables* | *Sales* | *Inventories* | *Receivables* |
| April | 50 | 15 | 10 | 100 | 100 | 100 |
| May | 55 | 20 | 12 | 110 | 133 | 120 |
| June | 60 | 18 | 15 | 120 | 120 | 150 |
| July | 55 | 15 | 12 | 110 | 100 | 120 |
| August | 65 | 18 | 14 | 130 | 120 | 140 |
| September | 70 | 20 | 15 | 140 | 133 | 150 |

The above Table on Index numbers compiled for two or more variables gives the trend ratios, which depict the relationship between them. Thus, by looking at the Table on index numbers, it is more easy to tell the favourable and unfavourable trends than by looking at the Table on absolute figures. Sales have improved in August and September, when the receivables have also increased. Inventories showed variations between 100 to 133 in each of the months but receivables showed increases, compared to sales in almost all the months. The implication of these trends is that credit sales have increased relatively to cash sales.

Similar comparisons can be had over longer periods of a few years, particularly in respect of capital employed and net profits or gross block to sales and debt to equity.

## Working Capital Management

Working Capital Management is concerned with the management of current assets and liabilities. Definitionally, these assets and liabilities are of short-term nature, confined to less than one year generally. Net working capital is current assets minus current liabilities, financed by short-term funds like bank borrowing or trade credits. Working Capital Management is thus efficient management of short-term funds. The Balance Sheet comprises of two components, namely, short-term and long-term or fixed and floating parts. The fixed part consists of gross block (fixed assets) and long-term liabilities. Examples of Gross Block are land, factory buildings, plant and machinery and also equipment and investments and loans are also part of long-term funds to some extent. A part of it may of course be of short-term nature also, as in the case of investments in Treasury bills and other short-term instruments.

The bifurcation of assets into short-term and long-term and similar bifurcation of liabilities is fictitious and arbitrary. Sometimes short-term funds are rolled over into long-term and long-term funds are used for short-term working capital requirements. There is always internal adjustment of funds between fixed and floating areas, and slippages of one into the other. As such the above classification is just a matter of convenience and nicety for discussion.

The objective of any funds flow statement prepared on the basis of net working capital concept, is to depict the ebb and flow of funds as working capital and the factors explaining such movements. Such a statement is called schedule of working capital.

All funds flows are ascertained as changes as between two balance sheet dates in the various components of them both fixed and floating. The working capital statement is based on the record of variations in current assets and current liabilities of the balance sheets as on two distinct time periods. As definitionally the net working capital is the difference between the current assets and current liabilities (excluding bank borrowings), an increase in current assets will lead to a rise in needed net working capital. But an increase in current liabilities will result in a fall in net working capital requirements.

An example of the format for the flow of funds statement is given below:

**Statement 33:2** **Funds Flow Statement**

| *Sources* | *Uses* |
|---|---|
| Net Profits | Net Losses |
| Increase in long-term liabilities | Decrease in long-term liabilities |
| Decrease in Fixed assets | Increase in fixed assets |
| Increase in Equity or debt | Refund of debt and borrowings |
| Increase in short-term liabilities | Increase in current assets |

In the above statement, all increases in liabilities are sources and a decrease in liabilities a use of funds. All increases in assets are use of funds and a decrease in assets a source of funds. Here in the above table only few items of balance sheet data are shown for illustrative purposes and hence, the statement is not exhaustive.

Additional information from income and expenditure statement, taken into the flow of funds statement is net profits. In fact depreciation, reserves etc. are all sources of funds, if they increase and uses if they decrease. The losses in income and expenditure statement is an item of uses.

**Statement 33:3** **Example of Working Capital Statement — Compilation**

*(Rs. in Crores)*

| (A) Current Assets | *2003* | *2004* | *Increase* | *Decrease* |
|---|---|---|---|---|
| Cash | 50 | 54 | 4 | — |
| Debtors/Receivables | 1704 | 1453 | — | 251 |
| Advances/Prepayments | 46 | 15 | — | 31 |
| Inventory | 2220 | 1947 | — | 273 |
| Total Current assets | 4020 | 3469 | 4 | 555 |
| (B) Current Liabilities | | | | |
| Creditors | 790 | 823 | — | 33 |
| Bills Payable | 675 | 230 | 445 | — |
| Provision for taxation | 80 | 100 | — | 20 |
| Other borrowings | 1190 | — | 1190 | — |
| Total Current liabilities | 2735 | 1153 | 1635 | 53 |
| (C) Net working capital | 1285 | 2316 | — | — |
| Increase in working capital | 1031 | — | — | 1031 |
| | 2316 | 2316 | 1639 | 1639 |

In the above example, the data are taken from the balance sheet of a company. As it is a hypothetical example, the figures are rounded up. It will be seen from the above that current assets minus current liabilities give the net working capital. As between the two years, there was an increase in the net working capital, because, the gap between assets and liabilities had widened over the year. The difference is made up by additional bank borrowing to increase the net working capital needed by the company.

## Cash Flow Statements

Related to the broader term of funds flows, there are three related concepts, namely, cash flows, total resource flows and working capital flows. The term "flows" include both inflows and outflows. In the case of cash flows, funds inflows and outflows are on a cash basis and the statement turns out to be a statement of receipts and payment of cash.

As in the case of funds flows, all sources and uses of funds are computed if they involve cash inflows and outflows. Any changes in assets and liabilities over any period, say a year involving cash accretion or depletion will form part of the cash flow statement. These cash flows may be from operations, financial statements incorporating both long-term and short-term income and surpluses from investment and disinvestment operations.

Once all sources and uses as derived from the financial statements are computed, they are arranged in a tabular form, as follows:

Example:

**Statement 33:4** **Cash Flow Statement of X Y Z Co.**

*(Rs. in Lakhs)*

| | | | |
|---|---|---|---|
| **Opening Cash Balance** | 40,000 | | |
| Bank Balance | 40,000 | | |
| Add Cash inflows | | Outflow of cash | |
| (1) issue of shares | 15,000 | Decrease in debentures | 40,000 |
| (2) increase in debtors | 25,000 | | |
| (3) operating profits | 10,000 | Payment of income tax | 10,000 |
| | | Payment of dividends | 20,000 |
| | | Purchases of additional Tools and Mach. | 40,000 |
| | | Cash Balance at close (Bank and Cash) | 20,000 |
| | 130,000 | | 130,000 |

## Liquid Assets

As referred to earlier, working capital management refers essentially to management of current assets, namely, cash and marketable securities, which are most liquid, followed by the other items such as receivables and inventories. The value of the firm, among other things, depends on its state of liquidity, which ensures that the company can meet its day-to-day obligations as they fall due. Liquidity refers nearness to cash, easy convertibility of current assets with the least cost into money and the certainty of the price realised on the asset. While excess liquidity reduces the income as these assets have zero or less remunerative returns, shortfall of liquidity leads to insolvency. The firm can reduce the probability of insolvency by increasing the liquid assets and *vice versa*.

Bankruptcy cost represents a drain in the system to suppliers of capital. The brunt of the drain in the system falls on the owners of the firm, namely, equity holders. Costs are due to higher interest rates earned on other assets which are foregone by investing in liquid assets, whose returns are low. The differential in interest rates and loss of income due to maintaining liquid assets are the costs of avoiding bankruptcy.

There is a trade-off. The firm aims of maintaining an optimum level of liquid assets which will be just sufficient to ward off bankruptcy. Thus, in the absence of perfect markets the value of the firm can be affected by the degree of liquid assets maintained. Thus liquidity management assumes importance in the imperfect markets; as it affects the value of the firm, and maintenance of optimum level of liquid assets, not too many and not too less, becomes a critical issue in the management of the working capital of a company.

## Current Account

What is the adequate level of working capital is a function of total fixed assets and the method of financing them. Both short-term and long-term assets and liabilities are linked. The amount of current liabilities to be maintained is a function of the capital structure and its financing and the level of debt and on the other hand, it is a function of current assets and in particular inventories, which are essential part of the sales. What part of debt should be of long-term nature is again a management decision affecting the current liabilities. Thus, the whole mix of financial operations impinge on the level and mix of current assets and current liabilities. The distinction between short-term and long-term assets and liabilities is only an accounting one.

The decisions on working capital management are not thus unique and unrelated to other financing and investment decisions.

Confining to current assets and current liabilities which directly influence the working capital management, the components of current assets to which attention is focussed are as follows:

**TABLE 33.4**

- Current Assets
  - Cash
  - Marketable Securities
    - TBs
    - CPs
    - CDs
    - Repos
  - Receivables
  - Inventories

In cash management, the firm aims at minimising idle cash held and maximising the returns by alternative uses of cash. The minimising of the cash holding involves synchronisation of cash inflows with outflows as exactly as possible. The factors to be looked into are the following:

(*a*) Speed up the collection process — to receive cash or cheques which can be collected on the same day through electronic transfer system.

(*b*) Reduce the float, namely, the funds in the transit pending collection.

(*c*) The proportion of credit sale to total sales to be brought down.

(*d*) Collected funds to be speedily credited to the bank account, which operates disbursements.

A number of practices will also help efficient management of cash. The following are a few examples:

(*a*) Decentralised billing but centralised collection.

(*b*) Strategically convenient network collection centres.

(*c*) Concentration of banking whereby the flow of funds is accelerated by having various collection centres but centralised disbursement account, into which collected funds at various centres are expeditiously credited.



## Lock Box System

This is a method of accelerating the inflow of funds. The purpose of this is to eliminate time between receipt of remittance by the company and their deposit in the bank. A lock box arrangement is made on a regional basis, choosing the regional banks at centres selected for billing pattern. The customers are billed with instructions to put their cheques in the local box numbers. The local or regional bank picks up the mail daily and arranges to transmit the funds to the centralised disbursing account.

The methods by which disbursements can be slowed down are as follows:

(*a*) Wage payment to be made monthly instead of weekly — extending the periods.

(*b*) Management of bank balances with expected return of cheques for payment.

(*c*) Playing on the float by giving cheques more than the balance, depending upon the amount of cheques in transit for receipt.

(*d*) Use of zero balance accounts, whereby the local accounts can get funds for the centralised accounts as and when cheques are presented and normally maintains a zero balance in the account. As between branch accounts, the transfer of funds is through the low cost, speedy electronic system.

## Cash and Liquid Assets

Cash is the most liquid asset, followed by money market short-term government and semi government securities. In general, the marketable securities available are Treasury bills, Bills Discounting, certificates of deposits, repos, short-term government and semi-government bonds are more liquid and more easily encashable than other securities.

The optimal level of marketable securities or other liquid assets is a function of optimal level of cash, cash requirements and actual cash held, among others. Cash requirement is partly a function of the company's own estimated outflow during the next time period of a week or a month and the minimum cash balances to be kept with the bank in the current account. The optimal level of cash is determined by a forecast by use of any of the known methods of forecasting.

Any company keeps in its portfolio a number of liquid assets, namely, cash and marketable securities. The securities can be evaluated in relation to the default risk, marketability, maturity, coupon rate, taxability and option type features. The total quantum of marketable securities and the composition of this basket is determined by the cash flow pattern, actual cash held and liquidity characteristics of these securities. Companies which require cash at no notice or on the same day prefer to keep their securities as Treasury bills or one year government bonds or Repos, which can be sold readily to DFHI, STCI or RBI. In foreign markets, bankers acceptances, Euro dollars, short-term municipal bonds, floating rate preferred stock are also available for such holding as liquid assets by companies. In India, the markets for these securities are not well developed and the markets for Repos, Commercial Paper and certificates of deposits are just developing in their secondary market segment.

## Models for Determining Optimal Cash

Optimal level of cash would be decided by a trade-off between interest income and transaction costs. If the future inflows are uncertain, as it is in real practice, there is need for provision for near money assets which are also called liquid assets. If there are no transaction costs of converting marketable liquid assets into cash and no inconvenience and time costs involved, there is no need for a firm to hold cash. The need to hold cash arises because of uncertainty of payment flows, time and cost involved in converting liquid assets into cash.

Cash is held generally for transaction purposes, precautionary purposes and asset or wealth purposes. Transaction needs are for payment of daily wages of petty expenses of transport, stationery, entertainment, etc. Precautionary needs arise due to unexpected expenses due to accidents, unforeseen payments, sudden demands for dues payable, etc. Asset or wealth purposes are for speculative trading, investment payments, etc.

Transactions costs and convenience costs are positive generally, which means that conversion of marketable or liquid assets into cash takes time, money and inconvenience. In such scenario, firms have to compulsorily hold cash. The proportion of cash to be held is a matter of experience and is a function of average expected payments or outflows, the forecast gap between inflows and outflows, volume of transactions or daily expenditure, sales and advertisement expenses and other incidentals. There are two types of models which help the decision of how much cash to hold.

The alternatives to holding cash are the interest earning liquid assets or marketable securities. The optimum levels of cash and marketable securities are determined by the trade-off between interest income on the one hand and transactions costs, conversion costs and inconvenience costs. If the latter are more than the interest income, the firm would hold cash. If the transactions and other costs are zero, then firm would hold no cash. As between these extremes the real position stands at some cash and some marketable securities.



## Baumol Model

W.J. Baumol advocated a model for holding cash by a firm, namely, economic order quantity. In this model, the carrying costs of holding cash, namely, interest foregone on liquid assets is balanced by fixed costs of transferring marketable securities to cash and *vice versa*.

The graphical depiction of this model is presented below:

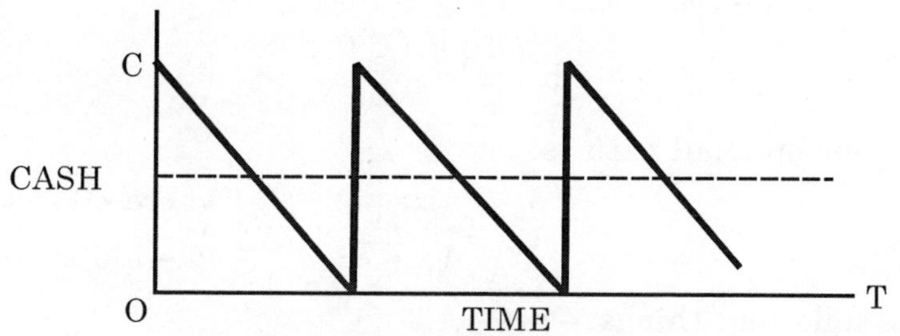


Inventory Model Approach

**Graph 33.2**

W.J. Baumol "Transactions Demand for Cash", QJE (Nov. 1952).

If a firm has an inventory of cash of Rs. 'C' when the amount is spent, it will replenish by selling marketable securities of 'C' value. Here, the transfer of funds from securities to cash occurs when cash reaches zero level. But in real practice, a cushion of cash is maintained always because of the lead time involved in the transaction of conversion of securities into cash.

To hold excess cash is a waste due to income foregone as interest. On the other hand there is another countervailing cost, namely, transaction costs, in converting securities into cash. The objective of the firm is to minimise the total costs — the sum of the fixed costs associated with transfers and the opportunity costs of earnings foregone by holding cash balances. These two costs are represented algebraically as:

$$b\left(\frac{T}{C}\right)+i\left(\frac{C}{2}\right)$$

where b is the fixed cost of a transaction which is independent of the amount involved.

$\left(\frac{T}{C}\right)$ represents the number of transactions during a period with T representing the total demand for cash over a period. $\left(\frac{T}{C}\right)$ multiplied by 'b' gives the total fixed costs for the period. $\frac{C}{2}$ represents average cash balance and when multiplied by interest rate (i) we obtain earnings forgone by virtue of holding cash. If we balance these two costs, namely, $b\left(\frac{T}{C}\right)$ and $i\left(\frac{C}{2}\right)$, we will aim at minimising the total costs. The optimal level of C is given by

$$C=\sqrt{\frac{2bT}{i}}$$

This equation is derived by taking the derivative of the following equation with respect to C is set to equal to zero:

$$b\left(\frac{T}{C}\right)+i\left(\frac{C}{2}\right)$$

The equation for optional cash is:

$$C^{\oplus}=\sqrt{\frac{2bT}{i}}$$

where $c^{\otimes}$ is the value where c is set equal to 0

It means the following things:

(1) Cash demand depends on the square root of the value of transactions; which implies that cash needed will increase less than proportionately to the transactions due to the economies of scale.

(2) Cash needed varies inversely with the interest rate (i) on marketable securities and directly with the fixed cost (b) of the transaction of conversion of marketable securities into cash.

## Example

Using the EOQ formula estimate the $C^{\otimes}$ given estimated cash payments (T) Rs. 30,000 per month and fixed cost per transaction (b) = Rs. 100 and interest rate (i) as 12% or 1% per month.

$$C^{\oplus} = \sqrt{\frac{2bT}{i}} = \sqrt{\frac{2 \times 100 \times 30{,}000}{0.01}}$$

$$= \sqrt{60{,}00{,}00{,}000} = 24{,}495$$

The optimal transaction size is Rs. 24,495 and the average cash balance is $\frac{24{,}495}{2} = 12{,}248$.

Here, the b is the transaction cost fixed uniformly for all transactions as per the assumption and i is the interest rate on money market instruments where liquid assets are traded.

It is also assumed in this model that the i is fixed and known. Cash payments are assumed to be steady over the specified period. Another limitation of this model is that cash payments are not completely predictable. E.O.Q. gives only a benchmark rule but not a precise rule governing the behaviour. Its assumptions and limitations are to some extent unrealistic.

## Miller and Orr Model

Morton H. Miller and Daniel Orr have presented a model which is useful if the cash balances fluctuate randomly. In cases when the demand for cash is stochastic and unknown in advance, then we have to use the stochastic models such as those of Miller and Orr. In these models there will be no unique specific limit of cash balances but there are two limits, one upper and the other lower limit for transfer of securities for cash and vice versa. As long as the cash remains within these limits, no transactions need to take place. These limits are set by the fixed costs associated with the securities transaction and the opportunity cost of holding cash.

Miller and Orr model specifies two control limits, as shown in the diagram below: h is the upper limit and zero is the lower bound.

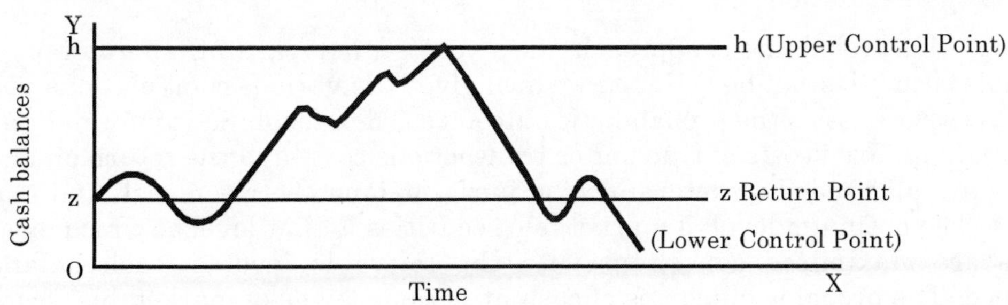


**Graph 33:3**

Take the 'h' as the upper limit and z as the lower limit. When the cash balances fall below z level and reaches zero level, then securities are sold and cash is replenished to the level of z. Above z level, cash balances may fluctuate upto a ceiling level of 'h' and above that level, cash is converted into marketable securities. The level of z and not zero is taken as the lower level if there are delays in transfer and leads in the transactions, or if a positive cash balance provides a level of comfort to the firm.

The optimal value of z, the point for the security transaction to take place is given by the formula as

$$Z = 3\sqrt{\frac{3\ b\sigma^2}{4i}}$$

Where b is the fixed cost of the transaction, $\sigma^2$ is the variance of daily cash flows and i is the interest on marketable securities.

'h' level then becomes '3 z'.

With such limits 'h' and 'z' the model minimises the total fixed and opportunity costs of cash management.

This model[@] is useful when the cash payments are uncertain but they range within set limits in a stochastic manner, unlike in the EOQ model, where the cash flows are predictable. Miller and Orr model is one of the simplest models to deal with the cash problem under the assumptions of stochastic cash flows. Here, the cash management involves the maintenance of the cash balances within certain limits.

## Probability Approach

Unlike the EOQ models and stochastic models, the probability models assume that cash demand is predictable within a range. Normally the cash flows are neither completely predictable nor completely stochastic. The required cash balances to be maintained is higher under the stochastic models than under the EOQ models. This is the effect of the unpredictability of the cash flows of the firm.

When cash flows are neither predictable completely nor unpredictable completely a probabilistic approach is employed. End of period cash balances, exclusive of the purchase or sale of marketable securities can be estimated for various cash flow outcomes to form a probability distribution.

Under the probabilistic approach the expected net earning at different levels of marketable securities can be estimated which gives the various combinations of cash and marketable securities as the probabilistic outcomes. The probabilistic information together with the data on fixed costs of transfer or transactions costs and the return on marketable securities are all needed to determine the initial balance between cash and marketable securities. The optimum level of marketable securities is that level at which expected net earnings are maximised consistent with the tolerable level of cash balance to be maintained. The probable outcomes of cash at various levels of marketable securities are set out and the most ideal cash balance situation is chosen, along with the level of marketable securities which is the optimum level for that outcome.

*Source:*

@ For further details, please see Meston H. Miller and Daniel Orr, "A Model of the Demand for Money by Firms", QJE (Aug. 1966).

## Stochastic Models

In cases where there is some uncertainty of cash payments, some authors have assumed that the demand for cash is stochastic. Also they are called control limit models, in the sense that the cash balances stay within these limits, otherwise transactions of conversion of securities into cash will take place. When the cash reaches the upper limit, as shown below in the chart, cash will be converted into securities. When the cash reaches the lower limit, securities will be converted into cash. Optimum cash balances lie within these two limits.

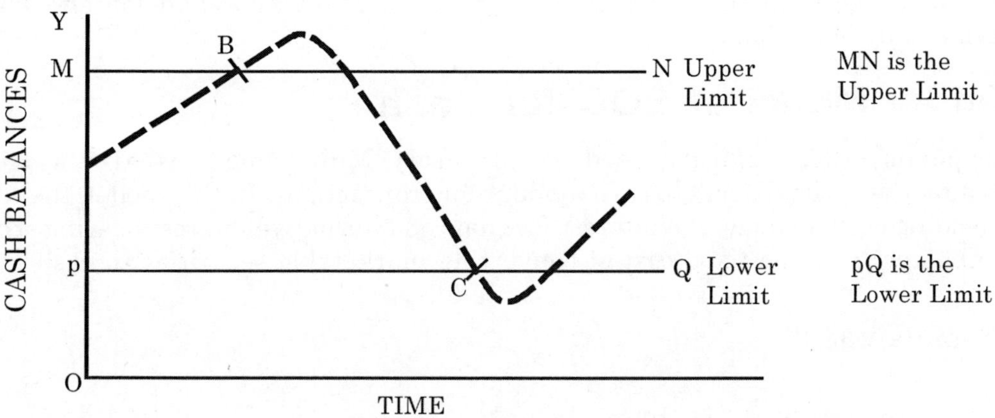


**Graph 33.4**

At the point 'B', cash is converted into securities and at the point 'C', securities are converted into cash. This theory has been propounded by Miller and Orr+ and variations of this model have been used by a number of other writers. The amount of OP is the core minimum that the company should always keep to offset any raid on the company. OP is like an insurance amount for the firm to be solvent. But the variations of cash between P and M are stochastic movements, depending on the business fluctuations of the company.

## Probability Merits

In actual practice, corporate experience shows that the cash flows of the firm are neither completely certain nor uncertain. There may be different degrees of predictability of these flows depending on the managerial efficiency and R&D support of the firm. In situations when cash flows are neither completely predictable nor unpredictable, firms can adopt a probabilistic approach.

In this approach, various probabilities are to be attached to possible outflows of cash and inflows of cash. For each of the levels of initial marketable securities, expected market earning and their pattern of inflow can be worked out. The optimal level of marketable securities is that level, where the expected net earnings are maximised.

+ Meston H. Miller and Daniel Orr, "A Model of the Demand for Money by Firms", QJE (Aug. 1966).

When the actual level of marketable securities goes above that level, the greater is the probability that some securities would be converted into cash. Conversely the probability of conversion of securities into cash or of cash into securities would be high, if the level, of net cash flows go above or below a point, which by practice the company knows as the normal and reasonable level. The theory of probability is applied to different scenarios of net cash flows.

In actual practice, the trade-off between holding cash and securities is decided by experience, the pattern of past flows, safe position for the company to be solvent, and a host of other factors. But the theoretical positions, exposed above are the bench marks for rational decision-making on the level of safe cash balance and for efficient cash management by the firm.

# Inventory Model of EOQ for Cash

Economic order quantity used in Inventory Management is also applied for determining the optimal average cash amount for transactions. In this model, the carrying cost of holding cash, namely, the interest foregone on alternative interest bearing securities is to be balanced by the fixed cost of converting marketable securities to cash and vice versa.

**Formula : 33.1**

In the following formula, the total fixed cost of the period is $b\left(\frac{T}{C}\right)$ and interest foregone by virtue of holding cash is $i\left(\frac{C}{2}\right)$ where b is the fixed cost of a transaction and $\frac{T}{C}$ represents the number of transactions during the period.

For T is total demand for cash over a period of time and C is the cash held during that period.

$\frac{C}{2}$ is average cash balance during the period and i is the interest rate on the alternative marketable securities for the period.

The formula for total costs, which is the sum of fixed costs associated with transfers and the opportunity cost of earnings foregone by holding cash balance is as follows:

$$\text{Costs} = b\left(\frac{T}{C}\right) + i\left(\frac{C}{2}\right)$$

If these above too components are balanced the total costs are minimised. Then the optimal level of 'C' is found by the formula:

$$C^{\otimes} = \sqrt{\frac{2bT}{t}}$$ where $C^{\otimes}$ is the value

when C is set equal to '0'

The present formula is derived from the above equation. This has been explained earlier as Baumol Model.

To illustrate with a numerical example, let us take the fixed cost per transaction as Rs. 100 and estimated cash payments for month is Rs. 6 lakhs. The interest rate on marketable securities (i) is 24% per annum of 2% per month.

Then applying the above formula

$$C^{\otimes} = \sqrt{\frac{2bT}{i}} = \sqrt{\frac{2 \times 100 \times 600{,}000}{0.02}}$$

$$= \sqrt{600{,}00{,}000 \times 100} = \sqrt{600{,}00{,}00{,}000}$$

$$= 77{,}459$$

If the interest rate is halved to 12% per annum or 1% per month, the optimum cash will rise by one and half times as seen below.

$$C^{\otimes} = \sqrt{\frac{2bT}{i}} = \sqrt{\frac{2 \times 100 \times 600{,}000}{0.01}}$$

$$= 109{,}544$$

The limitations are the unrealistic nature of the assumptions.[@]

Firstly, the fixed costs per transaction is more difficult to work out in reality than assumed.

Secondly, the assumption that cash payments are steady and continue to be so is unrealistic.

Thirdly, the assumption of certainty of cash payments over a period is a serious limitation to this model.

There are various degrees of uncertainty and to that extent dependability on this model is reduced. Even so, this Model provides a benchmark to go by for estimating the cash balance requirements of a firm.

❖ ❖ ❖

@ See W.J. Baumol, "The Transactions Demand for Cash," *Quarterly Journal Economics,* November, 1952.

# WORKING CAPITAL MANAGEMENT

# 34

## Receivables

Under the caption of working capital, we have discussed cash and liquid assets and all current liabilities and the treatment of working capital. The amount of Receivables held and the quality of these Receivable Accounts are a function of the firm's credit and collection policies. Economic conditions, money market conditions, credit policies of banks are the external factors, which influence the accounts receivable. The firm's credit and collection policies are partly determined by the nature of the commodities produced or dealt with in the market for such commodities and the comparable practices of the competitors.

As for the credit policy, the variables to be considered are the quality of trade accounts, length of the credit period, cash discount and any other special terms and the collection process of the firm. Credit policy influences and is influenced by sales. In general, a liberal credit policy can increase sales, but may lead to more bad and doubtful debts. Thus, the quality of accounts will be better by a selective credit policy but may reduce the sales. There is a trade off between profitability and Risk. Liberal credit policy will increase sales and profits but a discretionary credit policy will improve the quality and reduce risk. Liberal credit policy may lead to bad and doubtful debts and increase risk.

Credit standards determine the quality for assets. If the credit standards are relaxed, clerical and servicing work will increase and costs will rise. Sometimes, there is a probability of rise in bad debts. For increasing sales marginally, there may be need for relaxing the credit standards but profitability of additional sales has to be weighed against the additional costs of servicing, collection etc. Extension of credit sales may be worthwhile if there is idle capacity and fixed costs do not change for any additional production and sales of the product provided of course additional sales atleast cover the variable costs on a net basis.

## Credit Standards

Examples of relaxing credit standards are increasing the credit period and extending the facility to all and sundry without distinction, etc. Such a policy has to weigh the trade off between profitability on additional sales and opportunity cost of increased investment in receivables. Liberalisation of credit standards may increase sales and receivables but may lower quality and at the same time may affect the level of inventories. With increased sales due to liberal credit policy, increased inventory has to be maintained. Sometimes discounts may be given for cash sales, which will reduce profitability. But the same discount given to accounts receivables for early payment will not affect sales but reduce collection period and the cost of credit to the company goes down. In actual practice, change in credit policy is difficult, unless it is well planned out and is related to the level of production and capacity. If the production is reaching the capacity, credit policy can be tightened and quality standards are to be increased. If there is a large unused capacity, credit policy can be eased to increase sales. Some credit sales may lead to lowering of quality of accounts receivable. Another factor which influences the credit policy changes is the composition of total costs (fixed costs + variable costs) and the marginal costs. If at least marginal costs and variable costs can be covered despite the lowering of credit policy it becomes worthwhile to lower credit standards.

Easing of credit policy or change in credit standards may no doubt attract additional sales for new customers but old sales and old customers would also demand similar terms. This would mean, that there would be a general slowing down of the collection period, increased bad debts and defaults.

## Cost-Benefit Analysis

In granting lower credit standards one has to take into account profitability criteria, seasonal factors in demand with a constant rate of production and changes in market conditions through recession in general or through actions of competitors.

Firstly, the company has to compare the profitability of additional sales with the required return on the additional investment in receivables before giving more liberal credit terms.

Secondly, to stimulate demand in the case of seasonal goods, carrying costs of inventory can be brought down, by giving credits for enlarged periods for payment to come after the seasonal slack. Such seasonal datings are advisable if the warehousing costs plus the required rate of return on investment in inventory exceed the required rate of return on the additional receivables.

Another factor considered in credit policy changes is the level of collection expenditure. If after taking into account the costs due to enlarged credit period, and the discounts offered for earlier payments, it may be advisable to change the credit policy, if the marginal gains due to enlarged sales are equal to marginal costs. The additional expenses of collection of these lower quality accounts, emerging out of easing of credit terms have to be added to the marginal costs to compare with the expected marginal gains. In sum, the policy change will be warranted, if its impact on profits is positive, for which some research and sensitivity analysis are necessary. In particular, credit standing of the customers, their credit rating have to be considered to avoid default risk. Otherwise Default risk may swallow any expected additional gains from additional receivables. If there is incremental profitability on additional sales due to liberalisation of credit policy, it is worthwhile liberalising. On the additional sales, additional revenue from these sales has to be adjusted for bad debt losses and investment cost of additional receivables for extended period and additional collection charges, if any, to arrive at net incremental profitability.

## Collection Charges

Collection charges depend upon the collection procedure such as collection through telephone, mailing, faxing the invoice, reminders on or prior to due date or handing over the collection work to an outside agency. In some cases of sticky accounts, hardly 50% of the due is received because of the above incidental and consequential charges. In case cash discounts are offered for prompt payment of receivables, this is a cost item to be added in collection expenditure. It is found that total profits of the firm will increase at a diminishing rate with stricter controls on credit standards upto a point, after which they decline. Hence, it is not always advantageous for the company to observe stricter credit standards. Similarly, it is not always advisable to liberalise credit as net profits increase only upto a point and then decrease.

The optimal point with respect to credit standards is set by a number of variables. There is a point upto which credit terms can be made stricter. These points set the limits for policy decisions and can be estimated with some difficulty for each firm separately, depending on a number of factors, both internal and external to the firm.

## Credit Standing of Customers

The line of credit allowed to any customer is based on some scientific methods of assessment of credit worthiness of the customer. In evaluating a credit applicant, the credit analyst obtains all financial and other information regarding the customer applicant and after a thorough analysis and assessment, reaches a credit decision. As information is costly and time consuming the cost of securing additional information has to be weighed against expected benefits. For new account such analysis and assessment is more elaborate and comprehensive. For an old account, only additional and latest information on the customer is called for to decide whether to accept the order or not. The overall credit limits of all applicants and the individual limits are then decided in order to plan for an optimum level of credit limits and Receivables accounts for the firm.

## Impact of Credit Decision

The credit decision is a matter of importance for the financial position and liquidity of the firm. Many firms use computer aided analysis of the credit standing of the customer applicant. The computer through proper programming can provide data on applicant's history, past record of payments on schedule, current status, present financial position and future expected financial standing and the computer can apply a consistent framework and criteria for credit analysis and helping the credit manager with a decision, whether, to give credit and if so, the extent up to which credit can be granted. The computer, or the credit manager has to go through a sequential investigation process, before making a credit decision. Some of the exercises which are repetitive are processed through the computer and the application of human talent has to be the final deciding factor and this is left to the Credit manager on whose efficiency and expertise the fortunes of the firm depend to an extent, particularly with respect to the liquidity of the firm. The Macro decision of the overall level permissible for Receivables, the total credit limits, credit terms, standards to be applied are all thus set out by the credit manager. In international transactions, credit rating of the counter party is sought from the banker or from foreign consulates and embassies abroad which is also an expense item.



## Inventory Management

Sales are made out of inventory and production feeds the inventory. Too much of an inventory, not justified by sales will lead to wasteful use of funds. Too little of an inventory is also a danger as sales and continuity of sales to meet the emerging demand will be adversely effected. The potential customers are also scared off and the demand will flow out to competitors.

The Inventory has the following components: raw-materials, semi-finished or goods in process, and finished goods. In all these cases, too much and too little both lead to inefficiency and rise in costs and fall in profits. Only the optimum levels, which will balance the expected benefits with the costs will maximise the profits of the firm.

In view of the advantages of economies of scale, as large stocks facilitate larger production, and as large orders carry discounts, purchase department favours larger building up of inventories of raw-materials as well. There is thus a bias for larger stocks of inventory rather than smaller stocks. The finance manager should be concerned with the cost of funds tied up in inventory, carrying costs storage and handling charges, including insurance, if necessary.

There is thus, a trade off between higher costs involved in holding larger stocks than necessary and the risk of loss of production and sales and consequent loss of customers, potential or actual. Larger stocks also give flexibility in managing production levels. Lower the level of inventory, the less is the flexibility. The larger the level of inventory, the higher will be the costs, of carrying, handling and storing. There is an optimal level, which will balance these two opposing forces and which the firm should strive to achieve. In evaluating, the level of inventory, the Management must balance the benefits of economies of production, of purchase and increased demand as against the cost of additional funds needed for additional inventory and carrying costs, including handling and storage costs.

# Economic Order Quantity

In managing the inventory and to secure an optimum level of inventory, the firm has to take into account the Economic Order Quantity (EOQ). To determine the EOQ, we have to forecast usage, ordering cost and carrying cost. If the usage of inventory is steady and does not change from period to period, average inventory in units is stated as Q/2, where Q is quantity of Inventory. The carrying cost per unit (C) multiplied by average number of units of inventory Q/2 is the carrying cost of inventory.

Carrying cost = Carrying cost per unit × Average number of units of inventory

$$= C \times \frac{Q}{2} = \frac{CQ}{2}$$

Then we have to consider ordering costs. The total ordering cost is equal to ordering cost per unit order multiplied by number of orders per period. The number of orders for a period of time is the total usage in units (S) divided by Q. S/Q is thus, the number of orders per a time period and O is the ordering cost per unit. Thus, the total ordering costs are $\frac{SO}{Q} = \left(\frac{S}{Q} \times O\right)$

Total inventory costs = carrying costs + ordering costs

$$T = \frac{CQ}{2} + \frac{SO}{Q}$$

If Q is the order quantity in the above equation, it shows that there is a trade off between the economies of increased order size (Q) and the added cost of carrying additional inventory. If Q is higher, carrying costs are higher but ordering costs are lower. If Q is lower, carrying costs are lower, but order costs are higher. Because of this trade off, there is an optimum order quantity which balances the above two opposing trends.

Given the above basic equation, to determine the optimal order quantity Q, we differentiate the above equation to set the derivative equal to zero.

$$\frac{dT}{dQ} = \frac{CQ}{2} - \frac{SO}{Q} = 0$$

$$CQ^2 - 2SO = 0$$

$$Q^2 = \frac{2SO}{C}$$

$$Q^{\otimes} = \sqrt{\frac{2SO}{C}}$$

The formula $Q^{\otimes} = \sqrt{\frac{2SO}{C}}$ is the equation for the economic order size.

To illustrate the use of the above formula take (C) carrying cost per unit as Rs. 10, usage of inventory item is 2000 units (S) ordering costs are Rs. 100 for a given period (O).

Then applying the above formula

$$Q^{\otimes} = \sqrt{\frac{2 \times 2{,}000 \times 100}{10}} = \sqrt{40{,}000} = 200 \text{ units}$$

If the usage is 2000 units and order quantity is 200 units then the firm makes an order ten times to meet its requirements.

Graphically, the EOQ relationships are depicted below with order size on x-axis and costs on the y-axis. Carrying costs vary directly with the order size. Ordering cost vary inversely, with the size of the order. As a result, the total cost line declines at first and then rises, when the decrease in average ordering costs is more than offset by the additional carrying costs. At the point $O^0$ on the x-axis, the optimum point of economic order quantity which minimises the total costs is secured.

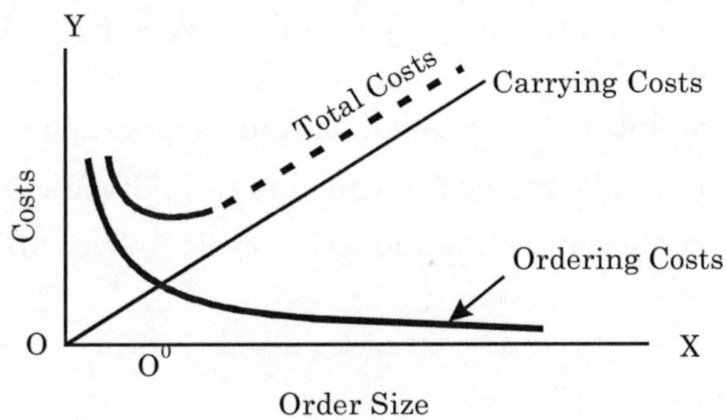


**Graph 34:1**

## Order Point and Safety Stock

In practice, the demand for inventory is not exactly known with certainty. Due to possible fluctuations in this demand, it is not possible to allow the stock of inventory to fall below a safe limit. Even if the inventory demand is known with certainty, there is a time lag between placing of order and its delivery. If the delivery time is 10 days; the new order has to be placed for the economic order quantity at a point when the safety stock level is expected to be reached in 10 days. The firm has to maintain the safety stock level for emergencies. We assume that the lead time for delivery is known and that the safety stock level is fairly certain by experience. Whatever is the cost of ordering, the firm has to maintain a certain minimum level as safety stock, which is adequate for the firm by experience.

The level of safety stock depends on various factors such as uncertainty of the demand for inventory, seasonal nature of demand for the product, varying time lags for delivery of stock to replenish inventory. Another factor which decides the minimum safety stock is the possible closure of production and consequent loss of the customers.

This is also called the cost of running out of stock and the risks involved in it. The greater the cost of carrying inventory, the more expensive is the maintenance of minimum safety stock. Thus, the decision on the amount of minimum safety stock involves the balancing of the probability and cost of carrying enough stock to avoid a possible stock out and closure of the plant for production. Here again the management faces a trade-off situation and has to carry out a cost-benefit analysis. The efficiency of management lies in how well they maintain the least cost economic order quantity of inventory with a safety stock and with no possible loss of production or orders and customers.

## Special Features of MNCs

Management of Receivables and Inventories is both an art and science. The basic principles of credit appraisal and collection of receivables are the same for all corporates, whether they are domestic or transnational in nature. The only difference lies in the greater expertise that is in-built in the multinationals, in management and the wider experience in different countries that they have and are exposed to.

But the factors influencing the credit policy to be followed, collection procedures, order quantity, ordering costs and carrying costs etc. vary from firm to firm, depending on a host of factors, namely:

(1) country's geographical, environmental and demographic factors.

(2) tastes, habits and cultures of the consumers and the clients.

(3) nature of the product and the production cycle and peculiarities of the product/products.

(4) the production process and technology used.

(5) nature and width of the market.

(6) marketing practices and trade customs.

(7) practices and policies of competitors in the field.

(8) local government regulations and the legal and regulatory framework that they have in the host country, etc.

In view of such diverse factors, no generalisation can be made of the collection and credit policies of a firm or of the inventory management techniques. The multinationals being experienced on a broader spectrum of operations, in a highly competitive environment, with greater financial strength and management expertise, have been found to operate in an optimal manner and on strict commercial considerations. They are more flexible and quick to change with the changing conditions of the policy and the environment. Their operations are more cost effective and efficient than the purely domestic companies.

## Financing of Working Capital

In the last chapter, we discussed mainly liquid assets and net working capital, which is the difference between current assets and current liabilities. In this chapter, we dealt with the optimum level of inventories and receivables, which are also current assets. Current liabilities are mostly decided by credit policy of the firm, and that of its suppliers. The input mix is determined by the production function and state of technology and the level of output and sales. The bills payable and creditors are mostly decided by the factors beyond the control of firm. The only way the Finance Manager can influence them is to look into alternative sources of supply of inputs and to choose the least cost combination of suppliers and their credit terms. Provision for taxation and other provisions are decided by the Government Policy and the management policy of the parent company. The local affiliate has to take them as given for its operations.

The gap between current assets and current liabilities is filled up by borrowing. The various alternatives for borrowings available to the firm are the domestic banks, foreign banks within the host country and the international currency markets through external commercial borrowings. But the RBI has barred the companies from ECBs for working capital purposes in the first half of 2004. In this context, the alternatives are limited to domestic banks and transfer of funds from other affiliates or parent company. The Finance Manager will look into the costs of each of the alternatives and choose the least cost alternative. For borrowing from banks the credit worthiness or credit rating of the firm will be taken into account, which is influenced by the firm's own liquidity position as reflected in the ratio of current assets to current liabilities. The ideal ratio is 2 : 1 and the Finance Manager knows by hindsight and experience, what ratio is acceptable to his bankers and this falls anything between 2:1 and 1:1. This sums up in brief the management aspects of working capital of the multilateral corporates.

❖ ❖ ❖

# PART VI

# MANAGEMENT OF LONG TERM INTERNATIONAL FINANCING

# PROJECT APPRAISAL AND CAPITAL BUDGETING

# 35

Any corporate unit has to plan for a Capital Budget for setting up a project or expansion and diversification with a view to maximising the shareholders' wealth. For making a public issue, companies generally get their projects appraised by a well-known agency like the banks, F.I.s and merchant bankers. Before going in for any project, the corporate unit has to weigh the alternative projects available to it, consider their costs and benefits or net profits accruing to the firm. The projects are then ranked in the order of their net profitability. The return on a project is compared to the required rate of return on investment, to consider its worthwhileness to pursue.

There are different methods of ranking the projects or considering the worthwhileness of investment. These methods are set out briefly below:

## (1) Pay Back Period

Pay back period is a method by which the number of years in which the project will repay the initial investment made, is considered. The smaller the number of years or the period of waiting for the company to get back the initial investment, the better will be the project. Given the same initial investment if project A pays back the investment in 3 years, while project B does the same in 4 years, the first one, namely, project A is preferred.

| *Example* | *Project A* | *Project B* |
|---|---|---|
| Initial Investment | Rs.1,00,000 | Rs.1,00,000 |
| Return in year 1 | 40,000 | 40,000 |
| Return in year 2 | 30,000 | 30,000 |
| Return in year 3 | 30,000 | 20,000 |
| Return in year 4 | 20,000 | 10,000 |

In the above example, project A is preferred as it takes lesser number of years to pay the initial investment than project B. If both the projects have the same Pay Back Period, then some other method is used.

Although, this method is simple to use and to understand, it does not consider the long-term benefits of the project, nor the written down value of the project. It does not take into account the time value of money and hence it is found to be defective and of limited value for preciseness.

## (2) ARR or Average Rate of Return Method

This is the average per annum return over the life cycle of the period relative to the investments made in it. Under this method, a project with a higher ARR is preferred to one with lower ARR. In the above example, data are applied as follows:

$$\text{ARR} = \frac{\text{Average Annual Profit}}{\text{Investment}}$$

$$\text{ARR for project A} = \frac{\text{Average Annual Profit}}{\text{Investment}}$$

$$= \left[\frac{1{,}20{,}000/4}{1{,}00{,}000}\right] = \frac{30{,}000}{1{,}00{,}000} \times 100 = 30\%$$

$$\text{ARR for project B} = \left[\frac{1{,}00{,}000/4}{10{,}00{,}000}\right] \text{or} = \frac{25{,}000 \times 100}{1{,}00{,}000} = 25\%$$

Because of higher ARR, Project A is preferred.

If both the projects have the same ARR, then the choice of the project becomes difficult under this method.

## (3) Discounted Cash Flow Method (D.C.F.)

In this method, the time value of money is considered. The future cash flows expected are discounted to the present time to know the discounted cash flow and compare it with the initial investments made. Today's cash outflow is thus, compared with today's value of all future cash inflows in a project. Net cash inflows in years 1, 2, 3 etc. are discounted to the present day by a discount factor, namely, the present value of one rupee in one year, two years, three years etc. All these cash inflows over the life cycle of the machine are discounted to the present time to compare it with the initial investment.

**Present Value of Re. 1 (from the Tables for the Purpose)**

one year hence 0.91

two years hence 0.83

three years hence0.75

four years hence 0.68

five years hence 0.62

Consider two projects, A & B with the following cash flows, to calculate the Net Present Value (NPV) Under D.C.F. method. The data in this method are given for illustration and are not the same as in the above illustration.

## Project A

| *Year* | *Cash flow* | × | *Present value of Re. 1* | *D.C.F. to the present* |
|---|---|---|---|---|
| 1 | 4,000 | × | 0.91 | 3,640 |
| 2 | 3,000 | × | 0.83 | 2,490 |
| 3 | 2,000 | × | 0.75 | 1,500 |
| 4 | 1,000 | × | 0.68 | 680 |
| | | | Total of Project 'A' | 8,310 |
| | | | Initial Investment | 8,000 |
| | | | NPV (Net Present Value) | 310 |

## Project B

| *Year* | *Cash flow* | × | *Present value of Re.1* | *D.C.F. to the present* |
|---|---|---|---|---|
| 1 | 1,000 | × | 0.91 | 910 |
| 2 | 2,000 | × | 0.83 | 1,660 |
| 3 | 3,000 | × | 0.75 | 2,250 |
| 4 | 4,000 | × | 0.68 | 2,720 |
| | | | Total of project 'B' | 7,540 |
| | | | Initial Investment | 8,000 |
| | | | NPV (Net Present Value) | – 460 |

## Rules of Selection of a Project

(1) When the NPV is zero, the project becomes break-even, as the IRR is equal to expected return on the investment.

(2) When the NPV becomes positive, the project becomes profitable. Those projects which have larger positive NPV are selected in that order.

(3) If the NPV is negative as in the case of the above project 'B', it is rejected.

## (4) Internal Rate of Return (IRR)

IRR is the actual internal rate of return on the project. It is the internally generated return on the investment in a project, out of the cash flows. Take the example of project 'A', referred to above. Its net positive present value is 310, at the rate of return of 10%.

In the present case, consider a rate of return of 30%, for the same cash flows.

| *Year* | *Cash flow* | × | *Discounting factor at 30%* | *D.C.F.* |
|---|---|---|---|---|
| 1 | 4,000 | × | 0.77 | = 3,080 |
| 2 | 3,000 | × | 0.59 | = 1,770 |
| 3 | 2,000 | × | 0.46 | = 920 |
| 4 | 1,000 | × | 0.35 | = 350 |
| | | | Total D.C.F. | 6,120 |
| | | | Initial Investment | 8,000 |
| | | | NPV | −1,880 |

IRR of project "A" is calculated as follows:

$$\text{IRR} = \begin{matrix}\text{Rate of Return}\\ \text{giving positive NPA}\end{matrix} + \left[\frac{\text{Positive N.P.V.}}{(\text{Positive NPV} + \text{Negative NPV})} \times \begin{matrix}\text{Difference Between}\\ \text{two rates}\end{matrix}\right]$$

$$+(10) \qquad + \left[\frac{310}{310+1{,}880} \times 0.20\right]$$

Return at Positive NPV is 10% — Actual NPV 310

Return at Negative NPV is 30% — Actual NPV − 1,880

Difference between two rates = 30 − 10 = 20%.

IRR for the above project "A" is

$$= 10 + \frac{310}{2{,}190} \times .20$$

$$= 10 + 0.028 = 10.028\%$$

Similarly IRR for the project "B" can be calculated, and compared for making a choice.

## (5) NPV and Relative NPV

NPV should be considered not in absolute sense but in the relative sense, relative to the level of investment. Thus, a number of projects of 'A' to 'D' may be available and each has a given level of investment and accordingly NPVs differ and absolutely NPVs in this case will be meaningless as shown below. Here relative NPV is given by the ratio of NPV to its investment.

| Project | Investment given | NPV Absolute | NPV ÷ Investment Relative |
|---|---|---|---|
| A | 1,000 | 250 | 25% |
| B | 2,000 | 400 | 20% |
| C | 3,000 | 500 | 16.6% |
| D | 2,500 | 450 | 18% |

If we take absolute NPV, then projects "C" and "D" may be selected; but if the relative NPVs are considered, which gives the actual return on investment in percentage terms, then projects 'A' and 'B' are to be selected. Thus, the criteria of choosing the projects has to be carefully selected to give the maximum profitability and increase the shareholders' wealth of the company.

## Capital Budgeting by MNCs

MNCs face a different set of factors from those faced by the domestic companies in the matter of foreign investment that they make. Briefly these problems which MNCs face are foreign government, regulations, tax regulations, exchange rate changes, inflation and differences between business risks of foreign and domestic projects. When an MNC has any business investment opportunities through mergers, acquisitions, joint ventures or subsidiaries, it has many business opportunities in many countries which are non-comparable. To bring them to a uniform level of comparability is a special task of the MNC. The first thing that the MNC does is to optimise the use of available information, while making adjustments to the cost of capital, and cash flow generated in each of the countries.

The basic objective of all investments of MNCs is to maximise the company value to the shareholders. Net present value is the most appropriate method adopted by most MNCs, but valued at constant dollars.

## NPV Formula

The net present value is defined as the present value of future cash flows, discounted at an appropriate rate of discount minus the initial cash outlay on the project. If only the NPV is positive, a project is selected. In the choice of a project among two of them, the one with greater NPV is chosen.

The formula for the NPV

$$NPV = \sum_{t=1}^{n} \frac{xt}{(1+k)^t} - Io$$

Io = initial capital investment

xt = net cash flow in period t,

k = project cost of capital or discount rate and t is the time period

NPV is most accepted method of use in the capital budgeting exercises. It focuses on the cash flows and the future flows discounted to the present time, which generally shareholders are interested in. As such it can satisfy the wealth maximisation criteria of MNCs.

Secondly, the NPV has the advantage of additivity in that the values of NPV for each of the projects accepted can be added for an overall view of the accepted projects of MNC.

## Incremental Cash Flows

What is more relevant for the MNC with its wide network of operations is the net increase in inflow due to an additional project rather than the NPV. The net inflow of a project is different from the inflow to MNC out of that project. The difference is due to cannibalisation of sales and profits. This refers to slicing off sales of an existing product of the company by the new product. To the extent that sales of a new product of a new project replace that of the existing product, the net contribution of the new project is lower due to cannibalisation.

In some cases, a new subsidiary in another country creates additional sales of the existing product of the company. This is the sales creation, which is the opposite of cannibalisation.

Besides, the MNC attributes an opportunity cost to any existing resource used by the parent for the affiliate in order to arrive at the net incremental cash flow from the project. Suppose the (MNC) parent company supplies its brand name to the affiliate, it will charge the affiliate for it at the opportunity cost in the form of a transfer price or a royalty, although, it does not cost anything additional to the MNC. Similarly, it will collect fees and charges for any services it renders for the affiliate and it is taken into account in arriving at net incremental cash flows.

## Adjustment for Taxes and Other Hurdles

Adjustment for taxes and other hurdles is done in net cash flows rather than the discount rate used. Some investments create additional business or increase the production and demand in other lines of business, while other investments reduce the production and demand in other lines. For example, many U.S. MNCs manufacture memory chips, despite losses made in this line of business, as without manufacturing some sort of memory chips, they believe that it is difficult to keep production technology competitive in chip business. On the other hand, Suzuki produced and sold new models but increase in new models had also decreased some demand for existing models.

These hurdles to investment in new projects are thus adjusted for in the cash flows to the parent company. The standard capital budgeting analysis for the MNCs involves calculating the expected after tax and after hurdle cash flows; associated with the prospective investment and then arrive at the net incremental cash flows which are more relevant to the parent company in their own currency. To discount these cash flows in a specific time frame, they use the weighted average cost of capital, which is calculated by taking the weights proportional to the source of capital that entered into the capital structure of the firm. Foreign investments in various countries have different risks and different debt-equity components in capital structure. Hence, the case for using a weighted average cost of capital is overwhelming.

Even so, some use the alternative approach of reflecting the business risks in the discount rate and apply *"all equity rate"* relevant to that country where investment is made. In this approach the value of the project is sum of the present value of cash flows adjusted for taxes, the present value of tax savings in debt financing and the present value of any savings on interest costs associated with country specific means of financing such as tax holidays or government guarantee for a minimum return given in some countries. Here in such cases, the discount rate used is the required rate of return on specific project which equals the risk free return plus the appropriate risk premium on the project's particular risk. Thus according to this school, each project has its own unique required rate of return. This unique rate is used to discount the future cash flows to the present to examine the worthiness of undertaking that project.

## MNC's Outlook

Two basic issues which MNCs look into before making foreign investment are:

1. Economic and political risk analysis.
2. Exchange rate changes and inflation risks.

These will be relative to each country and each project. MNCs prefer countries where there are no government and exchange controls and where there is economic and political stability. For, MNCs look into the project from the point of view of the returns to the parent company and not to the project per se.

Firstly, The value of the project is of course examined in terms of the present value of the future cash flows net of any transactions costs, costs of transfer and taxes to the parent company.

Secondly, the project cash flows are also assessed from the point of view of the subsidiary as if the subsidiary is a separate unit of account.

Thirdly, the project is examined for any of adverse or beneficial effects on the other affiliates of the MNCs, which are part of its total system.

Finally, the cash flows are analysed from the point of the project as such and for the parent company, in particular.

Incremental cash flows to the parent company is the final deciding factor for making any investment in a subsidiary. From parent company's post investment cash flows are to be deducted the pre-investment cash flows to arrive at the incremental cash flows to the parent company. The parent company uses the market prices or opportunity costs for goods and services supplied to the subsidiary for the project. The royalties and fees paid by the subsidiary to the parent company are taken net of taxes. The parent company adjusts for the global costs and benefits involved in a new project and considers the following

*(i)* Cannibalisation of sales of other affiliates

*(ii)* Creation of additional sales to other affiliates

*(iii)* Taxes and tax credits affecting the parent company

(*iv*) Costs and benefits involved in market and product diversification and addition to the potential of the parent company on a global basis

(*v*) Externalities and key link provided by this affiliate to the global service network.

Risk is avoided and if risk is taken, additional returns are to be secured for additional risk. If a foreign country has political and economic stability that is the first preference of the MNCs. If however, there is political and economic uncertainty as in the case of India and Latin American countries, in general the MNCs adjust their project appraisal by the following methods:

(*i*) Adjust the cash flows to reflect the impact of the country risk.

(*ii*) Raise the required rate of return by adjusting upwards the total risk and the additional return required for additional risk and

(*iii*) Shortening the pay back period of the project commensurate with the perceived country risk and its impact on the return to the parent company.

## Exchange Rate Changes and Inflation

The impact of inflation on the cash flows from the affiliate to the parent company is to deflate the cash flows by the expected inflation. Different flows are affected differently by inflation. Thus, depreciation tax rebate does not change with inflation, while revenues and variable costs or working capital are variable with inflation. As a result of inflation or any other factor, exchange rate may depreciate in the affiliate country. The cash flows required in the domestic currency which may be increased due to inflation will have to be adjusted for currency depreciation expected during the life cycle of the project. Each year's cash outflows or inflows are to be inflated or deflated due to expected depreciation for the currency before the future flows are discounted to the present day to arrive at the adjusted NPV. All these calculations will be in the form of net inflows or incremental inflows into the parent company accounts in the parent company currency as ultimately it is the maximisation of the wealth of the parent company that is aimed at by all foreign investments in the affiliates in the new projects or the existing projects.

The parent company has a principal cash outflow for the new project, in the form of initial investment outlay for plant purchase, equipment etc., and for working capital requirements. Subsequent cash outflows are for operating expenses or for rise in costs due to inflation or by rise in production. The return flow of funds take the form of dividend or interest paid to the head office, net of taxes, and after providing for tax shield for depreciation and interest charges. Interest subsidies or tax credits are also to be taken into account. Repayment of working capital loans and repayment of terminal value of the initial investment, net of any capital gain tax has to be repatriated back. Here, the cash flows initially made and cash flows returned back to the head office are at the respective exchange rates and the initial forecast will be on the basis of relative degrees of inflation in the respective countries, as projected at the time of project analysis. Basically the project appraisal by the parent company is in terms of the net gain to its shareholders, calculated as the additional or incremental flows for any given outlay, in the form of return on investment, as dividends, interest, fees, royalties etc. If it has exported anything to its affiliate, it will also receive payments in home currency to the parent company for any exports of goods and services. For loan towards working capital or capital expenditure, it will receive interest payments half yearly or yearly and dividend on equity capital half yearly or yearly. All these payments of dividends and interest income net of local taxes if any, are payable and get tax credits in the home country, if there is a double taxation avoidance agreement between the parent country and affiliate country.

The parent company charges the affiliate for its licensing for the use of the parent's name and for the use of its brands, it receives royalty, and for technical know-how and consultancy, it receives fees and charges. For any and all of its services, the affiliate has to pay to the parent company through the transfer price mechanism or as per the original agreement through normal price mechanism. The loans are granted from the parent company out of internal sources, which are charged on the basis of opportunity cost or on the basis of prevailing Euro-market rates.

To avoid or reduce political risks, many countries entered into investment guarantee agreements. This will prevent expropriation and blocked funds in the country of affiliates. If the expropriation is possible then country will be a high risk country and expected return will also be high. Then the expected present value of future flows will be discounted heavily. If the possibility of blocked funds is there, then the value of the project becomes zero. In all cases, where the fear of expropriation and blocked accounts are there, the expected project will not be viable and its net incremental flows will be zero and so investment in such countries will not take place. To the extent that some alleviating factors are there like the government guarantee for investment against expropriation and the rigour of exchange control is not high, then project may be set up with a high discount rate for the risk factors.

## Growth Options

Growth option is an attractive feature for the MNCs, which jump at any prospect of growth and expansion in any part of the world.

First of all, they wish to expand market with increased production and economies of scale, flowing from such investment. A potentially large market like India and China are sure bet for growth prospects. Growth prospects, size of markets, rate of growth of GDP and share in world trade are some of the positive factors attracting foreign investment. But the negative factors are political and economic instability, possible changes in economic policies, bureaucracy, red tape degree of controls, corruption etc. Besides, the degree of inflation and exchange rate depreciation are factors to be considered in deflating the expected cash flows from the new project.

## Use of D.C.F.

The calculation of NPV involves the use of D.C.F. method. This assumes that we know in advance the expected cash flows of project for the life period of the project. It also takes a uniform discount rate for the calculation. In the dynamic world, cash flows change year after year and they will not turn out to be as expected.

Further, the risk expectations might change at anytime with the result that the discount rate used will have to be changed every time these perceptions change.

The project appraisal is generally a static appraisal as at a point of time. The MNCs therefore, revise these projections every time, there are changed perceptions and atleast once in a year. This method of appraisal is problematic for strategic investments as those in R&D, factory automation, a brand name, or a distribution network, which provide multiple effects and cumulative growth prospects which are difficult to measure. Valuing projects with a discretionary follow up requires an expanded NPV rule, with its attendant options.

Where discretion is used, this is dependent on the following factors:

(1) The ability and possibility to defer a project with more time to reconsider the prospects.

(2) Risk of the project and the riskier projects carry a larger return. These are more attractive to MNCs. There is a trade-off between risk and return.

(3) Growth options are likely to be more valuable to the MNCs due to greater prospects of higher return.

(4) The level of interest rates or discount rate used for high risk projects is higher and the higher interest rates raise the value of the firm and attractiveness of the projects will be higher.

(5) Proprietary nature of the firm in the affiliate rather than the joint venture will be more acceptable, as share-options will reduce the returns to the parent company.

For an MNC nothing is more attractive than the perpetuation of their monopoly rights in their subsidiaries and affiliates. They therefore, prefer in any country fully owned subsidiaries. But in some countries like India, in some areas of production like oil drilling infrastructure projects, electricity, the government prefers joint ownership with local partners. This will reduce attractiveness of the projects for the MNCs and they come under second best category for the MNCs. The MNCs thrive on intangible assets and these assets take the form of skills, knowledge, brand names and the like, on which they get monopoly returns.

Capital budgeting exercise of MNCs need an adjusted NPV method, where adjustments are made to both cash flows and the discount rate used for discounting the cash flows. The changes in perceptions of risk, particularly the political risk requires a change in the discount rate.

Tax flows and tax factors like the tax deduction at source, withdrawal tax, tax credits etc., influence the cash flows in a positive or negative manner, depending on the nature of tax laws, and changes in them. The MNCs adjust their flows regularly as and when needed for these factors.

More information and better knowledge of the countries in which they operate will enable them to perceive the risks well ahead and change the foreign investment flows accordingly, uniformly lower discount rate or a higher discount rate is not applied but the rate is changed to suit to the changed political and economic environment in the host countries. Most MNCs take into account all available options — expansion, contraction and exit and they are quick to act on perceived options, which help them to gain most from their worldwide operations.

# Free Cash Flow Method (FCFM)

A study by PriceWaterhouseCoopers Ltd. (PwC) in the U.S.A. revealed that almost 80% of Fund Managers and Analysts rated the FCFM as the best tool for valuation. Since a long time Economic Value Added (EVA) method was popular in India and it was used by even FIIs in India. But the major flaw in EVA is that it misses the time dimension and cannot be used to give future projections.

Brand valuation and human resource valuation are the two other methods that have gained popularity in India in the recent past. Brand valuation figure was arrived at by taking the charge on capital at 5%. But this figure is low as the average inflation rate was about 8% in the 1990s. So some companies like BPL have raised the charge to 10% while arriving at the brand value.

H.R. valuation has gained prominence with a strong growth of the I.T. and software sector. Here the common approach used is the Levin and SWART model. But PWC has recommended the use of replacement cost approach for H.R. valuation.

In a survey conducted by PWC in the UK, Australia and Hong Kong, there emerged a common conclusion, namely, the use of FCFM is a better method than others. So many companies are understood to be shifting to FCFM for enhancing the shareholder's value. PWC being the leader in financial advisory service focuses on valuation as one of the major tools for advicing on mergers, acquisition, cross border investments. PWC offers valuation services in business valuations, valuation of intangibles, manpower valuation and assessment of compensation claims. These valuations are mostly done by FCFM, because of its greater use in future projections.

The uses of valuations range in purpose from shareholder value, analysis for making price projections for new issues, to restructuring, buy-outs, value reporting, dispute analysis and litigation support.

The chart below focuses on the value drivers of FCFM and vindicates its superiority in future projections as well as identify the company's strengths and weaknesses in the creation of shareholder value and opportunities for improvement in cash flow. Now that the corporates in India have been globalising their operations, market competition is forcing them towards, financial restructuring, capital strengthening, mergers, acquisitions and diversification and integration etc. In all these efforts, the valuation for a company assumes all the importance. The method of valuation has also become a critical factor in this process.

**CHART**

**Value Drivers**

The FCFM is based on 7 key value drivers:

- Sales growth
- Operating profit margin
- Cash tax rate
- Working capital
- Fixed assets
- Cost of capital
- Growth duration period

These value drivers are benchmarked against key competitors. This value builder analysis can be used to arrive at future projections as well as identify the company's strengths and weaknesses in the creation of shareholder value and cash flow improvement opportunities.

## Corporate Treasury as a Profit Centre

The basic principle of corporate planning and budgeting is that cost centres only should be separated from cost and profit centres, in the process of planning for optimisation of profits. The cost centres should aim at minimisation of costs while cost and profit centres should aim at maximisation of net profits. In many manufacturing organisations, production and stocking involve only costs. So are the departments of materials purchases, stationery department, R&D and advertising etc., which are all feeding departments involving only costs. Advertising and selling expenses are necessary for marketing of the products or services. R&D falls in a separate category which may appear as cost centre in the short-run but its benefits are long-run increase in profits through reduced costs and improved productivity. The same is the case with HRD and training Departments.

Traditionally the profit centres, in a direct sense are associated with the marketing and finance departments. Marketing involves both cash and credit sales, leading to profits, depending on the margin which is the difference between price and marginal cost of production plus selling cost. The finance department has also a major role in profit maximisation in keeping the financial input costs lower, capital structure as an ideal low cost exercise and in the choice of sources. Similarly cost effectiveness can be achieved in the optimum utilisation or distribution of funds. In principle marginal cost of funds in different uses should be equal and marginal cost should be equal to marginal benefit in each of the individual items of deployment of funds.

The principle of optimisation is to be applied both in the current account and capital account. In the former, the distribution of current assets and their marginal return have to be compared with the distribution of current liabilities and their marginal return. In the current account, cost reduction and profit maximisation is possible through choice of a proper mix of credit and cash sales, credit collection machinery and its costs and benefits. The quality of credit bills and the collection time and costs of collection are the relevant variables. Similarly, in the mixture of liabilities, the maturity pattern and nature of liability and the relative costs and benefits are relevant.

In the capital budgeting decision, the order of priority for investment decision is made on the basis of cost benefit analysis. The tools used are the average return versus average costs, pay back period of investment, discounted pay backs or returns or the internal rate of return or NPA approach. Capital investment decisions can be made on the basis of decision tree approach. In all these cases, the priority of investment and the worthwhileness of investment depends on the cost benefit analysis in some sense or other such as average costs or marginal costs etc.

In the case of trading companies and the finance companies, the approach has to be different from manufacturing companies. Pure trading companies may maximise their profits by keeping optimum margin between the purchase price plus value added and the sale price. The spreads have to be competitive with others in the same line of business whether it is trading company or a manufacturing company. In the present day competitive world, the price at which a product or service is sold is subject to the constraint of what the competitors have set for it. The product may be the same or a similar one and the objective or purpose for which they are intended may be the same.

In the case of finance companies the financial products may be loans, investments, lease, hire-purchase or other types of advances of money for other manufacturing and trading companies. The cost of service is to be covered along with a profit margin in almost all these activities of finance companies. There are degrees of differences, among the finance companies, namely, banks, commercial and co-operative, financial institutions — all India and state level and non-bank finance companies. Almost all these companies are involved in financing and investment activities. In all such cases, their operations involve trading and investment in many instruments in Treasury markets, namely, Money Market, government bonds, corporate bonds and Forex market. The sources and uses of funds reveal a flow statement of cash and funds. The deficits and surpluses in these have to be met and managed in a cost efficient and productive and profitable manner.

As much as banks, corporates can take to treasury operations of investment in government bonds and hold foreign exchange abroad for taking positions for genuine hedge operations, both in the spot and forward markets. These operations are more relevant to exports and MNCs. The strength of these operations can be demonstrated with the episode of September 1995 to February 1996 when the rupee came under pressure and fell from Rs. 31 to Rs. 36 as against dollar. Again following the weakening of the Asian currencies, rupee came under pressure in November-December 1997, when the rupee fell from Rs. 36 to Rs. 40. Banks are the conduit for these operations of corporates, taking up position in the dollars spot and in the forward markets.

The operations in gilt-edged market expanded following the reforms since 1992. Auction sale of new instruments of government securities and market related interest rates offered on the government bonds are only some of the examples of free market in the gilts. Availability of Repos in this market, permitting some primary dealers to operate as wholesalers and commercial banks to spread the retail network are measures, intended to expand the gilted market. FIIs are allowed to operate in the gilted market as much as mutual funds and corporates since 1996. The flexible use of interest rate policy following the activation of bank rate and freeing of banks' interest rates and PLR from RBI controls gave right signals for free markets in India and freedom to operate in these markets within the prudential norms set by banks themselves. The RBI moves in 1997 in the direction of capital account convertibility gave further fillip for free operation of corporates in the Forex market subject to some limits.

In meeting their deficits and surpluses, Treasury operations are involved. With such cash flow and funds flow to manufacturing and exporting units, wherever, management of funds or cash is involved, there is the Treasury operation which is not the same as the art of a Finance Manager, who manages the funds of the company in a least cost combination in sources and maximisation or optimisation process in utilisation of funds.

❖ ❖ ❖

# INTERNATIONAL CAPITAL FLOWS

# 36

## Introduction

One of the important methods of financing trade is through aid and credits. Larger trade is possible through larger aid and it is in this context that a study of the mechanics of capital flow is relevant in international finance. Foreign resources are, however, not an unmixed blessing as some costs are involved such as amortisation, interest payments, political and economic interference of donors, etc. But economic development of any country depends on the rate of investment and pattern of allocation of funds. The rate of investment depends on the available domestic savings and foreign resources. The latter in turn depends on the foreign aid, loans, grants and other forms of assistance, including technical collaboration and assistance. In the initial stages of development, domestic incomes and savings would be low and hence the reliance on foreign assistance. Historically, even the USA and Soviet Russia and a host of other countries have depended upon foreign capital for economic development of their countries at one stage or the other. In the modern industrialised world, flow of technology as between countries may partly depend upon the flow of foreign aid and foreign private investment.

The importance of foreign aid is emphasised in connection with easing of foreign exchange constraint in a country with sluggish export growth and exiguous state of foreign exchange resources.

Firstly, foreign aid fills in the savings gap (investment minus savings at home);

Secondly, it releases the foreign exchange constraint in the sense of making available input without having to pay for it immediately in foreign exchange. In more recent years when the domestic investment rate was as high as 26-28 per cent and the domestic savings rate was lower than that, we had to depend upon foreign savings, and the contribution of the foreign sector to the domestic economy cannot be over-emphasised in this context. Compared to eighties and seventies the investment rate was higher in the nineties. But the savings rate was not rising at the same rate in the domestic economy. The reliance on foreign resources was felt necessary.

## Theory of Foreign Capital Flow

The general theory of capital movement applies to autonomous private capital flows but not to the flow of foreign aid which are induced flows and it is particularly true in the case of developing countries. According to the traditional theory, private capital of a long-term nature moves across borders to take advantage of differences in yield and diversification and opportunities for investment. The latter would depend upon differences in factor endowments and in factor proportions employed in the various productive process in different countries. Thus, capital from capital-rich countries would flow to the capital-poor countries where the return is high, and where there are investment opportunities. The pattern of flows under foreign aid does not depend upon the pure economic factors nor on pure commercial considerations as referred to above, but more on politico-economic factors.

There are various theories on the subject of aid for development, such as Balanced Growth Theories (Nurkse and Lewis); Unbalanced Growth Theories (of Hirschman and Streeten) or Dualistic Theories (of Higgins, Ranis, Fey etc.) or Bottleneck Theories (of Wickesell and Singer) or Two-gap Theories or Single-gap Theories (of H.B. Chenery, Strout, etc.)[1]

The effect of aid on the foreign exchange market is to increase the supply and ease the pressures of demand, to facilitate the transfer mechanism in the currency markets and to obviate the need for frequent changes in the exchange rates, pending the process of structural adjustment in the domestic economy. The inflow of foreign funds would, however, increase the money supply which may not lead to inflationary pressures so long as funds are efficiently and productively used in the development process.

The effect of aid on the economic development can be explained through a macro production function which includes imports, exports and/or foreign investment as a function of development or *vice versa*. The contribution of foreign sector is felt in the product market — input and output markets through expenditure on products at home and abroad. It is also felt in the factor market by the "augmentation effect" on domestic resources, the "bottleneck-relieving effect" so far as the foreign exchange constraint is concerned and the "acceleration effect" through the interdependence of the factors in the

*Sources:*

1. Vide, V.A. Avadhani, *Imports and Capital Formation in Under-developed Countries,* Sudhir Publications, 1978.

factor markets.[2] Thus, the availability of foreign resources for the purpose of investment would accelerate growth by helping the co-operating factors at home to be fully deployed and by accelerating the rate of investment. This would enable the necessary technical innovation and accelerate the entrepreneurial function. Imports and foreign resources augment domestic economic growth theoretically by a multiplier process through any of the effects referred to above. The mechanism may work either through input markets or output markets or through interactions of all the product markets and factor markets. The basic postulate is that foreign resources fill in the gaps, make available non-available and complementary resources and augment the investment process.

## Aid Requirements

The amount of aid required is estimated either by the savings gap approach or by the foreign exchange gap approach. Under the former, given the warranted investment and the domestic savings rate, foreign resources required are derived by deducting one from the other. The foreign exchange gap, namely, the difference between exports and imports, is also used for assessing the foreign resources needed for development. A third approach is spill-over gap to be filled in as it arises due to inflation, time-lags and faulty estimations. The actual amount of foreign funds required would depend upon a host of politico-economic factors. The important economic factors available are domestic savings, targeted rate of investment and incomes, incremental capital-output ratio and the estimated gap in resources.

The criteria for granting aid by the donor countries are the available exports surplus of those countries, domestic savings, investment rates, their national incomes and their own requirements at home. The donor countries have firstly the problem of transfer of resources in the foreign exchange market as large scale transfer of resources involves the movement of the exchange rate against them.

Secondly, such aid flows would also affect the domestic money supply both in the donor country and the donee country. The outflow of funds from India would reduce the money supply while the reverse holds good for the inflow of funds. Such inflows and outflows effect the expenditures at home and outputs and incomes of the people. They also produce redistribution effects, shifting incomes from one sector to another with different average and marginal propensities to consume and save.

## Criteria Governing Aid

The donor countries not only look into their own capacity to grant aid but at the recipient country's capacity to absorb aid. The latter is judged by the efficiency and productivity in the resource allocation in the pattern of planning and investment and in priorities of allocation, the methods of raising resources and the overall performance of the economy. The other criterion is to judge on the basis of needs of the recipient country which are examined in relation to the relative population, average standard of living, natural resource endowments, planning efforts, etc. The self-efforts of the country at raising domestic savings and investment, long-term prospects of growth of output and of

2. *Ibid.*

exports and repayment capacity of the recipient country, its allocative efficiency etc., are also looked into.

There are certain adverse effects as well as beneficial effects of transfer of funds through aid. The beneficial effects arise out of increased foreign investment, increased output incomes and employment etc. These effects are experienced in varying degrees both by the donor and donee countries. With a view to increase the effectiveness of aid, the donor countries insist on a correct measurement of the absorption capacity of the donee country. The absorption capacities are measured in various ways, including the level of productivity, the marginal and average propensities to save and capital-output ratios in the recipient country, import substitution and export promotion policies adopted at home and the planned and actual marginal investment ratios.

The criteria for donor countries to give aid are their level of *per capita* income, availability of domestic savings and balance of payments surpluses. The donor country should have a comfortable resource position in the domestic capital market and an easy foreign exchange reserves position without heavy balance of payments pressures.

India's economic development had relied heavily on foreign assistance in the initial stages. During the successive Five-Year Plans, the proportion of external assistance to total finance of the plans increased up to 1969-70 and reached a maximum of about 36 per cent in the annual plan periods (1966-67 to 1968-69). It was only about 10 per cent in the First Plan, 24 per cent in the Second Plan and 29 per cent in the Third Plan. After 1969-70, the reliance on external aid declined as part of the government's deliberate strategy of reducing our reliance on foreign sources. In the subsequent two Five-Year Plans of 1969-74 and 1975-80, the proportion of foreign assistance to total plan outlay was brought down to 13 per cent and 10 per cent respectively. In fact, during the Fifth Plan period of 1975-80, amortization and interest payments on foreign debt worked out to about 50 per cent to 60 per cent of the gross aid during that period. The importance of net foreign aid in the planning process has declined thereafter. During the Sixth and Seventh Plan periods (1980 to 1990), the proportion of foreign aid to total plan outlay would be not more than 8 per cent to 10 per cent. During eighties, aid flows from bilateral and multilateral sources financed up to 35% of current account deficit. But during nineties net inflow of external aid was declining. There was a large stock of unused aid with India; the composition of resource inflow changed into more private trade credits and commercial borrowing abroad, due to drying up of aids during nineties and later on. Aid has become negative due to larger repayment than inflows of aid in recent years.

## Types of Aid

Various types of aid were granted to India, depending upon their nature and purpose. Two major types of aid are tied and untied. Tied aid is that which is linked to a country or project for specific use in the project and the country mentioned therein and untied aid is one that is not tied to any project, programme or country. Untied aid constitutes about one-third of the total in the case of India. Tied aid works out to be a major component of foreign aid granted. The tying may be to a project specified in India or to a specific programme of the Government of India or to a currency or country for import of the corresponding goods and services mostly from the donor country.

There can be single or double tying of aid. Single tying relates to tying only once to a project or programme or currency of a country. If tying is to both currency and project, it is called double tying.

Another broad classification of aid may be military aid and economic aid. Military aid is given by a friendly country for strengthening the political ties with the recipient and is not solely based on economic or commercial considerations. Thus, the US aid to NATO countries and to Pakistan is based on military considerations. Economic aid for development by the developed countries is also partly based on political affinities with the recipient country. Such aid can be bilateral or multilateral. While bilateral aid is from one government to the other, multilateral aid is through international financial institutions for use in the import of goods and services from any country.

In the case of India, bilateral aid constitutes the bulk of the total aid. The aid utilisation depends upon the type of tying, the form and nature of the aid. Tied aid and bilateral aid are usable only for specific purposes or projects and in specified countries. This would lead to a lower rate of utilisation of such aid. On the other hand, multilateral aid is usable anywhere and hence its rate of utilisation will be high. In India, the degree of utilisation of foreign assistance is about 75-80 per cent of the total aid which is mainly due to the big component of bilateral assistance in it. Major donor countries are the USA, France, West Germany, USSR and the UK, Japan in the bilateral group. The international institutions which provide multilateral assistance to India are IMF, IBRD and IDA. More recently, assistance from petroleum-producing countries in West Asia had increased. The multilateral assistance from institutions worked out to about 30% of the total external debt of the Government of India, as reflected in the composition of external debt, as at end March 2004. External debt as percentage of GDP stood at 21.2% in US dollars as of end 2013.

## Forms of Aid

Among the various forms of aid, loans account for the bulk of it, namely, 80-90 per cent and the rest is accounted for by grants. Until 1970-71 commodity assistance in the form of PL 480 and PL 665 Aid (laws of USA for disposal of excess foodgrains) used to figure as aid to India and constituted about 20-25 per cent of the total aid. Part of the PL 480/665 assistance was repayable in rupees and part in convertible currencies. In the seventies India had not relied on any aid for foodgrains but had built a sizable buffer stock of foodgrains at home by itself. Until the Third Five Year Plan (1965-66), loans accounted for 60-65 per cent, grants for 5-10 per cent and commodity assistance for 25-35 per cent. At present about 80-85 per cent of the total aid to India is on loan basis and 15-20 per cent in grants. Some of the loans are from the international bodies on a multilateral basis. Assistance from the IDA and ADB is on soft terms, namely, at lower rates of interest and on long repayment schedules, which is ideally suited to economic growth for a poor country with low *per capita* incomes like India. Aid tantamounts to capital flows across countries mostly for balance of payments and investment in the recipient country.

## Desirable Pattern of Flows

Aid and trade are linked together and trade is better than aid for allocation of resources and their productive use at home. If aid facilitates the larger flow of trade, particularly on a multilateral basis, it is desirable to depend on aid. For the purpose of development long-term aid on soft terms and in particular untied aid would be most beneficial for the receiving country. Internationalisation and institutionalisation of aid are desirable for the benefit of the receiving countries so that donor countries do not feel the political hegemony over the recipient. As such, UNCTAD was advocating institutionalisation of aid, increasing aid flows up to at least 1 per cent of GNP of developed countries and aid on softer terms. More recently such aid has dried up due to increasing domestic economic problems of donor countries. Besides, as trade is better than aid, the long-term strategy of growth of the aid recipient country should be such that aid utilisation is effective, and productivity and output are increased so that the country can grow on its own momentum without foreign aid after a time. It should be possible for the country to service foreign debt (for amortization and interest payments) through their normal export performance annually. For this purpose, trade has to expand more than aid after a point by which servicing of foreign debt could be facilitated. The long-run interests of a country would, therefore, be in greater exports and imports and growth of the economy and not in continued dependence of foreign aid.

Aid channelled through a third country is called indirect aid. Thus, USA might provide India with technical and financial assistance with a condition that India should pass it on to Nepal. Third country currency assistance is also passed on if the loan is through the currency of a third country who is neither the donor nor the recipient, and such aid would benefit the third country also by easing the pressures on its foreign exchange as the loan is utilised in that third currency and country.

## Advantages and Disadvantages of Aid

Aid is not an unmixed blessing. It has both advantages and disadvantages and the extent of reliance on aid is to be decided by each country on its own merits. Advantages of aid in general are many, if used productively and efficiently by the recipient country.

Firstly, it would provide larger imports than possible by exports or country's foreign exchange reserves.

Secondly, import of essential consumption requirements can be met by aid and this would promote domestic consumption and inflationary pressures are kept under control.

Thirdly, by facilitating the import of capital goods for investment, growth in the economy is accelerated. By proper planning and investment, debt burden can be kept under control and enough export potential can be generated to service the debt burden. Aid also facilitates fuller utilisation of capacity, through imports of spare parts, raw materials etc. If, on the other hand, aid is frittered away in ostentatious consumption or unproductive enterprises, then the burden becomes heavy. Similarly, if aid is tied, the project costs would be higher as supplies cannot be got from the cheapest markets and the recipient country would lose. The same is true if aid is on a bilateral basis when the alternative avenues of supplies of goods or services are cheaper and the recipient country has to pay a higher price for the goods imported and for the services rendered from abroad with the result that the debt burden becomes heavier.

The type of aid and terms of aid are, therefore, crucial variables for determining the debt burden and the advantages and disadvantages of aid. Debt servicing becomes a burden if aid is tied or the terms of aid are onerous. Aid is no doubt a necessary but not a sufficient condition for growth. Doubts are cast on whether foreign funds would really supplement domestic savings rather than supplant. Foreign funds might not always lead to investment and growth if used for balance of payments purposes, delaying the process of adjustments in the economy. It is important, therefore, that aid is phased out and is productively used so that after a period of time, dependence on aid is reduced and debt servicing would not be a burden.

During the last few years, repayment of principal and interest exceeded the gross external aid with the result that there is net outflow on this account, in India.

## Debt Burden of Government

The outstanding external debt of the Government of India was around $ 230 billion, as on March 31, 2009 and $ 390 billion in 2013. The servicing of such debt involves two burdens — money burden and real burden. (1) Money burden is in finding the resources for payment of interest and repayment of loan instalments and (2) Real burden involves the transfer of such resources abroad involving the foreign exchange loss or outflow from the country. Real burden is the loss of physical resources, on top of the transfer burden leading to adverse movements in its foreign exchange rates. As per World Bank Debt Tables, India's foreign debt is mostly of long-term nature from private non-guaranteed sources. Debt stock GDP ratio was 21.2% and Debt service ratio was 5.9% in 2013 (for total external debt). Short-term debt as percentage of our reserves stood at only 18% in March 2009. Our reserves cover up to 15 months of imports into India. These factors show that our foreign debt burden is not heavy.

## Foreign Investment in India

An adjunct to aid is the private foreign investment and foreign participation in domestic ventures. Foreign investment in India takes the form of (i) Direct investment of capital in India by branches of foreign companies or subsidiaries of foreign companies, or (ii) Creditor capital, or (iii) Portfolio equity holdings by non-residents. All these three forms can be found in official as well as in private account in India. But foreign investment on official account constitutes the bulk of our net foreign liabilities. Besides, such investment was mostly in long-term loans from foreign governments. There is also direct investment by branches of foreign companies of foreign-controlled rupee companies or creditor capital (supplier's credit or trade credit). Private foreign investment in India took mostly the form of suppliers' credit to commercial and industrial enterprises and long-term loans or credit. The data on foreign assets and liabilities of India are published from time to time by the RBI in its bulletins.[3]

3. "International Banking Statistics in India", *RBI Bulletins*.

The private foreign investment policy of the Government of India was to encourage foreign capital inflow and foreign technical know-how into areas clearly demarcated for them as desirable. Where the country has adequate technological know-how, foreign investment is discouraged. No foreign investment is permitted in strategic industries like ammunition, atomic energy, defence items, etc. In areas of key industries such as chemicals, fertilisers, cement, paper and pulp where there is scope for foreign investment and technological know-how, foreign investment is permitted for the purpose of encouraging import substitution. More recently, foreign investment by oil-producing countries has been encouraged to flow into India, provided such investment does not exceed 49-51 per cent of equity of the Indian venture and takes the form of loans and equity participation for foreign collaboration. This norm is relaxed in the case of 100 per cent exporting units. The industries which are export-oriented such as hotels, hospitals, etc., are the permitted avenues of investments for the oil-producing countries. The government has also given consent where necessary for foreign technical collaboration with Indian industry and for investment by non-residents in Indian enterprises, upto some limits. Purpose-wise and agency-wise or country-wise external assistance provided by foreign countries to India is published yearly by the RBI. FII inflows/outflows are also published regularly by the RBI.

Foreign investment in India is also encouraged as a vehicle of transfer of technology not indigenously available or to promote export-oriented production in India. Investment in India by developed countries is encouraged: (1) In the form of portfolio investment, (a) In the export-oriented units, (b) In priority areas of cement, fertilisers, petroleum product, paper etc., (2) Investment in hotels and hospitals etc., and (3) Investment in portfolio form in some other activities.

## Latest Foreign Investment Policy

Foreign investment in India is encouraged by many methods:

1. Through NRE accounts and FCNR accounts, which bring in deposits in NRI foreign currencies or external rupees for use by banks in India.
2. Direct investment and portfolio investment by NRIs in the shares and securities of Indian companies.
3. Investment by foreign institutions — FFIs, FIIs and OCBs is permitted up to 51% of equity of Indian companies.

Under the liberalisation policy of July 1991 and thereafter automatic approvals are granted for foreign investment in high priority industries up to 51% useful for import of capital goods or for foreign technology agreements. Trading houses engaged in export business are also allowed foreign investment up to 51% of equity. Even existing companies whose foreign holding is less than 51% are permitted to issue fresh equity if foreign holding is less than 51% and permitted to issue fresh equity to foreign companies/nationals. Procedures for granting permit by the RBI and by the Secretariat for Industrial Approvals and by Foreign Investment Promotion Board (FIPB) have been streamlined and simplified. Foreign Investment Promotion Council (FIPC) was also set up in 1977 to help promotion of foreign investment into India.

Since 1992, these measures were further liberalised. The earlier stipulation that dividend payments outflow by companies with 51% equity must be balanced by export earnings over a period of seven years was dispensed with. FFIs are permitted by the SEBI to invest and operate in the Indian capital and stock market. The holding by any FFI in any single company is subject to a ceiling of 5% and all FFIs together in any single company can hold up to 24% of equity later raised to 30% or 40%. Foreign banks and foreign security firms are now allowed to operate in India subject to necessary approvals. The investment by NRIs and OCBs is permitted up to even 100% in the new issues of capital or in convertible debentures of private or public limited company in the specified priority sector industries.

There will be no lock-in period for any of these investments except those which have been allotted on a firm basis under the preferential quotas to FFIs. The NRIs have been granted repatriation facility as well. The FFIs investing under the 24% quota are given the benefit of a flat rate of tax of 20% on dividend and interest income and 10% on long-term capital gains, before taking out the funds. NRI investment in sick companies and in 100% EOUs will continue to be allowed to which was added the investment of 100% in power generation in 1992.

The FERA was diluted by removing the Sections 26 (7) 28, 29 and 31 whereby FERA companies are put on par with the Indian companies. They can undertake any activity in India and acquire and dispose of property etc. They are allowed to use their trademarks in India. The FERA is replaced by FEMA, reducing the control aspect in 1999.

The investment and disinvestment under portfolio investment were made easy and automatic if they are put through the stock exchanges in India. To keep pace with technological revolution in computers, an Electronic Hardware Technology Park was set up for foreigners to have 100% equity participation, duty free import of capital goods and a tax holiday for 5 years.

NRIs are allowed to invest in any venture, firm, company or partnership up to 100% on non-repatriation basis without prior approval of the RBI. Liberalisation was also seen in the RBI exchange controls on the ADs. They are permitted to borrow abroad upto limits and release foreign exchange for remittance of dividends, interest etc., to NRIs/OCBs and for Indian nationals going abroad for medical purposes or education, travel etc. Foreign investment is made through stock and capital markets. Foreign Direct Investment (FDI) is now defined to include equity capital of unincorporated enterprises, reinvested earnings of foreign companies, intercorporate debt transactions between entities, in addition to equity capital investment in related entities. FDI inflow in 2002-03 was lower than in the preceding year ($ 4660 million as against $ 6131 million in 2001-02 (see Table on next page). There was also an outflow in the form of Indian investment abroad of $ 1049 million in 2002-03, as against $ 1390 million in 2001-02.

The table gives an idea of the impact of new policy on foreign investment inflows since 1991, following economic reforms.

**TABLE 36.1**

**Foreign Investment Inflows**

*(U.S. dollar in millions)*

| *Item* | 2010-11 | 2011-12 | 2012-13 |
|---|---|---|---|
| Direct Investment | 11834 | 22089 | 19819 |
| Portfolio Investment | 30393 | 17170 | 26891 |
| Total Inflows: | 42227 | 39259 | 46710 |
| of which GDRs | 3238 | 11928 | 14839 |

*Source:* Annual Reports RBI.

## NRI Schemes

From time to time, the rates of interest and the terms of acceptance, maturity periods, etc. of NRI deposits are amended to suit to the changing international money market conditions. After the launching of economic reforms, many FERA conditions have been diluted. In May 1993, FCNR scheme was amended to give more freedom to banks to borrow under the scheme. Under the FCNR (BANKS) Scheme, banks can borrow through deposits of "6 months and above but less than 1 year." The regular FCNR scheme will continue to operate for deposits of one year but less than 3 years", and "3 years and above." The depositor under the scheme continues to have exchange cover in the sense that he can take back the funds in the currency and the rate at which he has deposited. This cover was given up by the RBI later on. The interest rates were brought down to around LIBOR in international markets.

## Foreign Currency (Non-resident) Accounts (Banks) Scheme

This new scheme was introduced in April 1993. As in the existing scheme, repatriation of funds will be freely permitted under the new scheme. The exchange risk cover will be provided by the banks and not by the RBI. However, the banks are now freed from the regulations of CRR and SLR requirements and from controls on the rates and quantum of lending. The other terms and conditions including the deposit rates will be identical with the existing FCNR scheme. The present NRI deposit schemes are FCNR (B), NR (E) RA, and NR (NR) RD. These are discussed in the next chapter also.

## International Investment Position

The RBI has been presenting the data on foreign assets and liabilities of India, based on surveys. In 1997, the IMF prescribed the proforma for compiling the IIP to be comparable among nations. The IIP presents the stocks of external sectors assets and liabilities, under the broad heads of Direct Investments, Portfolio Investments, other investments, including reinvestment of reserves of foreign companies and reserve assets. Some important categories included in the present presentation of data are as follows:

(1) Loans by Direct Investors to Direct Investment Enterprises.

(2) Buyers' credit.

(3) Investments of non-resident governments and international institutions.

(4) Reinvestable reserves portfolio of foreign companies.

## Indian Aid to Other Countries

India also extends assistance to other countries in the form of loans and grants. The loans are in the form of suppliers' credit or trade credits mostly of a long-term nature. These loans and grants are mostly to neighbouring countries like Nepal, Bhutan, Sri Lanka, Bangladesh etc.

More recently, Indian private investment abroad is permitted by the government either in the form of technical and consultancy project exports, construction projects or turnkey projects. Indian ventures abroad are of three categories:

*(i)* Direct investment by Indian companies or suppliers' credit by Indian exporters;

*(ii)* Joint ventures along with some developed countries in a developing country or even in a developed country; and

*(iii)* Consultancy and project exports.

## Joint Ventures

Joint ventures are joint collaborations in the field of manufacturing, processing and marketing by two or more countries. A joint enterprise can be brought about by an agreement at joint ownership, control and management of a venture located at home or abroad between a local firm and a foreign firm. Such contracts involve also a common licence, or sharing of a trade patent or manufacturing formula or management contract.

In the case of India, such joint ventures by foreign companies are obliged by government policy to share with Indian equity a proportion of ownership capital extending from 25 per cent to 75 per cent depending on the nature of the manufacturing activity and its importance to the Indian economy. Even without joint venture, foreign individuals, firms and companies (of Indian origin) are now permitted to invest in Indian companies. This was designed to encourage private foreign capital inflow into India. NRIs can now invest up to even 100% in Indian ventures on a non-repatriation basis.

Indian joint ventures may also result in our investment in foreign countries. Such investment may take the form of equity participation in share capital, sharing of technical and managerial expertise, setting up of a turnkey project or export of capital goods, plant and machinery. Indian joint ventures extend to both developed and developing countries and investment in a third country also.

## Government Policy Guidelines

For Indian entrepreneurs to enter into joint ventures abroad, they require the prior approval of the Indian government. There is an Inter-ministerial Committee on Joint Ventures abroad. The Committee comprises the representatives of Ministries of Commerce, External Affairs, Finance, Industry, DGTD and the Department of Company Affairs.

Applications have to be made in a prescribed form for the purpose under Section 27 of the FERA and Section 372 of the Companies Act, to the Ministry of Commerce which provides secretarial assistance to the inter-ministerial Committee. This committee is guided by certain norms, referred to below:

(1) Exchange Control and other governmental rules of the host country should be complied with.

(2) Indian participation in the venture should be in the form of export of know-how, consultancy, plant, machinery and capital goods.

(3) Granting of rupee loans by Indian participating companies and raising of foreign exchange loans abroad are permitted.

(4) Generally, cash flows for equity participation are not permitted, except in special cases.

(5) Necessary project reports, cash flow and profitability projections should be submitted to prove the technical and financial viability of the project undertaken by the joint venture.

(6) RBI clearance of foreign exchange release would then follow depending on the terms on which the project is cleared by the government.

The plant, machinery and other goods exported under the above scheme would be entitled to all export incentives which are currently available to exporters. These exports are permitted on deferred payment basis or under loans, or lines of credit. Inward receipts for service fees, royalties, consultancy etc., are to be as per the Exchange Control guidelines or capitalisation if that is permitted by the terms of government approval.

Indian investment centres abroad help the prospective entrepreneurs in formulating such schemes of joint venture or other forms of foreign investment. They help to locate foreign participants, disseminate market intelligence and act as intermediaries between Indian entrepreneurs and foreign participants.

But it is understood from the studies conducted by the Indian Investment Centres abroad that many approved projects could not be fructified. Some of them were abandoned before the projects were launched due to late realisation of the difficulties and non-viability of the project or due to inadequate financial support. A few were also given up after launching due to differences with collaborators, objections from the host country or non-fulfilment of agreed conditions by the foreign collaborators. It would thus, appear that the mortality rate of the Indian ventures abroad is rather high.

India became a member of Multilateral Investment Guarantee Agency, set up in 1988. It provides investment assurance and advisory services for foreign private investment. This helps the investment flows into India without politico-economic risks.

## Nature of International Flows of Capital

Capital Account of Balance of payments of any country comprises of capital flows in and out of the country on account of government sector, private corporate sector and banking sector. Some of these flows are for genuine trade and current account flows for transactions purposes and for hedge purposes. But there are speculative flows to take advantage of interest rate differentials and exchange rate changes expected. As it is difficult to distinguish capital for transactions purposes and speculation purposes, they are all clubbed together. Some capital flows are for investment and some for working capital purposes. They are generally, identified under heads of Direct and Portfolio Investment, into equity and debt, short-term trade credits for working capital of corporate sector and banking capital which includes, in the case of India NRI, deposits as well, in addition to capital flows for long-term purposes such as project finance.

In the case of MNCs, the sources of finance is discussed in a separate chapter. The international capital flows include inter-company transfers of funds among subsidiaries or affiliates both in the form of equity and debt. Banking funds include those for working capital, trade credits and loans from banks abroad in the currency markets to banks in the home country and its corporates. External Commercial Borrowings (ECB), include foreign currency convertible bonds, ADRs, GDRs, floating rate and fixed rate bonds, etc. Government flows of capital include the government to government loans, external assistance and loans from international agencies, like IBRD, IFC, ADB etc.

## Banking Sector

In India, there are 93 banks authorised to deal in foreign currency and foreign exchange. These reported more liabilities than assets. The liabilities include FCNR deposits, NRE accounts, inter-bank borrowings, bonds, floating rate notes, FII's accounts, NRNR deposits, NRO rupee deposits and non-resident special rupee accounts, exchange earners foreign currency accounts (EEFC), rupee liabilities to non-residents foreign currency liabilities to branches abroad, residents and non-residents abroad.

International assets of banks include the following items, among others: Foreign currency loans to residents and non-residents, outstanding export bills, foreign currency lending and deposits with banks in India and abroad, overseas foreign currency assets, remittable profits of foreign branches of Indian banks, assets in Indian rupees with non-residents or loans to non-residents in Indian Rupees, etc.

The above foreign assets and liabilities of Indian banks are reported by RBI, in their Monthly Bulletins.

**Table 36.2**

**International Banking Statistics**

*(Amount outstanding)*

| | *Amount Outstanding as at end Dec. 2003* | *(as at end of 2009) (Rs. Crores)* |
|---|---|---|
| International Assets of Indian Banks (of both Indian and Foreign Origin) | Rs. 108,112 crores | 2,29,356 |
| International Liabilities of Indian Banks | Rs. 210,283 crores | 3,86,608 |

*Source:* RBI Bulletin, Nov. 2009

The above data are presented to give illustration of banking flows of funds, internationally.

Yet over the last few years, There was a net inflows due to as increase in foreign loans which include partly the loans on non-government account also.

## Government Sector

Similarly, the flow of funds on government account can be presented in a similar form to understand the magnitude of funds involved. The Table below gives an example for the selected year of the flows under the head of external assistance.

**TABLE 36.3**

**External Assistance (*2002-03, 2008-09)***

*(Rs. in Crores)*

| | *2002-03* | | | |
|---|---|---|---|---|
| | *Inflows* | *Outflows* | *2008-09* | *2013-14* |
| Loans | 13,448 | — | 23,687 | 317.72 |
| Grants | 1,715 | — | 2,786 | 34.11 |
| Repayments | — | 24,290 | 11,067 | 262.05 |
| Interest payments | — | 4,534 | 4,829 | — |
| | 15,163 | 28,824 | 10,577 | 8978 |

It will be seen from the above Table that there is a net outflow of funds on government account, as outflows are more than inflows. But this is due to our high level of foreign exchange reserve leading to prepayments of many foreign loans by the government of India Yet over the last over few years, there was a net inflows due to an increase in foreign loans, which include partly the loans on non-government account also. In the case of banking data, referred to above, there is a net inflow of funds, as the liabilities are more than assets in respect of banking sector.

## Corporate Sector

In the case of corporate sector also there is a net outflow on account of commercial borrowings as can be seen from the following Table on the composition of capital flows in respect of India for the year 2003-04. Net capital inflows in India showed a steadily rising trend since the economic reforms were started in India in 1992. These inflows rose from U.S. $ 3,876 million in 1992-93 to U.S. $ 16,736 million in 2003-04 U.S. $ 107,993 million in 2007-08. The breakdown of these flows are shown in the following Table for illustration:

**TABLE 36.4**

**Composition of Capital Flows**

| *(in Percentage to Total)* | *2003-04* | *2007-08* | *2012-13* |
|---|---|---|---|
| 1. Non-debt Creating Inflows | 72.5 | 58.29 | |
| (a) Direct Investment | 21.1 | 31.7 | 19,819 |
| (b) Portfolio Investment | 51.4 | 27.2 | 26,891 |
| 2. Debt Creating Inflows | 1.4 | 38.9 | |
| (a) External Assistance | –12.0 | 1.9 | 4,734 |

| | | | |
|---|---|---|---|
| (b) External Commercial Borrowings (ECB) | –8.4 | 21.02 | 27,270 |
| (c) Short-Term Credits | 7.1 | 15.9 | 21,685 |
| (d) NRI Deposits | 16.4 | 0.2 | 14,842 |
| (e) Rupee Debt Services | –1.7 | –0.1 | –1.8 |
| 3. Other Capital (including Banking Capital) | 26.1 | 2.2 | 16,571 |

*Source:* RBI: Annual Reports.

Minus sign in the above Table indicates outflow and the rest are inflows. Debt creating flows are mostly negative as Indian corporates and government are repaying debt of high cost nature in preference to direct and portfolio investment in India. This is as per the government policy guidelines. The only positive debt items are short-term credits for working capital of corporates and NRI deposits. The RBI has been discouraging these inflows of NRI deposits by lowering the interest rates payable on them and encouraging banks to lend to NRI and other non residents out of these NRI deposits. The obvious conclusion from the above discussion is that the agencies for international flows from the domestic economy are government, banks and corporates and that most of these inflows are in the nature of non-debt creating inflows of direct and portfolio investments.

## World Trends

These trends in international output flows into India are in tune with those of world trends on net capital flows into Emerging Market economies. Only private direct investments and portfolio investments indicate positive inflows, while other private capital flows of banking nature and on government account present picture of net outflows. Debt capital flow is declining, while those of equity nature are rising. This trend is mostly attributed to the MNC activities in Emerging Market economies, which are showing growing importance globally and imperatives of the domestic economic and political conditions.

The Table below presents the data on the Net Capital inflow into Emerging Market economies for the year 2004 for illustration

**TABLE 36.5**

**World Net Capital Inflows**

*in U.S. $ billion*

| | *2004* | *2009* |
|---|---|---|
| I. Net Private Capital flows | 196.6 | – 190.3 |
| (a) Net private direct investment | 186.4 | 312.8 |
| (b) Net private portfolio investment | 28.8 | – 234.5 |
| (c) Net other private capital flows (mostly of debt nature) | – 18.6 | – 268.5 |
| II. Net Official flows | – 58.6 | |

*Source:* IMF World Economic Outlook, 2009.

## Agencies Involved

MNCs are the most important agency for international capital flows in more recent years. Apart from MNCs, the international banks and domestic banks operating in the international markets are responsible for international capital flows, particularly to developing countries, like India. There are of course, traditional agencies of importance for international capital flows, namely, the multinational agencies and regional agencies for flow of finance for reconstruction and development as for example IMF, IBRD, IFC, ADB, etc. Some governments like those of U.S., Germany and Japan are also lending on a bilateral basis.

Among the agencies involved in international capital flows, MNCs account for direct investment and Foreign Institutional Investors (FIIs) and Foreign Financial Institutions account for portfolio investment in equity and debt. Reference was already made to the role of banking sector and government in the international currency markets and capital markets. In India, FIIs play an important role in the stock and capital markets. As per the SEBI data, net investment by FIIs were influenced by global factors such as interest rate changes and inflationary expectations as also by the expected domestic corporate growth and economic fundamentals. But, it was found that the stock market trends were perceptibly influenced by inflow and outflow of funds by FIIs, both in terms of prices of stock and volume of trading as also the volatility of the market.

The role of banks and FIIs as the intermediaries in the flow of funds across borders is a well-known fact to need any special discussion. But the basic players are the corporates, both domestic and foreign and governments to some extent. But in India, governments are not a dominating force to reckon with, due to its comfortable liquidity conditions in the domestic economy and external conditions, as reflected in huge external current account surpluses, surfeict of Forex reserves and comfortable balance of payments position. In fact, India is a creditor country with the IMF and has been repaying its high cost of external debt for the last few years.

The role of international and regional banks in the international flows of capital is discussed later separately. Here, mention maybe made of the role of the MNCs, in India, in particular. With the trend to globalisation of markets, MNCs have become an important force to reckon with. Their operations have both merits and demerits. Among merits, mention may be made of the favourable impact of their entry into the country in the form of increasing efficiency and productivity, growth in output, income and employment in the nation. They bring in scarce resources of capital, technology and enterprise and make better use of our plentiful resources of labour expertise, management talent and natural resources as inputs. Business Process Outside (BPO) is being increased in India by U.S. and U.K. and international mobility of factors has increased.

## Capital Flows and Growth

Over the last decade, official financing for development of developing countries has come down, as can be seen from the Table on the next page. The role of bilateral assistance has become negative, while that of multilateral assistance has come down. In this context, the private capital flows through global corporates, FIIs and FFIs have become critical and filled up the gap. India has become a creditor country with the IMF and has prepaid costly external debt. Net inflows into India declined sharply, particularly in the second half of 90s and early 21st century and reliance was placed on commercial borrowings and non-resident deposits.

**TABLE 36.6**

**Net Official Flows to Developing Countries**

*(US $ billion)*

| | *1995* | *2002* |
|---|---|---|
| 1. World Bank Group (IBRD and IDA) | 6.3 | 1.5 |
| 2. Major Regional Development Banks | 5.1 | 1.9 |
| 3. IMF | 16.8 | 14.5 |
| 4. Total Multilateral Flows | 28.2 | 21.3 |
| 5. Total Bilateral Flows | 10.5 | –5.1 |

(Total multilateral flows include "others", not included here. Regional Development Banks include Inter American Development Bank, Asian Development Bank, European Bank and, Reconstruction and Development and African Development Bank)

*Source:* Global Development Finance, World Bank, 2003 and Report on Currency and Finance 2002-03, RBI.

The capital flows have been historically associated with growth of developing countries. Many developed nations have depended on foreign capital for their growth. These capital flows took the form of grants, loans and other forms of assistance in kind or finance. Assistance in kind took the form of export of commodities like wheat as in the case of U.S. aid to India in sixties under PL 480. External aid played a significant role in India's planned investment until 1980s. External assistance has a concessional element, even if it is in the form of loans. In the eighties and nineties, the annual external assistance has come down drastically.

The amount of concessional financing has come down to all developing countries from U.S. $ 5.5 billion in 1995 to U.S. $ 1.8 billion in 2002. The lower flow of official aid was attributed to structural changes in global capital flows, lack of matching resources and lower absorption in the receiving countries. Due to high debt servicing the outflow was more than the inflow during the recent years in the case of India.

Thus the amount of capital flows depended on a number of factors like pace and level of utilisation, stage of growth and debt servicing capacity of the receiving country. Empirically, the RBI studies showed that inflows into India depends on the level of development, represented by Gross Domestic Product (GDP) and debt service rates in the previous period. Both the variables were found to be significantly related to capital flows for the period studied, 1970-71 — 2002-03. In the recent past external assistance has emerged as a major financing item in the capital account of the Balance of Payments, in India. But in the quinnannium, 1998-2003, there were net outflows of funds from India, reflecting the change in government policy, towards managing external debt, through attracting more capital flows in the form of FDI, and portfolio investment of a non-debt creating nature. The foreign funds inflow was encouraged into selected sectors of the economy, when foreign technology and capital were needed.

The government policy changes in respect of both monetary and fiscal policies are also a reflection of larger capital inflows due to current account convertibility of rupee, gradual liberalisation of foreign investment policy and capital account controls. The larger inflows led to huge accumulation of foreign exchange reserves and appreciation of the rupee *vis-a-vis* the dollar during 2003 and 2004, which was unprecedented in the monetary history of India.

In the global operations of MNCs, international finance managers have to keep an eye on these emerging global forces, in their planning and budgetary exercises and in the actual financing and investment decisions. In the fast changing dynamic world, the Finance Manager has to update his policies from time to time.

The motives of foreign investment would continue to dominate in the future world and the need for capital and advanced research technology is indispensable for the growth of the poorer countries in Asia and Africa. The MNCs bring in certain definite advantages to both the host countries as well as home countries referred to earlier. They increase employment, expand the flow of goods and services and improve the living standard of the people across the world. Thus, had it not been for the MNCs, the developing countries would not have been able to acquire these inputs necessary for development and this assures the continuance of the importance of the MNCs in the future world pattern of production and trade. They brought in much needed capital and latest technology, which Promoted the growth of the in economies in developing countries. They filled in the gap, caused due to decline multilateral and Bilateral external assistance.

The liberalised policy of foreign flows into Indian industries and dilution of FERA by FEMA encouraging MNC to operate and expand in India are promoting the competition and making our economy more competitive and efficient.

The multinational corporations have revolutionised the system of world production and sales. Their activities have brought to question the traditional trade theory, based on comparative costs and locational advantages. The transnational company may produce at one corner of the world and supply the finished goods at another corner of the world at a cost lower than that when produced locally with its traditional comparative cost advantage and locational superiority.

The growth of MNC activities has changed the patterns of trade based on skill endowments and transport cost. Some more recent theories such as "Neo-technology" and "Neo-factor proportions theories" base their explanation of trade patterns on market imperfections, differences in technology, skill levels, economies of scale and product differentiation. These take into account the role of MNCs and technological dynamism in LDCs. Professor Gray's generalised theory also incorporates the effects of MNC's operations on world production and trade.

## Multinational Financing Agencies and World Bank

In the post-war world, international capital markets have dried up as a source of finance due to war ravages on the domestic economies and various degrees of exchange and trade controls imposed by the respective countries on domestic economic considerations. But the need for finance was also great for rehabilitation of the productive system in the case of developed countries and for economic development of the poorer countries. To start with, government-to-government loans, grants and other bilateral assistance gained ground soon after the war. At this time, multilateral institutions for promoting trade and aid were designed by the founding fathers of the Bretton Woods Conference in 1944 in the form of International Monetary Fund for short-term lending and International Bank for Reconstruction and Development IBRD for long-term lending. Both these institutions started functioning in 1946. In this chapter, discussion is concentrated on IBRD and other term-lending institutions in the international financial system. The original largest subscribers to these institutions are the US, the UK, China, France and India.

Leaving aside their structural and organisational aspects, their functional aspects involved both lending and guaranteeing. The World Bank (IBRD) guarantees in part or whole, loans made by private investors through private channels and make direct loans out of Bank's own funds or out of borrowed funds from governments or private investors or banks. If the banks lend to a private party, that party's government is expected to guarantee the loan. The basic objective of World Bank was to relieve poverty and provision of basic social services and then promote economic growth.

The sources of their lendable resources are the members' subscription paid in gold and their own currencies and borrowing from the private capital markets by issue of its own bonds such as in the US, Canada, Switzerland, the UK etc. These funds in the members' currencies or in the borrowing country's currency are to be used with the concurrence of the concerned country. The main object of the World Bank is to facilitate the flows of long-term aid in the form of loans at low rates and promote economic growth in developing countries. The Bank accordingly borrows and lends at low rates, keeping only a small margin for its own operations thereby keeping down the interest rate burdens for the borrowing country. Secondly, the Bank is promoting multilateralism in aid flows and thus in trade flows by institutionalising these flows through itself. Thirdly, the Bank by imposing conditions for assistance, developed a tradition for efficient allocation of funds in the recipient country, pursuit of right policies and proper management of the economies. Fourthly, it is helping the balanced growth of the economies of developing countries and of world trade through multilateral channels. Fifthly, it is aiding the member countries with technical and managerial help and training their personnel in their Economic Development Institute. Sixthly, it is helping to create an international stake in the borrowing and non-borrowing members in the regular servicing of loans, as the members have to share the risk of loss as well as actual losses in the Bank's lending operations. Prompt and regular repayments and servicing of loans are thus the responsibility of all members.

The Bank has been giving programme and project assistance to member countries, both developed and developing countries. The bulk of its assistance is going to the developing countries at present. Its principal emphasis is on basic public services and infrastructural facilities like railways, communications, electric power, agriculture, industry, etc. In Fiscal year 1998, a new policy specifying the minimum size of liquid assets portfolio was implemented.

## The International Development Association (IDA)

The International Development Association (IDA) is an affiliate of the World Bank set up in 1960 designed to promote economic development and productivity by extending softer loans than the World Bank could to the poorer low-income member countries. Most of the IDA loans are long-term, extending upto 50 years and at low interest rates of 2 per cent to 4 per cent. The repayment terms are also designed to suit the borrower and moratorium is granted upto about 25 years. These loans are for important development projects in the developing countries on flexible terms, so as not to adversely affect their balance of payments position. As these loans are of multilateral nature, they can be used in any country. IDA may unlike IBRD not insist on government guarantee in advancing to private parties. IDA may, provide both technical and financial assistance required for development projects.

The resources of IDA are from the initial subscriptions, additional subscriptions if any and borrowings from members of supplementary resources. Only 10 per cent of the subscriptions of the members are paid up and the rest of the 90 per cent in respect of the developed countries (Group I) was paid up over a period of 5 years in freely convertible currencies. In the case of developing countries included in Group II, they paid 90 per cent of the subscription in national currencies which cannot be used without their consent.

In 1975, IBRD had started a third window for long-term loans to developing countries on terms, intermediate between soft loans of IDA and World Bank. This assistance is for 25 years at a rate of 4.5 per cent for developing countries with per capita incomes under $ 375. An interest subsidy fund was also started with contribution from some oil-producing and developed countries in order to lend funds at subsidised rate.

## International Finance Corporation (IFC)

The International Finance Corporation (IFC) was set up in 1956, as an affiliate of the World Bank. Its membership and management are kept separate. The object of IFC was to promote flows of private capital without government guarantee. Thus IFC would lend capital in the form of investment in debentures or other senior securities along with private parties in the member countries. It will encourage private management of such concerns and encourage domestic entrepreneurship. To keep the funds rotating, it may sell off its investments in any company of a member country in favour of some domestic investors in that country. IFC has not been investing in venture capital (equity), but only in loan capital.

The IFC has been encouraging the flow of private capital and growth of private enterprise in member countries. It is on the lookout for promising firms in these countries or for commercially viable proposals for investment. It would encourage domestic management and private domestic and foreign capital to flow into the selected ventures through its involvement in its technical and financial help for the projects. This was channelised through private financial institutions like ICICI in India.

## The Bank for International Settlements (BIS)

The Bank for International Settlements (BIS) was set up in 1930 consisting of the European central banks as members. In 1970, Japan and Canada joined as members. New members could be admitted only on invitation from BIS. The objectives of the BIS are to promote co-operation among the central banks in their international financial operations and to act as a trustee or agent in regard to international settlements entrusted to it by the member countries.

One of the original tasks entrusted to it was to co-operate in carrying out of the "young plan" under which it was entrusted with the duty of receiving and distributing the German Reparation Payments to member countries. The statutes under which BIS was set up had laid down the transactions which it may undertake such as purchase, sale, exchange of gold, bills of exchange and short-term financial obligations of member countries and acceptance of deposits from central banks. The Bank was prohibited from issuing its own notes, accepting bills of exchange, making advances to governments or to acquire ownership of any real property, etc.

The Bank's main sources of funds are the short-term and sight deposits of member central banks. Its dealings are mostly with the central banks of member countries with its interventions in the various exchange markets. Its arrangements with commercial banks of member countries are incidental to its main dealings with the central banks.

The services provided by it to member countries are as follows:

(1) Gold operations in international markets;

(2) Foreign exchange purchase or sale operations;

(3) Purchase and sale to central banks of the short-term marketable government securities of member countries;

(4) To act as trustee and agent of the member country; and

(5) To act as fiscal agent for the European Payments Union.

It provides a forum for exchange of information as between central banks. It would extend credit and help ease pressures on any member's currency and promote co-operation among member countries. Since 1964 multilateral surveillance of the balance of payments adjustments of the Group of Ten is being carried out through the BIS. The BIS extends highly qualitative and confidential service to member countries of a very valuable nature. India has joined the BIS on invitation early in the Nineties.

## Asian Development Bank (ADB)

ADB was originally sponsored by the ECAFE, a body of the UN for the Asian and Far East region. It was set up by subscriptions from many countries in Asia and outside and started operations in 1966 as a development bank for helping the poor nations of Asia in their development efforts. It aims at raising funds from private and public sources for development purposes and assist the member states in the region with financial and technical aid, loans and equity participation etc. It is located in Manila, Philippines.

The main donors are Japan, Australia, U.S.A. etc., and India is also a member receiving assistance. It has Ordinary Capital Resources (OCR) and Asian Development Fund (ADF) for providing financial assistance and the latter for soft loans to poorer countries.

The assistance of ADB takes the following forms:

(1) Government and government guaranteed loans to private and public companies and corporations.

(2) Direct private sector lending.

(3) Equity investment in private sector corporate units.

(4) Equity underwriting in member countries.

Loans take the form of project loans, programme loans, sector loans, credit lines, technical assistance loans and unguaranteed private sector loans.

Financial assistance has gone to the following sectors of the economy in the order of importance:

(1) Energy sector, power and electricity generation.

(2) Transport and communications sector.

(3) Social infrastructure.

(4) Agriculture and agro-based industry.

(5) Financial Sector.

(6) Industry and non-fuel minerals.

The ADB has also provided technical assistance and loans for this purpose to various projects and programmes. India has been one of the major beneficiaries of assistance from ADB. Its assistance has been a great help for the economic development of the poor Asian countries. This is particularly so, in respect of aid from the soft loan window of the Bank, namely, Asian Development Fund, which has been replenished from time to time from the rich donor countries like Japan and U.S.A.

## Other Regional Development Banks

During the last two decades, many regional financing bodies have cropped up to finance the development projects in almost all regions. The functions of these bodies are development and financing and financing takes the form of loans and equity to local companies both in public and private sector. They also supply management and consultancy services to those companies who have a deficiency in this regard. They lend to support projects that promote regional corporation and economic integration.

The major regional development banks are the following:

**(1) European Investment Bank (EIB):** The EIB offers to lend development loans to less developed counties in European common market. Its services are extended to associated members of Africa, which are poor developing countries.

**(2) Inter-American Development Bank (IADB):** It is a body set up to assist the Joint Projects and foreign owned projects in Latin America. The preferred projects for financing are agriculture and infrastructure, power, roads, dams, etc.

**(3) Atlantic Development Group for Latin America (ASGLA):** It is an international private investment company dedicated to the socio-economic development of Latin America. It provides not only finance but the much needed entrepreneurial expertise and technical services.

**(4) Asian Development Bank (ADB):** It is funded by the Western developed countries and Japan in addition to subscriptions of the member countries. It guarantees loans to private sector and also provides equity and loan capital to the government and semi-government bodies as also to the private sector bodies, entrusted with the projects in the core sector, agriculture, power financial, etc. This has been already discussed earlier.

**(5) African Development Bank:** This body lends to government and semi-government bodies in poorer countries in Africa and provides assistance in the form of technical assistance and consultancy in addition to loans (equity and debt) for project financing.

**(6) Arab Fund for Economic and Social Development (AFESD):** It is a multilateral Arab Fund that actively assists and develops the projects in Arab League countries. It takes the responsibility for project feasibility study, project implementation, consultancy and related services.

Other bodies include Bank for International Settlement at Basle for cooperation and assistance among central banks of countries referred to already. European Bank for Reconstruction and Development (EBRD), was founded in 1990 with an initial capital of about $ 13 billion. It is intended to finance the structural reforms of the East European countries, privatisation and shifts to market oriented economy from state controlled and state run economy.

There is also Islamic Development Bank for assisting only the Islamic countries in Asia and Far East and Mid West. The funds are generated from the surpluses of the oil producing countries and are used for assisting projects in the poorer Islamic countries.

These development funds did nothing except to perpetuate the state-run planned projects and increase the state economic activity rather than private sector activity. The ADB and some other regional bodies assisted only projects approved and run by the government and semi-government bodies. They did nothing to encourage private enterprise, competition and market oriented economies. The recent IMF loans for structural reforms are mostly used for financing the balance of payment disequilibria and not to promote privatisation and private enterprise.

The post war success stories of Japan, West Germany, Taiwan, South Korea, Hong Kong and Singapore owe their success to reliance on private enterprise, and sound economic policies to promote efficiency, and establish market oriented competition and openness of the economies. Their export led growth was a success as opposed import led growth followed by India and many other Asian neighbours. Baker plan of 1985 insisted that aid should flow only to finance market reforms and to encourage private enterprise. It did not succeed at that time but later, eighties and nineties saw many countries dismantling their restrictions and moving to more market oriented economies for their growth. Particularly nineties is the period when many countries including Russia, China, India etc. have plunged into free market oriented economies, privatisation and globalisation, which encouraged the growth of MNCs, the world over.

❖ ❖ ❖

# FOREIGN INVESTMENTS (DIRECT AND PORTFOLIO, GDR AND ADRs)

37

## Introduction

This chapter deals with the long-term borrowings of a company. At the macro-level, a country which has a large external debt, prefers to issue equity or equity-linked instruments. These would reduce the debt servicing burden and improve the credit rating of the country. India is not having a large external debt and bulk of its external debt is in the form of medium and long-term debt. Global depository Receipts are equity-linked instruments, representing the equity shares of a specific number (of 1 to 10 shares) denominated in a foreign currency and traded abroad. Indian government encouraged the companies to go for foreign borrowings and in particular, equity.

Some of the Asian countries have large external debt, particularly of short-term nature and this will lead to some problems of debt servicing, depreciation of the currency and even currency crisis as in the case of Asian currency crisis of 1997, involving many developing countries of South Asia.

International finance has now become an important source of funds of both short-term and long-term nature for the corporates in India, due to current account convertibility of the rupee, introduced in 1994 and globalisation of the Indian markets. The decision to raise funds in India or abroad is a question of cost and easy availability and the capital structure requirements of the corporates. International finance has become an alternative to domestic sources. The access and entry into foreign capital markets and the rates at which one can borrow and whether one can borrow or not depends on the credit rating of the company and the country, capacity to service that debt as measured by its export earnings or foreign exchange earnings, the timing and the state of the domestic and foreign markets. The actual decision to resort to foreign finance, the extent and terms of borrowing, repayment schedule etc., will vary from company to company and country to country. A company which becomes eligible to raise funds abroad achieves a global status and recognition of institutional investors abroad and they are mostly MNCs. The foreign institutions and pension funds etc. supply the funds for various reasons, such as diversification of their asset portfolio due to differences in country risks, potential for capital appreciations and gain in Return on Investment (ROI). But their investments are made after an in-depth study of the country and currency risk and fundamentals of the company, under question. The investors abroad are again of different categories, namely, foreign security firms, pension funds, provident funds, country off shore funds, mutual funds and foreign financial institutions.

## Globalisation of Indian Markets

In India, with the recent economic and financial reforms, markets have become free, and competitive and globalised. The FIIs and FFIs, including foreign security firms are allowed to operate in Indian financial markets. The convertibility of the rupee on Current Account facilitated the inflows and outflows of funds. The policy of Foreign direct investment has been liberalised in India so as to promote that investment both in equity and debt subject to some limits, in the Indian corporates. These policy changes widened the avenues or sources of funds as also the instruments through which they can raise funds from abroad.

## External Debt of India

India's external debt was at a peak of $ 99.01 billion in 1991, which was brought down in stages to $ 94.32 billion at end March 1998 but rose to $ 112 billion at end March 2004 and to $ 229 billion in 2009 and $ 390 billion in 2013. The reduction was brought about by design and plan to reduce external dependence and to keep the debt service ratio within manageable limits. The latter rise was due to inflows of NRI funds.

The debt service ratio which reached a peak of 35.3% in 1990-91 declined steadily to 18,3% of the current receipts in 2003-04. The external debt to GDP ratio also has down from a high of 37.7% in 1991-92 to a low of 22% of GDP at end March 2009.

Short-term debt which became unpopular since the Mexican crisis, has declined. The short-term debt comprised 10.2% of the total external debt in 1991 and fell sharply to 4% at end March 2004. This decline was brought about in a planned manner despite the freedom given to corporates to make commercial borrowings abroad for their resource requirements.

There is another structural change in the pattern of debt. Not only the long-term debt is rising but also the share of concessional debt is declining. Many sources of external debt from multinational agencies and international bodies have dried up and India had to fall back on more costly commercial lines of credit. The share of concessional debt declined from 45.3% at end March 1995 to 18.2% at end March 2009. In view of the drying up of concessional lines of borrowing, care has to be taken to keep the debt levels at reasonable level, so as not to raise the burden of debt servicing.

The following Table presents the composition of external debt:

**Table: 37:1**
**Composition of External Debt** *(in U.S. $ million)*

| | *March end 1999* | *March end 2004* | *March end 2009* | |
|---|---|---|---|---|
| Multilateral | 30,555 | 29,614 | 39,566 | 51,642 |
| Bilateral | 17,486 | 17,489 | 20,589 | 25,065 |
| IMF 287 | 287 | 60 | Nid | 7,310 |
| Trade credits and Commercial borrowing | 28,509 | 26,874 | 77.280 | 1,20,893 |
| NRI/FCNR Accounts | 12,344 | 31,171 | 41,554 | 70,823 |
| Total long-term debt (excluding rupee debt) | 93,902@ | 1,07,857 | 1,80,514 | |
| Concessional debt as % of total | 37.9 | 35.8 | 18.2% | 11.2 |
| Sort-term debt as % of total | 4.4 | 4.2 | 21.5% | 44.8 |
| Debt stock to GDP ratio | 23.7 | 17.6 | 22.0% | 21.2 |
| Debt service ratio | 18.00 | 18.3 | 4.6% | 5.9 |

*Note:* Some items like rupee denominated debt are not included and hence totals do not tally.
*Source:* RBI Reports on Currency and Finance and annual Reports

External debt stock rose in 1998 due to floating of the Resurgent Bonds for $ 4.2 billion in August 1998, following the Pokhran test. But this was once-for-all shot and the debt burden is planned to be kept within limits. Debt to GDP and debt servicing ratios have declined since 1991. The strategy to keep short-term debt low has paid rich dividends as India did not suffer much capital outflow during the Asian Currency crisis. Higher exports and encouraging foreign direct investments are the only methods to manage the external debt position with the manageable limits.

# DATA ON FOREIGN INVESTMENT

**Table 37.2**
**Total Foreign Direct Investment**

| *Year* | *Amount in million of U.S. $* |
|---|---|
| 1994-95 | 1,314 |
| 1995-96 | 2,133 |
| 1996-97 | 2,821 |
| 1997-98 | 3,557 |
| 2000-01 | 4,029 |
| 2001-02 | 6,151 |
| 2002-03 | 4,660 |
| 2003-04 | 4,675 |
| 2005-06 | 8,961 |
| 2008-09 | 35,168 |
| 2010-11 | 11,834 |
| 2011-12 | 22,067 |
| 2012-13 | 19,819 |

*Source:* RBI Annual Reports

**Table 37.3**
**Total Foreign Portfolio Investment**

| *Year* | *Amount in million of U.S. $* |
|---|---|
| 1994-95 | 3,824 |
| 1995-96 | 2,748 |
| 1996-97 | 3,312 |
| 1997-98 | 1,828 |
| 2000-01 | 2,760 |
| 2001-02 | 2,021 |
| 2002-03 | 979 |
| 2003-04 | 11,377 |
| 2005-06 | 12,492 |
| 2008-09 | −13,855 |
| 2009-10 | 32,398 |
| 2010-11 | 30,293 |

**Table 37.4**
**Outstanding Balances under Various NRI Deposit Schemes**

| *(in US $ million)* | *1997-98* | *1998-99* | *2002-03* | *2003-04* | *2008-09* | *2013* | *2014* |
|---|---|---|---|---|---|---|---|
| FCNR (B) | 8,467 | 8,323 | 10,193 | 10,961 | 13,211 | 15,188 | 41,823 |
| NR (E) RA | 5,637 | 6,220 | 14,716 | 20,559 | 23,570 | 45,924 | 53,908 |
| NRNRD/NRO | 6,262 | 6,758 | 3,449 | 1,746 | 4,773 | 9,710 | 9,114 |
| | 20,369 | 21,301 | 28,358 | 33,266 | 41,554 | 70,522 | 1,03,844 |

# Foreign Investment into India

The major effort of the government to attract foreign direct investment in India was outlined in the Industrial Policy Statement of 1991. Since then there was a sustained growth of direct investment inflows from U.S. $ 97 million in 1990-91 to U.S. $ 3904 million in 2001-02 and U.S. $ 4660 million in 2002-03. Companies registered in Mauritius, U.S.A., U.K., Germany and Japan account for the bulk of the foreign direct investment. Industry-wise, the major areas or industry groups are computers, engineering and services.

Foreign funds for portfolio investment varied from year to year, depending on the interest rate differentials, expected returns on investment and expected exchange rate changes. They rose from a low amount of U.S. $ 4 million 1991-92 to a high of U.S. $ 38.24 million in 1994-95. Following the Asian Currency Crisis in 1997-98, there was a net outflow in 1998-99, after which there was a revival of inflows to reach U.S. $ 11377 million in 2003-04. There was a decline in 2008-09 due to world wide recession.

**Table 37.5**
**Composition of the Capital Account Inflows (in % ages)**

| | *1997-98* | *1998-99* | *2002-03* | *2003-04* | *2008-09* | *2010-11* |
|---|---|---|---|---|---|---|
| (a) Non debt creating inflows | 54.8 | 28.2 | 44.6 | 72.5 | 231.0 | 22% |
| (b) Debt creating inflows | 52.5 | 62.7 | –6.6 | 1.4 | 87.2 | 55% |
| (c) Others Including Banking Capital | – 7.3 | 9.1 | 62.0 | 26.1 | –218.2 | 23% |
| | 100 | 100 | 100 | 100 | 100 | 100 |

Of the debt creating flows, bulk of it is due to external commercial borrowing.

## Commercial Borrowing

Since the reforms were started in 1992, commercial borrowing has increased substantially. This has taken the form of commercial bank loans from abroad, securitised borrowings such as through IDRs, GDRs, ADRs, FCCBs etc., loans from International Financial Institutions, I.F.C., etc. and self liquidating loans.

Short-term loans are in the form of borrowing for working capital from banks and by corporates from the money market abroad through foreign commercial banks and foreign investment banks, buyers' credit from abroad, suppliers' credit from abroad, export credit component of bilateral credit from country to country and export credit for defence purposes.

International capital market encompasses all lendings and borrowings, both private and government, in foreign currencies, from foreign banks, investment agencies, pension and provident funds and a host of other government, financial and private institutional agencies.

Government to government borrowings, multilateral agency borrowing and bilateral borrowings as between countries are all the methods of government borrowings. In addition to short-term borrowings from the IMF, there are borrowings from NRIs and foreign residents of Indian origin and OCBs in the form of their term deposits with banks. In recent years, the extent of reliance on the foreign funds by the government has come down. The private sector borrowings have also declined during 1996-99 due to recession in domestic industries, depression in currency markets of Asia and a slow down of world output and world trade growth. Foreign financial markets have witnessed a trance due to debt crisis and currency crisis of some less developed countries.

## Global Instruments

The two major categories of equity-linked instruments used in international borrowing are IDRs International Depository Receipts and ECB. The various types of IDRs are ADRs, EDRs and GDRs. ADRs are American Depository Receipts, created in the U.S.A. wherein a U.S. Depository bank would hold a predetermined number of foreign securities and issue against them tradable ADRs, thus turning them into dollar denominated instruments. They are convertible at the option of the holder into the underlying shares. The issue of ADR requires the SEC clearance in USA for which the details of the issuing company has to be provided to them. The ADRs are optionally convertible into underlying securities but not compulsorily. ADRs are tradable only in the U.S.

The Global Repository Receipts GDRs are instruments of equity-linked nature which can be traded in multiple markets, outside the domestic market of the issuer. A GDR represents one or more equity shares with a right to the holder for conversion into underlying shares. The underlying shares are already listed on domestic stock exchanges. The holders of GDRs do not carry any voting rights but only dividends and capital appreciation.

If these are EDRs, they are the International Depository Receipts the Global Depository Receipts, European Depository Receipts, which are issued in Europe by an Indian company with an European bank holding the securities of issuing company and Depository Receipts are issued on the basis of the foreign securities held with it and these EDRs are tradable in Europe, where the clearing system called Euroclear and CEDEL is used.

A GDR is tradable both in Europe and America, as it raises capital both in Europe and America, through a uniform security. In 1990, Rule 144A was adopted by SEC to facilitate secondary market trading in non-fungible unregistered securities among the qualified institutional buyers. This eliminates the registration requirements of the U.S. Securities Act of 1933, with the SEC. The right of conversion into underlying securities is optional and converted securities do not carry any exchange risk, unless they are sold in the issuing company's country. Issue of GDRs raises foreign funds, enhances the issuing company's image and broadens market into a global stage.

## Other Equity Linked Instruments

In addition to these instruments of ADRs, GDRs and EDRs, many companies are issuing similar equity-linked instruments like straights, FRNs and VRNs, warrants and convertibles. These instruments are advantageous to both the issuing company and the investor. Being quoted in dollars, the foreign investors do not have to bother about the currency of the issuing company. GDRs become fungible and tradable on its own without bothering about the underlying security. In the event of the holder of GDR converting into the underlying securities, the custodian of foreign securities will release these securities to local market, for sale and the proceeds are converted into dollars at the prevailing exchange rate after deducting 10% tax on the proceeds, repatriates the net amount of the proceeds to the foreign seller of these underlying securities in the domestic market of the issuing company.

The advantages of ADRs or GDRs are the lower cost than on domestic issues. It expands the market through a more diversified and liquid exposure. It postpones the debt servicing burden as they are considered as equity.

GDRs are fungible instruments, denominated in dollars. The investors in GDRs avoid problems of unfamiliar settlement and clearing system and confusing tax procedures of the country of origin. They are traded as if a dollar denominated security is traded in America or Europe, without having to bother about the underlying security. The two-way fungibility of ADR, GDRs in 2001 has helped conversion of ADR/GDR into domestic shares and vice versa. This has brought about more alignment of domestic market with foreign markets, and improved the liquidity of these shares.

## New Global Instruments

As referred to earlier global new issues are in the form of GDRs, ECBs, Straights, FRN, VRN, Warrants and Convertibles. Straights are Euro-bonds in the form of debt instruments with a fixed maturity period and a fixed rate of interest. FRN are Floating Rate Notes and short-term borrowing with a floating rate of interest depending on the

Treasury bond rate or some other benchmark interest rate. Similar is the case with the Variable Rate Notes (VRN) which may have variable interest rate varying with LIBOR or SIBOR.

Warrants and convertibles are similar to equity-linked debt instruments issued in the domestic market. Warrants issued with a bond are detachable and tradable separately. It carries a right of conversion at a fixed future date and at a price which is more favourable than the market price.

ECB or Euro-Convertible Bond is a quasi equity instrument, issued outside the domestic market with an option to convert this debt instrument into one or more equity shares at a predetermined price. Till conversion it carries an interest paid in dollars but this rate is lower than on a fixed coupon bond and the difference reflects the conversion value of the bond. If the company is doing well, stock prices will be rising and the investor in ECB captures the premium. The company as well as the investor benefits from this method. The company can benefit by securing funds when it is not ready to service equity and hopes to earn enough after a period to service larger equity due to conversion of ECB When it is difficult to issue equity, it is the next best alternative to the company. The investors bear less risk and earn a fixed return after which they enjoy the benefits of equity holders.

A convertible or GDR is preferable to both debt and equity under certain conditions of continued market sluggishness. The conditions of the financial position of the company is also a factor to decide whether, the issue should be GDR, ECB or a pure debt or equity or a combination of both in different proportions. Most of the conversions are optional to the holder of the instrument, and generally they carry both put and call options. Call option is not exercised by the company only during some specific period say upto 2 to 3 years and is exercised at specified market prices of the underlying shares, say when it goes up to a trigger level of around 125-140% of the bond conversion value. The put option is exercised by investor, if market conditions are unfavourable, but the terms of issue lay down a range of specified time and price for exercising this option.

ECBs are bearer securities and no registers are kept. They can be bought and sold over the counter, and interest is paid to the coupon holder of the bond. Quotations are available on the screen through the communications network such as Reuters. They are priced at a higher premium than GDRs, as they contain some debt element, while GDRs are only another form of equity-domestic stocks converted into foreign currencies and priced accordingly.

A GDR has lower leverage effect and no interest cost. It dilutes the EPS. It is traded like equity only, involving no foreign exchange risk or cash redemptions. An ECB on the other hand is debt until conversion. It does not dilute EPS, until conversion. It enables the company to enjoy tax deductibility of interest payments, leverage to equity and safer for the company. It is preferred in volatile market conditions with a downward protection of debt value in the secondary market than in the case of GDR. The addition of sweeteners to composite issues like GDR, ECB or Eurobonds with warrants etc. are resorted to if the conditions of market are unsuitable for issue for straight debt or equity and the company's financial position does not warrant a straight debt or equity issue.

## GDR Features

GDRs being equity, will have no maturity as in the case of ECB. The currency in which it is denominated is generally dollar and its listing is done in Europe and USA, namely, London, Luxemburg, New York, etc. Unlike the ECB it will have no coupon rate, but the price is decided on the basis of the market price ruling in the immediate past. The commission paid on GDR is generally more at say 3-5% as against 2-5% in the case of ECBs.

The issue expenses include management fee (of around 0.5% to 1.0%) underwriting fee (of around 1 to 2%) selling expenses (of around 2 to 3%), leading to a total commission of around 5% in the case of GDRs. The same will be lower at around 3% in the case of ECBs for the simple reason that they are easier to sell due to less risk involved in ECBs.

GDRs do not give any rights of voting unlike equity shares issued domestically. They are something like non-voting shares of equity. The domestic shares are held with a domestic bank, as a custodian. Besides, there will be depository bank in Europe or America, who issues the GDRs for sale to the lead managers and underwriters and who are responsible to the investors for the underlying shares, for collection of dividends, rights, bonus and other entitlements to be given to the investors of GDRs on a pro rata basis. The custodian is responsible to the depository bank and has to arrange for sale of underlying shares in the domestic market and remit the foreign exchange proceeds to the depository bank to be paid to the ultimate investor. The custodian has to observe the domestic exchange control and tax laws, as applicable to these transactions.

## Pre-issue Operations

The pre-issue work involves the preparation of the strategy, obtain internal approvals, legal and statutory clearances and finalises the size of issue, terms and depository, custodian, etc. The whole process will take about three months. This period includes also the time taken for preparation of offer circular, agreements and covenants with all the concerned parties, and lodging of application with the Stock Exchange and clearing system, say the CEDEL or Euroclear, pre-marketing survey or book building, fixation of price, road shows or investor meets abroad and syndication of the issue, entering into final agreements, foreign listing and trading approvals to be received and closing of the issue, and receiving the payments in foreign currency and delivery of share entitlements, in the form of GDRs. After the market operation is over, a tombstone advertisement is given in newspapers to record the issue.

## Domestic Statutory Clearances

As part of the statutory requirements, the issuing company has to get the approval of the general body by a special resolution for the issue of GDRs as additional equity in foreign markets. This is as per the requirement of Section 81 of the Companies Act, whereby the authorisation is given for issue of additional equity upto specified amount. This new equity along with the existing equity should be within the authorised capital, as otherwise the capital clause of the Articles of Association and Memorandum of the company has to be amended by the general body in their annual or special meeting.

The other statutory requirements are as follows:

The issuing company has to approach the Ministry of Finance Department of Economic Affairs (DEA) with a request for permission to enter the global market. This is as per the requirements of FERA Guidelines. The company has to provide the government with project report, sources and uses of funds, projections of financial position of the project and justification for approaching the global market.

The government specifies the approval for the fixed amount, within a price range and to follow a queuing procedure as is laid down generally for proper timing and to avoid bunching of issues. The Ministry of Finance approval is to be followed by the approval of RBI under FERA for record of external receipts and payments and then by the Department of Company Affairs, under the Companies Act, for exemption from procedures of local issue and non-applicability of Section 187c. Filing of prospectus with the Domestic Stock Exchange Concerned, ROC, and SEBI, etc. has to be completed for record and for listing and for satisfying the statutory guidelines in this regard.

The issuing company has to enter into formal agreement after the government clearance, with the Lead Manager who will be responsible to appoint the co-managers or form a syndicate of Managers and underwriters and steer the issue clear to success. The choice of the global Lead manager is critical to the issue and it depends on the research capability, past track record, and proper pricing of the issue. The potential investor groups and underwriters provide a feedback of the price and likely market absorption. The road show and investor meets are necessary for this purpose.

## Central Role of Lead Manager

Due diligence exercise of the Lead Manager is another landmark in the issue process. For this a meeting is held by the Lead Manager with the legal advisers and auditors of the issuing company and manager's overseas legal Advisors. Senior executives and the company secretary will be interviewed on a confidential basis to check the accuracy of the details given in prospectus and the veracity of the financial data. The Lead Manager will also investigate through his research team the statements made in the offer document before they can give due diligence certificate to the SEBI, as required by the Act and guidelines.

After this exercise, the Lead Manager will undertake another critical activity of canvassing the issue through a network of managers and underwriters by passing on the information to the institutional clients, regular investor funds and international bankers and foreign security firms. A good public relations exercise and a high profile coverage of the international financial press are necessary, and desirable. For this purpose, road shows at selected cities and financial centres of the world are held where the Lead Managers answer queries, give clarifications and provide them with a package of reports such as Lead Manager's Country Report, summary of the past performance data, annual reports for the past three years and the prospectus of the present issue, etc.

The syndication process and the feedback reports will be the basis on fixing the launch date when the issue is open for subscription. As the subscriptions are pre-arranged, the cheques are issued on the same date or on the next date, when the issue will be closed.

If there is a shortfall, the underwriters will put in the funds in the proportion of their underwriting obligations. If there is oversubscription there will be refunds in a proportionate manner or exercise the American "green shoe option" of retaining over subscription. This option of retaining over subscription should not lead to excess supply and drop in prices after the issue is listed. In some cases, the issue is sold on "Bought out deal" basis, when the Lead Manager takes over the whole amount and distributes among his institutional clients by sending them firm allotment advises on the basis of cheques presented by them.

The issue is closed and the relevant stock exchange has confirmed the agreement to listing and this is followed by a series of agreements to be signed with the stock exchange, mandatory market maker, as per listing agreement and the depository abroad and the custodian in the domestic market.

The issuing company, after the signing of all the agreements, issues equity shares to be registered in the name of the depository as per the agreement with them by the issuer company and share certificates are physically lodged with the custodian, as per the agreement entered into with them. Once the issue is listed, trading starts; it is the responsibility of the market maker to see that the price does not drop below the issue price, as that would damage both the company and the global Lead Manager. After listing, care has to be taken for proper matching of supply with demand and maintain a stable price range of the issued securities or GDRs as the case may be.

# BORROWING THROUGH EURO-ISSUES

## Government Guidelines

As per government guidelines of November 1993, Foreign Currency Convertible bonds are defined as bonds issued and subscribed by NRIs, and foreigners in foreign currencies. These are convertible into ordinary shares of the issuing company itself in a proportion stipulated in the beginning. These convertible bonds and GDRs are treated as direct foreign investment. This type of foreign investment in any company is subject to a ceiling of 51% of the paid up capital of the company. Each GDR is equal to 1 to 10 shares of the issuing company and subject to conversion or redemption as per the terms of issue.

As per the government guidelines of May 1994 a company or a group of companies will not be allowed to borrow more than two times during any financial year and a minimum gap of 12 months is necessary between two issues. Out of the proceeds of the issue 85% are to be used for import of capital equipment, machinery etc. and 15% for other general purposes. The GDRs have no lock-in-period and are traded as if they are shares in foreign markets. The GDRs are the resulting instrument of credit from overseas depository banks which are authorised by the issuing companies in India to issue outside the country GDRs to non-resident foreigners and NRIs against the deposit of shares of the issuing company in India. These shares are held by denominated domestic custodian bank. The GDRs are negotiable and all transactions in GDRs are exempted from Indian taxes, so long as the transactions are completed outside the country.

As per the fresh guidelines, issued in October. 1994, the time limit of 12 months for use of the Euro issue funds from the date of their issue was removed. The interest and dividends paid on these instruments are subject to deduction of tax at source of 10%. But capital gains tax for transactions done outside India is exempted.

The rates of interest on these instruments issued varied with the credit rating of the company, market conditions and a host of other factors and generally on the basis of LIBOR plus.

The off shore funds were also raised by UTI, SBI and some financial institutions. The funds arising out of these issues are in foreign currencies and are invested abroad upto 80% and the rest of 20% is invested in India. The foreign investment and securities firms like Merril Lynch, Robert Fleming, Morgan Stanley, Baring Securities, etc. acted as Lead Managers and many foreign banks have helped in this process.

## Issues in Foreign Markets

Indian companies are allowed to borrow abroad in the Euro-currency markets and foreign capital market since 1992. Thus, short-term paper is issued in the form of Euro currency notes at rates linked to LIBOR. These rates are cheaper than those in India. Besides, Euro-currency bonds of medium to long-term nature are issued as debt instruments. Some of these bonds are convertible into equity shares of Indian companies at a future date. Foreign currency bonds are debt instruments while GDRs are equity instruments of Indian companies, denominated in foreign currencies, quoted and traded in foreign markets. Only companies with high credit rating are allowed to borrow abroad either through FCBs or GDRs. With the globalisation of the market, Indian banks as much as Indian companies have been taking recourse to foreign funds more frequently.

During 1998-99, resources mobilisation by the Indian corporates through Euro issues registered a significant decline. Only three issues aggregating Rs. 2,105 crores were floated, as against seven issues for an aggregate amount of Rs. 4,387 crores floated in 1997-98, reflecting the industrial recession at home and depressed market conditions abroad. Amounts raised through GDR and ADR by Indian corporates stood at $ 831 million in 2000-01 which fell to $ 477 million in 2001-02 and to $ 459 million in 2003-04, but rose to Rs. 613 million in 2004-05. The amounts shot upto a high of $ 6645 million in 2007-08 but declined to $ 1162 million in 2008-09 due to world wide recession in that year.

## Banks and Indian Companies

In recent years with privatisation and globalisation of the economy, the corporate sector began to increasingly depend upon the new issues market and domestic and foreign capital markets. Their dependence upon banks and financial institutions including the Public Sector began to decline. Now that the Indian companies are having access to foreign markets through Indian and foreign banks abroad and foreign financial institutions, they started borrowing abroad since 1992. Given the low interest rates in international markets, the Indian companies with good credit rating would benefit through foreign currency issues and convertible bonds, and global depository receipts. Although,

GDRs are issued in foreign currencies either in the form of shares or bonds they will be denominated in rupees upon conversion into shares of the issuing company. Banks have a crucial role in the above process. GDRs are traded abroad and are mostly on discount in the foreign markets.

## Banks and Foreign Capital

Under the present liberalised financial scenario, banks' role has become more important in the economy. Banks help the external sector by financing of exports and export production, financing of imports and providing foreign exchange for outward and inward remittance, and funds flow both for current and capital account transactions. They take more foreign exchange risks, foreign credit risk and provide necessary funds to public, business and government. They facilitate the growth of exports and import financing and provide hedge against foreign currency risk. Among banks, the multinationals and foreign banks are more involved in the external sector and with their contacts and counterpart agencies abroad, they are in a better position now to provide services in the external sector and in foreign exchange. They are helping Indian corporate sector to raise funds abroad as equity or debt in the Euro currency market and through foreign financial institutions in the form of GDRs and Euro bonds. The banks and corporates are now allowed to deal in foreign exchange more freely than before, due to relaxation of FERA and keep accounts abroad or borrow from abroad. Some public financial institutions and banks, including UTI have floated offshore funds to raise finance in foreign currencies of which atleast 20% should be invested in Indian corporate sector.

In the issue and marketing of these bonds, as much as GDRs and offshore funds etc., the major investment and security firms like Merril Lynch, Robert Fleming, Morgan Stanley, Baring Securities etc., have acted as the Lead Managers.

## Exchange Rate and Banks

Rupee was first devalued by around 18% in July 1991, in two instalments. This was followed by abolition of cash compensatory support scheme, earlier made available to exporters as an incentive, but to keep incentives for exports to grow, a new scheme of exim scrips to exporters was introduced. These were made transferable and entitled the holder to freely import foreign goods needed for domestic production. This export incentive scheme became unnecessary when in March 1992, the rupee was made partially convertible on trade account upto 60% of the export proceeds. The rest of the 40% was to be sold to the banks at the official rate of exchange by exporters. This led to the introduction of Liberalised Exchange Rate Management System (LERMS). The experience with this by banks has proved to be beneficial to trade and encouraged the government to move to more liberalised system. Later in March 1993, rupee was made fully convertible on trade account to boost the exports, with 100% of exports converted at the market rates. The export incentives such as Exim Scrips were withdrawn. In March 1994, full rupee convertibility on current account was also announced with the result that the banks in India have to operate in a free foreign exchange market, exposing themselves to greater risks.

# POLICY ON EXTERNAL COMMERCIAL BORROWINGS (ECB)

External commercial borrowings include commercial bank loans from abroad, buyers' credit, suppliers' credit, securitised instruments such as FRN, FRB, FCCB, credit from official export credit agencies, multilateral financial agencies, IBRD, ADB, IFC etc.

The access to these methods of borrowings is liberalised from time to time with an annual ceiling. Higher priority is given for borrowing for projects in the infrastructure and core sectors and export sector. Development financial institutions are also expected to borrow for meeting the needs of medium and small-scale units.

All corporates and institutions are permitted to raise ECBs upto 20 million U.S. dollars with an average maturity of 3 years, for all corporate objectives except real estate and stock market investments. Corporates with foreign exchange earnings are permitted to raise upto thrice the average amount of annual exports during the previous three years, subject to a ceiling of U.S. $ 100 million without end use restrictions. Holding companies and promoters are permitted to raise ECB upto a ceiling of U.S. $ 500 million to finance equity investment in a subsidiary or J.V. implementing the infrastructure projects. Interest rate spreads are linked to LIBOR and maturity periods.

Corporates can draw on ECBs for 8 years and above but less than 16 years upto an amount of U.S. $ 100 million and above 16 years upto an amount of U.S. $ 200 million. Long-term debt instrument should not include any "Put" or 'Call' options which may reduce the stated maturities. All financial intermediaries, including DFIs are required to observe the maturity criteria for on-lending and extend the loans within 12 months of drawing on them. They can also lend for rupee expenditure and ECBs can be used for import of capital goods and services and project related rupee expenditure.

All the infrastructure and greenfield projects are permitted to avail of ECBs upto 35% of the total project cost and for telecom projects, upto 50% of the project cost. Greater flexibility is allowed for power projects and other infrastructure projects, based on merits. Banks and FIs cannot provide guarantee for ECB. Long-term borrowing was encouraged to reduce the outstanding short-term debt of India.

The RBI is the sanctioning authority for short-term loans upto 3 years and the other cases have to go to the Ministry of Finance. Roll over of an ECB, or inter-corporate swapping of ECBs is not permitted. Corporates can however undertake liability management for hedging the interest rate and exchange rate risk on their underlying foreign currency exposure without prior approval through interest rate swaps, currency swaps, coupon swaps and forward rate agreements.

These ECB guidelines and procedures are periodically reviewed in the light of conditions of external debt servicing, foreign reserves position, market conditions and sectoral requirements. In view of surfeit of foreign exchange reserves since 2003-04, there was a policy of restraining ECB by corporates to the minimum necessary for working capital and FDI in desired sectors. Later on ECB funds were not allowed to be used for working capital purposes.

## Changes in ECB Guidelines

ECB would be allowed to all corporates, except banks, FIs and NBFCs. FIs are eligible to the extent of their participation in the restructuring to textile and steel sector. End use restrictions were removed in January 2004, but replaced in April 2004. They are not allowed for working capital or other corporate uses of short-term nature, for repayments of rupee loans or for further lending. The money cannot be used for investment in capital market or the real estate.

There are also restrictions on the interest rate spreads. For maturities of 3 to 5 years, the maximum spread is 200 basis points above six months LIBOR. For ECBs above 5 years of maturity, the maximum spread is 350 basis points above LIBOR and those above 7 years the maximum spread is 450 basis points above LIBOR. Interest rates on ECBD were tightened from January 2010 by making loans upto 5 years at 300 points above LIBOR and for loans above 5 years at 500 points above LIBOR.

The automatic route upto \$ 20 million will be there for ECBs between 3 to 5 years and upto \$ 500 million for ECBs above 5 years. Proposals for short-term credit above U.S. \$ 20 million are considered by the RBI on merits. These restrictions were liberalised after 2004 step-by-step. Earlier repayments of ECB by corporates were allowed without any limit in more recent years. As the policy is changing from time to time, one has to update the information from financial press, or from the RBI publications.

# THE RULE BOOK — NRI INVESTMENTS

## Direct Investment without Repatriation Benefits

(1) General permission for all NRIs (not OCBs) expect for investment in a concern engaged in agricultural/plantation activity or real estate business.

(2) Investment permitted in both the primary as well as secondary market issues.

(3) Interest and income allowed to be repatriated upto US \$ 1000 or its equivalent in full and one-third of the balance income earned during financial year upto US \$ 100 or its equivalent in full and two-third of the balance income earned during the financial year 1995-96, the entire income earned during the financial year 1996-97 and onwards. Repatriation is possible after payment of income-tax, since 1996-97.

## Direct Investment with Repatriation Benefits

(1) There are two direct investment schemes: the 40 per cent scheme and the 100 per cent scheme.

(2) Under the 40 per cent scheme, NRIs are allowed to invest in shares and debentures of companies with repatriation benefits to the extent of 40 per cent of the new issue. There is no ceiling on remittance of interest or dividend.

(3) Under the 100 per cent scheme, NRIs can invest in high priority industries listed in Annexure III to the Statement on Industrial Policy upto 100 per cent of the new issue. Dividend and interest can be freely remitted.

## Other Investments

(1) NRI can invest in sick industrial units upto 100 per cent by subscribing to existing shares or new issues. The investment has a lock-in period of three years. This was relaxed on a case-by-case basis.

(2) In certain high priority industries in which foreign investment upto 51 per cent is permitted on repatriation basis, NRIs can pick up the balance 49 per cent on repatriation basis.

(3) NRIs can invest upto 100 per cent in shares or convertible debentures of companies engaged in real estate development. Dividend can be freely repatriated, but the investment carries a lock-in of three years.

(4) Permission for investment in non-convertible debentures has to be obtained from the Reserve Bank.

(5) 100 per cent investment in export oriented units and export trading activities is permitted.

(6) Under the Portfolio Investment Scheme, NRIs are allowed to acquire shares and debentures through the stock exchanges in India by making an application to the Reserve Bank. There is a ceiling of 5 per cent of the paid-up share capital of the company which can be raised to 24 per cent if the company concerned passes a resolution to that effect in its general body meeting. Individually NRIs can invest upto 1 per cent of the paid-up share capital or the series of convertible debentures. The earlier lock-in period of one year has been withdrawn, for their portfolio investments.

## Foreign Financial Institutions (FFIs)

Foreign Financial Institutions (FFIs) have been permitted by SEBI to operate in India since 1993. They got registration from SEBI and from the RBI under FERA. The registration is valid for 5 years.

## Who are FFIs?

These are Foreign Institutions such as pension funds, mutual funds, investment trusts, AMCs, Institutional Portfolio Managers, etc., who operate generally in all money and capital market instruments abroad. They are now operating in Indian money and capital markets as well, but through accepted brokers.

The criteria for granting registration to the FFIs are their track record, professional competency, financial soundness and their experience in their own countries.

# Foreign Institutional Investors (FIIs)

## Activities Allowed

The general permission from the Reserve Bank will enable the FIIs to:

**(1)** Buy, sell and realise capital gains on investments made through the initial corpus remitted to India;

**(2)** Subscribe/renounce rights offerings of shares and invest on all recognised stock exchanges through a designated bank branch;

**(3)** Appoint a domestic custodian for a custody of investments held;

**(4)** Open foreign currency denominated account/(s) with a designated bank;

**(5)** Open a special non-resident rupee account to which all receipts from the capital inflows, sale proceeds of shares, dividends and interests could be credited;

**(6)** Transfer sums from the foreign currency accounts to the rupee account and *vice versa,* at the market rates of exchange;

**(7)** Make investments in securities in India out of the balances in the rupee account;

**(8)** Transfer repatriable (after tax) proceeds from the rupee account to the foreign currency account/(s).

**(9)** Repatriate the capital, capital gains, dividends, incomes received by way of interest, etc., and any compensation received towards sale/renouncement of right offerings of shares.

FIIs are, however, advised to ensure that the designated branch of their bank/the custodian are authorised to deduct applicable Indian taxes and that they arrange to pay the tax and remit the net proceeds at market rates of exchange;

- Register the FII's holdings with the concerned company without any further clearance under FERA.

## Portfolio Management

Portfolio investments in primary or secondary markets, however, will be subject to the following ceilings:

(a) The holding of a single FII in any company should not normally exceed five per cent of the total issued capital of the company. For this purpose, the holdings of an FII group will be counted as holdings of a single FII (the limit raised to 10%).

(b) The total foreign holding in any company should not exceed 24 per cent of its issued share capital. Foreign holdings include holdings of all registered FIIs and holdings through NRI portfolio investments, i.e., NRI corporate and non-corporate investments (the limit is also flexible).

(i) Direct foreign investments, i.e., foreign investments under financial collaborations are permitted up to 51 per cent in all priority areas; and

(ii) Investment through alternative routes, such as, offshore single/regional funds, global depository receipts and euro-convertibles, are outside the above ceilings.

FII investments by way of preferential allotments are permitted up to 15 per cent of the equity of the company provided the aggregate FII/NRI/OCB investment does not exceed 24 per cent of the equity of the company. This can be raised by passing a resolution in the general body meeting of the company, upto 51% in certain priority sectors.

## NRIs Investments

The NRIs can invest in Indian Corporate Sector in two forms:

(a) Direct Investment,

(b) Portfolio Investment.

There are two schemes of Direct Investments, namely, upto 40% in selected industries and upto 100% in EOUs and sick companies.

The Portfolio Investment does not put any limits on the operations of NRIs, provided they operate through stock exchanges and registered brokers.

Bank deposits, real estate, the primary and secondary stock market are a few of the main avenues of NRI investment in India with their repatriability and regulations prescribed by the Foreign Exchange Regulation Act (FERA).

Following the Government of India's decision to divest a portion of shares held by it in public sector enterprises (PSEs) the RBI has also permitted NRIs/OCBs to purchase the shares of PSEs on repatriation basis.

❖ ❖ ❖

# FINANCING OF DEBT AND EQUITY INVESTMENTS (THROUGH GLOBAL MARKETS)

# 38

Foreign flows through official channels from the government and international financial bodies (IBRD, IFC, etc.) have dried up in the last two decades. The international capital markets of London and New York which used to supply bulk of foreign capital before the fifties have also fallen flat on supply of funds. The gap left by these sources was filled up by international currency markets, namely, Euro-dollar, Euro-sterling and other convertible currencies since the seventies after the fall of dollar as an international currency with the IMF and the consequential reforms effected in the international monetary system. The Euro-currency markets used to supply funds of short-term nature, rolled over into medium-term in some cases. This was in the form of debt initially, but swept into equity route through ADR/GDRs. But bulk of the equity funds have started to flow into Emerging Market economies, particularly into Asia through MNCs. The direct and portfolio investments began to grow in importance over the last two decades. In India, they started to flow in after the economic reforms were started in 1992, when the markets were opened up in the country.

## World Trends

The Table 38.1 presents the data on world trends of net capital flows into emerging market economies. These net flows are in the form of direct investment, portfolio investment and other long-term and short-term investment flows, including official and private

**Table 38.1**
**Net World Capital Flows**

*(in U.S. dollar billion)*

| *Year* | *Private Direct Investment* | *Private Portfolio Investment* | *Private Capital Flows Total* |
|---|---|---|---|
| 2000 | 174 | 21 | 61 |
| 2001 | 185 | –87 | 61 |
| 2004 | 186 | 29 | 197 |
| 2009 | 313 | – 234.5 | – 268.5 |

*Source:* IMF: World Economic Outlook, April 2009.

borrowing. As these data are from IMF report on world economic outlook, these are authentic flows of capital, as reported officially by member countries. Besides, as there are investment flows, short-term working capital funds and speculative funds are excluded. Emerging Market economies include all developing countries in transition to full convertibility of currencies.

The data begins with 1997, which witnessed the Asian Currency Crisis due to speculative capital outflows. The subsequent flows were stabilised after reaching a high in 2001, for direct investment. The column on total capital flows do not tally with the other two columns, as the data on other capital flows, which were mostly negative were not presented. The details of the other private capital and their nature is not clear from the data. Only positive inflows are presented as the objective is to study the trends of inflows at global level and not outflows from developing countries, as the latter are for monthly repayments for investments and to developed countries.

## Trends in India

So far as India is concerned, the data on equity and debt are as shown in Table 38.2 These data exclude the government RBI and NRI, but include the reinvested earnings, under direct investment. The data on both portfolio investment and direct investment are presented. Direct investment can be either in equity or debt, data in respect of which are

**Table 38.2**
**Foreign Investment Flows in India**

*(in US dollar million)*

| | *2000-01* | *2001-02* | *2002-03* | *2003-04* | *2008-09* | *2010-11* |
|---|---|---|---|---|---|---|
| Total Direct Equity | 2400 | 4095 | 2700 | 2,387 | 35,168 | 717.74 |
| Equity | 423 | 1072 | 1042 | 925 | 27,995 | 596.94 |
| Reinvested Earnings | 1350 | 1646 | 1498 | 1,800 | 6426 | 344.56 |
| Debt and Other Capital | 279 | 390 | 462 | 488 | 747 | 277.40 |
| Total Portfolio Equity | 2760 | 2021 | 979 | 11,377 | – 13,855 | 13,781 |
| GDR and ADRs | 831 | 477 | 600 | 459 | 1,162 | 55,361 |
| FIIs | 1847 | 1505 | 377 | 10,918 | – 15,017 | 14,842 |
| Offshore Funds | 82 | 39 | 2 | – | – | 5,041 |
| Grand Total | 6,789 | 8,152 | 5,639 | 16,052 | 21,313 | 10,085 |

*Source:* RBI Annual Reports

presented in the Table 38.2. These data are derived from the Tables presented by the RBI in their Annual Reports. The totals may not therefore tally with the individual columns.

It will be seen that these data are from RBI and may not tally with that of SEBI on portfolio investments by FIIs. The totals will not tally with components as the Table is meant to give an idea of private capital flows into non-governmental corporate sector. As the flows of NRIs are not significant, it makes no difference whether they are of equity or debt nature. In the data on direct equity, debt capital is excluded and shown separately under the head of debt and other capital, which is of non-equity nature. The data shows that debt flows are insignificant, as compared to equity flows in India. These data representing the macro picture for the Indian Economy, do not reflect the ideal or the actual debt equity ratio of the MNCs at the micro level. The data represent the policy of the government of encouraging only the inflows of equity nature and not of debt nature for two reasons. One is that the India's external debt has to be kept low and stable and second is that India has surfeit of exchange reserves, which should discourage huge inflows of foreign funds.

From the macro angle, the government considers equity is more welcome, as the servicing of it is not an obligation on the company or the nation. The debt involves an obligation of interest payments, which constitutes an outflow committed. As equity is ownership capital, it brings in with it foreign technology and enterprise along with the capital.

## Micro Picture

From the micro angle of a firm, the foreign capital is cheaper source of finance than domestic capital. It broadens the equity base and brings in global status and standing in the financial sense. The grant of ESOPs to foreign employees and acquisitions of foreign smaller companies will improve the international status and access to long-term funds and to international currency markets. The corresponding argument for ADRs and GDRs is that they are tradable abroad and broaden the equity base eventually. But the obligations of these companies for acquiring international status are the transparency of operations, good corporate governance and liquidity for their stock.

## Costs of Capital

If the international markets are integrated, stock prices move on identical lines and are correctly priced, if the information flows are perfect to reflect true fundamentals of the company. The choice of the firm lies not only in the cost of capital, cost of issue and costs of conversion in the Forex market for domestic use. The costs of issue include the payments to the managing bank, underwriting agency and other intermediaries. The cost of capital depends on the average return on equity in the industry in which the firm is involved in the case of equity capital, whether it is raised from local sources or international markets or from parent company or other subsidiaries through inter-company transfers. The corporate tax rates on taxable profits, withholding taxes on payments, if any, and government rules and regulations if any, in this regard are relevant factors.

If it is debt capital, the costs include the cost of issue and costs of servicing the debt through interest payments.

In the case of GDRs and ADRs, the costs are more due to payments for services of the depository, custodian and other intermediaries, in addition to interest payments to the holders of issue. The instruments of equity and debt are weighed in the form of costs, advantages and disadvantages and taxes payable. In the global market, the choice of equity versus debt depends mostly on the management policy, in addition to the environmental, economic and financial factors and government policy guidelines of the country of location of the firm and that of the parent company. Management policy depends on a host of other variables and changes from firm to firm and country to country.

## Management Policy

Basic fundamentals of the firm dictate minimisation of costs and maximisation of profits. Bearing these criteria in mind the parent company formulates its policy for itself and its subsidiaries. Prima facie, the state in which the firm is empirical, namely, whether it is set up recently or in initial stages or advanced stages of growth. Until the breaking point and upto profitable stage, it is equity finance which is preferred, as servicing of debt is a burden on revenue and it is size of operations, which is considered. If the size of operations is large, larger equity is necessary, as debt raising capacity depends on the creditworthiness or credit rating of the firm in the eyes of lenders and bankers, which in turn depends on the equity stake of owners of the firm. The profitability or the net cash inflows is the factor influencing the management policy on equity versus debt. Each has its own merits and demerits and the choice depends on the situation in which the company is placed. Taxation is a factor, which favours debt which is an expense item and is not taxable. The costs of issue of equity and debt and the costs of servicing these are the final deciding factors for the management policy.

## Merits and Demerits of Equity

Equity has both advantages and disadvantages. Equity helps to build the base of ownership of the company. The burden of servicing it can be postponed in the initial stages of the company and in times of hardship of lower cash inflows and lower profits. Equity brings the credibility and creditworthiness to the company, as it represents the stake of stockholders, who are the owners of the company. The higher the creditworthiness, the better is the credit rating of the company to raise debt capital from the public or the banks. Equity stake proves the bonafides of the parent company which supplies equity in the initial stages, followed by other sources, domestic and foreign, which is possible after the firm has reached the profitability stage.

Equity has disadvantages also. It increases the average cost of capital for the firm. It is a more risky asset, than debt from the point of view of investors. It attracts the tax on dividends, as profits or as a withholding tax on dividends. It is ownership capital and management will have a greater burden of servicing it and to see that the share holders' wealth is increasing and share price is quoted at a premium. Equity does not provide the gearing which debt capital provides. Expansion of equity base requires growing profitability of the company. Equity is therefore, the choice of the company only under certain conditions, which vary from company to company and the nature of the industry and country, in which the company operates.

## Merits and Demerits of Debt

Debt has the advantage of a fixed liability in the form of servicing it with interest payments. It has the advantage of changing the maturity period. While equity is indefinite in maturity, debt will have a fixed maturity. Debt provides the gearing advantage to equity, as the capital employed can be raised and profits can be realised on a given equity base but with a larger capital employed. Debt is long-term or short-term depending on the needs of the investment whether it is for working capital or for long-term fixed asset acquisition by the firm. Debt has the advantage of reducing the tax liability, as servicing of debt is an expenditure item reducing the net operating income which is taxable, as profits. Whether debt is raised from banks or FIs will depend on the purpose, maturity period, etc. Similarly, whether debt is to be raised from domestic or foreign sources will depend on the interest rate, maturity periods, currency of borrowing, exchange rate stability and government policy of the county of the location of the firm. There are various forms in which debt can be raised by a firm for long-term purposes.

*(1)* Debentures of various coupon rates and maturity

*(2)* Bonds of various coupon rates and maturity

*(3)* Fixed Rate Bonds

*(4)* Floating Rate Bonds

*(5)* Discount bonds/deep discount bonds

*(6)* Convertible bonds/option oriented bonds

*(7)* LIBOR related Bonds from Euro-Markets

*(8)* Euro currency Bonds/ADRs/GDRs, etc.

Debt for short-term purposes can be raised through

*(a)* Syndicated credits, consorted by two or more banks, domestic or foreign.

*(b)* Term loans for short and medium-periods of one to five years.

*(c)* Note Issuance Facility which has committed underwritten facility to borrow.

*(d)* Money market instruments like commercial bills, commercial paper, certificates of deposit etc.

Working capital borrowing is discussed in a separate chapter.

The disadvantages of debt are also important. It raises the risk of the firm due to interest liability and creditor's priority for repayment and interest payment over servicing of investors in equity. Whether profits are made or not, debt has to be serviced. It reduces the credit rating of the company and constitutes a burden on stockholders. They are a drain on the net cash inflow. It is a liability of the company irrespective of its profit earning capacity.

## Empirical Position

Data on finances of Foreign Direct Investment companies in India are published by the RBI from time to time. There are in other words, the foreign MNCs and the data relate to their firms in India. The latest data relate to the year 2006-07, of 524 major foreign companies published in the RBI Monthly Bulletin, February 2009

These data show that debt to equity ratio is small relatively, consistent with the government policy of keeping the debt inflows lower than equity at macro level. Debt as per cent of equity for these foreign companies stood at 36.5%. Internal sources of funds occupy a minor share of 41.6% in total sources of funds. Internal sources include reserves, surplus and provisions. External sources include paid up capital raised through new issues and trade dues and other liabilities. Their net borrowings are negative due to larger repayment than fresh borrowings, only in respect of non bank sources.

An analysis of their sources and uses of funds shows that gross fixed assets formation to total uses is high at 46% in 2006-07. Increase in bank borrowings to total external sources is low at 7% of the total. This would indicate that MNCs in India depend more on their own sources or those of affiliates or parent company through inter-company transfers, rather than bank borrowings. Their liquidity and profitability ratio are also sound in true financial sense. The ratio of current assets to current liabilities is 1:2 and current assets to total net assets is 44.3%. Gross profits after tax to net worth is at 19.5% and gross profits sales ratio is 14.4%. Ordinary dividends to ordinary paid up capital is 36.9%. This financial picture of the MNCs at macro level is note worthy and creditable as compared to the domestic companies.

Each firm's position varies with the country, of origin and the industry in which it is operating. The micro firm's financial policy depends on the economic and financial environment and the parent company's management policy. The optimum mix of debt to equity and external borrowing etc. are all variables, changing from company to company and country to country.

## Determinants of FDI

At the macro level, the determinants are the policy framework of the RBI and government, financial infrastructure, business outlook and expectations of the economic fundamentals. Most studies concluded that they are relatively stable. During the period 1992-97, however, highest volatility as measured by the coefficient of variation was in bank loans, followed by portfolio investment and FDI in that order. From the host country point of view, the major factors influencing the FDI flows are as follows:

(1) Policy framework — economic and political stability, entry and exit policies, tax and tariff policies, structure of the market, competition and opportunities for patents and franchise, etc.

(2) Market size and per capita income, environment constraints, consumer preference, etc.

(3) Resources seeking for inputs, natural factor endowment, labour availability, wage structure, skilled labour and managerial talents.

(4) Physical infrastructure, roads, power, communication, media, legal safeguards.

(5) Efficiency grounds which include cost of resources like interest rates, availability of credit, costs of raw materials, intermediates, accessories, parts, etc.

(6) Business facilitation, investment incentives, tax holidays, investment promotion policy, corruption and red tape in bureaucracy, social amenities and export and import facilities like offshore banking, special economic zone, export processing zones, etc.

FDI inflow rose steadily in the 90s due to economic and financial reforms initiated in India. It rose from $ 97 million in 1990-91 to $ 6.1 billion in 2001-02 and stood at $ 5.5 billion in 2004-05 and rose sharply $ 38.3 billion in 2008-09. The invested earnings of FDI companies constituted 32% of the total FDI, and debt flows worked out to 10%. So the debt equity ratio was low at macro level due to policy imperatives.

It was only since 1991, when the reforms were started that the Indian economy witnessed sustained FDI inflows. The fact that these flows are more in China than India would indicate that China has a larger market size, larger per capita income, better infrastructure, better literacy rates and education and competitive efficiency in the markets which attracted larger FDI inflows into China. The tax system and administrative procedures were simpler and less corruption and red tape in China were an added advantage.

The above facts suggest that FDI inflow not only depend on globalisations like economic growth and world trade, inflation etc., but on the policy framework in the recipient country and its economic fundamentals including open ness of the economy, liberalisation, privatisation, competitive efficiency, market size, etc.

Empirical studies on major factors influencing inflows and outflows of FDI in India over the period 1970-71 to 2002-03, shows that, *inter alia*, the inflows are dependent on the world economic growth proxied by world GDP growth as a 'push factor' and the ratio of fiscal deficit to GDP in the domestic economy, which is a proxy for credit rating of the economy. The latter has a negative impact on inflows, while the former has a significant positive impact. The open ness of the economy which is proxied by exports plus imports ratio to domestic GDP is found to influence the outflows of FDIs. It was also found empirically that there is a unidirectional causal relationship running from FDI to export growth in the case of India.

To sum up, FDI inflows increased significantly only since 1990s, with the initiation of reforms in India. The major factors are the world GDP growth and the policy framework and openness of the Indian economy. Investment climate improved by the efforts at liberalisation, privatisation, disinvestment process, along with the growth of the competitive efficiency in the economy. The inflows are mostly from Mauritius and U.S.A. and into growth industries like engineering, chemicals, software and services sectors. There is a large scope for improving the infrastructure, competitive efficiency and openness of the economy and for reducing corruption and red tape and tax liabilities and tax burden in India.

## Determinants of Portfolio Investment

Portfolio investments took the form of GDR/ADRs, FII flows and offshore funds. On an average GDR/ADR inflows were about one-third of the total inflows, going upto 2/3rds in some years. Offshore funds were on an average less than 5% of the total portfolio investment. They have a seasonality factor in that they are more concentrated around February (or January to April) of every year, which is explained by tax saving investments and money from year end bonuses. The flows generally take place from advanced countries or those with better infrastructure to less developed and developing countries, depending on various factors. Besides, seasonality, they have a high volatility. Even so, cross country comparison shows that they are more stable in India (69.4% for the period 1995-2002) than in Mexico, Indonesia and other developing countries. This is explained by better investment climate in India during this period.

FII investment fluctuated more widely with outflow in some years. FIIs are allowed to invest in both equity and debt market. As per SEBI data the proportion of debt to equity investment stood at only 6% in 2002-03. ADR/GDRs are in the form of debt initially, but convertible into equity at a later stage. The debt equity ratio in these flows is difficult to judge prima facie, but equity is more than debt in general.

Among the determinants of the portfolio flows mention should be made of risk, return framework. A combination of domestic, regional and global forces work on the pattern of flows. The FII flows are positively correlated with the B.S.E. sensex, indicating the domestic stock market return. The alternative opportunity cost was measured by LIBOR and the risk on Nasdaq, which are significantly related to FII inflows. Foreign portfolio investment was larger than foreign direct investment inflows. The gross inflows were US $ 110 billion in 2006-07 and rose to $ 236 billions in 2007-08, before declining to $ 129 billions in 2008-09 due to world wide recession. Taking the outflows also into consideration, there were net (positive) inflows in both 2006-07 and 2007-08, but there was a net outflow in 2008-09, following global financial crisis.

❖ ❖ ❖

# MEASUREMENT OF PORTFOLIO RISK

# 39

## Introduction

This chapter deals with nature and measurement of Risk in Investment by the corporates, in the markets especially in the stock and capital markets, in the host country or foreign countries. The corporates are treated as individual investors and the risk factors involved in these investments are dealt with in this chapter. All international transactions are risky, whether in stock and capital market or in banking and financial sector or in goods and services. The degree of risk however, varies on the basis of the features of the assets, investment instrument, the mode of investment, or the issuer of the security, credit rating of the counter party, market risks in commodity market and financial markets.

## Risk and Uncertainty

Risk and uncertainty go together. Risk suggests that the decision-maker knows that there is some possible consequence of a financial decision, but uncertainty involves a situation, where the outcome is not known to the decision-maker. But basically, whether the outcome is known or not, the transactions involve both risk and uncertainty. For our discussion, the word "Risk" is used to comprise all elements of variability of return, uncertainty of the outcome, time periods and loss or gain in transactions.

Some risks can be controlled by the investors and some by the issuers of securities by planning. Others cannot be so controlled and they are to be borne compulsorily by the company.

# SYSTEMATIC AND UNSYSTEMATIC RISKS

## Risks are Classified into two Major Categories

(1) Systematic Risks are out of external and uncontrollable factors, arising out of the market, nature of the industry and the state of the economy and a host of other factors. (2) Unsystematic Risks emerge out of the known and controllable factors, internal to the issuer of the securities or companies. The former is measured by Beta and the latter is reduced or eliminated by portfolio diversification.

## Examples of Systematic Risks

**(1) Market Risk:** This arises out of changes in Demand and Supply pressures in the markets, following the changing flow of information or expectations. The totality of investor perception and subjective factors influence the events in the market which are unpredictable and give rise to risk, which is not controllable.

**(2) Interest Rate Risk:** The return on an investment depends on the interest rate promised on it and changes in market rates of interest from time to time. The cost of funds borrowed by companies or stock brokers depend on interest rates. The market activity and investor perceptions change with the changes in interest rates. These interest rates depend on nature of instruments, stocks, bonds, loans, etc., maturity of the period and the creditworthiness of the issuer of securities. But basically the monetary and credit policy which is not controllable by the investor affects the riskiness of investments due to their effects on return, expectations, and the total principal amount due to be refunded.

**(3) Purchasing Power Risk:** Inflation or rise in prices lead to rise in costs of production, lower margins, wage rises and profit squeezing etc. The return expected by investors will change due to change in real value of returns. Cost-push inflation is caused by rise in the costs, due to wage rise or rise in input prices. Demand-pull forces operate to increase prices due to inadequate supplies and rising demand. The increase in demand may be caused by changing expectation of future interest rates and inflation or due to increase in money supply or creation of currency to finance the deficits of the government. This element of purchasing power risk is inherent in all investments and cannot be controlled by the issuer or company.

## Examples of Unsystematic Risks

**(1) Business Risk:** This relates to the variability of the business, sales income, profits, etc. which in turn depend on the market conditions for the product mix, input supplies, strength of competitors, etc. This business risk is sometimes external to the company due to changes in government policy or strategies of competitors or unforeseen market conditions. They may be internal due to fall in production, labour problems, raw material problems or inadequate supply of electricity etc. The Internal Business Risk leads to fall in revenues and in profit of the company, but can be corrected by certain changes in the company's policies.

**(2) Financial Risk:** This relates to the method of financing, adopted by the company, high leverage landing to larger debt servicing problems or short-term liquidity problems due to bad debts, delayed receivables and fall in current liabilities. These problems could no doubt be solved, but they may lead to fluctuations in earnings, profits and dividends to shareholders. Sometimes, if the company runs into losses or reduced profits, these may lead to fall in returns to investors or negative returns. Proper financial planning and other financial adjustments can be used to correct this risk and as such it is controllable.

**(3) Default or Insolvency Risk:** The borrower or issuer of securities may become insolvent or may default, or delay the payments due, such as interest instalments or principal repayments. The borrower's credit rating might have fallen suddenly and he became default prone and in its extreme form it may take to insolvency or bankruptcies. In such cases, the investor may get no return or negative returns. An investment in a healthy company's share might turn out to be a waste paper, if within a short span, by the deliberate mistakes of management or acts of God, the company became sick and its share price tumbled below its face value.

## Other Risks

In addition to the above major risks, both in controllable and uncontrollable categories, there are many more risks, which can be listed, but in actual practice, they may vary in form, size and effect.

Some of such identifiable risks are the *Political Risks,* following changes in the government, or its policy shown in fiscal or budgetary aspects, etc., through changes in tax rates, imposition of controls or administrative regulations etc., *Management Risks,* due to errors or inefficiencies of management, causing losses to the company; *Marketability Risks* involving loss of liquidity or loss of value in conversions from one asset to another say, from stocks to bonds, or *vice versa.* Such risks may arise due to some features of securities, such as callability; or lack of sinking fund or Debenture Redemption Reserve fund, for repayment of principal or due to conversion terms, attached to the security, which may go adverse to the company.

All the above types of risks are of varying degrees, resulting in uncertainty or variability of return, loss of income, and capital losses, or erosion of real value of income and wealth of the investor. Normally, the higher the risk taken, the higher is the return. But sometimes the risk is caused by acts of God and there may be no return at all.

## Risks Measurement

Total risk of any investment is total variance of returns on that investment. This can be represented by spread or range of variations or fluctuation, creating uncertainty of the return and its amount. Range is the spread or breath of variations. The concepts of variance, standard deviation, dispersion over the mean covariance and beta coefficients etc. are also used to explain the measure of risk. In the context of portfolio of assets, or investment in any assets, risk is inherent in all such dealings. This risk primarily arises first out of parting of your funds or loss of liquidity. Money lent or parted always has an element of risk. This element is the same as the concept of total risk.

Some investments in bank deposits and post office deposits or certificates or insurance, PF, etc., are less risky, but they are also not devoid of any risk. Risk may take the form loss of time, cost involved in realisation of cash or theft of certificates etc. These are very elementary forms of risk, attached to any investment.

## Range of Variation

One measure of risk is the variability or range of variability of return. If the returns for example fluctuate from zero to 20%, it is a high risk investment, which might arise due to wrong choice of companies or securities invested in. The default prone bonds, or equity shares of some sick or sick prone companies may show such a wide range of fluctuation in returns. Generally equity investments are subject to such variability of returns, within a wide range and hence called most risky investments. The range is a relative term and can be expressed as a percentage change. Risks in relation to portfolios are different from risk of individual securities. Risk in relation to portfolio is discussed in a latter chapter. Can you estimate the risk of time?

Risk can arise from credit default or interest rate changes. Credit risk is assessed and measured by what is called credit rating.

## Why Credit Rating?

There was an enormous increase in the demand for capital by companies and investors had no way to know the credit quality of the companies whether they were strong financially, weak in some respects but more importantly whether they were frauds. Generally, equities are not rated as their risk is not measurable and they being the owners of the companies have to take the residual risk. But when companies issue bonds or debentures or any debt instruments, they can be rated. Here again the company is not rated but the instrument, issued by the company is rated, for its capacity to service that instrument.

Credit rating is essentially giving an expert opinion by a rating agency on the relative willingness and ability of the issuer of a debt instrument to meet the debt servicing obligation in time and in full, whether it is counter party credit, market in goods or finance.

These rating grades are quite common with Triple *AAA,* as least risky. *AA* less risky, *A* more risky, *B* just adequate to service and *C,* inadequate to service and highly risky and D is default prone. The agency rating will add their own prefix or suffix to those grades to indicate their stamp of rating. Thus in India, at present there are some rating agencies, namely, CRISIL, ICRA, CARE, Duff and Phelps and FITCH and it is now made compulsory that companies issuing debt instruments to get the ratings and publish them. If a company is not satisfied with a rating of an agency, it can go to another agency. International credit rating agencies for country's sovereign rating are Moodys, Standard & Poor, Duff and Phelps and Japanese Bond Research Institute.

Among debt instruments in capital markets, bonds, debentures preference shares and different categories of debt instruments are to be rated. Besides, among the money market instruments, Commercial Paper and short-term instruments of less than one year and fixed deposits of one to three years are also rated. When rating is done analysis of the company's financial and operational aspects is carried out on the basis of the data available at that time.

## How to Minimise the Risks?

The company specific risks (unsystematic risks) can be reduced by diversifying into a few companies belonging to various industry groups, asset groups or different types of instruments like equity shares, bonds, debentures etc. Thus, asset classes are bank deposits, company deposits, gold, silver, land, real estate, equity shares etc. Industry groups are tea, sugar, paper, cement, steel, electricity, electronics, computer software etc. Each of them have different risk-return characteristics and investments are to be made, based on individual's risk preferences. The second category of risk (systematic risk) is managed by the use of Beta of different company shares.

## Measurement of Risk — Beta

In simple language, Beta is percentage change in the scrip return divided by the percentage change in market return. Here the appreciation in the scrip price relative to the market price index is considered. Leaving aside the mathematical formulae for calculating the Beta over the period of time, one can take readily available Betas of well traded companies from Financial Journals like Dalal Street, Capital Market, ICFAI Journal etc. If Beta is 1, the scrip risk is the same as the market risk. If Beta is greater than 1, the scrip risk is more than the market risk, and if Beta is less than 1, the scrip risk is less than the market risk. The defensive or risk averse investors should invest in scrips with Beta less than 1. Aggressive risk takers would prefer scrips with Beta greater than 1.

## Risk Return Analysis

All transactions are risky. The higher the risk taken, the higher is the return. But proper management of risk involves the right choice of investments whose risks are compensating. The total risks of two companies may be different and even lower than the risk of a group of two companies if their risks are offset by each other. Thus, if the risk of Reliance is represented by Beta of 1.90 and of Dr. Reddy's at 0.70 the total of these two is 1.30, on average. But the actual Beta of the group of these two may be less than that due to the fact that covariances of these two may be negative or independent.

# WHAT IS PORTFOLIO RISK?

As the investors acquire different sets of assets of financial nature, such as gold, silver, real estate, buildings, insurance policies, post office certificates, NSC or NSS etc., they are making a provision for future. The risk of each of such investments is to be understood before hand. Normally, the average householder keeps most of his income in cash or bank deposits and assumes that they are safe and least risky. Little does he realise that they also carry a risk with them — the fear of loss or actual loss or theft and loss of real value of these assets through the rise in price or inflation in the economy. Cash carries no interest or income and bank deposits carry a nominal rate of 4% on savings deposits; no interest on current account and a maximum of 8% on term deposits of one year and above. The liquidity on fixed deposits is poor as one has to wait for the period to maturity or take loan on such amount but at a loss of income due to penal rate. Generally risk averters invest only in banks, P.O. and UTI and mutual funds. Gold, silver, real estate, nidhis and chit funds are the other avenues of investment for average householder, of middle and lower income groups. If the investor desired to have a real rate of return which is substantially higher than the inflation rate he has to invest in relatively more risky areas of investment like shares and debentures of companies or bonds of government and semi-government agencies or deposits with companies and firms. Investment in chit funds, nidhis, company deposits, and in private limited companies has the highest risk. But the basic principle is that the higher the risk, the higher is the return and the investor should have a clear perception of the elements of risk and return when he makes investments. Risk Return Analysis is thus, essential for the investment and portfolio management. This is applicable to corporates and MNCs in that they make investments and manage a portfolio.

## Management of Portfolio

Many times the investors go on acquiring these assets in an *ad hoc* and unplanned manner and the result is high risk, low return profile which they may face. All such assets would constitute his portfolio and the wise investor not only plans his portfolio as per his risk return profile or preferences but manages his portfolio efficiently so as to secure the highest return for the lowest risk possible at that level of investment. This in short is the portfolio management.

Corporates manage their portfolios on the basis of the same principles of Risk-Return Analysis to maximise their trading income or non-operational income. These investments in the money market are mainly aimed at liquidity adjustment and optimum income realisation. Other investments in the capital market, if any, are mainly for finance and investment companies, which may also be MNCs. These investments are generally meant for income, capital gains and other benefits and rarely for speculative purposes. Hedges are available in the futures and option markets. Many manufacturing and trading companies are found to make investments in affiliates, subsidiaries etc. Their investments in projects are assessed as per the principles, discussed in an earlier chapter on Capital Budgeting.

❖ ❖ ❖

# RISK MEASUREMENT IN INVESTMENTS

# 40

In International Financial Management, the corporate executive is concerned with investment function, in addition to finance function. In any investment, whether at domestic or international level, risk is inherent and one has to bear it. Risk reduction risk measurement and related aspects are discussed here at the theoretical level.

## CAPM

As international equity investment faces many risks, measurement and management of that risk becomes important. Theoretically, CAPM Capital Asset Pricing Model applies to international investment as much as domestic investment.

The CAPM was developed to explain how risky securities are priced in market and this was attributed to experts like Sharpe and Lintner. Markowitz theory being more theoretical, CAPM aims at a more practical approach to stock valuation.

It is no doubt based on the mean-variance approach to risk for assessment of investment as developed by Markowitz. It explains the behavioural pattern of investors in building up portfolios.

The CAPM is based on certain assumptions, some of which are common to CAPM and MPT. CAPM is in fact developed as part of MPT (Modern Portfolio Theory). The assumptions are first set out below:

(1) The investor aims at maximising the utility of his wealth, rather than the wealth or return. The difference between them is that individual preferences are taken into account in the utility concept. While some have preference for larger risk which will have increasing marginal utility for wealth, for others, with less preference for risk, the incremental wealth will be less attractive if it is attached with more risk. Thus, the preference of investors for risk return will be taken into account in this model.

(2) Investors have similar expectations of Risk and Return. Without these consensus standards, the estimates of mean and variance may lead to different forecasts with the result that the efficient portfolio of each will be different from that of the others. There will be innumerable efficient frontiers, each dependent on the set of preferences of individuals for risk and return. If investors do not have similar expectations, there will be no homogeneity in their conception and no single efficient frontier line will apply to all.

This in turn will imply that the price of an asset, which is the best estimate of the present value of future returns will be different for different investors. This assumption is therefore, unrealistic for application in the real world.

(3) Investors make investment decision on a rational basis, depending on their assessment of risk and return. Risk is measured by two factors, mean and variance. In the CAPM we assume that rational investors diversify away their diversifiable risk, namely, unsystematic risk and only systematic risk remains which varies with the Beta of the security. While some use the Beta only, as a measure of risk, others use both Beta and variance of returns (total risk) as the sources of reward or expected return. As these perceptions of risk and reward vary from individual to individual, under CAPM we get a series of efficient frontier lines while in the case of MPT, there will be a single efficient frontier line, as the conception of risk and return expectation is assumed to be homogeneous in the latter.

(4) Investors will have free access to all available information at no cost and no loss of time. If the information is not the same for all, no common efficient frontier line can be drawn. Besides even if the information is not available at the same time different conclusions can be drawn regarding expected return and risk and no single price of the capital asset can be conceived.

(5) Investors should have identical time horizons which again is highly unrealistic. Investors have different time horizons and their estimates of stock value will therefore, differ, even as the estimated earnings are the same per year. Continuous time models are sometimes used to get over the above difficulty or again one can approximate a single period model as a proxy to multi-period model on the assumption that returns are the same over time and time has no relevance to expected returns and that expected returns are again independent of the past and current information.

While the above assumptions are common to both CAPM and MPT, some assumptions are specific to CAPM. Thus, there is a risk free asset, which gives risk free return. Investors can borrow and lend unlimited amounts at the same price. This assumption of risk free asset transforms the curved efficient frontier line to a linear one. Risk can be reduced by adding a risk free asset, or borrowing at the risk free rate.

Besides, it is also necessary to assume in CAPM that total asset quantity is fixed and all assets are marketable and divisible. This assumption implies that the liquidity requirement of investors is ignored and there will be no new issues, which are both unrealistic.

After the brief review of the above assumptions we can summarise the requirements for CAPM as follows:

Risk is measured by variance of expected returns. There are two components of risk — systematic (non-diversifiable) and unsystematic (diversifiable). For diversifiable risk, the investor makes a proper diversification to reduce the risk and for the non-diversifiable portion, he uses the relevant Beta measure to adjust to his requirement or preferences. Due to the possibility of risk free asset and lending and borrowing at the free rate, the investor has two components of the portfolio — risk free assets and the risky market assets. His total return is summation from the above two components.

Under CAPM, the equilibrium situation arises when all frictions, like taxes, divisibility transaction costs and different risk-free borrowing and lending rates are assumed away. Equilibrium will be brought about by changes in prices due to changes in demand and supply.

## CPM Line

Figure below depicts the capital market line with riskless rate of return. Point P is the riskless interest rate. Preferred investments are plotted along the line PMZ, by combination of both risky assets and risk free asset along with the borrowing and lending. The slope of the PMZ is the measure of the reward for risk taking. P is the risk free return, Em — T is the measure of the risk premium — a return for the risk taking. The reward for waiting is the risk less interest rate, OP, and second reward is the return per unit of risk borne, measured by the slope 'α' of the PMZ line. The internal rate can be considered as price of time and the slope of capital market line as price of the risk (See Figure 40.1).

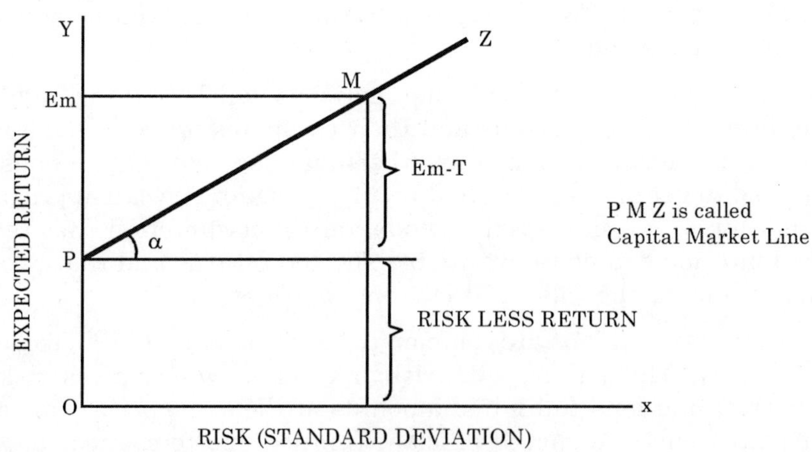


**Fig. 40.1**

The equation of CML, connecting the risk less asset with the risky portfolio is

$$Re = Rf \frac{RM - Rf}{\sigma m} \times \sigma e$$ These terms are explained later.

$\sigma m$ is total risk of the market and $\sigma e$ is risk of the scrip or portfolio.

If the borrowing and lending rates are different, then OQ becomes the borrowing rate and OP will be the lending rate, as shown below. The efficient frontier line with differential borrowing and lending rates will be as shown below: (Fig. 40.2)

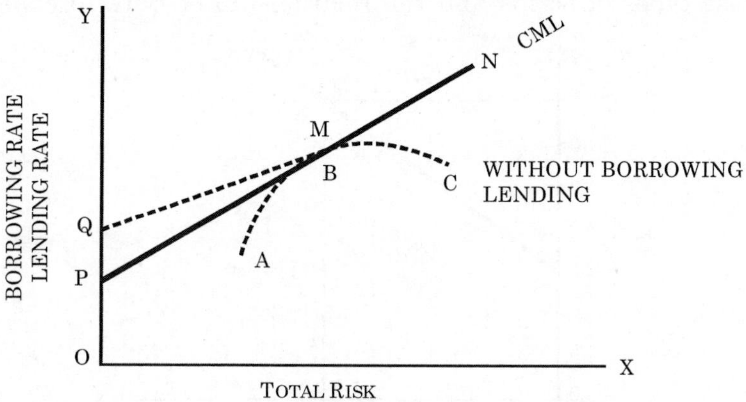


**Fig. 40.2**

QMN is line with the borrowing of OQ and PMN is with the lending of OP and ABC is the efficiency frontier line without borrowing and lending. The curved line will become linear; if once the riskless asset of borrowing and lending at fixed riskless rate is introduced.

The CML as described above reflects the relationship of total risk and expected return. Total risk includes both systematic and unsystematic risks. It may also include the risk free assets to reduce the total risk. The CAPM has two components of the capital market return, which are the reward for waiting or riskless return, and the reward per unit of risk borne as measured by the slope of the CML line.

The investors will have their choice of efficient portfolio somewhere along the line of CML, as all efficient portfolios would be on it. Those which are less efficient will be below the line PMN, in the chart above. The risk free rate can be thought as the price of time and the slope of the capital market line as the Price of Risk.

## Security Market Line (SML)

Unlike the CML, which considers the total risk as a measure of variability of returns, SML takes into account only the systematic risk, which is market related and is not possible to reduce or eliminate by diversification. Beta is the measure of risk of a security relative to the whole market, and is used in the SML.

Since the unsystematic risk is already taken care of by diversification in the construction of an efficient portfolio, it is desirable to develop an alternative to CML which will use Beta as the independent variable and can be adopted for use in portfolio management and in purchase of individual securities. Such a line is called Security

Market Line, which depicts a linear relationship between expected return and the systematic risk.

The SML curve drawn below shows a positive slope, indicating that the return and risk are positively related. The higher the risk, the higher is the return. The Beta of market portfolio, as represented by the BSE or NSE index is always one. But the company scrip can have Betas higher than 1 or lower than 1. Those with Betas less than 1 are defensive securities and those with Betas above 1 are called aggressive scrips. The graph below shows these types of scrips and the relationship of Beta to expected return.

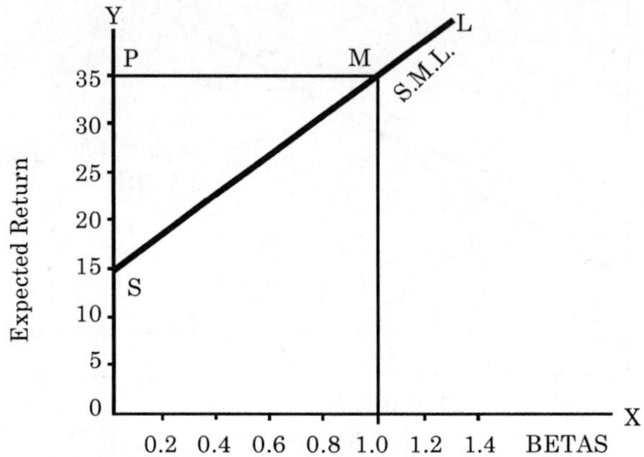


**Fig. 40.3**

SML is Security Market Line, OS is the risk-free return, OP is the return of the market, whose Beta is 1; those below Beta 1 are defensive and others are aggressive scrips in the market.

SML can be represented symbolically by an equation as;

Ri = Rf + Bi (Rm – Rf),

Ri is the return on the security, i,

Rf is Risk-free return,

Rm is Market Return.

Bi is Beta of Scrip i related to Market Risk ,

If Rf = 10, Rm = 20 Bi = 1.5, which is more risky than the market average, then

Ri = 10 + 1.5 (20 – 10)

= 10 + 15 = 25.0% which is higher than the market return

Suppose the Bi is less risky than the market at 0.75 then

Ri = 10 + 0.75 (20 – 10)

= 10 + 7.5 = 17.5%, which is lower than the market return

From the above equation, we can estimate the expected return on a security. It is represented as something like a premium or discount on the market return and can be compared. It can be a return on a security as distinguished from a portfolio. If the

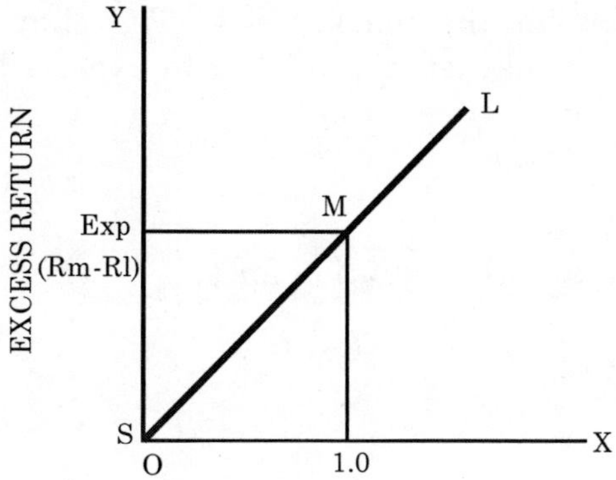


Fig. 40.4

security is correctly priced it will have Ri = Rf = 0 and SML curve goes through the origin (see chart on the left) Ri – Rf measures the excess return which varies with the risk taken. Within the chart it is seen that Rm – Rf is excess return if market Beta = 1. The security market line implies that the individual assets and portfolio should be on SML, if they are correctly priced. Beta values should then correctly represent the contribution to the risk of the security to the portfolio. All assets lying above the SML are undervalued and those below the SML are overvalued. If we buy undervalued securities, the returns will be more and *vice versa.* It will thus be seen that SML curve assumes a critical importance in portfolio selection and individual investment decision.

## CAPM Analysis

The expected return of a portfolio in equilibrium is equal to risk free rate Rf, plus risk premium which is related to its Beta. Thus, Rp – Rf = risk premium and this is equal to $B_{PM}$ (Rm – Rf) where Rp is expected rate of return and Rf the risk free return.

These symbols are the same as explained above. This leads us to the market model, which relates the expected excess return of the portfolio to the excess return of the market. This is an explanation of the risk premium which gives excess returns. The chart 40.5 presents the relation of E [(Rm) – (Rf)], to the E (RP – Rf) viz., in words, excess

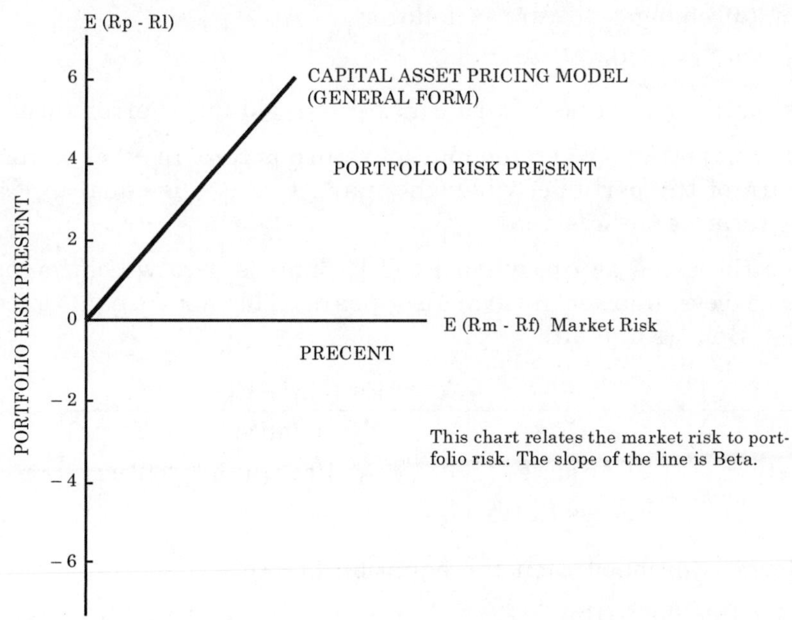


Fig. 40.5

returns on a portfolio to the portfolio's excess risk over the market risk. The chart presents CAPM in a general form with expected excess market risk related to expected excess return.

## Market Model

Risk premium form is the one shown in Fig. 40.5 and the equation for this is where T is risk free return.

$$\underset{\text{for portfolio)}}{\underset{\text{(Premium}}{\text{RpT}}} = \underset{\text{Beta}}{\beta\text{pm}} \times \underset{\text{for market}}{\underset{\text{Premium}}{(\text{Rm} - \text{T})}}$$

Beta relates the portfolio risk premium to market risk premium. If Beta is one they are the same. "T" is risk free return.

Market Model can be presented in the form of a regression equation. Taking the above equation for risk premium of the portfolio, let us introduce a new concept of risk adjusted excess return which is generated by the expertise of the portfolio manager, represented by the $\alpha$p. This can be graphically represented as the y-axis intercept for the regression line. $\alpha$p can be zero, positive or negative, depending on the performance of the portfolio.

When this model is presented in the risk premium form, the equation is

$$\text{Rp} \square \text{Rf} = \alpha\text{p} \square \text{Rf}\ (1 \square \beta\text{pm}) + \beta\text{pm}\ (\text{Rm} \square \text{Rf}) + \text{rp}$$

Let, $\alpha\text{p}^{\text{o}} = \alpha\text{p} \square \text{Rf}\ (1 \square \beta\text{pm})$

As the risk of the portfolio remains unaffected, $\beta$pm of the characteristic line remains unchanged but $\alpha$p changes to $\alpha\text{p}^{\text{o}}$ as follows:

$$\alpha\text{p}^{\text{o}} = \alpha\text{p} \square \text{Rf}\ (1 \square \beta\text{pm})$$

$\alpha\text{p}^{\text{o}}$ is risk adjusted excess return and $\sigma$p is residual or error term.

$\sigma$p is return on portfolio when the market return is zero. In other words, $\alpha$p represents the excess return of the portfolio, when the market return is equal to riskless rate and rp is the error term or the residual.

$\alpha\text{p}^{\text{o}}$ can be the same as $\alpha$p, when Rf $(1 \square \beta\text{pm})$ is zero which happens when $\beta$pm is 1; then the excess market return disappears. The above equation now becomes; $\text{Rp} - \text{Rf} = \alpha\text{p} + \text{Bpm}\ (\text{Rm} - \text{Rf}) + \text{rp}$.

$$\text{R}_\text{p} = \frac{\text{Rf}}{\begin{pmatrix}\text{Riskless}\\ \text{Return}\end{pmatrix}} + \frac{\alpha\text{p}}{\begin{pmatrix}\text{Risk}\\ \text{Adjusted}\\ \text{Excess Return}\end{pmatrix}} + \frac{\beta\text{Pm}(\text{Rm} - \text{Rf})}{\begin{pmatrix}\text{Systematic}\\ \text{Risk Premium}\end{pmatrix}} + \frac{\text{rp}}{\begin{pmatrix}\text{Error}\\ \text{Term}\end{pmatrix}}$$

If error term is dropped then the equation becomes

$$\text{Rp} = \text{Rf} + \alpha\text{P} + \beta\text{pm}\ (\text{Rm} \square \text{Rf})$$

The above equation states that if the risk adjusted excess return on a portfolio is positive $\alpha\text{p}^0 > \text{o}$, then the portfolio return is greater than what is normally expected, indicating superior return. If $\alpha p^0$ is positive, the Portfolio Manager has shown his expertise in beating the market by showing return higher than the market return.

We have seen that the slope of SML curve is $\beta$. If we have a perfectly diversified portfolio in the CAPM, the error term disappears. If at the same time expected risk adjusted excess return $\alpha^0 p$ of the portfolio is zero which is assured under Market Efficiency Theory, then the slope of the characteristic line is Beta of the portfolio. Thus, under condition of perfect markets, the slope of the regression line is Beta and excess returns disappear ($\alpha p^0 = 0$).

## Uses and Limitations

In real world, investors get higher return for higher risk and they are more concerned with company related risks than with the market related risks, except in the case of trained investment analysts. Companies are found to use CAPM to determine the cost of equity for the firm, to estimate the required return for divisions or lines of business and to determine the hurdle rates for corporate investments and to evaluate the performance of investment division in terms of costs and returns. These hurdle rates of return are in general the required rates of return and the corporates assess the past performance of the costs and related returns for each of the divisions. In the case of public utilities, the CAPM can be used to estimate the costs and rates to be charged to cover the costs. The CAPM is used to regulate the public utilities from the point of view of costs.

Historical return and Betas are used to select the proper risk in investments in the portfolio. CAPM is used to select securities, construct portfolios and evaluate the performance of the portfolio. It is thus a useful tool for investment analysis and portfolio management.

The limitations of the theory are also pointed out by many critics. This theory is unrealistic for any average investor, who goes by the fundamental factors influencing the company, its earnings, dividend and bonus record. Empirical tests of the Model have not proved very useful. The Model is built on *ex-ante* factors while in reality the expectations of the future vary from person to person. Data and analysis are to be based on *ex-post* factors while anticipations of future risk and returns are *ex-ante* and both may not be related. The CAPM is in fact not testable exactly as the exact composition of the market is known and is used in testing. The empirical tests conducted by Richard Roll and others were only tests on samples whether the proxy market portfolio was efficient or not. The use of surrogatives and proxies have not proved the theory as really useful and practical.

CAPM theory is thus, a nice theoretical exposition but in actual world, it does not conform to the real world risk-return trends and empirical tests have not given unequivocal support to the theory. It is also found that there are many non-Beta factors influencing the returns. The calculation of Beta is itself of doubtful validity as the historical Betas may not reflect the future risks or returns. In the short-run in particular, projections on the basis of Betas or returns and risk have been found to be unreliable and results contrary to CAPM Theory were noticed. Thus, CAPM is a good theoretical tool but with its own limitations in practical applications.

## Duration (Example)

Q. An investor wants to purchase a Bond with maturity 3 years, coupon rate 11% and par value.

(A) If the investor is requiring YTM 15% of equivalent risk what is the price he should pay?

$$P = \left(\frac{11}{1+0.15}\right) + \frac{11}{(1+0.15)^2} + \frac{111}{(1+0.15)^3} = 9.56 + 8.32 + 72.98 = 90.86$$

(B) If the bond is selling at a price of Rs. 97.59 what is its YTM?
YTM is to be estimated by trial and error method. Consider 12% as YTM. Then

$$\left(\frac{11}{1+0.12}\right) + \frac{11}{(1+0.12)^2} + \frac{111}{(1+0.12)^3} = 9.82 + 8.77 + 79.01 = 97.59$$

Hence, YTM is 12%

(C) What is the duration of Bond, if the YTM is 12% and expected return is 10.06%?

| *Duration* | *Value* | *% age Value* | *Weighted Duration* |
|---|---|---|---|
| 1 Year | $9.82 = \left(\frac{11}{1.12}\right)$ | 10.06 | 0.1006 = 1 × 0.1006 |
| 2 Year | $8.77 = \left(\frac{11}{(1.12)^2}\right)$ | 8.99 | 0.1798 = 2 × 0.0899 |
| 3 Year | $79.01 = \left(\frac{111}{(1.12)^3}\right)$ | 80.95 | 2.4285 = 3 × 0.8095 |
| Total | 97.60 | 100.00 | 2.7089 |

The duration in the case of value bond of YTM of 12% and expected return 10.06% was shown above. Then the weighted duration of the portfolio is 2.7089.

The Market Model and CAPM may not give similar results as expected excess returns and risk premiums, in the two models are not identical.

Say $\alpha p = 4\%$, $Rf = 6\%$ (riskless return)

$\beta$ Beta = 2, Rm (expected market return) = 10%.

Expected Risk Premium (Rp – Rf)

Market Model = $\alpha P^{\alpha} + \beta pm\ (Rm - Rf)$

(Rp – Rf) = 4 – 6 (1 – 2) + 2 (10 – 6)

4 + 6 + 8 = 18%

Where, $\alpha P^{\alpha} = \alpha P - Rf\ (1 - \beta m)$

4 – 6 (1 – 2)

## CAPM Example

$(Rp \square Rf) = \beta Pm\ (Rm - Rf)$

$= 2\ (10 - 6)$

$20 - 12 = 8\%$

In the exceptional case when the portfolio is in equilibrium, the expected risk premium of the portfolio under both models should be identical. That happens when $\alpha p^0 = 0 + \alpha p - Rf\ (1 - Bpm)$

Then under Market Model

The excess premium $= 0 + 2\ (10 - 6)$

$= 2 \times 4 = 8\%$

and under CAPM

$Rp - Rf = 2\ (10 - 6)$

$20 - 12 = 8\%$

If the risk free rate is 10%, expected return on NSE Index is 18%, standard deviation is 5% (SD). Construct an efficient portfolio to secure 16% return. The efficient portfolio consists of market securities and risk free securities invested in the proportion of W and 1 – W respectively, then

$Rp = W\ (Rm) + (1 - W)\ Rf$

$16\% = W\ (18\%) + (1 - W)\ 10\%$

$16 = 18W + 10 \square 10W$

$16 \square 10 = 6 = 18W \square 10W = 8W$. Thus, $8W = 6$

and $W = \frac{6}{8} = 75\%$ $\quad 1 \square W = 25\%$

Investment in market securities is 75% of the amount and 25% in risk free securities. The portfolio risk in this case is

$$Rp = Rf + \frac{(Rm - Rf)}{\sigma m\ \sigma p}$$

$$16 = 10 + \frac{18 - 10}{5} \sigma p = \left[16 = 10 + \frac{8}{5} \sigma p\right]$$

$$16 \square 10 = \frac{8}{5} \sigma p$$

$$6 \times 5 = 30 = 8\ \sigma p$$

$$\sigma p = \frac{30}{8} = 3.75$$

If now an amount of Rs. 10,000 is to be invested and expected return is 20%, construct a portfolio and calculate its risk

$$Rp = 20 = W \times 18 + (1 \square W)\ 10$$

$$20 = 18W + 10 - 10W\ (viz.,\ 10 + 8W)$$

$$10 = 8W$$

$$W = \frac{10}{8} = 1.25$$

Since it is more than 1, borrow 0.25 or 25% of Rs. 10,000 to invest in market portfolio. Thus own funds are Rs. 10,000 and borrowed funds are Rs. 2,500, with a total of Rs. 12,500.

Risk on the portfolio is calculated as follows:

$$20 = 10 + \left(\frac{18-10}{5}\right)\sigma p = 10 + \frac{8}{5}\sigma p$$

$$\therefore\ 20 - 10 = \frac{8}{5}\ \sigma p$$

$$\sigma p = \frac{10 \times 5}{8} = \frac{50}{8} = 6.25\%$$

## Diversification

The traditional theory laid down diversification as a technique of selection of securities in a portfolio. This is called "Random diversification" or "Simple diversification," on the basis of straight rule of "two is a better than one." Simple diversification on random basis was found to be more remunerative by researchers and these number of scrips in a portfolio of individuals is to be around 10 to 15 securities.

Rational basis of why diversification and how to achieve optimal diversification were studied by later researchers, of which Markowitz is reputed to be the pioneer. "Naive diversification" or "Superfluous diversification" may result from random and indiscriminate selection of securities, which does not lead to any reduction of risk. Thus, cycle and tubes are related industries and one invests in those two types of industries which are highly correlated in a positive manner, the risk will be increased by diversification rather than reducing. Naive diversification thus, means that diversification in name only which does not reduce the risk. Thus, an investor may have 10 scrips in steel, mini steel and ferrous metals, which will only increase risk. But an investor having 10 scrips spread in cycles, electronics, sugar, steel, auto, etc., will have less risk as these industries are not auto-correlated and their risks are independent of each other or even negatively related.

It was thus, left to Markowitz and later researchers to show that diversification is a tool to reduce unsystematic risk and how it can be reduced by a study of variances and covariances of securities return, as against the market returns.

## Why Diversification?

It is never prudent to put all ones' eggs in one basket, as it may lead to total ruin if the basket itself is broken or lost. The human behaviour is normally risk averse which means that for psychological reasons, he distributes his assets in a variety of risk classes, some in cash, some in bank deposits, insurance, provident fund, pension fund etc. These are all examples of the normal human behaviour of diversifying the asset holdings to reduce risk, provide for contingency and take all precautions against total loss.

(a) Thus, the average investor never puts all his savings in one form or in one security for self-protection and for psychological reasons.

(b) Money kept idle or in some investments which do not give adequate return will be a loss to investor, as he loses the value of money over time. By logic of common sense, investors try to satisfy most of their objectives of savings by putting money in various avenues and that means diversification. The various objectives are income, capital appreciation, safety, marketability, contingency, liquidity and hedge against inflation and for future provision of larger incomes. His choice of investments will cater to these requirements which lead to diversification of investments.

Even without the theoretical basis of covering or reducing the unsystematic diversifiable risk, the investor in the traditional theory used to adopt some methods of diversification.

Further discussion on diversification is presented in the next chapter.

## Example on Measurement of Risk

*Calculation of Standard Deviation and Variance*

As diversification is meant for reduction of risk, its measurement is relevant here.

**Table 40.1**

| *DCM* | | | *Escorts* | | |
|---|---|---|---|---|---|
| *Return* | *Probability* | *Weighted Average Return* | *Return* | *Probability* | *Weighted Average Return* |
| 8 | 0.15 | 1.20 | 9 | 0.30 | 2.70 |
| 9 | 0.20 | 1.80 | 10 | 0.40 | 4.00 |
| 10 | 0.30 | 3.00 | 11 | 0.30 | 3.30 |
| 11 | 0.20 | 2.20 | | | |
| 12 | 0.15 | 1.80 | | | |
| | | 10% | | | 10% |

Average return is the same in both cases but risk is different. DCM has a range of variation from 8% to 12% while the Escorts has a variation from 9 to 11. So Escorts is preferred by the investor.

## Calculation of Standard Deviation

**TABLE 40.2**

*Example DCM*

| *Return* | *Mean* | *Difference (d)* | *Square of Deviation ($d^2$)* |
|---|---|---|---|
| 8 | 10 | − 2 | 4 |
| 9 | 10 | − 1 | 1 |
| 10 | 10 | 0 | 0 |
| 11 | 10 | 1 | 1 |
| 12 | 10 | 2 | 4 |

$\Sigma d^2 = 10$

$\sigma$ = Standard deviation is $\sqrt{\frac{\Sigma d^2}{N}} = \sqrt{\frac{10}{5}} = \sqrt{2}$

$\sigma$ standard deviation = $\sqrt{2}$ = 1.41

$\sigma^2$ = variance is 2

## Example Escorts

| *Return* | *Mean* | *Deviation* | *Square of Deviation* |
|---|---|---|---|
| 9 | 10 | 1 | 1 |
| 10 | 10 | 0 | 0 |
| 11 | 10 | 1 | 1 |

$Sd^2 = 2$

$\sigma$ = standard deviation = $\sqrt{\frac{\Sigma d^2}{N}} = \sqrt{\frac{2}{3}} = \sqrt{0.66}$

$\sigma$ = $\sqrt{0.66}$ = 0.82

$\sigma^2$ = variation = 0.66

Risk on the Escorts is lower in the above example.

## Simple Diversification

Take two securities of TISCO and Reliance

| *Security* | *Expected Return* | *Proportion of Investment* |
|---|---|---|
| TISCO | 20% | 25% |
| Reliance | 25% | 75% |

The return on the portfolio by combining them would be $Rp = W_1R_1 + W_2R_2$. $R_1$ and $R_2$ are returns and $W_1$ and $W_2$ are weights of two investments.

$$Rp = 0.20\ (.25) + 0.25\ (0.75)$$

$$= 5\% + 18.75\% = 23.75\%$$

Here, no consideration is given for risk and covariance of risk on the securities, invested in the portfolio. This can be demonstrated by taking an example of Markowitz diversification.

## Markowitz Diversification

Before discussing the Markowitz diversification, what the researches of investors and investment analysts have found is to be set out briefly.

Firstly, they found that putting all eggs in one basket is bad and most risky.

Secondly, there should be adequate diversification of investment into various securities as that will spread the risk and reduce it; if the number of them say 10 to 15 is adequate to enjoy the economies of time, scale of operations and expertise utilised by the investor in his analysis.

Reference was already made to Naive diversification, which is a spread of investments into many securities but will not reduce the risk, like buying ten securities all in the shipping industry, which is risky industry in itself. Besides some researchers have found that there is an optimisation process for diversification to reduce the unsystematic or company related risk by choosing such companies which are not closely related or not owned by the same family group in the same industry group. This optimisation process also leads to an investment in 10-15 companies well chosen for differences in their characteristics, nature of the product market, pattern of production etc.

An example of weighted return on a diversified portfolio is given below:

## Example

What is the expected return of a portfolio, comprising of the following securities:

| *Security* | *Expected Return* | *% of Fund, Invested* |
|---|---|---|
| 1. DCM | 10% | 25% |
| 2. Shriram Fibres | 15% | 25% |
| 3. J.K. Synthetics | 20% | 50% |

$Rp = W_1\ R_1 + W_2\ R_2 + W_3\ R_3$

Rs are expected returns and Ws are weights

$Rp = (10 \times 0.25) + 15\ (0.25) + 20\ (0.50)$

$= 2.5 + 3.75 + 10.0$

$=$ 16.25%. This is the expected return on the portfolio.

❖ ❖ ❖

# PORTFOLIO DIVERSIFICATION AND RISK REDUCTION

# 41

## Introduction

International operations of corporates involve investment and portfolio management at the international level, in addition to the finance function and other functions that the corporate executive performs. In portfolio management, diversification and risk reduction are vital factors for maximisation of wealth of the shareholders, at the world level.

## What is Diversification?

Diversification is a technique of reducing the risk involved in investment and in Portfolio Management including International Investment. This is a process of conscious selection of assets, instruments and scrips of companies/government securities, in a manner that the total risks are brought down. This process helps in the reduction of risk, under category of what is known as "Unsystematic Risk" and promotes the optimisation of returns for a given level of risks in Portfolio Management.

We have seen that in the case of unsystematic risk, the method of lowering the risk is to diversify into a number of companies and a number of industries, for selection of scrips in the portfolio. This diversification may take any of the following forms:

(1) Into different *types of assets,* like gold, real estate, government securities, corporate securities, etc.

(2) Into different *instruments* or security type bonds, stocks, debentures, government securities, etc.

(3) Into different *industry lines,* namely, plastics, chemicals, engineering, cement, steel, fertilisers, etc.

(4) Into different *scrips of companies,* viz., new companies, growing companies, new product companies etc.

(5) Into different types of nations or countries.

## Principles

The principles involved in diversification are as follows:

A single company/industry is more risky than two companies/industries. Two companies in say, steel industry are more risky than one company in steel, and one in Tyres and Tubes.

Two companies, one in steel and the other in chemicals are less risky than two in either steel or chemicals. Similarly, two companies or two industries which are similar in nature of demand or market etc., are more risky than the two in dissimilar industries. Statistically speaking, their variance/covariance should be different. It is proper diversification which involves two or more companies/two or more industries whose fortunes fluctuate independent of one another or in different directions, or into two or more countries of different stages of growth.

## Random Diversification

The traditional belief is that diversification involves "not putting all eggs in one basket." This policy involves as many baskets as possible; carried to the extreme it is good to have as many companies as possible, and as many industries as possible in one's portfolio. But this is a misconception as economies of scale operate in the reverse direction (involving diseconomies) with the result that monitoring and review of the portfolio become inefficient, costly and cumbersome and outweigh the benefits of diversification.

There are some accepted methods of effecting diversification:

**(1) Randomness in Selection of Companies and Industries:** The probability of reducing risk is more with a random selection as the statistical error of choosing wrong companies will come down due to randomness of selection which is a statistical technique. This involves placing of companies in any order and picking them up in random manner.

**(2) Optimisation of Selection Process:** Given the amount of money to be invested there is optimum number of companies, where money can be invested. If the number is too small, risk cannot be reduced adequately and if the number is too big, there will be diseconomies and difficulty of supervision, analysis and monitoring will increase risk again. There is thus, a optimum number of companies to be chosen for a given amount of investment.

**(3) Adequate Diversification:** Many traditional approaches emphasise on the need for adequate diversification. This involves as many industries and companies or securities as possible to get the best results. This principle believes in the possibilities of reducing risk to even zero, if there are adequate number of companies and industries. Markowitz emphasised however that what is needed is not only the number of securities to be chosen but the right kind of securities to be chosen. Thus, even if there are a large number of companies they may not reduce risk adequately if they are positively correlated with each other and the market, in which case, they all move in the same direction and many risks will not be reduced and may even increase.

**(4) Markowitz Diversification:** Markowitz emphasised the need for a right number of securities — not too many or too less — and securities which are negatively correlated or not correlated at all. The purpose of diversification is to reduce the unsystematic risk arising out of company's policies and performance. Thus, many of such risks can be reduced by a proper choice of companies and industries. Neither random selection, nor adequate number of securities can guarantee this. One can see from the chart 41.1 that for an individual investor a number of around 10-16 companies can secure reduction of risk to an optimum level if they are properly selected as per Markowitz. For mutual funds or finance companies this number may be higher. The graph shows both systematic and unsystematic risks and the horizontal line of systematic risk cannot be reduced by diversification, but to a large extent unsystematic risk can be reduced by a right choice of companies and to a limited number.

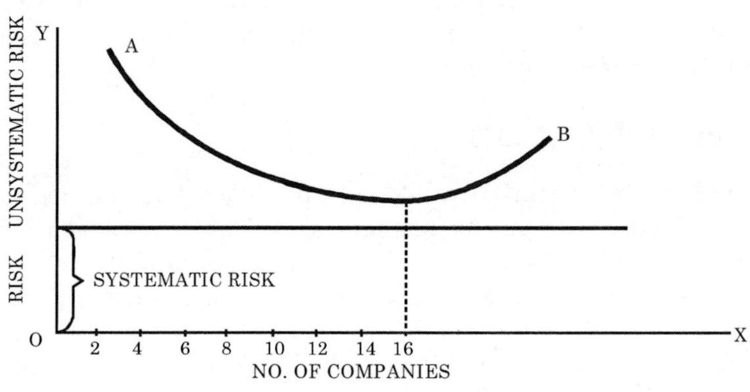


**Chart 41.1**

## International Diversification

The benefits of diversification are well perceived by Portfolio Managers, that many in developed countries, started investing in foreign bonds, stocks and other instruments. They found that they can extend diversification principle to foreign stocks, bonds etc., to improve returns for a given risk by adopting proper techniques of diversification.

## Why International Diversification?

(1) The size and character of international equity and bond markets are so widely varying; so it will increase the scope for larger investment and larger diversification.

(2) The returns in local currencies of some foreign countries are higher than in domestic markets. Thus, for example in Singapore, Malaysia, Taiwan and India the returns in local currencies are higher than in U.S. economy.

(3) The economic trends, business conditions and local profitability and earnings ratios differ widely among countries that the EPS in some developing countries is higher and give opportunity for better diversification and higher returns, through international investments.

(4) International investment is advantageous due to larger investment avenues now open in the first place and secondly due to the imperfect correlation among the international markets. The total risk of a portfolio including the international investment will be lower than with only domestic investment. The degree of volatility, and all risk measures, indicate that these risks vary among the countries and in different degrees and the possibility of covariance, or high correlation will be low.

The frontier of efficiency portfolios can be widened, by inclusion of foreign investments in a portfolio. Thus many International Portfolio Managers prefer to invest in India and so will be the case of Indian Portfolio Managers, if they can diversify into international investments. There are some directions however which will increase risk in such investments.

## Risks in Foreign Investments

(1) Political and social developments may create problems in an unpredictable manner.

(2) Economic and monetary policies may change to their disadvantage. Foreign exchange controls, double taxation, appropriation of foreign assets etc., stand in the way.

(3) Risks of currency fluctuations may pose danger to larger profits depending upon the management in exchange rates. The currency risks are important because the foreign investor when he wants to take home his profits, the desired currency is his local currency, and this has to take into account the exchange rates. The gains or returns out of foreign investments might be offset by opposite and adverse movements in exchange rates. These factors create more risks.

(4) Unforeseen international developments such as wars, political and ideological conflicts etc., might create additional risks.

(5) Foreign information is difficult and foreign accounting and reporting systems differ. All the above factors make the international diversification as desirable provided some active policy of management of portfolio is preferred and even global diversification is achieved. These are factors influencing the global diversification which provide opportunities of risk hedge, due to the diversities in their economies and markets:

Thus, leaving the domestic frontiers, the foreign economies may themselves provide a picture of varying degrees of economic and business fluctuations, high and low inflation rates *vis-a-vis* the GDP growth rates, etc.

Thus $\frac{P}{E}$ multiple of some markets as in India may be higher than in U.S.A. But the growth rate of India is higher than U.S.A. with the result that potential for growth is higher here. Besides EPS in different countries may vary widely and these have to be studied in terms of domestic EPS, foreign EPS, adjusted for forward exchange rates, foreign interest rates, inflation rates *vis-a-vis* the GDP growth rates, so that the international investor knows which markets are attractive internationally, and he can pursue a policy of international diversification to secure offsetting of risks — that is investment risks in Brazil, offsetting investment risks in Germany and yet the returns in total portfolios are higher, when taken back in U.S. dollars. The various markets behave with different degrees of risk/return features such that when the U.S. returns are lower, their returns may be higher in foreign markets thus reducing the total risk of portfolios including foreign investments.

# FFI's INVESTMENT IN INDIA

FFIs were permitted to operate in the Indian capital market since September, 1992, in a bid to globalise the markets. Since January 1993, FII investment started in India. By March 2000, there were 503 FFIs registered with the RBI/SEBI, operating in India. The cumulative amount of their investment upto March 2003 was more than $ 19 billion, but after 1996 the inflow slowed down and its impact was felt on the market. FIIs' net investments in equity and debt in the Indian markets rose from Rs. 42,918 crores in 2004-05 to a high of Rs. 65,073 crores in 2007-08, before declining to negative amount (or outflows) of Rs. 46,382 crores in 2008-09 due to world wide recession and bearish risk trend in markets. In a study published in RBI's Annual Report, 1995-96 it was revealed that BSE Sensex is significantly related ($\gamma = 0.49$) to lagged net investment by FFIs. Such studies are also available in World Bank studies and IMF Studies, which also revealed the significant impact of foreign flows into capital markets of developing countries.

[Ref. Claesseus S. and S. Gooptu, Eds. (1993) "Portfolio Investment in Developing Countries." W.B. Discussion Paper No. 228 and Schadler S. and Carkovic M. Eds. (1993) "Recent Experiences with Surges in Capital Inflows", IMF occasional paper No. 108, IMF.]

These flows influence the market through demand pressures, affecting the interest rates and stock prices, money supply, domestic savings and investment activity in the domestic economies.

## NRI Investment in India

NRI investments in India can take any of the following three forms:

*(i)* Avenues for Personal Investment.

*(ii)* Direct Investment Schemes.

*(iii)* Portfolio Investment Schemes.

**(A) Personal Investments Scheme:** NRI or Foreign Citizens of Indian origin can acquire any of the following investments in India without RBI's prior permission. These are:

Government Securities, P.O. Savings and National Plan Certificates, UTI units, and their schemes, company deposits, mutual fund schemes. New issues of equity, equity shares, debentures, both on repatriation and non-repatriation basis, immovable property for residential purpose, India Development Bonds, housing and real estate development schemes to the extent of even 100%.

The investee company and not NRI has to take prior permission of the RBI in the above cases. Repatriation is permitted if only funds have come from NRE/FCNR accounts and not NRO accounts. The shares of companies their deposits and debentures and Commercial Paper are all available for investment on a non-repatriation basis, under this scheme.

**(B) Direct Investment Scheme:** There are two schemes of 40% and 100% of investment, under this category 40% scheme is for investment in shares and debentures in companies engaged in industrial and manufacturing activity, Hotels, Hospitals, shipping companies, computer software, oil exploration, etc. There is no ceiling on the amount of remittable dividend, but the investee company has to take RBI permission in this regard.

100% scheme is for real estate development, township development, construction of residential buildings, houses etc., development of roads, building materials, bridges and infrastructure facilities, house finance and air taxi operators. They can invest upto 100% in debentures (NCDS), sick industrial undertakings without repatriation. The 100% investment is also permitted for OCBs (overseas corporate bodies with 60% participation of NRIs). They can make investments in 100% export oriented units, EPZ, and high priority industries with foreign equity participation of 51% with the rest to be left (49%) to NRIs.

Original investment can be repatriated after 3 years from the date of the issue. Actual income or dividends, can be freely repatriable, subject to payment of tax (at a flat rate of 20%). OCBs are permitted to repatriate after 3 years at 16% net profit and air taxi operators only after 5 years and out of accumulated foreign exchange earnings only.

NRIs can invest in high priority industries listed in Annexure II to the latest statement on Industrial Policy. The general guideline is that FIIs, FFIs, etc. can invest in any corporate upto 51% of equity, subject to changes as permitted for their investment upto even 100% of equity.

**(C) Portfolio Investment Scheme:** NRIs can freely invest and disinvest without any lock-in period in the cases of the investment in domestic mutual funds, without any limit, and in paid up capital and debt capital upto 5% for each individual subject to an overall ceiling of 10% for all NRIs and OCBs, which can be raised upto 30% now if the company passes a resolution to that effect in the General Body Meeting.

The ADs who have the accounts of NRIs can be used as the medium for portfolio investments on the stock exchanges. RBI's approval is to be secured by the NRI through that particular AD. There is no lock-in period and RBI's approval is valid for 5 years. Capital gains and dividends etc., can be repatriated after payment of taxes (at a flat rate of 20%), if the funds have come through NRE and FCNR accounts. NRI investments in other than banks like NBFC are not permitted as in April 2004.

Sale and transfer of shares is also permitted by the RBI without prior permission in respect of government securities, debentures of corporates, and those on non-repatriation basis. However, RBI prior permission is required for transfer to other NRIs, residents, either by private placement or through any private agency. Those on repatriation basis require permission of the RBI. Rights entitlements and bonus issued are subject to RBI's permission which has to be sought by the company. General permission of RBI is available only for those on non-repatriation basis.

These provisions are subject to constant changes, which are reported in the financial press on a daily basis.

## Passive International Investment Strategy

In passive strategy, an International Index fund is the ideal method of investing abroad. Thus, the offshore funds of India, or other international funds of China, Brazil, Mexico, etc., can be used as the index funds, for passive investment. They can alternatively trade in only major world markets, like U.K., Japan, Germany, France, and Switzerland, after a study of their market behaviour. This strategy of investing in balanced portfolio of a large number of countries, with a high degree of diversification may improve the returns on such positions.

Risk in a foreign portfolio in terms of standard deviation of the continuously compounded annualised return is formula 41.1, as shown below:

$$Vt = [V_l m^2 + V_c^2 + 2P\ V_c\ V_m]\ ½$$

Vc = Exchange Rate risk, $V_m$ is total portfolio risk in local market terms, fully hedged, $V_t$ = total portfolio risk in base currency terms, without currency hedging. p = correlation between exchange rate return and portfolio return in local market terms. The above formula indicates that total portfolio risk in foreign markets is lower, if there is a good negative correlation between local currency returns and local market returns in stock market.

The factors influencing such foreign portfolios are: (i) Foreign asset local returns, (ii) Foreign currency returns, (iii) Domestic asset returns, and (iv) Correlation coefficient between these variables.

The return on a fully hedged foreign investment is

$$R = L\ r + F_p/d$$

R = Return an foreign investment fully hedged.

Lr = Local asset returns, $F_p/d$ is the forward premium/discount (U.S. short-term rate and foreign short-term rate).

## Active International Investment Strategy

Active strategy is oriented to identifying relatively attractive and unattractive national markets. Such identification is followed by ranking these markets abroad and weightage in one's portfolio is given by such ranking in terms of the attractiveness of the local markets. This identification involves some analytical and predictive powers both in the investment markets and currency markets. The operation of such active strategy is depicted below.

**TABLE 41.1**

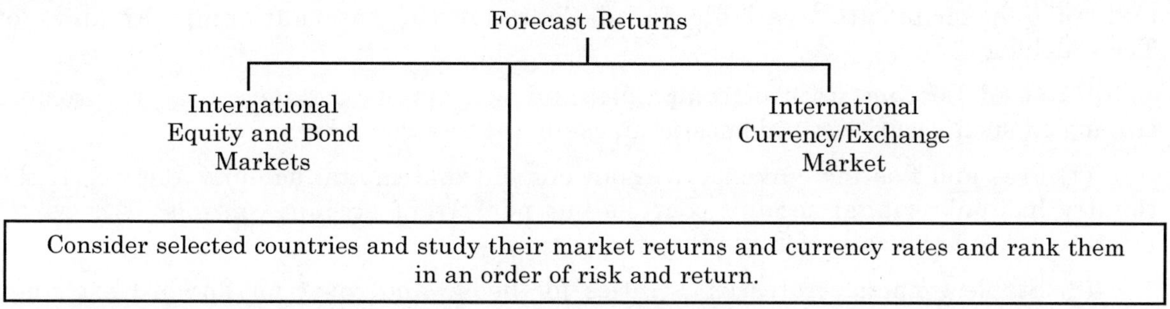


Adjust for hedging of currency rates and market returns so that, an optimum Portfolio with higher return and lowest risk is built.

## Return Forecasts

An exercise of importance in active Portfolio Management is to forecast the returns in equity market and in currency markets.

If say the foreign equity return is 20% as against 10% of domestic return, foreign investments may look attractive but if that 20% return is lost by adverse currency rate fluctuations or high local tax rates then it is not worthwhile investing abroad.

Example of return forecast Table is given below:

**TABLE 41.2**

| *Country* | *Currency Forecast Return* | *Equity Market Forecast Return* | *Net Return %* |
|---|---|---|---|
| UK | 1.1 | 18.2 | 19.3 |
| France | 1.0 | 13.6 | 14.6 |
| Germany | 4.7 | 13.9 | 18.6 |
| India | –5.0 | 20.0 | 15.0 |

Equity market returns are high in India but tax rates and currency rate variations create negative return so that investment becomes unattractive in India, as seen from the above Table. In considering various markets the Portfolio Manager takes into account various economic and political factors and not merely equity returns. A few examples of there factors are given here:

(1) EPS market index and $\frac{\text{P}}{\text{E}}$ multiple.

(2) Relative growth of the economy and the market. If market earnings growth is higher than the growth rate of GDP it is potentially good market.

(3) If the market capitalisation is low relative to GDP and potentiality of growth of market capitalisation is high, such markets are again attractive to foreign investors.

(4) Monthly volatility and annual volatility of prices, should not be very high for attracting foreign investment.

(5) Liquidity and settlement process in the markets — whether deliveries are prompt and enough scrips are available for delivery at the international standards of T + 3 delivery.

(6) Good floating stock of companies and wide public holding so as to promote trading in such securities in domestic markets of those countries.

(7) Free and floating currency without current and capital account controls. If the country has only capital account controls but no current account controls, it is partly attractive as in the case of India.

(8) Stable exchange rates or facilities for hedge and cover for forward exchange position are available in these markets.

If the above features are prevailing in a good measure, and are favourable, such countries are worthwhile and attractive for foreign portfolio management. The breadth of the market in terms of the available number of traded companies and their floating stock are also considered in addition to the expected returns and risks involved in trading in such markets.

International diversification is desirable to improve return and reduce risks. The optimisation process with international diversification is more complicated and active investment strategy will give better returns than passive strategy. Some prior conditions should also be satisfied for optimisation process.

## Evans-Archer Study and Diversification

Advantages of diversification are seen in both returns and risk. Returns can be improved and risks lowered by proper diversification of securities, in those which have negative covariance or are independent. In the chart 41.2, stocks 4, 5 and portfolio 4 & 5 are having the same expected return of 14% but the standard deviation (σ) of the portfolio 4 & 5 is less than the standard deviation of 4 or 5 alone. By combining 4 and 5 into a portfolio, the investor has reduced the risk without any loss of return.

Take stocks 5 and 6, and a portfolio of 5 & 6. Since the return of any portfolio is the weighted average of individual security returns, the expected return of the portfolio is 12, while that of stock 5 is 14% and of stock 6 is 10% [average is ½ (14 + 10) = 12.] But the risk or standard deviation of a portfolio is not simply a weighted average of individual securities. Standard deviation, portfolio 5 and 6 plots to the left of a straight line connecting 5 & 6 — which means that there is less risk in the portfolio than in the weighted average combination (linear line).

Besides, the securities need not be equally weighted as in the above example. If one can design different combinations, he may reach the efficient frontier line which has least risk for a given return.

In this chart, as seen above, returns can be improved and risk reduced by diversification. The optimum points of different combinations, giving the least risk for a given level of return will constitute the efficient frontier. Beyond the frontier line, one cannot reduce the risk further, due to diseconomies or difficulties of reducing the risk further. Reduction of risk takes place due to the fact that securities' returns are not perfectly correlated in the portfolio.

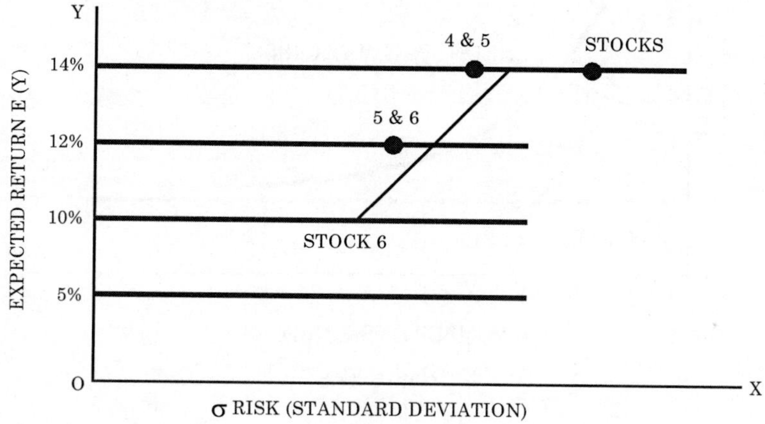


**Chart 41.2**

## Naive Diversification

This refers to the diversification by simply picking stocks at random. This may or may not reduce risk to the optimum level. As the number of stocks in a portfolio is increased randomly, it is possible to reduce the risk upto a point and that too only in respect of the non-systematic risk. The market related systematic risk cannot be reduced by diversification.

## Evans and Archers' Study@

*Evans and Archer* studied the data of 470 NYSE firms during 1958-67 and showed that if the maximum risk of a single stock is 21%, it can be reduced to the extent of approximately 9% and the rest of 12% representing the systematic risk, cannot be diversified away. That is the market risk which the investor has to bear and by using the concept of Beta referred in another chapter, he can take that much risk, that he can tolerate as per his preference or aversion.

In the below chart 41.3 the average standard deviation of returns for a single stock was about 21%. When portfolios of only two stocks, selected were formed, the average standard deviation of this portfolio is about 16% (not shown in the chart). The average standard deviation (σ) of the portfolio of three stocks was 15% and so on down the line, until, the risk is reduced upto 8 stocks in his study. Most of the diversification benefits were achieved even by the use of 8 stocks portfolio. If all the 470 stocks were grouped together into one portfolio, the standard deviation was 11.6%. Thus, in his study of 470 stocks, of the total risk he reduced only upto about 9%, and 12% is the systematic risk or market risk could not be reduced.

*Sources:*

@ J.L. Evans and S.H. Archer "Diversification and the Reduction of Dispersion — An Empirical Analysis," *Journal of Finance,* December 1968.

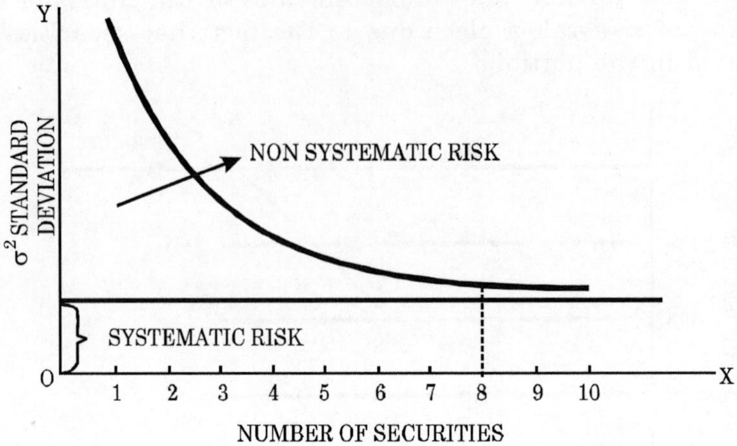


**Chart 41.3**

Thus, Evans and Archer study showed the optimum level upto which risk can be lowered and that will lower depending upon stocks chosen and the time period.

❖ ❖ ❖

# MULTINATIONAL TAXATION

# 42

Taxation in various countries, on their domestic and foreign incomes are an important factor and part of the environment, which influences the global operations of MNCs. Taxation has an impact on almost all decisions such as foreign investment, capital structure, financing costs, dependence on foreign sources of finance, managing the exchange risk etc. In short, all important decisions of the MNCs, like the Investment Decision, Financing Decision and Dividend Decision are influenced by taxation.

## Need for Tax Planning

International Tax planning is therefore necessary to reduce the impact of taxation and maximise the after tax cash flows, in which any company is interested. Tax planning involves and necessitates flexibility of the multinational corporation in structuring foreign operations, spread of its operations and arranging for remittance of cash flows and pattern of and sourcing of finances for its operations. Planning involves the knowledge of the prevailing system of taxation in all countries in which it is operating. The tax system encompasses all taxation of goods and services, imports and exports, tax treatment of foreign source incomes, tax credits, tax havens, incentives and rebates, bilateral tax treaties for avoidance of double taxation etc.

The basic principles of international taxation are equity, justice and neutrality. Equity means that all tax payers in similar situations and with similar income are subject to the same rules. Thus, the dividend income should be subject to the same tax rate whether received from India or abroad or from domestic companies or foreign companies. Tax neutrality refers to the neutral impact of the taxation on financial and investment and dividend payouts of the corporates. There should be uniformity in both the tax rate applicable and in the determination of taxable income in respect of all companies. Taxation should not interfere, according to this principle with the flow of capital, labour and thus change the production structure across borders and thus, change the allocative efficiency of the market forces influence the overall productivity and profits and world welfare. Besides, the other principle of taxation is fairness and justice in tax treatment of any income and from any source. Justice refers to the absence of bias, or discrimination in taxation as between any two categories of tax payers. But all these principles are violated by most tax systems of the world. Domestic and foreign companies are treated differently and sometimes tax holidays and incentives are given for domestic investment in the domestic soil.

## Bilateral Tax Treaties

Some saving considerations to the violation of the principles of taxation on international business are the agreements for avoidance of double taxation as between countries and availability of foreign tax credits in the domestic tax system. The general discriminatory tax treatment of multinationals is modulated by bilateral network of tax treaties, designed to avoid double taxation of income by two Taxing Authorities. Thus India has entered into these tax treaties with many of our trading partners like USA, UK, Germany and other developed countries and also some developing countries. Foreign tax credits give credit in domestic taxation for foreign incomes taxed already by foreign countries. These include both direct and indirect foreign tax credits. Direct credits relate to those directly imposed and collected on foreign branches or subsidiaries while indirect tax credits are those deemed to have been paid such as withholding taxes paid.

The home country gives credit for the taxes paid by the subsidiary or affiliates in foreign country on the incomes transferred back to the home country. This tax paid in foreign countries can be reduced by shifting the taxable income from high tax country to low tax country and offsetting losses of some subsidiary against profits of other subsidiary, in the income shown in the home country.

The Look Through Rules in U.S. apply to Controlled Foreign Companies (CFC), and if all of the CFC's income is operating income, all its payments to its U.S. parent will be deemed to be operating income, regardless of whether the remittances are royalties, fees, rents and interest and dividends. Thus, the high taxed dividends can be averaged with low or no tax paid interest income and royalties.

## Allocation of Income

MNCs know how to allocate incomes and expenses as between the parent company and affiliates and among affiliates to take advantage of different tax systems in different countries. If there is differential tax rates in the home country between the domestic income and foreign income there is a tendency for the MNCs to show less income from domestic sources *vis-a-vis* foreign sources, if the latter are taxed at a lower rate. Similarly, the affiliates' income which is taxed at a lower rate in home country (USA) is shown as higher taxable income. If there are two affiliates — one cash rich in a low tax rate country like Switzerland and the other in India, and the Indian affiliate borrows from Euro market in Singapore, the Indian affiliate can get its funds from the cash rich affiliate in Switzerland. Indian affiliate pays interest income to cash rich Swiss affiliate. Now Swiss affiliate converted the possible dividend income into interest income, which is advantageous to the US parent company. Under the existing law, it is preferable for the U.S. parent company to transfer certain interest, R&D, and general and administrative expenses incurred in the USA to the books of foreign subsidiaries. Under the 1986 law in the USA, interest expense is allocated on the basis of corresponding assets. The head office now borrows for the affiliates and pays interest on it but the interest is allocatable to the affiliates, on the basis of funds used by them out of the parent company's borrowings.

The allocation of R&D expenses is also relevant to the U.S. law, as is the general and administrative expenses. Under the current law in the U.S., 50% of expenses on R&D in the U.S. is allocatable to the U.S. source income and the other 50% can be apportioned between the U.S. source and foreign sources, depending on the basis of either sales or gross income.

Gross income minus deductions for tax credits or rebates is equal to net taxable income. The total from all sources including that from parent company remains the same but what changes by these allocations is the taxable income from each of the foreign subsidiaries and the total taxable income from foreign sources.

The tax law in the parent company is most relevant for the tax planning of the MNC. Thus, in the U.S. as per the latest law, U.S. operational income is taxed more heavily than, the foreign operational income. Then the U.S. parent spends on most of the expenses of the affiliates as permitted by law and reduces their own income and shows higher foreign operational income which is taxed at a lower rate in the U.S.

## Transfer Pricing for Tax Planning

The general vehicle of such adjustments of income is through transfer price mechanism. But the fixation of transfer price and other accounting practices of MNCs should conform to internationally accepted and generally accepted accounting principles. Accordingly, transfer price is based on arm's length transaction with a third party. This subject was discussed already in earlier chapters. The objective is to have maximum net after tax profit inflow for the parent company.

## Use of Inter-Company Loans

Inter-company loans or transactions are used as a vehicle for reducing the tax liability of the sum of the parent and subsidiaries' income. There can be shifts of income from high income tax centres to low income tax centres. The parent company can give non-interest bearing loans to subsidiaries. Some services can be performed by one affiliate to another at no charge or high charge depending upon the exigencies of taxes. Similarly there can be transfer of machinery and equipment at nominal charges or no charges. The sale of inventory and valuation of assets could be at very low costs to show low income for tax purposes. On the same basis, the transfer of intangible property such as trademarks, patents, formulas, licences etc. can be highly undervalued or overvalued as the actual pricing of them is next to impossible.

By any of such methods, the tax liability of each of the affiliates and the total for all affiliates and subsidiaries of MNC can be reduced by a proper tax planning. The legal provisions and practices in each of the affiliate countries as also in the parent country have to be kept in mind in the process. The objective is maximisation of after-tax wealth of parent plus affiliates. The tax provisions in particular relating to incentives and rebates or tax havens will be taken full advantage of in this process. The differential taxation of different types of incomes such as interest, dividends, fees, royalties etc. and withholding taxes if any and tax rates as applicable in different affiliate countries will be taken into account by the parent company in its tax planning efforts and in its objective of maximisation of wealth of equity holders.

## Tax Incentives

Various governments offer a number of tax incentives to the exporters on the basis of their export performance. Export income is partly or wholly tax exempt. Besides, interest rate on post shipment and/or pre-shipment finance will be lower than the normal rates. There will be tax exemption for inputs going into exports and exporters will be given liberal licences to import their requirements. Export oriented units and export processing zones are exempt from Excise and Customs Duties as in India.

MNCs make an examination of possible locations which are tax havens. Of these, the factors taken into account for selection, as for example are the following:

(1) Economic policies of the government.
(2) Political stability of the government.
(3) Attitudes to foreign investment and business
(4) Tax treaties executed with parent country,
(5) Tax heavens, EPZ, tax rebates etc.
(6) Banking facilities in the host countries
(7) Existence of or absence of exchange controls
(8) Infrastructure facilities
(9) Bureaucratic red tape, corruption, and other malpractices.

## Organisational Set up of MNC

The form in which the organisation is to be set up outside the country may be a branch, a subsidiary or a joint venture project. Each has its own advantages and disadvantages for tax purposes. For example, a branch is advantageous, if the parent country allows the losses of the branch to offset the profits of the parent company in taxation for the parent income. Another factor is whether the host country will allow the tax-free use of working capital funds. The parent company takes into account all alternative tax haven countries for the choice of location for branches, subsidiaries and joint ventures. What form of organisation is best suited and which location gives the best banking and infrastructure facilities and many more such considerations are examined before the MNC makes a final decision about the choice, most suitable to it.

The various tax havens of the world can be grouped into the following four types:

Type I countries that exempt from income taxes and wealth and gift taxes, all foreign income or local income from foreign subsidiaries.

Type II countries which tax the foreign companies but at lower rates..

Type III countries which tax all incomes from the domestic sources but exempt all income from foreign sources.

Type IV nations which give special tax incentives like tax holiday in selected sectors of industry.

Countries of Type I are the Bahamas, Bermuda and the Cayman Islands. These tax havens in the Caribbean have no tax treaties and foreign owned companies are given guarantees of long-term nature against any taxes. The incorporation fees and other initial expenses are also low in these countries.

Countries of Type II are British Virgin Islands, the Netherlands, Antilles, etc. In these countries, tax rates are low such as a 12% income tax rate or a withholding tax on dividends.

Type III country, has its best example in Hong Kong where the domestic source income has a nominal tax rate of 15% but foreign source income is tax free. There is no tax on capital gains or dividends remitted to foreign countries. Panama is another country of this type where foreign source income of all types is tax exempt. The incorporation laws are also liberal.

Type IV of countries are PUERTO Rico and Republic of Ireland, which exempts all export income. In Europe, the tax haven countries are Switzerland, the Netherlands and Liechtenstein.

## Tax Reliefs and Rebates in India

In India, there are more than 150 deductions, exemptions, allowances and rebates scattered all over the Income Tax Act. Mostly, these reliefs are covered under chapters VI A and VIII of the I.T. Act to a large extent. These include, among others, LIC premia, PF, PPF, NSCs, donations, rents paid, profits of industrial units in backward areas. SSI unit profits, export turnover, profits of units set up in specified industries after a certain date. Section 80I deals with deduction from interest and dividends exemption from tax to inter-corporate dividends and others such as tax relief related to physical disability and old age etc. Donations for charitable and other welfare purposes comprise the largest single tax relief. The export turnover of companies is another major factor for tax relief of a large component. Exemptions of export earnings and tax holiday for projects set up in some backward areas or poor infrastructure and other selected sectors have relevance to MNCs. So are the units set up in EOU, SEZ, etc. which get many tax reliefs.

A study of the Income Tax Department, whose results were published in August 1999, but relates to the returns submitted for 1996-97, for all types of individuals, HUF, registered firms and companies, shows that these reliefs of all types deprive the Exchequer of 12.4% of the gross income of the assessees. The major deductions are claimed under 50 heads of tax-relief avenues which are provided in the Act. The gross income of the assessee is total income admitted by the assessee prior to the admissible deductions. The reliefs relate to various heads of income like salaries, rental income, interest and dividend income and other categories. Nearly 12-13% of the total returns account for those who show a returned income of Rs. 1 lakh and more and contribute more than three-fourths of the total tax payable.

## Tax Credits

Many tax treaties are entered into on a bilateral basis between India and other countries. If India for example imposes a withholding tax of say 10% of income repatriated to the parent company in U.S., the U.S. tax authority gives credit for this tax already paid on this income and there will be no double taxation, as there is a tax treaty between India and USA. If the Indian corporation tax is higher say at 35% and US tax is lower at 30%, and if the excess tax credit cannot be used, then the US parent company prefers a branch in India rather than a subsidiary. Under the present system, the income of the branch forms part of the parent company and the total income is taxed at a lower rate in the USA.

The tax treatment of the branch and that of subsidiary are different in some countries. If the branch incurs a loss, it is possible to carry back and forward tax losses and credits. The total tax credits available in all countries where the parent company has branches or subsidiaries is generally taken into account in total.

## Tax Havens

A branch is preferred for only selling and marketing arrangements. So long as the branch can show losses, these offset the profits of the parent company and no tax is payable so long as there is no net profit. The U.S. parent company then sets up a wholly owned subsidiary in a tax haven country like Bermuda or Virgin Islands. This subsidiary takes over the business of the branches once these become profit centres. As this wholly owned subsidiary, namely, *Alpha* is registered outside, say in Bermuda, and does not pay any taxes, the excess funds are ploughed back for expansion and no dividend comes to the U.S. parent company for payment of taxes in the U.S. If the operations of the *Alpha* company grows, to a large extent, it will set up with its excess funds a subsidiary in Latin America. With the semi-finished goods from Bermuda being converted into finished goods in Latin America, by its subsidiary say *Gamma,* the Latin American subsidiary takes over manufacture and sale of finished goods in Latin America. Although it pays its local taxes, its payments to Alpha company as dividends are tax free in Bermuda, which is used to set up manufacturing activities in Irish Republic. As Irish Republic gives tax free treatment to all exports, from that country the subsidiary set up by Bermuda Company *Alpha* in Irish Republic will sell its goods in European Commonwealth and gets tax free income, which is again used to expand its business in Europe. As long as the parent company gets no dividends, in the U.S.A., the *Alpha* company, set up by it in Bermuda, continues to grow and expand its worldwide network in Latin America, Ireland, Europe (Switzerland) and even in Hong Kong and Singapore in Asia. Only when any dividends are received for its original investment by the parent company, in the US, will it pay any tax to the US Authorities.

## Investment Decisions on Tax Planning

The complexities involved in tax planning for the MNC are thus very deep. Global tax planning involves the following decisions, namely:

(1) what should be the organisation for the foreign operations of the MNC — branch, subsidiary wholly or partly owned — or joint venture partly or wholly owned and any changes in the organisational structure, country-wise.

(2) Deciding on the optimal use of tax havens, bilateral tax treaties, tax incentive vehicles like foreign sales corporation (FSC), which is a form of tax saving mechanism in the USA.

(3) Finally the MNC has to decide when, how and from where the funds have to be brought back to the U.S.A.

In any tax planning, the global executive should know his environment in each of the country in which the corporate operates. This environment includes tax treatment of different types of income, tax havens, tax credits due to bilateral tax treaties etc.

The type of organisation and the various financing and investment decisions in different countries are based on home and host countries' policies concerning taxation of foreign source income, bilateral tax treaties leading to tax credits, the various country tax rates and the tax differentials etc. The MNC tries to build up an empire outside the home country, so long as the tax rates are as high as 35% to 50%, in the home country and bring back funds only when it is absolutely necessary.

## Corporate Goals

The corporate goal is not necessarily the tax minimisation. But there may be more important objectives as maximisation of shareholders' wealth, wherever in the world, that wealth is located. The corporate investment policies in each of the countries, sourcing of financing, accessing of blocked funds and distribution of available funds among the various affiliates and repatriation of excess funds to the home country in the form of dividends or any other form will all depend on the home country's tax-policy, tax rates, availability of tax credit and tax policies — in the various affiliate countries. Ultimately all tax planning aims at maximisation of the wealth of the shareholders of the MNC.

## Investment Incentives

Advance taxes are payable by all those whose tax is not deducted at source by employers. That means, self-employed, businessmen and service oriented job holders like consultants have to pay advance tax in three or four instalments on a quarterly basis, say September, December, March, etc.

Some countries give investment incentives as in the case of P.F. in India, Srilanka & Pakistan. Sops are given to non-residents by some countries. In India, non-residents are taxed on income received, accrued or earned in India, at a rate of 20% for income on investments and at a rate of 10% on long-term capital gains. Most countries which have double tax avoidance treaties tax only on the income, originating for the country in question. Non-residents are taxed at concessional rates in Sri Lanka, Pakistan, Japan and Malaysia. Even UK and France provide some exemptions and concessions to non-residents in respect of their tax payments.

## Global Trend — Tax Rates on Corporates

A study of the global trends in corporate tax rates show a steady and declining trend. The reason for this trend is increasing entry of MNCs into many emerging countries and hence, competition among countries to show attractive tax picture for foreign companies. As new technologies make it easier for MNCs to move business activities and capital around the globe, countries are under increasing pressure to maintain competitive tax regimes.

In general, the tax rates in developing countries are lower than in developed countries with a view to attract corporates to come into those countries. Average tax rates in Latin American Countries is even lower. Among the OECD countries, corporate tax rates fell in Denmark from 34% to 32%; in France from 41.66% to 40% and in Japan from 51.6% to 48%. If many developing countries like Argentina, Pakistan and India raised rates as between 1998 and 1999, it was due to revenue considerations. Pakistan raised the rate from 30 to 35% and India raised it for 1999-2000 from 35% to 38.5% by adding a surcharge of 10% in the Budget for revenue purposes. This was lowered more recently.

Among the European Union countries, the trend is to lower the corporate tax rates. Since 1996, the average corporate tax rate among the EU countries dropped by about three percentage points to 36% approximately.

With the introduction of a common currency Euro, in the E.U. countries, the pressure for competitive tax rates has become more severe. Thus, the E.U. countries are now in the process of streamlining the corporate tax rates along the participating countries.

Some countries have an effective rate different from nominal rate. For example, both in India and Bangladesh tax holidays and tax rebates are available for export companies, EOUs and EPZs, etc. Companies in infrastructure, I.T. software, telecom, etc. in India enjoy a lower effective rate or even a complete tax holiday for new companies. On the other hand, in India there are two different tax rates for domestic companies and foreign companies respectively. This differential treatment for foreign and domestic companies was given up in 2004 but given an incentive for foreign companies by lowered the surcharge on corporate tax rate of 30% + 2.5% of surcharge as against 10% for domestic companies.

## Grey Areas in International Tax Planning

Transfer pricing, thin capitalisation and taxation of e-commerce are getting more relevance in the realm of taxation due to growing trend of globalisation. Transfer pricing is to be based on the principle that taxation would aim at making the transfer transaction as if it is made between unconcerned parties. As far as thin trading is concerned, the aim of the authorities is to look at the connected party loans and interest payments on loans to a parent company, if the concerned parties or the head office and branches are separate entities and/or arm's length basis is maintained in the terms of these transactions. The other grey areas are taxation of e-commerce, lack of legislative provisions for dealing with malpractices in transfer pricing and lack of tax treaties among many countries. The application of these rules gives rise to many complications. Intra-group arrangements often involve a network of rights and responsibilities between numerous companies in different legal jurisdictions. Many transactions in the network are unique and there will be no direct comparable transaction as between unconcerned parties. Comparison of a single part of that network on a stand alone basis, so as to achieve its similarity with corresponding arm's length transactions is difficult, if not impossible.

Tax authorities have to be familiar with the multinational rules, published by the O.E.C.D. But these model treaties, guidelines, commentaries, etc., have the effect to the extent that they are incorporated in the domestic legislation. OECD conventions are not binding. Suo motto and absence of legislative backing makes the tax authorities look arbitrary in their assessment. These grey areas in globalised investment and trading may lead to legal hassles. Under the European Treaty, the EC Directives have direct applicability to member states. India has to incorporate them in law and practice.

## Transfer Pricing Methods — Measures to Plug Tax Loopholes

At present, the onus of proof lies on the Tax Department which should be laid on the company. Second, the companies should be put under an obligation to maintain detailed accounts justifying the transfer price for any service or good, as in the case of the practice in the U.S. and U.K. Lastly, some proper methods acceptable to the I.T. Authorities should be set out as guidelines to the companies. Two proper methods are feasible: one is transaction method which is comparable uncontrolled price for similar transactions (CUP) which uses the data or information at which similar transaction between unrelated parties is priced. The other method acceptable should be the resale price (RPM) based on cost plus method which uses information on costs, gross margin in unrelated party transactions. Right now there is no data on prices of imports and exports of the goods and services in which MNCs are dealing. A data bank and MIS Departments to be built for this purpose by the Customs and Excise Departments.

The I.T. Act does contain some provisions to deal with cases of inflated expenditures and reduced incomes by corporates. But no regulations classifying and elucidating those provisions exist and these provisions are not enforced properly by the authorities. Right now sections of I.T. Act, namely, 40 A (2) and section 92 deal with such malpractices as inflated expenditure and reduced taxable profits. But it was reported recently, that the Ministry of Finance has laid down norms on transfer prices relating to their practices and procedures acceptable to the I.T. Department.

Till recently, the tax rates in India were slightly higher on foreign companies and their branches in India than the companies of Indian origin. This used to force them to open joint ventures or subsidiaries with registration in India to avoid higher rates of taxation. This has also discouraged, the setting up of units for Business Process Outsourcing (BPO) in India. Only in 2004, the Central Board of Direct Taxes Appellate Authority has indicated that foreign companies and Indian companies should be treated on par for purposes of direct taxation. This is in tune with the principles of equity and OECD approved code of conduct in international taxation. This method of taxation will encourage foreign companies to enter into India for operations, manufacture and outsourcing which will promote employment and income in India. As in 2009-10, foreign companies and domestic companies are taxed at the same rate of 30% but with only 2 1/2% surcharge for foreign companies as against 10% surcharge for domestic companies.

❖ ❖ ❖

# BIBLIOGRAPHY


1. James C. Van Home : *Financial Management and Policy,* Prentice Hall of India Pvt. Ltd.

2. Alan C. Shapiro : *Multinational Financial Management,* Prentice Hall of India Pvt. Ltd.

3. Ian H. Giddy : *Global Financial Markets*, A.I.T.B.S. Publishers and sDistributors.

4. Bhaskar Majumdar : *Concept and Practice of Global Finance,* Bharat Publishing House.

5. Sanjaya Lall : *The New Multinationals,* John Wiley and Sons.

6. I.L.O. : I.L.O., "*Multinational Enterprises and Social Policy.*"

7. Smith Roy C. and Ingo Walter : *Global Financial Services,* New York, Harper.

8. Levi Mawice : *International Finance: Financial Management and the International Economy,* McGraw-Hill.

9. George Abraham and Ian H. Giddy : *International Finance Handbook,* Wiley Publishing, New York.

10. Lessard Darald R. : *International Financial Management: Theory and Applications,* New York, Wiley Publishers.

11. Walmsley Julian : *Global Investing: Euro Bonds and Alternatives,* Macmillan.

12. Dufey, Gunter and Ian H. Giddly : *The International Money Market,* Englewood Clifts, Prentice Hall.

13. Eiteman David, Arthurstonahill and Michael Moffett : *Multionational Business Finance,* Addison Wesley, 1991.

14. Buckley A. : *International Capital Budgeting* Prentice Hall, (1996).

15. Bishop P. and Dixon D. : *Foreign Exchange Handbook,* McGraw-Hill Inc.

16. Ardiep F.D. : *Derivatives*, Harword University Press, (1996).

17. Grabbe O.J : *International Financial Market Elsevier* 1986.